P9-CRA-299

FINANCING BUSINESS FIRMS

FINANCING BUSINESS FIRMS

by
CHARLES L. PRATHER, Ph.D., Pd.D.
Professor of Banking and Finance
The University of Texas

1961 ~ REVISED EDITION
RICHARD D. IRWIN, INC.
HOMEWOOD, ILLINOIS

REVISED EDITION
First Printing, September, 1961

Library of Congress Catalogue Card No. 61–14496

PRINTED IN THE UNITED STATES OF AMERICA

to KATHERINE
~~~ CHARLES
and JOHN
~~~

Preface

ALTHOUGH the subject matter in this book is customarily taught in college courses entitled "Corporation Finance," the title "Financing Business Firms" was selected because the theories and principles of business finance apply to unincorporated business firms as well as those that are incorporated. In treating the subject matter, about the same amount of space has been devoted to financing short-term and intermediate as to financing long-term capital needs of business firms.

Financing with "funds from operations" has been given a more prominent place in this edition because students are puzzled when they read about "tax bankrupt" corporations on one hand and the rapid growth of American business firms on the other.

As indicated in the table of contents, the subject matter is divided into eight parts with chapter groupings we have found helpful in teaching. In the first six parts, the problems of "going concerns" are emphasized, and they are entitled Nature and Organization of Business Firms, Financial Statements and Financial Planning, Funds from Operations, Short-Term and Intermediate Loan Capital, Owners' Equity, and Long-Term Debts of Business Corporations. In the last two parts, special problems of business finance are considered and these include Business Promotion and Expansion, and Recapitalization, Reorganization, and Liquidation of Business Firms.

In writing each chapter, the problem was not so much deciding what should be included as what should be excluded. The following appeared in the preface of the first edition: "Since details pertaining to the earnings and financial conditions of corporations whose securities are in the hands of the general public are available in investment manuals, much of this type of information was omitted." We have been told, however, that investment manuals are not always available in sufficient numbers; hence more illustrations and procedures are included in this edition. The end product is a bigger book and—we hope—a more useful one without being too cumbersome.

Quotations are used in the questions and problems at the end of each chapter, for these have proved stimulating and useful in teaching business policy. Emphasis is on new quotations but a few of the old ones have been retained.

The author is indebted to those who have read and criticized the first edition and the current manuscript in whole or part. These include Jack W. Cashin and Donald E. Vaughn, whose major contribution is related to Chapter 25, of the University of Texas; Billy J. Hinton of Baylor University; Edward A. Jordan, formerly of the University of Connecticut; and Reginald W. Gregory of Merrill Lynch, Pierce, Fenner & Smith. The author renews his note of appreciation for the help of Sydney M. Robbins, now of Columbia University, and Girvin H. Sanderson, now of Baylor University, for their help in preparing the manuscript for the first edition. Finally, the author is most grateful to his wife, Katherine F. Prather, and Jack W. Cashin for the many tedious hours spent in helping to put the manuscript in final form.

CHARLES L. PRATHER

THE UNIVERSITY OF TEXAS
March, 1961

Table of Contents

PART IV: SHORT-TERM AND INTERMEDIATE LOAN CAPITAL

PART V: OWNERS' EQUITY

PART VI: LONG-TERM DEBTS OF BUSINESS CORPORATIONS

PART I

Nature and Organization of Business Firms

BUSINESS FINANCE is a study of the methods and procedures whereby business firms acquire and utilize the funds needed to operate. Because of the diversity in type and size and the large number of business units, the subject is of necessity a comprehensive one.

The legal form of organization under which a firm operates will greatly influence many of its activities; hence, a thorough study of the advantages and disadvantages of the various forms of organization is imperative. Each form is superior to the others in some respects, and the selection of a particular one is largely a matter of balancing one set of advantages against another.

A business corporation differs from the other two most common forms (proprietorship and partnership) in that it is a legal entity. Consequently, a corporation tends to be a more permanent but more complicated form of organization encountering problems not associated with the others.

This section presents the background of business finance, legal forms of organization, and the organization and management of corporations.

CHAPTER 1

Nature of Business Finance

IN THE United States, the focal point of economic activity centers in business firms. Traditionally, business is conducted for the sake of profit or possible profit, but today many decisions of business firms indicate an awareness of the effect of their policies on outside interests such as labor groups, customers, government agencies, and the general public. Perhaps this placement of "good public relations" first and "profits" second merely indicates a realization that, in the long run, it is "good business" to work for the well-being of the community, the nation, and the economy as a whole.

This chapter deals with the scope of business finance, definition of terms, social importance of business finance, economic problems of business units, and classification of business firms.

SCOPE OF BUSINESS FINANCE

A business firm is defined as a financially responsible business organization with an established place of business, owned by one or more persons, and subject to a single set of operating policies. A business firm may control one or more plants or outlets and may be engaged in one or more forms of business activity. Today, there are more than 4,600,000 business firms in the United States. These include all firms—those with a few thousand dollars in assets at one extreme and the billion-dollar business firms at the other (such as the American Telephone and Telegraph Company, the world's largest nonfinancial business corporation).

The major function of the finance officer of a business firm is to see that funds are available to carry out the plans of management. It will be necessary for him to know everything about the operations of the business that provide cash and necessitate expenditures not only in the present but also in the future. More broadly, successful financial management entails not only knowledge of the sources of funds but also their proper application in the productive process. If a private business fails to meet expenses and to earn enough to attract capital for expansion, it ceases to grow, withers, and dies. During periods of national emergency such as wars, business management may give less weight to the profit objective than to other objectives; but in the long run, the profit motive is recognized as the "spark plug" of the American free enterprise system.

Perhaps there has been no time in history when modern industry has offered a greater challenge to college graduates than at present. Training in accounting and law as well as in finance are recommended because financial executives must be in a position to maintain internal control of business activities, to institute and keep general and cost accounting systems, to keep records of the assets and income of their companies, and to give greater accountability to stockholders, the government, and the general public.

Business enterprises draw heavily upon all fields of finance. Monetary economists provide information as to monetary management, national income, general prices, interest rates, and the money market. Investment bankers are the middlemen through whom large business firms sell their securities and thus raise capital funds for business expansion and other purposes. Commercial banks are providing business enterprises with intermediate and long-term credit as well as with short-term funds. Much of the savings of the nation that is invested in business enterprises reaches individual firms through specialized institutions that are playing an important part in the capital market (private pension funds, savings institutions, trusts, and life insurance companies).

Many large business firms have their own statisticians who analyze their companies' operation or make special studies as required by management. In addition, these statisticians interpret information obtained from the Bureau of Labor Statistics, the Office of Business Economics in the United States Department of Commerce, the Federal Reserve System, mercantile agencies, and other public and private sources. The type of business, in turn, will determine the type of trained personnel necessary for its operation—engineers, marketing specialists, chemists, and so on.

In the field of business, the current demand for personnel is for the specialist who can see the forest as well as the trees. In an exact science, the equations and reactions are known and predictable; but in business management there are human equations which cannot be solved mathematically. Being an art rather than a science, business management, including financial management, depends upon judgment factors that cannot be taught. This means that a book on business finance can only provide facts, indicate problems, and describe some of the ways in which they have been and may be handled.

DEFINITION OF TERMS

It is significant to note that certain institutions were excluded from the discussion of the scope of business finance. Although privately owned business enterprises include banks, insurance companies, and other financial institutions, in this presentation of the subject matter of business finance they will be treated as sources of business funds, as servants of rather than as parts of "business." Also, the financing of farms was not discussed because farmers have special financial problems which are best studied separately from those of other business enterprises.

A definition of business which emphasizes the profit motive excludes many forms of co-operative and mutual institutions organized for the benefit of their members rather than for profit. Such institutions are found in most fields of industry, including agriculture, finance, manufacturing, marketing, and personal services. Other nonprofit associations or corporations that such a definition excludes are athletic, aesthetic, benevolent, civic, cultural, educational, fraternal, patriotic, religious, scientific, and social organizations.

Governments and government-owned corporations and agencies are organized to provide services, not to make a profit. Many of them are subsidized in varying degrees by direct government contributions; others may be expected to pay expenses from their earnings, but even here, their financial problems are fundamentally different from those encountered by private business enterprises. Business finance also excludes the activities of lawyers, physicians, and others engaged in professional practices. Usually the amount of capital needed by those engaged in professions is small relative to the investment required by nonprofessional businesses with a comparable income. If the reader thinks that the subject matter of business finance is being unduly limited, let him be reminded that even with this limited definition there are over 4,600,000 business firms in the United States.

Business finance deals primarily with raising, administering, and disbursing funds by privately owned business units operating in nonfinancial fields of industry. The terminology used in business or corporation finance is very similar to that found in investment literature and many of the problems dealt with are identical; however, the point of view is different. While a book on business finance treats such subjects as types of stocks and bonds as do books on investments, in business finance these topics are dealt with from the viewpoint of business enterprises rather than from that of investors. In business finance, capital, financial planning, and financial management are emphasized.

"Capital" may be defined as the product of past industry used to aid further production. This definition not only separates capital from land but also separates producers' goods from consumers' goods. Businessmen may speak of capital as meaning the total assets needed to operate a business without distinguishing between land and capital—the tools of production. The accountant's definition stresses net worth, the excess of "total assets" over "total liabilities." The legal definition of capital is even more restricted than that of the accountants, being "capital stock." Thus, capital of a corporation would be the amount paid in at the time of issuance of stock, "the amount invested in the business." But even this definition needs to be qualified because sometimes shares of stock are sold for more than par value, or more than "stated" value if the stock has no par value (the difference is accounted for as "capital surplus" and not included in "capital stock").

Sometimes the word capital is used in the sense of invested capital or capital structure—meaning stocks, bonds, and other forms of long-term indebtedness. Obviously, current liabilities are excluded; hence, there are arguments in favor of linking the idea of capital to the financial structure—the total of all liabilities and owners' equity. Business decisions are made by individuals, and when any one individual uses the term *capital* he will be using it in terms of his own experiences. Thus to an individual the term *capital* may include leases, savings accounts, bonds, mortgages, and stock certificates (intangible personal property) as well as physical assets such as land and buildings (real property) and tangible forms of mobile wealth such as animals, automobiles, machinery, and furniture (tangible personal property).

All of the foregoing concepts of capital have a place in business finance, but it is more accurate to make distinctions such as *net* capital investment, capital goods, total assets of a business firm, net worth, capital stock, capital structure, financial structure, and property and property rights. Capital expenditures may be considered in terms of *gross* capital investments. When considered from a national point of view, *gross* domestic investment is the output of new capital goods and inventories; *net* capital investment is gross domestic investment minus an allowance for the depreciation of capital goods used up or consumed in the productive process. Similarly, *gross* business savings include undistributed profits of business firms plus their depreciation allowances; *net* business savings include only undistributed profits.

While there are some who feel that in business finance capital expenditures should be considered only on a net basis, the majority now take the position that there is a place for both the gross and net presentation of the subject matter.[1] Certainly, the finance officer of a business firm will estimate the funds available to meet the needs of his company to include all funds from operations whether they are accounted for as depreciation allowances or as undistributed profits after federal income taxes.

SOCIAL IMPORTANCE OF BUSINESS FINANCE

Public interest in the problem of financing business units has increased in recent years because of (1) wide public ownership of American business corporations, (2) the increase in size and complexity of business units, and (3) attacks upon capitalism (an economic system wherein the means of production are privately owned and operated for profit).

The wide public ownership of American corporations may be illustrated by American Telephone and Telegraph Company, with 2,900,000 shareholders. General Motors Corporation, United States Steel Corporation, General Electric Company, and Standard Oil Company of New Jersey are among the many other favorites of American investors. Statistics suggest that about 15,000,000 persons own stock of American public corporations. This group is not restricted to those with high incomes, since approximately 50 per cent

---

[1] National Association of Manufacturers, *Major Tendencies in Business Finance*, Economic Policy Division Series, No. 77 (New York, January, 1958).

of these are from families with total annual incomes of between $5,000 and $10,000. In addition, about 1,500,000 others own shares of privately held corporations (companies with fewer than 300 shareholders whose stock is usually not available to the general public). Moreover, an estimated 110,000,000 Americans have an indirect investment in stock because of savings placed with life insurance companies, retirement funds, mutual savings banks, savings and loan associations, and other financial institutions which have investments in stock.[2] Although corporations seem to dominate the American business scene, there are more than 3,800,000 single proprietorships and 700,000 partnerships currently operating in the United States.

There is an increasing appreciation of the fact that financial developments are of vital concern to virtually all Americans because thereon may depend the uninterrupted continuation of our high standard of living. Moreover, the current leadership of the United States in the affairs of the western world has been traced by some directly to its material strength. In the words of Professor Nevins, "The architects of our material progress—the men like Whitney, McCormack, Westinghouse, Rockefeller, Carnegie, Hill, and Ford—will yet stand forth in their stature as builders of a strength which civilization found indispensible."[3]

While generalizations concerning the sources of strength of the American economy are of interest, it seems more appropriate to recognize the ability of the American people to use the country's material resources. For illustration, Professor Maclaurin writes, "My own conviction is that any industry today which fails to incorporate a research conception will languish and die. The inclusion of such a conception into an industrial structure seems to me more important, both to industry itself and to the public, than the degree to which the industry is monopolistic."[4] Others would stress the existence of free institutions which encourage free thinking, free enterprises, and development of human resources.[5]

[2] New York Stock Exchange, *Share Ownership in America: 1959* (New York, 1959), p. 5.

[3] "Rewriting History is Urged by Nevins," *New York Times*, September 20, 1953, p. 67.

[4] W. Rupert Maclaurin, "Technological Progress in Some American Industries," *American Economic Review*, Vol. XLIV, No. 2 (May, 1954), p. 189.

[5] The extent to which the American public accepts without question the large annual salaries paid top executives of business firms may be cited as an index of the public regard for business in the United States. Of the 644 top officials of large corporations in 1959, 28 earned in excess of $300,000, 50 earned from $200,000 to $300,000, 290 from

National Income by Industrial Origin. Today, the yardstick against which economic changes are measured is national income or gross national product. Thus college presidents are noting the lag in expenditures for higher education as compared to the increase in national income, and those who analyze the national debt burden are noting how it is declining in terms of national income. The statistics of gross national product, subdivided into business, general government, household and institutions, and rest of the world, given in Table 1, demonstrate the degree to which American business firms

TABLE 1

GROSS NATIONAL PRODUCT BY LEGAL FORM OF ORGANIZATION FOR SELECTED YEARS

(In Billions of Dollars)

	1947	*1952*	*1957*
Business	250.3	308.7	357.7
General government	22.8	33.2	33.2
Household and institutions	8.2	10.4	13.9
Rest of the world	1.1	1.3	2.2
Total	282.4	353.6	407.0

Source: United States Department of Commerce, Office of Business Economics, *U.S. Income and Output*, a Supplement to the *Survey of Current Business* (Washington, D.C.: U.S. Government Printing Office, 1958), pp. 136–37.

dominate the current production of goods and services.

The statistics of national income by industrial origin given in Table 2 direct attention to (1) the predominance of private enterprise as a source of national income and (2) the current importance of manufacturing and trade industries as compared to farming, mining, transportation, and other industries. In 1947, agriculture, forestry, and fisheries accounted for almost 10 per cent of national income; by 1957 this percentage declined to less than 5 per cent.[6] As a source of national income, manufacturing leads all other divisions, accounting for over 30 per cent; communications and public utilities account for less than 4 per cent (see Table 2).

$100,000 to $200,000, and 276 from $33,000 to $100,000. At the top of the list was Frederic G. Donner, chairman of the General Motors Corporation, whose salary of $201,350 was supplemented by bonus payments of $469,000. (*New York Times*, May 3, 1960, p. 53.) "Take home pay" is reduced sharply by personal income taxes. Reports of remuneration figures of chief officers of corporations are filed with the Securities and Exchange Commission.

[6] Today agricultural workers number about the same as in 1871, but they feed a population 5½ times as large and produce large farm surpluses. See also, U.S. Department of Commerce, Office of Business Economics, *U.S. Income and Output* (Washington, D.C.: U.S. Government Printing Office, 1958), p. 211.

TABLE 2

NATIONAL INCOME BY INDUSTRY DIVISION FOR SELECTED YEARS
(In Billions of Dollars)

	1947	*1952*	*1957*
Agriculture, forestry and fisheries	19.3	19.5	16.2
Manufacturing	58.7	100.1	112.5
Wholesale and retail trade	37.3	49.8	59.6
Finance, insurance and real estate	15.2	27.6	34.6
Transportation	11.5	15.8	17.3
Communications and public utilities	5.1	10.1	13.3
Services	18.9	29.2	39.4
Government and governmental enterprises	18.6	35.3	42.9
Other	13.4	22.4	28.1
Total	198.0	309.8	363.9

Source: United States Department of Commerce, Office of Business Economics, *U.S. Income and Output*, a Supplement to the *Survey of Current Business* (Washington, D.C.: U.S. Government Printing Office, 1958), pp. 132–33.

Those who are gainfully employed may be divided into two groups—those producing goods and those producing services. Within recent years, the service industries (wholesale and retail trade; finance, insurance and real estate; transportation; communications and public utilities; services; and government and governmental enterprises) have produced a greater share of national income than the goods-creating industries (manufacturing; agriculture, forestry, and fisheries). Occupational changes which have taken place during the last century reflect increasing reliance on the use of machinery and other labor-savings devices in agriculture, manufacturing, mining, transportation, and other industries. Because of further development of automation, fewer workers will be needed in most industries, but future production will require an increase in savings as well as in personnel from the professional groups (engineers, scientists, accountants, and other specialists).

Role of the Government. Although most business firms are privately owned, the government exerts a strong influence on economic activities. Governments not only prescribe many of the rules under which business firms operate but also influence the allocation of resources and national income. A considerable part of business income is socialized through taxation (over one half of the net income of American business corporations is paid to national, state, and local governments). While socialization of a large percentage of business income raises serious problems, it is a less drastic step than that taken by many countries wherein the means of production are socialized and operated by the state.

TABLE 3

SOURCES AND USES OF CORPORATE FUNDS FOR SELECTED YEARS*
(In Billions of Dollars)

	1947	*1952*	*1957*
Sources			
Internal sources, total	16.6	17.8	28.5
Retained profits†	11.4	7.4	8.8
Depreciation	5.2	10.4	19.7
External, long-term sources, total	6.3	9.4	12.1
Stock	1.4	3.0	3.4
Bonds	3.0	4.9	7.5
Other debts	1.9	1.5	1.2
Short-term sources, total	9.5	3.6	−.5
Bank loans	1.4	1.6	.6
Trade payables	4.5	2.7	−1.1
Federal income tax liabilities	2.1	−3.1	−1.9
Other	1.5	2.4	1.9
Sources, Total	32.4	30.8	40.1
Uses			
Increase in physical assets, total	24.1	23.7	34.4
Plant and equipment	17.0	22.4	32.7
Inventories (book value)	7.1	1.3	1.7
Increase in financial assets, total	8.6	6.3	3.8
Receivables	7.6	5.8	3.3
Consumer	1.4	2.2	0.9
Other	6.2	3.6	2.4
Cash and government securities	1.0	.1	−1.8
Cash, including deposits	2.2	.8	−.1
U.S. Government securities	−1.2	−.7	−1.7
Other assets	.0	.4	2.3
Uses, Total	32.7	30.0	38.2
Discrepancy (uses less sources)	.3	−0.8	−1.9

* Excludes banks and insurance companies.
† Includes depletion allowances.
Source: U.S. Department of Commerce, Office of Business Economics, *U.S. Income and Output*, a Supplement to the *Survey of Current Business* (Washington, D.C.: U.S. Government Printing Office, 1958), p. 195.

The federal government is thought by many to be responsible for maintaining stability and growth in the economy. Unless private enterprise achieves these ends, there is a strong likelihood of more government action. The national economic policy of the United States was expressed by Congress in the Employment Act of 1946 which states that it is the "responsibility of the Federal Government to use all practical means consistent with its needs and obligations and other essential considerations of national policy, with the assistance and cooperation of industry, agriculture, labor, and State and local governments, to coordinate and utilize all its plans, functions, and resources for the purpose of creating and maintaining, in a manner calculated to foster and promote free, competitive enterprise and general welfare, conditions under which there will be afforded useful employment opportunities, including self-employment, for those able, willing, and seeking to work, and to promote maximum employment production, and purchasing power."

ECONOMIC PROBLEMS OF BUSINESS UNITS

The organization of the productive system of the United States into many separately owned and operated business units causes many economic problems. Although composed of millions of business units, the economy of the United States is characterized by industrial concentration and large firms. About 75 per cent of all business firms have fewer than four employees, and 99 per cent have fewer than 500 employees. At the other extreme, 1 per cent of United States business firms provide employment for 60 per cent of the working population. Other standards for measuring the size of business units—total assets, fixed investment, sales, and income—support the same conclusion, that there is a predominance of large firms in the transportation, public utility, and manufacturing industries. Small firms are most numerous in the service, contract construction, and wholesale and retail trades industries (see Table 4).

TABLE 4

NUMBER OF BUSINESS FIRMS IN OPERATION FOR SELECTED YEARS*
(In Thousands of Firms)

	1951	*1955*	*1959*†
All Industries	4,067.2	4,286.6	4,589.2
Mining and Quarrying	37.0	38.8	42.0
Contract construction	377.3	429.8	475.9
Manufacturing	322.8	326.1	331.0
Transportation, communication, and other public utilities	180.7	193.4	211.8
Wholesale trade	268.6	291.9	317.0
Retail trade	1,820.9	1,874.5	1,956.3
Finance insurance and real estate	326.9	359.5	403.3
Service industries	733.0	772.6	851.9

* Statistics are of January 1.
† Estimates for 1959 are based on incomplete data.
Source: "Rise in Business Population," *Survey of Current Business*, Vol. XXXIX, No. 5 (May, 1959), p. 18.

To some, the term "big business" has a sinister connotation which is due largely to abuses of the past. At the present time, however, the ethical standards under which large business firms operate are higher than those which govern small firms. The reason is obvious: big business is carried on under the same nation-wide publicity associated with "big government" and "big labor unions." In addition, many large business corporations are dependent on smaller firms—for illustration, General Electric depends upon 42,000 small business firms and the "big three" in the automotive industry (General Motors, Ford, and Chrysler) obtain over 50 per cent of the parts for each car assembled from small-parts manufacturers.

A business firm cannot operate without assets such as cash, stocks of raw materials, equipment, and buildings. After operations have begun, other assets such as accounts and other receivables, work in process, and finished goods will appear. Acquiring and maintaining these assets is essentially a problem of obtaining and applying funds—a problem that may be present in any type of economy.

A business firm begins operations by directing a flow of funds into the channels of production and trade which create and move goods or services to consumers. In paying for these goods or services, consumers direct a return flow of funds to the business firm. Whether considered from the viewpoint of the economy as a whole or from that of an individual business firm, this flow of money is to business as the flow of blood is to the human body. The dual function of financial management is to raise funds and to use these funds and others already invested in the enterprise to make a profit.

For the establishment, operation, and expansion of any modern business firm, both investment and short-term capital funds are needed. Investment or long-term capital funds are most frequently required to finance the acquisition of capital assets—plant, machinery, permanent equipment—and to provide minimum working capital. Later, capital funds may be needed for plant replacement or expansion, new machines, and other capital acquisitions. For a "going concern," capital is committed for a long period of time and the interests of investors and lenders are represented by so-called "long-term instruments of finance," including stock certificates which normally have no maturity date and/or long-term obligations such as long-term promissory notes, mortgages, debentures, and bonds of various types.

Most business firms need to supplement long-term capital funds with short-term funds to finance seasonal and unexpected activities. Prior to World War II, the long-term debt of private business corporations usually exceeded their short-term debt; since that time the opposite has been true. At the end of 1958, the total short-term debt (original maturity of less than one year from the date of issue) of private corporations was $150.4 billion and their long-term debt (original maturity of one year or more from the date of issue) was \$143.9 billion, compared with \$155.7 billion and \$134.1 billion, respectively, just one year before.[7] This increase in the relative importance of short-term debt has also characterized other sectors of the economy (farm debt, consumer debt, government debt, and other nonbusiness debt). If debts having a maturity of more than one year are divided into intermediate (those having maturities of from one to five years from the date of issue) and long-term (those having maturities of more than five years), the decline in the relative importance of long-term debt is even more spectacular.

Sources of Business Funds. Normally, business firms, whether proprietorships, partnerships, or corporations, finance the major part of their needs for capital from internal sources that are accounted for as retained earnings and depreciation allowances (see Table 3). Both are bookkeeping items, but depreciation allowances represent a cost of doing business while retained earnings show profits that have been earned by a business concern and not distributed to its owners. All of the items in the liability and net worth sections of a balance sheet have been instrumental in obtaining or retaining assets used by a business firm (see Chapter 4). For illustration, if \$1,000 is retained from sales receipts and is accounted for as retained earnings or as a depreciation allowance, it remains available for use by the firm.

The savings of individuals supplemented by bank credit constitute the main external sources of funds used by business firms. It is difficult to trace the sources of savings used by business firms because a large part of modern savings enter investment channels through institutions such as life insurance companies, savings and loan associations, banks of different kinds, pension funds, investment houses, and governments. Some savings used by business firms also originate abroad. Individuals save when they buy insurance policies, make deposits in banks and savings institutions, make principal payments on mortgages, and buy stocks and bonds. Usually several transactions are required before such savings are used by business firms in their operations. When a surplus is used by a government to retire outstanding bonds, some of the recipients of these funds may invest them in corporate bonds. Thereby, a government surplus would ultimately become a source of business funds to the issuing corporation. Similarly, funds used to retire a mortgage obligation or to pay the

[7] "Public and Private Debt in 1958–59," *Survey of Current Business,* Vol. XXXIX, No. 5 (May, 1959), p. 12.

premium on an insurance policy may be utilized to finance the purchase of an item of business equipment such as an electric computer. The importance of internal and external sources of funds to large companies is indicated by Chart 1.

CHART 1

SELECTED SOURCES OF FUNDS FOR LARGE CORPORATIONS
(Percentage Distribution 1946–53)

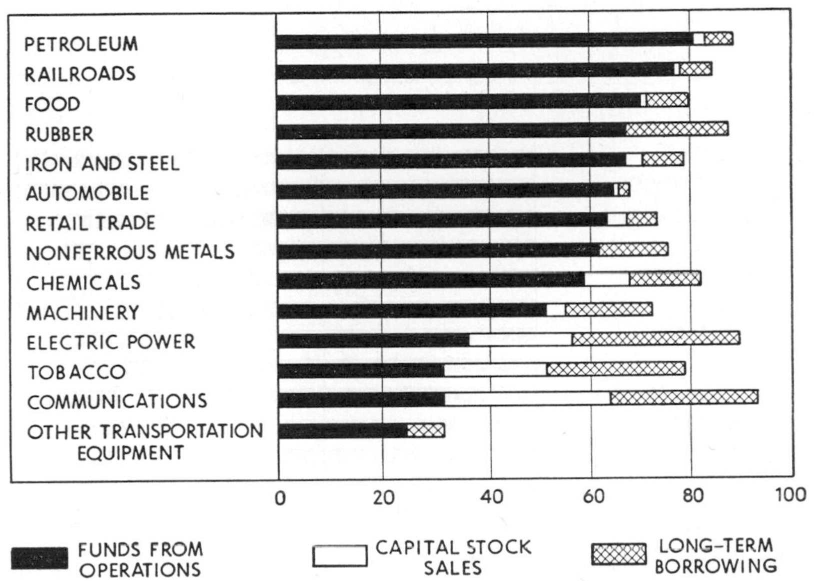

Source: Board of Governors of the Federal Reserve System, *Federal Reserve Bulletin* (August, 1954), p. 816.

Uses of Business Funds. The funds of business firms are used to acquire plants, equipment, inventories, and other assets (see Table 3). Plants include all nonresidential buildings used in production such as power plants, office buildings, foundries, factories, and stores. In addition, some business firms have long-term investments in mines, land, and railroads. Equipment includes machinery, implements, and other installations in business buildings or plants which are used to further production. Investments which are classified as short-term investments (current assets) include raw materials, goods in process of production, and finished products. Changes in investments in inventories reflect changes in economic activity or in prices and are sometimes given a major role in explaining fluctuations in the business cycle.

Credit extended by business firms to their customers is classified as accounts receivable by the creditor firms and as accounts payable by the debtor firms. Receivables, government securities, and cash balances are known as financial assets (see Table 3) and, like inventories, are subject to fluctuations which reflect changes in economic conditions or financial policies of management. Some firms invest in the securities of other corporations for purposes of control. The selected uses of funds by large companies is indicated by Chart 2.

CHART 2

SELECTED USES OF FUNDS
(Percentage Distribution, 1946–53)

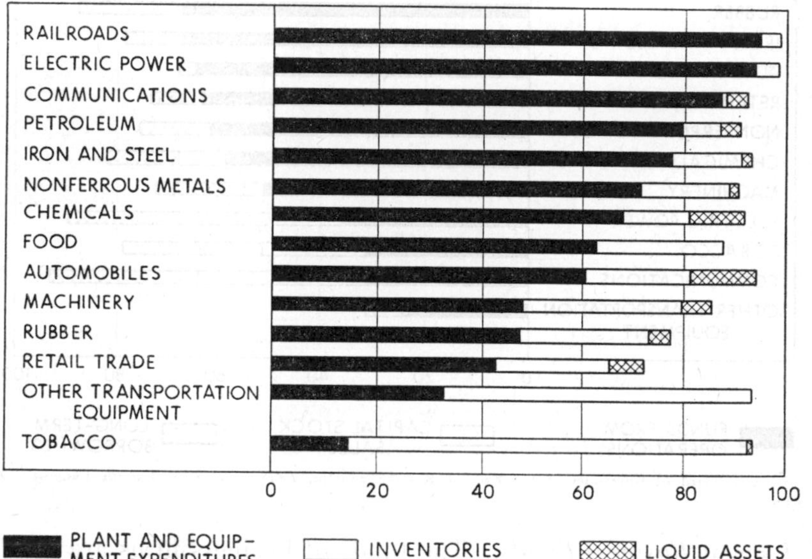

Source: Board of Governors of the Federal Reserve System, *Federal Reserve Bulletin* (August, 1954), p. 814.

CLASSIFICATION OF BUSINESS FIRMS

Classification by Type of Industry. Business firms are often classified according to the industry in which they operate or the type of product involved. The statistics presented in Table 4 exclude governmental units, agriculture, and professional service firms. Although many firms produce a variety of commodities, each is counted only once according to its major activity. A person who is self-employed is included if he has a place of business or if he has at least one employee. Approximately 40 per cent of all business firms have no employees, 75 per cent have fewer than 4, and only 5 per cent employ 20 or more. Sixty per cent of all business firms are in the retail trade and service industries, the major industries that serve consumers.[8]

During the last decade, the number of business firms in the contract construction industry and the finance division have shown the greatest percentage increase, and the number of firms engaged in the service industries, wholesale trade, and transportation has increased at a rate above the average for all firms. In the retail trades, the number of firms in the general merchandizing and food fields has declined, but this decline has been more than offset by the increase in the number of service stations, motor vehicle and automobile accessory dealers. The number of firms engaged in manufacturing has increased less than those of other major industries.

Public Utilities and Railroads. Public utility companies are classified according to the services provided, with the chief groups being electric light and power companies, communications companies, electric railroads, and natural and artificial gas companies. Newcomers in the field of communications are radio broadcasting and televising companies. Although the characteristics of these companies vary greatly, all are subject to public regulation by the federal, state, and/or local governments.

While public utility companies provide services or commodities that may be regarded as necessary to the modern way of life, they usually function most economically under conditions of monopoly. Under ordinary conditions of monopoly, they would be in a position not only to discriminate among customers but also to collect exorbitant fees; hence the people, through their legislative bodies, have made provisions for regulation of public utility companies. The problem is "How much regulation?" and this is answered by the courts.[9]

Railroads are similar to public utilities in many respects, being subject to the same type of general regulation by federal and state

---

[8] General service industries include hotels, motels, and other lodging places; laundry, dry cleaning, and garment repair firms; barber and beauty shops; automobile and miscellaneous repair shops; motion picture and other amusement firms; and other personal service firms. See also "Rise in the Business Population," *Survey of Current Business* (May, 1959), p. 16.

[9] The right to receive profits is an essential attribute of property, and if there is a ruling that unduly limits profits, the courts may rule that it is "confiscatory" and therefore illegal. The Fifth Amendment to the Constitution limits the power of the federal government by declaring that no person shall be "deprived of life, liberty, or property without due process of law." The Fourteenth Amendment similarly limits state governments by forbidding states from depriving "any person of life, liberty, or property without due process of law."

governments. Railroads are by far our most important common carriers. The transportation field also includes corporations which operate airlines, water transportation facilities, and pipelines. In addition, there are many supporting service companies. Regulation of railroads and other transportation companies is subject to the same sort of review by the courts as that already noted for public utility companies. Firms in the fields of railroads and public utilities require large capital investments relative to other businesses with comparable annual receipts and employees.

The rapid growth and stable incomes enjoyed by public utility companies has made it possible for them to raise new funds without difficulty in the capital markets. Railroads have been less fortunate in that their incomes have been less stable due largely to competition from other carriers as well as privately owned automobiles, trucks, and airplanes. Modernization of terminals and other buildings and repair of roadbeds has been financed largely with funds from operations accounted for as depreciation allowances. New equipment has been financed in part by the sale of equipment obligations. Wide fluctuations in earnings of railroads make financing with loan capital more hazardous.

At the present time, railroads have main-line mileage and terminal facilities in excess of that needed to care for the trade. This overexpansion could be corrected in part by consolidations which would permit disposition of some facilities and also permit savings in capital outlays and operating expenses. This, however, would not cure all of the ills of the railroads. Many of the rate schedules under which railroads operate are unrealistic and do not permit effective competition with other carriers. Railroads are frequently required to maintain unprofitable passenger and other services, and the railroads are hampered more than most industries by custom and practices which create inefficiencies in operations (featherbedding, etc.). Eventually, the American public may have to choose between a more efficient private operation or a subsidized or public operation of the nation's railroad industry.

Rate regulation of public utility and railroad companies has had an effect on their financial structures and methods of financing. Although companies in these fields are permitted to earn a reasonable return on their investments, they must depend to a greater extent than other large companies on the capital market for new funds (rather than on retained earnings) in order to finance expansion. When long-term debts mature, railroads and public utility companies customarily refinance with new bonds or capital stock issues. In contrast, manufacturing companies may finance expansion to a greater extent with net earnings and retire bonds with assets set aside for this purpose in a "sinking" fund. Although the growth of manufacturing, wholesale and retail trades, and other industries has reduced the relative importance of public utility and railroad companies, the financial problems of these companies are much more important than suggested by the amount of national income which they originate.

Manufacturing Industries. One of the most significant of all changes in the American economy during the present century has been the rapid growth of manufacturing. Since manufacturing corporations account for more than 30 per cent of the national income originating in private sources, the financial well-being of these firms as a group is essential to that of the United States economy. Within the manufacturing industries there are many groups having distinct economic problems which are reflected in their financial policies and capital structures. The most important among the groups in the industrial field are those which manufacture iron and steel products; machinery, except electrical; foods and kindred products; automobiles and automobile equipment; chemicals and allied products; electrical machinery; transportation equipment, except automobiles; textile-mill products; printing, publishing, and allied industries; apparel and other finished fabric products; products of petroleum and coal; paper and allied products; nonferrous metals and coal; stone, clay, and glass products; lumber and timber basic products; furniture and finished lumber products; rubber products; leather and leather products; and tobacco products.

Trades and Other Industries. As a source of national income, the wholesale and retail trades are second only to manufacturing (see Table 2). Over 40 per cent of all business firms are in the retail trades alone (see Table 4). Most of their capital is provided by owners and may be supplemented by funds borrowed from banks and other lenders. While most business enterprises in this field are small, the growth of chain stores has resulted in the creation of firms that are national, regional, and/or state-wide in their scope of operations. These firms are able to finance more easily in both the capital and money markets.

The financial problems of firms in the general service industries are somewhat kindred to those of small retailers. In the aggregate, income from "services" is greater than from agriculture, forestry, and fisheries combined. Some of the service industries are on a personal household basis requiring little or no capital financing; but others require a great amount of capital. The latter include hotels and other lodging places, motion picture theatres, educational services provided by private institutions, hospitals and religious organizations.

Other industries that include private business firms having major financing problems are the building and mining industries. As a source of national income, contract construction companies are almost as important as companies in the transportation field. Although mining is considered a basic industry, incomewise it is the least important of major industries.

SUMMARY

Business finance is a study of the ways whereby private nonfinancial business enterprises organized for profit obtain and use the funds needed for acquiring the assets used in modern business. In recent years, interest in the problems of financing business units has increased because of the increase in size and complexity of business units and the wide public ownership of American corporations. Business finance is of social importance because of the effect of financial developments on national income and our standard of living. While private enterprise is the source of 75 per cent of the gross national income, the government plays an important role by prescribing many of the rules under which business concerns are organized, financed, and operated and by influencing the allocation of resources and national income in many ways.

The business population of the United States consists of over 4,600,000 firms. The chief sources of funds with which they operate are the savings of individuals and institutions, retained earnings, and bank credit. Industries are commonly classified as public utilities, railroads, manufacturing firms, trades, and other industries. As a group, manufacturing companies originate over 30 per cent of the national income. About 60 per cent of all business firms are in the retail trades and service industries where small business units predominate. Business finance deals with both long-term and short-term financial problems of business concerns from the view point of business management. Financial management is involved whether a firm is a sole proprietorship, a partnership, a corporation, or any other form of business organization.

Although the productive system of the United States consists of many separately organized and operated business units, there are vast concentrations in particular industries. Regardless of the size of the business unit, each business firm must acquire and apply funds to its operations. Funds may be obtained from the business itself (internal sources) or may be obtained from outside the business (external sources).

Business firms are commonly classified according to the industry in which they operate or the type of product they produce. Firms in different industries are faced with different problems and even firms in the same industry will have to cope with different problems because of difference in size, capital structure, managerial policies, and other factors. Transportation and public utility companies are subjected to rate regulation which affects both their financial structures and methods of financing.

Manufacturing firms, which account for less than 8 per cent of the total number of business firms, originate more than 30 per cent of national income; while firms in the wholesale and retail trade industries, which account for almost 50 per cent of the total number of business firms, originate less than 17 per cent of national income.

Much has been written about competition between the government (and government owned institutions) and private enterprise; however, in spite of this competition, more than 75 per cent of the gross national income still originates in private sources in the United States. Furthermore, one of the outstanding characteristics of the American economy is the ease of starting a new business. The normal increase in business population is closely related to changes in the gross national product (the market value of the output of goods and services produced by the nation's economy). This means that there will tend to be a net increase in the number of business units when there is an increase in the dollar value of the nation's business.

While the volume of business done by existing firms may increase, it does not follow that their proportionate share of the nation's business will be any greater than it was before the increase in the gross national product. Also important is the fact that there is a place among the giants of modern industry for newcomers in both new and old industries. While growth in size tends to reduce the number of business units, an increase in the division of labor in our modern economy opens new opportunities for enterprising individuals in certain industries. This is demonstrated by the fact that the number of business firms per 1,000 population is now nearly

26½ as compared to 21 in 1900. Nevertheless, in many industries it is not easy for individuals to start new business firms.

QUESTIONS AND PROBLEMS

1. Identify: (*a*) business firm, (*b*) "business," (*c*) business finance.
2. Give reasons for the increase in public interest in the problems of business finance. Discuss each.
3. What conclusions may be drawn from the facts that retail and wholesale trades have the largest number of business units and originate only about 16 per cent of national income, while manufacturing firms which are considerably fewer in number originate over 30 per cent of national income?
4. Why are large firms associated with transporation, public utility, and manufacturing industries, and small firms with service, construction, and wholesale and retail trade industries?
5. Is there justification for the distrust of "big business" sometimes encountered? Are the ethical standards under which "big business" operate as high as those under which small business firms operate? Explain.
6. Distinguish between (*a*) internal and external sources of business funds, (*b*) savings and bank credit as sources of business funds, and (*c*) long-term and short-term sources of funds.
7. What has been the effect of rate regulation of public utility and railroad companies on their financial structures and methods of financing? Is there justification for treating the financing problems of both as a group? Explain.
8. On what basis is the exclusion of financial institutions such as commercial banks, savings institutions, and life insurance companies from the study of business finance justified?
9. Do the statistics of business firms per 1,000 population now as compared with 1900 suggest that there are fewer opportunities for one to start his own business? Explain.
10. Explain: "For the decade beginning January 1, 1950, there was an increase in total business population from 4,009,000 firms to 4,659,000. This is an average net increase of 65,000 new businesses per year . . . Virtually all new businesses established are small businesses."—(*Fourteenth Semiannual Report of the Small Business Administration for the Six Months Ending June 30, 1960* [Washington, D.C.: U.S. Government Printing Office, 1960], p. 7.)
11. "The Company [Houston Lighting and Power Company] asked the Houston City Council last September to grant it rate increases designed to bring in additional revenues . . . Some kind of permanent financing is expected this year . . . The form of the financing will be either preferred stock or debentures instead of common stock. . ." (*Wall Street Journal* [New York], January 18, 1961, p. 10.) Why is it necessary for this company to ask for a rate increase while other firms are free to raise the prices of their products at will?

12. "Failure to adequately share the fruits of technological gains with all consumers . . . because of excessive concentration of corporate and union power, is a most serious problem." ("Romney Urges Sharing Gains with Consumers" [George Romney, president, American Motor Corporation], *American Banker*, January 10, 1961, p. 9.) Comment on this quotation keeping in mind the "sinister" aspect of "big business."
13. Discuss the managerial policies suggested by this statement: "Since 1936, business concerns have been permitted to make tax-deductible contributions to educational institutions. But it was not until after World War II that corporations really became interested in such aid. Now, corporations aid to education is widely considered as a good business investment." (*New York Times*, January 9, 1961, p. 142.)

CHAPTER 2

Legal Forms of Business Organization

THE THREE most common legal forms of business organization are sole or individual proprietorships, partnerships, and corporations. Other types of business organization, such as joint-stock companies, business trusts, associations organized under special state laws, and "estates," are less commonly encountered. Approximately 70 per cent of all business firms in the United States are organized as proprietorships, 18 per cent as partnerships, and 11 per cent as corporations (see Table 5).

This chapter presents statistics of business population classified according to the legal forms of organization, discusses individual proprietorships, partnerships, and corporations, and introduces

TABLE 5

NUMBER OF FIRMS BY TYPES OF ORGANIZATION AND INDUSTRY
(In Thousands)

Industry	*Individual*	*Partnership*	*Corporate*	*Others*	*All Types*
Mining and quarrying	17.6	7.1	7.8	0.8	33.4
Contract construction	219.4	43.4	17.3	0.4	280.5
Manufacturing	149.7	77.9	97.2	5.8	330.6
Transportation, communication and other public utilities	137.5	13.5	22.1	5.9	178.9
Wholesale trade	86.7	49.6	54.3	3.8	194.4
Retail trade	1,201.4	339.2	100.4	15.6	1,656.6
Finance, insurance and real estate	186.6	49.0	76.4	31.7	343.7
Service industries	668.7	111.4	36.2	5.2	821.5
All Industries	2,667.6	691.1	411.7	69.2	3,839.6

Source: United States Department of Commerce, Office of Business Economics, *Survey of Current Business*, Vol. XXXI, No. 6 (June, 1951), p. 10.

some of the tax problems associated with each type of organization. In selecting the legal form of organization under which to operate, the organizers of a business firm should estimate their financial needs and select the form which best satisfies those needs. However, statistics of business population and business transfers indicate that many firms change their form of organization after commencing operations.

INDIVIDUAL PROPRIETORSHIPS

An individual or sole proprietorship is defined as a business enterprise owned exclusively by an individual who makes the decision to enter business, contributes or purchases the original assets, controls the operation of the venture, and assumes liability for the debts of the business to the full extent of his business and personal wealth. The enterprise cannot be completely disassociated from the owner who makes the final decisions as to business organization, policies, and practices. All others working for the business are employees. Individuals may be permitted to share in profits without disturbing their status as employees, but if they are permitted to assume responsibilities other than those for which they are compensated, their status may be treated as that of partners. The legal problem is one of distinguishing between what constitutes an employment contract and what constitutes a partnership agreement. Under provisions of state employment acts, payment of salaries to proprietors or to partners does not make them employees, but both are considered to be self-employed and therefore required to make social security payments.

Ease of Organization. Usually, a proprietorship form of business organization may be formed without legal formalities. Although most fields of business activity are open freely to individuals, in some industries (such as banking) statutes require incorporation. On the other hand, the laws of some states prohibit incorporation of firms offering certain types of professional and other services (for illustration, insurance agencies may not be incorporated in Texas). To an increasing extent, all business enterprises are being regulated and an individual proprietorship is no exception. Before embarking on a business venture, a license is commonly required and there may be inspection fees of various types. Nevertheless, the relative ease of organizing a business as a sole proprietorship is one of the major arguments in favor of this form of business organization.

Managerial Aspects. Since the business activities of a single proprietor are treated as the activities of an individual, the proprietor as a citizen may conduct business in any state in the Union. Thus, the need to qualify in a foreign state (any state other than the one wherein incorporated) is avoided, except when licensing is involved. The nature of services offered, the product manufactured, or the goods sold may be changed at the discretion of the owner (provided the necessary license, if required, may be obtained). In a single proprietorship, managerial decisions may be made promptly rather than being delayed by consulting others. The owner assumes all risks and receives all profits after taxes, and this stimulates his giving full attention to the affairs of his business.

Impermanence of Life. The life of a single proprietorship business is coexistent with that of the owner; when he dies, his heirs become the owners. Often the business will be terminated because legal questions that arise concerning the estate hamper the continued operation of the business by some member of the family. If the business is continued, the need for ready cash to meet the expenses of estate administration plus heavy estate taxes may cause a serious drain on the business assets. A proprietor may carry life insurance to care for such cash needs, but under current laws, premiums paid for life insurance by a single proprietor may not be deducted as a business expense (as is true for corporations). Without provisions having been made for taxes and other estate expenses, the legal representative of the decedent's estate may be forced to liquidate the business assets. Since the market for such property under forced sales is largely confined to competitors who are looking for bargains, usually only a fractional part of the value of the business is recovered.

Problems of Financing. The resources of a single proprietor are limited to the capital he may contribute to the business and the amount he may borrow. Usually, the primary source of new capital is retained earnings, but an individual proprietor may be able to supplement his capital funds by obtaining credit from those from whom he buys (trade credit), commercial and savings banks, insurance companies, finance companies and factors, local and state development credit corporations, and certain governmental agencies (all of which will be considered in later chapters). Proprietors most commonly pledge real estate to obtain funds for long-term needs. In addition to the general assets and earning power of the proprietor (mortgagor), the lender (mortgagee) will have the pledged real estate as security for the loan. The expenses associated with this form of borrowing are considerable since title search, appraisal, brokerage fees, commissions, recording fees, and other charges are included.

Unlimited Liability of Proprietors. In a proprietorship, the debts of the business enterprise are at the same time the obligations of the owner as an individual. He has unlimited liability, and in case his business fails, his home and personal property may be sold by the receiver to meet the obligations of the business. It is the owner who makes contracts, borrows money, and decides on policies; it is the owner (and not the business) who is liable for the results. Of course, a proprietor may avoid some personal risks by keeping title to his home, car, and other forms of valuable property in his wife's name. Although such practices are harmful to the credit standing of the owner, they are not unusual. Because of this situation, creditors often insist on the signatures of both husband and wife on promises to pay. From the viewpoint of the creditor, this has the dual advantage of increasing the volume of personal assets that may be attached in case of failure and of facilitating settlement in case of death of the proprietor.

The statutes of all states provide for exemption of certain kinds of property of debtors from seizure through judicial process for the benefit of creditors. The kinds of property most commonly exempt include homesteads up to a specified valuation; personal property such as household articles, tools, and clothing of a certain value; and wages of employees, laborers, and mechanics up to a certain amount. A debtor may waive his right to exemptions by failure to claim them when filing his schedule of assets or by specifically surrendering them by signing a waiver-note running to a particular creditor. In some states a waiver of exemption may be declared void because it is deemed to be against public policy.

Although it has been claimed that unincorporated business firms have better credit standings because of unlimited liability of the owners, a survey made of interest rates charged by commercial banks shows that the rates for unincorporated firms are slightly higher than for incorporated firms of the same size. It may be that bankers are more impressed by the quality of management of incorporated firms than that of single proprietors or partners, or it may be that bankers are aware of the inherent instability of unincorporated business units due to their limited lives. Under certain circumstances there are tax advantages associated with the single proprietorship form of business organization.

PARTNERSHIPS

A "partnership," as defined in the Uniform Partnership Act, is "an association of two or more persons to carry on as co-owners a business for profit." The amount of property contributed, the risks assumed, and the amount of time and effort spent by each partner in the common undertaking will depend in part upon the type of partnership. Most partnerships are either general or limited partnerships. In a general partnership, all partners are personally liable for all obligations of the firm. In a limited partnership, in addition to general partners there are one or more partners whose liability is restricted to his or their investment in the firm. In a few states, statutory provisions have been made for partnership associations wherein partners have no liability for the debts of their associations beyond their original investments, and in a few other states, provisions have been made for mining partnerships wherein the nature of a partnership is further modified.

Business firms classified as partnerships make provisions for sharing profits and losses, proprietory interests, managerial decisions, and contributions to the capital of the partnership. Other evidence of a partnership organization include the intent of the parties, as indicated by written contracts, and conduct toward strangers, as indicated in public statements, correspondence, letterheads, and life insurance made payable to the partnership as beneficiary. This does not mean that all of the features listed must be present in every partnership. In some cases, a partner may make no capital contribution but may provide services, a patent, or something else of value; in other cases, sole control may be vested in one party without destroying the partnership.

General Partnerships. A general partnership is a common-law form of organization which receives its binding force from general acceptance and precedent as distinguished from statutory law. But, in order to secure greater uniformity among states, the Uniform Partnership Act was drafted by a committee of the American Bar Association and subsequently adopted by most states. The act defines the nature of partnerships; states how a partnership is to be formed, changed, and dissolved; clarifies the relationship among partners, between partners and the firm, and between the partnership and creditors (including the rule of marshaling explained below); and provides for the relationships of incoming and outgoing members and the rights and liabilities of the estates of deceased or bankrupt members.

A general partnership agreement entails a contractual relationship which may be written, oral, or implied, but for most satisfactory results, all partnership agreements should be drawn and signed by all partners. The partnership form of business organization has the advantage of permitting two or more persons to combine their abilities and resources to carry on a business enterprise. Thus a good production man with training in engineering may find it advantageous to have one partner who is a good salesman and another partner who is a good business executive. Even though a single proprietor could obtain managerial skills by employing competent persons, a partnership has the advantage of being able to pool the capital funds of the various partners, and this may contribute to a better credit rating than any one of the partners could attain as a sole proprietor. Partnerships permit the retention of the personal touch in business, but the larger the number of partners, the greater the danger of friction among them.

Each partner is a general agent of his firm and a partnership may be held to business contracts executed by any one of them. While a partnership agreement may limit the authority of a partner, the firm may still be held for a contract made in violation of this agreement if the contractor had had no prior notice of the limitation on the partner's authority. A contract which customarily calls for the signatures of all partners would be an exception. Thus, if a bank loan is made on the signature of only one partner when the usual procedure calls for the signatures of all, the bank's claim against the individual partners would be weakened. Nevertheless, the ability of any one partner, as a mutual agent, to pledge the assets of the partnership and also to involve the personal assets of all partners is a serious hazard assumed by partners. Because of this mutual agency, each partner has the right to approve of persons who are to become partners, known as the right of *delectus personae.* The Uniform Partnership Act permits a partnership to own real estate in its own name, but as a general rule, the partnership is not a separate entity.

Partners are jointly and individually responsible for the debts of the firm, and any agreement among partners as to the liabilities to be assumed in the case of business failure is not binding on the general public. If a judgment obtained against a partnership is not covered by its assets, the judgment may be exercised against the assets of the individual partners. But the individual partners may have personal debts as well as business debts. In this case, the answer by the courts as to who has priority is based on a procedure known as the *rule of marshaling.* Briefly, this rule states that business creditors must first exhaust business assets before they can exercise their claims against the personal assets of general partners, and personal creditors of partners have a claim against personal assets of partners ahead of firm creditors but cannot attach business assets until firm creditors have been paid. Thus, business creditors have priority in seizure of business assets. If personal creditors are satisfied out of personal assets, business creditors may seize and sell any remaining personal assets. If business creditors are satisfied in full out of business assets, personal creditors may seize and sell any remaining business assets.

Unlimited liability is most hazardous to the partner who has a relatively small investment in a business and a large amount of personal assets. A wealthy person should be wary of investing in a general partnership, because in case of business failure, business assets may not cover obligations and the unpaid creditors may seize his cash, securities, home, and other personal assets in amounts sufficient to satisfy their claims. If one partner pays more than his fair share, he may obtain a "right of contribution" from a court of equity against his copartners for the excess, but in practice, this may be meaningless. If a wealthy person is to join a partnership, it should be on a limited partnership basis. However, even this is hazardous because the courts may rule, under certain circumstances, that a limited partnership is a general partnership and that all partners have unlimited liability.

Limited Partnerships. A limited partnership is a business firm consisting of one or more general partners and one or more special, silent, or limited partners. By written agreement the liability of each silent or limited partner is limited to his investment in the firm. Nevertheless, if the contribution of a limited partner is property that has been overvalued (for example by $20,000) by him, he may be held liable for the amount by which it was overvalued in case of business failure. In order to be effective against outside creditors, the provisions of the statutes under which a limited partnership is formed must be followed strictly. All except the states of Arizona and Florida have made statutory provisions for limited partnerships and about thirty states have adopted the Uniform Limited Partnership Act. The limited partnership form of business organization is not new in the United States, having been introduced by the French colonists along with the Civil Law of France. Since limited partnerships are provided for by state laws rather than by federal laws, a limited partnership is such only in the state wherein it is organized. The same firm members may organize a firm under statutes of two or more states, but the firm would be a general partnership in all other states.

In a limited partnership the rights and privileges of each partner must be in writing, and the agreement must be signed by all partners. In addition, this agreement must show specifically the status of each partner, whether "general" or "limited," and the amount of capital or an evaluation of other assets contributed by each. In order to make the agreement binding on outside creditors, a copy must be filed with a designated public official (usually the recorder or county clerk where the firm's main office is located). Usually, the title of the firm must contain the word "limited" or its abbreviation, "Ltd." The Uniform Limited Partnership Act requires that, at the time of organization, the partnership agreement or notice thereof be published a designated number of times in the local newspapers. The purpose of this requirement is to protect creditors of the firm.

The limited partnership form of organization permits participation in business ventures by silent partners—men and women who supply capital resources but who are unable or unwilling to assume managerial responsibilities and unlimited liability associated with general partnerships. The capital contributed by limited partners is important to the firm because it increases the equity of the firm and provides a better credit basis. Although the interest of the limited partner is transferrable, it is less salable than shares of corporations or similar organizations.

A limited partnership may be used as a means whereby young men without capital resources may obtain financial assistance from others without going into debt or incorporating. A limited partnership is sometimes a reorganized general partnership, created when a partner wishes to retire from active participation but desires to maintain his investment in the firm. Only general partners are authorized to sign for the partnership and to transact business, and unless specifically permitted by law, names of silent partners may not be used in a firm's title.

From the viewpoint of the firm, the limited partnership has the advantage of attracting and keeping capital resources that otherwise might not be available; but from the viewpoint of the general partners, the limited partnership offers no relief from unlimited liability for obligations of the business firm. Individuals who are looking for such relief may best incorporate their business or organize a partnership association (see below). The partnership type of business organization is best adapted to businesses where the disadvantages of unlimited liability are small and family ownership is predominant. There are tax advantages associated with the partnership form of business organization which are discussed at the end of this chapter.

Mining Partnerships. A mining partnership is a special type of partnership provided for by the statutes in some states wherein mining and oil drilling are important industries. Unlike the more common forms of partnerships, in a mining partnership an owner may dispose of his interest without the consent of other partners. If a mining partnership is used, one of the partners is usually designated as the manager; he alone may bind all of the other partners to full liability for all debts incurred in the business venture.

The chief advantage of the mining partnership is that it permits a continuity of operations not present in ordinary forms of partnerships. The speculator, who expects a quick return on an oil drilling or mining venture, may sell his interest and move on to another undertaking without disrupting the drilling or mining activity in progress. After a partner has disassociated himself from the partnership, he is no longer responsible for the debts of the partnership and his capital is freed for other purposes. In the meantime, the managing partner is free to operate the firm without disruption because of changes in ownership.

Partnership Associations. A partnership association is a special kind of limited partnership that gives owners limited liability for the debts of the association. Shares are transferable but new shareholders are not entitled to vote without the approval of a majority of the old shareholders. A partnership association is managed by a board of directors elected at the annual meeting of shareholders. Michigan, New Jersey, Ohio, and Pennsylvania are the only states that have statutory provisions for the organization of partnership associations. As in the case of a limited partnership, there is a tendency to treat a partnership association as a general partnership outside the state of origin. For federal income tax purposes, a partnership association is treated as a corporation, therefore this form of organization offers few advantages not possessed by the corporate form of business organization.

Joint Ventures or Syndicates. A joint venture or syndicate is a temporary form of partnership consisting of two or more persons, partnerships, or corporations organized for the purpose of completing a specific undertaking. The joint venture or syndicate is used widely in the fields of real estate and investment banking.

CORPORATIONS

The Corporation, a Legal Entity. A corporation is an artificial person created and endowed by law with some of the rights and privileges of natural persons; hence a corporation is a legal entity distinct and separate from the natural persons who own or manage it. Being a legal entity, a corporation possesses rights and privileges as provided for by the laws of the state under which it is organized and as guaranteed by the Constitution of the United States.[1]

A corporation customarily has the right to buy and sell, to own and hold property, to make contracts, to sue and be sued, and otherwise to exercise the powers conferred upon it in its own name, much in the same way as a natural person. However, these rights may be limited by a corporation's charter. For illustration, it may be limited as to the kinds of things that may be bought and sold, the type of property that may be owned, and so on for other activities.

Although a corporation is treated as an "artificial person," it is not a citizen and does not come under the provision of the Constitution which states that "the citizens of each State shall be entitled to all privileges and immunities of citizens in the several States." So, a corporation that enjoys certain privileges in its state of origin may not enjoy similar privileges in other states without permission of the latter. A corporation is treated as a person under the Fifth and Fourteenth Amendments which prohibit the federal government and state governments from depriving any person of "life, liberty, or property without due process of law." However, a state constitution

[1] In the field of finance, there are many corporations which operate under federal charters as provided for by Congressional acts, and it has been proposed that all corporations engaged in interstate commerce be required to obtain federal charters. Among the institutions organized under federal charters are commercial banks, central banks, mortgage banks, credit unions, savings and loan associations, production credit associations, and foreign banking institutions. Outside the field of finance, there are a few corporations that have federal charters. While some advocate more widespread federal chartering of business corporations, others favor state chartering of all commercial banks as well as business corporations.

may provide that no irrevocable charters be granted and that those granted hereafter shall be subject to the law of the state as amended from time to time.

Being an artificial person, may a corporation like a natural person be guilty of crimes and subject to fines, death, and other penalties? Although agreement is not unanimous, the answer seems to be "yes." While a corporation cannot be placed in prison, it may be fined and its charter may be revoked, which is comparable to the death sentence. In practice, a corporation acts only through its individual agents—directors, officers, and employees—functioning within the scope of their authority. Nevertheless, it is the corporation rather than the agents which receives blame or credit for wage cuts or increases, for poor or good quality goods, and so on. So, the "institutional fallacy" in business, as in government, lives on with mankind—as though it were unimportant—relegated to the background. However, the courts may set aside the legal entity aspect of a corporation and hold the stockholders, directors, and/or officers responsible if the corporation is being used to evade the law, defraud creditors, or in other ways to act contrary to public policy. Thus in some cases, the liability of participants (owners and managers) in a corporation may be no different from that of single proprietors or partners.[2]

The Corporation, a Capital-Raising Device. The corporation has been described as a capital-raising device. The five main reasons why corporations are able to raise millions of dollars in capital funds are (1) the capital of a corporation is divided into shares, (2) owners have limited liability for the debts of their corporation, (3) incorporation permits separation of personal and business debts, (4) corporations may have perpetual charters and long lives, and (5) ownership is freely transferable.

1. The capital of a corporation is divided into shares represented by stock certificates. Each share represents a fraction of the capital (about 1/235,000,000 of the capital in the case of the American Telephone and Telegraph Company). This division of ownership into small units makes it possible for small investors to buy common stock. Shares, the ownership of which entails varying degrees of risk, may be issued to meet the needs of different classes of investors.

---

[2] In the "price-fixing" and "bid-rigging" case involving the electrical equipment manufacturing companies, the companies were fined and many of their executives were given jail sentences (generally thirty days) and also personal fines which are customary in antitrust cases. See *New York Times* (February 7, 1961) pp. 1 and 7.

This ability to issue different classes of stock also permits the management of a corporation to obtain other desired results, such as facilitating control by the use of voting and nonvoting stock.

2. From the viewpoint of investors, the most important feature of the corporate form of business organization is that stockholders generally are not liable for the debts of the corporation. This means that stockholders' personal assets may not be seized by creditors to pay for business debts. Since all business ventures involve some risk, the avoidance of the personal liability risk alone may be sufficient justification for operating a business as a corporation. However, it must be remembered that modern business is carried on to a considerable extent with borrowed funds; if incorporation works to the advantage of stockholders in that their liability is usually limited to the amount of their investment, it may work to the disadvantage of creditors.

When a corporation is liquidated and the assets are not sufficient to meet its obligations, both the creditors and the owners may lose, but losses of stockholders will be limited to their original investment with two possible minor exceptions. Stockholders may be assessed an amount equal to the difference between the par or stated value of the shares and the amount paid for them at the time of issue if less than par or stated value. In some states, statutes also provide that stockholders may be assessed an amount up to but not exceeding the par value of their stock for unpaid wages of labor. The risk involved in the first of these two minor exceptions to the limited liability rule may be eliminated by buying only fully paid and nonassessable stock.

It has been stated that because of the limited liability of stockholders for the debts of their corporations, corporate managers have been reckless in administering the financial affairs of their firms (paying themselves excessive salaries and placing assets beyond the reach of creditors). Although this may have been true in some cases, corporate management has a good record in its treatment of corporate affairs including the interests of creditors and stockholders. In the case of large corporations, the position of creditors has been strengthened by protective provisions in lending agreements which are discussed in detail in later chapters. In the case of small corporations, creditors can usually protect their rights by dictating the terms of loan agreements. For illustration, the limited liability of owners of a small corporation may be nullified in whole or part if the officers and chief stockholders, as individuals, are required to endorse a promissory note of their firm or sign a legal form called a *guaranty* which may be "limited" or "continuing." A limited guaranty is restricted to a particular note or a fixed period of time; a continuing guaranty covers current and future obligations and remains in effect until revoked by the guarantor. The purpose of requiring personal endorsement and/or guarantees is to place the debt-paying ability of another party behind the corporation's obligation.

Corporations may be required to pledge some form of valuable property. If the chief stockholders or officers have made loans to their corporation, a commercial bank may, before making a subsequent loan, require them to subordinate their claims to that of the bank. In case of bankruptcy, the holders of subordinated claims may be required to file them along with other creditors under an agreement that surrenders their portion of the proceeds of the bankruptcy settlement to the bank.

3. For small companies the so-called advantage of limited liability for debts of the corporation may mean little in practice. However, of all incorporated business firms in the United States, about one third are in the retail trades and service industries where the average-size business unit is small. This may be explained in part by the desire of the incorporators to free the business enterprise from the possible crippling effects that might follow if one of the owners were to suffer a severe financial loss. In other words, the real reason for incorporating a small business firm may be to protect the business from the personal debts of owners (rather than the other way around, usually presented in giving the advantages of and reasons for incorporating).

An owner may want to protect his business from personal financial losses caused by (1) death, causing legal fees and estate taxes; (2) judgments resulting from automobile accidents not covered by insurance; (3) divorce and other marital difficulties; and (4) lawsuits and other personal difficulties. Even if the firm is incorporated, personal financial difficulties of an owner may lead to the sale of his stock, and this may have a disturbing effect because of change in ownership; but the assets of the corporation, which have the same status as those of a second party, may not be taken by a stockholder except as provided by law (as in dissolution when owners share on a prorata basis or according to contract if there are two or more classes of stock).

For large corporations, the separation of personal and business debts may be important if a relatively large amount of stock is held by one shareholder. In case of death of such a shareholder, estate and inheritance taxes may necessitate the sale of the stock which would tend to have a depressing effect on its market price and which may cause existing management to lose control of the corporation. There are ways whereby management may anticipate such situations, such as carrying life insurance on such a stockholder in order to have funds to acquire the stock if it is to be sold by the heirs. In some cases, large stockholders avoid estate and inheritance taxes by leaving stock in trust with the income therefrom to be used for educational, welfare, religious, or other semipublic purposes (for illustration the Cullen, Ford, Mellon, and Rockefeller foundations).

4. Corporations are thought of as having a permanent form of organization because most states permit them to have perpetual charters. In states where charters are limited to a definite number of years, they may usually be renewed without difficulty. In fact, corporations are not perpetual and thousands disappear each year because of mergers, consolidations, and voluntary or involuntary dissolution. Thus, what is meant by permanence of existence of the corporate form of organization is that the life of the corporation, unlike that of a proprietorship or partnership, is not legally related to that of owners. Being legal entities, corporations may be held responsible for obligations in their own names entirely, divorced from the uncertainties of human life. This statement should not be interpreted to mean that the death of a key officer, director, or stockholder is unimportant to the affairs of a corporation. In practice, the "permanence of a corporation" simply means that this form of organization tends to be more permanent than other forms. Therefore, incorporation does facilitate financing.

Banks and other lenders seem to show a preference for making loans to business firms organized as corporations, as indicated by the fact that corporations are granted unsecured loans more often than are unincorporated business firms of comparable size. However, factors other than the form of organization are the determinants of whether a business loan will be secured or unsecured. Furthermore, while it is true that lenders may insist that proprietors and partners pledge property and arrange for business insurance to protect them and that chief heirs be co-makers on promissory notes, these same protective devices may also be applied to key personnel of corporations. In the final analysis, the credit worthiness of any business firm depends upon its ability to meet its obligations regardless of its legal form of organization.

5. The use of freely transferable shares permits a stockholder to buy, sell, or dispose of his interest in a corporation without approval of other owners of the corporation (usually not true for general partnerships). This feature of transferable ownership is an important factor in raising large capital funds because many individuals are willing to make only temporary investments in a company. There are a few exceptions to the general rule that stockholders may be free to dispose of their interest in a corporation without the approval of the corporation. In some cases, employees may acquire stock under an employee ownership plan that requires them to sell the stock back to the corporation if and when they cease being employees; in other cases, a stockholder may be required to keep the stock acquired under an "incentive plan" for a specified number of years.

Common stock has no maturity date (assuming the corporation has a perpetual charter); therefore, most individuals would find stock ownership unattractive if title to shares could not be sold freely. Security dealers and brokers provide facilities for buying and selling shares, and this marketability adds much to their investment appeal.

The very ease of transferring ownership may later prove disadvantageous to those initiating and managing a business enterprise. Only by owning and controlling a majority of the voting stock can those who were responsible for promoting and sponsoring the firm during the early stages of its existence be certain of retaining control. The management of a large firm may be able to perpetuate its control in various ways, such as the use of voting and nonvoting stock, the use of trusts, and the wide dissemination of ownership (see below).

It is easy for family-owned corporations to bring other members into the business by gifts and other transfers of stock, but there are clearly defined rules covering the admission of new partners which may militate against admitting other members of a family into a partnership. Compared to partnerships, the corporate form of organization (with limited liability of stockholders) may give more financial security to older owners who wish to become inactive but still desire to retain their investments. While it may be asserted that the limited partnership form of legal organization provides many of the advantages attributed to the corporate form, there is always the possibility that a "limited" partner may be treated as a general partner in a lawsuit or claim against the partners.

Classes of Business Corporations. There are many kinds of corporations, but this text considers only those that meet the test of a business firm as defined in Chapter 1. Agricultural, financial, professional, governmental, and mutual and other non-profitseeking organizations such as churches, private schools, fraternal organizations, athletic and other clubs are excluded.

Business corporations are often classified according to the industry, following the general pattern as summarized in Table 5. In each of these categories, business corporations may be subdivided according to their chief product and/or service. Sometimes they are classified on a geographical basis; for example, railroads may be called "eastern," "western," "northern," or "southern" depending on the territory served. Business corporations are also classified according to the nature of their operations, as operating, holding, and operating-holding or holding-operating companies.

Corporations may be classified according to the place of incorporation, with those chartered within the state of operation being called "domestic" corporations and all others operating in that state being called "foreign" corporations. Sometimes, corporations having charters issued by governments outside of the United States are called "alien" corporations.

Business corporations are also classified according to ownership; those whose stock is widely held are called "public" corporations and those whose stock is held by an individual, a family, or a few individuals are called "private" or "closed" corporations. This classification may be confusing unless one remembers that the reference is to business corporations which by definition exclude those owned by the government.

Only if corporations are small or if the stock is held by a small group are the actual owners in a position to exercise all of their time-honored prerogatives of ownership. For good or for evil, management has passed into the hands of officers and directors or other control groups who are free to pursue policies largely without interference from the "legal" owners. On one hand, this concentration of control may make for greater efficiency, but on the other hand, it may result in the business enterprise being operated for the benefit of managers (as in the case of one tobacco company whose president paid himself a salary of a million dollars a year over the protest of stockholders).

OTHER LEGAL TYPES OF BUSINESS UNITS

Joint-Stock Companies. A joint-stock company, like a corporation, has capital divided into equal shares evidenced by freely transferable certificates and has continuity of existence apart from the lives of its members. But, like partners of a partnership, shareholders of a joint-stock company have unlimited liability and are individually and collectively responsible for the debts of the company. This means that if the obligations of a joint-stock company are not satisfied by liquidation of the business assets, a judgment may be obtained against the property of the individual shareholders.

The chief disadvantage of the joint-stock company is the unlimited liability of shareholders. While this disadvantage may be overcome in part by inserting a clause in each contract stating that the contractor shall look only to the assets of the company for satisfaction, there are many noncontractual types of claims that may arise wherein the shareholder would not be protected; this alone is usually enough justification for organizers to follow the necessary legal procedure called for in incorporation. As a result, joint-stock companies are an uncommon type of business organization in the United States.

The tendency for the federal government to tax joint-stock companies as corporations and for states to pass laws providing for their control has deprived this type of business organization of its two major advantages over corporations—the tax advantage and freedom from regulation. As compared to partnerships and proprietorships, a joint-stock company has the advantages of greater permanence, greater ease of raising capital, and greater freedom for shareholders as evidenced by easily transferable shares.

Business Trusts. A trust is an agreement between a trustor and a trustee whereby title to property is transferred from the trustor to the trustee who holds and manages it in the interest of a beneficiary or beneficiaries. Trusts are widely used in the field of finance, where trust companies and trust departments of commercial banks accept and administer property left in trust for the benefit of individuals, schools, hospitals, and charitable and other organizations. Although there are many other applications of the trust principle, the one of immediate interest to students of business finance is its use to control business enterprises; when so used, it may be referred to by titles such as business trust, Massachusetts trust, express trust, voluntary association, and common-law trust.

Business trusts are organized under deeds of trust which resemble the articles of association of joint-stock companies and the charters of corporations. The trust form of business organization permits a business enterprise to raise capital funds by selling trust certificates to investors. The similarity of trust certificates to stock certificates is so great that investors may be unaware of the fact that they are beneficiaries of a business trust rather than part owners of a corporation. Some business trusts raise funds by public sale of bonds, debentures, and/or notes; hence their financial structures resemble those of corporations.

For the purpose of perpetuating management, the business trust is superior to other forms of business organization. At the time of creation, the promoters may designate themselves as trustees, and this group will be responsible for the operation of the business trust until its termination. If one of the trustees dies or becomes unable to serve, the remaining members of the board of trustees choose his successor. This may be desirable from the viewpoint of the board of trustees, but it may not be desirable from the viewpoint of the shareholders because the business trust may fall into the hands of trustees who, if they do not conduct the affairs of the business properly, are difficult to remove in the absence of malfeasance. In addition, the modern tendency is to levy the same income, franchise, and/or license taxes on business trusts as on corporations, so there is little if any tax advantage in operating as a business trust instead of a corporation.

TAX CONSIDERATION

In selecting the legal form of business organization under which to operate, consideration is given to tax as well as nontax factors. While the amount of property taxes paid does not vary greatly with the legal form of organization and the assessment of fees against a corporation in each state in which it operates is only a minor consideration when choosing the form of organization, there may be considerable variation in the amount of federal income tax liability on business income when operating under different forms of organization.

Ordinary Income. Business income of individual proprietorships and partnerships is treated as personal income of the owners and as such is subject to the progressive tax rates in the federal personal income tax schedule. Currently, the personal income tax for single (unmarried) taxpayers starts at 20 per cent for taxable income above $2,000 and increases to a rate of 91 per cent for taxable income above $200,000. A corporation is treated as a separate taxpayer and is subject to two tax rates—30 per cent of all taxable income plus 22 per cent of taxable income above $25,000.

For purposes of illustration, assume that an unmarried taxpayer has taxable income of $10,000 other than his income from a business of which he is the sole proprietor.[3] If the business produces a net income of $300,000, this is taxed as additional personal income and is subject to the personal tax rate applicable. The additional income tax resulting from business income would amount to $254,280. If the same firm is incorporated and it produces $300,000 of taxable income, the corporate tax liability is $150,500 ($90,000 plus $60,500). If this income after taxes ($149,500) is distributed as dividends to the owner, he would pay an additional personal income tax of $111,707. Total taxes paid on business income would be $262,207. The above illustrates the principle of double taxation. As a general rule, if a business wishes to distribute all of its earnings to the owners, there is a tax disadvantage rather than a tax advantage in operating as a corporation.[4] However, if a business wishes to retain a large portion of its earnings for expansion or other reasons, there will be a tax advantage to incorporation.

The above illustration does not consider the likely probability that the corporation would pay the owner a reasonable salary. The amount paid in salaries to owners is a deductible expense to a corporation and hence escapes corporate income taxation. In fact, if the profits equal the amount paid as salaries, the total tax will be the same regardless of whether or not a firm is incorporated. Although the example used herein is an oversimplification of the problem—it does not, for instance, even consider the effect of possible state income taxes—it demonstrates the need to compare the tax advantages of operating as an unincorporated business with those of operating as a corporation.

Nonincorporated Firms Taxed as Corporations. For a small business firm with taxable income of $25,000 or less, a case can

[3] The assumption of $10,000 of other taxable income eliminates the need of computing personal deductions and other tax adjustments. It does change the tax bracket slightly, but does not alter the principle involved.

[4] Token relief from "double taxation" is permitted in that the first $50 received as dividends from domestic corporations is excluded from income and a limited credit is allowed against income taxes. In the above illustration, both of these credits are applied.

usually be made for being taxed as a nonincorporated business; however, when taxable income is higher, each case must be studied on its merits. For different reasons, a business firm may want to operate as a nonincorporated business even though the tax burden may be greater. Congress has provided some relief in Section 1361 of the Internal Revenue Act of 1954, which permits qualified proprietorships and partnerships with fifty or fewer members to be taxed as corporations. In order for an unincorporated firm to qualify as a corporation for tax purposes, its tangible assets must be a material income-producing factor (most commercial, manufacturing, and similar companies can qualify) or at least 50 per cent of its gross income must be obtained from buying and selling real estate, securities, and/or commodities (that is, they must be brokers or dealers in their fields).[5] In allowing qualified partnerships and sole proprietorships to use the corporate form of business as a tax shelter, Congress recognized another aspect of the tax problem—how business firms manage their incomes.

Tax on Retained Earnings. Congress, in permitting corporations to retain earnings, did not intend that this be used as a device for avoiding personal income taxes on dividends. The Internal Revenue Code provides for a special tax (often referred to as a surplus tax) on retained earnings of corporations if the intent is to avoid personal income taxes on dividends. (The rate is 27½ per cent on the first $100,000 of excess retained earnings plus 38½ per cent on additional amounts.) A corporation may accumulate an earned surplus up to $100,000 over a period of years without penalty, and if there is an accumulation in excess of this amount, the burden of proving that the purpose is tax evasion rests with the Treasury. Assuming that a corporation cannot support its position that an amount of $200,000 is needed but can show that $190,000 is needed, the special tax would be levied on the $10,000. Before reaching the penalty point, the corporation should declare a dividend (this would be taxable as personal income of stockholders).

Corporate Income Taxed as Personal Income. While some qualified unincorporated business firms find it expedient to be taxed as corporations, owners of some corporations prefer to have the taxable income of their corporations taxed but once as personal income. This line of reasoning was accepted by Congress, which changed the

---

[5] Electing to be taxed as a corporation is irrevocable unless there is a change in ownership by more than 20 per cent and permission of the Commissioner of Internal Revenue Service is obtained. The tax on income from personal holdings (dividends, interest, etc.) is levied directly on the sole proprietor or partners.

tax law in the Technical Amendments Act (effective for the first time in 1959) to permit corporate income to be treated almost as if it were personal income. If certain conditions are met and proper election is made, the tax on a corporation's income will be levied on its shareholders in direct proportion to their stock ownership. A corporation which is paying out most of its earnings as dividends may wish to qualify under this provision. Thus the corporate income tax will be eliminated and the burden of double taxation avoided.

The provisions of the Technical Amendments Act of 1958 may benefit owners of some business firms operating as corporations for commercial reasons despite the fact that there may have been tax advantages in operating as sole proprietorships or partnerships. These provisions may also result in incorporation of some business firms which have been operating as proprietorships or partnerships in order to avoid the corporate income tax. That this has actually been the result is shown by the fact that during the first seven months of 1959, over 119,500 new corporations were organized (44 per cent more than during the previous year). One reason given for this surge to incorporate was the change in the tax law that encouraged sole proprietorships and small partnerships to incorporate.

Cost of Fringe Benefits. Owners of business firms consider not only the more obvious advantages and disadvantages associated with various forms of organization but also such items as the tax treatment of "fringe benefits" under differing forms of legal organization. A stockholder of a corporation who works for the corporation is an employee, while a partner in a partnership who works for the business firm is not classified as an employee. Under present law, formal profit-sharing and pension plans are for the benefit of employees, and under qualified plans, the costs are deductible from earnings for federal income tax purposes. Furthermore, an employee pays no tax on the amount of the contribution made by the corporation on his behalf until he starts to draw benefits from the plan. Partners and sole proprietors, being owners instead of employees, do not receive this tax treatment. The same principle applies to premiums paid for group health and accident insurance—more discrimination in favor of the corporation and its employees.

SUMMARY

Business firms are classified in many ways, some of the more common being according to legal form of organization, type of industry, chief product, geographical location, method of operation, and nature of ownership. Legal forms of organization include (1) sole or individual proprietorships; (2) partnerships of various types including general, limited and mining partnerships, and joint ventures or syndicates; (3) corporations, which may be subdivided or classified in a number of ways; and (4) miscellaneous types of organizations. There are advantages and disadvantages inherent in each form of legal organization and these must be considered carefully by the organizers of a business firm when selecting the form under which to operate.

The factors considered by organizers when selecting the legal form of organization include ease of organization, simplicity of management, ease of financing, and liability of owners for the debts of the business firm. After the business firm has been in operation for some time, problems as to changes in management and in ownership may develop. Sooner or later a business firm must give serious consideration to the possibility of lowering its federal income tax liability. At this point, the owners of the firm may decide to change the legal form of organization, elect to be taxed as a corporation if unincorporated, or elect to have the corporate income treated as if it were personal income. Although a small unincorporated firm may qualify as a corporation for tax purposes, incorporation may offer a number of advantages, such as limiting owners' liability for the debts of the firm and giving greater permanence to the business.

While the organizers of a small business firm may have considerable choice as to the legal form under which to organize, a large firm usually finds it necessary to incorporate because of financial, managerial, and tax problems. The corporate form of organization is best suited to raise large sums needed to finance large business firms because new capital may be raised by the sale of capital stock or bonds in the capital market. In addition, corporations usually have perpetual charters and legal entities separate from the individuals who own them; hence, stockholders are not responsible for the debts of their corporations and they may withdraw from ownership merely by selling their shares.

QUESTIONS AND PROBLEMS

1. Note the rights and responsibilities associated with sole proprietorship.
2. Do the financial needs of a business have an influence on those who are selecting the legal form of business organization? Why?
3. (*a*) In terms of the number of business concerns, what is the relative importance of each of the three major forms of business organization

and all others (see Table 5)? (*b*) In what industries are individual proprietorships relatively most important? (*c*) In what industries are corporations relatively most important? Why?

4. From a sample page in the classified section of your telephone book, note the names of the business firms and estimate the number organized as (*a*) individual proprietorships, (*b*) partnerships, and (*c*) corporations.
5. Identify: (*a*) general partnerships, (*b*) limited partnerships, (*c*) mining partnerships, (*d*) partnership associations, and (*e*) joint ventures or syndicates.
6. How does a partnership association differ from the other forms of legal organization? If it has financial advantages over the others, why is it not more common?
7. What are the financing advantages and disadvantages of the sole proprietorship form of business organization?
8. "The limited partnership form of organization permits participation in business ventures by silent partners." What contribution do "silent partners" most commonly make?
9. What is the "rule of marshaling?" What is its financial implication to wealthy individuals participating in general partnerships?
10. Distinguish between (*a*) private or closed corporations and public corporations, and (*b*) domestic and foreign corporations.
11. (*a*) What is meant by "double taxation of corporate earnings?" (*b*) Refer to the example cited in subsection entitled "Ordinary Income," under "Tax Consideration." Compute the personal federal income taxes applicable.
12. "Corporations tend to be more efficient in raising capital for business purposes than are unincorporated business firms." Explain.
13. Discuss the limited liability feature of incorporation from the viewpoint of (*a*) owners, (*b*) creditors, and (*c*) the corporation.
14. What are the advantages of separating personal and business debts from the viewpoint of (*a*) owners and (*b*) the business firm?
15. "Under the Technical Amendments Act of 1958, small corporations may choose to be taxed as partnerships. As a result, there was a record number of new business incorporations during 1959; . . ."(*Fourteenth Semiannual Report of the Small Business Administration for the Six Months Ending June 30, 1960* [Washington, D.C.: U.S. Government Printing Office, 1960], p. 7.) What managerial policy is suggested by this quotation?
16. Explain: "All of the above dividends . . . represent ordinary dividend income and are subject to the Federal income tax and to the $50 exclusion from gross income and the 4% credit against income tax . . ." (The Dow Chemical Company, in *2nd Quarter Dividend Remittance,* Statement to common stock shareholders, January 14, 1961.)

CHAPTER 3

Organization and Management of Corporations

THE CORPORATE form of business organization has become so important that the subject matter of business finance is sometimes limited to a discussion of the financial problems and policies of corporations. Among large business units in most major fields of industry, the corporate form is predominant because the managerial functions of business organizations tend to increase in complexity with increases in size. The managerial organization of a small corporation, however, is virtually the same as that of a proprietorship or partnership, and if the stock of such a corporation is owned and controlled by one person, it differs little from a proprietorship. If the stock of such as corporation is owned by a few individuals who are at the same time directors and officers of the company, their relationship to the firm is essentially the same as it would be in a partnership. In fact, many business firms change their legal forms of organization with little or no change in staff.

ORGANIZATION OF BUSINESS CORPORATIONS

In the United States, most business corporations are organized under state business corporation acts. These have existed in some form since the passage of the first general incorporation act by the state of New York in 1811. Previously, the small number of private business firms organized as corporations (probably no more than 250) operated under charters granted by special acts of state legislatures. During this period, it was assumed by some that only a few kinds of business enterprises—such as banks, insurance companies, canal companies, turnpike companies, and municipal water supply companies—could operate efficiently under the corporate form of organization. In addition, there was a widespread belief that corporations were monopolistic in nature and that their creation was contrary to the public interest. This attitude may be traced, in part, to the fact that most of the charters under which the thirteen original colonies were settled were monopolistic.[1]

In 1804, a decision of the Supreme Court of the United States limited the powers of a corporation to those derived from its charter, reducing the misgivings of those who feared the monopolistic nature of corporations.[2] The state could limit the activities of a business corporation by enumerating in its business corporation act the purposes for which corporations may be organized, and then requiring incorporators of a business to select but a single one of these purposes. In order to keep the business corporation act in line with economic developments, it was necessary for each state's legislature to add new "special purpose clauses" from time to time. All but a few states have abolished this "doctrine of limited corporate purposes" because it was a serious handicap to individual corporations which were expanding along vertical lines and producing a variety of products. In general, corporations may be organized for any purpose not forbidden by law and for as many purposes as the incorporators desire (the general purpose clause). Now the charters are drawn so that they offer little difficulty to corporations wishing to engage in diverse activities.

Customarily, corporations have implied rights which are incidental to the operation of any business. Acts committed outside the scope of a corporation's charter, called *ultra vires* acts, may be binding on the corporation. Thus a court may uphold certain acts of a corporation even though some interested party, such as a stockholder, may claim that the corporation had no authority to so act

---

[1] The trading and colonization companies that had charters giving them monopolistic trading and colonizing privileges in the New World (with the date of the first charter in parenthesis) included London Company (1606), Plymouth Company (1606), The Council of New England (1620), The Governor and Company of Massachusetts Bay (1629), The United East India Company (1602), New Netherlands Company (1614), The Dutch West India Company (1621), and the New Sweden Company (1637). Individuals also shared monopolistic privileges with chartered companies in the New World. They included Sir Walter Raleigh (1584), Cecilius Calvert (1632), William Penn (1681), the Earl of Clarendon and seven other proprietors—"Grant of Carolina"—(1663), and James Oglethorpe (1732).

[2] *Head & Amory* v. *The Providence Insurance Co.*, 2 Cranch 127, 2 L.Ed. 229.

(sell bonds, purchase a plant, etc.). By the same reasoning, the courts may require corporate management to fulfill certain contracts even though having entered into such contracts may have been outside the scope of the corporation's authority.

The general purpose clause has extended the capacity of corporations and has reduced the importance of the *ultra vires* principle. Now, some modern business corporation laws contain provisions such as "all corporations shall have and possess general corporate capacity and want of such capacity shall never be made the basis of any claim or defense at law or in equity." Such provisions tend to eliminate "the doctrine of inherent incapacity" and to increase the corporation's responsibility toward the general public.[3]

Over the years, legislation has tended to broaden the powers and privileges of corporations and to make incorporation easier; however, the chief reason for the increase in the number of corporations has been the economic growth of the United States. The greatest rate of increase in the number of corporations took place around the turn of the century. This increase was due primarily to the development of transportation and national markets, the growth in manufacturing industries, and the development of financial markets for securities of business corporations. In the current century, the trend toward large-scale enterprises appeared in the wholesale and retail fields without abating in others. As a result, the corporation became the typical form of business organization for big business in the United States as well as in other industrial countries such as Canada and Great Britain. Passage of the Technical Amendments Act of 1958 has increased the popularity of the corporate form of business organization among small business firms.

THE CORPORATE CHARTER

In most states, three or more natural persons, twenty-one years of age or older, may act as incorporators of a business concern. Customarily, incorporators use a standard form provided by the appropriate state official (usually the Secretary of State). When com-

[3] Nevertheless, the use of "lack of authority" as a defense or claim may be asserted by shareholders (1) against the corporation to enjoin the doing of any act or acts such as the transfer of real or personal property by or to the corporation, and (2) in suits against incumbent or former officers or directors of a corporation for exceeding their authority. Likewise, the State, through the Attorney General, may use the "lack-of-authority" argument in action to dissolve a corporation and to enjoin a corporation from transacting unauthorized business.

pleted and approved, this standard form becomes the "charter" of the corporation.

Articles of Incorporation. Customarily the articles of incorporation must contain the name of the corporation; purposes (types of business) for which the corporation is formed; period of duration, which may be perpetual; shares of stock, and classes thereof, which are to be issued; post office address of the initial registered office; name and address of each incorporator and also of the original board of directors, if required; statement that the corporation shall not commence business until at least a stated amount has been paid in cash, property, or labor for shares issued ("commencement capital"); and other provisions, not in conflict with the basic law, that the incorporators wish to include in the articles of incorporation.

If the Secretary of State finds that the articles of incorporation conform to the law, he collects the required fees; indicates on each of the forms received the month, day, and year "filed"; issues a certificate of incorporation (the charter), to which he affixes one of the endorsed copies of the articles of incorporation, and gives it to the incorporators or their representatives; and files the second copy of endorsed articles of incorporation in his own office.[4] Upon issuance of the certificate of incorporation, corporate existence begins; however, merely receiving a franchise (the right to be) is not enough to meet the legal requirements of modern business corporation acts. Usually a corporation is prohibited from doing any business or incurring any indebtedness (except that incidental to its organization) until it has received the amount of value stated in the articles of incorporation for the issuance of shares ("commencement capital"). Failure of the board of directors to adhere to this rule makes the directors liable for that part of the capital not paid in.

The last step provided for in the formation of a business corporation is the organization meeting of the board of directors. If the original board of directors is named in the articles of incorporation, the first meeting of the board is called by the incorporators. If the original board of directors is not named in the articles of incorporation, the incorporators call a meeting of the original shareholders for the purpose of selecting the board of directors. In either case the basic responsibility for selection of officers and getting the corporation functioning rests with the board of directors.

---

[4] In some states, copies of the articles of incorporation will be filed in the recording office of the county in which the chief office of the corporation is located.

Nature of Charter. A corporation's articles of incorporation, after proper certification, constitute its authority to do business and is commonly referred to as its charter. To say that it is the grant or guarantee of rights may be misleading because business corporation acts do not require that corporate powers be enumerated in the charter. In its broadest sense, the charter of a corporation consists of the certificate of incorporation together with the limitations and modifications thereto imposed by the constitution of the state of incorporation, the Constitution of the United States, and the state and federal statutes passed pursuant thereto.

A business corporation charter is, in effect, a contract between the corporation and the state. If and when this contract is to be changed, the consent of both parties is usually required. Providing that legal requirements are met, the role of the state is largely passive. In practice, state business corporation acts usually contain provisions whereby a corporation may amend its charter by following about the same procedure as that required for original incorporation (that is, filing the properly approved documents with the Secretary of State and paying the registration fee). To protect the rights of existing shareholders, an amendment will have had the approval of the required number of shareholders (usually two thirds) entitled to vote thereon.[5]

While business corporation acts contain provisions whereby corporations may amend their charters freely, sight must not be lost of the fact that state legislatures usually insert a "reservation of power" clause into the law (such as, "The legislature shall at all times have power to prescribe such regulations, provisions, and limitations as it may deem advisable, which regulations, provisions, and limitations shall be binding upon any and all corporations subject to the provisions of this Act and the Legislature shall have power to amend, repeal, or modify this Act at pleasure"). This "reservation of power" clause virtually gives state governments power to amend the charters of corporations. However, if the law is changed to the disadvantage of existing corporations, it may be tested in federal courts under the "due process clause" contained in the Fourteenth

---

[5] Business corporation acts also contain provisions covering procedures for (1) merger of domestic corporations wherein one corporation absorbs the other, (2) consolidation of domestic corporations wherein a new corporation absorbs the assets of the old corporations, (3) merger or consolidation of domestic and foreign corporations, (4) voluntary dissolution of a corporation either by incorporators before it has commenced business or by consent of shareholders, and (5) involuntary dissolution by the decree of the appropriate court.

Amendment. Despite the enactment of "reservation of power" clauses, the sanctity of the corporate contract (established in the Dartmouth College case, 1819) has not been nullified.

Choice of State of Incorporation. Usually, a small corporation will find it advantageous to incorporate in the state in which it plans to operate. As might be expected, New York, because of its economic prominence, issues more charters than any other state. However, large corporations, certainly those which plan to operate in several states, ought to choose the state which offers the greatest advantages. The promoters of corporations such as United States Steel, General Electric, General Motors, and others that were first organized as holding companies may have been influenced by provisions in a state law permitting one corporation to own stock in another. At one time this was one of the main reasons for choosing New Jersey or Delaware as the state of incorporation; but, because revisions of states' business corporation laws have broadened the general powers of most business corporations to allow such stock ownership, this reason is declining in importance.

Greater uniformity among states' business corporation laws and increased federal regulation of financing, accounting, and other practices of corporations have reduced the advantages obtained from incorporating in one state as opposed to another. Also, a model business corporation act, drafted by the Committee of the American Bar Association, has influenced states' business corporation acts and tended to make them more uniform. The financing of public utilities, railroads, and other corporations have been greatly changed by a series of acts passed by Congress during the years following the depression of the early 1930's. Some of these laws, those which are pertinent to our subject, are discussed in later chapters.

The movement toward standardization of legal requirements does not mean that the choice of the specific state in which to incorporate is unimportant. For illustration, Corn Products Company shifted its charter from New Jersey to Delaware at the time (1959) it merged with Best Foods. The company desired to operate under the "more clearly defined" corporation provisions as set forth in the Delaware Code of 1953, as amended. In addition to certain procedural advantages, management stressed certain tax savings and the avoidance of the escheat laws in New Jersey (which permits the state to take into custody cash obligations such as dividends, interest, and wages which have been unclaimed for five years). Since 1900, corporations doing a national or regional business have favored Delaware, Maryland, and New Jersey as states in which to incorporate for various reasons.[6]

Since the early 1930's, Congress has made additional provisions for regulation of large business units, including requirements to disclose information when financing in the open market and to make reports when securities are listed on national securities exchanges. In addition, provisions have been made for national supervision and for more stringent regulation of communications companies and railroads and other transportation companies. At various times, bills have been introduced in Congress which would require federal incorporation of large corporations. A law which would set standards for the organization and operation of all large companies would be advantageous; but, for political reasons, the present system will probably be continued (state chartering and federal regulation of financial and other practices of a business firm).

The modern trend among states is to enlarge the powers of tax officials to levy taxes on foreign corporations on the business done in the state; hence, the tax advantages of financing in certain states is no longer as great as it had been in the past. Some corporations which have outgrown their charters shift incorporation to one of the favorite states. Presumably, corporation lawyers are influenced less by differences among states' corporation taxes and fees than by factors such as a friendly and tested legal atmosphere, location in an industrial state, proximity to New York and Washington, customs and their own backgrounds and experiences, and recommendations of boards of directors or stockholders.

Choice of Corporate Name. One of the first legal steps in incorporation is to file "An Application for Reservation of Corporate Name" with the Secretary of State or a state official serving in the same capacity. Because of court decisions and statutes, there are rules that must be followed in selecting a corporate name. Customarily, the corporate name (1) must contain the word or abbreviation of the word *corporation, company, incorporated,* or *limited* in its title; (2) shall not be the same or deceptively similar to the name of a domestic or foreign corporation registered in the state—or one in process of being formed or registered; and (3) shall not

---

[6] For summaries of state laws pertaining to tax codes, look under *Tax Systems* in the most recent publication of Commerce Clearing House, Inc., Tax Research Department.

contain any word or phrase which would indicate or imply that the corporation is organized for purposes other than those stated in the articles of incorporation.

Usually, the corporate name is selected to indicate one or more of the following: name of the owners, incorporators, or someone related to the business currently or in the past (to give a personal touch)—for illustration E. I. du Pont de Nemours & Company and Richard D. Irwin, Inc.; name of the product or nature of the business (so that the company and product will be thought of simultaneously)—for illustration Bulova Watch Company, Incorporated, Ideal Cement Company, General Motors Corporation, and General Electric Company; and area served or geographical location of the corporation—for illustration Western Massachusetts Company, Oneida, Ltd., and The North American Company. Names of corporations frequently emphasize two of the above—for illustration Libbey-Owens-Ford Glass Company, California Ink Company, Inc., and The Dow Chemical Company. Sometimes names will emphasize all three —for illustration Ford Motor Company of Canada, Loew's Boston Theatres Company, and United States Hoffman Machinery Company.

Draft of Bylaws. The bylaws are the secondary laws or regulations made by a corporation, an association, or an unincorporated society. In the absence of charter or statutory provisions, stockholders have the exclusive right to enact bylaws, but the statutes may vest this power in the board of directors unless reserved to the shareholders in the articles of incorporation. The original bylaws are usually drafted by a lawyer and may contain any provisions for the regulation and management of the affairs of the corporation which are not inconsistent with the articles of incorporation, the business corporation act under which the corporation is organized, and the state and federal constitutions. The bylaws may limit the powers of the corporation but may not extend the powers beyond those found in the articles of incorporation and the law. Although there are no legal forms that must be followed in drafting bylaws, there are statutory provisions that must be followed with reference to rights and privileges of shareholders; the number, election, filling of vacancies, responsibilities, and so on for the board of directors; appointment of officers; and handling of certain financial affairs of the corporation. Provisions required or permitted by a business corporation act may appear in the bylaws or in the articles of incorporation.

Bylaws customarily contain details providing for the location of offices and places for the transaction of business; annual and special meetings of stockholders which includes such details as notices, qualification of voters, number constituting a quorum, and methods of voting; number of directors, term of office, directors' meetings, and limitation on powers of directors; standing committees; designation of officers and their functions; form of stock certificates, method of transfer, stock records, and other routine matters pertaining to the issuance and transfer of shares; definition of the fiscal year, time for dividend payments, restrictions on salaries and other matters pertaining to the financial affairs of the corporation; provisions for amendments; and any additional provisions. The bylaws, together with the charter, constitute the managerial and operational plan of a corporation.

STOCKHOLDERS OF CORPORATIONS

Provisions for governing corporations have been compared to those of cities, states, and other political subdivisions, but the analogy best fits the city manager form of government. Stockholders, as voters, elect the board of directors, who in the city manager form of government would correspond to the city council. As a group, the board of directors is responsible for managing the affairs of the corporation. The members of the board of directors choose one of their number as the chairman of the board of directors, who corresponds to the mayor in the city manager form of government. The board of directors is responsible for selecting the chief executive, the president, who corresponds to the city manager in the city manager form of government. The selection of other executive officers will vary, being delegated to some extent to the chief executive and subject to confirmation by the board of directors—or city council.

Stockholders. A stockholder is a holder of record of shares in a corporation (the record of this must be written or printed). Customarily, a stockholder's interest is evidenced by a certificate signed by the president and the secretary of the corporation.[7] If there are several classes of stock or shares, modern business corporation acts customarily require that the certificates, representing each class, state the relative rights of the owners either on the face or back. In addition, the stock certificate usually shows the name of the state

---

[7] Sometimes, the business corporation may permit a vice-president and assistant secretary to sign in place of the president and secretary. Usually, facsimiles of officers' signatures are permitted and may be used when certificates are countersigned by a transfer agent or registrar other than an employee of the corporation. Otherwise, the issuance of new stock certificates resulting from a stock dividend or a new issue might be delayed for months.

under whose laws the issuing corporation is organized, name of the person to whom issued, and the par value of each share represented by the certificate or a statement that the shares are without par value.

For the purpose of determining the stockholders entitled to vote and to receive dividends, when declared by the board of directors, a corporation or its agent keeps a stock transfer book containing the names of all stockholders to whom it has issued stock certificates. In order to prevent fraud, the New York Stock Exchange requires that the transfer of title be certified to by a trust company (called the registrar) located in Manhattan for all securities traded on the New York Stock Exchange.

The stock transfer book is seldom up-to-date because many shares are being bought and sold daily on stock exchanges or in the over-the-counter market. If a stockholder sells his stock, a new certificate is issued to the new stockholder and the old certificate is cancelled. In some cases, title to a stock certificate may be kept in the name of a broker or dealer ("street name") in order to facilitate trading in the security (such as buying and/or selling on margin). For voting and dividend payment purposes, the bylaws of a corporation usually provide a record date and the closing date of the transfer book so that the list of those entitled to vote and receive dividends may be prepared in advance. The stock records of a corporation are open to inspection by stockholders.

Stockholders' Meetings. Stockholders' meetings may be held at the registered or principal office of the corporation or at such places within, or outside of, the state of origin as permitted by the state's business corporation act and as provided for in the bylaws of the corporation. There are two kinds of stockholders' meetings: "annual" and "special." The day for the annual meeting is specified in the bylaws and may be, for example, "the fourth Tuesday in April." Annual meetings are held for the purpose of selecting new directors, hearing reports of officers, answering questions of stockholders, and voting upon matters brought before the stockholders.

Special meeting may be called by the holders of no less than one tenth (or some other specified percentage) of the shares entitled to vote at the meetings, the board of directors, the president, or such officers or persons as may be designated in the articles of incorporation or bylaws. If a special meeting is to be held, the purpose or purposes for which it is called must be indicated. Such meeting may be called to secure approval of a new stock issue or some other proposal of the board of directors that necessitates action prior to the next annual meeting. The business corporation act prescribes that, in order to conduct business, a quorum (usually a majority) of shareholders must be present or be represented by proxyholders.

Provisions for Voting. Under common law, each shareholder has one vote irrespective of the number of shares owned, but this method of voting is not in keeping with the risks assumed in stock ownership of business corporations. Therefore, modern corporation law usually provides that each outstanding share is entitled to one vote if it is not of a class of stock that is denied the right to vote by the articles of incorporation, as it may be for preferred stock. This method of voting prevents minority representation on the board of directors, because a group owning or controlling 50 per cent of the voting shares plus one can elect its slate of candidates for directors.

In some states, statutory provisions are made for cumulative voting (also by the federal government for national banks) in order to give minority stockholders representation on boards of directors if they want to use this voting privilege. In cumulative voting, a stockholder may cast votes equal to the number of shares held (assume 100), times the number of directors to be elected (assume 10), for any one candidate (thus, 1,000 votes), or he can divide them among two or more candidates. If we assume that there are 1,000 shares of voting stock outstanding, the stockholder owning 100 shares could elect himself or his candidate to the board of directors. By taking the number of votes to be cast times the number of directors to be elected, a stockholder or group of stockholders could compute how best to prorate their votes among candidates so as to elect the largest possible number of directors.[8]

Generally, management is opposed to cumulative voting because it favors special groups and does not represent the interest of all stockholders indiscriminately. Sometimes cumulative voting permits a minority group to elect a majority of the directors, which is not the intent of the cumulative voting provision. In order to accumulate votes intelligently, a group must have an estimate of (1) the

---

[8] To insure election of one director, a stockholder or group of stockholders must have the number of votes computed as follows:

$$\frac{\text{Number of voting shares} \times \text{Number of directors to be elected}}{\text{Number of directors to be elected plus 1}} \text{ plus 1 (one).}$$

If 1,000 shares are to be voted and ten directors are to be elected, a minimum of 910 votes will be needed to elect one director.

$$\left(\frac{1{,}000 \times 10}{10 + 1} + 1 = 910\right).$$

number of shares that will be voted (in person and by proxy), (2) how the independents will vote, and (3) the plan of the opposition as to accumulating votes. It is possible under cumulative voting to give one candidate so many votes that those votes in excess of the number needed for election would have elected a second candidate. Foreknowledge of the extent to which independents are supporting a candidate would permit diversion of votes to other candidates. In case no prior list of candidates is prepared and there is no knowledge that some shareholders plan to cumulate their votes, management may spread its votes over its slate of candidates and end up with minority representation on the board of directors.

Cumulative voting is not the usual procedure and the wisdom of authorizing it has been questioned. Some states have repealed their laws requiring mandatory provisions for cumulative voting by business corporations. While better representation is usually desirable, it is not necessarily assured by selecting board members from minority groups; such board members may have few of the characteristics which would qualify them for directors. There have been instances in which such directors seemed to take the position that they were obliged to disagree with management regardless of the merits of the issues.[9]

Proxies. A shareholder may vote in person or by proxy (one who is authorized to act for another). In corporation law, it is customary to provide that a proxy must be in writing and properly signed by the stockholder or by his duly authorized attorney-in-fact. Management usually solicits proxies from shareholders for each meeting in order to assure enough representation to hold an official meeting, to obtain votes to support managerial policies, and/or to elect directors who have been nominated by them. Under the terms of the Securities Exchange Act of 1934, the Securities and Exchange Commission regulates the conditions under which proxies may be solicited by mail or other channels of interstate commerce.

Although regulations of the commission pertaining to solicitation of proxies have changed from time to time, they do include these requirements: (1) a clear statement identifying the solicitor of the proxy (usually this is the existing management); (2) names of auditors to be named at the meeting for which the proxies are being solicited; (3) a statement of matters that the minority interests are

---

[9] See also Leland C. Whetten, *Cumulative Voting for Directors: Its Origin and Significance* (Atlanta: Bureau of Business and Economic Research, Georgia State College of Business Administration, 1959).

expected to raise at the proposed meeting; (4) a statement as to the action management proposes to take on items affecting officers and directors (such as profit-sharing plans; bonus, pension, or retirement plans; and rights or options to purchase securities) and a space to indicate how the proxyholder is to vote; (5) names of officers, directors, and members of the nominating committee and data on the cost of soliciting proxies; and (6) information about stockholdings and about the slate of candidates for directorship.

Customarily proxies are solicited only by management, however, a stockholder may appoint any person planning to attend a meeting to vote his shares.[10] Sometimes, one or more groups other than management may solicit proxies, although without strong financial backing, such groups are usually unsuccessful in their attempt to obtain enough votes to elect their own candidates for directorship. Corporations pay the expenses of soliciting proxies for management—but not for minority groups. In a "proxy fight," such as the successful one in 1954 to gain control of the New York Central Railroad by Robert R. Young and associates, the expenses of soliciting proxies may run into millions of dollars.

Prior to the stockholders' meeting, a minority group will need to control or acquire a relatively large block of stock. This may necessitate purchasing shares at relatively high prices which would add to the cost of obtaining control. If and when there is a change in management resulting from a successful proxy fight, it is more often due to having the support of a few large stockholders than to obtaining the support of small stockholders who traditionally follow management. However, if small stockholders hold the balance of power, a strong appeal may be made to them through newspapers, pamphlets, and letters; in some cases, use is made of proxy soliciting firms.[11]

---

[10] In 1959, in a move to strengthen stockholders' rights, the New York Stock Exchange ruled that all "actively operated" companies listed on the Exchange (excluding nine railroads operated under lease and two companies operated by trustees classified as non-operating) must solicit proxies from shareholders and allow them to vote on matters to be considered at the annual meeting. Previously, 28 companies did not solicit proxies and stockholders could vote only by going to the meetings or by finding their own proxies to represent them. There is no ruling by the Securities and Exchange Commission requiring proxies to be solicited. *Wall Street Journal* (New York), April 3, 1959, p. 20.

[11] Proxy fights are usually most common during depression years, and the record number in 1958 was attributed not only to the business recession but also to the publicity given proxy fights in recent years. Charges of violation of proxy rules by both sides usually leads to court action and delays which are to the advantage of one or the other group. Some proxy fights are compromised and result in split boards of directors. A partially successful fight is often followed by another proxy fight the next year. *New York Times*, January 12, 1959, p. 81.

Proxies are printed with spaces for the signatures of stockholders and for marking "for" or "against" votes on matters to be voted upon at the proposed meeting (see Illustration 1). If no preference is indicated, a committee for management customarily votes as indicated in the proxy statement. In recent years, corporate management has frequently requested stockholders to vote on matters pertaining directly or indirectly to remuneration of personnel (such as bonus and stock option plans, and pension and retirement plans) and to changes in capitalization of corporations. As a result of proxy regulation by the Securities and Exchange Commission, many items

ILLUSTRATION 1

SHAREHOLDER'S PROXY

Libby, McNeill & Libby SOLICITED BY MANAGEMENT

PROXY FOR 1959 ANNUAL MEETING

The undersigned hereby appoints Charles S. Bridges, John B. Iglehart and Brooks Whitehouse or any of them, proxies, with full power of substitution, to vote all of the stock of the undersigned at the annual meeting of stockholders of Libby, McNeill & Libby to be held at 57 Exchange Street, Portland, Maine, on Wednesday, September 16, 1959, and at any and all adjournments, (a) for the election of directors, (b) for ( ) or against ( ) the proposed Stock Option Plan and the related amendment to the charter of the Company providing that the shares issued under the Plan need not first be offered to the holders of common stock, and (c) according to the discretion of the proxies on any other business that may properly come before the meeting.

Unless contrary instructions are indicated, the proxies are to vote in favor of proposal (b).

Dated ...., 1959 Please Sign Here } ....
....

Please sign name as shown on reverse side. If joint tenants, all should sign.

appear on proxy statements at the request of minority groups. These have included such things as proposals to limit officers' salaries, to limit pension benefits, to have a woman director, to have regional meetings of stockholders, and to permit cumulative voting.

BOARD OF DIRECTORS

Legally, the board of directors of a business corporation manages the corporation's affairs. The directors, collectively, act for the corporation under powers found in the articles of incorporation, bylaws, and statutes, and those established by custom. The board of directors operates under some of the legal rules pertaining to trusteeships and under others applicable to agents. Directors are expected to act in good faith, to exercise ordinary care, and to show prudence and diligence in the management of the corporation's affairs.

Corporation law customarily states that the board of directors must "manage" the corporate affairs of the company, but this principle is a legacy of the past, when corporations were small and owned by a few stockholders who were at the same time either directors and officers of their company or relatives and friends of the chief executive. The position of the board of directors of public corporations has changed from that of "managers" to that of "advisors," with active management delegated to executives. Nevertheless, directors must "direct" or be held legally responsible for the mistakes of their corporations. A board of directors "directs" the affairs of their corporation by selecting the chief officers, backing up their decisions, specifying the powers and duties of the chief officers in the bylaws or by resolution of the board of directors, determining salaries of officers and principal employees, deciding major policies for the corporation, and following up to see that the desired results are obtained.[12]

A director is supposed to act in the interest of his company, to represent the stockholders, to guide management, and to refrain from unwarranted personal gain at the expense of the company merely because he is a director. A director need not be a technical expert in regard to the affairs of the company, but he is expected to show the same prudence that an ordinary man exercises in the management of his financial or business affairs.

Directors of most corporations are elected annually, but they are customarily re-elected; consequently, the tenure of their directorship is indefinite. Usually, a board of directors will have but one vacancy each year; more vacancies may occur due to dissension within the board. Nevertheless, death, illness, resignation, and other factors cause the composition of any board of directors to change substantially over a period of ten or fifteen years. A common complaint about boards of directors is that too many board members are too old. As a result, some corporations have a compulsory retirement age which is usually older (70) for board members than for officers and employees (65). Former executives may then be kept on the board after they have been retired as officers, although one danger in having too many directors above the age of 65 is that death or illness may cause too many vacancies during a relatively short period.

In recent years an increasing number of corporations have provided for terms of office of directors of more than one year and for

[12] Sidney J. Weinberg, "A Corporation Director Looks at his Job," *The Harvard Business Review*, Vol. XXVII, No. 5 (September, 1949), pp. 585–93.

staggered terms so that only a specified number of directors are elected each year. For illustration, the term of office of Corn Products Company directors is three years, with one third of the fifteen directors elected each year. Thus, the majority of the directors will have experience in their positions. This procedure in selecting a board of directors is also important in perpetuating management's control when challenged by minority groups through the means of cumulative voting. Except for three states whose laws require annual election of directors, classified boards—those resulting from staggered elections—have wide legal sanction, and the laws permitting classified directorates are of long standing (Maryland, 1868; Illinois, 1871; and Pennsylvania, 1887).

As in politics, a successful candidate for the board of directors must have the support of some powerful group; in the case of corporate elections, successful candidates are usually those nominated by and supported by existing management and large stockholders. Management usually wants directors who can help the corporation and may consider such problems as achieving a balance between "inside" and "outside" directors when selecting the slate of candidates to be elected.

Inside directors are those who are active officers of the corporation; all others are classified as outside directors. The advantages claimed for having inside directors are these: they are best informed as to the details of the business and so are in the best position to make policy decisions; with key executives on the board, the various functions or divisions of the business will be represented at board meetings; the presence of key executives when decisions are made will prevent any misunderstanding as to their meaning when such decisions are executed; since key executives have full-time positions with the corporation, they will be on hand whenever meetings are called; inside directors have but one position and one loyalty, and therefore their primary economic interest will be the corporation's well-being; and the loyalty and executive position of key officials will be strengthened by making them directors.

While the foregoing arguments in favor of a board of directors made up of "insiders" are impressive, they reflect misunderstanding as to the functions of a board of directors. The administrative danger is that "log-rolling" and "pork-barrel" decisions may result when insiders pass on the affairs of a particular department. There may be lack of constructive criticism from other inside directors for fear of retaliation, and if directors are critical, there might be factional fights among different groups. In either case, a decline in efficiency would tend to result. All directors should be on the same footing when voting, but when a board is made up of "insiders," a director may hesitate to oppose policies favored by another director who is his superior in the corporation. From the viewpoint of shareholders, the most dangerous aspect of having "insiders" determine the corporation's policies without review by impartial directors is that directors may use the corporation for selfish purposes to the detriment of stockholders. Employee-directors not only determine their own salaries, pensions, and other forms of remuneration, but also pass upon their own qualifications to be retained as officers. Even when a corporation has no public shareholders, there may be need for outside directors who feel a responsibility to customers, employees, and others.

Since World War I, representatives of management on boards of directors have increased; however, at the present time, a trend toward selecting more outside directors seems to be developing. Recently, some oil companies have placed outside directors on their boards for the first time. In general, manufacturing corporations' boards of directors have more employee-directors as members than do nonmanufacturing corporations' boards of directors.

The motive behind selecting "big names" to serve as members of corporations' boards of directors is to add prestige to the corporation. However, this "window-dressing" practice is objected to because such members tend to be so overburdened with directorships and other activities as to make them ineffective as directors. It would be well for most corporations to have a plan whereby any director unable to attend meetings and to perform other functions effectively would be retired automatically. It has been recommended that corporations use the services of "professional" directors who would give all of their time to being directors of one or more corporations and who would be paid for their services. In Great Britain, where professional directors are used widely, it is claimed that they have a broader point of view and are less involved in factional strife than inside directors.

Small corporations interested in obtaining the advice of "experts" sometimes place them on their boards of directors. Such companies probably have more to gain from outside directors than do large companies. The fees paid to directors are small; if a company can obtain the advice of accountants, advertising men, architects, bankers, engineers, lawyers, and real estate men in exchange for placing them on the board of directors, it may be advantageous to do so. Actually, there is no reason for a member of a board to provide his professional services at less than cost to a firm on whose board he sits. In fact, the reverse is often true; there are many firms which find themselves handicapped by having a particular attorney, accountant, or banker because he is a member of the firm's board. In most instances, a business firm will find it advantageous to hire experts as the need arises and ask its board to perform only its traditional role of policy making. Sometimes corporate management has no choice but to accept representation of creditors on the board of directors. Commercial and investment bankers often make representation on the board of directors a condition of making a loan or underwriting a bond issue of a corporation.

The need for better human or public relations has been advanced as a reason for selecting directors to represent groups whose good will is essential to the well-being of a corporation. When financing with credit, the practice of having banker or underwriter representation on the board of directors has been noted; there may be just as much need for obtaining the goodwill of other groups such as labor, customers, suppliers (who advance trade credit), the government, and women. The assumption is that better relations will result when special groups are aware of the problems of management and the progress of the company. The main objection to these arrangements is that favoritism may be shown to the disadvantage of stockholders and the general public. On the other hand, suggestions made by such directors may lead to improvement in financing practices, personnel and labor policies, products, services, and buying policies.

The suggestion that corporations use representatives of the government as directors has been rejected as being impractical. Businessmen are fearful of government domination on the one hand and the general public is fearful of businessmen's domination of government on the other hand. The fear of "conflict of interest" is so great as to force federal government appointees to dispose of their corporate stocks before they are confirmed by the United States Senate.

The suggestion to have women represented on boards of directors seems to have merit. Today, women are in the majority among stockholders of most large corporations and they are the chief buyers of services and products placed on the market. While many corporations have women directors, director candidates ought to be selected on the basis of merit regardless of sex, position, religion, etc. To select a woman as a director simply because she is a woman would open the gate to claims for representation because of race, religion, politics, and other special reasons. In selecting director candidates the objective is to select directors that best fit the needs of the corporation.

In theory, directors represent the interests of shareholders by maximizing their long-term gains; but, if directors were to broaden their objectives to include labor and other groups, the interests of stockholders would tend to be harmed. Special interest groups such as labor, customers, suppliers, management, the general public, and others usually have their own methods of protecting their interests: labor has its unions; customers and suppliers may deal with competitors; management is well represented on boards of directors; and the public has the aid of federal, state, and local legislative bodies and regulatory agencies. Although there is no quarrel with the more professional attitude of businessmen in regard to their social responsibilities, so-called "business statesmanship" and "growing benevolence" toward special groups may not be serving the public interest, which is primarily concerned with purchasing the products of industry at noninflated prices.

There is no answer to the question of the proper size of a board of directors, but some of the largest manufacturing and public utility corporations have no more than sixteen members on their boards of directors.[13] A board that is too large is unwieldy and must depend on working committees to administer the corporation's affairs. A board of directors is too small when it does not permit adequate representation of different groups and when a burden is thrown on individual members.

A majority of directors usually constitutes a quorum; however, the articles of incorporation or bylaws may require action on some matters to be taken by a greater number of directors. Sometimes the bylaws require a director to disqualify himself on action in which he has a personal interest (such as making a contract with a second firm in which he has a financial interest). Directors meetings are regular and special. Regular meetings are provided for in the bylaws (usually monthly) and may be held with or without notice; special meetings require notification of directors as provided for in the bylaws. Unless required by the articles of incorporation or by-

[13] The average number of members on boards of directors in the American Institute of Management's "excellently managed companies" is thirteen, and for different subdivisions the numbers are as follows: banks, twenty-two; insurance companies, sixteen; public utility companies, thirteen; and manufacturing companies, twelve. *Manual of Excellent Management* (New York, American Institute of Management, 1957), p. 23.

laws, the purpose or purposes for which a meeting is called need not be specified in the notice of such meeting. However, best results are obtained when an agenda is prepared for each meeting and an advance notice with supporting information is sent to each director.

The "prudent man theory" requires each director to attend meetings, read and understand reports, and act legally and judiciously in the interest of creditors, stockholders, and the general public. Failure to do so may mean the loss of the director's personal fortune; even after his death his estate may be involved in litigation resulting from action by creditors, stockholders and others. Unless specifically authorized, directors as such receive no salaries from their corporations, but the corporations' bylaws usually provide that the directors are to receive a specific amount of compensation ($200 for American Telephone and Telegraph Company) plus traveling expenses for each meeting attended. While there is a tendency to remunerate directors' services more generously, directors are probably the most underpaid persons in American business.[14]

The efficiency of a board of directors depends on many factors, the most important of which is the ability of the members to work as a team. Factional differences are difficult to avoid; if they are allowed to become deep rooted, the entire staff of the organization may become involved. Such a situation is certain to breed inefficiency. One of the primary responsibilities of the chairman of the board of directors is to prevent the development of factions and dissension among board members. It is his responsibility to handle impartially and diplomatically any hostilities which may appear.

In every organization someone must be responsible for replacing officials when they reach retirement age. This is usually the responsibility of the board of directors under the leadership of the chairman. Some companies are handicapped because of executives who are legacies of former directors or officials. Nepotism tends to be a threat in any organization unless there are rules against it.

A second objectionable managerial practice is that of obtaining top executives from other business firms—a violation of the cardinal principle of good personnel management, that of promoting from within. The value obtained from recruiting executives from outside is usually offset by losses incurred by the effects of this prac-

[14] Among the larger companies, the most common fee for attending meetings is $100, but fees of as little as $10 are not uncommon. These token payments are but part of the directors' compensation because most directors also receive retainer fees ranging from $400 to $15,000, and "inside" directors also receive their regular salaries plus "fringe" benefits as officers of their corporations.

tice on the existing staff members who, as a consequence, find little incentive to work for promotion. Well-managed corporations give attention to developing future leaders within their organizations and rarely find it necessary to go outside for top executives. It is understandable when companies in financial difficulties make changes in top management by recruiting outsiders for key positions, and sometimes changes in top management are forced by stockholders through the device of electing new boards of directors.

OFFICERS OF CORPORATIONS

Business corporation acts customarily require a minimum of three or four officers—president, secretary, treasurer, and usually a vice-president. Additional officers, assistant officers, and agents may be appointed or selected by the board of directors. Officers derive their powers from statutes, articles of incorporation, bylaws, resolution of the board of directors, and custom or usage. The specific functions of each officer will vary from corporation to corporation, depending upon the size of the corporation, the nature of the business, personalities of the officers, and other variables. Sometimes, two or more offices will be held by the same person, but statutes usually specify that the offices of president and secretary must be held by different persons. The bylaws of a corporation usually give the board of directors the power to remove officers at any time, but the statutes customarily give protection to those who have contracts with their corporations (rights to unpaid salaries, pensions, bonuses, stock-purchase options, and other privileges may be at stake).

In managing the affairs of the corporation, statutes usually require the president and the secretary or treasurer to sign certain reports. In performing the day-to-day business of a corporation, the president may be merely a specialist who holds his position because of special ability in finance, law, selling, or manufacturing. In some cases, the president may be the general manager in charge of co-ordinating the activities of many specialists under his supervision. In other cases, the president is elected to his position because of large holdings of stock in the company, in which case the actual management of the corporation may be in the hands of an executive vice-president or general manager. Although the powers of the president and other officers are customarily provided for in the bylaws, the courts have held officers responsible for not exercising powers customarily given to such officers.

Corporations are customarily required to have at least one vice-president, but a corporation's board of directors may make provisions for two or more vice-presidents. In large corporations, the title "vice-president" is usually given to the heads of different departments or divisions (as used here, the word "division" is more inclusive than "department," for example "Chevrolet" and "Buick" divisions of General Motors). When there are several vice-presidents, one will be designated as the executive or first vice-president to indicate that he is to act in place of the president during the latter's absence. Usually there is nothing in the title of other vice-presidents to indicate the duties of the holder, but sometimes it is combined with a second title to indicate the responsibilities of the officer (for illustration, "vice-president and treasurer," "vice-president in charge of sales," etc.).

The secretary is the recording officer of a corporation or any other business organization. The secretary is usually responsible for keeping a record of the names of all stockholders; he acts as secretary at stockholders' and directors' meetings; he is in charge of mailing notices of meetings; and he is entrusted with the corporate seal. The secretary may be in charge of the stock record book; if so, he is responsible for preparing a list of those eligible to vote and to receive dividends—if and when voted by the board of directors. The functions of the secretary are more directly related to—and he is in closer touch with—stockholders than any other officer.

Financial administration of business corporations may follow one of three organizational patterns: (1) in large corporations, there is a financial vice-president with the treasurer and controller subordinate to him; (2) in middle-sized companies, the treasurer and controller are responsible directly to the president; and (3) in small companies, the treasurer is the chief financial officer to whom the controller or chief accounting officer is subordinate.

There is no uniformity among large business firms as to specific activities which are primarily financial and therefore the ones to engage the attention of a financial executive. Among managerial activities that receive high ratings are those related to participating in long-range planning, accounting operations, revising and approving terms of contracts for capital acquisitions, preparing long-range budgets, giving advice on expenditures for purchases of capital assets, and supervising cashiers. Thus, in the minds of financial executives, the activities pertaining to financial planning rank high in importance. At the same time it has been indicated that day-to-day activities of finance officers, which pertain to working capital management, are highly significant.[15]

For obvious reasons the responsibilities of all financial executives have increased during the last twenty years. As a result, the financial management of large firms may be placed under a vice-president in charge of finance. Usually his functions are to coordinate the activities of all financial executives and to work closely with the finance committee of the board of directors.

The treasurer is one of the three officers sometimes specifically required by business corporation acts. He is usually the chief financial officer of a small business enterprise and his duties vary with the size and type of business of his company. The functions of the office of treasurer include supervising care of petty cash funds; payment of dividends and interest; purchase and sale of securities; establishment of surety bond requirements; claims from and against customers; custodianship of funds, securities, insurance policies, and other financial papers; general and employee insurance programs and payrolls; purchase, sale, and lease of property; payment of real estate and personal property taxes and assessments; and loans and capital-financing transactions.

The treasurer is responsible for establishing and maintaining banking relations, formulating and administering credit and collection policies, reviewing financial contracts, maintaining proper equity positions and working capital ratios, supervising maximum and minimum limits of inventories and their rate of turnover, and investing surplus funds of the company. The treasurer or an assistant treasurer must sign or cosign checks, contracts, stock certificates, and other documents. The treasurer may be responsible for analyzing and interpreting economic conditions and recommending policies to be followed. However, in larger companies, this analysis work is usually done by a separate department under an economist or statistician.

The controller has charge of general and cost accounting systems, internal auditing, and development and operation of the budget. The controller is expected to assist management by preparing financial facts and figures and giving advice as to how they may be used in planning and administering operations. Then, by keeping operations under constant review, he reminds management of its own rec-

[15] J. Fred Weston, "The Finance Function," *Journal of Finance,* Vol. IX, No. 3 (September, 1954), pp. 265–81.

ord and also reduces the danger of error and fraud. The controller may also be responsible for preparing the financial statements and for the tax accounting work of his business firm.

Most important among the tax accounting problems are those associated with federal income tax laws (which along with other federal tax laws have been codified and consolidated in what is called the Internal Revenue Code). The intent of the federal income tax law is to tax income—receipts that represent gains to the taxpayer—but the law provides that certain kinds of income need not be reported and makes other qualifications so that taxable income may not be the same as accounting income. While many of the tax problems have legal aspects, they are primarily accountants' problems. The controller may be given the responsibility for making statistical studies required by management, preparing reports required by the Securities and Exchange Commission and other governmental agencies, and familiarizing appropriate departments with government orders, regulations and requests and checking for compliance.

Current and post audits by an officer or an agency independent of the firm's executives and directly responsible to the board of directors are also important. Some companies employ an auditor, who is directly responsible to the board of directors, to check on the activities of the controller, treasurer, and other officers. In addition, the board of directors customarily employs an auditing firm to make periodic reports on the business affairs of the firm. Since management of "public" business corporations may be separated from ownership, a type of audit desired by the former may not be satisfactory to the latter. Thus the recommendation has been made that stockholders select the auditing firm. Although this practice is required in certain foreign countries, it is not common in the United States. If stockholders are indifferent—and there is little evidence to the contrary—an arrangement whereby stockholders are to select the auditing firm would not be practical. However, a compromise plan has been worked out by some corporations (for example, General Motors Corporation) so that the board of directors selects the auditing firm and the stockholders approve or disapprove at the annual meeting.

SUMMARY

The smaller the business unit and the simpler its organization, the closer will be the relationship between owners and managers. At one extreme, there is the sole proprietorship wherein ownership and management are embodied in one individual; at the other extreme, there is the large corporation wherein the gulf between ownership and management may be bridged only by the board of directors. A corporation's charter, together with its bylaws, constitutes the managerial and operational plan of a corporation.

The business and other affairs of a business corporation are managed by a board of directors elected by shareholders from a list of candidates usually selected by management. In selecting director candidates, management must not only weigh the pros and cons of using "inside" and/or "outside" directors, "big name" directors, professional directors, and representatives of creditors, labor, customers, suppliers, and the government, but must also decide on the number of directors, tenure of office, and limitations as to age of directors. However, in the final analysis, the objective is to select directors best fitted to meet the requirements of the corporation. An important factor in the efficiency of a board of directors is the ability of the members to work together as a team with the chairman of the board as its captain.

Business corporation acts customarily require corporations to have a minimum of three or four officers—president, secretary, treasurer, and sometimes a vice-president. These officers may be appointed or selected by the board of directors, and they derive their powers from the state statutes, articles of incorporation, bylaws, resolutions of the board of directors, and custom or usage. In large corporations, a controller may be appointed to supervise the operation of the general and cost accounting systems, internal auditing, and development and operation of the budget. In addition, an outside auditing firm is customarily employed and is responsible to the board of directors to check on the business affairs of the corporation. In general, the work of finance officers pertains to the planning function of business, while the work of accounting officers pertains to the control function of business.

QUESTIONS AND PROBLEMS

1. "A corporation gives promise of preserving its 'going concern value' by continued existence in spite of death or retirement of any particular owner." Is this "going concern value" financially important?
2. Define or explain: (*a*) special chartering acts, (*b*) general incorporation laws, (*c*) single purpose corporation, (*d*) *ultra vires* acts, and (*e*) "doctrine of inherent incapacity."
3. "The New York Central Railroad finally is going to try to become a Delaware Corporation. . . The railroad at present is incorporated in the

states of New York, Pennsylvania, Ohio, Indiana, Illinois, and Michigan." (*New York Times*, June 11, 1960, p. 33.) Why would it seek a Delaware charter?

4. What provisions pertaining to financing are usually found in a corporation's (*a*) charter and (*b*) bylaws?
5. Do corporate names have value? How are they protected?
6. Discuss: (*a*) how the common-law provision for voting differs from voting provisions of most corporations, and (*b*) the advantages of cummulative voting for minority groups.
7. Discuss: (*a*) the compensation of directors relative to the risks they assume, (*b*) the "prudent man theory" as it pertains to directors, and (*c*) the relationship between directors and officers of a corporation.
8. Business corporation acts customarily require a minimum of three or four officers. Identify them and outline their duties and responsibilities.
9. (*a*) What are the usual duties of a controller of a corporation? (*b*) How do the duties of the controller differ from those of the auditor of a corporation?
10. Comment on the following: "A New York stock broker and director of Pierce Industries, Bernard Fein, filed a stockholder's suit accusing the Pierce chairman of causing the company great financial loss in transactions involving the chairman's family." (*Wall Street Journal* [New York], January 12, 1961, p. 15.)
11. What are the advantages to a corporation of having a classified board of directors (one in which the terms of office are staggered and only a portion of the board is elected annually)?
12. What advantages are claimed for an inside board of directors? What are the disadvantages of such a board? Whose interests are most apt to be overlooked by an inside board?
13. Why is securing an audit of a corporation's books of interest to the corporation's (*a*) directors and (*b*) stockholders? As a rule, are stockholders asked to pass upon an auditing firm? Do they show any evidence of being interested in an audit?
14. The board of directors of General Electric is made up of nineteen members; in addition to three top officers, other members "come from a wide variety of fields of endeavor, including agriculture, banking, finance, international trade, manufacturing, marketing, mining, research and education, textiles and transportation. They are also widely representative in a geographical sense and in the diversity of their ages." (General Electric Company, "The Work of Your Board of Directors," *Share Owners Quarterly*, January 26, 1959, p. 2.) What policy in selecting new directors is suggested by the foregoing quotation?
15. Assume that a small businessman owns 51 per cent of his company's stock, that his wife owns 20 per cent, his son 10 per cent, and the remainder is owned by four able business acquaintances who are in disagreement with the policies of the company. What can the small businessman do about this situation?

16. "Running a successful small corporation in a competitive market is a difficult job . . . As chief executive, you must make decisions dealing with all phases of your firm's operation—administration, finance, production, control, marketing, personnel, and so on." (C. T. Richardson, "How Directors Strengthen Small Firms," *Management Aids for Small Manufacturers,* May, 1958, p. 1.) What qualities should be emphasized in selecting new directors by an owner who is seeking help through additions to his board of directors?

PART II

Financial Statements and Financial Planning

FINANCIAL statements are the media through which data concerning a business firm's operations are transmitted to those interested in such information. The most widely used financial statements are balance sheets and income statements; however there are several others that are used for budgeting, planning, and other specific purposes. While it is not necessary to be a trained accountant to utilize financial statements, an understanding of their contents and limitations is essential.

Among the various managerial uses of financial statements is that of financial planning, which is essentially a problem of determining the capital needs of a business and establishing policies that will tend to work toward the fulfillment of those needs. A business firm encounters needs for both working and fixed capital. One of the primary goals of financial management is that of maintaining adequate working capital, without which a firm cannot efficiently and profitably carry on its activities.

Fixed capital needs are those associated with financing fixed assets, and it is fairly common to rely on long-term debt for this purpose. While long-term debt may tend to improve the net working capital position, it may result in excessive fixed charges against the earnings of the business. This section deals with financial statements and the working capital and fixed capital needs of business firms.

CHAPTER 4

Financial Statements of Business Firms

TO A LARGE extent, many of the problems facing a business firm are understandable only in terms of the information disclosed in its financial statements. This is especially true as businesses increase in size and complexity. While it is sometimes assumed that small firms can operate effectively with few if any financial statements, this is rarely the case.

All business firms must rely upon adequate financial statements in solving three basic problems. The first major problem confronting practically all businesses is that of acquiring assets and promoting products or services. In this matter, a prosperous going concern has an obvious advantage over a newly organized one in that it has earnings which may be retained and used to finance expansion or to meet operating needs. The second problem which business firms face is that of using existing assets efficiently and profitably. The provisions which must be made for meeting expenses for wages, materials, and other items make this an operating as well as a financial problem. And the third problem, to be dealt with from the time a business firm is organized, is that of paying state and federal income taxes. Because of the complexity of the laws and rules and regulations of state taxing agencies and the Internal Revenue Service, tax accounting has developed to a stage where it is almost a separate field of endeavor.

Management uses financial statements as the basis for analysis and appraisal of financial weakness and strength within the business firm. Bankers and other lenders check financial statements when passing on the requests of business firms for loans. Regulatory agencies require corporations which are financing in the open market to furnish prospective investors with financial statements that disclose their current financial positions. And firms whose stocks are bought and sold on national exchanges must file financial statements periodically with the Securities and Exchange Commission. It is not necessary to be a trained accountant to understand the meaning of items appearing in financial statements. This chapter deals with the two most important of these statements—the balance sheet and the profit and loss statement—and with financial reporting.

BALANCE SHEET—ASSETS

A balance sheet shows the assets, liabilities, and net worth items of a business firm at a given time. The term "claims of owners" is often substituted for "net worth" and the term "equity" may be used in place of the term "claim." The basic premise on which the balance sheet is based is that total assets of a business firm equal its liabilities plus the claims of owners (ASSETS = LIABILITIES + CLAIMS OF OWNERS). Although the claims of owners are residual, the balance sheet may be arranged so as to emphasize them (CLAIMS OF OWNERS = ASSETS—LIABILITIES); nevertheless the orthodox arrangement is to present assets first, followed by liabilities and equity of owners. Losses will decrease owners' equity and may even cause insolvency, a situation wherein assets are less than liabilities; however this situation does not upset the balance between assets and claims to assets because owners' equity will be replaced by a deficit, or a minus owners' equity position.

A position statement or balance sheet of a business firm portrays its financial position as disclosed by its records at a particular time. While it is true that there is general agreement among accountants on many points of theory and procedure—and consequently the results achieved by different accountants are fairly uniform—at the same time both accounting theory and procedure are constantly changing and noticeable differences in practices will be found at different times. A balance sheet of a business firm has many uses, but it also has many limitations and may need several adjustments before a meaningful analysis can be made. For illustration, if price levels are changing rapidly, historical costs will not reflect current values, and adjustments will be necessary before pricing and other policies can be established. A simple balance sheet is presented in Table 6.

TABLE 6

COMPANY X BALANCE SHEET

(December 31, 1960)

ASSETS		LIABILITIES AND OWNERS' EQUITY	
Current Assets:		*Current Liabilities:*	
Cash	$ 10,000	Notes payable	$ 20,000
Marketable securities	10,000	Accounts payable	30,000
Accounts receivable	40,000	Taxes payable	2,000
Inventories	70,000	Other accrued liabilities	8,000
Prepaid expenses	5,000	Total Current Liabilities	$ 60,000
Total Current Assets	$135,000		
Fixed Assets:		*Long-Term Liabilities:*	
Land	$ 30,000	Mortgage note payable	$ 10,000
Buildings	40,000	Bonds payable	30,000
Equipment	20,000	Total Long-Term Debt	$ 40,000
Total Fixed Assets	$ 90,000		
Other Noncurrent Assets:		*Owners' Equity:*	
Investments	$ 10,000	Retained earnings	$ 35,000
		Capital	100,000
		Total Owners' Equity	$135,000
Total Assets	$235,000	Total Liabilities and Equity	$235,000

Definition of Assets. In a broad sense, an asset is any item of value owned. The assets of a business firm are its total resources, both tangible and intangible, plus incurred costs which are expected to benefit the firm in the future. Obviously cash, receivables, stocks of goods or inventories, equipment, buildings, land, patents, and goodwill—as well as other resources or items which have economic value—are classified as assets; however the justification for classifying a cost factor as an asset is less obvious. Sound accounting principles require that costs which benefit the income of a particular period be charged to that period. Consequently, an item such as prepaid expense is carried as a current asset until charged off, and costs that will affect income over a long period are classified as deferred charges until amortized or written off over a period of years. If all costs were written off in the period in which payments were made, the income for that period would be understated.

Current Assets. Current assets include cash and other assets that are expected to be turned into cash within a year in the ordinary course of business. When the operating cycle is longer than one year, current assets may include items that do not meet the time qualification of this definition. The operating cycle of a business firm is the time required to convert raw materials into finished products, to sell them, and to collect payment thereon. A wine producer, for example, would have an operating cycle extending over several years. However most business firms use one year as the basis for classifying assets regardless of the length of the operating cycle. The chief items included in current assets are cash, temporary investments, receivables, and inventories.

The item *cash* includes demand deposits (checking accounts) in banks in the United States and in foreign countries, cash receipts not deposited in banks, and currency kept on hand to meet current needs. The statistics presented in Table 7 show that manufacturing companies in the United States have over 5 per cent of their total assets in the form of cash. During the normal course of business, a firm sells assets and/or services and receives currency and/or checks in payment. Although most banks give immediate credit for checks deposited, some out-of-town checks may take several days for collection and banks usually expect their customers to keep balances large enough to cover them. Some of the checks deposited may be improperly drawn, written in amounts in excess of balances, and returned as "bad checks"; therefore, a business firm must make allowances for such items when estimating its desirable cash balance. The actual amount of deposits in commercial banks is considerably inflated as indicated by the item "cash items in process of collection" on the combined statement of assets of insured commercial banks (which amounted to $16.2 billion at the end of 1959).[1]

Business firms must spend money in order to make a profit on operations; therefore there will be an outflow of funds in payment for goods, labor, utilities, and other necessary items. This outflow will rarely be matched by an inflow; consequently, a business firm is likely to have a deficiency of cash from trading operations at some times and a surplus at others. In anticipation of a period of cash deficiency, a firm may build up its cash balance or it may borrow; during other periods, the same firm may have a surplus of cash which can be invested temporarily in a marketable security to earn an investment income.

A business firm keeps part of its assets in the form of cash not only to care for normal trade needs but also to meet periodic interest payments, installments on debt obligations, dividends, taxes, and

[1] *Annual Report of the Federal Deposit Insurance Corporation for the Year Ended December 31, 1959* (Washington, D.C.: U.S. Government Printing Office, 1960), p. 136.

other payments. In addition, a firm ought to be prepared for unexpected declines in revenues caused by factors such as a slump in sales, difficulty in collecting receivables, strikes, and other emergencies. While it would be uneconomical to hold cash in sufficient amounts to care for every possible emergency, it is desirable to have some reserves to finance unusual situations. Most business firms also keep cash balances with their banks to avoid or minimize service charges on checking accounts, to meet compensatory balance requirements on lines of credit, to improve their credit standings, and to retain good relationships with their banks.

It is expensive for a business firm to keep assets in the form of cash because of the resulting loss of earnings; therefore a good finance officer will seek temporary investments for funds not needed immediately in the current operations of his business firm. There are many "near money" forms of investments (savings accounts, commercial bills or bankers' acceptances, open-market commercial paper, and short-term United States Treasury obligations) which make it possible to earn an income from short-term investments pending income tax payments, dividend disbursements, interest and installment payments on debts, and anticipated seasonal needs for cash.

Among the different forms of temporary investments, short-term government securities are the most important. Large corporations which have ready access to the money and capital markets are the chief business-firm investors in marketable United States Treasury bills, certificates of indebtedness, notes, and government bonds which are approaching maturity. In addition, business firms also purchase special issues of government securities such as tax and savings notes (see Table 7).

Some corporations purchase commercial paper and bankers' acceptances in the open market. Sometimes business firms make loans to employees and officers, but this practice may be forbidden by statutes or by the bylaws of corporations because it could lead to abuses which could result in losses to the firm. If such loans are made, it would be wiser to treat them as personnel services rather than as an outlet for surplus cash. A better policy for business firms would be to help employees to establish a credit union and provide it with free secretarial help, supplies, equipment, and office space.

The chief financial officer of a business firm may hold cash or other assets as required by action of the board of directors or by contracts with creditors or others. The fact that a board of directors

TABLE 7

FINANCIAL STATEMENT OF MANUFACTURING CORPORATIONS, EXCEPT NEWSPAPERS
Second Quarter, 1960 (In Millions of Dollars)

	All Assets	*Per Cent*
ASSETS		
Cash on hand and in bank	14,083	5.6
U.S. Government securities, including Treasury savings notes	12,531	5.0
Total Cash and U.S. Government Securities	26,614	10.6
Receivables from U.S. Government, excluding tax credits	2,621	1.0
Other notes and accounts receivable (net)	37,694	15.0
Total Receivables	40,315	16.0
Inventories	60,530	24.1
Other current assets	6,261	2.5
Total Current Assets	133,720	53.2
Property, plant, and equipment	186,956	74.4
Deduct: Reserve for depreciation and depletion	89,861	35.8
Total Property, Plant, and Equipment (Net)	97,095	38.6
Other noncurrent assets	20,493	8.2
Total Assets	251,307	100.0
LIABILITIES AND STOCKHOLDERS' EQUITY		
Short-term loans from banks (original maturity of 1 year or less)	8,416	3.3
Advances and prepayment by U.S. Government	1,857	0.7
Trade accounts and notes payable	19,519	7.8
Federal income tax accrued	9,330	3.7
Installments, due in 1 year, on long-term debt:		
(*a*) Loans from banks	782	0.3
(*b*) Other long-term debt	1,139	0.5
Other current liabilities	12,404	4.9
Total Current Liabilities	53,447	21.2
Long-term debt due in more than 1 year:		
(*a*) Loans from banks	4,455	1.8
(*b*) Other long-term debt	25,584	10.2
Other noncurrent liabilities*	3,332	1.3
Total Liabilities	86,818	34.5
Reserve not reflected elsewhere*	2,207	0.9
Capital stock, capital surplus, and minority interest	66,770	26.6
Earned surplus and surplus reserves	95,512	38.0
Total Stockholders' Equity	164,489	65.5
Total Liabilities and Stockholders' Equity	251,307	100.0
NET WORKING CAPITAL		
Excess of current assets over current liabilities	80,273	

* Effective with the report for second quarter, 1960, corporations were requested to include federal income taxes with other noncurrent liabilities. The effect of this has been to shift approximately $800 million from reserves not reflected elsewhere to other noncurrent liabilities.

Source: Federal Trade Commission—Securities and Exchange Commission, *Quarterly Financial Report for Manufacturing Corporations*, Second Quarter, 1960, pp. 12 and 34.

has appropriated part of retained earnings (earned surplus) for some special purpose, such as air conditioning a building, does not mean that cash will be available when needed (as when the air-conditioning equipment is to be purchased and installed). Therefore, the board of directors may pass a resolution directing the chief financial officer to "fund" the reserve by segregating cash in a special deposit in a bank or to buy marketable government securities so that cash will be on hand or readily available when the need arises (as when a purchase is to be made).

Special funds may also be created when debt contracts call for setting aside a specified amount periodically for the retirement of the debt on or before maturity. A board of directors may also direct the chief financial officer to create a fund for payment of federal income taxes and other liabilities such as employee benefit and pension payments. Some of these special funds are an outgrowth of managerial decisions; others are due to "collective bargaining," and still others are traced to some responsibility placed on management by governmental agencies. Among the accounting reserves for which special funds are commonly created are vacation wages payable, incentive compensation, profit-sharing and bonus payments, contributions to benefit and welfare programs, annuities and other outlays for past services, social security and federal income taxes withheld, and employee deposits for purchase of savings bonds or other securities. The administration of assets segregated in special funds is different from that of assets in general funds even though the purposes may overlap. Investments in securities other than government securities will be accounted for as other current or noncurrent assets.

Corporate management usually sets the same standards for its temporary investment of funds as do commercial banks. This means that temporary investments are usually in short-term securities of the highest quality so that they may be sold for cash without loss or delay. Temporary investments of business firms are usually shown on their balance sheets at cost; however, some firms carry such investments either at market or redemption value or show these values by a notation on the balance sheet.

The amount of credit extended by a business firm to its customers at any one time is indicated by the volume of trade accounts, bills, and/or notes receivable. The most common types of receivables are those which result from sales of goods or services, but there may be others such as claims against insurance companies, for losses sustained; the government, for tax refunds; common carriers, for goods damaged; officers, employees, or subsidiaries, for prior advances; and stockholders, for unpaid stock subscriptions or assessments. Trade practices usually govern terms of sales when credit is given.

While terms offered may be standardized, buyers do not react uniformly; as a result, business firms must have efficient collection policies in order to avoid losses and the tying up of large amounts of cash in receivables. Accounts receivable customarily appear on the balance sheet in a form that indicates the total claims outstanding less allowances for doubtful accounts; loans and bills receivable may appear as the total outstanding less discounted notes and bills.

Most credit sales are made on an "open-account" basis with the seller keeping a bookkeeping record of claims and the buyer keeping a similar record of accounts payable. Each will have copies of invoices and shipping papers as evidence of the existence of the credit or debt. In some cases, sellers expect buyers to give promissory notes as evidence of obligations. These promissory notes may be of the installment type which are used most commonly when financing sales of durable goods. Although a bill of exchange or trade or bankers' acceptance may be used in domestic trade, it appears most commonly in foreign trade financing. The accounts receivable item on a balance sheet represents the amount of unpaid sales billed to customers after proper allowances have been made for uncollectible notes, bills, or accounts. Among manufacturing corporations in the United States, about 16 per cent of total assets are in the form of receivables (see Table 7).

An inventory is an itemized list of goods or stock of goods on hand with their estimated value. Measured in dollar amounts, inventory is usually the largest item among the working capital assets of a business firm (see Table 7). However, the investment in inventories is apt to be small for service companies. For a manufacturing company, inventories will consist of supplies, raw materials, work in progress, and finished goods; these are valued according to some accepted rule such as "cost or market, whichever is lower."

Unless a firm choses to speculate, its objective in inventory management should be to provide adequate stocks of goods of proper quality needed for production and sale. The actual amount will depend on the nature of business operations and on purchasing policies, but the minimum amount must be enough to keep production of sales up to schedule. The inventory management problem becomes more difficult as the number of steps and parts used in production increases and the production process lengthens. For an individual business firm, inventory control may consist of setting minimum and maximum amounts of inventories that should be kept on hand in terms of production or sales. Purchasing policies as to inventories reflect anticipated seasonal, cyclical, and trend demands for goods; therefore changes in the volume of inventories in the hands of business firms are an important index of anticipated business conditions.

Other current assets include prepaid expenses and deferred charges, such as outlays for interest, taxes, rent, insurance, supplies, travelling expenses, and other short-lived expenses. In addition, there will be a cost item for that portion of deferred charges which have been amortized during the current operating period.

Fixed Assets. Fixed assets are those of a somewhat "fixed" or permanent nature (a life expectancy of more than one year) that are used by the business firm in its normal operations. They consist of items that cannot be sold without disrupting business operations. Fixed assets may be classified as tangible or intangible. The former include items such as land, plants, and equipment used in operations. They have the common characteristic of long life and, as in the case of equipment, are used for the purpose for which their creative utility was manufactured. (Trucks, machines, and other equipment in possession of dealers in such items are classified as inventory pending their sale to ultimate users.) With the exception of land, valuation of tangible assets on balance sheets is usually followed by an allowance for depreciation which, when deducted from the valuation figure of the asset, gives a net value. New plants, equipment, and other fixed assets are first valued at cost.

Intangible fixed assets increase the profit potentiality of a business firm; but, as the word *intangible* suggests, they are not of a physical or material nature as are the tangible assets listed above. This classification includes such items as goodwill, patents, trademarks, licenses, franchises, and other items that may be presumed to endow the firm which owns them with extra rights, privileges, or advantages. Intangibles may be valued at cost, but the valuation of some may be an arbitrary one chosen by the firm.

Other Noncurrent Assets. Some assets are neither current assets nor fixed assets as these terms have been defined. For illustration, an investment in common stock of a subsidiary company would not be classified as a current asset or as a fixed asset. Although common stock could be sold within a year, it does not follow that it would be sold in the normal course of business. Among the other forms of long-term investments owned by a business firm which are classified as noncurrent assets are preferred stock, bonds, mortgage notes, other securities, and real estate not being used in business operations. Investments should appear on the balance sheet at current market values. Other noncurrent assets owned may include cash surrender value of life insurance policies wherein the business enterprise is the beneficiary, advances to subsidiary companies, and other items not classified as current or fixed assets.

Long-term investments which are usually held for long-term purposes include securities of subsidiaries and affiliated companies held for control purposes and investments earmarked for redemption of bonds and preferred stock, construction of new plants, and payment of pension and other benefits to employees. Permanent investments are usually valued originally at cost with provisions for amortization of the premium or accumulation of the discount if bonds are purchased above or below par. Treasury stock (a company's own stock which has been issued and reacquired), which usually appears on balance sheets as a deduction from the net worth section, is listed by some companies as an asset when it is held for some specific purpose such as payment of a bonus under an incentive plan.

Real estate and other forms of property not currently used by a business firm in its operations may be held in anticipation of future expansion, as a speculation, or for income purposes. While the cash surrender value of any life insurance policy wherein the business firm is the beneficiary usually appears as a miscellaneous asset or investment, it sometimes appears as a current asset (illustrating the variations in accounting practices).

Deferred charges, which are classified as noncurrent assets, are similar to prepaid expenses, but their nature justifies their being amortized over a period of years. Deferred charges may include prepaid insurance policies that are to be in effect for several years, research and experimental costs that are expected to affect income for a number of years, advertising expenditures that will benefit the firm for a period of time, costs of factory layouts or removal to new locations, discounts, and expenses associated with long-term capital financing.

BALANCE SHEET—LIABILITIES

The claims of creditors and owners against a business firm, sometimes referred to as creditors' and owners' equity, have been identified as the sources of a business firm's assets. The word *liabilities* is sometimes used to include the claims of both creditors and owners; more properly it includes only those debts owed creditors, and these may include provisions for obligations which are not ascertained. Capital stock, deferred credits to income, and surplus are balance sheet liabilities only insofar as they represent balances to be accounted for by the company. Generally, liabilities are considered current when they are due within one year (or within the operating cycle of the firm) and noncurrent or long-term when maturities are delayed for more than one year.

Current Liabilities. The short-term liabilities of a business firm include amounts owed to banks on short-term business loans, accounts payable chiefly to trade creditors, sums due customers because of their cash advances or prepayment of goods ordered or services rendered, amounts due the federal government for accrued income taxes, installment payments due on long-term loans, and any other debts due within the present period.

Business firms commonly borrow from their banks, and those loans which call for repayment of the principal within the year are classified as short-term liabilities. Small companies are relatively more dependent on their banks for loan capital than are large companies. The policies of business firms concerning bank borrowing are considered in a later chapter. At times, some of the notes payable represent funds borrowed from officers of the firm.

Accounts payable result chiefly from purchases of goods on credit, and to the seller they are accounts receivable. Evidence of trade credit may be in the form of book accounts, notes receivable, or bills receivable. Other notes payable may be included in this section of the balance sheet, but more properly they would be noted separately or would appear under other current liabilities.

Customers of business firms, including the federal government, may make cash advances (loans) or prepay for goods ordered. When the production period is several years (as for an atomic submarine, diesel engine, or battleship), the sales or purchase contract may specify cash advances or periodic payments during production in order to ease the financial burden on the manufacturer.

The United States government does not collect corporate income taxes on a pay-as-you-go basis; therefore a business firm's tax liability will accrue and will appear on its balance sheet as a short-term liability. Federal income taxes should be estimated on the basis of estimated monthly profits and should appear as an allowance or reserve for federal income taxes. Some corporations show their tax liability minus the value of government securities held to pay them, thus understating both their assets and their liabilities.

Installment payments on term loans, serial bonds, mortgage notes, and other long-term obligations or preferred stock which are due within a year are classified as current liabilities. Segregation of such amounts helps to determine the net working capital position of a business firm and must be done in computing a firm's current ratio.

Among the "other current liabilities" are deferred expenses, deferred income, and dividends. Current liabilities are obligations which mature within one year and which are normally liquidated out of current earnings; however, through oversight or intent, at the end of the year there may remain unpaid taxes, interest, salaries, wages, and other items that have to be accounted for as deferred expenses or accrued liabilities. To omit them would be to overstate working capital and net worth and to understate liabilities.

Deferred income represents funds received but not yet earned. Usually that portion of income which has been earned is included in the profit and loss statement. Failure to include an item on the balance sheet to account for the unearned portion would overstate income and understate liabilities. Dividends declared by a corporation's board of directors which are payable on a specified date are included among current liabilities until the date of payment.

Long-Term Debts. Long-term debts include term bank loans, mortgage loans, bonds, notes, purchase-obligations, and other debts which have a maturity of more than one year. As the maturity date approaches, the long-term obligations become current obligations unless provisions are made for refinancing them with other long-term debts. The policies entailed in financing with long-term bank loans, bond issues, and other long-term credit instruments are discussed in later chapters.

Contingent Liabilities. Contingent liabilities are conditional obligations dependent upon something that may or may not occur. Among the circumstances that may give rise to contingent liabilities are those which involve discounting notes and receivables with recourse (which means that if the obligor does not pay, the company is liable); contracting for future delivery; having lawsuits or claims for damages pending or unsettled; signing a promise to pay as an accommodation endorser; having disputed state and/or federal income tax claims pending; and guaranteeing or signing warranties of products. If the contingent liability is remote, it may be disclosed in a footnote to the balance sheet. When the amounts involved are substantial, failure to recognize contingent liabilities results in a distorted picture of a business firm's financial affairs.

Reserves Not Reflected Elsewhere. In the balance sheet of manufacturing companies (see Table 7), the word "reserve" appears in three different places—as a deduction under "property, plant and equipment"; in "earned surplus and surplus reserve"; and under total liabilities as "reserve not reflected elsewhere." In all three cases, the term "reserve" has a meaning other than the popular one (an asset kept for some future use, such as money set aside for an emergency). Instead, the term is used to indicate the accumulated adjustment of the valuation of assets to which they are related, as for plant and equipment (called valuation reserves); to show allowances for liabilities the amount and/or time of payment not being shown on the balance sheet date (called liability reserves); and to account for debiting the retained earnings account and crediting the various reserve accounts, thereby scattering and hiding retained earnings throughout the liability and equity sides of the balance sheet (called surplus reserves).

Fortunately, in modern accounting the word "allowance" is replacing the word "reserve" in indicating the valuation of assets such as "allowances for depreciation," "allowances for doubtful accounts," etc. In place of the item "reserve for taxes" and other liabilities for which the amount and/or time for payment are uncertain at the time of preparing the balance sheet, items such as "estimated federal income tax" may be used for so-called liability reserves. There is justification for use of the word *reserve* in the third category as noted below, but students should be familiar with the other two because all three types appear on position statements.

BALANCE SHEET—OWNERS' EQUITY

Customarily the amount of equity that owners have in a business firm is indicated by two main accounts, one indicating contributed capital and the other indicating retained earnings. In the case of a corporation, contributed capital comes primarily from stockholders—the owners of the corporation. There may be gifts of assets from others, but that is unusual. Generally, contributed capital will be accounted for in capital stock and capital surplus on the balance sheet. Capital stock is the recorded value of the shares issued to the owners of the business corporation.

Surplus is defined as the excess of a corporation's assets over the sum of its liabilities, plus capital stock. Like the word "reserve," the word "surplus" is used less frequently in modern accounting because the popular meaning of the term (an asset that remains when a use or need has been satisfied) is not applicable. A surplus account is an equity item, not an asset item. Surplus accounts are most commonly divided into two classes: "capital surplus" and "earned surplus," or simply "retained earnings" or "earnings retained in the business."

Capital surplus may result from (1) sale of stock at a premium (the excess over par or stated value is placed in this section), (2) gifts or donations of assets or stock to the corporation, (3) profits from repurchasing shares at a discount, (4) reduction in par or stated value of shares, (5) writing up the value of assets, and so on. Often a statement of capital surplus, explaining changes in this account, is used to supplement the information presented in a balance sheet. An example of such a statement is found in Table 8.

TABLE 8

GENERAL MOTORS CORPORATION STATEMENT OF CONSOLIDATED CAPITAL SURPLUS
(For the Nine Months Ended September 30, 1960 and 1959)

	1960	*1959*
Capital surplus at beginning of the period	$553,273,244	$499,289,887
Paid-in capital in excess of par value of newly issued common stock of $1⅔ par value sold under provisions of:		
General Motors Savings-Stock Purchase Program (967,523 shares in 1960 and 811,052 shares in 1959)	43,459,250	38,900,611
General Motors Stock Option Plan (28,807 shares in 1960 and 18,123 shares in 1959)	967,435	608,631
Capital surplus at end of period	$597,699,929	$538,799,129

Source: General Motors Corporation, *GM Shareholders' Quarterly* (Third Quarter, 1960), p. 5.

Earned surplus or accumulated earnings retained in the business result from the ordinary operations of the business and may include gains from other sources. When not restricted by appropriation to some surplus reserve account, earned surplus is available for dividend payments. As a matter of policy, the board of directors of a business corporation may reduce this "free surplus" by creating reserve accounts for redemption of a bond issue, for planned expansion, contingencies, and so on. Only the bookkeeping records would be changed; there would be no decline in net worth but the earned surplus account would be scattered in part among different reserve accounts. After achieving the purpose for which the reserve account was created, the amount would be returned to the earned surplus account. For illustration, immediately prior to debt retirement, the pertinent accounting items may be as follows:

ASSETS		LIABILITIES AND EQUITIES	
Cash	$ 1,000,000	Debt	$ 1,000,000
Other assets	25,000,000	Capital stock	20,000,000
		Reserve for debt	1,000,000
		Earned surplus	4,000,000
Total	$26,000,000	Total	$26,000,000

After the debt has been paid and the reserve account has been transferred back to earned surplus, the pertinent items would be as follows:

ASSETS		LIABILITIES AND EQUITIES	
Assets	$25,000,000	Capital stock	$20,000,000
		Earned surplus	5,000,000
Total	$25,000,000	Total	$25,000,000

Unless surplus accounts have been "funded" by having specific assets set aside for the purposes indicated, cash may not be available to finance the purposes for which the bookkeeping reserves were created. However, this does not invalidate the practice of creating them because it may be desirable to construct a balance sheet in such a manner that it will reflect the financial plans of management as well as the financial position of a firm. Perhaps the most significant thing to note in regard to new reserves appearing on modern balance sheets is that many are created for the benefit of employees and officers (this may indicate that management is more aware of the importance of good employee–management relations or it may reflect the effectiveness of labor union activities).

Minority Interest. When the item *minority interest* appears on a balance sheet, it represents the investment of minority stockholders of subsidiary companies whose assets have been consolidated with those of the parent corporation. Technically, minority interests represent a portion of the ownership of a corporation and may appear among the capital accounts. A more common procedure, however, is to present this item separately between liabilities and the capital accounts.

INCOME STATEMENTS

A balance sheet presents a statement of assets, liabilities, and proprietorship interest of a company as of a particular day and does not indicate how the position of the company was achieved. An income statement summarizes the transactions between the balance sheet dates, providing the means of "bridging the gap." It contains a comparison of the revenues of a period, which may be a year or a fraction thereof, with the expenses that were incurred to gain those revenues. Thus: REVENUES − (EXPENSES + LOSSES + TAXES) = INCOME. Then to complete the story of the business firm's development, one must use the surplus account which shows extraordinary income and expense items for the period which are not treated as current income or current expenses.

Again, it is important to recognize that there is some disagreement among accountants as to what an income statement should include. One group holds that only normal costs, expenses, and losses identifiable with a given period should be charged against the revenue of that period, while "unusual, nonrecurring or extraordinary gains or losses," when material (that is, large relative to net income), should be carried directly to the earned surplus account. Another group holds that all gains and losses realized during the income period must be included in the income statement. While the Securities and Exchange Commission recognizes the importance of having all items of profit and loss shown in an income statement, it does permit charging extraordinary items to surplus when it is appropriate. A fairly common type of income statement is similar to the hypothetical statement for "Y" Company.

Y COMPANY

INCOME STATEMENT FOR THE YEAR ENDED DECEMBER 31, 1960

Gross sales	$412,000
Less: Returns, allowances, and discounts	12,000
Net sales	$400,000
Cost of goods sold	300,000
Gross profit on sales	$100,000
Operating expenses:	
Wages	$ 42,000
Other expenses	4,000
Bad debt allowance	6,000
Depreciation allowance	8,000
Total Expenses	$ 60,000
Net profit from operations	$ 40,000
Income from other sources	$ 5,000
Less other charges	1,000
Interest	600
Total	$ 3,400
Income before income taxes	$ 43,400
Less allowances for income taxes	15,000
Net income for period	$ 28,400

There are many variations of the simplified form of the income statement in annual and other reports of corporations issued to stockholders, but the orthodox form may be more useful because it is designed to show functional responsibility. In the orthodox income statement, the first item is gross sales, gross revenue, gross billings of customers, or sales of products and services. Amounts for returns of goods, discounts, and allowances are deducted from gross sales to arrive at net sales. If the deduction is unusually large percentagewise, it may indicate a defective product or unwise sales policies such as overselling customers or giving excessively liberal discounts and adjustments, or it may mean that the business situation has worsened and that buyers are taking advantage of credit terms in returning goods they fear they may not be able to sell.

The objective of any business firm is to make a profit on net sales. To find out if this objective has been reached, the first step is to adjust for the cost of goods sold by taking an inventory at the beginning of the period, adding purchases and costs of hauling (freight in), and deducting the value of the inventory at the end of the period. The difference between net sales and the cost of goods sold is gross profit on sales. The next step is to deduct selling and administrative expenses. These expenses cover the cost of doing business excluding the cost of merchandise and financing. These may appear under two items—selling expenses and administrative expenses—or they may be separated in some detail—salaries; office supplies; heat, light and power; general taxes; bad debts; and depreciation of plant, equipment, etc. At this stage there should be some indication of the success or failure of management in carrying on the business because the amount remaining will be net operating income or profits from operations.

Other income will then be added to net operating income, including income from investments, rentals, and miscellaneous sources. Deductions from this amount will include interest on notes and other credit obligations, and other expenses not actually incurred in operations. Further adjustments may be made for past income periods, and the result will be net income before federal income taxes. After these taxes are computed and deducted, what remains is net income. The disposition of net income is reflected in the earned surplus account. A surplus statement may be presented as a continuation of a composite income statement as follows:

Net profits after income taxes	$28,400
Deduct: Cash dividends charged to surplus	10,400
Net Profit retained in the business	$18,000
Add: Earned surplus and surplus reserves at the beginning of the period	$80,000
Add: Other direct charges or credits to surplus (net)	−400
Earned surplus and surplus reserves at the end of the period	$97,600

Customarily, in income statements issued by corporations to their stockholders, there is a comparison of earnings for two or more income periods plus the amount earned per share. This is illustrated by Table 9.

TABLE 9

STATEMENT OF CONSOLIDATED INCOME

"Z" Chemical Corporation and Wholly Owned Subsidiaries

	6 Months Ended May 31, 1960	*6 Months Ended May 31, 1959*
Net sales	$74,994,900	$74,732,200
Income before provision for income taxes	12,731,800	13,947,700
Provision for income taxes	6,344,000	7,050,000
Net income	6,387,800	6,897,700
Preferred dividends	106,250	106,250
Earned per share of common stock	$.86	$.93

Often income statements are so prepared as to express profits and other items as a percentage of sales. An example of this treatment is found in Table 10, which is a composite income statement for the second quarter of 1960 of all manufacturing companies except newspapers.

TABLE 10

COMPOSITE INCOME STATEMENT OF ALL MANUFACTURING COMPANIES EXCEPT NEWSPAPERS

(Second Quarter, 1960)

	Millions of Dollars	*Per Cent of Sales*
Sales (net of returns, allowances, and discounts)	88,092	100.0
Deduct: Costs and expenses (net of purchase discounts)	80,926	91.9
Net profit from operations	7,166	8.1
Add: Other income or deductions (net)	255	0.3
Net profit before federal income taxes	7,421	8.4
Deduct: Provision for federal income taxes	3,340	3.8
Net profit after taxes	4,081	4.6

Source: Federal Trade Commission, Securities and Exchange Commission, *Quarterly Financial Report for Manufacturing Corporations* (Second Quarter, 1960), pp. 12 and 23.

To obtain the fullest benefit from income statement analysis, other facts may be needed. For illustration, it may be desirable to know the disposition of the net income produced. Consequently, a statement of income retained is often prepared as a supplement to an income statement. An example of such a statement is found in Table 11.

FINANCIAL REPORTING

Management would find it impossible to make intelligent business decisions without financial reports, and without such reports a highly complex economy such as that of the United States would be unable to function. Because of variations in accounting practices, it is important to know the basis on which financial statements are prepared as well as to understand the meaning of the captions appearing on such statements. A practice followed by all good students is that of reading footnotes in textbooks; it is equally important for users of financial statements to read the footnotes that accompany them.

TABLE 11

General Motors Corporation and Consolidated Subsidiaries Statement of Consolidated Net Income Retained for Use in the Business
(For the Three Months Ended March 31, 1959 and 1958)

	March 31, 1959	*March 31, 1958*
Net income retained for use in the business (earned surplus) at beginning of the period	$3,763,550,405	$3,701,791,427
Net income for period	293,482,419	184,601,266
Total	$4,057,032,824	$3,886,392,693
Less Cash Dividends:		
Preferred stock—$5.00 series	$ 2,294,555	$ 2,294,555
Preferred stock—$3.75 series	937,519	937,520
Total preferred dividends	$ 3,232,074	$ 3,232,075
Common stock:		
March 10 ($0.50 per share)	$ 140,328,923	$ 139,478,936
Total Cash Dividends	$ 143,560,997	$ 142,711,011
Net income retained for use in the business (earned surplus) at end of the period	$3,913,471,827	$3,743,681,682

Source: General Motors Corporation, *GM Shareholders' Quarterly* (March 31, 1959), p. 5.

The amounts reported in financial statements often do not reflect market values because the financial statement figures are usually based on original costs or valuations which are not necessarily the same as current values because of changes in general prices and other factors. Downward adjustments in valuation figures are permitted to reflect loss of value due to obsolescence, bad debts, and other factors, but these adjustments may be more or less than needed (these adjustments as well as the original estimates of value may be nothing more than someone's opinion). In accounting, certain assumptions are necessary which would be "indefensible if they were not indispensible."

Financial statements are usually prepared on the assumption that the business will continue to operate over a period of time and that if the business does not expand, it will earn at least enough to prevent insolvency. If the concept of a "going concern" needs to be modified, the assets must be reappraised downward, for property sold at bankruptcy prices should have lower valuations than the valuations assigned under standard accounting practices.

Consistency of treatment is essential so that comparisons of successive statements will be meaningful. It is desirable for certified public accountants to state that financial reports have been "prepared in conformity with accepted accounting principles and that they have been applied on a consistent basis."[2] However, changes are permitted provided there is full disclosure of changes in procedures. While the decision as to treatment of many items in an income statement are made by management, certain regulatory agencies have considerable influence on financial reporting. For illustration, income is determined for tax purposes in accordance with the Internal Revenue Code and related regulations and decisions; but for rate making purposes, it is determined by the Interstate Commerce Commission, public utility commissions, and other regulatory agencies. In other cases, the reported profits differ because identical companies may be using alternate methods which are in keeping "with generally accepted accounting principles." For example, a company using the "last-in, first-out" method of inventory valuation will show less net annual income during a period of rising prices than a company using the "first-in, first-out" method of inventory valuation. Likewise, a company that uses the "diminishing-balance" method of depreciation will show less income in the early years than a company using the "straight-line" method of depreciation (see Chapter 7). As a result of using different methods of inventory valuation and depreciation, the reported profits for two identical companies during a particular year may vary by millions of dollars; the fact that profits would be about the same over a period of time would not change the effect of using different permissible accounting methods for a particular year.

Considerable progress is being made in the development of accounting principles and standardization of procedures under the leadership of the American Institute of Certified Public Accountants, American Accounting Association, individual members of the accounting profession, and practitioners. Management is responsible

---

[2] From Libby, McNeill & Libby, *Annual Report for the Year Ended July 2, 1960*, p. 13. Note the following: "In our opinion the accompanying consolidated balance sheet and statement of consolidated income and earnings retained in the business present fairly the financial position of Libby, McNeill & Libby and subsidiary companies at July 2, 1960 and the results of their operations for the fiscal year then ended, in conformity with generally accepted accounting principles applied on a basis consistent with that of the preceding fiscal year. August 5, 1960, Arthur Young & Company."

for the financial reporting of the corporation which it represents, the New York Stock Exchange is responsible for the reporting practices of listed companies, and the Securities and Exchange Commission is responsible for statements intended for investors.

One of the chief duties of the Securities and Exchange Commission is to see that investors receive financial statements that are informative, complete, and least likely to mislead. Under several acts, the Commission is permitted to define accounting terms, to prescribe the form in which required information is to be set forth, and to determine the methods to be followed in preparing financial reports.

The Securities and Exchange Commission has prescribed uniform systems of accounts for companies subject to the provisions of the Public Utility Holding Company Act, formulated rules governing accounting and auditing of securities brokers and dealers under the Securities Exchange Act, and promulgated rules contained in a single comprehensive regulation (Regulation S—X) covering form and content of financial statements filed with the commission in compliance with various acts. Generally, the commission follows the principles that have been developed by business and the accounting profession.

The Interstate Commerce Commission requires common carriers to use a uniform system of accounts prescribed by the commission, the primary purpose being to facilitate regulation (but the basic procedures were established in 1914 and have not been modernized). Reports required include comparative balance sheets and income or profit and loss statements, supporting schedules, and operating and other statistical data—including the number of employees, compensation paid them, and services which they render.

SUMMARY

The financial, administrative, and income tax accounting statements of business firms are among the tools used by management in financial and business planning. The balance sheet contains information about the owners' equity, retained earnings, and investment of borrowed capital. In the orthodox balance sheet, assets are classified as current assets; investments and miscellaneous assets; real estate, plants, and equipment; deferred charges; and goodwill, patents, etc. On the liabilities side of the balance sheet are current liabilities, fixed indebtedness, reserves, capital, and surplus.

The income statement, designed to report on income and income-producing activities, shows the results of a business concern's operations over a period of time. The major items in the income statement are net sales less allowances for costs, interest, and depreciation; net income; amount earned on common stock; and amount earned per share of common stock. The surplus statement is a report of the net income retained for use in the business over a period of time. The major items in such a statement are net income retained for use in the business—earned surplus at the beginning of the period, less cash dividends on preferred and common stock, and net income retained for use in the business—earned surplus at the end of the period.

Variations in accounting practices may cause overstatement or understatement of costs, expenses, profits, and other items found in balance sheet and income statements. Thus, changing circumstances (especially those occasioned by changes in the value of money) require adjustments in accounting practices if a true picture of the position of the business enterprise is to be portrayed in its financial statements. As protection against "window dressing," the New York Stock Exchange, the Securities and Exchange Commission, and state and federal regulatory agencies require that financial statements be audited by responsible independent public accountants. The Internal Revenue Service specifies accounting procedures for income tax accounting purposes and exerts a substantial influence on financial accounting and reporting.

QUESTIONS AND PROBLEMS

1. (*a*) Distinguish among operating, financial, and income tax accounting statements. (*b*) What are the most important financial statements?
2. Distinguish between "current" and "fixed" assets.
3. Identify: (*a*) chief forms of current assets, and (*b*) types of receivables.
4. For what purposes may special funds be created? Do they help to explain why business firms have short-term investments in government securities?
5. (*a*) Should a business firm's investments in corporate securities be considered as available working capital? (*b*) May loans to employees be considered a proper outlet for funds? Why?
6. What is meant by an inventory? What should be the objective of inventory management?
7. Identify: (*a*) current liabilities. (*b*) long-term indebtedness, and (*c*) contingent liabilities.
8. What are "reserve accounts?"
9. List and explain the items usually appearing under "capital" on a balance sheet.

10. Financial statements are usually prepared on the assumption that the business will continue to operate over a period of time. If this assumption needs to be revised, how will valuations be affected? Why?
11. Identify the different items appearing on the profit and loss or income statement.
12. In computing net income for a period, items which are material (large relative to income) should be excluded if misleading inferences would be drawn when included in reporting net income. What is the importance of this principle if used by management?
13. Comment on each of the following:
    (*a*) "These companies maintain their accounts in accordance with Uniform System of Accounts prescribed for telephone companies by the Federal Communications Commission." (American Telephone and Telegraph Company, *1959 Annual Report* [New York, 1960], p. 23.)
    (*b*) "In our opinion, the accompanying balance sheet and statement of earnings and earnings reinvested in the business present fairly the financial position of The Chesapeake and Ohio Railway Company at December 31, 1958 and the results of its operations for the year then ended, in conformity with principles of accounting prescribed or authorized by the Interstate Commerce Commission applied on a basis consistent with that of the preceding year. Peat, Marwick, Mitchell & Co." (The Chesapeake and Ohio Railway Company, *Annual Report for the Year Ended December 31, 1958* [Cleveland, 1959], p. 32.)
    (*c*) "The Company and its subsidiaries have consistently followed the practice of publishing their accounts without deduction for depletion of metal mines, and no such deduction is included in these financial statements." (The Anaconda Company, *Annual Report for the Year Ended December 31, 1959* [New York, 1960], p. 22.)
    (*d*) "For the year 1959 General Motors provided $919 million for United States and foreign taxes on income . . . In addition provisions for other taxes such as state and local taxes and the Corporation's share of social security taxes . . . brought GM's total tax bill . . . to $1,250 million . . ." (General Motors Corporation, *Fifty-First Annual Report Year Ended December 31, 1959* [New York, 1960], p. 28.)

CHAPTER 5

Working Capital Needs of Business Firms

CAPITAL, when defined in terms of assets, includes all of the resources owned by a firm. For purposes of financial management, assets of a firm are usually divided into working capital assets, which include cash and those which will be converted into cash within one year in the normal course of business; fixed capital assets, which not only include land, buildings, and equipment, but also include intangibles and investments; and other noncurrent assets.

There are two concepts of working capital. The first is synonymous with current assets, and the second refers to the excess of current assets over current liabilities. This second concept, though commonly used by credit analysts and others interested in determining the debt paying power of a business, seems illogical to most businessmen who see working capital as the medium through which assets of a firm are acquired. For purposes of clarity, this text will employ the term *working capital* to mean current assets (cash and other assets that will shortly be converted into cash in the normal operations of a business) and will use the term *net working capital* to mean the excess of current assets over current liabilities.

Current assets, because of their form, have great flexibility and can be used immediately (cash items) or after a short period (noncash items) to achieve various business objectives. Consequently, the management of working capital is not only one of the most vital, but also one of the most interesting aspects of financial management.

Over the years, financial managers have come to recognize two important and sometimes difficult-to-achieve goals: one is the maintenance of a proper relationship between working capital and sales; the other is an avoidance of an overinvestment in inventory (sometimes called the "graveyard of business firms"). By paying proper attention to these two objectives of working capital management and by avoiding excessive investment in fixed assets (which is discussed in the next chapter), the danger of insolvency is minimized. This chapter deals with the nature of working capital assets and the financing of their acquisition, as well as with some of the more important working capital ratios used by managers.

WORKING CAPITAL

Every business firm needs funds with which to finance its working capital assets. Such funds may be obtained from proprietors, from investors through the sale of securities, from lenders, from suppliers of goods and services, and from the firm's own operations; usually, two or more of these sources of funds are used, and for a firm already in operation, the last is the most important source. It has been suggested that the term *circulating capital* should be substituted for the term *working capital* in order to emphasize the circular-flow nature of funds invested in working capital assets.

Concept of Circulating Capital. At the beginning of a business venture, cash is provided by owners and lenders. A part of this cash is invested in tools, machinery, furniture, equipment, buildings, and other forms of fixed capital assets which are not to be sold throughout the year during the normal course of business. The remainder of the cash is kept available as working capital to meet the current requirements of the business enterprise, such as purchases of services, raw materials, merchandise, and other things needed to operate the business. From these expenditures, merchandise or inventories of finished goods will become available—thus completing the first phase in the circular flow of working capital (see Illustration 2).

The finished merchandise of any business firm will be priced and sold to other business firms or to consumers on terms common to firms within the particular division of the industry. Credit sales will be accounted for as accounts receivable, which normally have maturities of thirty days after the billing date. Terms usually permit generous discounts for cash remittances within a specified period; therefore, most accounts receivable are paid within two weeks after the billing date. When payment is received, the circular flow of working capital is complete—that is, from cash to merchandise to accounts receivable and back to cash. If the business firm is profitable, the sum of cash obtained at the end of each cycle will be greater than the amount originally paid out. Each cycle should provide a gross profit, and the amount of net earnings for the year will depend, in part, on the number of times that working capital is turned over. The flow of working capital through the different stages

ILLUSTRATION 2

Circular Flow of Working Capital

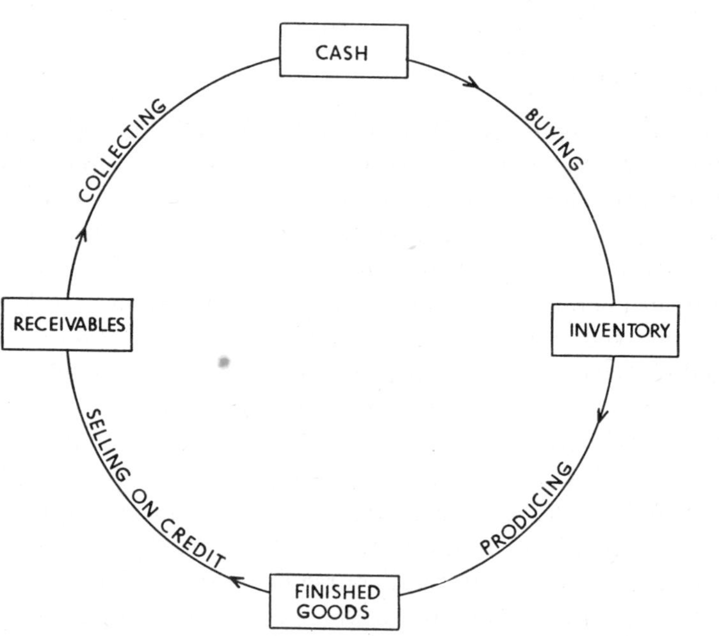

of business operation does not always proceed smoothly. For illustration, if merchandise is difficult to sell or if receivables are impossible to collect, working capital becomes congealed or frozen.

Permanence of Working Capital. Working capital may be classified as permanent, regular or normal, and seasonal or variable. Permanent working capital is the minimum amount of current assets needed to conduct a business even during the dullest season of the year. This amount will vary from year to year depending on the growth of the business firm and the stage of the business cycle. Permanent working capital should be supplied by owners, obtained with long-term credit, and from operations—retained earnings; but some business firms depend on trade creditors, commercial banks, finance companies, and others for a large part of their permanent working capital needs.

Seasonal or variable working capital is the additional amount of current assets (particularly cash, inventories, and receivables) required during the most active business seasons of the year (see Illustration 3). Normally, business firms which are subject to seasonal working capital needs borrow short-term funds from commercial

ILLUSTRATION 3

CAPITAL NEEDS OF BUSINESS FIRMS

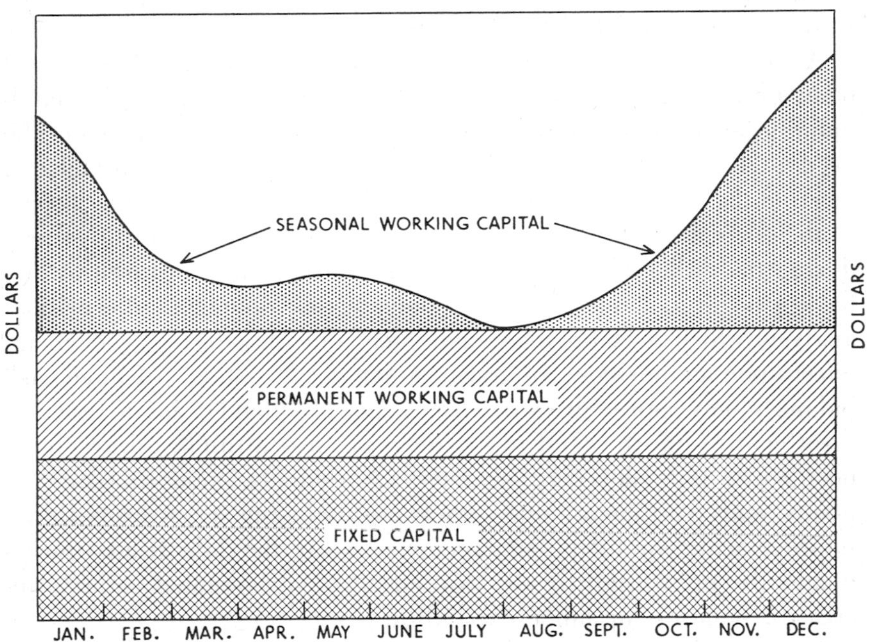

banks or other lenders to finance enlarged payrolls, inventories, and accounts receivable. A business firm usually anticipates seasonal needs for funds by arranging for a line of credit at the beginning of the calendar or fiscal year. A line of credit is merely an understanding with a bank that it will lend up to a certain amount if the credit standing of the customer does not deteriorate sharply. In some cases, management may arrange for a definite loan commitment, a contract to make cash available under specified conditions. Although good banking connections are not reflected in the balance sheet of a business firm, their presence may be as important as assets which do appear there.

In computing working capital needs, finance officers can be fairly accurate in estimating the need for cash to meet periodic obligations such as interest payments on loans, cash dividends which have been declared, federal income taxes, debt retirement installments, and sinking fund obligations. But additional working capital needs may arise because of more remote circumstances such as strikes, stoppage of work, public improvements that interfere with normal trade (street closing, traffic re-routing, and so on), accidents, fires, floods, and other happenings. A business firm may protect itself against some of these hazards by carrying insurance; in addition, it may want to keep a more-than-normal amount of working capital in the form of cash and marketable securities.

A business firm may avoid borrowing to finance seasonal and other needs by keeping current assets in amounts equal to its maximum needs. This policy, it is true, would free management from the need to borrow for short-term purposes and from the anxiety of meeting the company's obligations; however, it would result in part of the current assets being idle, or bearing but a low rate of return, during the dull business season. While most firms would enjoy not having to go to banks and other lenders for financing, the critical analysis which accompanies such financing may have a beneficial effect upon the business. In addition, the very existence of huge cash balances may cause pressure for larger dividends; invite government control efforts; tend to create a careless attitude toward business costs, thus delaying changes in products, modernization of plants and equipment, and other cost-reducing or sales-building improvements; or tempt management to use the idle funds uneconomically or wastefully by authorizing unwarranted salary increases, bonuses, or other expenditures.

On the other hand, working capital in amounts exceeding the usual needs of a business have proven beneficial in some cases. For example, following World War II, the existence of excess working capital assets permitted many business firms to use substantial sums for research, replacement of obsolete equipment, purchase of other companies, and expansion of their operations. The accumulation of excess cash and near cash assets during good times may permit a business corporation to adopt a more stable dividend policy over a long period of time.

Irrespective of the arguments in favor of and opposed to the accumulation of excess amounts of working capital assets, the trend among business firms is toward the achievement of greater liquidity of assets. Repeated experience with business fluctuations, wide price movements, and rapid technological changes have caused management of major companies to follow conservative working capital policies.

FACTORS INFLUENCING THE AMOUNT OF WORKING CAPITAL

There are a number of factors which influence the amount of working capital needed by a business firm. These include the characteristics of the industry in which the firm operates, the size and age of the firm, variations in terms of purchase and sale contracts, and the cyclical and seasonal nature of the business of the company. The last of these is the chief factor determining the amount of temporary working capital needed by a particular firm. Public utility companies—chiefly gas, light, power, and water companies—have regularity of income and small investments in inventories other than supplies. On the other hand, they must invest large amounts in plants and equipment. Thus, their short-term investments compared to their long-term investments are relatively small.

Generally, inventories are small for service industries, but they constitute the most important short-term asset of mining companies, manufacturing firms, and retail and wholesale trade companies. (By definition, services include all outlays for which no physical goods are received in return.) The funds needed by a business firm which provides personal services consist mainly of outlays for supplies needed in operations, till money for change, and bank accounts for payrolls and other current expenses.

Working capital assets of manufacturing corporations are substantial, amounting to over 50 per cent of the total assets (see Table 12), but a typical business firm operating in the retail trade field leases its store space and has even a larger percentage of its total assets in the form of current assets. A business firm whose expenditures entail large seasonal variations needs more working capital to finance raw materials, wages, and other items than another firm with little or no seasonal variation in output. Thus a company producing a variety of items may be able to use its assets more economically than a company which produces only one item, even though both firms may be in the same industry.

Another factor which is important in determining the amount of working capital needed is size. The amount needed will be relatively large per unit of output for a small company that is subject to higher overhead costs, less favorable buying terms, and higher interest rates —and that operates with poorer technological methods and occupies

TABLE 12

WORKING CAPITAL ASSETS OF MANUFACTURING COMPANIES EXCEPT NEWSPAPERS
FIRST QUARTER, 1960
(In Millions of Dollars and Percentages of Total Assets)

Items	*Dollars*	*Per Cent*
Cash on hand and in banks	13,842	5.6
U.S. Government securities (including savings notes)	13,469	5.4
Total Cash and U.S. Government Securities	27,311	11.0
Receivables from U.S. Government (excluding tax credits)	2,689	1.1
Other notes and receivables (net)	36,534	14.7
Total Receivables	39,223	15.8
Inventories	60,102	24.3
Other current assets	6,179	2.5
Total Current Assets	132,815	53.6

Source: Federal Trade Commission—Securities and Exchange Commission, *Quarterly Financial Report for Manufacturing Companies, First Quarter 1960* (Washington, D.C.: U.S. Government Printing Office, 1960), pp. 12 and 34.

a less favorable competitive position than a comparable middle-size or larger firm in the same field. Small growing companies tend to be hard pressed in financing their working capital needs because they seldom have access to the open market as do larger, established business firms.

Working capital needs will vary among businesses in the same industry because of differences in purchase and sale terms. For illustration, a retailer who buys for cash and sells on credit will need more working capital than a retailer who buys on credit and sells for cash (the latter may even be operating on the proverbial shoestring). Buying practices and sales terms affect both the quantity and quality of assets. A department store which caters to the "carriage trade" by carrying a quality line of merchandise and offering extensive charge accounts will usually have a slow turnover of assets, a high margin on sales, and relatively large accounts receivables. A second department store which stresses "cash and carry" operations will usually have a rapid turnover, a low margin on sales, and little or no accounts receivables.

Risk is an important factor in determining working capital needs because the greater the uncertainty of receipts and expenditures, the greater the need for working capital. A business firm producing an item which sells for a small unit price and which necessitates repeat buying—such as canned foods or staple dry goods—would be subject to less risk than a firm producing a semiluxury item which sells for a relatively high price and is purchased but once over a period of years—such as jewelry, furniture, automobiles, and household appliances.

Among the other risks of carrying on business operations are those associated with the business cycle. The extent to which a particular business firm is affected depends upon the factors previously noted—the nature of the industry, purchase and sale practices, size, and the product handled. Well managed business firms may change their policies to coincide with expected changes in business activity. For illustration, they may adjust their inventories to correspond to current and expected sales. Cash sales and prompt collections may be emphasized during the peak of the business cycle and de-emphasized during depressions (or the reverse in some cases). Ease of financing may also be a factor in working capital needs, and some business firms may be forced to reduce expenditures when loan credit becomes restricted. At such times, an increase in the turnover of working capital assets may make credit restriction less burdensome.

ANALYSIS OF NET WORKING CAPITAL

One of the primary goals of financial management is that of maintaining adequate net working capital, the excess of current assets over current liabilities. If a firm has inadequate net working capital, it may encounter difficulties in meeting its obligations. While it is a common and proper practice for financial management to concern itself with cash statements, a net working capital statement may be more revealing. For illustration, a cash statement can create the illusion of adequate cash merely by postponing payment, while net working capital, being a residual amount, is less subject to manipulation.

Management may note changes in net working capital by an analysis similar to the one which follows:

Sources of funds during the year	
From operations:	
Income	$1,000,000
Plus expenses of a nonfunded nature previously deleted	500,000
Total Funds from Operations	$1,500,000
New financing with debts	500,000
New financing with stock	500,000
Sales of fixed assets	100,000
Total Sources	$2,600,000
Application of funds during the year	
Retirement of long-term debt	$1,000,000
Purchase of fixed assets	1,600,000
Dividends on stock	100,000
Net change in funds	−$100,000

The above statement is known by a variety of names, such as a statement of changes in net working capital, statement of financial operations, or statement of funds (funds as used in this statement is synonymous with net working capital). It illustrates, among other things, the relationship between long-term financing and changes in net working capital. Funds from operations include not only income but also allowances for depreciation and similar charges which are costs of doing business; since these are not cash outlays, they do not reduce funds available for use. This statement shows a decrease in net working capital even though income from operations suggests a profitable year. Management may find this statement helpful not only in indicating changes in a company's net working capital but also as material upon which to base a decision concerning cash dividends, expansion programs, salary increases, and other fund-using programs.

If more detailed information is desired, a statement of changes in working capital instead of net working capital may be prepared. Such a statement will emphasize changes in the specific assets which constitute working capital. An illustration follows:

	Jan. 1	*Dec. 31*	*Change*
Cash	$ 400,000	$ 350,000	$− 50,000
Accounts receivables	600,000	625,000	+25,000
Inventories	800,000	750,000	−50,000
Total Current Assets	$1,800,000	$1,725,000	$ −75,000
Current liabilities	500,000	525,000	+25,000
Net working capital	$1,300,000	$1,200,000	$−100,000

From the above, it can be seen that the change in net working capital is the same as that revealed in the previous statement; however, this statement is more specific in that it points out the change in each asset affecting working capital.

Need for Adequate Net Working Capital. As was stated previously, one of the primary requisites of sound financial management is that of maintaining an adequate amount of net working capital (current assets less current liabilities). The proper amount of net working capital depends on many factors, but one method of testing for adequacy is to compute net working capital turnover as follows:

$$\frac{\text{ANNUAL NET SALES, \$678,000}}{\text{NET WORKING CAPITAL, \$110,000}} = 6.2 \text{ TIMES.}$$

A turnover of 6.2 indicates the amount of business done (sales) by each dollar of net working capital during a year. A business firm [illegible]e net working capital turnover is too high is subject to financial [illegible]n when there is a decline in receipts or an increase in expenditures. Such things as delay in collecting accounts or a strike can have disastrous results if net working capital is inadequate.

TABLE 13

SELECTED STANDARD RATIOS OF BUSINESS FIRMS

Line of Business	*Net Sales to Net Working Capital (Times)*	*Net Profit on Net Working Capital (Per Cent)*	*Current Assets to Current Liabilities (Times)*	*Collection Period (Days)*
Manufacturers				
Breweries	8.26	15.37	2.71	18
Cotton cloth mills	3.58	7.35	4.62	37
Drugs	3.35	31.48	2.85	38
Furniture	4.90	12.90	3.17	41
Stoves, ranges, ovens	4.64	12.68	3.74	41
Wholesalers				
Dry goods	4.71	4.54	3.17	49
Fresh fruits and produce	15.80	9.02	2.77	15
Groceries	10.71	8.51	2.81	15
Lumber	4.92	4.57	3.36	43
Women's wear	5.67	1.67	2.57	58
Retailers				
Department stores	3.95	6.98	3.57	x
Groceries & meat chain	18.42	6.41	1.71	x
Hardware	4.00	5.51	3.35	x
Lumber, building materials	3.35	6.26	4.21	67
Shoes	5.01	11.32	2.70	x

x not computed

Source: Roy A. Foulke, *Current Trends in Terms of Sales* (New York: Dun & Bradstreet, Inc., 1959) Selected from Tables for 72 Lines of Business Activity, pp. 48–59.

If net working capital turnover is too low, it probably indicates that the firm is not using its resources efficiently and that profits are consequently lower than necessary. Financial managers, in an effort to test the profitableness of net working capital, compute the profit per dollar of net working capital (divide net profits by net sales). Usually a low turnover will be accompanied by low profit per dollar of net working capital. Such a situation requires corrective measures and may result in retirement of long-term debt, expansion of business, or distribution of funds to owners (larger dividends).

An increase in business will normally require an increase in most of the current assets (cash, inventory, receivables, etc.). The safest financial policy would entail an increase in net working capital preferably by increasing equity capital. If an increase in equity capital is not feasible, net working capital can be increased by resorting to long-term debt (term loans, bond issues, or other long-term arrangements).

If a business firm needing additional funds borrows from a commercial bank for a three-month period, there is no change in its net working capital; but, if it were to borrow for a five-year period, net working capital would increase by the amount of the loan. These situations may be illustrated by the following examples:

	Company A	*Company B*
ASSETS		
Current Assets:		
Cash	$ 20,000	$ 20,000
Accounts receivable	40,000	40,000
Inventories	100,000	100,000
Other current assets	20,000	20,000
Total Current Assets	$180,000	$180,000
Fixed assets	100,000	100,000
Total Assets	$280,000	$280,000
LIABILITIES AND NET WORTH		
Current Liabilities:		
Notes payable at bank	$ 10,000	
Accounts payable	50,000	$ 50,000
Other current liabilities	10,000	10,000
Total Current Liabilities	$ 70,000	$ 60,000
Long-Term Debt and Equity:		
Mortgage loan		$ 10,000
Bonds		120,000
Net worth	$210,000	90,000
Total Liabilities and Equity	$280,000	$280,000

Supplementary information to Company A financial statement.

Annual net sales for year	$678,000
Net profits after taxes	$ 21,000
Net working capital	$110,000

Net working capital for Company A is $110,000 ($180,000 – $70,000) and for Company B, $120,000 ($180,000 – $60,000). If Company A repays the bank loan when due, its current assets will be reduced by $10,000 and its current liabilities by the same amount, so its net working capital will remain the same. But Company B has improved its net working capital position by long-term borrowing.

If the amount of long-term debt is divided by net working capital, it will give the percentage of the company's funded debt that has been invested in current assets. For Company B this percentage is found as follows:

$$\frac{\text{Funded Debt, \$130,000}}{\text{Net Working Capital, \$120,000}} = 108.3 \text{ Per Cent.}$$

The higher the funded debt–net working capital ratio, the greater the amount of current assets being financed with long-term debt. A percentage in excess of 100 indicates that net working capital current assets are less than the funded debt and that the equity of the owners as well as part of the funded debt is tied up in noncurrent assets. This situation would indicate a heavy long-term debt structure which could cause difficulties in financing sinking fund requirements and meeting debt maturities. A percentage of 25 or less may be fairly normal for retail and wholesale trade companies and a somewhat higher percentage would be normal for manufacturing companies (see Table 14).

TABLE 14

SELECTED STANDARD RATIOS OF BUSINESS FIRMS

Line of Business	*Current Debt to Inventory (Per Cent)*	*Inventory to Net Working Capital (Per Cent)*	*Funded Debt to Net Working Capital (Per Cent)*	*Net Sales to Inventory (Times)*
Manufacturers				
Breweries	129.0	46.8	44.2	19.5
Cotton cloth mills	38.7	81.0	24.1	4.2
Drugs	90.0	62.8	26.4	5.5
Furniture	72.2	68.7	23.0	5.9
Stoves, ranges, ovens	54.9	72.6	27.8	5.2
Wholesalers				
Dry goods	65.8	68.6	17.4	6.2
Fresh fruits & produce	201.9	28.9	50.9	66.7
Groceries	55.8	98.2	22.8	10.9
Lumber	63.2	70.2	23.7	5.2
Women's wear	155.7	43.9	41.5	7.4
Retailers				
Department stores	59.2	67.1	32.7	5.7
Groceries & meat chain	82.6	155.1	53.1	14.1
Hardware	49.6	83.4	32.6	3.2
Lumber, building materials	56.6	66.3	25.2	5.5
Shoes	47.7	117.9	21.1	3.9

Source: Roy A. Foulke, *Current Trends in Terms of Sales* (New York: Dun & Bradstreet, Inc., 1959), Selected from Tables for 72 Lines of Business Activity, pp. 48–59.

The old adage "Beware of top-heavy liabilities" is just as pertinent today as in the past. Businessmen who are heavily in debt sometimes borrow funds on terms that violate the requisites of sound financial principles, thus increasing the danger of insolvency. The elimination of top-heavy debt situations would curtail business failures sharply. Debts may be reduced by (1) using cash obtained from liquidation of assets (which is not always practical), (2) obtaining funds from sales of capital stock (which is not always feasible), and (3) using funds from operations such as earnings (which cannot be obtained overnight). So the correct policy for management is to watch its debts and to prevent the development of a top-heavy debt structure.

Liquidity Ratios. Business management recognizes the need to be able to meet obligations as they come due and most business firms construct various ratios that indicate their current debt paying ability. Among the most widely used for this purpose is the current ratio which is found by dividing current assets by current liabilities. For Company A this would be:

$$\frac{\text{Current Assets, \$180,000}}{\text{Current Liabilities, \$70,000}} \text{ or } 2.57\,.$$

After repaying the bank loan, Company A would have a current ratio of $\frac{\$170,000}{\$\ 60,000}$ or 2.83. While repayment of the current debt does not change the net working capital of the company, it causes the company to have a more favorable current ratio.

Generally a current ratio of 2.73 is satisfactory, but there is no single correct ratio, as is shown by Table 13. However, a current ratio of at least 2.0 is considered desirable in most lines of business. A low current ratio may be improved in several ways: repaying current debts, borrowing for terms of more than a year, collecting tax refunds, converting noncurrent assets into current assets, increasing investments in current assets, and retaining earnings. On the other hand, the current ratio may be reduced by short-term borrowing, buying goods and materials on account, accruing federal income taxes and other expenses, converting current assets into noncurrent assets, paying cash dividends, and decreasing profits.

The chief advantages of having a high current ratio is that it protects a business firm from difficulties that might arise because of accounts receivable becoming noncollectible or inventories unsalable. When there is insufficient cash to meet maturing liabilities, a business firm is at the mercy of its creditors. Bankers are interested in making loans that will be repaid; therefore, a business firm with a weak current ratio may find it impossible to borrow additional funds when the need for them is greatest.

The chief value of the current ratio is that it provides an index of the ability of a business firm to pay its short-term debts. As is true for all ratios, the use of current ratios requires intelligent analysis and comparison to those of other companies in the same field (see Table 13). Although at one time a current ratio of 2 to 1 was considered adequate, further analysis has indicated that the quality of current assets and also current liabilities varies from time to time for a particular company and from company to company (depending on the nature of the business). For illustration, for different business firms the types of goods that make up inventories vary from raw materials and semi-manufactured goods, to merchandise held for sale. The last may range from highly marketable goods whose value may be established readily to goods having only a special market. The dollar value of goods carried as inventory may have little or no relationship to reality; also, because of different methods of valuation, any comparison of the inventory positions of different companies may be misleading.

Conversion of inventories into cash entails two steps, sales and then collection of receivables. Neither is assured. Inventories tend to be largest during business booms and this gives a misleading impression of the liquidity of a business firm. Deliberate liquidation of inventories by a business firm to improve its cash position would ordinarily occur under pressing financial circumstances irrespective of the need to maintain an adequate stock of goods for efficient operations. Thus, a current ratio of 2 to 1 or a higher current ratio may not reveal a satisfactory liquidity ratio during some phases of a business cycle. Since inventories are the least liquid of working capital assets, a comparison of current assets minus inventories to current liabilities may give a more meaningful ratio than the current ratio. This so-called quick asset ratio of Company A would be $\frac{\$180,000 - \$100,000}{\$70,000}$ or 1.14 times, which is larger than the rule-of-thumb ratio (1 to 1).

In the final analysis, the best test of the liquid position of a business firm is its ratio of cash plus securities (mainly government obligations) to current liabilities. Although government securities are not cash, many of them are either short term or approaching maturity. Others may be tax anticipation notes that can be used to pay income taxes. Unlike inventories and receivables, government securities held by a business firm may be sold readily to obtain cash when needed without disrupting business operations.

Other modifications of the current ratio emphasize the quality of current liabilities. Some current liabilities may be due within a day or two and others at the end of the year, some may be owed to open-market creditors and payable at maturity, and others may be bank loans which are customarily renewed or extended on request at maturity. Each type of liability may have a different effect on the future working capital position of a business firm.

Excessive Investment in Inventories. Avoidance of excessive investment in materials, merchandise, and supplies is an elementary rule of financial management, and probably no rule of financial management is more frequently violated. Usually an inventory is not only the largest but also the least liquid of a firm's current assets. Proper analysis of an inventory requires the use of several ratios, one of which is the inventory–net capital ratio which for Company A is as follows:

$$\frac{\text{INVENTORIES, \$100,000}}{\text{NET WORKING CAPITAL \$110,000}} = 0.91\,.$$

Comparison of standard ratios of a business firm to those of other companies in the same line of business indicates whether a firm has too little or too much so invested. However, the dollar value of inventories is influenced not only by the stock of goods but also by the accounting method used in its evaluation, such as actual costs which are indicated by code or number for each item in stock or a derived cost method. Derived cost methods include: (1) average costs, found by averaging unit prices as taken from inventories or dividing total costs of goods to be accounted for by the number of units; (2) standard costs, which prices each unit at a "standard" or uniform cost previously determined; (3) "first-in, first-out," or FIFO, which assumes goods are sold in the order acquired, and (4) "last-in, first-out," or LIFO, which assumes that goods acquired last are sold first.

The method of accounting for inventories may affect not only their book value but also the net profits of the company. The use of the last-in first-out method tends to stabilize income, and the opposite is true for the first-in first-out method. Under the last-in first-out method, goods, materials and supplies are valued at current replacement costs rather than at actual purchase costs. During periods of rising prices, this results in inventories being carried at more conservative values, serving in effect to increase costs of goods sold and reduce reported profits and income taxes. However, if inventories at year-end are smaller than a year earlier, some of the tax advantage is lost because a taxable profit must be reported on that part of the inventory not replaced after being used up or sold. However, when the last-in first-out method is used during periods of falling prices, reported inventories remain high, losses are concealed, and taxable income is relatively large. A proposed new Internal Revenue Service rule that would permit all inventories to be pooled would reduce the tax impact resulting from falling prices —a combined inventory method would permit increases in some "pools" to offset decreases in other "pools" for tax purposes.[1]

One way to check the freshness of the stock which makes up the inventory is to compute the net sales–inventory ratio, also called the inventory–turnover ratio. This is found by dividing net sales for a year by the inventory carried on the books at the end of the year. When sales are $678,000, the turnover of inventory for Company A would be as follows:

$$\frac{\text{Net Sales, \$678,000}}{\text{Inventory, \$100,000}} \text{ or 6.8 Times.}$$

A more meaningful inventory turnover ratio would result if the figure for "cost of goods sold" were compared to inventory, or if the dollar amount of inventory were computed at retail prices before being compared to net sales. As customarily used, there is a comparison of sales at retail prices to inventories at wholesale prices. (Some department stores carry inventory at retail prices.) Neither of these methods of adjusting values to the same price basis may be practical; therefore a third method of adjusting the inventory–turnover ratio has been suggested—dividing the uncorrected ratio by the mark-up plus 1. If the mark-up in prices is 50 per cent, the corrected ratio for Company A would be:

$$6.8 \div (0.50 + 1) = 4.5 .$$

The inventory-turnover ratio, like other ratios, is computed for comparison of one period to another or one company to a second; therefore it is of value irrespective of the method used, provided the ratio is computed in the same way each time. However it is not an accurate measure of physical turnover of goods because accuracy could only be obtained by counting every item in stock and comparing it to the physical sales of those same items.

Inventories may be checked against current debt to determine the amount of equity that short-term creditors have in inventories. The current debt to inventory ratio helps to answer the question as to who is financing stock in trade—the owners and long-term creditors, or

[1] *Wall Street Journal* (New York: December 7, 1960), p. 1.

trade and other short-term creditors. For Company A this ratio would be

$$\frac{\text{Current Debt, \$70,000}}{\text{Inventories, \$100,000}} = 70 \text{ Per Cent},$$

an unsatisfactory ratio for most retail firms but a satisfactory ratio for some manufacturing firms and wholesalers (see Table 14).

Another ratio used to test the quality of current assets is the inventory–current assets ratio. If this percentage is low, it means that current assets are made up largely of cash, receivables, and other more liquid assets; if the percentage is high, it means that less liquid assets predominate. A business firm having a low inventory–current assets ratio may be in a more satisfactory position with a current ratio of 2 to 1 than a second firm having a high inventory–current assets ratio with a 3 to 1 current ratio. Actually, the use of this ratio would tend to give the same results as the acid test or quick assets ratio. This suggests that it may be better to use a few ratios and to understand their significance than to compute a large number which overlap.

The conclusion usually drawn from inventory ratios is that the more rapid the turnover, the smaller will be the amount of working capital needed in terms of net sales and the larger will be total profits (unless the apparent rapidity of sales is due to an excessive markdown in prices, understocking, and other factors). Holding more inventories than needed is a form of speculation which is usually criticized, but sometimes speculation in inventories is profitable (as for many firms that bought in excess of current needs at the outbreak of World War II and the Korean War).

Receivables. Business firms which sell on credit have the problem of screening customers as to credit worthiness and of collecting notes or accounts receivable after making sales. The device most commonly used to test the promptness with which receivables are collected is one which expresses the result in terms of days required for collection. If one half of the sales of Company A are credit sales, the formula would be

$$\frac{\text{Accounts Receivable, \$40,000} \times 360}{\text{Net Credit Sales, \$339,000}}$$

or 42 days, the number of days accounts are outstanding. The same results would be obtained by dividing annual credit sales by 360 days to obtain the average credit sales per day and then dividing the total accounts receivable by the average credit sales per day. Some analysts prefer to use 365 days rather than 360 days, but this is of minor importance since the collection ratio is only a rough index of how long funds are tied up in credit sales. An analysis of individual accounts is required to determine which accounts are past due and how long they have been overdue.

When a business firm does not keep separate records for credit sales, any inventory ratio based on total sales loses some of its meaning. Most business firms know the approximate percentage of credit sales to total sales. Assuming the figure for Company A is 50 per cent, the ratio would be computed as follows:

$$\frac{\text{Accounts Receivable } \$40{,}000 \times 360}{\text{Total Sales, } \$678{,}000} \times \frac{100}{50} = 42 \text{ Days.}$$

One criticism of the collection ratio is that the amount of receivables outstanding at the end of the year is not likely to be representative since receivables are usually at a seasonal low at that time, while credit sales for the year have no seasonal factor affecting the total. A more accurate method would be to use daily averages of receivables, but such an average would be difficult to compute. If the accounting records do not reflect some unusual factor at the time of the balance sheet statement, the collection ratio will indicate roughly whether collections are improving, deteriorating, or remaining the same. When compared to the collection ratios of similar firms in the same line, they will indicate the relative position of the company among its competitors. Receivables, like inventories, tend to expand when the volume of business is rising, but they are not cash until they are collected; slowing down of collections is often a factor in tightening financial conditions.

When the collection period is longer than that of the average for companies in the same line or industry and the collection ratio is increasing as compared to that of previous years, it is time for management to review its credit and collection policies. A business firm may not be in a position to stop credit sales to all overdue customers, but it may curtail the amount of credit extended to such customers. A credit policy which is too rigid relative to that of competitors may destroy future business, but one which is too liberal may be even less desirable. If the volume of receivables is too high, it may be necessary for some individual accounts to be written off in order to show a realistic situation. However, if the fault lies with those responsible for collecting accounts receivable, a vigorous collection policy may turn some of the past-due accounts into cash. Although loans to officers, employees, and outsiders are sometimes included among receivables of business firms, they should be carried in a separate account as nonbusiness receivables. The important point is for management to watch not only its own collection period but also that of its competitors (see Table 13).

SUMMARY

The working capital of a firm is its circulating capital, which flows from cash to inventories, to production, to receivables, and back to cash. If the business is profitable, the amount of cash at the end of each cycle will be greater than at the beginning of the cycle. The number of times the working capital is turned over during a year will be a factor in the firm's net earnings. Some of the working capital or current assets of a firm will be in cash on hand, time deposits in banks, United States government obligations, and loans and other investments. The remainder will be in receivables and in inventories. Financial management includes the administration of fixed and current assets, which necessitates co-ordination of selling and credit policies. Inventory management includes requisitioning, purchasing, storekeeping, accounting, and auditing as well as determining the kinds and amounts of goods to purchase and/or produce.

In analyzing a particular business firm's working capital position, management may use ratios such as the inventory–turnover ratio, inventory–net working capital ratio, inventory–current debt ratio, collection ratios, and current ratios. When these ratios are calculated on the same date each year over a period of years, they will indicate significant trend changes in a firm's position; when these ratios are compared to those of comparable firms in the same lines of business activity, they will indicate changes in a firm's competitive position.

Thus a business firm may use ratio analysis not only to reveal changes in its position over a period of years but also to compare its current position to the position of other firms in the same industry. Dun and Bradstreet, Inc. make regular computations of working capital ratios for different groups of manufacturers, wholesalers, and retailers. These ratios provide a standard against which a company may check its own ratios. However, ratio analysis does not show the existence of lines of credit and loan commitments that business firms may have with their banks, and this ability to borrow may mean that a business firm is considerably stronger than ratio analysis would suggest.

QUESTIONS AND PROBLEMS

1. Distinguish between (*a*) the two concepts of working capital, and (*b*) permanent and seasonal working capital.
2. A policy of keeping current assets in excess of usual normal needs would free management from the need to borrow. What are the disadvantages of such a policy?
3. Explain the "circular-flow nature of working capital."
4. Why is the over-investment in inventory sometimes called the "graveyard of business firms?"
5. Identify: (*a*) current ratio, (*b*) quick asset ratio, (*c*) receivables–turnover ratio, and (*d*) inventory–turnover ratio.
6. Explain the following: "Since 1941 the Company has used the 'last-in, first-out' (LIFO) method of inventory valuation which provides a cushion against inventory losses when costs decline." (Libby, McNeill & Libby, Semi-Annual Report for the Six Months Ended December 31, 1960 [Chicago, Feb. 3, 1961], n.p.)
7. What are the main factors that influence the amount of working capital needed by a business firm?
8. Since each business has its own time sequence for working cash to flow from sales and back to cash, how does the cash flow for a lumber and building supply company compare to that of a restaurant? (See J. P. Jones, "Watch Your Cash" in Small Business Administration, *Management Aids for Small Manufacturers*, July, 1959.)
9. In preparing a statement of funds such as that presented in this chapter, what is the justification for including depreciation allowances as a source of funds?
10. Account for the difference in the collection period between (*a*) wholesale grocers and wholesale dry goods firms, and (*b*) breweries and furniture manufacturers (see Table 13).
11. Account for the difference in the net sales to inventory ratios between (*a*) retail groceries and meat chains and department stores, (*b*) wholesale dry goods and fresh fruit and produce firms, and (*c*) manufacturers of furniture and breweries (see Table 14).
12. "The financial condition of the company is good. At the year-end, net working capital—the excess of current assets over current liabilities—was $70,439,000 higher than at the end of 1958. The ratio of current assets to current liabilities at the close of the year was 4.14." (Reynolds Metals Company, *32nd Annual Report 1959* [Richmond, Virginia, 1959], p. 7.) Do you agree that the company's financial condition is good? Why?
13. Analyze: "In contrast to individuals, businesses have stepped up their savings in the form of retained earnings over the past two years. Many businesses have, nevertheless, had to turn to banks to accommodate their working capital needs." (The Chase Manhattan Bank, *Business In Brief* [July–August, 1960], n.p.)

CHAPTER 6

Fixed Capital Needs of Business Firms

BUSINESSMEN are constantly confronted with financial problems throughout the operations of their business firms. After obtaining funds with which to start a business, managers will face problems arising from expansion and the need for extra funds during months when expenditures are above normal. When planning to expand a business on a permanent basis, questions which must be answered include: Why is capital needed? How much is needed? How can it be obtained? How can it be repaid if it is borrowed?

The basic problem in financial control is to use resources of the business firm profitably while preserving its solvency. The main funds used in financing are those generated by the operations of the business firm (funds from operations), those provided by creditors, and those contributed by owners of the firm. Business firms depend to varying degrees on all of these sources of funds in their operations, and each one has its advantages and disadvantages or limitations.

The assets of business firms are classified as current, fixed, and other noncurrent assets. Because of their nature, the problems associated with current assets are more dynamic than those pertaining to fixed assets, but the latter may be more troublesome. One of the most elementary principles of sound financial management is to avoid excessive investment in fixed assets. Whether the investment in such assets is excessive depends on its relationship to tangible net worth. Tangible net worth represents the excess of assets over liabilities as reported in the balance sheet and it is found by subtracting all debts and reserves from total tangible assets.

In practice, the problem of financing fixed assets is closely related to that of financing current assets. If fixed charges resulting from financing fixed assets are too large, there may be a violation of the second principle of sound financial management—that "net working capital must be in proper proportion to sales." This chapter deals primarily with financing fixed assets.

NATURE OF FIXED CAPITAL ASSETS

Fixed capital assets are defined as the relatively permanent assets which a firm acquires for use in producing goods or services. Although fixed capital assets are not for resale during the ordinary course of business, this does not mean that they may not be disposed of if they have outlived their usefulness to the firm. The basic distinction between fixed and working capital assets is the use made of them. For illustration, a truck would be a working capital asset (inventory) to a truck dealer but a fixed capital asset to a trucking firm.

Classes of Fixed Capital Assets. The three classes of fixed capital assets are tangible fixed assets, intangible fixed assets, and fixed investments. Tangible fixed assets include land, buildings, equipment, machinery, rolling stock of railroads, trucks, mineral resources, and so on (except where the firm is a dealer in such items). All types of tangible property are included provided that they meet the standards set for fixed capital assets as defined above. Intangible fixed assets include all forms of intangible property regarded as a relatively permanent part of the assets of the business firm. Intangible fixed assets include goodwill, patents, copyrights, trade-marks, mailing lists, leases, and so on.

The part of a business firm's investments in securities which are of a relatively permanent nature are fixed capital assets. Such investments may include loans to and holdings of stocks and bonds of subsidiary and allied companies. Some of a business firm's investments in securities may result from a policy of investing funds set aside for expansion or replacement of plant and equipment. Other investments may be earmarked for sinking funds created to redeem the firm's securities or for pension funds for employees and/or officers.

Recovery of Fixed Capital Investments. The use of the word *fixed* to designate noncurrent assets may give the erroneous impression that these assets are permanent. At the time of acquisition, fixed assets may have an estimated life of two, five, ten, or more years. If the estimated life is five years, the cost of the asset customarily will be spread over a five-year period through depreciation or depletion charges. What remains of the cost at any one time will be the value appearing on the balance sheet (net value—cost of the capital asset less reserves for depreciation). Although the usual business practice is to prorate the original cost of a depreciable fixed asset over its useful life, some fixed capital assets are not subject to depreciation. Land may not be depreciated, but natural resources being exploited may be. A patent or lease having a limited life may be amortized, and "goodwill" may or may not be written off, depending on whether or not it resulted from an expenditure that will benefit the company for only a particular period of time. Specific policies followed in regard to depreciation depend on management.

Expenditures for raw materials, labor, and so on constitute a direct element in the cost of production, and expenditures for fixed capital assets enter into the cost of production by periodic allocation of their cost to expenses in the form of depreciation. Normally all expenditures for current services and inventories—but only a fraction of those for fixed capital assets—will be recovered from sales within one year.

Funds obtained from sales will not be affected by the amount of depreciation charges or allowances; however, these allowances will affect the amount that must be added to income in computing funds from operations. One general rule is that any current revenue reduction arising from the amortization of long-term assets must be added to income to arrive at the figure for funds from operations. Assuming the illustration below to be a conventional income statement, funds from operations may be found by adding net income and depreciation allowances ($10,000 + $20,000 = $30,000). A second method of obtaining funds from operations is to deduct from revenue those expenses, losses, and taxes which utilize funds ($100,-000 − $70,000 = $30,000).

Sales		$100,000
Less:		
Labor, etc.	$70,000	
Depreciation	20,000	
Total expenses		90,000
Net Income		$ 10,000

First Procedure		*Second Procedure*	
Income reported	$10,000	Sales or revenue	$100,000
Add back expenses not using funds	20,000	Subtract expenses using funds	70,000
Funds from operations	$30,000	Funds from operations	$ 30,000

Over a period of time, investments in fixed assets will be liquidated out of cash receipts from sales, and funds, formerly tied up in fixed assets, will be available for replacement of fixed or long-lived assets, financing working capital needs, retirement of debt, paying dividends, and so on. Thus funds from operations which are accounted for as depreciation allowances are available for spending.

To simplify presentation, depreciation allowances are sometimes referred to as a source of corporate funds which we know originate in sales. This same confusion exists when the statement is made that business firms finance with stocks and bonds. Actually, they finance with cash obtained from the sale of stocks and bonds. The capital account, bond indebtedness, and depreciation allowance items on a balance sheet are ink scratches—bookkeeping items; but, when these are referred to as sources of funds, there should be no misunderstanding.

Total Expenditures for Fixed Assets. When funds retained as depreciation allowances are spent for fixed assets, they are included in the statistics of total capital outlays for a period. From an accounting point of view, the amount of capital assets of business firms would remain the same, but there would be a change in the composition of working and fixed capital assets. For illustration, a truck that has been fully depreciated will have been written off the books; but, over the truck's useful life, the business firm will have retained earnings in an amount equal to its cost. Normally such funds will be used by the business firm rather than kept idle in anticipation of replacement.

Over the course of years, a going concern will have "written off" all of its original depreciable assets until none of them remain. Unless there have been changes in the nature or size of the concern's business, it may be assumed that all of the fully depreciable assets have been replaced with new assets of the same sort. Although the items accounted for as assets have changed, the total amount of assets may be the same. Assuming total fixed assets were $100,000 at the beginning of a firm's operations, the amount might be the same five years hence. The accounting records may suggest that nothing of significance has taken place; but, if more efficient machines and better processes have been acquired out of depreciation and other allowances, the productive capacity of the firm may have increased substantially by the use of so-called replacement capital.

During recent years, total capital outlays for plants and equipment have been at an annual rate of $30 billion. The size of expenditures for plants and equipment may give the impression that business leaders are unduly pessimistic when they emphasize the lack of capital—and particularly venture capital—brought about by high corporate and personal income taxes. If, in reporting expenditures, adjustments were made to show that four dollars out of every five spent for new plants and equipment were required to replace capital values currently used up, the reported capital expenditures of thirty billion dollars would be less impressive because only one fifth (about six billion dollars) represents net expansion.

Because of inflation—a characteristic of most of the years since the depression of the early 1930's—accounting allowances for depreciation in business reports may be less than the current cost of replacing the fixed capital assets consumed. For example, a plant that cost one million dollars in 1935 may require an expenditure of three million dollars to replace it in 1960 (see also Chapter 7). These problems are the most serious for business firms in industries where expenditures for fixed assets are high relative to those for working capital assets.

Relative Importance of Fixed Capital Assets. The amount of fixed assets relative to total assets will vary widely among business firms because of differences in the nature of their operations. In general, firms in the service and merchandising industries have relatively small investments in fixed capital assets and relatively large investments in working capital assets. If a retailer leases his business building, equipment, and furnishings, most of the firm's total assets will be in cash, inventories, and receivables. If a real estate company owns a hotel together with its equipment and furnishings, the real estate company's investments in fixed capital assets will be large, while those of the company that operates the hotel will be small.

In contrast to the relatively small investments in fixed capital assets of most service and merchandising firms are the relatively large investments in fixed assets of public utility, railway, and real estate companies. The latter firms need relatively small amounts of working capital assets—cash, inventories, and receivables—because they provide services which are paid for with cash or receivables that are quickly convertible into cash; but their investments for fixed capital assets—buildings, machinery, and equipment—are relatively and absolutely large.

The relative importance of fixed capital assets in other industries, including manufacturing, will be somewhere between the two extremes—service and merchandising firms on one hand and public utility, railway, and real estate companies on the other. Some manufacturing companies have their capital assets divided almost equally between fixed and working capital assets.

BREAK-EVEN POINT

Usually there is less danger of underinvesting in equipment, plant, and other fixed assets than in overinvesting in them; therefore, the relationship between a corporation's investments in fixed assets must be in proportion to its tangible net worth. As would be expected, fixed assets are of major importance in the heavy goods manufacturing industry and of relatively little importance in light goods manufacturing industries such as the garment trade industry. Since tangible net worth represents the excess of tangible assets over liabilities as reported on the balance sheet, the method of financing as well as the amount of fixed assets is significant. Tangible assets include all assets less patents, copyrights, trademarks, leaseholds, goodwill, franchises, and similar assets; liabilities include all debts such as accounts payable, notes payable, term loans, mortgages, bonds, accrued expenses, and reserves for taxes and contingencies. The fixed assets figure used by management in the comparison between fixed assets and tangible net worth is net fixed assets (fixed assets minus accumulated depreciation). For a building, the book value may appear as:

Building	$50,000
Less accumulated depreciation	10,000
	$40,000

Irrespective of the level of output, a business firm will be subject to certain fixed expenses such as property taxes, depreciation charges, insurance, heat, light, and general administrative expenses. Other expenses will change with the increase in volume of business, including those for materials (cost of goods sold), labor, and other variables which are related directly to the volume of business. In addition, there are other expenses that have characteristics of both fixed and variable, such as those for advertising, commissions, and manufacturing expenses other than for labor and materials. When management has expense figures segregated, the break-even point (a balance of revenues and expenses) is found by dividing the total fixed and semivariable costs by the margin of income dollars over the variable expense dollars.

Charts of break-even points may be constructed for individual business firms by indicating the number of sales on the X axis and cost of output and income on the Y axis. There are three break-even points; cash, financial, and profit break-even points. The cash break-even point is the point where the total revenue curve intersects the total cash outlay curve (excluding interest and dividends). The financial break-even point is the intersection of the total cash revenue curve and the total cash outlay curve including interest and dividends. The profit break-even point is the intersection of the total income curve (including accruals) and the total cost curve (including accruals). When the term "break-even" point is used, the profit break-even point is meant (see Illustration 4).

ILLUSTRATION 4

BREAK-EVEN POINT

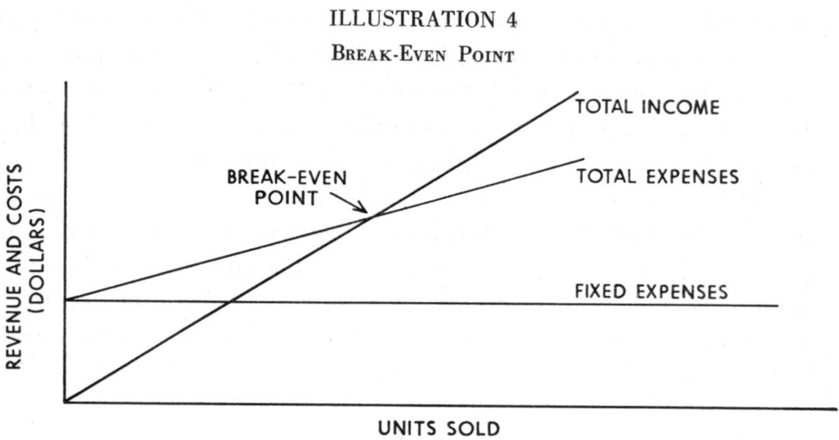

When the fixed assets of a business firm are excessive, fixed and semifixed charges (for insurance premiums, property taxes, maintenance charges, and interest and other payments) become burdensome during a period of declining income. High fixed costs tend to make the break-even point too high and a profitable level of sales too difficult to achieve and to maintain. If a business firm permits its fixed assets to get out of line with those of its competitors, the situation could be financially disastrous.

If two business firms each have net sales of $100,000 and variable costs of $8.00 per unit of sales, but Firm A has fixed costs of $15,000 and Firm B fixed costs of $8,000, the break-even points would be:

Firm A $\$15{,}000 \div \left(\dfrac{\$100{,}000 - 80{,}000}{100{,}000} \text{ or } 20\%\right) = \$75{,}000$

Firm B $\$\ 8{,}000 \div \left(\dfrac{\$100{,}000 - 80{,}000}{100{,}000} \text{ or } 20\%\right) = \$40{,}000$

Firm A, with the higher break-even point, not only would have more difficulty in remaining "in the black" but also would be less profitable ($5,000 as compared with $12,000):

	Firm A	*Firm B*
Net income	$100,000	$100,000
Fixed costs	$ 15,000	$ 8,000
Variable costs	80,000	80,000
Total Costs	$ 95,000	$ 88,000
Net earnings	$ 5,000	$ 12,000

With an increase in sales from $100,000 to $200,000, Firm A with its higher fixed costs may experience a decline in its variable per unit cost from $8.00 to $7.00 because of more efficient use of its larger plant and equipment, while Firm B with the same increase in sales may experience an increase in its variable per unit costs from $8.00 to $9.00 because of less efficient plant and equipment. Now the break-even points would be:

$$\textit{Firm A} \quad \$15{,}000 \div \left(\frac{\$200{,}000 - \$140{,}000}{200{,}000} \text{ or } 30\%\right) = \$50{,}000$$

$$\textit{Firm B} \quad \$\ 8{,}000 \div \left(\frac{\$200{,}000 - \$180{,}000}{200{,}000} \text{ or } 10\%\right) = \$80{,}000$$

Now Firm B, with the higher break-even point, has also become less profitable:

	Firm A	*Firm B*
Net income	$200,000	$200,000
Fixed costs	$ 15,000	$ 8,000
Variable costs	140,000	180,000
Total Costs	$155,000	$188,000
Net earnings	$ 45,000	$ 12,000

If the amount of sales falls below the break-even point, the business firm must cut costs, increase income, or do both in order to become profitable. Thus construction of a break-even point chart may be an aid to management in bringing expenses in line with income, re-evaluating its sales program, and determining policies as to prices, merchandising, wages, and credit. Although break-even charts are most helpful in managing working capital assets, they also may be of benefit in appraising proposed capital expenditures which would tend to change the cost situation of the business firm.

PLANS FOR CAPITAL EXPENDITURES

Long-range planning of investments is an integral part of any system for evaluating capital additions. The time period for which capital budgets are made will vary among business firms because of the peculiarities of individual firms. For illustration, because of the nature of their products, public utility companies have less difficulty in financing future capital needs than do industrial firms. While a public utility company may project its capital needs for as long as twenty-five years, an equally successful firm in a different field may not be able to project its fixed capital needs for more than five years. Most long-term capital plans are on a tentative basis until the time for actual expenditures approaches.

Capital planning by a business firm is based on the anticipated growth of the economy as a whole, as well as of the specific industry in which the firm is operating, and on the anticipated place of the firm within the industry. Specific proposals for capital expenditures must be considered in terms of anticipated increased revenue or cost savings. This in turn raises questions as to total cost of acquisitions, length of service life, operating expenses, maintenance costs, and tax-free depreciation allowances. Usually there is some discrepancy between anticipated costs and anticipated income because there are changes in the price level as well as routine miscalculations of costs and receipts. Changes in corporate income taxes, wages, and other costs over which management may have little or no control are factors that affect the profitability of fixed-asset expansion, but changes in market demand due to inventions must be anticipated by management.

Fixed capital expenditures are usually classified as major and minor; the former would include those for plant sites, buildings and expensive machinery and the latter those for small additions to plants, inexpensive machinery, and other miscellaneous items which are capitalized (tools and small items may not be capitalized but rather treated as current expenses irrespective of their useful life). Capital expenditures may also be classified as labor-saving or necessities or as replacement assets or for expansion. Top management has a primary interest in major capital expenditures, but all are important.

Replacement investments are usually more pressing than those for expansion, but policies in this regard are complicated by the fact that some fixed capital assets may never become completely obsolete or entirely worn out. In making decisions as to when such assets are to be replaced, the cost of replacement should be weighed against the anticipated savings and/or increased revenue derived from greater efficiency of new fixed assets. When such replacement investments result in an increase in output, the expenditure may contain an element of expansion. When new capital assets are designed to produce new products, estimates must be made not only of costs but also of the effect of the new products on the market for old products of the company. Expansionary investments in capital assets are those which are expected to result in an increase in output and income. Customarily the board of directors of a corporation makes decisions pertaining to capital expenditures of this type. A vital question in this regard is whether the market will absorb the additional output in the near future in sufficient quantities to justify the outlay.

In planning capital expenditures, priority is given to projects which are the most urgent, but evaluating the urgency of items may be largely subjective. This may result in different department heads presenting more or less persuasive arguments along with misleading data. Management is often faced with real emergencies, and under such conditions the degree of necessity may take precedence over other apparently more profitable capital outlays.

In many cases when there is a need for replacement, business management may resort to some rule of the thumb in arriving at decisions such as giving preference to utilizing projects that have a required pay-back period of from two to five years (rather than from ten to fifteen years), to replacing assets when their usefulness is exhausted or their book value is approaching zero, to replacing company cars because the policy calls for their replacement every two years, or to replacing a machine because a considerable sum of money could thereby be saved. A corporation may set up an arbitrary rate of return on investments to be used as a guide for the acceptance or rejection of proposed capital investments. For example, a proposal for the acquisition of a machine that permits an annual cost savings of 20 per cent may be approved and proposals for those that permit lesser amounts may be rejected. A single rate of return expected for all fixed assets may not be realistic; therefore different rates may be set for different types of assets. As a matter of policy, machines may be replaced when major overhaul is required and fixed assets may be replaced when operating costs on them move upward.

In an expanding economy, there are usually more investment opportunities than available capital, but not all investment decisions can be made on the basis of profitability. Sometimes capital investments must be made in order to stay in business (replacing property that has been destroyed by fire). Other investments may be made—such as safety or health measures to protect employees or the public—to meet requirements of a governmental agency. There may be other capital expenditures by a company for the welfare of employees or the community in which it is located, such as for public meeting rooms to be used for community functions or swimming pools for employees and their families. While capital expenditures of this type may be relatively small, they may be given priority in capital budgets despite the fact that no direct profits therefrom are anticipated. Sound judgment is a characteristic of successful management and a great deal of thought has been given to the development of rules to be used in evaluating proposed capital additions. Two of the most widely used types of analysis are considered in the next section.

SELECTION OF CAPITAL PROJECTS

The most important aspect of the problem of financing fixed capital assets is the ability to justify any capital expenditure on the basis of return. Since the cash return on fixed-asset expenditures is over a long period of time, there is more risk in these expenditures than in those for inventories and other working capital assets.

The "pay back," "cash recovery," or "pay-off" period (or time) is the most widely used method of measuring the value of proposed investments. This is the estimated time needed for the cumulative net earnings from an asset to equal the investment in the asset. If the net cost of a fixed asset is $50,000 and the cash inflow (net earnings before depreciation charges and after corporate income taxes) resulting from the investment averages $10,000 per year over a ten year period, the cash recovery period would be five years.[1] Management may consider an investment wherein the payback period is five years to be preferable to one wherein it is ten years—with both having the same useful life—because the first would entail less risk. The preferred investment in Table 15 would be Opportunity C because the payback period (cash flow) would be two and one-half years as compared to five years for Opportunity A and almost eight years for Opportunity B.

Management may be justified in emphasizing projects having short

[1] Depreciation charges are excluded because they are noncash items, but income taxes represent a real cash outlay and they are deducted from the amount of usable funds generated by the project (as for interest payments on borrowed funds and other expenses that reduce cash earnings available for reinvestment).

payback periods when the capital wastage is difficult to predict and the possibility of short economic life is great.[2] Such a policy would be particularly helpful to a company whose funds from operations are limited and whose interest rates on borrowed funds are high. In other words, the payback analysis emphasizes liquidity as a goal of capital expenditures, but its use may result in exclusion of some profitable capital investments.

TABLE 15

Discounted Cash Flow Analysis

	Opportunity A		Opportunity B		Opportunity C	
Year	*Cash Flow*	*Present Value (8 Per Cent)*	*Cash Flow*	*Present Value (8 Per Cent)*	*Cash Flow*	*Present Value (8 Per Cent)*
1	$ 10,000	$ 9,259			$20,000	$18,518
2	10,000	8,573	$ 1,000	$ 857	20,000	16,146
3	10,000	7,938	1,000	794	20,000	15,876
4	10,000	7,350	5,000	3,675	15,000	10,025
5	10,000	6,806	10,000	6,806	10,000	6,806
6	10,000	6,302	18,000	11,344	10,000	6,302
7	10,000	5,835	18,000	10,503		
8	10,000	5,403	18,000	9,725		
9	10,000	5,002	18,000	9,004		
10	10,000	4,632	18,000	8,138		
	$100,000	$67,100	$107,000	$60,846	$95,000	$73,673

The payback method entails a cash flow analysis but it does not measure the profitability of an investment. Sometimes the return on the investment is regarded to be the reciprocal of the payback period —assume five years, which gives a reciprocal of 20 per cent (1.00 ÷ 5)—but this is incorrect. The payback analysis ignores depreciation allowances, projects gross revenue and expenses only for the anticipated payback period, and fails to cover the useful life of the capital asset beyond the payment period. Generally, this method of analysis is not inclusive enough to be used as a comprehensive guide to capital investment; however it is reasonably satisfactory when time is a factor and when investment proposals covering items having the same useful life are to be screened.

Management may consider the discount cash flow method of analysis in evaluating alternate capital investment opportunities. In this

[2] One of the major petroleum companies has a three-year payback period for "big" risks, three and one half year payback period for "normal" risks, and a four-year payback period for "limited" or "small" risks.

method the discount factor is applied to determine the present worth of future income, recognizing the difference in the value of money over a period of time. After expenditures and receipts are estimated and arranged according to the years during which they are anticipated, the data are used in conjunction with present value tables to show the present worth of the cash flow. If one assumes that there are three investment opportunities having the same cost ($50,000) and with cash proceeds as given in Table 15, the preferred investment would be Opportunity C.

A key problem in using the discounted cash flow analysis is the rate of return, with a high rate sharply discounting the value of cash received in the future and a low rate increasing its estimated value. A 4 per cent rate would make investment Opportunity B in Table 15 more attractive and would reduce the attractiveness of Opportunity C. Customarily companies will have available a profit–investment ratio which may be used quickly in considering an investment opportunity. Because of varying circumstances, usually no fixed criterion is set up for all conditions.

In weighing the profitability of proposed capital expenditures, consideration should be given to the effects of federal income taxes because various projects may affect a company's tax position differently. Capital investments are not deductible in the year paid or incurred for tax purposes, so these costs are recovered by way of depreciation allowances. Thus an investment in which accelerated amortization is permitted for tax purposes may be given priority over a second project wherein tax credit in the early years is less. Proper planning and timing of capital investments materially affects the amount of taxes and therefore the amount of income. Because the current Internal Revenue Service regulations permit tax-loss carry back to the three previous years and their being carried forward five years, sometimes investment in properties wherein there is a loss may be advantageous.

FINANCING CAPITAL EXPENDITURES

In financing capital investments the cost of capital is basic; therefore the expected return from a proposed investment must be measured against the cost of borrowing or of obtaining equity capital. This problem is closely related to sources of funds such as those generated internally through normal operations of a business firm or those derived through various media of external financing. The major sources of external financing of fixed capital assets are divided into two main divisions—those giving rise to equities and those creating debts. The first group presents problems associated with financing with common and preferred stock and the second, those associated with bonds, mortgages, equipment trust certificates, and term loans. Many companies have enjoyed the advantages of financing with debts because interest payments are included as costs in computing corporate income taxes, while dividends are not. In addition, because of inflation, debt repayment is accomplished with dollars having less value than those borrowed. In order to retain a sound financial condition, business firms must have long-term capital expenditure plans so as to avoid weak debt–equity ratios and the necessity for financing with equities when market conditions are unfavorable.

In acting on proposals for changes in fixed capital assets, management will consider the effect on working capital needs. If acquiring a new plant or equipment increases the need for new supplies, materials or inventories, and labor, and/or increases cash needs for insurance payments, taxes on property, and other costs, it is conceivable that the acquisition of new fixed capital assets could result in a profitable business firm becoming unprofitable. On the other hand, economies resulting from capital expenditures could have the effect of sharply reducing labor costs and working capital needs and thereby increasing profitability.

In recent years, the use of sales and lease-back arrangements as methods of financing capital improvements have increased sharply. Among the advantages of leasing assets are the conservation of a business firm's capital funds and the avoidance of larger debts. The lease arrangement may permit the utilization of the latest models and types of equipment together with servicing of the equipment by the lessor. Such rental payments are deductible as an expense for income tax purposes. These advantages must be weighed against the disadvantages which may include a higher cost–use ratio and difficulties of breaking lease arrangements when equipment or other capital assets being leased are no longer needed. The advantages and disadvantages of lease arrangement vary for different firms and each firm must weigh them against alternate methods of financing.

A specific decision as to whether to lease or buy necessitates analyzing the cost of the asset, its estimated salvage value, and the rate of return on the proposed purchase (which should be the same as the current net earnings). In a lease arrangement, no initial capital outlay is required and the salvage value must be omitted as part of the receipts expected when the lease expires. The rental expenditure is the additional cost that is used under the lease arrangement. Normally, profits derived from purchased assets are greater than from leased assets, but the margin may be so minor as to make ownership of assets unimportant. Leasing is usually preferred when more attractive investment outlays are possible or when capital is difficult to obtain.

CORPORATE SECURITIES

Since the end of World War II, funds for financing capital needs of business corporations have come chiefly from internal sources—reductions in cash, receivables and investments, and increases in undistributed profits and depreciation charges. When outside sources were used, business firms either sold stock or borrowed.

Capital Stock. Capital stock, whether common stock or preferred stock, represents ownership in a corporation. The chief difference between preferred stock and common stock is that the former usually has a prior claim to earnings, and in case of liquidation, to assets of the corporation. Claims of both classes of stockholders are junior to those of bondholders and other creditors. Of the securities that constitute the capitalization of a corporation, common stock is usually the largest in amount. The holders of common stock assume the greatest risk, but their potential for gain in the form of dividends and capital appreciation is greater than that of any other security holder. In addition, common stockholders usually have more voting rights and may exercise more control than holders of other classes of securities of their corporation.

Relatively few industrial companies issue preferred stock. When preferred stock is issued by corporations, the amount is usually small compared with the amount of common stock outstanding. The rights and privileges of preferred stockholders depend on charter provisions of the issuing corporation and on the terms of the specific issue. When preferred stockholders are given preference over common stockholders as to earnings, the amount of dividends is usually limited to a fixed percentage or fixed dollar amount per share (as 6 per cent or $6.00 per share). Usually, the voting rights of preferred stockholders are curtailed, thereby limiting their influence over the policies of corporate management.

From the viewpoint of the issuing corporation, there are many advantages in financing with capital stock. Stock has no maturity date and the corporation is not required to repay any of the funds acquired by an issue of stock unless there are special provisions made for this purpose, as may be the case with preferred stock (see Chapter 19). While stockholders usually expect to receive dividends, there is no legal obligation to pay dividends unless voted by the board of directors. In case of need, a corporation may pass or omit dividends in order to conserve cash and other current assets for other purposes.

Bonds. A bond is evidence of a debt on which the issuing company usually promises to pay a specified amount of interest (usually every six months) and to repay the principal on the expiration or maturity date. A corporation may raise part of its long-term capital funds by financing with bonds, and the holders of such bonds are creditors of the corporation whose claims to earnings and assets are superior to those of stockholders. From the viewpoint of the corporation, interest is a fixed charge and failure to meet interest obligations usually means that the corporation is insolvent in the equity sense. In addition, the contract under which bonds are issued may require the corporation to make provisions for the retirement of a fixed percentage of the bonds each year (as by annual contribution to a sinking fund) which increases the costs and hazards associated with bond or debt financing. Bonds are issued by both strong and weak companies—by the former from choice and by the latter from necessity because it may be the only adequate source of funds available to them.

A corporation may choose to issue bonds rather than preferred or common stock for several reasons. For one reason, the supply of loanable funds may be more abundant than equity capital because institutional investors are given greater freedom by regulatory agencies when investing in bonds rather than in stocks. Since insurance companies, savings institutions, and other institutional investors are dominant among the buyers of new corporate securities, the capital market is usually more favorable to bond financing than stock financing. To be sure, there is a great deal of popular interest in the stock market, but this is primarily a secondhand market wherein already distributed shares are bought and sold and wherein no new capital is obtained by issuing corporations. Although corporations may raise new capital by the sale of stock, established firms usually find it easier to raise long-term funds by the sale of bonds because of a more favorable market for these securities.

A second advantage of bond financing is that interest on indebtedness is deductible from earnings as a cost in computing taxable income of a corporation. If the tax rate were 50 per cent, there would be a substantial saving which would, in effect, reduce the cost of obtaining funds by one half. This saving is apparent when a comparison is made between Case A and Case B below, wherein 5 per cent bonds are substituted in Case B for 5 per cent preferred stock in Case A. As can be seen from the following example, the actual tax saving is 52 per cent of $500,000 or $260,000:

Case A

Common stock	$40,000,000
Preferred stock (5%)	10,000,000
Preferred stock dividend	500,000
Income before federal income tax	5,000,000
Federal income tax	2,594,500
Income available for dividends	1,905,500

Case B

Common stock	$40,000,000
Bonds (5%)	10,000,000
Bond interest	500,000
Income before federal income tax	4,500,000
Federal income tax	2,334,500
Income for common stock	2,165,500

A third factor that may cause corporate management to issue bonds rather than stock is that creditors do not normally have voting privileges. In case of a stock issue, if a large block were to be purchased by an outside group, management's control may be threatened. This danger of loss of control seems to be especially important to corporations whose shares are closely held by officers and members of boards of directors. However, it is relatively unimportant to large companies whose shares are widely held and voting is chiefly by proxy in favor of management (as long as profits and dividends are satisfactory).

Capitalization. The total amount of securities issued by a corporation is referred to as the amount of its capitalization. Thus a company which has issued the three standard types of corporate securities would have common and preferred stock carried on the books at par or stated value and bonds carried at their par or face value. However, in order not to misrepresent the amount of equity capital in the business, corporate surplus should be included along with the book value of securities. In some cases, surplus accounts represent the bulk of stockholders' equity. There is also justification for including long-term debts in forms other than those represented by bonds in a corporation's capital structure. To a considerable extent long-term bank and insurance company loans are being substituted for corporate bonds in financing business firms. Some claim that current liabilities should also be included because in an analysis of risk associated with debt financing the best single measure would be the ratio of total debt (including current liabilities) to net worth.

One conclusion that may be drawn from the fact that the assets of business firms differ is that the methods of financing will also differ. One may go a step farther and conclude that the composition of assets of a business firm will determine to a large degree the methods to be used in financing. If this conclusion were valid it would mean that all business firms in the same line or industry would have identical capital structures. Obviously, this is not the case. In practice, the financial structure of a business firm will be influenced by both external factors such as the line of business and internal factors such as those controlled by financial management. For illustration, a business firm having stable earnings, such as a public utility company, may adopt a less conservative financial structure than one whose income is subject to cyclical flows, such as a company engaged in manufacturing durable goods.

In analyzing a business firm's financial structure, the starting point is the industry despite the fact that there is considerable variation among companies in the same industry. In such an analysis an answer must be found to the question, "What is the long-run purpose of financial management?" The purpose may be to maximize profits or earnings or the long-run value per share of common stock. While these purposes are interrelated, they are not identical because maximum profits per share may be obtained under conditions of financial risk which will increase the rate at which earnings are capitalized and give a lower market price than would be true in case of a second company wherein financial risk is less and earnings are capitalized at a lower rate. For illustration, Company A which is financing one half with debt and one half with common stock may find that its earnings of $12 per share are being capitalized at 20 per cent ($12 ÷ .20 = $60), while Company B which is financing exclusively with common stock may find that its earnings of $12 per share are being capitalized at 15 per cent ($12 ÷ .15 = $80).

Other things remaining the same, the risk assumed by a business firm increases as the proportion of debt to equity in the capital structure increases. If a firm's total debt is $500,000 and its tangible net worth is $1,000,000, the ratio of total debt to net worth is 1 to 2 or 50 per cent ($500,000 ÷ $1,000,000 = .50), and if the debt were to increase to $1,000,000 with no change in equity, the ratio would become 1 to 1 or 100 per cent. In financing a business firm, the aim is not to avoid debt entirely but to achieve a proper balance between debt capital and equity capital (that is, a satisfactory debt-liability ratio). Presumably there is an optimum capital structure for every business firm in every industry, and this would reflect both external and internal factors. Obviously, the relationship between debt and equity in the financial structure of a business firm will change with changes in earnings, interest rates, capital market conditions, and market price of the company's stock.

Trading on Equity. Since debts increase the hazards of doing business, why do business firms ever use debt financing? The answer is that it is profitable to borrow at one rate (assume 5 per cent) when earnings on funds are at a higher rate (assume 12 per cent). Financing with debts is an easy way to increase earnings on common stock without increasing owners' investment, provided the earnings on the borrowed funds are in excess of the interest paid on them.

Trading on equity usually refers to financing with debt, but it may include financing with preferred stock and/or other securities which are senior to common stock in claims to earnings. The effect of trading on equity on the per-share earnings of the common stock of a company is called leverage, and it may be advantageous or disadvantageous to common stockholders. It is a financial strain to meet interest payments on loan capital when earnings are falling or are at a low level, but this situation can change rapidly. The leverage effect of financing with senior securities on earnings per share of common stock is suggested by the illustration below, wherein there are changes in the debt structure and assumed earnings for different years. After subtracting interest payments, the remaining profits are divided by the number of shares of common stock outstanding to obtain earnings per share. (In order to emphasize the leverage factor, federal income taxes are ignored in the illustration.)

Year		*1958*	*1959*	*1960*
Total profits		$8,000	$10,000	$20,000
Case A				
Common stock (2,000 shares)	$200,000	$4.00	$5.00	$10.00
Case B				
Bonds (5%)	$ 50,000			
(Deduct $2,500 interest from profits)				
Common stock (1,500 shares)	$150,000	$3.67	$5.00	$11.67
Case C				
Bonds (5%)	$100,000			
(Deduct $5,000 interest from profits)				
Common stock (1,000 shares)	$100,000	$3.00	$7.00	$15.00

Operating Leverage. The earnings accrued to common stock are affected not only by the amount of capital leverage but also by the degree of operating leverage. A great deal of operating leverage is present when the fixed costs of a business firm do not vary materially with changes in the volume of sales or production (that is, fixed costs are spread over more units of sales or output). This is illustrated by the hypothetical case given below, wherein an increase in sales of 20 per cent from 1958 to 1959 resulted in an increase in earnings of 25 per cent and an increase in sales of 50 per cent from 1959 to 1960 resulted in an increase in earnings of 150 per cent:

	1958	*1959*	*1960*
Sales	$50,000	$60,000	$75,000
Variable expenses	12,000	20,000	25,000
Nonvariable expenses	30,000	30,000	30,000
Net earnings (before income taxes)	8,000	10,000	20,000

RATIO ANALYSIS

Ratios are devices that show the relationship between two items and they are used to measure financial changes or financial conditions. They may also be used to compare items that are part of the same financial statement or to compare items on two different financial statements of the same business firm. Ratios are also used to compare conditions of one business firm to others in the same industry.

By dividing fixed assets by tangible net worth, the percentage of fixed assets financed by owners will be shown. As this percentage approaches 100, an increasing percentage of the working capital and other nonfixed asset financing needs are being cared for with credit. Although a high percentage may be a normal situation for public utility companies, for most other companies a high percentage generally suggests the need for greater financing with equity capital.

By drawing upon the income and balance sheet statements, management may find out the amount of profit being realized on capital by computing the ratio of net profits to tangible net worth as follows:

$$\frac{\text{Net Profits after Income Tax, \$5,000}}{\text{Tangible Net Worth, \$50,000}} = \text{10 Per Cent.}$$

By comparing this percentage to that of the preceding year or to that of another company in the same industry or line of trade, management has a profitability index of its efficiency relative to the preceding year or to other companies during the current year. The same financial statements may be drawn on to compute statistical ratios frequently used by management. One of these is the turnover of tangible net worth, which is as follows:

$$\frac{\text{Net Sales, \$250,000}}{\text{Tangible Net Worth, \$50,000}} = \text{5 Times.}$$

This ratio indicates the turnover or activity of the business firm's equity. It can be too high when sales are being expanded by cutting prices and selling at too small a margin of profit, or it can be too low when sales volume is out of line with the amount of tangible net worth. By checking against the company's record for previous years and against the current record of competitors, management is given information as to the company's strength or weakness.

In order to check on how burdensome debts may be at a particular time, management may compare total debt to tangible net worth as follows:

$$\frac{\text{Total Debt, \$40,000}}{\text{Tangible Net Worth, \$50,000}} = \text{80 Per Cent.}$$

This means that for every dollar being provided by owners, eighty cents is being provided by creditors. For most business firms, this would be an uncomfortable situation, and it would suggest that the business firm is not being financed conservatively. While this percentage may be normal for some wholesalers and retailers—and even low for some public utility companies—it would be high for most manufacturing firms. One objective of financial management is to avoid insolvency—a situation wherein total assets are less than total liabilities; thus the greater the tangible net worth relative to total debt, the greater is the margin of protection.

SUMMARY

Fixed capital assets are the relatively long-lived assets acquired for use in producing goods and services. They consist of tangible assets (land, buildings, equipment, machinery, etc.), intangible assets (goodwill, patents, trade-marks, leases, etc.), and fixed investments. The cost of fixed assets is spread over their estimated useful lives and recovered through depreciation charges. Break-even point charts may be used by management in seeking an answer to the question, "Has the company invested too heavily in fixed assets?" "Pay-back" and "discounted cash flow" analyses are used by management in the selection of projects to be developed, but there are some capital projects that are justified for reasons other than profits associated with the specific outlay.

Funds from operations which are accounted for as depreciation allowances are available for spending. "Debt" and "equity" securities are used to obtain cash from external sources. Corporate securities include capital stock (common and preferred), which represent ownership, and bonds, which represent debt. While there are advantages in financing with equity capital exclusively, corporate management may issue bonds when loan funds are more abundant than venture capital and because interest paid on them is deductible as a cost in computing federal corporate income taxes. An additional reason for issuing bonds may be to preserve control by existing management of the corporation. However, there is more risk entailed in financing with debts than with equities because interest payments are a fixed charge, and while dividends on preferred stock may also be considered a fixed charge, its claim to earnings does not have the priority of debt obligations.

The composition of the assets of a business firm will affect the methods used to finance them; thus the capital structure of any business corporation will depend on both internal and external factors including the relative importance of fixed and working capital assets, stability of earnings, tax advantage of debt financing, interest rates in the capital market, and others. With changes in these factors, changes in debt and equity relationships in a corporation's financial structure may be advisable.

Trading on equity refers to the practice of financing with senior securities (preferred stocks and bonds). While such a practice increases the possibility of high returns to the owners of common stock, it also increases the risk. The extent to which a firm may engage in trading on equity depends in part upon the stability of its earnings; consequently the practice will be associated with some industries more than with others.

Ratio analysis may be used by financial managers in examining the fixed asset and debt relationship of a firm. The main advantage to a ratio analysis is that, being a percentage figure, it permits comparison of firms of unequal size.

QUESTIONS AND PROBLEMS

1. Identify the classes of fixed capital assets. How does a business firm recover its investments in fixed capital assets?
2. How does the relative percentage of fixed assets affect a business firm's financial policies?
3. In recent years, "funds for financing fixed capital needs of business corporations have come chiefly from internal sources." What does this

mean? Explain why "funds available as depreciation allowances are now larger than in the past."

4. How may management be aided in its selection of capital expenditures by (*a*) a break-even point analysis, and (*b*) the discounted cash flow analysis?
5. Why may leasing instead of purchasing fixed assets be advantageous to a firm? What effect will a lease arrangement have on a firm's need for long-term funds?
6. Compare the advantages of financing fixed assets by capital stock issues with bond issues. Why do relatively few industrial firms issue preferred stock?
7. Explain the managerial policy suggested by the following: "Total capital expenditures during 1960 amounted to $15,315,000. This compared with provisions for depreciation on $8,835,300. Capital expenditures will be higher in 1961, many of the 1960 construction projects having gotten under way late in the year." (Hooker Chemical Corporation and Subsidiaries, *Annual Report for the Year Ended November 30, 1960* [New York, 1961], p. 4.)
8. Identify: (*a*) trading on equity, (*b*) capital leverage, and (*c*) operating leverage.
9. What ratios may be used to test the effectiveness of fixed-asset policies of management?
10. How is the break-even point affected by the relationship between fixed and variable costs? How does the composition of the assets of a business firm affect the relationship between fixed and variable costs?
11. How would the financial structure of a corporation whose long-run purpose of financial management is to maximize profits differ from that of a second corporation whose purpose is to maximize the long-run value per share of common stock?

PART III

Funds from Operations

FUNDS UTILIZED by a business concern may be derived from both internal and external sources; however, those generated by a firm's operations (internal sources) are by far the most important. Funds from operations are available for many uses such as reinvestment, retirement of debt, and distribution to owners in the form of dividends.

Depreciation, a method of recapturing capital investments, not only affects income during a period but also constitutes an expense which does not require a cash outlay. Retained earnings—profits earned by a business but not distributed to the owners—are an important source of funds to many firms and have been used to finance much of the business expansion accomplished in recent years.

Dividend policy embraces more than the distribution of profits to owners and properly compliments policies relative to retained earnings and depreciation. While few would dispute the rights of owners to profits from business operations, in many instances the retention of part of the earnings is to the best interest of all.

This section, FUNDS FROM OPERATIONS, covers depreciation allowances, retained earnings, and dividends and divided policies.

CHAPTER 7

Depreciation Allowances

BUSINESS firms finance with cash; the concept of financing with depreciation allowances may be misunderstood unless it is realized that the term *depreciation allowances* is used to cover returns from sales which are retained in the business. In this respect, financing with depreciation allowances is similar to financing with retained earnings. Strictly speaking, business firms do not finance with owners' equity or debts because these items represent sources of funds.

Retained earnings constitute a major part of the funds used to purchase plants, equipment, and other business assets. The amount of profits available to a corporation for such reinvestment is determined by income after taxes and dividend payments. Chart 3 indicates the relative importance of undistributed profits and depreciation allowances in corporate financing in recent years. The bars in this chart labelled "depreciation" show, in addition to depreciation allowances, depletion of natural resources, amortization of intangible assets, profits or losses on noncurrent assets, and accumulations of bond discounts on bonds payable.

Funds from operations may be computed either by (1) adding back to income those expenses which did not use funds or (2) subtracting from revenues those costs which did use funds (see Chapter 6).

SIGNIFICANCE OF DEPRECIATION ALLOWANCES

The funds from operations which are considered under the heading "depreciation allowances" are a return from sales that may be retained in the business; but, instead of being treated as earnings, they are regarded as replacement capital which may be used to replace fixed assets. The cost of material things which are used up in the productive process are customarily charged against current income, while the cost of a fixed asset is prorated over its useful life. In theory, all production costs must be recouped from funds received; therefore, fixed capital assets are gradually converted into cash in the productive process. These funds are available for reinvestment, retirement of debt, or distribution to stockholders. Thus,

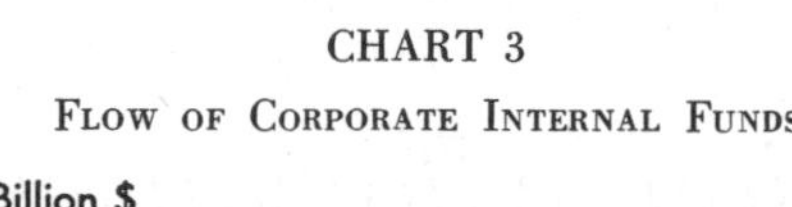

CHART 3

FLOW OF CORPORATE INTERNAL FUNDS

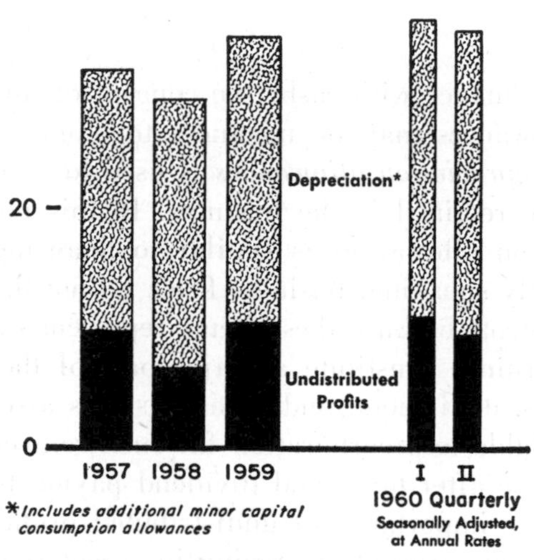

Source: U.S. Department of Commerce, Office of Business Economics, *Survey of Current Business* (October, 1960), p. 11.

funds from operations accounted for as depreciation allowances (or charges) are of interest to financial managers as well as to accountants.

Because of the growth in the nation's productive facilities, increases in costs of plant and equipment, decreases in useful life expectancy of assets, and increases in use of methods of depreciation that result in faster write-offs, depreciation allowances have increased materially in recent years. Current methods of calculating depreciation tend to further reduce profits, thereby reducing the ratio of profits to sales and making comparisons of current with past profitability of business firms less meaningful. However, it appears that in the aggregate the effect of varying depreciation upon net income from one period to another has been "only a fraction of 1 per cent of pretax totals."[1] Any change which increases the amount of depreciation charge will tend to reduce corporate taxes. Profits, whether measured before or after taxes, are influenced more by cyclical changes in business than by depreciation allowances; consequently, the short run influence of depreciation allowances on profits of business firms, compared to other factors, is of minor importance.

When considered from an accounting viewpoint, depreciation accounting is a systematic procedure for allocating the costs of fixed or long-lived assets over their useful lives. The concept of "useful life" recognizes not only physical deterioration but also obsolescence caused by technical or other changes. The allowance or reserve for depreciation is merely an asset valuation account—a bookkeeping entry—not a cash reserve. Depreciation itself is any loss in value and is not necessarily related to earnings. Depreciation takes place irrespective of the accounting procedure in use and depreciation can not be a source of funds. Funds obviously are not created by charging depreciation. However, depreciation affects income and must be added back, as was shown in a previous chapter, to compute funds from operation. Depreciation accounting indicates the estimated current value of fixed capital assets; for illustration, the estimated current value of a business structure which originally cost $1,000,000 may appear on the balance sheet as follows:

Building	$1,000,000
Less: accumulated depreciation to date	300,000
Building less depreciation	$ 700,000

Financial management must make provisions for the replacement of plants and equipment, and such replacement becomes a major problem when technological changes are improving replacement assets and their costs are increasing. Management may replace assets by foregoing dividend payments or by resorting to public financing if necessary; however, failure to make provisions for adequate depreciation is financial mismanagement at its worst. When depreciation allowances are deducted as a cost for tax purposes, it means that the company is permitted to recover its investments in fixed assets tax free. While depreciation allowances do not create funds, they affect the net profit figure and result in tax savings (conserving cash rather than creating it).

[1] U.S. Department of Commerce, Office of Business Economics, *Survey of Current Business* (October, 1960), p. 12.

Although a depreciation charge does not entail a cash payment to anyone, it is a legitimate expense item (one without which profits cannot be earned). Whether tax free or not tax free, realistic depreciation allowances represent the recovery of investments in plant and equipment. Most financial writers recognize depreciation allowances as a "source of funds" as they do retained earnings or the proceeds from the sale of bonds or stock. Since depreciation allowances and retained earnings pertain to funds from operations, one point of distinction that is made incorrectly is that the former belong to the company while the latter belong to the stockholders, and that as a policy matter, depreciation reserves represent something that may be spent rather freely by management.

A company's engineers are interested in depreciation allowances because they are concerned with having new equipment equal or superior to that used by their competitors. While the engineers are thinking in terms of replacement of plant and equipment, the accountants are thinking in terms of allocation of costs of fixed assets. Thus the viewpoints of the engineers and those of financial management are similar.

Depreciation allowances are of interest to economists because of the effect of expenditures of funds from operations on national income and tax receipts of the federal and state governments. They recognize that more productive efficiency often results when funds accounted for as depreciation allowances are spent, because the new capital equipment purchased may be more efficient than that replaced. If only replacement values were to result from spending depreciation allowances for plants, equipment, and machinery, this spending would still have an important effect on the national economy.

Economists contend that liberal depreciation allowances not only assure the maintenance of the capital value of a business firm but also increase or stabilize national income. During depressions, funds retained from operations would be available in larger amounts for expenditures when such outlays for plants and equipment would be most helpful to the economy. (Note cyclical changes in new plant and equipment expenditures indicated in Chart 4.) The larger the expenditures for plants and equipment were during depressions, the smaller these expenditures would have to be during boom periods, when such expenditures would be least helpful. Even if these funds were not spent for fixed assets, they would be available for other purposes. The funds represented by depreciation allowances are in excess of $20 billion annually, and spending these funds at a steady rate has a stabilizing influence on the national economy.

While some criticize proposed liberalization of depreciation allowances because it would result in a temporary loss in government

CHART 4

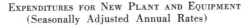

EXPENDITURES FOR NEW PLANT AND EQUIPMENT
(Seasonally Adjusted Annual Rates)

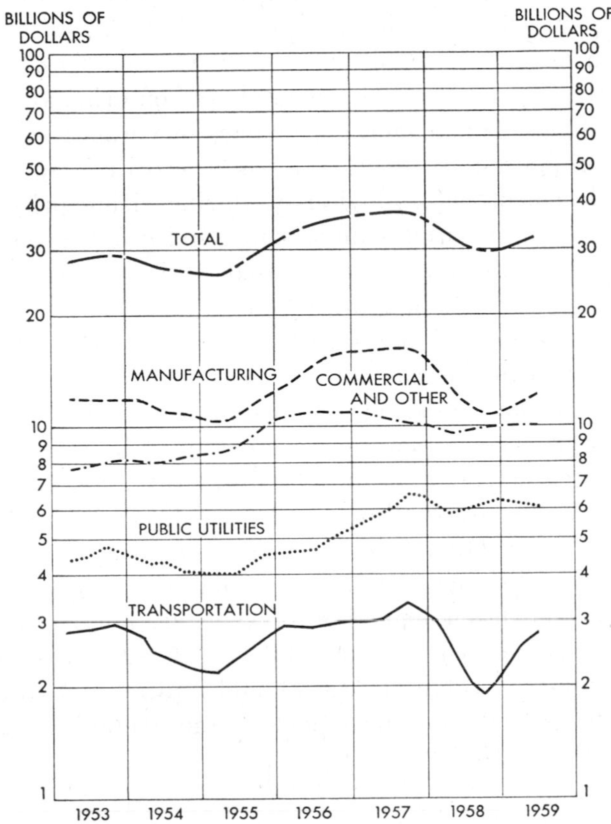

Notes: Estimates for first and second quarters of 1959 are based on anticipated capital expenditures as reported by business between late January and early March, and have been adjusted, when necessary, for systematic tendencis in anticipation data.

Source: Federal Reserve Bank of St. Louis, *Monthly Review* (April, 1959), p. 39.

income, others contend that more liberal depreciation allowances would result in more liberal replacement of capital policies which would cause an increase in expenditures and output, thereby assuring a larger base on which to collect future income taxes. They further contend that inadequate depreciation allowances would impede modernization, resulting in a decline in production.

Depreciation allowances that do not permit tax-free recapture of investments in fixed assets before the end of their useful lives lead to inequities among taxpayers, and those taxpayers having large investments in plants and equipment suffer most. When general prices are rising, this problem is a serious one because it results in funds retained from depreciation accruals, based on traditional costs, being inadequate. Replacement needs must be met either by using retained earnings or by raising funds from external sources. A realistic depreciation policy recognizes two problems: the rate of depreciation and the base for depreciation allowances.

Usually depreciation allowances are based on original cost, which introduces numerous managerial problems that would be avoided—or at least minimized—if they were based on value depreciation or current replacement costs. Obviously, during rising prices, historical cost–depreciation value is understated and profits are overstated. Although the gap is never fully closed, it is lessened when new costs are recognized. The last-in first-out (LIFO) method of treating inventories has lessened the impact of rising prices on reported profits, but this principle has not been accepted for long-term assets.

As a result of the increasing cost of replacing fixed assets, charges against current income may be increased with a corresponding credit for replacement of property. Most evaluation concepts provide for capital recovery through depreciation allowances, but a newer concept is to estimate replacement costs of a proposed capital addition while allowing for higher replacement costs caused by higher prices and technological improvements. For illustration, assume that a machine costing $11,000 has an estimated useful life of 10 years, salvage value of $1,000, and replacement cost of $21,-000 would necessitate a replacement charge averaging $2,000 per year $\left(\frac{\$21,000 - \$1,000}{10} = \$2,000\right)$.

Governmental acceptance of some form of replacement cost accounting would lead to better financial management by permitting full depreciation tax free. This would reduce the need for financing with borrowed funds or stock sales with the accompanying possible dilution of equity of present investors, and it would permit more rapid replacement of equipment and facilities which are becoming obsolescent or wearing out. Irrespective of the tax aspect, a realistic depreciation policy for fixed assets would lessen the unwarranted optimism of management, stockholders, and employees caused by misleading information on the volume of profits.

BASIC CONCEPTS AND POLICIES

Depreciation. The term *depreciation* refers to both physical depreciation and functional depreciation or obsolescence. Physical depreciation refers to decline in value of man-made physical assets due to wear and tear, exposure to the elements, and/or time, while functional depreciation or obsolescence refers to decline in value of assets due to loss of utility; that is, they are rendered out of date as newer processes, discoveries, and products appear. Both physical depreciation and normal obsolescence are treated as current expenses.

Although fixed assets may be in excellent physical condition, they may become out of date almost overnight; in fact, there are cases in which fixed assets have become obsolete while still in process of construction. While accountants can readily compute the useful life expectancy of some fixed assets, no one can foresee or estimate accurately the useful life of all fixed assets; thus special reserve accounts may be created out of current earnings or surplus to deal with unpredictable obsolescence.

Depletion refers to the using up or exhaustion of natural resources which are not replaceable—petroleum, ore, stone, and so on. At any one location, there is a limit to the amount of natural resources available and the portion extracted cannot be replenished. Although the assets for which depreciation and depletion allowances are set up are dissimilar, the problems associated with depreciation of fixed assets and depletion of natural resources are similar.

Amortization refers to the method used in allocating the cost of intangible assets over their estimated useful lives. The original valuation of intangible assets may be difficult to determine because there may be no related costs that measure the value of assets such as patents, copyrights, and leases. After determining the original valuation, this amount may be allocated over the useful life of the asset by one of the methods used to depreciate tangible fixed assets (see below). The useful life of an intangible asset such as a patent, lease, or franchise may or may not coincide with its legal or contract life (for illustration, a new patent may make the one held obsolete); therefore management may follow a policy of rapid amortization. However, for tax purposes, the amortization and write-off period must be the same; if the assets become obsolete, the difference is chargeable to earnings in the year that this occurs.

If a fixed asset is to be used for five years, the original cost should be allocated over that period of time. Each year, in reporting its income and expenses, a business concern should deduct an allowance or depreciation expense for each deductible asset. Depreciation accounting has as its chief purpose the distribution of the cost or basic value of tangible assets in a systematic and rational manner. Annual costs, due to the deterioration of long-lived assets, must be computed and included in the operating statement for each year. For illustration, if a business firm spends $3,200 for a truck having a useful life expectancy of five years and a scrap value of $200, the firm ought to recover $3,000 ($3,200 – $200) in the selling price of its goods or services over five years.

Whether or not it is recognized, a family operating on a budget has a problem of adding something as an annual expense for the loss in value of the home, furniture, car, and other fixed assets. Few families take depreciation into account in budgeting, but if a business firm were to follow a like practice, the consequences would be serious. Accurate accounting is imperative for a business concern because management must know the financial status of the firm in order to pay the right amount of federal income and other taxes, plan expenditures intelligently, price goods and services properly, and give accurate reports to owners and others.

When a business firm reports income for tax purposes without making adequate deductions for depreciation of fixed assets, its costs are understated, its income is overstated, and its income tax payments are higher than they should be; conversely, when a firm deducts the total cost of newly acquired fixed assets at the time of purchase, costs are overstated, income is understated, and if this procedure is permitted for tax purposes, taxes will be underpaid.

When business income is reported without proper deductions for depreciation of fixed assets, the overstated business income for the year may encourage unwise expenditures. Management may feel justified in making cash disbursements for salary increases, dividend payments, year-end bonuses, and other things when such disbursements are not warranted. Unless records are kept of all expenses, including depreciation charges, the earnings retained in the business may be used in expansion of the least profitable phase of the business.

When business income is reported without deductions for depreciation of fixed assets, management may assume that profits are satisfactory and resort to price cutting or more liberal trade credit terms to increase sales on items which actually entail a loss. Had depreciation costs been deducted, management would have realized that its prices were already too low and that the correct policy was to raise prices. Unless a business concern recovers the cost of operations in the selling price of its products, a decline in its competitive position and ultimate insolvency must be anticipated.

When business income is reported to owners and others without deductions having been made for depreciation of fixed assets, management is making two mistakes—reporting too large net income and too large value for assets. At best, income and asset valuation figures are estimates; even when a systematic accounting system is used, there is still a margin for error. When, over a period of time, income and asset valuation figures are overstated by any substantial amount, expenditure policies based thereon could lead to insolvency of the business firm.

When going business concerns use the depreciation device they are recognizing the fact that capital invested in fixed assets is being changed into capital invested in current assets. This gives financial management more leeway in making disbursements without affecting the total assets of the business concern. Assets are available for purposes such as financing working capital needs, which may make borrowing unnecessary; paying off loans, which would reduce both total liabilities and total assets but would not reduce net worth or equity; and paying cash dividends, which would reduce assets and earned surplus of the business firm.

The retention of assets as depreciation charges also permits management to shift production from one line to another—from farm machinery to railroad equipment or from baby carriages to machine guns—without having to resort to outside sources for capital. During World War II, when many business firms shifted from peace to war production, financing was facilitated by the liquidity resulting from recapture of fixed assets through depreciation allowances.

Write-offs. Some business firms may write off the costs of fixed assets when they are acquired and then carry them on their books at a nominal figure (such as one dollar). While this procedure will overstate current charges, it will overstate profits in later years because no annual depreciation charges will be deducted in computing profits. If the process were a recurring one, the costs and gains would offset each other; therefore the income statement would show an accurate picture of earnings from year to year. But policies in regard to "write-down" and "write-off" of capital assets as expenses ought to be uniformly consistent so that the progress of the business firm will be portrayed clearly. Undervaluation or overvaluation of assets, and overstatement or understatement of liabilities may result in "secret reserve accounts" or in "secret losses."

Although writing off costs of newly acquired assets seems like an ultraconservative practice, just the opposite is the case insofar as future income is concerned. Since there will be no depreciation allowances to deduct from gross income, annual net income will be overstated. This overstatement of net earnings may mislead a board of directors, none of whom may be trained accountants, into voting a cash dividend when it may be unwarranted or even illegal. This practice would also result in inaccuracy in the valuation of assets as reported on the balance sheet, but this may be minor compared to the effects of misrepresentation of net income.

The assumption that understatement of the value of assets is an ultraconservative accounting practice belongs to the era in which investment analysis stressed assets as the security for debts, balance sheets were the chief financial statements, and profit and loss or income statements were of minor importance. Nevertheless, to the extent that values of fixed assets are shown on the books at less than true value, an understatement of values takes place and so-called "secret reserve" accounts exist. If losses occur, the book value of assets may be "written up"; thus total assets will exceed total liabilities and the solvency of the business concern will be maintained. However, most of the business concerns undergoing reorganization or liquidation arrived at this impasse because of inability to meet their obligations. So it is much more important to maintain the earning power of a business enterprise by computing and reporting all costs of doing business accurately, thus avoiding weakening the firm by paying unwarranted cash dividends.

The policy of overstating the value of fixed assets, which most commonly occurs when there are intangible assets, is also misleading and may cause legal difficulties if a corporation's board of directors assumes that the corporation is solvent and votes a cash dividend. If a corporation follows a depreciation policy commensurate with its valuation policy, all earnings may be retained with beneficial results; however neither understatement or overstatement of the value of assets is recommended.

Insurance Policies. The extent to which a business concern should earmark a portion of gross income for anticipated loss of value of assets depends in part upon the concern's policy as to insurance. If its policy is one of insuring every possible hazard including sales credits, the cash outlay for insurance will be recognized for what it is, an expense that must be deducted from gross income before reporting net income or earnings. However, if a corporation goes to the other extreme and carries no insurance of any kind, would it be justified in ignoring the possible losses which have been recognized as an appropriate expense? In practice, most business firms follow a policy of carrying fire and other forms of insurance and making allowances for bad debts and other normal business hazards. In addition, a business concern may adopt a policy of "self-insurance" to cover extraordinary losses and hazards. The costs will be revealed by charges against operating expenses, and the cumulative effects will be shown on the balance sheet as reserve accounts created for special purposes.

Replacement Depreciation. It has been contended that a realistic balance sheet will show appreciation as well as depreciation in fixed assets. A sharp increase in prices that would increase the dollar value of fixed assets would also increase the cost of replacement, and this would necessitate larger annual allowances for depreciation. So, a balance sheet that shows an increase in the money value of assets and a corresponding increase in the surplus account of a corporation ought to show an increase in the annual provision for depreciation in the income statement.

The sharp increase in prices following World War II brought the problem of providing for replacement of fixed assets at higher prices into national prominence. The contention of management was that corporations would not have sufficient income with which to pay higher taxes, higher salaries, and higher dividends unless the purchasing power of invested capital remained intact. Thus, because of higher prices, a plant that cost $10 million and may have been depreciated at the rate of $1 million per year would cost $20 million to be replaced. Use of the old rate of depreciation would mean that only $10 million would be available (ignoring salvage value if any). Therefore, larger amounts of gross income must be retained to offset the deficiency. Because more dollars are needed to maintain the plant and equipment when the value of money decreases, less net income ought to be reported; this decline in net income should be reflected in tax and dividend payments, officers' salaries and bonuses, and perhaps wages of employees.

Repair, Maintenance, and Retirement. Repairs, replacement, and retirement of fixed assets may be charged to operating expenses, which would result in the value of fixed assets being prolonged and the allowances for depreciation being reduced. Customarily, provisions are made in the operating budget for purchase of small tools and repair parts and for ordinary maintenance and repairs. This raises the question of why all replacement, maintenance, and other costs should not be charged to current income. For illustration, if a trucking firm purchases one truck each year, the cost of each truck (assuming no change in price) would be equal to the depreciation charge of the units purchased in previous years; therefore, the firm may deduct the cost of one truck each year instead of deducting an annual depreciation for each truck. This method of bookkeeping may be allowed in cases wherein the same dollar amounts of fixed assets are acquired each year.

The use of replacement and maintenance charges as a substitute for the more systematic depreciation allowance method did not work well when used by railroads and public utility companies because, during depression years, they did not buy the annual quota of new equipment. Then, they had no charges to deduct as a substitute for "depreciation allowances"; consequently, they had to pay higher taxes when they could least afford to do so. This method is not systematic and it has been abandoned by most business firms.

Some public utility companies use a retirement system in which credits to reserves are based on an assumed rate of property replacement; others use a revenue method wherein credits to reserves are a fixed percentage of revenues (reduced by the amount spent for maintenance of the property). The reserves accumulated under these methods do not measure the estimated depreciation of the associated properties and are being used less and less in favor of simpler straight-line depreciation methods.

METHODS OF COMPUTING DEPRECIATION

Among the more common methods of computing depreciation allowances are (1) straight-line, (2) compound interest, (3) constant percentage of book value, (4) sum-of-the-years' digits, (5) unit of production, (6) sales or profits, and (7) composite life and group.

1. The straight-line method of depreciation is based on the assumption that the fixed assets lose the same amount of value each year during the estimated useful life of the assets. For illustration, if a $1,000,000 plant has an estimated useful life of 20 years and no salvage value (the cost of demolishing the plant may be equal to the price obtained for the rubble of brick and steel), the annual

depreciation charge would be $50,000. The straight-line method makes no allowances for the fact that normally the depreciation rate is greater the first year than later years (but this may be offset by smaller maintenance charges the first year and larger charges during the later years). Nevertheless, the straight-line method usually underestimates capital consumption during the early years and overestimates it during the later years. However, this method is not difficult either to compute or to understand and is more widely used than other methods, particularly in the depreciation accounting on buildings. Among the companies in the privately owned division of the electric utility industry, 92 per cent are using the straight-line method.[2]

2. The compound interest, annuity, or sinking-fund method is the most logical of any in use for computing depreciation allowances because it recognizes that depreciation allowances, as liability items, have their counterpart in asset values which are employed in some way in the business. If assets are to be retained at the rate of $50,000 a year to replace a $1,000,000 plant at the end of 20 years (20 × $50,000 would be $1,000,000), presumably the $50,000 retained the first year and each $50,000 retained in subsequent years will be gainfully employed. Should these earnings be ignored in computing depreciation charges?

Management may compute the annual depreciation allowance for the $1,000,000 plant discussed above by the following steps: (1) from an annuity table, select the interest rate which, for purpose of illustration, may be assumed to be 5 per cent; (2) note the amount that $1 per annum payment compounded at 5 per cent is worth at the end of 20 years ($33.0659541); and (3) divide the value of the depreciable asset, $1,000,000, by this figure ($1,000,000 ÷ $33.0659541 = $30,245). The result is about $30,245 which would be the annual allowance for depreciation. Thus the sinking-fund method provides that the amount of depreciation allowance is, when cumulated at a given rate of interest compounded annually, a sum that will equal the original value of the plant.

The compound interest method is sometimes critized because it is difficult to compute and does not provide adequate depreciation for the first years. There is little merit in the first criticism but the second is particularly pertinent when rapid functional depreciation or ob-

[2] Federal Power Commission, *Electric Utility Depreciation Practices 1958, Class A and B Privately Owned Companies* (Washington, D.C.: U.S. Government Printing Office, 1960), p. 1.

solescence of assets must be anticipated. The interest or sinking-fund method has been used in the public utility field, but it is being replaced by the straight-line method. The results achieved by the compound-interest method are usually the reverse of those obtained by the constant percentage of book value and sum-of-the-years' digits methods. When the compound interest method is used the accumulated reserves are lowest during the first period and grow increasingly larger as the impact of compound interest increases and as the property being depreciated ages.

3. The constant percentage of book value or declining balance method provides for rapid charge-off of fixed assets during the early years of the useful life of such assets but never reaches 100 per cent (mathematically, it could continue indefinitely). For illustration, if a $1,000,000 plant is depreciated by 20 per cent the first year, by 20 per cent of the remaining book value the second year, and so on, the base is declining progressively from $1,000,000 the first year to $800,000 the second, $640,000 the third, and so on. The depreciation charge would be $200,000 the first year, $160,000 the second year, $128,000 the third year, and so on. Unless the percentage rate of depreciation is high enough to be realistic, a substantial part of the cost will remain at the end of the useful life of the asset.

In case of long-term investments, a percentage rate of depreciation double that used in the straight-line method would be unsatisfactory; therefore, a still higher percentage rate for long-term investments would be in order. For relatively short-term assets, the declining balance method offers more rapid recovery of investments than does the straight-line method of depreciation. For illustration, when the useful life of an asset is ten years, at the end of five years the declining-balance method would recover more than two thirds of the cost when the depreciation rate is 20 per cent, while the straight-line method would recover only one half of the cost.

4. The straight-line method is criticized because it does not recognize the need for more rapid depreciation during the early years of the useful life of an asset and the declining balance method is criticized because it always leaves an undepreciated terminal value. Both criticisms are met by applying the depreciation rate in the sum-of-the-years' digits method which keeps the same base but applies a different percentage rate of depreciation.

The sum-of-the-years' digits method of depreciation is computed as shown by the following hypothetical illustration: If the useful life of an asset is 5 years, the sum-of-the-years' digits is 5 + 4 +

3 + 2 + 1 = 15 and the depreciation allowance is 5/15 the first year, 4/15 the second, 3/15 the third, 2/15 the fourth, and 1/15 the fifth and last year of the useful life of the asset. The sum-of-the-years' digits method was among the methods specifically authorized in the 1954 Federal Income Tax Code and it is being used extensively in equipment-depreciation accounting.

5. The unit of production method of depreciation is one of several methods which links the depreciation allowance to the use of the fixed asset. In this method, depreciation may be computed by taking the probable working life of a fixed asset in terms of hours of output and dividing this figure into the cost of the asset minus estimated salvage value (giving depreciable value). For illustration, if the service life of a machine is 10,000 hours, the depreciation charge would be found by dividing 10,000 into the depreciable value figure assumed to be $1,000. Thus, the depreciation charge would be 10 cents for each hour of operation, and if the machine is used 2,000 hours in one year, the depreciation charge for the year would be $200.

If depreciation is computed in terms of output, which is assumed to be 5,000 units, the depreciation charge per unit of output would be 20 cents. If the machine is used to produce 4,000 units during a year, the depreciation charge would be $800. When a "use" method is used to depreciate transportation equipment (cars, trucks, etc.), the basis may be mileage rather than hours or output. When depreciation is computed in terms of hours of operation, output, or mileage, the depreciation charge is highest when use is greatest; however, the fact that assets depreciate even when they are not being used is ignored.

6. When the aim of management is to stabilize reported earnings, allowances for depreciation may be computed as a percentage of total sales or profits. Using this method will result in costs being understated during bad years and overstated during good years, and profits being overstated in bad years and understated in good years. Thus, the earning statement for any particular year will be inaccurate and the inaccuracy will be cumulative if there are several years of either high sales and high profits or low sales and low profits or losses.

Relating depreciation allowances to gross earnings permits a business firm with a small margin of profit to have the same depreciation allowance as a firm with a large margin of profit; linking depreciation allowances to net earnings would result in no depreciation charges when there are no profits. In the public utility field, companies are sometimes permitted to set aside a percentage of gross revenue for depreciation, maintenance, and repair.

7. The composite life method may be used to compute depreciation charges for several types of property having varying depreciable values. The objective is to arrive at an annual rate of depreciation which can be applied to different types of property rather than one for each type. By prorating the annual depreciation charge for each type of property on the straight-line basis and dividing the total of these items by the total cost of all assets, one may arrive at a rate that is applicable to all fixed assets. This is simply an average of several straight-line computations and results in some percentage figure, such as 3 per cent, that is applied to all fixed assets. The composite life method permits realism in bookkeeping that is not present when one rule is applied to a factory made up of things such as walls, windows, roof, fixtures, and equipment—no two of which are subject to the same rate of deterioration.

The group method of depreciation is based on the straight-line or some other method of depreciation which is applied to a group of similar but not identical properties such as gasoline stations owned and operated by one business concern. One depreciation reserve account is used by the firm and if any unit (station) is disposed of for any reason, the entire amount, minus salvage value, is charged against the reserve for depreciation. The group method of depreciation, like the composite method, simplifies bookkeeping procedure.

METHODS OF COMPUTING DEPLETION

Depletion is the reduction in the value of wasting assets (natural resources) through conversion into salable products, and a depletion allowance or reserve is the accounting charge to income that reflects the decrease in the value of these assets. Depletion for a year is found by multiplying the number of units removed (as 100,000 barrels of oil) by the unit cost of each unit. Before the unit cost can be computed, the amount of natural resources or wasting assets available must be evaluated; this is often a difficult matter. If the property is purchased from a second party for $1,000,000 and the company's technicians estimate that there are 10,000,000 units, the cost per unit would be 10 cents. When the number of units removed during a year is multiplied by 10 cents, the product is the depletion charge for the year. If the oil or mineral rights were not purchased from a second party, the cost figures will have to be based on the capitalized value of discovery or development costs and all other expenditures that led to the acquisition of the assets. Then, engineers and other scientists may calculate the amount of the product that can be extracted profitably. With the passage of time, this calculation of total production may have to be revised upward or downward, which would entail a decrease or increase in the depletion rate.

For income tax purposes, depletion may be computed without regard to the cost of the asset being depleted. The tax policy in case of physical assets is to permit business firms to recover their investments tax free, but in wasting-assets industries there is uncertainty as to whether the assets (gas, oil and others) can be replaced and considerable expense is entailed in attempting to do so.

The Internal Revenue Code permits varying depletion allowances ranging from 5 to 27½ per cent of *gross* income for different extractive industries, provided the amount deducted does not exceed 50 per cent of the *net* income from the property prior to depletion. Percentage depletion rates now apply to about 100 minerals. Here are some of these rates: 5 per cent on sand, gravel, and oyster shells; 10 per cent for coal; 15 per cent for a large number of other minerals; 23 per cent for sulphur and uranium; and 27½ per cent for gas and oil. In practice, the controlling rate is often based on 50 per cent of net income, which is uniform for all minerals. Usually the percentage depletion method results in larger deductions than the per unit of product or output method. The effect of this has been to encourage companies in oil, gas, and other fields to finance exploration and development of natural resources. The percentage depletion method is applicable to all minerals except soil, sod, dirt, turf, water, mosses, and minerals from sea water or similar inexhaustible sources.

FEDERAL REGULATION AND RAPID WRITE-OFFS

Since the end of World War II, depreciation allowances have increased steadily and today they account for the most important single source of corporate funds. Purchase of assets at higher prices and use of new accounting techniques for depreciation of plants and equipment have resulted in the depreciable asset base being larger and depreciation allowances being greater. Added impetus to the use of funds accounted for as depreciation allowances occurred in 1950, when rapid amortization provisions were introduced into the federal income tax law for investments in defense-related expansion, and in 1954 when the same principle was applied to new facilities.

These changes were significant in their influence over timing depreciation as a cost, but they had no effect on total depreciation allowances (which can never exceed 100 per cent of the depreciable value of an asset).

Despite the many methods of computing depreciation allowances, the influence of the Federal Income Tax Code has resulted in considerable uniformity in methods used by companies in the same industry. In computing federal corporate income taxes, "reasonable" depreciation charges are deductible as expenses. In the past, in rulings upon "reasonableness of such charges made by a particular company," the Bureau of Internal Revenue (now, the Internal Revenue Service) was influenced by practices which were current in the industry within which the company operated.

The 1954 Federal Income Tax Code recognized certain specific methods of computing depreciation allowances; as a result, an individual company could use a specific method without being required to justify its use on the basis of the industry's practice. Under this code, if and when the corporate income tax rate reaches 52 per cent, each extra dollar deducted as an expense will mean a tax saving of 52 cents. However, no more than the depreciable value of a fixed asset may be deducted as an expense over the life of the fixed asset. Therefore, a most important aspect of the method used for tax purposes is one of timing—how rapidly the tax saving may be taken and under what circumstances (when tax rates are high or when low). Although the method used to compute depreciation allowances for tax purposes may differ from that used in financial reporting, usually the same method is used for the sake of economy.[3]

The Internal Revenue Service permits business firms to make "reasonable allowances for the exhaustion, wear and tear of property used in trade or business, including a reasonable allowance for obsolescence." The administrative provisions permit making agreements in writing with respect to depreciation rates. Such rates stand until significant new developments occur; then, if changed, the burden of proof rests upon the party initiating the change. Recent changes in the Internal Revenue Code have recognized specific depreciation methods. A business concern now has a wider choice and is no longer limited to the method commonly used in its industry.

---

[3] United States Treasury Department, Internal Revenue Service, *Bulletin F* (1959) contains tables of useful lives of depreciable property. The schedules of useful lives is out of date and a "comprehensive and extended survey of the subject is being made." When completed, a new revision of *Bulletin F* is promised.

The 1954 Federal Income Tax Code contains provisions which liberalize depreciation allowances in addition to recognizing specific methods of depreciation. Business firms may now deduct as much as two thirds of the cost of equipment and new plants, with a service life of three years or more, during the first half of the property's useful life. The 1954 code specifically permits the use of the declining balance method in an amount equal to 200 per cent (formerly 150 per cent) of a corresponding straight-line method. Other methods for accelerating depreciation allowances may be used, provided the accumulated allowances do not exceed two thirds of the cost of the fixed assets during the first half of the useful life of the asset.

To obtain the added facilities needed for defense and war purposes, the federal government is dependent, at least in part, upon private capital and private initiative. Business leaders may hesitate to engage in war and/or defense production for fear that, at the end of the emergency, they will be burdened with plants, equipment, and other assets for which they have no need during normal periods. Under customary depreciation procedures, a business concern would be required to spread depreciation charges over the normal life of such assets—ten to twenty years. Such charges would depress net earnings for as long as they are being made; however, if the premise that the assets will be unnecessary at the end of the emergency is valid, their true rate of depreciation is not ten to twenty years but the period of the emergency. This principle has been applied to depreciation charges at different times, including both World Wars and the Korean War period.

A business concern that is expanding because of defense or other essential government contracts may obtain a "certificate of necessity" from the Defense Production Administration that is binding on the Internal Revenue Service. A certificate of necessity permits the depreciation of fixed assets over a five-year period with the annual amount deducted before computing corporate income taxes. One of the chief benefits of this plan is that it shortens the payback period and reduces the risk of capital loss. At the same time, there may or may not be a tax advantage if the fixed assets have a useful life that extends beyond the depreciation period.

The value of tax reduction concentrated over five years is much greater when high rates are in effect (for example, when the normal tax plus excess profit taxes may be—at a combined rate—as high as 77 per cent) than at a later period when rates are lower. Since the assets still in use after the depreciation period will not be subject to depreciation, the tax burden will then be larger. Whether or not an over-all tax saving has been effected will be determined by comparing the tax reduction during the accelerated depreciation period with the additional taxes paid after the end of that time. A tax saving may occur because tax rates are likely to be higher during an emergency than after one. Customarily, business concerns consider rapid depreciation of assets to be advantageous if for no other reason than that it represents a postponement of tax payments. In effect, this postponement amounts to an interest-free loan.

Changes in the 1954 Federal Income Tax Code imply partial acceptance of the principle of rapid depreciation (which has also been recognized in the tax codes of Canada, Australia, the United Kingdom, and other countries). In addition to the opportunity given business firms to recapture their investments in a shorter period of time, the effect on the economy as a whole has been stressed.

Under a ten-year depreciation plan, a business concern with depreciable assets of $10,000,000 would have $1,000,000 each year for reinvestment in fixed assets; but, after a shift to a five-year depreciation plan, the firm would have $2,000,000 each year for reinvestment in fixed assets. If all of the $2,000,000 is an allowable deduction as an expense in computing federal corporate income taxes, the business concern's tax would be sharply reduced (by $520,000 when the rate is 52 per cent). If and when all fully depreciated assets are replaced by new assets, the process is started over again; but, if the assets that have been written off are not replaced, the book value of depreciable assets would be zero, there would be no allowances for depreciation, and corporate income taxes would increase. Therefore, management now has a greater incentive to modernize plants and equipment than in the past, when allowable depreciation charges were less.

At the same time that new equipment is being purchased with funds retained in the business (part of which originate in tax savings), some of the assets that have been written off will continue to be used in production. Then total output may be increased because of the use of better tools and machines and an increase in the amount of capital goods in use. Although neither of these changes will be shown on the balance sheet of a business concern, both will be reflected in the profit and loss statement and reported net earnings before federal income taxes. As a result of the increase in national income, both corporate and personal tax payments should increase (which is perhaps the most important tax argument in favor of adoption of more rapid depreciation methods).

In addition to the Internal Revenue Service, there are other governmental agencies that have an influence on depreciation policies of business corporations. The Federal Power Commission, Interstate Commerce Commission, and state regulatory agencies are interested in depreciation policies of corporations in the public utility and transportation industries. Since depreciation charges are a cost of doing business that must be recognized along with other costs in fixing reasonable charges for service (rate-making), these supervisory agencies must pass on depreciation charges.

In the public utility field, emphasis is on regular depreciation of fixed assets over their estimated useful life so that the valuation of property for rate-making purposes reflects accrued depreciation accurately. In some cases, companies have been required to write off book values that were in excess of original costs against earnings and surplus.

Concerning the railroad industry, the Interstate Commerce Commission was formerly more tolerant of the policy of using current maintenance and replacement of fixed assets as a substitute for depreciation of assets; but, in this industry as elsewhere, standard plans are being set up for depreciation of structures, equipment, and other fixed assets. To a greater degree than in the past, railroad companies are using assets retained as a result of depreciation allowances for modernization and replacement purposes.

SUMMARY

Depreciation and similar allowances are used to allocate the cost or basic value of fixed assets over their useful life. Among the methods used are (1) straight-line, (2) compound interest, (3) constant percentage of book value, (4) sum-of-the-years' digits, (5) unit of production or output, (6) sales or profits, and (7) composite life and group.

The greater use of capital assets and the accelerated rate of decline in their useful life have resulted in more rapid depreciation practices; these have been encouraged in individual cases by issuance of "certificates of necessity" and, in general, by changes in the Federal Income Tax Code which permit the use of more rapid depreciation methods. As a result, "funds from operations" have tended to increase and to provide more assets for purchase and modernization of plants and equipment. "Funds from operations" include not only depreciation allowances but also net earnings retained in the business.

Profits not paid out as cash dividends and assets retained because of depreciation allowances are sources of funds that may be used to finance the purchase of assets. However, corporate savings result from retained earnings which include only profits after all taxes are paid. In order to measure the effects of using "funds from operations" upon the productive capacity of a business firm, it is necessary to recognize that more efficient equipment is being installed to replace the worn-out and discarded equipment. Because of modern improvements, better processes, and technological changes, the rate of increase in output is more rapid than the increase in net capital investment. This aspect of betterment, leading to greater productivity, may not be reflected in valuation of assets on the balance sheet; however, it is reflected in the profit and loss statement, income or operating statement, corporate income tax statement, and earned surplus account.

QUESTIONS AND PROBLEMS

1. Identify: (*a*) depreciation, (*b*) depletion, and (*c*) amortization.
2. What are the effects on reported net income for the current year when there are inadequate provisions for depreciation? Compare this to the practice of treating new acquisitions of fixed assets as current expenses at the time of purchase.
3. (*a*) How do depreciation charges affect the valuation of assets on a balance sheet? (*b*) What is meant by the statement that liberal depreciation allowances not only may assure the maintenance of the capital value of a business firm but also may increase or stabilize national income?
4. (*a*) What are the advantages claimed for "rapid write-offs" of fixed assets? (*b*) Does "rapid write-off" have any effect on reported future income? Explain.
5. Explain the differences between percentage depletion and cost depletion. Why is percentage depletion permitted for tax purposes in extractive industries?
6. What adjustment to reported net income must be made in order to determine "funds from operations?"
7. "The shift to the use of newer formulae in calculating depreciation charges has a special, somewhat distorting effect on book profits." (U.S. Department of Commerce, Office of Business Economics, *Survey of Current Business* [October, 1960], p. 11.) What are the "newer formulae?" Account for the effects described in the above quotation.
8. Compare the straight-line method and the declining balance method of computing depreciation. What are the advantages and disadvantages of each?

9. How does the sum-of-the-years' digits method of computing depreciation differ from the declining balance method? For what reasons is the sum-of-the-years' digit method superior?
10. Explain the compound interest method of computing depreciation. What is the justification of such a method?
11. Explain the unit of production method of computing depreciation. It is sometimes said that this method fails to make an allowance for functional obsolescence. Why is this so?
12. "Corporations have had to use retained earnings to pour in billions of dollars each year simply to make up for the inadequaucy of depreciation." (First National City Bank, *Monthly Letter, Business and Economic Conditions* [December, 1960], p. 137.) What method of handling depreciation would remedy this situation?
13. "Revise the tax laws relative to depreciation to permit the earlier replacement of obsolete equipment. This will help to make American industry the most efficient, low-cost industry in a highly competitive world." (H. V. Prochnow, *A Time For Critical Decisions* [First National Bank of Chicago, 1959], p. 18.) Why?
14. "The provision for depreciation and amortization of property amounted to $78.4 million for the year ending May 31, 1960. The Company uses the declining balance method of computing depreciation wherever applicable." (Dow Chemical Company, *Sixty-Third Annual Report* [August, 1960], p. 16.) Is the company justified in using this method of computing depreciation? Explain.

CHAPTER 8

Retained Earnings

IN THE United States, corporate profits before income taxes now amount to almost $50 billion annually; however, because nearly 50 per cent of pretax earnings are paid out as taxes, only about one half of corporate earnings are available for corporate uses and dividend payments. Retained earnings originate in the operations of business firms and may be used for several purposes: to finance working capital and fixed capital needs, to allow business expansion, and to retire debt and preferred stock. Usually, business management has greater freedom in spending funds accounted for as retained earnings than funds from outside sources—such as banks and insurance companies—because the latter are usually borrowed for specific purposes and the terms under which they are obtained from lenders may contain provisions which limit their uses.

Business profits are hard to measure accurately because of the difficulty of making proper allowances for depreciation, bad debts, and other legitimate charges against current earnings; accounting practices pertaining to the treatment of unusual gains and losses; fluctuations in prices that affect the dollar value of sales; and other factors. Presumably, the "earned surplus" or "earnings retained in the business" account will be equal to past earnings of a business firm, minus cash dividends which have been paid out. However, it is a common practice for the board of directors of a corporation to apportion part of the retained earnings account among different surplus reserve accounts. This procedure results in distributing the retained earnings account throughout the equity side of the balance sheet and hiding a portion of retained earnings under different reserve titles. This chapter deals with the importance of retained earnings, reserve accounts, funds, income stabilization, and the use of ratios to indicate changes in income positions.

IMPORTANCE OF RETAINED EARNINGS

When a corporation finances with retained earnings, it does not follow that the amount of cash on the asset side of the company's balance sheet has increased by an equal amount but rather that the stockholders' share of total assets has increased. (It is not unusual for profitable companies which are expanding rapidly to be short of cash.) Although retained earnings are funds from operations, they are not identifiable with any specific asset or group of assets.

It should be clear that business firms do not finance with liabilities and net worth items (bookkeeping entries) but rather with cash and other assets. This does not mean that a distinction among the sources of funds is unimportant. The need for proper depreciation accounting has been emphasized, and it is also important to recognize the need for treating funds accounted for as retained earnings differently from those borrowed or obtained through the sale of stock. For legal reasons, management must distinguish between borrowed and contributed capital and between contributed capital and retained earnings. Management must not only safeguard the interest of creditors but also know whether it can legally declare a cash dividend.

An important aspect of financing with funds accounted for as retained earnings is the effect that it has had on the size of corporations. While some writers emphasize combinations of two or more firms in explaining the size of business corporations, others are equally as positive that the most important factor in the growth of business units is financing with retained earnings. Some corporations, created by combinations of several business concerns forty or fifty years ago, have reached their present size chiefly by financing with retained earnings. For illustration, the following firms have financed at least 60 per cent of their growth with retained earnings since their organization: United States Steel Corporation (1901), Ford Motor Company (1903), P. Lorillard Company (1911), Deere and Company (1912), B.F. Goodrich Company (1913), and Chrysler Corporation (1925). Although the factors are interrelated, internal growth, in its broadest sense, includes financing expansion of plants and equipment with stocks and bonds as well as with retained earnings, in contrast to external growth resulting from mergers, consolidations, and so on. According to a special study of seventy-four major corporations, increase in size has been attributed primarily to internal and relatively little to external growth.[1]

Although financing with funds accounted for as retained earnings has characterized American business finance, the retention of earnings has been criticized because it permits tax avoidance by large stockholders, as they have no personal income taxes to pay on earnings which are not disbursed to them in the form of dividends; it deprives some stockholders of funds which they could spend or invest in other securities; and it permits corporations to keep resources idle or uneconomically employed.

The criticism of the policy of retaining earnings, which was particularly bitter during the early 1930's, led to the passage of the Undistributed Profits Tax of 1936. This act was revised in 1938 and repealed in 1940, but Section 102 of the Revenue Act imposes a punitive tax upon corporations that retain earnings to an unreasonable extent for the purpose of permitting tax avoidance by shareholders. If assets are being retained to care for future expansion, a business firm should be able to justify the retention if questioned by the Internal Revenue Service; however, of the companies which have been penalized under Section 102, the majority have been small corporations. The stock of such companies is usually held by a small number of stockholders who may attempt to withhold the distribution of earnings as a means of preventing higher personal income taxes. On the other hand, small companies are more dependent on retained earnings as a source of funds for expansion than are large corporations, and what may appear to be excessive retention of earnings in the short run may be justified in the long run. Business firms whose profits from operations are subject to wide cyclical fluctuations need adequate "reserves" in order to avoid financial difficulties during recessions.

Beginning with the Revenue Act of 1954, Congress, recognizing the unfairness of Section 102 to small corporations, made the following provisions: it increased the amount of earnings (to $100,000) that may be accumulated without fear of penalty and placed the burden of proving tax avoidance upon the Treasury; also, it made the penalty levied applicable only to those earnings above the amount reasonably needed in the business. (This act also gave unincorporated firms the option of being taxed as corporations and later

[1] J. Fred Weston, *The Role of Mergers in the Growth of Large Business Firms* (Berkeley and Los Angeles: University of California Press, 1953), p. 90.

corporations were given the option of being taxed as partnerships.)

Although some maintain that corporations should obtain funds through the sale of securities in the open market, such financing is not always practical. Small corporations are handicapped by the high cost of such financing and the narrow market for their securities. A large corporation may object to diluting its equity with new stock issues and to making its capital structure top-heavy with new bond issues. The increase in costs and prices since World War II means that more capital is needed to carry on business operations. In addition, corporate income taxes absorb a substantial portion of gross income, a part of which would have been available for corporate financing under prewar conditions. Even under the most favorable circumstances, a new business firm must adopt conservative dividend policies in order to retain an adequate share of gross earnings for contingencies, replacement, and expansion (it is not surprising that many of the corporations in the electronic industry have never paid dividends to their shareholders).

A corporation's management is responsible for preserving its solvency. To this end, retaining earnings to increase a corporation's net worth or to reduce its debts is desirable. Business corporations are subject to variations in earnings and it would be foolhardy not to retain part of them during periods of high profits to care for the needs of a "rainy day," when cyclical, seasonal, or social factors cause earnings to decline sharply.

Retention of earnings by corporations represents an involuntary form of investment by stockholders; but, over a number of years, this reinvestment of corporate profits should result in a higher rate of earnings per share, which will tend to be reflected in dividends paid in future years. If management has a choice of either retaining earnings and distributing a stock dividend or paying a cash dividend and then giving stockholders pre-emptive rights to purchase new shares, the first alternative may be more advantageous to stockholders not only because stock dividends are usually not taxable as income when issued but also because capitalization of retained earnings would tend to strengthen the corporation and to facilitate adoption of a stable dividend policy.

Corporation savings may be the least expensive way of obtaining equity capital because corporate earnings paid out as cash dividends may be subject to an average tax of 33 per cent as personal taxable income and a much higher rate as marginal income (91 per cent when taxable personal income exceeds $200,000). If stockholders were to receive 100 per cent of corporate earnings after taxes as dividends, the net worth of the corporation would be reduced by a minimum of one third of what it would be if all earnings were retained.[2]

A policy of financing with retained earnings is a form of savings necessary to the growth of a business firm, but the importance of such a policy varies among firms in different industries and among companies within each industry (see Table 16). During some years,

TABLE 16

SOURCES AND USES OF CORPORATE FUNDS BY INDUSTRY
Year Ended June 30, 1960 (Billions of Dollars)

	Manufacturing and Mining	*Railroads*	*Other Transportation*	*Public Utilities and Communication*
Sources				
Retained profits*	5.9	−0.2	−0.1	0.4
Depreciation	11.0	1.0	1.2	3.3
External long-term‡	1.5	−0.1	0.5	3.7
Short-term**	3.5	0.1	0.4	0.8
Sources, Total	21.9	0.8	2.0	8.2
Uses				
Plant and equipment	14.7	1.1	1.9	8.7
Inventories (book value)	4.8	†	0.1	†
Receivables and miscellaneous assets	3.7	†	0.2	0.2
Cash & U.S. Government securities	−1.9	−0.1	†	−0.1
Uses, Total	21.3	1.0	2.2	8.8
Discrepancy (uses less sources)	0.6	0.2	0.2	0.6

* Includes depletion charges.
† Less than $50 million.
‡ Includes stocks, bonded debt, long-term bank loans, mortgages, and other long-term debt.
** Includes short-term bank loans, trade payables, federal income tax liabilities, and miscellaneous liabilities.
Source: U.S. Department of Commerce, Office of Business Economics, *Survey of Current Business* (October, 1960), p. 17.

a corporation may disburse more cash dividends than were actually earned after corporate income taxes. This means that a corporation may dis-save as well as save—disperse retained earnings of previous years during periods of low net profits in order to maintain a stable dividend policy.

SURPLUS ACCOUNTS

Business management, in administering retained earnings and other income, makes use of two types of bookkeeping items, "sur-

[2] See also Walter A. Morton, "The Structure of the Capital Market and the Price of Money," *American Economic Review*, Vol. XLIV, No. 2 (May, 1954), p. 447.

plus accounts" and "reserves accounts." The surplus account may be thought of as showing asset values that are not represented by claims of creditors and the capital account as representing the contributions of shareholders. The surplus account is equal to total assets minus liabilities and the par or stated value of the company's capital stock. Some of the factors which affect the amount of the surplus account tend to increase it while others tend to decrease it.

Formerly, it was customary to divide surplus accounts into subdivisions to indicate origin; today most business firms have two items under surplus accounts—"earned surplus" (also called "retained earnings account") and "capital surplus." The bookkeeping sums representing changes in the book value of assets that are charged against or credited to each of these accounts depend to some extent on their origin. Customarily, "earned surplus" is credited for "net income" and charged for "net loss" during the current year. When appropriations are made from earned surplus by a corporation's board of directors for special purposes, there will be a decrease in reported earned surplus by the amount of the bookkeeping entry for the reserve account, but there will be no change in the "net worth." Ordinarily, when a cash dividend is paid, the surplus account is charged and the assets of the corporation are reduced.

The "capital surplus" which is closely related to the "capital account" is used to show changes in capital stock that cannot be reflected so readily in the capital account statement because of bookkeeping in terms of par value or stated value and other changes that are not related to the normal operation of the business firm. The capital surplus account is used when recording the excess resulting from original issues of stock above par or stated value; sales of treasury stock at a profit; redemption or retirement of capital stock, scrip, warrants, and so on at less than par; donation of stock; conversion of another class of stock where values in excess of par are to be recognized; stock assessments; forfeited subscriptions; cancellation of indebtedness; and any surplus from appreciation of assets, combinations with other companies, and so on. The capital surplus account will be charged when there are losses resulting from transactions of these types, such as redemption of preferred stock at more than par value, sale of treasury stock at a loss, and so on. Other transactions that may affect the capital surplus account are changes in goodwill, appropriations transferred thereto or therefrom, extraordinary gains or losses, and adjustments of prior years for depreciation, taxes, and other items; but more often, these adjustments will be made in the earned surplus account (see Table 17). For all intents and purposes, capital surplus is a permanent part of net worth of a business firm, and although permitted by the laws of some states, the declaration of dividends from capital surplus is not a wise policy.

TABLE 17

INCOME AND SURPLUS OF ALL MANUFACTURING COMPANIES EXCEPT NEWSPAPERS (In Millions of Dollars)

Income and Surplus	*First Quarter 1959*	*First Quarter 1960*
Sales (net of returns, allowances, and discounts)	80,695	85,699
Deduct: Costs and expenses (net of purchase discounts)	73,673	78,478
Net profit from operations	7,022	7,221
Add: Other income or deductions (net)	138	259
Net profit before federal income taxes	7,160	7,480
Deduct: Provisions for federal income taxes	3,338	3,489
Net profits after taxes	3,821	3,991
Deduct: Cash dividends charged to surplus	1,839	2,001
Net profit retained in the business	1,982	1,990
Add: Earned surplus and surplus reserves at the beginning of period	85,533	91,844
Add: Other direct charges or credits to surplus (net)	−42	−212
Earned surplus and surplus reserves at end of period	87,474	93,622
Depreciation and depletion included above, including accelerated amortization of emergency facilities	2,503	2,674

Source: Federal Trade Commission—Securities and Exchange Commission, *Quarterly Financial Report for Manufacturing Corporations, First Quarter 1960*, p. 34.

The laws of some states, having protection of creditors as their purpose, prohibit the payment of cash dividends if a corporation's capital is impaired. Even in the absence of statutory prohibition the courts may accept the common-law concept that the capital of a corporation is like a trust fund and that the payment of cash dividends except out of earnings (current or past) is illegal. Sometimes a part of the earned surplus is earmarked for this purpose and labelled "reserve for dividends."

The "earned surplus" account presumably indicates in part the past profitability of a business firm and the amount of earnings retained in the business, but this may not be the case because of payment of stock dividends; financial reorganizations, mergers or other combinations; spin-offs (distribution by a parent corporation of the controlling stock in a subsidiary corporation to the stockholders of the parent corporation); and undisclosed assets. Unless the current income statement is bypassed, the retained earnings statement will contain only entries to show the declaration of dividends, transactions concerned with retiring capital stock, and transfers of income or losses.

Management may adopt a policy of charging or crediting the retained earnings section with extraordinary losses or gains, or in some cases, even with some of the more normal expenses or receipts which should never be permitted to reach the retained earnings statement. Although surplus accounts are only bookkeeping items, they are used to avoid legal embarrassment and may permit management to show a solvent position during financial crises even though the corporation may not be able to meet its obligations as they mature. Millions of dollars of fixed assets may be charged off against surplus and the books will show that total assets still exceed total liabilities.

Reserves. In the use of retained earnings, management may debit the earned surplus account and credit one or more reserve accounts. While it is not necessary to do so, this procedure has the advantage of indicating to the stockholders and others management's intention in regard to the uses of retained earnings. Being bookkeeping items, these reserves do not affect assets and they are not reserves in the sense of something being held to meet a possible or certain future needs (such as a cash reserve of a bank, a family reserve of food, troops held uncommitted, and so on).

The connotation that may be drawn from identifying part of the earned surplus with a specific purpose is that the remainder of the earned surplus is not being used productively and should be distributed as cash dividends to stockholders. It is often argued that the effect of creating "reserve accounts" will be to reduce the pressure for cash dividends by hiding retained earnings under different reserve accounts, and to place stockholders on notice that retained earnings so earmarked are not available for dividends; but the effect may be just the opposite. Policy may be served equally well if creation of proprietory reserve accounts is either avoided entirely or kept to a minimum. However, when the board of directors, by resolution, appropriates the surplus for a specific purpose, it prevents the use of surplus so impounded for dividend declaration and also calls attention to the need for which the appropriation was made.

A second policy which may be even more dangerous to a business firm than the creation of needless "reserve accounts" is to "fund" them. By this is meant not only the creation of bookkeeping entries but also the isolation of corporate assets to finance specific things for which the reserve account was created. For illustration, management may not only create a reserve account for air conditioning a building at a cost of $40,000 at some future time but also may to deposit $40,000 in a bank to finance it. This means that there is a reduction in cash available for current financing; also, if many such funded reserve accounts are created, the economic life of the business firm may be endangered. Such a policy could force a corporation to borrow when it would have had sufficient assets to finance current needs if they were not tied up in bank deposits and short-term investments. Funds may be held for future needs without being earmarked for a particular purpose and reserve accounts may be created without being funded; in either case, more flexible management of assets would be possible.

When the purpose for which a surplus reserve has been created is achieved, the surplus reserve is usually erased. For illustration, a surplus reserve of $500,000 for a new building will be erased on completion of the building and the $500,000 will be transferred back to earned surplus. The company's books will show a change in assets—a new building will replace cash and other assets. As noted previously, this change could have taken place without the creation of the reserve account.

Any number of surplus reserve accounts may be created, and those which appear on a particular balance sheet reflect the policy of management. Surplus reserve accounts reflect the policy of management in regard to retirement of long-term debt and preferred stock, self-insurance, replacement of plants, and other contingencies. However, the device of creating surplus reserve accounts is applicable to all individual situations that are a normal or extraordinary part of business affairs (but it is not recommended).

Earned surplus may be used to absorb losses, write off inflated assets, and correct inaccurate accounting estimates. For illustration, allowances for depreciation are proper charges against earnings that should never reach the surplus, but sometimes it may be found that deductions from earnings have not been sufficient and an appropriation from surplus is necessary to supplement the regular allowances for depreciation. If a certain sum of money is needed to settle a damage claim against the corporation, it may be more desirable to charge the earned surplus account than to charge current income. Management may have overstated the net worth position of the business firm by overstating the value of assets or understating the amount of liabilities, in which case the only remedy may be to rewrite the balance sheet. In arriving at the true value of the corporation, the earned surplus may be sufficient to absorb the losses, but sometimes it will also be necessary to rewrite the capital surplus and the capital account.

Management may also follow accounting procedures that will hide profits in various ways, creating "secret reserves." It is not unusual for a nominal figure such as one dollar to be written down for goodwill, patents, and other intangibles. The same results may be achieved by overstating liabilities and expenses—such as depreciation charges, omitting accrued assets or prepaid expenses, and improperly charging capital expenditures to operating expenses. Management may correct such situations by reappraising assets to show that they have been undervalued or by eliminating liability items as being no longer needed.

Surplus reserves and reserve funds are not the same; surplus reserves are carried on the equity side of a balance sheet while reserve funds are set up as assets. Usually management has complete freedom in the use of retained earnings, but there are exceptions. Debt contracts or provisions in the articles of incorporation of a corporation may require the creation of sinking fund reserve accounts and retention of all or part of net profits after taxes under certain circumstances. When financing with preferred stock, bonds, and/or term loans, management is frequently required by contract to refrain from paying dividends on common stock and from purchasing the corporation's shares if the company's current ratio falls below a specified figure, its net tangible assets drop below a stated amount, its earnings are less than twice the interest charges, or its earnings do not exceed dividends on preferred stock by 50 per cent (earnings equal 1½ times preferred stock dividends). When a corporation fails to meet the financial standards set by debt contracts or charter provisions, net profits must be retained in the business.

If the sinking-fund reserve account is required to be funded, the corporation surrenders assets to a sinking-fund trustee who uses them to retire the debt for which the sinking fund was created. If sinking-fund reserves are created but not funded, liquid assets may not be available when debts mature; therefore, even in the absence of contractual obligations, management may find it desirable to fund reserve accounts for retirement of debt and preferred stock.

The funds that are appropriated to retire debt and/or preferred stock are not deductible as an expense before computing federal and other income taxes; they are derived from net profits after all costs of doing business are met and after provisions have been made for estimated federal income taxes. Retiring debt at book value reduces the assets of a business firm but does not reduce its net worth because it reduces liabilities by an equivalent amount. After a debt has been retired with assets withdrawn from the business, the sinking-fund reserve (the bookkeeping item) is eliminated and the amount is transferred on the books back to the earned surplus account. The decrease in debt will be offset on the books by a decrease in assets.

The procedure for retiring preferred stock is the same as for retiring debt, except that the part of equity represented by preferred stock is reduced. If bonds and/or preferred stock to be retired are acquired at a discount or premium from book value, the difference from book value is adjusted in the surplus account. (The surplus will be credited for the amount of the discount or debited for the amount of the premium.)

Insurance reserve accounts are created for all types of insurance and they are similar to sinking-fund reserves in that they are usually funded. They may have captions such as "self-insurance" or "general insurance" or may be labelled for particular purposes such as accident, casualty, employer's liability, fire, public liability, tornado, or workmen's compensation. Unless insurance reserves are excessive, they cannot be transferred back to surplus until the business firm is liquidated, and as a rule, they cannot be considered as part of the net worth.

In addition to surplus reserve accounts, there are "valuation" and "liability" reserve accounts which represent current costs of doing business and which are properly charged against current income. These reserve accounts are basically different from surplus reserve accounts which in principle do not affect net worth or current income. In practice, the distinction between valuation and liability reserve accounts on the one hand and surplus reserve accounts on the other hand sometimes breaks down. Although the modern practice is to use some word other than "reserve" to show estimated changes in asset values and expenses wherein the date of payment or the amount is uncertain, the word "reserve" may appear almost anywhere on the balance sheet (that is, it may appear in the asset section, current liability section, above the stockholders' equity section, within the stockholders' equity section, or in notes to financial statements and letters to stockholders).

Quite commonly balance sheets of business firms will show reserves or allowances for accounts receivable. The reasoning is that all accounts receivable are not collectible and that accuracy in reporting their value and income necessitates a reduction from the gross amount. A similar practice may be followed in regard to inventory wherein there is a possibility of future decline in prices, obsolescence, and other factors. The importance of reserves or allowances for depreciation, depletion, and amortization has been discussed previously.

Among the other reserves or allowances are those which deal with liabilities whose amounts and time of payment are uncertain. Some business firms create reserves or make allowances for federal income taxes wherein there is uncertainty as to the amount. Reserve accounts may appear for contingencies such as employee benefits, insurance, guarantees or warranties, contract completion, coupon redemption, endorsement of commercial paper, and so on. In considering the estimated losses for which funds may be needed, management may appropriate retained earnings and create a surplus reserve account showing them below the current liability section of the balance sheet rather than within the stockholders' equity section or among current liabilities.

INCOME STABILIZATION AS A MANAGEMENT POLICY

In the foregoing discussion on income, surplus, and reserve account items, the element of managerial judgment was emphasized. Some of the methods of overstating and understating net income and asset values have been presented, but this should not be interpreted as a general desire to manipulate reports so as to mislead stockholders and others. In most cases, one of the objectives of management is to achieve stability in net income consistent with the profit motive of business concerns. Business firms benefit from stability of income because it permits obtaining capital at lower costs, budgeting of cash more accurately, paying maturing obligations with greater ease, and taking cash discounts. The amount and stability of corporate profits is important to a business firm because of its influence on its source of external funds.

There are advantages in presenting an all-inclusive income statement over the practice of permitting extraordinary items to bypass it. If management is to perform its job wisely it may be best to depend on current reports of operations which have not been distorted by special adjustments. In their treatment of depreciation, depletion, and amortization allowances, nonrecurring profits and losses, inventory valuation, and reserves for specific purposes or contingencies, accountants may present a picture that could mislead top management or the board of directors.

One of the most important factors in the stability or instability of a corporation's income is the nature of its product. Income stability is usually associated with companies which produce low-cost necessities and staple consumer goods of a nondurable type. However, if such goods are produced for a highly competitive market, a slight change in demand may result in heavy losses because of changes in inventory prices and volume of sales. Income instability is usually associated with companies producing durable capital goods, storable raw materials, high-priced durable consumer goods, and luxury or fashionable goods.

Usually, companies which produce storable raw materials and durable capital goods show the greatest fluctuations in income. This is illustrated by the experiences of metal and metal-producing industries, the demand for whose product is extremely cyclical—extremely large during boom periods and extremely low during depressions. The variations in income of producers of durable consumer goods are similar to those of metal producers, but fluctuations may be less extreme. Because the demand for luxury items such as furs and jewelry depends on consumer buying power, the incomes of firms in these fields tend to coincide with or follow the business cycle. Since the demand for durable capital goods is usually subject to cyclical fluctuations, companies producing such goods attempt to stabilize earnings by maintaining prices, producing new products, exploiting new techniques, and advertising more extensively to keep or broaden their markets. Because of the rapid change in demands for products, due in part to new discoveries and new processes, an increasing number of corporations are seeking stability by diversifying products. In the manufacturing industry, profits of large corporations tend to be more stable than those of smaller concerns, but profits are still sensitive to cyclical changes.

The influence of corporate income taxes on net profits is most significant for large corporations. Since the expiration of the federal excess profits tax in 1954, corporate income taxes have been made proportional to taxable income, the exception being that the first $25,000 of taxable income earned by any corporation is exempt from the federal surtax. (The federal statutory rate is 30 per cent for all corporate income plus 22 per cent for all taxable in excess of $25,000; in addition, most states levy a tax at a rate of 2 per cent or more.)

Generally, retained earnings increase during boom years and decline during recessions because of dividend policies as well as fluctuations in earnings. For illustration, the total amount of retained earnings during the first six months of 1959 was three times the amount retained during the cyclical low of the corresponding period in 1958. While the disbursements of cash dividends tend to be fairly stable from year to year, the pay-out ratio was about 50 per cent during the 1950's, which was low compared to pre-World War II standards. This change is dividend policies is associated with management's increased reliance on funds from operations to finance capital expansion. Management has not forgotten the distressing experiences of the 1930's; this explains in part the present-day emphasis on liquidity—the holding of cash and United States government securities.

INCOME POSITION AS INDICATED BY RATIOS

Ratios for use in determining the financial positions of business concerns have been developed by credit men and security analysts. The objectives of these ratios are to reveal "window dressing" in financial statements as well as to show financial position based on information given in financial statements. Alert management has turned to ratio analysis as a device for self-appraisal. Investment and income analysis is no better than the information on which it is based, and some of the pitfalls that must be faced have already been suggested. The analyst, on examining a balance sheet, may find that there are items between liabilities and stockholders' equity sections that should be classified as either credits or equities; that allowances for fixed asset depreciation may appear in the equity section rather than as a subtraction from fixed assets; and that treasury stock, treasury bonds, bond discount prepaid interest, and operating deficits appear as assets. Pertinent valuation problems exist in the areas of fixed assets, investments, intangibles, and inventories. Items such as goodwill, patents, and organization, development, and bond-issue costs may be omitted entirely in computing the asset position, even though such items affect future revenues. In addition, inventory valuation may be more difficult if the last-in, first-out method is used.

Income appraisal raises questions of measurement of depreciation, cost of goods sold which is affected by the inventory procedure used, and items that may have been included as an expense for the period or spread over several accounting periods (maintenance, repairs, research, and development expenditures). There are two major groups of ratios: one to measure the liquidity and debt-paying ability of business corporations, which were considered in earlier chapters, and another to measure the earning positions of business firms, which are discussed below.

Operating Ratios. In considering the earning position of a business firm, management may compute operating ratios such as cash discounts, net revenues, expenses, and taxes as percentages of sales. This is illustrated by Table 18. The operating ratio which is usually

TABLE 18

OPERATING INCOME STATEMENT

	Amounts	*Operating Ratios*
Sales	$20,000	100.0%
Less cash discounts	500	2.5
Net revenues	$19,500	97.5%
Expenses and taxes		
Cost of goods sold	$ 6,000	30.0%
Selling expenses	4,000	20.0
Administrative expenses	5,000	25.0
Income taxes	1,500	7.5
Total Expenses and Taxes	$16,500	82.5%
Net income ($19,500–$16,500)	$ 3,000	15.0%

emphasized is the ratio of total expenses to total revenues, which is 82.5 per cent in the illustration given in Table 18 (total expenses divided by total revenues).

Although there are other factors to be considered, a low operating ratio is desirable. Because financial charges—interest and principal payments on long-term debt—are disregarded in operating expenses, a company may show a low operating ratio and still be in an unfavorable financial position because of heavy fixed charges.

The operating ratio may be a valuable tool to management; for illustration, if the corporation's operating ratio is high compared to other companies in the same industry, the reasons may be found and corrected. The trend of operating ratio, as found by comparing the ratio from year to year, may be more significant than the actual operating ratio at any particular time—if it is increasing, an analysis would be made to find the cause, and this would entail examining each component of operating expenses in relation to gross revenue. The larger the difference between the operating ratio and 100 per cent, the larger is the margin of operating profit.

A margin of operating profit that is considered adequate varies from industry to industry and even among companies in the same industry. For illustration, in the railroad industry the operating ratio —all operating expenses to operating revenues—is elucidated by an analysis of the "maintenance ratio," which shows the percentage of railroad operating revenues used for maintenance including depreciation, and the "transportation ratio," which shows the percentage of railroad operating revenue used for transportation expenses. In addition, there are performance ratios—average tons per loaded freight car, train miles per train hour, car miles per car day, and so on.

Public utility operating ratios will reflect the basic nature of each service provided (light and power, gas, water, gas and oil pipelines, or telephone), the mode of operation (hydroelectric or coal), and regulatory policies. Depreciation charges are an important expense factor in the operating expenses of both railroad and public utility companies. The per cent of annual depreciation to gross property is indicative of the rate of annual depreciation charges. Earnings reflect both economic conditions and regulatory policies. The operating ratio may be but 50 per cent for a well-run hydroelectric company and as high as 75 per cent for a gas company. Operating ratios for industrial companies are even more variable than those for the public utility group.

In addition to operating ratios, other ratios are used to check the efficiency of business firms. If the ratio of net income to net sales of a business firm should drop from 15 to 10 per cent, management may seek for answers in changes in other ratios. The answer may be found in a rise in selling expenses from 25 to 30 per cent, in an increase in administrative expenses, or elsewhere. The ratio of net income to net sales is not in itself an adequate index of the adequacy of profits; other ratios are needed to supplement it.

Earning Ratios. Earning ratios are of interest to different groups, such as stockholders, creditors, and others; therefore a number of different earning ratios may be computed. The most inclusive of these ratios is the all asset earning ratio which is found by dividing net income before deduction of interest by the average total assets used during the period. Interest payments are not deducted, book figures may be adjusted, and the average may be found by taking the adjusted figures for the beginning and end of the year. Income taxes may be deducted, depending on the use to be made of the ratio. This ratio purports to measure the efficiency of the firm by measuring the per dollar earning on the resources of the firm, including those obtained with borrowed funds.

A stock-equity earning ratio is found by dividing the earnings of stockholders by the average stockholders' equity. A high stock-equity earning ratio may be due to the leverage factor, the financing of a business firm with debts (the dangers of this procedure have been discussed elsewhere). The average of stockholders' equity may be found by taking the figures for the beginning and end of the year and dividing by two. The intent of this ratio is to measure the efficiency of management in the use of stockholders' investments in the firm. However, of greater interest to stockholders and investors are the figures that indicate earnings per share, to be found by dividing the earnings assignable to stockholders by the number of shares outstanding. Since the number of shares may change during a year because of stock splits, stock dividends, and sales of stock, adjustments may have to be made before making comparisons with previous years. Although not an earning ratio, dividends per share are also of interest to investors. This figure is found by dividing total cash dividends by the number of shares outstanding.

The number of times interest is earned over a year (the fixed charge ratio) is of particular interest to bondholders because it reveals the percentage of earnings available to meet their interest claims. The fixed charge ratio is found by dividing net income of the corporation before deduction of interest charges by the total interest payments. Earnings may be considered as unsatisfactory to bondholders unless they cover interest on bonds two or three times.

SUMMARY

The importance of retained earnings as a device to insure the solvency of a corporation is widely recognized, but the full impact of the use of retained earnings as a basis for internal growth has often been neither understood nor appreciated. The administration of retained earnings and other income gives rise to two types of bookkeeping items, *surplus accounts* and *reserve accounts*. The two items generally found under surplus accounts are *earned surplus*, also called *retained earnings account*, and *capital surplus*. There are three classes of reserve accounts, namely asset or valuation reserves, liability reserves, and surplus or proprietorship reserves. Sinking-fund reserve accounts may be created to fulfill debt-contract requirements; they may or may not be funded. If funded, assets must be surrendered to a sinking-fund trustee and the corporation loses the use of such assets.

If the net income of a corporation is subject to wide fluctuations, management may create large secret reserves by showing intangibles such as goodwill and patents, real estate, and other assets at nominal values. There is also a possibility of charging capital expenditures as operating expenses and using accelerated depreciation methods to create secret reserves equal to capital improvements or assets fully depreciated. Moreover, even though expected outlays may be small, large contingent and other reserve accounts may be employed, and these have the effect of creating secret reserves. If and when heavy losses occur, undervalued assets may be revalued and excessive reserve accounts may be eliminated and the sums transferred to the surplus account. Management may analyze its company's financial statements by computing certain ratios that will indicate its current position and its operating efficiency. Over a period of years, specific ratios will indicate the influence of changes in the cost of labor and other materials, depreciation charges, and whether expansion of sales has occurred at the expense of profits.

QUESTIONS AND PROBLEMS

1. How important are funds accounted for as retained earnings in explaining the growth of American business enterprises?
2. What are the more common criticisms of a policy of retaining earnings?
3. In answer to the admonition to corporations to finance to a greater extent by sales of additional stocks and bonds, the following statement was made: "the practical fact is that retention of earnings or 'corporate savings' is the simplest, cheapest, and most natural way to build a business and enlarge the base of the equity investment." (First National City Bank, *Monthly Letter, Business and Economic Conditions* [December, 1960], p. 137.) Do you agree? Explain.
4. Retention of earnings, it has been said, represents an involuntary form of investment by stockholders. In what way do stockholders benefit from retained earnings?
5. List and explain the factors which influence the stability of a firm's income.
6. Identify: (*a*) operating ratio, and (*b* fixed charge ratio. Are they important? Why?
7. Comment on the policy suggested by the following: "The board of directors of the New York Central Railroad decided yesterday to pass dividends for the first quarter of this year, although preliminary indica-

tions are that the big carrier will wind up in the black for 1960." (*New York Times* [January 13, 1961], p. 39.)

8. Distinguish among surplus, valuation, and liability reserve accounts.
9. Explain why depreciation allowances are a much more important source of funds than external long-term financing in the manufacturing industry as compared with public utility companies (see Table 16).
10. Which income and expense items influence the earned surplus and surplus reserve accounts (see Table 17)?
11. Analyze: "Under the most restrictive of the provisions relating to payment of cash dividends on common stock in the Company's indentures, loan agreements and certificate of incorporation, approximately $19,-500,000 of earned surplus at November 30, 1960 was unrestricted, but in no event may any such dividends be paid if net current assets are reduced below $12,000,000." (Hooker Chemical Corporation, *Annual Report for the Year Ended November 30, 1960* [New York, 1961], p. 10.)

CHAPTER 9

Dividends and Dividend Policies

DIVIDENDS may be classified into three groups: (1) those which reduce the assets of a corporation, such as cash and property dividends; (2) those which increase the liabilities of a corporation, such as scrip or bond dividends; and (3) those which neither decrease assets nor increase liabilities of a corporation, such as stock dividends. Of the various types of dividends, those payable in cash are most important, and when the term *dividend* is used without qualification, reference is made to a cash dividend.

The almost continuous prosperity of the period since the end of World War II, together with the policy of rebuilding plants and equipment, have permitted payment of higher cash dividends to shareholders during the last three or four years. In historical prospective, the dividend-earnings ratios of most companies have remained low, but the rapid build-up of equity funds has permitted the distribution of stock dividends and the voting for stock splits at an unusual rate. Dividends are socially important through their influence on the sources of investment funds. This chapter deals with general and legal aspects of dividend payments, basis for dividend policies, dividend payment practices, cash dividends, stock dividends, and property and scrip dividends.

GENERAL AND LEGAL ASPECTS OF CASH DIVIDEND PAYMENTS

Often the subject matter pertaining to the use of profits of business corporations is treated as if profits from current operations were applied as follows: first, segregated to meet special purposes; second, retained in general surplus accounts for expansion; and third, after other needs are fully cared for, distributed to stockholders as dividends. Individual business firms seem to follow a policy of using profits to provide for anticipated needs of the business firm, but sometimes the payment of cash dividends may take precedence over retention of net earnings for other purposes. Cash dividend payments have been more stable than either corporate income after

CHART 5

Corporate Income, All Industries 1929–53
(In Billions of Dollars)

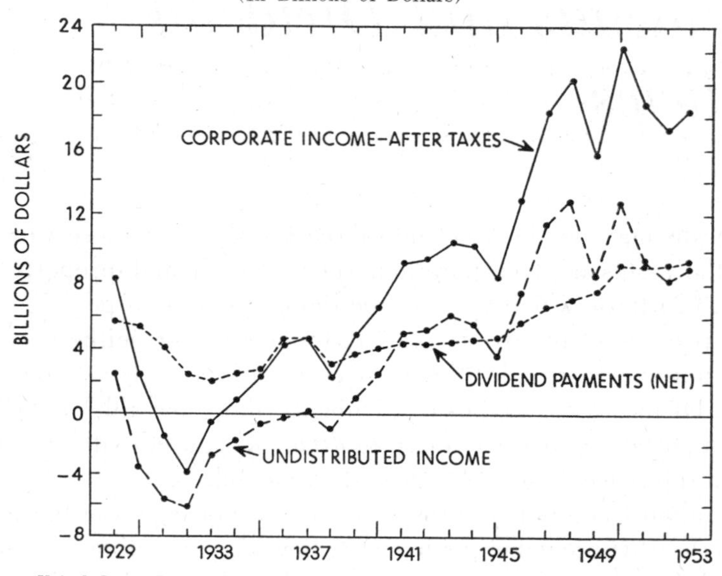

Source: United States Department of Commerce, Office of Business Economics, *National Income, 1954 Edition* (Washington, D.C.: U.S. Government Printing Office, 1954), pp. 188–93.

taxes or income retained in business. Sometimes dividends to stockholders come first, as illustrated by the fact that from 1931 to 1933, when most corporations were operating at a loss, dividends were being paid (see Chart 5).

During the early 1930's, corporate management was bitterly criticized because of policies relative to net earnings, the retention of which was described as being unfair to shareholders; however, the record suggests that in most cases the criticism was not justified. When cases are brought before the courts, directors are usually upheld in retaining earnings of a business; in fact, the courts have overruled the payment of dividends as voted by directors more often than they have overruled the retention of net profits.

In recent years, stockholders have been referred to as "the forgotten men in business finance," but these critics of dividend policies are seemingly unaware of not only the legal and other problems faced by corporate management but also the record of dividend payment which shows that corporate management has been more generous in disbursing net profits over the years than is generally supposed. When the payment of dividends is being considered, a board of directors must be sure that the distribution is legal as well as expedient under current and anticipated circumstances. Cash dividends are charged against surplus, indicating that stockholders' equity is reduced; although the withdrawal of cash is not a cost in the accounting or income tax sense, the assets of the corporation are reduced. The effect is to reduce cash and decrease retained earnings by an equal amount.

Legal Restrictions. The first and basic fact that management must take into account before declaring dividends is to be sure that realized earnings are available for distribution and that their payment will not impair the paid-in capital of the firm. Irrespective of what the financial statements show in the way of earned surplus and current net profits, the courts may and often have questioned the valuations given assets by accountants. As a result of revaluation, a corporation which seemed to have sufficient profits to pay a dividend may be shown to be insolvent (assets being less than liabilities). Payment of cash dividends when a corporation is insolvent, or would be made insolvent by such payment, is illegal; directors are responsible, jointly and severally, for such illegal dividend payments.

In order to pay a cash dividend in some states, a corporation must be more than solvent in the bankruptcy sense; that is, it must have a specified minimum amount of capital. In New York and Pennsylvania, dividends that impair capital are illegal; in Delaware and Ohio, dividend payments may be made only if an excess of net assets over capital as well as liabilities remains after such payments. (In effect, the laws in the four states are the same.) In other states the payment of cash dividends is legal only when paid out of net profits.

Legal phraseology varies from state to state, and a corporation's board of directors must be sure that a proposed cash dividend payment is legal under the statutes of its state of incorporation. In borderline cases, it may be wise to omit a cash dividend because valuations of assets as they appear on the corporation's books may be upset in court proceedings. More specifically, management ought to be sure that, even under the most critical court review, negative answers would be given to these four questions regarding payment of a cash dividend: (1) Would it impair the corporation's capital? (2) Would it impair the claims of creditors? (3) Is the corporation insolvent? (4) Would the payment cause insolvency? These questions are merely applications of common-law rules; namely, "capital may not be paid out to stockholders until creditors are satisfied" and "dividends should only be paid out of profits."

Most business corporation acts provide for procedures whereby a director may oppose a cash dividend so as not to be held responsible for the payment if legal action is taken by creditors or others to recover from directors the cash paid out as dividends. Usually a director is bound by the vote of the majority; however, if he files written dissent from the action taken on the payment of a cash dividend and his dissent is included in the minutes of the meeting, he is not liable for any subsequent action taken to recover the cash paid out.

Some state laws provide for modification of the basic rule requiring that cash dividends be paid out of surplus or net profits only. For illustration, an exception is usually made for a consuming- or wasting-assets corporation exploiting natural resources; part of such a corporation's cash dividends may be a return of capital. A consuming-assets corporation may be permitted to pay cash dividends in an amount not exceeding its total depletion and amortization reserves; however, the cash dividend may be illegal if it is made when the corporation is insolvent or if its payment causes insolvency.

Corporations in some fields are supervised by federal or state regulatory agencies and their prior approval may be required before a dividend is paid. For illustration, the Public Utility Holding Company Act of 1935 requires registered holding companies and their subsidiaries to obtain approval of the Securities and Exchange Commission before paying a dividend out of capital or earned surplus.

Contract Restrictions. Before declaring a cash dividend, a corporation's board of directors must be careful to comply with restrictions on payment of dividends as found in debt contracts or other contracts. Most frequently, such restrictions are found in long-term debt contracts, but they may also be found in intermediate and short-term debt contracts such as term loan agreements, V-loan contracts, and short-term debt agreements.

A corporation's board of directors may also be denied the right to declare dividends on common stock because of contracts pertaining to prior rights of preferred stockholders over common stockholders to the earnings of the corporation. In some cases, clauses in a corporation's charter or bylaws may make it illegal to pay dividends on common stock unless certain financial standards have been met and are maintained. This may be illustrated by the requirement that net current assets must be 150 or 200 per cent of the par value of the outstanding preferred stock before dividends may be paid. In other cases compliance with a sinking-fund requirement for retirement of debts or preferred stock may prevent the declaration of dividends. The purpose of these restrictions is to insure the maintenance of a business firm's liquidity and solvency—a logical objective of management. The foregoing precautions should be taken even when there are no restrictions being imposed by debt and preferred stock contracts or by statutory provisions.

The Human Element. Although dividend payments may be discussed in legal, financial, or economic terms, in practice it is not possible to keep the human element out of decisions made by directors. The fact that directors are responsible for improper payments may have a dampening influence on any proposal to pay a cash dividend. Corporations are regarded as continuing business enterprises, but stockholders may withdraw by selling their interest to others if they are dissatisfied with current and/or anticipated dividend policies. A board of directors must protect the interests of both creditors and stockholders; therefore, protection of capital assets must come ahead of dividend payments. However, if stockholders are to be induced to provide venture capital, in the long run the return on stock must be equal to a normal interest payment plus enough to compensate for the risks assumed. (Many investors depend entirely on dividends for income.)

Directors may vote a cash dividend in order to aid in the sale of blocks of stock offered by persons close to management or to secure a more favorable price for a new issue of securities. In buying stock, many investors are influenced more by dividend payments than by earnings of a corporation. Directors may vote for a cash dividend in order to obtain more favorable terms in a proposed merger or consolidation, or to make conversion of bonds or preferred stock more attractive. Usually, directors vote for cash dividends because they regard their payment to be in the best interests of the corporation and the stockholders. On the other hand, directors may vote against paying a cash dividend in order to depress the market price of the stock so that shares may be acquired at "bargain prices," to permit large stockholders to avoid personal income tax payments, or to avoid "giving away" assets of the corporation if dividend payments are so regarded by directors.

The decision as to when and under what circumstances stockholders are to share in the earnings of their corporation is left to the board of directors; once a cash dividend has been declared, it becomes a liability of the corporation. (Cash dividends, declared but not paid, are a current liability during the interim between the record date and the payment date). A board of directors may be under pressure to declare dividends when the earned surplus is large and current profits are satisfactory; preferred stockholders may feel that their dividends should be paid if current earnings are adequate even if the financial position of the corporation is weak. Stockholders have met with little success in attempting to force directors to vote dividends through court proceedings. One of the best known of these cases (an exception to the general rule) was the action brought by stockholders of the Ford Motor Company in a Michigan state court in 1916 which resulted in the board of directors being ordered to declare a dividend aggregating $19,000,000. While dividends entail a distribution to stockholders of something belonging to the corporation, it should not be forgotten that the corporation is owned by the stockholders.

BASIS FOR DIVIDEND POLICIES

A dividend policy, which is a settled course of action governing the payment of dividends, should be based on the long-run welfare of a business firm. This view is not in conflict with the interests of stockholders because the well-being of a corporation and its owners ought to be the same in the long run. Usually, there is a different dividend distribution for each class of shareholders, the general rule being that each shareholder within a class of stock must be treated alike. Hence, a corporation may have one dividend rate for common stock, a second rate for one class of preferred stock, a third rate for a second class of preferred stock, and so on for other classes of preferred stock.[1] Dividend policies are influenced by legal and other restrictions; earnings, capital structure, and anticipated

[1] For illustration, the Philadelphia Electric Company reported cash dividend payments for 1959 as follows: $4.68 per share on 4.68 per cent preferred stock, $4.30 per share on 4.3 per cent preferred stock, $3.80 per share on 3.8 per cent preferred stock, $1.00 per share on $1 dividends preference common stock, and $2.24 per share on common stock. Philadelphia Electric Company, *Annual Report for the Year 1959* (Philadelphia; 1960), p. 28.

financial needs of the corporation; and the wishes of stockholders, management, and directors.

In anticipation of a meeting of the board of directors, at which dividend payment on stock is to be considered, the chief financial officer of the corporation customarily prepares all the facts that should be considered in deciding on the action to be taken. If a company has been paying a regular dividend, the problem may be one of justifying its continuance, paying an extra dividend, reducing or increasing the current dividend rate, or omitting the dividend.

Working Capital Position. In voting a cash dividend, a board of directors creates a current liability; when these dividends are paid, there will be a loss of working capital assets. Because other current liabilities may be coming due at the same time, need for cash and other assets must be projected. If a cash dividend would divert funds needed for operating purposes or for meeting current liabilities, it might be unwise to use working capital for dividend purposes. However, management may feel that it is important to maintain a stable dividend policy and may borrow to do so. The theory is that if retained earnings and current profits justify payment of a cash dividend, the issue should not be decided solely on the basis of a corporation's cash position. Corporations frequently borrow to discharge obligations for payrolls, goods, and income taxes. If the payment of dividends is considered to be a moral obligation (as the payment of interest is a legal obligation), then dividends should be paid regularly. But if a cash dividend would weaken the corporation's working capital position unduly, it should not be paid.

Fixed Capital Position. A factor to be considered in the payment of a cash dividend is the effect on the corporation's long-run program for expansion. If a company has reached the limit of its physical productive capacity and must expand to prevent the loss of all or part of its market to competitors, it may either finance expansion in the open market or retain earnings and forego or reduce dividend payments. Investment in fixed assets usually necessitates considerable risk, so management may be reluctant to finance from outside sources—especially with debts.

When capital structure of a corporation is top-heavy with debt, using all or part of net profits to build up equity is sound financial policy. Among the major corporations, railroad companies have been most consistent in using net profits to reduce their fixed debts in recent years. The ability of a corporation to finance fixed charges depends upon both the amount and stability of its income; when debts are created during prosperity the charges thereon may become excessive during depressions.

If outside financing is necessary, management may find it desirable to pass all cash dividends in order to improve the corporation's borrowing position with creditors; but if a new stock issue is being considered, management may want to pay cash dividends at the old rate or even at an increased rate. A cash dividend on stock makes it a more attractive investment and helps to establish a favorable market for it. As measured by standards prevailing before World War II, cash dividend payments have been conservative since 1945.

Nature of Net Earnings. Corporations having stable incomes are in a better position to adopt settled dividend policies than those whose earnings fluctuate widely. For illustration, public utility companies may have a more stable dividend policy than mining companies or those manufacturing durable producers' goods. Until a company is well established, it may have no dividend policy; after becoming established, it should distinguish between normal or regular and extra dividends.

In some states, dividends may be paid only with current earnings, and the dividend payments of corporations organized under such statutes tend to be more variable than those of corporations chartered in other states which permit earnings of prior years to be used for dividend purposes. Limiting dividend payments to current earnings (considered by some authorities to be the best index of a corporation's ability to pay dividends) would tend to have the effect of forcing stockholders to give more attention to the affairs of their corporations.

Retained Earnings Plus Net Current Earnings. In most cases, a corporation's ability to pay dividends depends upon its net current earnings plus earnings which have been retained from preceding years. Thus profits may be retained during prosperous years and paid out when earnings decline and stockholders' income needs may become compelling. Such a practice would be in keeping with national economic policies which have as their purpose the stabilization of national income through fiscal and monetary policies (less spending during business booms and more spending during depressions). Corporations that are able to establish and maintain a regular dividend policy tend to attract investor-stockholders (rather than speculators).

Tax Aspect. Cash and property dividends received by stockholders are taxable as cash or at fair market value of the property distributed. In general, stock dividends are tax free; however, there may be exceptions. For illustration, when a shareholder has an option of accepting cash or stock as a dividend on common stock and when a preferred stockholder receives stock in lieu of dividends for the current or a preceding year, the stock is taxable at fair market value.

The high tax rate on personal income has been a factor in the reluctance of boards of directors to declare cash dividends. Federal tax rates on individual personal income in the 1954 Revenue Act contain graduated rates by brackets ranging from 20 per cent to 91 per cent for taxable income (normal and surtax taxes were eliminated). An individual director may vote against declaring a dividend in the hope that the income tax rate will decline or that his personal income will find him in a lower income bracket at some future time when dividend payments are resumed. If earnings are retained, the net worth and productive capacity of a company tend to increase and the market price of its stock tends to appreciate; then, if the taxpayer sells his stock, he will be subject to a capital gains tax at a maximum rate of 25 per cent irrespective of his income bracket. When the capital stock of a corporation is owned by a few stockholders who are also directors or officers, it is reasonable to assume that the corporation may retain most of its earnings and pay few cash dividends. However, as pointed out in the preceding chapter, there are limitations on the tax-free retention of earnings.

CASH DIVIDENDS

Mechanics of Dividend Declaration and Payment. A cash dividend declaration is effected by a resolution by a majority of directors at a regular or special meeting. Usually the minutes of meetings at which dividends are declared are covered in more detail than those of other meetings of the board of directors. The minutes contain a record of the information received from the chief financial officer on the net profits of the company and the amount of earned surplus. When the board of directors declares a dividend, the individual directors want the record to show that they acted on the assumption that the payment is legal and they want a resolution drawn to show that the dividend payment is justified. The declaration gives the name of the stock on which the dividend is to be paid, the amount per share, the date and time when the names of stockholders are to be determined for dividend purposes (such as at the close of business on December 15, 1960), and the date on which the dividend checks are to be dated and mailed to stockholders.

For illustration, dividends on common and preferred stock of Sperry Rand Corporation were reported as follows:[2]

	Record Date	Payment Date	Per Share
Common:	May 14, 1959	June 25, 1959	$ .20
	Aug. 13, 1959	Sept. 24, 1959	.20
	Nov. 16, 1959	Dec. 31, 1959	.20
	Feb. 11, 1960	Mar. 24, 1960	.20
Preferred:			
	May 14, 1959	July 1, 1959	$1.12½
	Aug. 13, 1959	Oct. 1, 1959	1.12½
	Nov. 16, 1959	Jan. 2, 1960	1.12½
	Feb. 11, 1960	April 1, 1960	1.12½

A corporation not only must have the legal right to declare a cash dividend but also it must have cash available to use in payment. The bylaws of a corporation may prescribe the dates for cash dividend payments—quarterly, semiannually, or annually—or may merely state that "the directors may from time to time declare dividends upon the capital stock from net profits or surplus of the company." Only when all stockholders agree and the board of directors does not object may a valid dividend be declared without the prior approval of the directors. Although such so-called "consent dividends" are rare, they are sometimes made by "closed" corporations (those owned by a few stockholders). The advantage to the board of directors in permitting stockholders to declare a consent dividend is that responsibility for any adverse development caused by the payment thereof would be shifted from the board of directors to the stockholders.

Designation of Cash Dividends. Cash dividends may be called regular, irregular, extra or special, interim, final, or liquidating (or they may have no label attached).

Regular dividends may be quarterly, semiannualy, or annually (in rare cases, even monthly).[3] If a board of directors designates a dividend as the "regular quarterly dividend of $1.00 per share of common stock," it indicates that the policy of management is to maintain that rate. "Regular" dividends are most frequently related to preferred stock; however, when a corporation has a long record of

[2] Sperry Rand Corporation, *Report to Stockholders For The Year Ended, March 31, 1960* (New York, 1960), p. F. 7.

[3] Monthly dividends are popular with women stockholders and those who have reached retirement age. From the viewpoint of management, the greatest drawback to paying monthly dividends is the cost of sending checks. Among the corporations that distribute monthly dividends are William Wrigley, Jr., Company, 70 per cent of whose 12,000 stockholders are women; Colorado Central Power; and Miles Laboratories (861 stockholders). Usually corporations enclose "stuffers" (advertising leaflets) with each check mailed, and the extra mailing costs may be more than offset by the advertising value.

paying a specified dividend on common stock at regular intervals, it is known as a "regular dividend." One of the best illustrations of this is the $2.25 quarterly dividend which had been paid on the common stock of the American Telephone and Telegraph Company from 1922 to 1959, when the stock was split one for three and a quarterly rate per share was fixed at 82.5 cents. Companies that have paid at least one dividend each year for many years include National City Bank of New York (now the First National City Bank of New York), since 1813; Hartford Fire Insurance Company, since 1873; American Telephone and Telegraph Company, since 1881; General Electric Company, since 1899; and a score or more other major companies, for over fifty years.

Irregular dividends are those paid in varying amounts, usually associated with companies whose earnings fluctuate widely (big earnings, big dividends and low earnings, low or no dividends). Irregular dividend policies are usually unpopular with shareholders, but those who hold stock in companies with such policies should expect fluctuations in cash dividend payments. It may even be that the average return for stock of these companies will be larger over a period of time than dividends paid by companies having a regular dividend policy. In some cases, there are many advantages in a "flexible" dividend policy.

When a corporation's earnings justify an additional dividend, it may be designated as an "extra" dividend. This practice does not commit the board of directors to a future increase in the dividend rate and places stockholders on notice that they are not justified in assuming that the extra dividend will be declared on the next dividend date. When an extra dividend is paid, it is usually distributed along with the regular dividend as a year-end dividend. If the extra amount were to be prorated and distributed along with each regular dividend, it might be considered as an increase in the regular dividend rate. A "special" dividend, whether in the form of cash or property, may be in the same category as an extra dividend, but usually the connotation is that some event not likely to be recurrent has made it possible.

Some American corporations have adopted the English terminology, calling dividends paid throughout the year "interim" dividends. Interim dividends may be paid as often as seems appropriate through the fiscal year. A final or year-end dividend is one paid at the end of the fiscal year. This terminology is used along with the concept of interim dividends.

When a cash dividend represents a return of capital, it may be termed a "liquidating" dividend. Liquidating cash dividends may be paid when a consuming- or wasting-assets corporation pays a cash dividend (part of the amount may represent profits and part a return of capital); a corporation is overcapitalized and returns part of the capital to owners; and a business firm is being liquidated either voluntarily or involuntarily under supervision of a federal court or otherwise.

STOCK DIVIDENDS

A stock dividend is one distributed in stock of the same kind as as that on which the dividend is declared. Although a corporation could distribute a different class of stock as a stock dividend, this is rarely done. The distribution of a stock dividend results in an increase in the corporation's capital account and in a decrease in its surplus but has no effect on its total net worth. When stockholders are given a choice of being paid a cash dividend or receiving a stock dividend and cash is chosen, the corporation sells the stock and remits cash.

During the 1920's, the practice of distributing stock dividends was fairly common. Some corporations, particularly in the public utility industry, distributed stock dividends on an annual basis (for illustration, 10 per cent); and large distributions, referred to as "cutting the melon," were fairly common occurrences. During the 1930's, the practice of issuing stock dividends declined; since World War II, however, it has become increasingly prevalent. Stock dividend distributions are closely associated with rising security markets and expanding companies. Since the stock distributed is of the same class as that held by the recipients, there is no change in the proportionate ownership interest among stockholders; however, if the stock is distributed to a class of stockholders other than the original holders of the stock—such as common stock being distributed to preferred stockholders—the relative position of the two classes of stockholders will be affected. Periodic and extraordinary stock dividends entail legal and accounting problems even though the total assets of the corporation remain unchanged following their distribution.

Legal Aspects of Stock Dividend Distributions. Unless authorized but unissued stock is available, the distribution of a stock dividend requires an amendment to the articles of incorporation because it changes the capital stock of the corporation. When such distributions are expected to be of a periodic nature, the board of directors may obtain an amendment to the charter authorizing the issuance of stock in excess of current needs. This authority would permit the board of directors to issue new stock as a dividend out of "authorized but unissued" stock. Because stock dividends do not reduce a corporation's assets or increase its liabilities, their distribution is subject to less scrutiny than the payment of cash dividends. However, stock dividends may be misinterpreted by investors; therefore the Securities and Exchange Commission opposes their issuance if misrepresentation seems to be implicated. This may happen when a stock dividend is made at the end of the year under conditions that lead investors to assume that it is being paid out of current earnings like a year-end cash dividend. It should be made clear that a stock dividend is nothing more than capitalization of earned surplus and no current liability is created as in the case of the declaration of a cash dividend.

In 1953, the New York Stock Exchange adopted a rule that prevented corporations whose stocks are listed on that exchange from paying a cash dividend, plus distributing a stock dividend, if the cash dividend plus the value of the stock at market price is in excess of the earnings per share for that year. This means that if earnings per share of common stock are $5 after all expenses are met, including provisions for income taxes, no more than a cash and/or stock dividend of $5 per share (valued at the market price of the stock) may be paid and/or distributed for the year.[4] In 1955, this rule was changed to permit capitalization of the stock dividend out of earned surplus regardless of when earned.

Restrictions on payment of dividends in loan agreements usually specifically exempt the distribution of stock dividends. This emphasizes the fact that they take nothing away from the debtor and do not weaken the creditor's claim against the debtor. Thus, the conclusion may be drawn that nothing except paper is given stockholders when a stock dividend is declared. Since no assets are received in return, it is difficult to agree with statements of management that "stock dividends provide an automatic method of financing without burden to the corporation or stockholders" or that "stock dividends provide a method of giving a satisfactory return to stockholders." Although stock dividends are opposed by many financial observers

---

[4] Among those affected were the stockholders of the International Business Machine Corporation. In 1953, the corporation was forced to rescind a 5 per cent stock dividend because it had a market value in excess of the company's earnings for that year.

and business executives, they are in wide use at the present time because it is felt that it gives stockholders "something" and "conserves cash."

Surplus and Stock Dividends. In order to make the new stock issued as a stock dividend fully paid and nonassessable, the surplus must be capitalized in an amount equal to the par or stated value of the stock dividend. The amount of surplus transferred to capital stock is the "consideration" required by most business corporation acts. If the total par value of stock issued as stock dividends is $1 million, this amount must be transferred from earned surplus to capital account. In effect, the corporation has purchased more of its stock for distribution to its stockholders and the stock has been paid for with retained earnings removed permanently from the surplus account. This reduction in surplus could mean that stockholders are farther removed from cash dividends during periods of low earnings because that part capitalized is no longer available for dividend payments.

Effect on Owners' Equity. When stockholders receive a stock dividend, there is no change in their proportional equity. The number of shares have been increased but the book value of the corporation's assets represented by owners' holdings has remained unchanged. If a stockholder owns 100 shares, representing 1 per cent of the corporation's capital, and receives a stock dividend of 10 per cent, he still owns 1 per cent of the capital stock. While he will have more shares, each share will represent proportionately less equity but his total proportional interest will be unchanged. This generalization is subject to minor qualification because of the provision for fractional shares. For illustration, if a stock dividend is declared on the basis of one new share for every twenty held, a fractional share may be issued for shares not multiples of twenty. Usually fractional shares have no voting or dividend rights and they sometimes lose their value unless they are surrendered for full shares within a specified period of time. Therefore, in order to avoid a loss, owners of fractional shares must either sell them or buy other fractional shares to make up whole shares. Failure of a stockholder to use his fractional share would mean that he would lose part of his equity and that other stockholders' equity would be increased by that amount. To prevent this injustice, particularly to small shareholders, modern corporate practice is to issue only whole shares and to pay a cash dividend in lieu of fractional shares.

Accounting for Stock Dividends. In accounting for a stock dividend, a corporation customarily informs shareholders of the amount of earned surplus which has been capitalized. Usually this capitalization is at the same rate as the par value (or stated value if no-par stock), but it may be more for two reasons:

(1) Management may want to maintain the same relationship between capital stock and capital surplus as existed prior to the stock dividend, such as 4 to 1; therefore the earned surplus will be capitalized for $12.50 for each $10 par value share, with $10 carried to capital stock and $2.50 to capital surplus.

(2) If the stock dividend is large, management may want to anticipate the effects of the new stock issued on the fair market price of each share by selecting what is expected to be a fair market price and charging earned surplus with that price for each new share. If a stock dividend of one share for each share held is assumed, the stock dividend would tend to lower the fair market price by about 50 per cent—for illustration, from $60 to $30. In this case, the earned surplus may be charged with $30 for each new share issued; if the par value is $10, $20 would be credited to capital surplus and $10 to capital account. If the stock dividend is small, assume 5 per cent (1 share for each 20 held), the earned surplus may be charged at a price per share equal to the average market price during the preceding year or a figure near the current market price.

Periodic Stock Dividends. Since World War II, stock dividends have been distributed to supplement or replace cash dividends in order to conserve cash and at the same time to appease stockholders calling for more dividends. (The necessity for conserving cash may be due to a weakened working capital position because of business expansion or for other reasons.) Although stock dividends give stockholders nothing which they did not already have, the extra shares may be sold; therefore stockholders may consider the receipt of a stock dividend preferable to receiving no dividends. When stock dividends are distributed in lieu of cash dividends, the adverse effect on the market price of the stock may be less severe than if dividends had been omitted. The stockholder may sell his new shares, thereby reducing his equity, but he could have sold old shares that represent the same amount of equity with the same results. Nevertheless, one of the arguments in favor of a stock dividend is that it offers stockholders an easy way to supplement their incomes.

If a cash dividend is also paid on each share, increasing the number of shares would distribute the total cash dividend payment over more shares, help to obscure large profits and the amount of financing with retained earnings, and lower the price earnings ratio of the stock. Regular stock dividends necessitate extra expense for printing and distributing new stock certificates and bookkeeping problems for both the company and shareholders.

The chief justification for a regular stock dividend is that it condones financing with retained earnings, which was discussed in the preceding chapter as an inexpensive way of financing. Stock dividends are less expensive than cash dividends but may be more expensive than omitting dividends. Usually business firms continue to pay the same cash dividend rate on stock after a stock dividend distribution, and so the cash outlay is larger because the number of shares has increased. If the intent of management is to increase the return to shareholders, this could be done by increasing the cash dividends rate. (Stockholders must pay brokerage fees when they sell stock and it may be an expensive way to obtain cash if their holdings are small.)

Usually, stock dividends are more popular with large than with small shareholders. Proceeds from the sale of stock dividends are taxed at the rate for capital gains, which is considerably below that on ordinary income, and this is important for those in the higher income brackets. Of course, if dividends were omitted entirely, stockholders would have the same tax advantage if they sold some of their shares for income. Since it is questionable that stockholders understand the nature of stock dividends, it is difficult to appraise their reactions to them; however most stockholders seem to prefer stock dividends to no dividends. If stockholders retain their shares and payment of regular cash dividends is resumed, their dividend receipts will increase. In addition, retention of earnings that might have been distributed as cash dividends should have a favorable effect on the market price of the stock in the future, permitting larger cash dividends than would otherwise have been possible.[5]

Irregular or Extraordinary Stock Dividends. By keeping the same par value or stated value, a corporation may issue an additional share of stock for each share outstanding and thus double the number of shares. According to the legal requirement discussed earlier, the earned surplus available must be sufficient to be capital-

[5] J. C. Bothwell, Jr., "Periodic Stock Dividends," *Harvard Business Review,* Vol. XXVIII, No. 1 (January, 1950), pp. 89–95.

ized in an amount at least equal to the aggregate of par or stated value of new shares. In voting a stock dividend, the existence of a large accumulated surplus is admitted; but management may prefer to increase the number of shares and retain the same dividend rate rather than to increase the dividend rate per share. (In a stock split, the par or stated value of each share is reduced; if the reduction is from $10 to $5, a new share may be issued for each share outstanding without changing the capital account or the earned surplus.)

One of the most common reasons for distributing a large or extraordinary stock dividend is to lower the market price. If a stock is selling for $160 per share and a stock dividend of three shares for each share outstanding is distributed, the market price would tend to fall to $40 per share. Actually, the price would tend to be pushed up by new buyers of stock in this popular price range. (Buying because of a rumor of a stock dividend often forces the market price to a higher level even before the stock dividend is voted by the board of directors.) However, the key to the market price is not the trading range into which the stock price falls, but corporate earnings and management's dividend policy.

Combination of Stock Dividend and Stock Split. The stock dividend of the General Electric Company in 1953 is an illustration of the combination of a large stock dividend necessitating the capitalization of earned surplus, with a stock split necessitating a change in stated value of common stock. With the approval of stockholders, the corporation's common stock was changed from a stated value of $6.25 per share to a par value of $5 per share and the surplus was capitalized for a total of $252,000,000. Two new shares were distributed for each old share held (each old shareholder then held three shares of five dollar par value stock for each share of no-par stock formerly held). The quarterly dividend rate was $1.00 on the old stock and $0.40 on the new; on the basis of the old stock, this amounted to $1.20 per share or a 20 per cent increase in the dividend rate.

PROPERTY AND SCRIP DIVIDENDS

Property Dividends. A property dividend is one paid with noncash assets of a corporation. A corporation may distribute its holdings of common stock in a second corporation by giving its stockholders their proportionate interest in their corporation's investment. Recently, Standard Oil Company of Indiana paid its stockholders an extra dividend in the form of one share of Standard Oil Company of New Jersey stock for each 50 shares of Standard Oil Company of Indiana held (with cash having been paid in lieu of fraction shares on the basis of the market price of Standard Oil of New Jersey stock on the record date).

Sometimes corporations distribute physical property, usually consumers' goods, among their stockholders. Such "surprise packages" not only please stockholders but also advertise the company's products. Although the Christmas packages and other courtesy gifts that some companies send to their stockholders have the same advertising value as property dividends, they should not be considered property dividends unless the distribution is in proportion to the number of shares held.

Scrip and Bond Dividends. A scrip dividend is one paid with promissory notes which may be in standard denominations or may be drawn for the exact amount that each stockholder is to receive. The notes may be payable on a specified date or in installments. Because the amounts are small, a great deal of clerical work is required to handle such "credits"; usually it would be less troublesome for the corporation to borrow from a bank in order to pay a cash dividend.

While corporations have broad powers to borrow or to go into debt for business purposes, management may be reluctant to create a bank debt to pay a cash dividend; however it should be even more reluctant to issue a scrip dividend. The theory behind a scrip dividend is that it permits cash to be retained temporarily. The scrip is usually sold by shareholders to banks and other investors at a discount, and the discount is usually greater than the interest rate that the corporation would have had to pay on a loan obtained to pay a cash dividend. Therefore, shareholders may object to receiving a scrip dividend in lieu of a cash dividend. Another objection to the payment of a scrip dividend is that a declaration of a scrip or bond dividend may be challenged by creditors because it would create a liability which may affect their rights.

A bond dividend is one paid with a long-term credit obligation. The theory behind paying a bond dividend is that it is more economical to finance in this way than to pay out cash and be forced to raise funds in the open market. Fortunately, the principle that a business firm should go into debt only for business needs is widely adhered to and distributions of scrip and bond dividends are rare. When a business corporation's financial position does not justify paying a dividend except with debts, dividend payments should be omitted.

SUMMARY

Although a corporation's board of directors is primarily responsible for declaring dividends, this power is subject to restrictions which have as their purpose the protection of creditors as well as the corporation's solvency. The limitations on dividend payments are found in common-law principles, statutes, rulings of regulatory agencies, corporate charters and bylaws, and debt contracts of various kinds. Decisions as to dividend payments may be influenced by the financial structure of a corporation, its working capital and fixed capital position, the attitude of stockholders and directors, income tax rates on individual incomes, legal aspects of provisions as to retained earnings, and—the basic consideration in all such decisions—the net profits and the amount of earned surplus available.

A cash dividend is a distribution of profits; a stock dividend is a distribution of capitalized surplus in the form of shares of stock; a property dividend is a distribution of property in the form of other securities or products of the corporation; and a bond or scrip dividend is a distribution of debt in the form of long- or short-term credit instruments. When corporate management adopts a specific policy as to the payment of dividends, it is known as a dividend policy.

Cash dividends may be regular, with the rate and the dividend date uniform over a period of time; extra or special and paid with a regular dividend (usually at the end of a corporation's fiscal year); or liquidating, representing a return of capital. The motives behind stock splits and stock dividend distributions may not be identical, but both entail legal and accounting problems. In order to make a stock dividend fully paid and nonassessable, earned surplus must be capitalized in an amount equal to the aggregate par or stated value of the stock issued. A stock dividend increases capital, decreases surplus, increases the number of shares outstanding, but has no effect on stockholders' proportional equity (except a minor adjustment for fractional shares).

The two chapters dealing with financing with funds from operations, depreciation allowances, and retained earnings are closely linked with cash dividend and other dividend policies. Presumably, management will always consider the immediate and future needs of a business corporation as well as opportunities to use funds profitably and the desires and objectives of stockholders. In making decisions as to cash dividend payments, management seems to weigh not only the immediate and future financial position of the corporation but also the impact of alternate procedures. In addition, consideration may also be given to the effect of plans for external financing, stockholder relations, and the market value of the company's stock.

QUESTIONS AND PROBLEMS

1. Identify the following types of dividends: (*a*) cash, (*b*) stock, (*c*) property, (*d*) bond, and (*e*) scrip.
2. What does Chart 5 suggest as to the order in which net earnings after income taxes are applied?
3. (*a*) What are the legal restrictions on the payment of cash dividends? (*b*) Are the restrictions on the payment of cash dividends equally applicable to a wasting-assets corporation? Explain.
4. Identify the following types of dividends: (*a*) consent, (*b*) regular, (*c*) extra or special, (*d*) interim, and (*d*) liquidating.
5. (*a*) In view of the fact that a declaration of cash dividends creates a current liability, why must a board of directors give consideration to the corporation's working capital position? Its fixed capital position? (*b*) What factors are favorable to the adoption of a regular dividend policy?
6. (*a*) Discuss the legal aspects of stock dividends. (*b*) What is the effect of such a distribution on surplus and on owners' equity? (*c*) Why is a large stock dividend sometimes considered to be a stock split?
7. Discuss the dividend policy followed by management as indicated by the following: "Dividends paid on the common stock amounted to $7.00 per share in 1959 compared with $6.00 in 1958. Three quarterly interim dividends of $1.50 each were paid in both years together with a year-end dividend of $2.50 in 1959 and $1.50 in 1958. . . Total dividends were . . . 79 per cent of earnings for the year, the same as the percentage for the ten-year period 1950 through 1959." (E.I. du Pont de Nemours & Company, *Annual Report for the Year 1959* [Wilmington, 1960], pp. 4–5.)
8. What dividend policy is suggested by the following: Corporate profit after corporate income taxes in 1960 are "estimated to have been off about a billion from 1959 . . . Thc 1960 payout ratio was 60 per cent of after-tax profits up from 55 per cent the year before." (*Survey of Current Business* [January, 1961], pp. 12–13.)
9. The board of directors of Sperry Rand Corporation declared a dividend in common stock of 2 per cent on common stock payable March 30, 1961 to shareholders of record at the close of business February 9, 1961. This dividend was in lieu of the quarterly cash dividend customarily paid in March and June. In view of the corporation's financial strength, was management justified in changing its dividend policy from "cash" to stock? (*Report to Stockholders, Nine Months Ended December 31, 1960* [New York, 1961], p. 2.)
10. Justify the tax policy indicated by the following: "A stock dividend of 1 share for each 50 shares held was paid on November 1, 1960 to hold-

ers of record on September 16, 1960. Counsel for the company have advised that this dividend, as distinguished from a cash dividend, is not subject to federal income tax." (The Dow Chemical Company, *2nd Quarter Dividend Remittance Statement to Common Stock Shareholders* [Midland, Michigan: January 14, 1961] p.

PART IV

Short-Term and Intermediate Loan Capital

AMONG THE most pressing needs of business firms are those associated with financing their operations. Businesses borrow for a multitude of reasons and from many sources. While the distinction among various types of credit is sometimes obscure, the type of credit needed will often influence the maturity, terms, and sources employed.

Approximately 90 per cent of wholesalers' and manufacturers' sales are made on credit; consequently, trade credit is an important, and sometimes the only, external source of funds available to a firm. However, the fairly common practice among trade creditors of allowing substantial discounts for prompt payment encourages borrowing from banks and other lenders to take advantage of these discounts. The selection of a commercial bank is an important consideration for a business firm. Unless a business selects a bank which is qualified and legally able to handle its banking needs, it will be unnecessarily handicapped.

Because most firms themselves extend credit to their customers, trade receivable financing has become an important aspect of total financing, and specialized firms such as factors and other finance companies have developed facilities to care for these needs. Working capital funds are obtained by some firms through the sale of commercial paper, but relatively few firms have the size or credit standing to permit them to take advantage of this low-cost form of credit.

Intermediate credit, that with a maturity of from one to five years, is often needed to finance equipment and is increasingly obtained by arranging for term loans. The growing practice of leasing instead of purchasing equipment frees a business from this particular need for funds and permits utilization of its borrowing capacity to achieve other goals.

This section covers the general nature of business borrowing, financing with trade credit, commercial banking relations of business firms, financing through factors and specialized finance companies, short-term open-market financing, and financing intermediate credit needs of business firms.

CHAPTER 10

~~~~~~~~~~~~~~~~~~~~~~~~~~~~~~

General Nature of Business Borrowing

THE GENERAL nature of business indebtedness and the relationship between creditors and business firms are considered in this chapter. Regardless of whether the contributions of creditors are in the form of money, merchandise, or services, they are generally temporary in nature. Creditors expect to be repaid according to the terms of the agreements under which advances are made. Some advances are made for less than one year, some for intermediate periods of from one to five years, and others for periods in excess of five years.

WHY AND HOW BUSINESS FIRMS BORROW

Business firms borrow in order to acquire assets, liquidate indebtedness, and replace their invested capital; they repay debts with funds obtained from conversion of assets into cash, funds obtained from other lenders, and/or capital funds obtained externally or accumulated internally.

Acquisition of Assets. Loans obtained for the purpose of acquiring assets are customarily subdivided into those used to obtain current assets and those used to obtain noncurrent or fixed assets. However, in practice, business firms may use funds advanced to finance current assets to acquire assets of a noncurrent nature and they may divert those obtained to finance fixed assets to financing current assets.

Traditionally, short-term loans are those the proceeds of which "flow through the business"—from raw materials to labor, then to
~~~~~~~~~~~~~~~~~~~~~~~~~~~~~~

overhead or inventory, then into accounts receivable, and finally into cash. From the viewpoint of commercial banks and other short-term lenders, short-term commercial loans are preferred to all others and they are generally made at the lowest interest rate charged by them. Usually a business firm will need additional funds during the season of the year when its operating activities are at their peak; then, when operating activities slacken, these funds will no longer be needed. Thus seasonal loans are those obtained to increase current assets during one period of a business firm's fiscal year, to be repaid when accounts receivable are collected during a later period.

In some instances, the seasonal indebtedness of a business firm may be related to specific purchases of merchandise under terms of payment embodied in letters of credit or acceptance agreements. A foreign or domestic trade supplier may be authorized to draw a time bill of exchange (draft) on the purchaser or his bank which will be honored by the drawee by acceptance (making the obligation his own by writing the word "accepted" on the face of the bill along with his signature and the date). Upon maturity, the bill of exchange will be presented to the acceptor for payment. If the draft was accepted by a bank, the purchaser will pay the bank with cash, usually obtained from the resale of the merchandise obtained from the trade supplier.

Practically all business firms make some use of seasonal loans, but they are used most extensively by firms whose volume of sales are characterized by a definite seasonal swing. Among the types of firms that usually need seasonal credit are manufacturers of seasonal goods, dealers in commodities that are produced and marketed during one season of the year, and retailers (such as clothing stores, shoe stores, apparel shops, and, to some extent, retail department stores). Many retailers have their greatest need for seasonal credit during the last quarter of the year.

Although it may be possible for a business concern to finance all of its seasonal and other demands for funds with its own resources, it would be a violation of the principles of good financial management—that no substantial portion of owners' equity should be kept idle during slack seasons in order to have sufficient resources to care for business needs during the peak season. When there is substantial variation in inventories and receivables during a business firm's fiscal year, the most economical way to finance them is with short-term bank loans or with funds obtained in the money market. Normally, seasonal working capital needs originate during one phase in the fiscal cycle of a manufacturing, merchandising, or service firm. However, in some cases the need for funds to finance working capital assets is more or less continuous. Quite often, these semipermanent types of working capital loans are in the form of sixty-day notes which are renewed periodically by the lender.

Some business firms finance their working capital needs with "revolving credits" arranged for through commercial banks, commercial finance companies, or other lenders. Usually a loan agreement of this type states the maximum amount of credit, final maturity of the credit, and restrictions on the borrower as to dividend payments, retirement of capital, and acquisitions of other business units. In addition, the business firm may agree to maintain a specified level of current assets, to carry a stated amount and type of insurance, and to follow other prescribed policies that would tend to assure the quality of the firm's credit. Customarily, an agreement of this type permits repayments and reborrowings according to the ability and needs of the business firm being financed.

The working capital loans of some business firms embody the major characteristics of term loans wherein borrowing is for more than one year and loan repayments are arranged on the installment plan. When obtaining a loan of this type, business firms often enter into term loan-like agreements which specify acts that a firm must perform and acts that are prohibited. Since the purpose of borrowing is to finance working capital assets, these loans may be classified as working capital loans.

Finally, a business firm may finance nonseasonal working capital assets by rotating its borrowings among several lenders (borrowing from a second lender to repay the first when that loan matures). This system permits the firm to clean-up its loans with each lender for a period of time during each year, but it does not disguise the fact that there is a continuity in the use of credit. A business firm that finances with nonseasonal working capital loans should realize that long-term funds are needed and that it would be more proper and safer to obtain them by an increase in either owners' equity or long-term debt. Although short-term assets being financed may be pledged as security for a loan, other factors determine whether the need is for short-term or long-term credit. If the need is for long-term funds, a loan providing for a longer maturity will permit the borrowing firm to either increase its equity, refinance the loan, or repay it without seriously impairing its working capital position.

Studies of loans made by business firms indicate that wide use is being made of semi-permanent types of working capital loans by some business firms, particularly those retailers who sell on the installment plan, firms which are growing rapidly, and other firms whose inventories and/or receivables are not being turned over rapidly enough to avoid financing with borrowed funds.

Business firms borrow from banks, commercial finance companies, and other lenders to finance equipment which includes almost all forms of tangible personal property. Funds obtained for such purposes are usually repaid on the installment plan with repayment over a period of time related to the useful or depreciable life of the equipment. Usually, repayment is made with funds from operations accounted for as depreciation allowances. The proceeds of a term loan are sometimes used to finance the purchase of equipment or interim needs between short-term and long-term outlays. Term loans are in the category of intermediate loans, having maturities in excess of one year at the time of origin.

The acquisition of land and the construction or purchase of plants and buildings are commonly financed with borrowed funds or loan capital. Large firms may finance such assets by issuing bonds or obtaining loans from insurance companies, private pension funds, and/or other institutional lenders. Smaller business firms rarely issue bonds, but they may obtain funds from the same sources as larger firms. In addition, they may obtain aid through the Small Business Administration and small business investment companies (see Chapter 25).

Repayment of Indebtedness. Business firms commonly borrow funds to repay indebtedness such as obligations to trade suppliers, the federal or state government (for tax liabilities), the public (when financing in the open market), banks, institutional investors, and participants in the business. Trade suppliers customarily permit business firms to take cash discounts on their accounts payable. These discounts are generally so generous that business firms find it profitable to borrow in order to take advantage of them.

Another legitimate reason for borrowing by business firms is to liquidate liabilities arising from accrued costs and expenses. While management usually makes arrangements to build up the assets of the firm so as to be able to meet income tax payments and other accrued expenses when due, current earnings may be invested in the form of inventories, receivables, or other noncash items. In such a case, it would usually be preferable to meet these liabilities by borrowing rather than by liquidating noncash assets, thus disrupting the normal operations of the business. Among the accrued expenses of a business firm, the quarterly federal income tax payment is usually the most important.

Obligations of business firms to the general public are usually associated with debts resulting from sales of bonds, debentures, notes, and bills in the capital and money markets. For various reasons, the managers of a business firm may want to liquidate these obligations with funds obtained from banks, life insurance companies, and other lenders. Conversely, business firms may want to repay loans from banks, life insurance companies, and others with funds obtained through open-market financing.

Business firms may arrange lines of credit with several banks in order to follow an established borrowing policy of being out of debt to each bank during a specific part of each year. In such cases the bank loans are not repaid out of cash from operations but out of cash borrowed from a second bank. The debt picture may be illustrated as follows:

MONTH	*Bank A*	*Bank B*	*Bank C*	*Bank D*	TOTAL
January	$500	...	$500	$500	$1,500
February	500	...	500	500	1,500
March	500	$500	...	500	1,500
April	500	500	...	500	1,500
May	500	500	...	500	1,500
June	...	500	500	500	1,500
July	...	500	500	500	1,500
August	...	500	500	500	1,500
September	500	500	500	...	1,500
October	500	500	500	...	1,500
November	500	500	500	...	1,500
December	500	...	500	500	1,500

The management of a business firm that finances by rotating loans among several banks is faced with the possibility that one bank may refuse to grant a loan when its turn comes; hence, after weighing the situation, management may decide to finance exclusively with one bank. The new loan contract may be written either on a term loan basis or a short-term loan basis with the right to renew at maturity.

Most closely associated with small business firms is another type of business borrowing: funds to repay indebtedness are obtained from principals in the business enterprise. Thus a small corporation may augment its assets by borrowing from its chief stockholders, officers, directors, or others closely associated with the firm. In most cases, a business firm will not be called upon to repay funds obtained in this way until the death or withdrawal of the creditor from the business firm.

Replacement of Invested Capital. A final reason for which a business firm may borrow is to replace part of its invested capital. A corporation may want to liquidate an issue of callable preferred stock outstanding with the proceeds of a bond issue or a term loan. The death of a large stockholder of a closely held corporation may necessitate borrowing by the corporation in order to acquire the stock from his estate, thus preventing its sale to outside interests which could gain control of the corporation. A similar situation may occur in the case of death or retirement of a partner in a business firm; that is, the remaining partner or partners may find it necessary to borrow in order to purchase the deceased or retired partner's net worth. In other cases, business firms may borrow in order to replace capital losses due to excessive dividend payments, operating losses, or other factors.

CHOICE BETWEEN DEBT AND EQUITY FINANCING

A business firm usually has some choice between financing with debts or with equities. One of the factors in the choice is the leverage principle inherent in debt financing; others include risk, flexibility or timing, control, and costs.

Leverage Principle. The leverage principle involves the proportion between total debt and owners' equity; hence, the leverage factor is present in all debt financing by business firms. Considerable borrowing is motivated by the desire to trade on equity, which assumes that the business firm will have net worth or equity sufficiently large to protect creditors. However, the borrower may be giving less consideration to the protection of creditors than to the leverage effect on the business profits.

There is no fixed or specific rule as to what constitutes the proper balance between debt and equity capital of a business firm except the general one previously noted that debts should not be excessive (or beyond the firm's ultimate ability to pay). However, in determining the debt–equity balance in any business firm's capital structure, the factors that must be taken into account include the degree of risk inherent in debt financing in the particular line of business involved, the ability of the business firm to generate funds (accounted for as depreciation allowances and earnings) that may be used to retire debt, the degree of liquidity of assets owned by the firm, the size of the enterprise, the ability to borrow in the money and capital markets, and the volume of business transacted by the firm. While the experiences of other firms in the same industry may be worth considering, in the final analysis, management must make an individual decision regarding the ratio of debt to owners' equity to be maintained by its firm.

The leverage principle may be explained in terms of long-term debt as illustrated by the balance sheets of two companies—one financing entirely with owners' equity and retained earnings and the other financing with long-term debt in addition to owners' equity and retained earnings. In order to emphasize the effects of debt in the capital structure, both companies are assumed to have the same volume of sales—on which they earn 5 per cent—and the same volume of assets.

COMPANY A

Current assets	$ 500,000
Fixed assets	500,000
Total Assets	$1,000,000
Current liabilities	$ 250,000
Long-term debt	......
Total Liabilities	$ 250,000
Capital stock	$ 500,000
Retained earnings	250,000
Total Liabilities and Capital	$1,000,000

COMPANY B

Current assets	$ 500,000
Fixed assets	500,000
Total Assets	$1,000,000
Current liabilities	$ 250,000
Long-term debt	500,000
Total Liabilities	$ 750,000
Capital stock	$ 200,000
Retained earnings	50,000
Total Liabilities and Capital	$1,000,000

Capital stock plus retained earnings amount to $750,000 for Company A and $250,000 for Company B. On net earnings of $100,000, Company A will earn 13⅓ per cent on its owners' investments ($100,000 ÷ $750,000). Company B with the same earnings must pay interest charges on its long-term debt amounting to $25,000 (assuming a 5 per cent per annum rate), leaving net earnings of $75,000. Company B will earn 30 per cent on its owners' investments ($75,000 ÷ $250,000) because the total investments of owners amount to only $250,000 as compared with $750,000 for Company A. (Because the emphasis here is on the leverage principle, no allowances have been made for corporate income taxes.) The conclusion that may be drawn from this illustration is that the greater the proportion of debt to equity in the capital structure of a business firm, the greater will be the effect of the leverage factor on the earnings assignable to owners; conversely, the smaller the proportion of debt to equity, the smaller will be the effect of the leverage factor on the earnings assignable to owners.

Risk Factor. Offsetting the leverage advantage of debt financing is the fact that it entails greater risk than equity financing. This difference in risk may be illustrated by assuming that the earnings of both Company A and Company B decline to $30,000. Now the earnings assignable to owners of Company A decline to 4 per cent ($30,000 ÷ $750,000), while those of Company B decline to 2 per cent ($5,000 ÷ $250,000). However, with only $5,000 remaining after interest payments, Company B may have difficulty in meeting the terms of its long-term debt contracts which usually contain provisions for the retirement of the principal, such as sinking fund contributions. It may be concluded that the greater the use made of borrowed funds, the greater will be the financial risks that a business firm assumes.

Flexibility. Business management has greater flexibility in regard to terms and timing when financing with debt obligations than when raising capital by equity financing. This is particularly pertinent when the need for funds is temporary or due to seasonal or cyclical factors. The minimum amount of working capital which any business firm requires constitutes a demand for long-term capital, but the additional amount needed during certain periods constitutes a demand for short-term capital.

In addition to the seasonal working capital assets needed by most business firms when production and sales are at their peak, some firms may have a nonpermanent demand for fixed assets which would justify borrowing. For illustration, when a development of a nonrecurring nature necessitates expansion of facilities, installation of new machines, or the purchase of additional equipment, it may be profitable to borrow rather than to increase the amount of equity capital (it is more difficult to retire equity capital than to retire debts, so the increase in equity capital may result in overcapitalization).

Because of the uncertainty of the future, business corporations follow financial plans wherein the instruments of credit either have definite maturity dates or are payable at the option of the company. Debt financing permits arranging maturities to coincide with the needs of the borrower (debt instruments may vary from those having a maturity of one day to those without a maturity date). However, with each increase in the amount of debt assumed by a business firm, additional financing becomes more difficult and usually more expensive; hence the debt contracted today may be the germ of future financial difficulties. While the earnings of a business firm are not affected directly by principal repayment, such payments are a burden in that they reduce the amount of cash available for expansion and other purposes, and any curtailment of such expenditures could cause a decline in future earnings.

Debt financing is usually less complicated than equity financing; arranging for a loan is simpler than arranging for a bond or stock issue, and arranging for a bond issue is usually easier than arranging for a stock issue. While both bond and stock issues are initiated by the board of directors of a corporation, when new stock is to be issued the approval of old stockholders is usually required (that is, an amendment to the corporation's charter is required).

Preservation of Control. Those in control of a corporation usually prefer to raise funds by borrowing rather than to risk losing control by selling stock. This desire to maintain control is particularly strong among owners of small firms who, after having built up their companies almost single-handedly over a period of years, are reluctant to share ownership with the general public. Even those in managerial positions of large corporations may object to the issuance of new shares because of the possibility of the stock being acquired by those unfriendly to existing management. However, whenever new financing is undertaken there is some danger that existing management will lose control in whole or part; even when financing with bonds is involved the underwriters of the issue may demand representation on the corporation's board of directors. The same demand may be made by the underwriters of an issue of common or preferred stock. Finally, most long-term loan contracts and term loan agreements embody provisions that limit the control of management.

The stockholders of large corporations rarely exercise their rights to vote except by proxy and they usually give their proxies to management. When existing management of a large corporation loses control it is usually because too large a percentage of stock has been acquired by a few stockholders who are unfriendly to management rather than because there has been an increase in the number of shares outstanding as a result of equity financing. However, there is less potential danger of loss of control when financing with bonds rather than with equities.

Costs. Usually it is less expensive and more convenient for a business firm to borrow than to issue stock. The well-known adage "borrow at 5 per cent, earn 10 per cent, and keep the difference," is merely a statement of the leverage principle of debt financing. The ability of a business firm to borrow at a lower rate than it can earn depends in part on the amount of protection that it is able to give the lender. It should be noted that the larger the proportion of debt relative to owners' equity, the greater is the lender's risk and the higher will be the cost of borrowing (when other things are the same).

One advantage in debt financing is that a business firm is permitted to deduct interest payments as a cost in computing federal income taxes. Theoretically, a firm could finance exclusively with income debentures; this would mean that earnings would be distributed as interest rather than as dividends and thus could be deducted as costs for income tax purposes. Since financing with debt seems to be more economical than financing with equities, why should not all of the capital needs of a business firm be satisfied with loan capital? The answer is that the future cannot be forecast accurately enough to justify the risks incurred in financing exclusively with loan capital even if lenders and borrowers could agree on such a contract (which would be almost impossible). While management of a business concern presumably would not borrow without having adequate assurance that the firm could meet its obligations, obviously this presumption is not entirely justified or there would be fewer business failures. The danger in borrowing lies in the inability of management to appraise the future earnings of the business firm with sufficient accuracy.

GENERAL PRINCIPLES OF DEBT FINANCING

The accumulated experience of business firms suggests certain general principles of debt financing. Many of these principles are applicable to borrowing in general, others to special industries, some to particular kinds of borrowing, and others to individual companies or types of companies. In general, debt policy is designed to protect owners from possible loss and "will vary with the willingness of management to risk such loss by trading on the equity. Industrials now carry a funded debt of about 12 per cent whereas the debts of railroads and utilities vary in range of 20 to 50 per cent or more of total capitalization."[1]

Earnings and Debt Costs. Regardless of the amount of property that may be pledged for a loan, in the final analysis it is the earning power of the obligor that measures the ability of the business firm to pay its debts. For any business firm, the best principle to follow in debt financing is to be sure that earnings over a period of years will

[1] Walter A. Morton, "The Structure of the Capital Market and the Price of Money," *American Economic Review*, Vol. XLIV, No. 2 (May, 1954), p. 443.

be sufficient to cover current interest charges and permit accumulation of funds to repay the principal. The higher the coverage of all debt charges (interest and sinking funds) and the more stable the earnings, the greater is the ability of the firm to borrow safely. Even if a company is planning to refund a debt when due (a common practice among public utility and railway companies), past and anticipated earnings are the best index of the company's ability to repay what it borrows.

In appraising earning power the future is stressed, and so the trend of earnings may be more indicative than actual past earnings. A business firm on the "upgrade" may be a far better risk than a second firm on the "downgrade" even though the past earning record of the first firm is not as good as that of the second. A comparative analysis of a company's financial statements over a period of years usually indicates the capability of its management. The prospects for the industry and other related factors must also be considered because both immediate and long-term earnings are important.

There are wide variations among industries in the relationship which ought to exist between earnings and interest charges. A public utility company may operate safely when net earnings are twice interest charges. An industrial firm, faced with competition and a fluctuating demand for its product (the "prince-pauper" type of enterprise), may find that net earnings that average three times interest charges over a number of years are inadequate at the depth of a depression. Companies with a high credit rating based on current and anticipated earnings have little difficulty in borrowing from institutional investors at low interest rates, while others with poor earning records find it difficult to borrow even at high interest rates.

Customarily, earnings after federal income taxes are stressed, but one fact that should be remembered is that all funds from operations may be used to meet interest and debt obligations. Among the ratios used to test the ability of corporations to meet their long-term debt costs is the number of time bond interest is earned, which gives the income security of the fixed debts:

$$\frac{\text{Net Income before Income Taxes}}{\text{Bond Service Requirements}}.$$

The net earning power of invested capital funds may be measured by dividing net profits on total investments by total investments:

$$\frac{\text{Net Profits on Total Investments}}{\text{Total Investments}}.$$

Asset Position. Working capital may be as important as earnings in estimating a business firm's ability to meet its obligations as they mature. Cash and other liquid assets indicate debt-paying ability. Commercial bankers and credit men are concerned chiefly with a borrower's ability to meet short-term obligations. Therefore the adequacy of working capital is analyzed more carefully in short-term lending than in long-term lending (see Chapter 5). Customarily, debts are paid with cash; hence, the liquidity of corporate assets and net working capital positions of business firms are of interest to all creditors. This corporate liquidity ratio is found by dividing current assets minus current liabilities by total investments:

$$\frac{\text{Current Assets—Current Liabilities}}{\text{Total Investments}}.$$

Often a business firm may borrow at a lower rate by pledging assets as security for a loan. In this case, the firm may have larger net profits with which to build up its net worth or retire its debt. Often clauses requiring the borrower to maintain certain ratios (current, fixed assets, etc.) are inserted in trust indentures, term loan agreements, and other debt contracts. Additional clauses may prohibit the borrower from paying dividends, except under certain conditions, and prohibit other actions that might dissipate the firm's assets. For long-term obligations, bond to total investment ratios are used to indicate the amount of asset security:

$$\frac{\text{Fixed Liabilities}}{\text{Total Investments}}.$$

Often long-term creditors emphasize the amount of fixed assets by using the following ratio:

$$\frac{\text{Fixed Liabilities}}{\text{Fixed Assets}}.$$

Business Cycle and Debt Financing. The economic history of the United States reveals that most financial failures occur during general business depressions. In any particular industry, the companies that financed to the largest extent by trading on equity (greatest debt relative to net worth) had the poorest survival records. As a precautionary measure, most business firms will find it advantageous to reduce their debts or increase their equity during the prosperous phase of the business cycle. In addition, it will be to their advantage to increase their holdings of cash and near cash assets so that they may have resources that can be used to meet maturing obligations if and when the need arises. Adequate cash or near cash resources permit expansion during depressions when prices and wages are lowest. A strong financial position also permits borrowing when interest rates are lowest and credit terms are most liberal.

The present debt policies of business concerns have been influenced by business experiences during the depression of the 1930's. Most of the railroad companies that failed during this period failed because of inability to meet fixed charges rather than because of operating losses; real estate companies had similar experiences; in other industries, the financial difficulties of many companies were due to high debt ratios. Because common stock can be sold easily in a "bull" market (during 1958–59 common stock was being sold at a lower earnings–price ratio than bonds), corporate management is now in a favorable position to obtain additional equity capital. But currently, because of low interest rates and the tax advantage of debt financing, corporate management seems to prefer financing with debts rather than with equities. The optimum debt ratio (debt as a percentage of total capitalization) varies with capital and money market conditions (see below) which reflect the attitude of investors during the phases of the business cycle.

Life Cycle and Debt Retirement. Most business enterprises pass through three stages—youth, middle age, and old age. In a later chapter, dealing with the promotion of new business firms, statistics are given showing the life expectancy of newly established business enterprises. It is concluded that a business firm should avoid debt financing until it is firmly established. During middle age, which is the firm's expansion and development period, moderate use may be made of loan capital. Most business enterprises—exceptions may be public utility and railway companies—should gradually retire long-term debts, preferably with retained earnings, before they reach "old age." Whenever an industry or an individual firm is faced with a decreasing demand for its services or products, debt reduction should be the primary objective of financial management.

Debt Policy. The debt policy of some firms is that of borrowing only as a last resort when funds cannot be raised economically in other ways. Other corporations have a policy of keeping long-term debt at a specified percentage of total capitalization (capital stock, surplus, bonds, debentures, and term loans) and current liabilities—with reference to current assets—at a ratio which is in line with the standard current ratio for the industry. The amount of debt financing by some corporations that seemingly have no established debt policy will reflect money and capital market conditions; dividend, retained earnings, and depreciation policies; and prejudices of the chief stockholders in regard to dilution of their equities. While no single debt policy fits the needs of all business firms, if the debt structure of an individual firm is greatly out of line with those of others in the same industry, its management may be criticized.

Finally, a debt policy capable of meeting a firm's needs at one time may be unsatisfactory at another. The chief cause of failures among firms in the building and railroad industries during the 1930's was overborrowing. In this connection, many companies which had no difficulty in meeting their interest and operating expenses went through bankruptcy because of the inability to meet sinking-fund requirements and maturing debt obligations. Most debt contracts contain an acceleration clause that causes the entire debt to become due and payable if any clause in the indenture or term loan agreement is violated.

Usually, business firms are strengthened when they can obtain and use borrowed funds productively; but, in times of adversity, interest charges and principal payments may permanently cripple a business. If a company cannot meet its obligations, it will either be reorganized or liquidated. Management, interested in the well being of its company, may find that it is more dangerous to finance with debts than with common stock or other forms of equity capital.

LEGAL ASPECTS OF BUSINESS DEBTS

Right to Go into Debt. Except for the common-law restriction that borrowing must be for the benefit of the company, business firms have an implied right to borrow unless specifically prohibited from doing so. Sometimes the articles of incorporation or bylaws of a corporation (or comparable documents of other types of business enterprises) place restrictions on the amount and conditions under which management may obligate its business firm. Restrictions limiting borrowing and other activities of management are also found in debt contracts such as mortgages, bond indentures, term loan agreements, collateral form notes, loan agreements when accounts receivable are assigned, and guarantees of various types.

When business concerns borrow, the lender inevitably assumes some risk of loss. When loans are negotiated, lenders may try to reduce these risks by requiring security, by limiting the loan period, by making certain specific provisions for repayment of the principal, by restricting the borrower's activities, and by making certain specific requirements of the debtor firm. At a later date, these requirements and restrictions may seriously handicap the activities of a business concern. Probably no banker or other lender would deliberately insert a clause into a debt contract that would interfere with the normal operation of a debtor business firm, but the history of business finance is replete with cases wherein normal operations of business firms were hampered by such clauses. So a borrower will try to obtain the privilege of repaying a debt at his option not only to be relieved of the debt but also to escape from the potentially crippling effects of the debt contract in the shortest possible time.

Execution of Forms. The rules applicable to the execution of contracts in general also apply to debt contracts, and usually banks and other institutional lenders have their lawyers draw up legally acceptable forms which are used for routine lending transactions. A business concern's legal counsel (or staff members) advise management as to the correct legal procedure in loan transactions; these are more detailed for corporations than for unincorporated businesses.

If a corporation is financing with a bond issue, its board of directors must provide proof of power to authorize such an issue (as provided for by charter, bylaws, and/or approval of stockholders and directors). For any type of borrowing, creditors usually request a resolution of the board of directors authorizing certain officers to sign documents, to pledge assets, and to act in other financial capacities for the corporation. There is a possibility that, after a resolution has been presented, the legality of a loan may be challenged by a stockholder or some other interested party; however, a creditor has the right to assume that the bylaws have been observed (regarding the presence of a quorum of directors, a properly conducted meeting, etc.). Certain powers possessed by officers of business concerns—to make contracts, incur liabilities, and borrow for normal business purposes—are binding on business firms. For illustration, notes of a corporation executed by its president and secretary are legal if the proceeds are used for business purposes.

Regulation of Security Issues. If a bond issue is to be offered to the general public, the legal procedures found in the Securities Act of 1933 and other federal or state laws which affect financing through public sales of securities must be followed. The legal aspects relative to issuance and retirement of securities are usually clear cut; the major problems of finance officers are those pertaining to the cost and ease of selling securities, and servicing and retiring debts. Management usually follows procedures that are customary in such cases. If new precedents are established, it is usually the major companies in the industry that initiate them.

Regulatory agencies (such as the Interstate Commerce Commission in the railroad field and the Securities and Exchange Commission in the public utility field) have influenced the techniques and procedures used by corporations in raising funds by borrowing. In some cases, this influence has had the effect of increasing private placement of debt to avoid registration requirements. When the Securities and Exchange Commission acts upon registration statements filed with it by business corporations, the purpose is to see that information supplied potential investors is complete and accurate. The right of an ordinary corporation to borrow is not questioned provided the required information is filed and the trustee meets the standards set forth in the Trust Indenture Act of 1939.

Laws to Protect Creditors. Businessmen have instigated the passage of laws designed to give business-concern creditors the same protection enjoyed by other creditors. Most of these are state laws; hence there are many variations among the commercial codes of various states. About three fourths of the states have special statutes covering "false financial statements" (which provide for punishment of those who issue false financial statements for the purpose of obtaining money or merchandise), and all states have "bad check" and "false pretense" statutes. The federal criminal code (Section 215) makes any one who uses the mail to defraud or to obtain money or property by means of false or fradulent pretenses subject to fine and/or imprisonment. States have also adopted laws covering warehouse receipts, negotiable instruments, and sales. Of the federal laws designed to protect creditors, the Federal Bankruptcy Act has been the most important in its effects.

While creditors customarily assume some risks, they want to make sure that these risks do not include the validity of their claims against debtors. While no intelligent lender would knowingly make a loan to an individual whose integrity he questions, nevertheless the case books in business law are replete with litigations involving the legality of the claims of creditors. Most lenders prefer to have debt obligations repaid with cash obtained during the normal course of the debtor's business; that is, they want to be assured of repayment without resorting to foreclosure and forced sale of the borrower's assets. Because most modern business is done "on credit," business concerns lose more from nonpayment of obligations than do other creditors.

FORMS OF BORROWING

There are various ways of classifying business borrowing, three of which are noted in this section. First, borrowing may be classified as short-term and long-term; second, as secured and unsecured; and third, as open-market and customer-loan.

Short-Term and Long-Term Borrowing. A short-term loan is one that matures in less than one year from the day it is negotiated, and a long-term loan is one that matures in one year or longer after it is negotiated. Sometimes, long-term borrowing is subdivided into (1) intermediate borrowing, to include obligations that mature within a period of from one to five years, and (2) long-term debts that mature after five years. The time classification of borrowing used by a business firm will vary according to the individual borrower. Thus, debts of five years may be considered short term by a firm that has most of its obligations in bonds having maturities of from 20 to 99 years, but may be considered long-term borrowing by a firm that customarily borrows for no longer than five years.

Secured and Unsecured Borrowing. When a business firm borrows, it gives a promise to pay which means that all of the debt-paying ability of the firm is pledged. In addition, the firm may give the lender a pledge of some specific asset which would mean that the loan is secured. If no specific assets are pledged the loan is classified as unsecured. If the asset pledged in a secured loan belongs to the firm, nothing has been added to the company's debt-paying ability. This is true because the promise to pay involves all of the firm's assets in case of financial difficulties. If the thing pledged belongs to a third party, such as a wealthy director or officer of the company, then something has been added to protect the credit of the business concern.

A specific lien on any of the company's assets protects secured lenders against the claims of others. In case of liquidation of assets in bankruptcy, secured creditors have a prior claim to the cash realized from the sale of the pledged assets in an amount equal to but not in excess of their claims. For any part of their claims not satisfied, secured creditors have the same status as unsecured creditors.

While pledging assets as a basis for borrowing strengthens the position of secured creditors, it weakens the position of unsecured creditors. The debt-paying ability of the borrower is the same whether or not something has been pledged. There are many reasons why business firms pledge assets for borrowing, the most common reason being that the lenders, upon whom the firms are most dependent for funds, demand it. The more common assets pledged are securities, real estate, equipment, inventories, and accounts receivables.

Experiences of commercial banks disclose that the interest rate on secured loans is higher than that on unsecured loans (indicating that security is required because there is more risk). Although banks make more secured loans than unsecured loans, the dollar value of unsecured loans is greater because large firms ordinarily (1) are able to provide complete financial information about their affairs, (2) have other sources of funds, and (3) have a better credit rating than small firms.

Open-Market and Customer-Loan Borrowing. Open-market borrowing entails raising funds through intermediaries in the money and capital market. The suppliers of the funds are the buyers of the credit instruments. Sometimes, a borrower foregoes the services of the middleman and sells credit instruments directly in the open market. For illustration, the General Motors Acceptance Corporation, the C.I.T. Financial Corporation and the Commercial Credit Company use their own note salesmen exclusively to sell their promissory notes.

In open-market borrowing, a business firm must meet the demands of the market which is made up of thousands of potential suppliers of funds. The larger business firms, known to investors because of their products and ratings in financial manuals, are the chief borrowers in the money and capital markets. Usually, the securities of such companies are marketable after the original distribution; this quality is desired by most investors.

The term "money market" is used to mean the place where the demand for and supply of short-term funds meet. For illustration, the New York money market is where funds originating throughout the world are drawn and where short-term funds may be obtained quickly. The New York money market is an important clearing center for financial institutions because it offers facilities for speedy investing and disinvesting in short-term government securities, bankers' acceptances, open-market promissory notes, call loans to security and commodity brokers and dealers, and other types of short-term obligations.

While the principal money market of the United States is in New York, there are thousands of other money markets throughout the country. Broadly speaking, there is a money market wherever a short-term lender and borrower meet. Nevertheless, a borrower is interested in the New York, Chicago, and other money markets as an alternative to borrowing in his own local money market, as a source of clues to current and expected financial and economic developments, or as a matter of mere curiosity. If money rates are tightening in the New York money market, the borrower may anticipate greater difficulty in arranging for new loans or renewing old ones on the same terms (such as amount and interest rate). Sales prices and mercantile credit terms will reflect central bank policies pertaining to general or special credit conditions. For illustration, if the policy of the Federal Reserve System is one of tightening credit, sellers will tend to review past-due accounts more carefully, to scrutinize new orders from customers more thoroughly, and to analyze their own inventory situations and production plans in anticipation of more competitive markets at the same or lower prices.

The concept of the capital market is so closely related to that of the money market that the two terms are often used interchangeably. However, the capital market is where the demand for and supply of long-term funds meet. It includes the primary market for new long-term credit instruments and stocks and the secondary capital market where outstanding stocks and bonds are bought and sold (securities exchanges) and customer-loan markets. Most of the borrowers in the money market are also borrowers in the capital market; they include the federal, state, local, and foreign governments, governmental agencies, business enterprises, individuals, and specialized financial institutions. The same overlapping with respect to borrowers in the money and capital markets is also true of lenders. Among the more specialized type of lenders are life insurance companies, savings institutions, trust companies, investment companies, and mortgage banks. Investment bankers, brokers, and dealers are middlemen in placing securities with institutional and individual investors. Since commercial banks are buyers of long-term as well as short-term credit instruments, they are of importance in the capital market.

Sometimes, it is assumed that the capital market is the one wherein long-term credit is obtained to acquire fixed capital goods and the money market is the one wherein short-term credit is obtained to acquire working capital assets. In practice, fixed capital needs are sometimes provided by the money market as well as by the capital market. If long-term funds are not available at a reasonable rate, short-term loans may be made. Of course, the borrower assumes the risk that such loans may have to be refinanced later under less favorable conditions. For over two decades, the interest rate advantage has favored the short-term borrower. In other words, there has been an upsweeping yield curve (namely, the pattern of interest rates as of one date has been progressively higher with each increase in maturity). While it may be logical to assume that an upsweeping yield curve is the normal pattern of interest rates, this has not been true in the past. Probably there have been just as many years during which the interest curve was downsweeping as upsweeping.[2] This means that the interest advantage associated will short-term borrowing, which has existed since 1933, may not be the characteristic of future money and capital markets.

Those who assume that the capital market is limited to financing fixed capital assets will find that, in practice, it is also used to finance working capital assets. For illustration, minimum working capital needs constitute a permanent demand for funds that may be obtained in the capital market. It is correct only in part to assume that a distinction may be drawn between capital and money markets according to the purpose for which funds are used.

In a customer-loan market, terms are negotiated by the borrower and the lender, such as the representative of a business firm and a commercial bank. Both large and small business firms borrow funds directly from banks and other lenders; while most of such loans are short-term, long-term loans are not uncommon (being over one third of all business loans made by commercial banks). Often, the latter are participated in by two or more lenders, including both commercial banks and life insurance companies.

SUMMARY

The procedures followed in borrowing differ with the type of business organization, the maturity of the loan, and—in the case of corporations—with the laws of the state of incorporation and the corporation's charter and bylaws. Before making a loan a creditor should check the validity of his claim against the debtor and otherwise protect himself against the assumption of unnecessary risks.

Even though circumstances vary among industries and among

---

[2] David Durand, *Basic Yields of Corporate Bonds, 1900–1942*, Technical Paper, No. 3 (New York: National Bureau of Economic Research, 1942), p. 17.

firms within an industry, there are some general principles of debt financing which may be applied in most instances. Care must be taken when committing a firm to interest payments and debt retirement obligations to be sure that these contracts can be met even if earnings should decline. Guides to debt financing include (1) the amount of debt relative to earnings and equity, and (2) the timing of debt contracts relative to the phase of the business cycle and the point in the life cycle of the business firm. In addition, consideration should be given to such specific guideposts as earnings relative to costs of debt servicing and retirement and the effect of pledging assets on the cost of financing and on the restrictions thereby placed on management.

Business firms borrow for the following reasons: there is greater freedom in arranging loans than in selling stock; it may be both expedient and cheaper to finance with debts rather than with stock issues; borrowing permits precise planning to meet requirements of most situations; they are motivated by the leverage effect on profits due to trading on equity; they may choose debt financing in preference to equity financing to avoid the risk of a change in managerial control; and in some cases, business firms may be able to borrow when they cannot obtain additional equity capital.

Business borrowing may be classified as short-term or long-term, secured or unsecured, and open-market or customer-loan. When giving a promise to pay a borrower pledges all of his debt-paying ability. Pledging assets does not alter the debt-paying ability of the borrower but it strengthens the position of the secured creditor and weakens that of the unsecured creditor. Other things being equal, weaker firms are required to pledge assets; therefore, banks' interest rates on secured loans tend to be higher than on unsecured loans. In open-market borrowing, funds are usually raised through intermediaries, while customer-loan borrowing involves negotiation between the borrower and lender.

QUESTIONS AND PROBLEMS

1. What is the common-law principle pertaining to business firms going into debt? Are business firms sometimes subjected to other restrictions which prevent their borrowing? Explain.
2. When corporations borrow, are forms required in addition to those used when sole proprietors borrow? Why?
3. Note the laws which have been passed to protect creditors. Are they of particular importance to businessmen? Why?

4. As a guide to borrowing policies, what is the significance of (*a*) earnings relative to debt charges and (*b*) amount of assets relative to debts?
5. Distinguish between money market and capital market.
6. Who are the chief borrowers in the (*a*) money market and (*b*) capital market?
7. What is meant by (*a*) an upsweeping yield curve and (*b*) a downsweeping yield curve?
8. Why do business firms find it advantageous to finance temporary needs by borrowing?
9. (*a*) Is it easier to borrow than to obtain additional funds from proprietors? (*b*) Is it cheaper in terms of costs of funds?
10. What are the disadvantages in the use of loan capital?
11. Distinguish between (*a*) short-term and long-term borrowing; (*b*) secured and unsecured loans; and (*c*) open-market and customer-loan borrowing.
12. What corporate policy is indicated by "Corporate security offerings in 1960 rose by $500 million from the preceding year's volume of $9¾ billion. The increase was entirely attributable to a $1 billion rise in sales of notes and bonds, while equity financing, both through common and preferred stock issues, declined from $2.6 billion in 1959 to $2.1 billion in 1960." (First National Bank of Chicago, *Business and Economic Review* [February, 1961], p. 6.) Is it wise to increase debts during recessions?

CHAPTER 11

Financing with Trade Credit

THE VOLUME of short-term credit is one of the most striking financial aspects of modern business. Approximately 60 per cent of the total debt of business corporations in the United States has a maturity of one year or less. Businesses have always used credit to finance the acquisition of goods, equipment and other assets, but the use of short-term and intermediate credit has increased substantially in recent years. This increase is accounted for, in part at least, by fundamental changes in the American economy which have brought about an expansion in service and merchandising industries and an increase in the use of high-cost equipment and machinery.

The sources of short-term and intermediate credit include business firms—a source of trade credit; commercial banks—a source of working capital funds; factors and specialized finance companies; and the open market. The role of business firms as suppliers of trade credit is discussed in this chapter, and other sources of short and intermediate term credit are discussed in those which follow.

ACCOUNTS RECEIVABLE

The working capital assets of most business firms include receivables (whether in the form of notes, bills, or accounts receivable) which bear no interest. They make up approximately 15 per cent of the total assets of manufacturing firms, and these receivables become accounts payable to the firms receiving the credit. As such they constitute a source of financing.

In the wholesale trade area, most sales are made on open accounts with the seller keeping bookkeeping records and copies of customers' orders, sales invoices, and shipping papers. Although a seller may require a buyer to sign a note or bill of exchange, this practice is rare except for sales of durable goods of high value and sales to foreign customers. The volume of accounts receivable of a business firm will depend upon the firm's volume of credit sales, terms of sale, paying practices of customers, collection policies, and the selection and screening of customers as to credit worthiness. Credit extended by suppliers to their business firm customers is called mercantile credit, and credit extended by business firms to their retail customers is called retail or consumer credit.

GENERAL ASPECTS OF MERCANTILE CREDIT

Mercantile credit extended by one business firm to another is a result of normal business operations such as the sale of goods by a manufacturer to a wholesaler, department store, dealer, or retailer. Of wholesalers' and manufacturers' sales, about 90 per cent are made "on credit." Mercantile credit is an important aspect of working capital financing. In addition, working capital is needed to care for retail sales to consumers. Although retail credit is relatively less important than mercantile credit, about 33 per cent of retail sales are made on a credit basis. Actually, credit may be present in many cash transactions because cash payments are often made with funds borrowed from commercial banks, credit unions, industrial banks and loan companies, small loan or personal finance companies, finance companies, and other financial agencies operating in the consumer finance field.

The amount of mercantile debt a business firm has at any one time depends upon many factors including its credit position, the trade in which it operates, the time of the year, and perhaps the phase of the business cycle. At one extreme, there are companies that have such a weak credit position that they can only buy on prepayment terms; at the other extreme there are companies that are so strong financially that they have almost unlimited credit. In addition to prepayment terms, there are "cash" terms and special credit terms applicable to individual orders, "lumped" orders, installment sales, and sales on consignment.

Prepayment Terms. Prepayment terms may call for (1) cash before delivery, (2) cash on delivery, or (3) sight drafts with a bill of lading attached which is surrendered on payment of the draft. Prepayment terms are standard practice in some lines, such as in the sale of automobiles and trucks by manufacturers to dealers with the use of sight drafts. Sometimes the prepayment terms are combined with others; for illustration, canners of fruits and vegetables most frequently use sight drafts with bills of lading attached and/or terms of 1½ per cent, 10 days, net 30 days (if paid within 10 days, the buyer may deduct 1½ per cent from the bill; otherwise the gross amount is due in 30 days) for large established accounts. (Some Florida canners offer an option of 2 per cent discount on sight drafts, or 1½ per cent, 10 days, net 30 days.)

In some cases, the use of prepayment terms may indicate an unsatisfactory credit condition. For illustration, the buyer may be a new firm whose credit has not been established or an old firm with a poor payment record. Also, prepayment terms may indicate some unusual reason for not wanting to give regular credit terms: perhaps the firm has filed a petition for reorganization or is being operated by a trustee or receiver. When prepayment is demanded before delivery of title to goods, the buyer will need cash; this may necessitate borrowing from individuals, finance or discount companies, or commercial banks.

Cash Terms. In the mercantile credit field, "cash terms" means that payment is to be made after receipt of the invoice for the goods —usually within ten days—to allow time for the buyer to examine the goods and to remit by check or draft. Actually, credit is present in so-called "cash" term sales. Sometimes the buyer may not remit promptly and what was assumed to have been a "cash" sale may become a sale "on credit." Usually, sales terms are a combination of cash and credit terms with the option left with the buyer. The following terms are fairly typical of those offered by various manufacturers: hardware and tools—2 per cent, 10 days, net 30 days; confectionary—2 per cent, 15 days, net 30 days; women's coats and suits—8 per cent, 10 days, net EOM (end of the month, usually considered the 25th but in some instances the 20th); curtains, draperies, and bedspreads—(to retailers) 2 per cent or 3 per cent, 10 days, EOM or net 70 days and (to jobbers) 2 per cent, 10 days, 30 or 60 days extra.

Credit Terms. There is no uniformity in credit terms quoted by business firms and the maturity of sales credit may vary from a few days to several months from the invoice date. Sometimes, the maturity of credit is related directly to the inventory turnover of the buyer; for illustration, meat is usually sold on one-week credit terms and beer on 15- or 20-day terms. However, maturity terms tend to be uniform throughout a given region within an industry and they may be influenced by state regulatory agencies (for illustration, beer may be sold only for cash delivery in some states, while in other states distributors are allowed 90 to 120 days for payment). When buyers are given credit terms that permit them to sell the goods purchased before the due date, it enables them to make remittances from cash sales and their working capital needs to finance inventories are lessened. However, the credit terms may permit the amount of the invoice to be discounted if payment is made within a specified period (2 per cent, 10 days, net 30 days, as the case may be). To offset the disadvantage to some buyers caused by geographical location, the time allowed for taking discounts may date from receipt or arrival of the goods rather than from the date of the invoice. A buyer who does not have cash usually finds it advantageous to borrow from his bank in order to save the difference between the interest charged by the bank and the amount of the cash discount. For illustration, a cash discount of 2 per cent on a purchase of $10,000 amounts to $200, while the 6 per cent interest on a bank loan for the same amount for 20 days would be only $33.33. When credit terms are 1 per cent, 10 days, net 30 days, the discount is equivalent to 18 per cent per annum. Generally, the shorter the net period the more profitable it is to take the discount even if it is necessary to borrow in order to do so.

In trades where buyers order several times per month, sellers may "lump" orders and allow credit terms which specify that the buyer will be billed for all purchases made during a given period on a certain date (for illustration, beginning, middle, or end of the month, or some specified date in the following month). In such cases, the credit period and provisions for cash discount will start from the specified date, called the billing date.

In order to encourage purchases of seasonal goods ahead of the normal period, manufacturers may arrange to make delivery and to date invoices according to what would be the normal delivery date. Seasonal dating terms are important in industries which have a high degree of seasonality in sales (for illustration, sporting goods, antifreeze, fuel oil, bicycles, heating and cooling equipment, and so on). Often, longer credit terms are granted when a new product is being promoted. Seasonal or promotional terms are helpful to both the seller and the buyer; they permit the former to provide for year-around production and minimum warehousing and provide the latter with inventories on credit or generous discounts if cash purchases are made. If further discounts are permitted when payments are made before the end of a long discount period or when cash payments are made and cash discounts are not standard terms, they are referred to as "anticipation" discounts.

When an account becomes delinquent, the normal practice is for the creditor to limit credit sales rather than to stop such sales. If the buyer is in a "tight spot" which seems to be temporary, no action may be taken by the trade creditor; but if the delinquency is prolonged, either the debtor may be asked to sign promissory notes when sales are made, or all future sales may be made on a prepayment basis until the delinquency is removed.

Consignment Terms. A manufacturer or wholesaler may ship goods on consignment, in which case the recipient or consignee sells the goods for the benefit of the consigner or owner. Since the consignee does not buy the goods, the cost of financing is borne by the consigner. In order to prevent the transaction from being interpreted as a conditional sale, the consigned merchandise must be clearly marked as the property of the consigner and/or kept apart from other merchandise in possession of the consignee. The proceeds from the sale of the consigned goods must be segregated from other funds of the consignee and remitted to the consigner according to prior agreement, minus commissions and other charges.

Cash-Discount System. The cash-discount system originated during the Civil War and reconstruction period when wholesale merchants were reluctant to sell on credit for fear of depreciation in the value of money. (From 1862 to 1879, the United States had a paper money standard, the United States note or "greenback" being the standard monetary unit.) Prior to the Civil War, promissory notes and trade acceptances were the basic credit instruments used in mercantile credit. During the "greenback" period buyers were often given the option of either signing a promissory note or trade acceptance, or paying cash less a discount—sometimes as much as 8 per cent. The latter was so attractive that the cash discount system gradually became standard practice and the promissory note and trade acceptance fell into general disuse. Following the greenback era, the open-book cash-discount system which had become deeply ingrained in American business finance persisted.

Improvements in transportation and communication facilities now permit rapid replacement of goods and make it unnecessary for buyers in most lines of trade to place orders for a six-months' or year's supply. Inasmuch as terms may be linked to the time required to move goods from the manufacturer or wholesaler through the retailer's firm into the hands of consumers, the need for long terms is declining; gradually the cash discount is being reduced and the time for which credit is extended is being shortened.

In the opinion of many, the cash discount has become a cumbersome method of adjusting prices downward. Some buyers regard the cash discount as a rebate for overpriced goods (an opinion supported by the fact that prices of goods are usually lowered when sellers eliminate discount terms in quoting sales terms). Abolition of the cash-discount system is also supported by the arguments that it would simplify bookkeeping and prevent disputes over taking unearned discounts.

Cash discounts, when computed on an annual basis, commonly amount to 24 or 36 per cent. This is far out of line with interest rates charged by banks and other financial institutions. But a seller may consider a cash discount as something more than just interest; if, as is contended, cash discounts have the effect of stimulating sales and expediting collections, they may be justified. Actually, if provisions for cash discounts result in higher prices, a buyer who pays cash is entitled to a discount. Logically, the burden of financing should fall on the one in possession of the goods.

Use of Promissory Notes. The current emphasis on recording credit extended by an entry on the seller's books (accounts receivable) and recording the indebtedness by an entry on the buyer's ledger (accounts payable) does not mean that the older credit instruments, promissory notes and trade acceptances, have entirely disappeared from the mercantile credit field. Promissory notes are still used in a few fields including wholesale jewelers (retailers are expected to settle bills in January and July), milling companies (selling flour to bakeries), dealers in raw and dressed furs, paper manufacturers (selling to publishers and printers), seed growers, and manufacturers of different types of equipment that are to be sold on the installment plan. Sales terms may vary among customers (for illustration, manufacturers' offers of fur garments to smaller retailers for preseason sales are usually made on a 4-month note basis, otherwise on net-60-day terms, and sales to department stores and large retailers are made on net 10 days, EOM terms—payable 10 days after the end of the month). The development of sources of credit information and improvements in collection techniques have permitted an increase in the length of the credit period, but improvements in transportation and communication have made possible more rapid turnovers of inventories, thus reducing the need for long mercantile credit terms.

Selling on the installment plan is not new—for example, manufacturers of agricultural machinery have used this method of selling to dealers for over a hundred years. However, the growth in the volume of producers' goods (machinery, equipment, and tools) used by manufacturers, farmers, and others necessitated expansion in installment sales; this expansion has been accompanied and facilitated by the development of specialized financial institutions. Usually, payment for producers' goods is arranged for on the installment plan, with the buyer signing a chattel mortgage note and/or a conditional-sales contract, and an installment note.[1]

Use of Sight Drafts and Acceptances. In some transactions, the seller attaches a commercial invoice, bill of lading, insurance certificate, and other papers to a trade draft or bill of exchange drawn by the seller on the buyer.[2] The terms of sale may call for payment or acceptance (endorsement on the face) of the bill of exchange before title to the goods is given to the buyer. If immediate payment is required, the buyer must finance the transaction with cash on hand or with funds borrowed from banks or other lenders before he obtains title to the goods (as evidenced by the bill of lading or warehouse receipt if the goods have been placed in storage). This is the customary procedure when manufacturers sell automobiles to dealers. In order to assure dealers a source of funds, automobile manufacturers took a leading role in organizing automobile finance companies (the three largest being the General Motors Acceptance Corporation, Commercial Credit Company and C.I.T. Financial Corporation). Being among the newer industries and selling a high-priced product, the automobile industry developed procedures that are among the soundest of all methods of financing trade credit (both wholesale and retail) by placing the financing burden on the one having possession of the goods being financed.

If trade drafts or bills of exchange are used, sight terms may be used (such as "30 days after sight"). In this case, after the buyer accepts the draft (for illustration, "accepted January 1, 1955, John Smith") he, the acceptor, is primarily liable for its payment when

---

[1] A chattel mortgage note is one secured by a chattel mortgage executed by the maker on specific personal property owned by him. An installment note is one in which the principal is payable in specific installments at specific times until the note is paid. Interest payments along with principal payments may or may not be required.

[2] Section 126 of the Negotiable Instruments Act defines a bill of exchange as follows: "A bill of exchange is an unconditional order in writing addressed by one person to another, signed by the person giving it, requiring the person to whom it is addressed to pay on demand or at a fixed or determinable future time a sum certain in money to order or to bearer."

it matures 30 days later. The trade draft has then become a trade acceptance. A trade acceptance is a bill of exchange drawn by the seller of goods on the buyer of such goods and accepted by the buyer. The seller may endorse the trade acceptance which has been returned to him and discount it at his bank or with an acceptance dealer. The bank or acceptance dealer may, in turn, endorse the bill and sell it in the bill market or to a Federal Reserve bank.

Trade acceptances are widely used in the export trade of the United States because of extra hazards, distance, time, custom, and other reasons. In domestic trade, trade acceptances have sometimes been used to collect past due open-book accounts. When requested to do so, the obligor may sign a trade acceptance which gives him an extension of credit but commits him to making payment on a definite date. (He may feel that he has nothing to lose because the account is already past due.) If the debtor places orders for additional goods, shipment may be made subject to acceptance or payment terms before transfer of title to the goods. In other cases, a slow-paying customer may be requested to sign a promissory note. In certain lines, when there is a departure from the customary method of selling on open-book accounts to acceptance terms, it may indicate a deterioration in the quality of the customer's receivables.

Other Forms of Business Credit. The sale of goods on credit is but one of several forms of credit extended by business firms to other business firms. In recent years, retailers and firms in the service and other industries have obtained cash funds and goods under lease arrangements. Suppliers sometimes provide small companies with cash at nominal interest rates or without interest costs; in some cases, large firms guarantee the credit of smaller firms, thereby making it possible for the latter to obtain funds at lower rates than they would otherwise have to pay. This arrangement benefits the supplier, who is assured an outlet for his products, and the creditor, who is assured an adequate supply of working capital.

SOURCES OF MERCANTILE CREDIT INFORMATION

The growth in the volume of mercantile credit has been accompanied by an increase in emphasis on the credit and collection work of business firms. All prospective customers are subject to some screening before being granted credit. Trade suppliers of credit base their decisions as to customers' credit worthiness on the records of the would-be creditors and on information supplied by customers themselves, mercantile agencies, and other suppliers of the prospective credit customers. The credit officer must determine the soundness of the financial structure of the prospective creditor firm, its payment practices, and its general credit worthiness. The most valuable source of information about an old customer may be the supplier's own salesmen, ledger records of the firm's purchases and payments, and the credit officer's judgment of the customer based on personal contacts, interviews, and other information. Some business firms use rule-of-thumb formulas to determine the amount of credit that will be made available to clients (such as a percentage of the customer's credit limit with other suppliers), but most firms base their decisions on their own credit appraisal of the particular customer. Usually, the amount of credit advanced will be determined by the needs and credit worthiness of each customer.

Customers. A customer desiring credit should be willing to supply the seller with financial statements—balance sheets and operating or profit and loss statements—and it is standard practice for well-organized business firms to prepare financial statements and to distribute them to those who are interested in the firm. Since the organization of the Securities and Exchange Commission in 1934, a great deal of progress has been made in standardizing accounting procedures; consequently, financial statements have become a more meaningful source of credit information. Making a false financial statement to obtain credit is punishable under both federal and state criminal law; thus the major problem of analyzing financial statements is usually that of appraising the quality of financial reports.

The financial statement which a supplier obtains from a customer may require supplementary information on certain items because the statement may be too brief, out-of-date, or inadequate in other respects. Printed financial statements are usually dated as of the end of a company's financial year and may not be representative of the current situation; therefore, credit officers obtain this supplementary information by personal interviews or direct correspondence. Some business firms supply their mercantile customers with financial-statement forms that are a combination of the balance sheet and profit and loss statement. Among the advantages of requesting information by mail on standard forms is that it gives the firm an opportunity to thank the customer for past patronage, or for his order or inquiry; and, at the same time, the request for financial information on an enclosed form may be explained as being the practice of the company or the trade.

If a customer has no printed financial statements, the supplier may be rendering him a real service by sending a standard form to be completed. Of course, forms may or may not be filled in or returned; and if they are returned, it may be necessary to request additional information about individual items. Suppliers may delay shipment of goods ordered until receipt of financial information requested. Today, established business firms are accustomed to receiving such requests from banks and their suppliers; and, if and when a customer is un-co-operative in giving information, it is usually interpreted as being a sign that he has something to hide. If an order given by such a customer is filled, it will usually be on a prepayment or cash basis. In other instances, only part of the order may be filled and the supplier will use the customer's ledger record as a guide to future sales and credit relations. Customarily, information supplied by customers is supplemented by information obtained from other sources. Inasmuch as most modern business is done on credit, buyers ought to be interested in making a good impression on their suppliers and other creditors; however a buyer may be reluctant to give information for fear that competitors and others will receive confidential information and use it to his disadvantage.

Mercantile Credit Agencies. Among the most widely used sources of credit information are the reports of mercantile credit agencies—organizations that specialize in gathering and supplying information concerning the credit, reputation, and financial standing of individuals and firms engaged in business. The information gathered by them is confidential and is so treated. Court decisions have held that credit reports furnished by an agency, like responses to a credit inquiry by one person to another, are "privileged communications" and that this defense may be used in legal action for libel. Court decisions, by reducing the likelihood of libel suits, have facilitated the development of mercantile credit agencies and the dissemination of credit information.

There are two types of mercantile agencies: general and specialized. A general mercantile agency reports on active commercial and industrial enterprises in all lines, while specialized agencies restrict their activities in one manner or another. Dun & Bradstreet, Inc., is of the general type and among the specialists are Lumberman's Credit Association, Inc., Produce Reporter Company, Jewelers Board of Trade, Lyons Furniture Mercantile Agency, and the National Credit Office, Inc.[3]

---

[3] A description of mercantile credit agencies may be found in H. V. Prochow and R. A. Foulke, *Practical Bank Credit* (2nd ed.; New York: Prentice-Hall, Inc., 1950), pp. 69–159, and in standard textbooks on credit and collection.

The services offered to subscribers by Dun & Bradstreet, Inc., include its *Reference Book,* which is issued six times a year and which contains the names of almost 3,000,000 commercial and industrial enterprises in the United States and Canada. Each firm is classified as to products and functions and is given a composite rating as "high," "good," "fair," or "limited." The composite credit appraisal is based on the degree to which the business firm meets eight conditions.[4] The *Reference Book* also contains an estimate of the financial strength of each business firm, which is usually measured by the firm's tangible net worth. Listings are classified by states and then broken down under cities, towns, and villages. Dun & Bradstreet, Inc., also prepares commercial credit reports on all enterprises listed in the *Reference Book* and sends these reports to subscribers on request. General credit reports are classified as "analytical," "specialized," and "synopsis."

Analytical reports cover the larger enterprises under these captions: personnel, history, method of operation, subsidiaries (when applicable), financial statements, trade investigation, and banking relations. The specialized reports cover the smaller and less complicated enterprises under the general headings of history, method of operation, financial information, and payments. The synopsis reports cover the smallest firms in the retail field, which comprise the majority of those rated in the *Reference Book.* The feature section in the synopsis report contains a brief analysis of the firm—its age, size, location, financial condition, paying habits, and condition and trend. Special reports are prepared on particular topics on a cost-plus basis at the request of subscribers, and other reports are prepared on customers whose orders are large or of an unusual nature.

In addition to Dun & Bradstreet, Inc., there are over one hundred other mercantile agencies in the United States. Some of these limit their activities to providing credit information on customers in particular lines of business or in certain territories.[5] Others provide

---

[4] The composite credit appraisal is an appraisal of (1) soundness of legal structure, (2) age of the firm, (3) capacity and experience of management, (4) presence or absence of criticized fires or failures, (5) willingness to submit financial statements, (6) soundness of financial position, (7) financial and business trends of the firm, and (8) the payment record of the firm.

[5] In the textile and apparel industry, mercantile agencies include National Credit Office, Inc.; Woods Service, Inc. (an affiliate of NCO); Credit Clearing Division of Dun & Bradstreet, Inc., which publishes the *Apparel Trades Book;* Credit Exchange, Inc.; Women's Apparel Board of Trade; Consolidated Credit Investigations; and other smaller agencies, many of which are located in New York City, the center of the clothing industry. In other fields, special credit agencies include the Lyon Furniture Mercantile Agency, which publishes the *Red Book* and *Weekly Supplement,* and the Jewelers Board of Trade, which publishes a *Rating Book* and a weekly *Service Bulletin* and issues Green

only special types of credit information (litigation lists and lists of individual inquiry agencies).[6] Services of specialized mercantile agencies are used to supplement those of general mercantile agencies. Some of the specialized credit agencies are subsidiaries of the more general agencies and others are independent.

Other Suppliers. Out of bitter experiences, suppliers have learned that they have a choice of co-operating with one another in exchanging credit information or suffering losses individually. By exchanging information about customers, suppliers prevent unscrupulous businessmen from operating indefinitely at their expense. By obtaining information from other suppliers about normal credit needs, lines of credit, paying habits, terms of sale, past-due accounts, and methods of payment, a credit man may reach an intelligent decision as to an order placed by a prospective customer. This information may be assembled by a local credit bureau or the credit department of a trade association, or may be obtained directly from other suppliers of the business firm.

When placing an order, the customer is usually asked for three or four business references. While these hand-picked names may be contacted, a credit manager usually contacts others who would logically be suppliers because of location or the nature of their product. In answering inquiries, others in the trade may give helpful leads. Inquiries may be made in writing, by telephone, or in person. In case of doubtful accounts, a direct exchange of information is particularly valuable. Group interchange of credit information has the advantages of economy and completeness because it eliminates duplication of effort and encompasses a larger number of sources of information. Information obtained from agencies may be less current than that obtained directly; therefore, both procedures may be followed. If the supplier is still uncertain, he may arrange for a special report from one or more agencies (credit bureau, trade association, and other reports on delinquent accounts will be of special interest).

The National Association of Credit Men supervises a national system of interchange of ledger information for sellers in the con-

---

Slips on individual customers and various developments. There are hundreds of trade associations that supply their members with credit information—see U.S. Department of Commerce, *National Associations of the United States* (Washington, D.C., 1949).

[6] The Credit Bureau of Greater New York publishes the *Daily Litigation Bulletin* which lists the commercial lawsuits in all industries in the metropolitan area. This service is strictly confidential and for the direct use of subscribers only. Among the individual inquiry agencies listed are the Retail Credit Company of Atlanta, Georgia, and its numerous branch offices, Bishop's Service, Inc.; Hooper-Holmes Bureau; O'Hanlon Reports; and Proudfoot's Commercial Agency, Inc.

tinental United States. It operates through 54 credit interchange bureaus, and a co-ordinating office, the Central Credit Interchange Bureau in St. Louis. The National Association of Credit Men also operates a foreign credit interchange bureau, a fraud prevention department, and the Washington service bureau; it sponsors several publications, a credit research foundation, and annual conventions.

Banks and Other Sources. When a supplier asks a new customer for the name of his bank, the supplier may then contact that bank for information as to the length of time the account has been therein, line of credit, payment habits, defaults, returned checks (because of insufficient funds), and general opinion as to the customer's character, capacity, and capital. Banks usually make trade inquiries about their borrower-customers from time to time; and so they feel obliged to answer suppliers' questions about their customers. But banks do not freely disclose detailed financial information about their customers; hence the information received from them may be fragmentary and vague. A large supplier may obtain more specific information indirectly through his own bank because banks do exchange detailed financial information. However, suppliers can only expect such service in rare cases where a large amount of credit is involved and then only a few times a year. For more detailed reports, suppliers may use the services of agencies, attorneys, or accountants.[7]

In addition to the preceding sources of credit information, there are many others such as legal records (county clerks' files and court records), investment services (Moody's Investment Service, Standard & Poor's Corporation, Fitch, H. H. Copeland & Son, and Institutional Utility Service), trade magazines, government publications, and newspapers.

FACTORS IN THE CREDIT DECISION

When an order is submitted for approval to the credit department of a business firm, the credit manager is usually inclined to approve it because the credit department is expected to operate in such a manner as to increase the profits of the firm. The credit manager does not determine credit policies but merely carries them out. The actual

[7] In order to locate an attorney from whom a credit report of an out-of-town customer may be obtained, a credit manager may consult an "attorney list" published by the Commercial Law League of America (Chicago), American Lawyers' Quarterly (Cleveland), the Commercial Bar (New York), the Columbia List (New York), etc.

The American Institute of Accountants' rules covering professional conduct require that the prior consent of the accountant's client must be obtained before the accountant makes information available to a third party regarding items other than those covered in reports and statements prepared by the member (see Rule 16).

credit policies of a business firm are correlated with its buying and other policies. Because refusal to grant credit could curtail or eliminate profits, a business firm's credit department will try to make arrangements whereby sales may be made in whole or part with a minimum of risk. Among the factors that influence a credit manager's decisions are his firm's profit margin on sales and the demand for its products, the credit position of the customer, general business conditions, and the possibility of working out special credit arrangements with submarginal customers.

Profit Margin. The first factor to note in all credit decisions is that some concerns or individuals may assume risks that others can not or ought not assume. While a loss of $10,000 may seem unimportant to a large firm, it may cause insolvency in a small one. Where risks are large anticipated profits should be large so that losses on one sale can be offset by profits on others. The general rule is the greater the profit margin on sales, the greater the risks that suppliers may take. This rule helps to explain the fact that it is easier to obtain trade credit than bank credit.

Demand for Product. When the market demand for the supplier's product is in excess of his production capacity, the supplier may be more selective in choosing customers. In accepting customers, factors in addition to the customer's credit standing may be considered. If the scarcity of the seller's product is due to some temporary cause (as illustrated by civilian-goods shortages during World War II), the seller may prorate available goods among old customers. On the other hand, if he is selling in a highly competitive market, he may sell to firms with poor credit ratings rather than risk losses due to idle plants, partially employed resources, and excessive inventories. In some instances, an expansion of credit sales makes it possible to hold together the labor force and staff and thereby to avoid the costs associated with recruiting and training personnel in the future. Therefore, the credit analysis verdict may be disregarded if the outlet is badly needed for sales purposes.

Credit Position of the Buyer. While the business position of the supplier is a factor in sales terms, the credit position of the customer is equally important. Credit men customarily refer to credit risks in terms of the three C's of credit: character, capacity, and capital.

Character refers to the willingness of a buyer to meet his obligations, and while the moral status of a business firm is difficult to measure, its record of fulfilling promises and the absence of fraud are important indices. But the past record may mean less than expected because management changes over a period of time and current management determines policies. In checking management of a business firm, the emphasis is on personnel. Certain things may suggest a lack of character in an individual—for illustration, involvement in fraud or actions that may have been fraudulent, indulgence in speculation, addiction to liquor, taking unearned discounts, and paying trade debts only after pressure has been applied. On the other hand, there are indicators of better than average moral risk such as length of time on a job and/or residence in one place, church and civic affiliations, and general reputation in the community.

The capacity of a business firm is reflected in its age and record, with old established firms enjoying a better credit rating than new ones. Comparative analysis of financial statements will indicate the current position of a business firm and the direction in which the business is moving. Usually, a business firm that is growing is a better credit risk than one that is declining, even though the financial analysis suggests that the second is in a better financial position than the first. However it is fairly easy for a small, rapidly growing concern to get into an overextended position. While its current ratio may be satisfactory, it may be short of cash. A firm's debt-paying ability is suggested by the current ratio, quick asset ratio, and cash as a percentage of total current assets. Financial statements will reflect the quality of a business firm's assets and the extent of its ability to meet current obligations, as well as the policies, foresight, and aggressiveness of its management.

When a business firm's ratios are constructed and compared to those of similar companies in the same field, they provide a measure of the company's efficiency. Three ratios in wide use are the current ratio, the inventory turnover ratio, and the ratio of receivables to net sales. There are at least twenty other ratios, many of which are more applicable to investment analysis than to credit analysis (such as net profits to sales, net profits to net worth, sales to net worth, and excess of net worth and funded debt over fixed and other assets).

Lines of credit with banks do not show on business firms' balance sheets, but they may be more significant than a high "current" or "quick" asset ratio. Presumably, assets in the form of accounts receivable will, when collected, provide cash to pay suppliers; but, if this cash is used to meet payrolls and to replace inventories, little cash may be available to meet trade obligations unless the volume of operations is reduced. If a firm's inventories represent an excessive portion of current assets, a high current ratio such as 4 to 1 or 5 to 1 may indicate less ability to meet current obligations than a second firm's current ratio of 1.5 to 1 if its current assets are made up largely of cash. Unless properly interpreted and carefully analyzed, credit ratios may have little meaning.

RETAIL CREDIT

Retail credit, which is credit extended by retailers to individual consumers, is usually treated separately from mercantile credit; however both require working capital which may be supplied by the same lenders. The problem of financing credit sales to customers is less serious to retailers than to suppliers and manufacturers because retailers have achieved a predominance of sales on a truly cash basis not achieved by mercantile firms. Except where sales of durable consumer goods predominate, retail cash sales are more important than credit sales. Per dollar of credit granted, retail credit is more expensive to administer than mercantile credit because (among other things) individual accounts are smaller. When retail credit is given, it may be on the basis of "end of the month" terms for billing, budget plans entailing three or more monthly payments, or installment contracts including installment notes.

Some retailers operate exclusively on a cash basis (for example, most chain stores in practically every line of trade). Some department stores sell not only for cash but also on charge accounts and installment plans. Service industries such as electric light and gas, telephone, and water companies, usually sell on an end of the month billing arrangement (sometimes with discounts for prompt payment). Although transportation companies are issuing credit cards to select customers, most of these services are supplied on a cash basis.

The relatively high cost of financing retail credit sales is due more to bookkeeping and collection costs than to losses incurred because of uncollectible accounts. Department stores and others justify open-book account credit on the basis of increasing sales. When firms sell durable consumer goods on the installment plan, it may be possible for them to shift part of the overhead (insurance and interest costs) to consumers in the form of service charges. The financing of receivables by retailers necessitates an increase in working capital which may be supplied by proprietors or by funds borrowed from banks, finance companies, or others.

SUMMARY

The increase in volume of short-term debt relative to long-term debt is due in part to the increased importance of the service and merchandising industries and a greater use of equipment and machinery in all industries. The sources of working capital assets include business firms, finance companies, factors, open-market lenders, and banks. Mercantile credit is an important aspect of working capital financing because about 90 per cent of wholesalers' and manufacturers' sales are made on credit. Mercantile credit terms include prepayment, cash, individual order, installment, and consignment terms. Although prepayment terms are standard practice in some lines, in others the use of prepayment terms may indicate an unsatisfactory credit situation.

Distributers and retailers are usually small firms and are the chief beneficiaries of trade credit. When they obtain assets on credit, funds are released to be used in other ways. Buyers may be able to convert goods into cash before the end of the credit period and thus operate on the proverbial shoestring. Even if the credit terms are shorter than the average turnover period, a smaller amount of capital is required for the operation of the business. The practice of future dating and giving promotional credit is increasing and this means that inventory financing by other firms is becoming more important. Many small firms, having established contacts with suppliers, are assured supplies in the event of temporary adversity.

When credit terms include a credit period of a given number of days from the invoice date, the buyer may be given an option of discounting the invoice price and remitting cash within a definite period of time or waiting until the end of the credit period and paying the invoice price (for illustration, 2 per cent, 10 days, net 30 days). The cash-discount system which originated during the Civil War gradually replaced the older trade-acceptance and promissory-note systems which had been standard practice. However, trade and bankers' acceptances are used currently in certain fields. When manufacturers sell automobiles to dealers the terms of sale customarily require payment of the bill of exchange before title to the cars is given the buyer. Trade and bankers' acceptances are also used widely in foreign trade.

The sources of mercantile credit information include customers, mercantile credit agencies, suppliers, banks, and others. The factors in credit-granting decisions include the supplier's profit margin and the demand for his product in addition to the more obvious one—the credit position of the buyer. In the mercantile credit field, business firms' accounts are rated for credit purposes on the basis of the customer's character, capacity, and capital. In addition, there are factors such as general and anticipated business conditions that will influence the terms on which credit is granted.

Although credit sales by retailers to consumers is not mercantile credit, such sales enlarge the demand for funds to finance working capital assets. Additional working capital assets are required to finance sales to business firms and consumers when buying is on credit terms; these funds may be supplied by proprietors or by lenders such as banks, finance companies, and others.

QUESTIONS AND PROBLEMS

1. Identify: (*a*) mercantile credit, and (*b*) retail credit.
2. Distinguish among the following mercantile credit terms: (*a*) prepayment; (*b*) cash; and (*c*) credit.
3. Analyze the cash-discount system. How is it linked to the volume of bank credit?
4. A manufacturer's credit to his customers may be evidenced by one or more of the three forms of "receivables." Identify each.
5. What are the most important sources of mercantile credit information?
6. Distinguish between a general and a specialized mercantile credit agency.
7. Explain how the following may be factors in making a credit decision: (*a*) profit margin, and (*b*) demand for product.
8. Show why the "three C's of credit" must be present in most credit transactions.
9. "Per dollar of credit granted, retail credit is more expensive to administer than mercantile credit." Why?
10. Is "window dressing" evident in the financial statement which follows? Does this mean that ratio analysis is unimportant? Why?

FINANCIAL STATEMENT OF FIRM X

	March 30	*Statement Day March 31*
Current Assets:		
Cash	$320,000	$ 20,000
Accounts receivable	150,000	150,000
Inventory	230,000	230,000
Total	$700,000	$400,000
Current Liabilities:		
Accounts payable	$150,000	$150,000
Notes payable	300,000	....
Total	$450,000	$150,000
Current ratio	1.56 to 1	2.67 to 1
Net Working Capital	$250,000	$250,000

11. The president of Standard Oil Company of New Jersey, Mr. M. J. Rathbone, stated in his speech at the annual meeting of stockholders, "Your company enjoys a prime credit status. This is in itself a highly important asset and an element of reserve strength which is a valuable adjunct to our strong cash position." (Standard Oil Company of New Jersey, *1960 Annual Meeting*, p. 6.) Explain.
12. "The place to look for possible causes of collection difficulty is not in your collection setup but rather in your credit granting policies and procedures." (Small Business Administration, "Improving Collections from Credit Sales," *Small Marketers Aids*, No. 49 [October, 1959], p. 1.) What sources of credit information may be used to avoid assuming potential collection problems?

CHAPTER 12

Commercial Banking Relations of Business Firms

BUSINESS FIRMS must have cash with which to operate and it is this need more than any other which explains why business firms establish and maintain financial relations with commercial banks. For the most part, business firms' cash receipts from receivables, sales, and other sources are deposited with banks before they are disbursed. Although a firm may keep some currency on hand as till money for making change and for minor disbursements, most of a business firm's payments are made with checks drawn on its bank account. In addition to maintaining checking accounts, business firms borrow from their commercial banks and use the other services offered by them. These services are so varied as to justify using the title "department store of finance" in referring to a commercial bank. This chapter deals with how business firms care for their cash needs, select their banks, and use the lending and other services offered by their banks.

CASH ASSET POLICIES

The cash items found on the balance sheet of a business firm include cash on hand and demand deposits and time deposits in banks. Although it would be more accurate to exclude time deposits, it is not unusual for all cash and near cash items to be included on the balance sheet under the caption "total cash and United States government securities." When assets that are not freely available for withdrawal to meet ordinary current obligations are included, the effect is to overstate the liquid position of the business firm.

Analyses of the demand deposit accounts of business firms reveal that the amounts reported as cash are exaggerated because some checks and other credit items that have been deposited have not been collected. In order to simplify bookkeeping procedures, banks customarily give immediate credit for all cash items with the understanding that depositors' balances will be sufficiently large to cover the "float."

Each checking account in a bank, whether that of an individual or a business firm, is analyzed to see that costs are covered because commercial banks must be compensated for expenses incurred in handling accounts. In addition to expenses incurred in making payments on checks written by business firms and others and those collected by them, some checks may be dishonored because of improper signature, insufficient funds, and other irregularities; the average cost of handling such items has been computed at 70.5 cents. After deducting for the foregoing costs plus the legal and other cash reserves [1] which the bank must keep against deposits, the usable amount of the deposit of the business firm is found. This amount is the base. for computing the earning credit assigned to the account. If the earning credit is insufficient to cover all costs, a service charge will be made. Therefore, many business firms follow a policy of keeping deposit accounts large enough to offset all service charges.

A business firm's day-to-day inflow of cash items deposited in its bank may be sufficient to offset the outflow from its deposit account; however, this is seldom the case because credit terms include end-of-the-month billing and cash discounts for payments within ten days (or within some other specified time limit). As a result of such credit terms, the cash outflow from accounts of most mercantile firms will be large during the first part of the month; meanwhile the cash inflow will be spread over the entire month. Hence, a business firm would need to accumulate large deposits during the month to meet the peak outflow during the first of the next month in order to avoid service charges.

Business firms may accumulate deposits in their bank accounts in preparation for meeting periodic payments of interest and dividends, state and federal income taxes, maturing notes and other

[1] See also, Country Bank Operations Commission and Bank Management Commission, *Current Trends in Bank Costs* (New York, American Bankers Association, 1949).

obligations, expansion of inventories and other assets, payrolls, and various other production and operational expenditures. Sometimes a business firm may keep its deposit balance in excess of its anticipated needs as a reserve to be used to meet unexpected developments, such as a decline in sales or production, or to take advantage of favorable opportunities for profit, such as acquiring assets at bargain prices, developing new products, and so on.

When business firms borrow from their commercial banks, one of the requisites for favorable credit terms is a satisfactory deposit account. In fixing interest rates on loans to commercial customers, banks are often influenced by the borrowers' average deposit balances—lowering or raising rates as deposit balances are high or low. Some commercial borrowers are required to keep a percentage of their lines of credit or loans on deposit at their banks. Such a compensatory balance has the effect of increasing the business firm's assets in the form of cash.

The managements of some business firms seem to lack any fixed policy in regard to cash; and, when a firm's cash balances are needlessly large, it may be due either to unusual profitability or to inertia on the part of management. However, the motive behind such a situation may be that of seeking prestige, displaying "wealth," desiring to become independent of banks for loan funds, or building up friendly relations with the bank. While such a policy of building up large cash balances may be required under certain circumstances and understandable under others, unused or idle balances are expensive in that they represent a loss of income. Such funds could be used in operations by some firms to earn as much as 15 or 20 per cent, or they could be invested in money market obligations which have the characteristics of safety, liquidity, and yield.

The treasurer of a business firm who is responsible for the cash position of the firm will find using a cash budget of value. On the basis of past experience, estimates may be made of expected cash receipts, outgo, and the cash balance remaining. When a business firm has established satisfactory relationships with its commercial bank, its problem of maintaining a satisfactory cash position will tend to be lessened because it will usually be able to obtain a bank loan before its cash position deteriorates seriously. To some extent, management may improve the firm's cash position by depositing checks promptly, centralizing deposit accounts, and taking advantage of cash discounts.

In most cases, business firms may anticipate their future needs for cash by holding near-cash items, that is, investments that are interest-bearing, short-term, and very liquid. These may include time deposit accounts at their banks and short-term government and commercial paper. In analyzing the liquidity of a business firm, its cash and near-cash assets are usually combined; but, over a period of time, the firm's holdings of cash and near cash assets will show considerable variation. When interest rates are high, more cash may be shifted to near cash items than when interest rates are low. In 1960, 5.6 per cent of the total assets of manufacturing firms were in the form of cash and 10.6 per cent in the form of cash and near cash; and, of these firms' current assets, between 11 and 12 per cent were in cash and over 20 per cent in cash and near cash assets.

SELECTION OF A BANK

The commercial banking system of the United States, being one of extremes, includes some of the largest private banks in the world and over 11,000 small banks with average resources of less than $10 million. The organization of an American bank may be such as to include many departments, each providing specialized services—checking, saving, loan, investment, trust, foreign exchange, and safe-deposit facilities—or it may consist of a single department which handles all of the bank's activities. The area served may either be nation-wide or limited to a single neighborhood. One large bank may stress serving large corporations almost exclusively, while another large bank may specialize in serving depositors and making loans to consumers, homeowners, and small and large business firms.

Any modern business firm needs good banking connections, and despite the fact that there are more commercial banks in the United States than in any other country in the world, a business firm's choice of a bank is usually limited to one in the area in which the firm is located. When there are several banks in a community, a business firm's choice will be limited to those banks which would welcome the account. While banks are important service institutions, they retain the privilege of accepting or rejecting applicants as bank customers. A business firm's deposit account could be too small for a large bank to welcome or too large for a small bank to service adequately.

Usually all banks within a community have the same service charges such as per item charges on checking accounts, exchange and collection charges and fees for cashier's checks, bank drafts, and transfers of funds by mail or telegraph; therefore, the cost of deposit accounts and other charges related thereto is seldom a factor in a business firm's selection of a bank. Location, personal regard for directors and officers, lending policies, and special services offered may be the determining factors in the selection. The special services may include a business advisory service, night depository, payroll services, management of pension funds and other trust services, safekeeping facilities, investment and security transfer services, foreign finance services, and business and credit information services. In addition to collecting cash items for business firms, banks may also collect matured notes, bills, bond coupons, and other obligations.

Businessmen prefer to deal with bankers who "know what they are doing" as evidenced by statements of policy, printed rules covering collection practices, service charges, etc. They also expect fair treatment, and the use of printed standard loan forms and loan agreements gives the impression of standard and uniform policies.

A business firm may prefer a "name" bank, a bank that is a member of the Federal Reserve System rather than a nonmember bank, and an insured bank rather than an uninsured bank (one that is participating in the Federal Deposit Insurance Corporation insurance coverage rather than one that is not participating). A factor in attracting business firms as customers may be the size of the bank, because this may determine the number and quality of services available and the maximum amount that may be borrowed. For illustration, the maximum unsecured loan that a national bank may make to one concern is an amount equal to 10 per cent of its capital and unimpaired surplus.

The borrowers from banks include many business firms whose earnings are above average but who are not able to finance all of their expansion with retained earnings because a large percentage of their cash will be invested in fixed and current assets. Any rapidly growing business firm tends to be short of cash because its current assets are usually tied up in accounts receivable and in inventories; in addition, such firms must make withdrawals out of cash to meet tax payments.

The typical business firm that borrows from a commercial bank is a repeat borrower who comes back for credit each year. This means that once the business firm has established satisfactory banking relations, it will be assured a source of future funds if other things remain the same. Thus, in selecting a bank, a business concern should consider its future as well as its current needs.

The typical loan-customer of a bank is a relatively small, moderately young, and rapidly growing business firm, but loan customers of banks also include many large, well-established business corporations. Because it is unusual for a business firm to shift its account from bank to bank, the firm's initial selection of a bank is usually the beginning of a long-term relationship.

The typical business firm has but one bank account, but there are many large corporations whose scope of operations makes it necessary to use the services of many banks in all parts of the country. A local business firm, which needs credit in excess of the amount that its bank is permitted to lend to one name, may seek funds from a larger bank outside the community or from two or more banks within the area. While the "10-per-cent rule" prevents any national bank from making an unsecured loan to one borrower in excess of 10 per cent of the bank's capital and unimpaired surplus, there are exceptions when loans are secured by pledges of designated types of property. (Although the forms and amounts vary, state-chartered banks are usually subject to similar loan limits.)

A bank may try to keep up with its customers' loan demands by increasing its capital stock and surplus by selling new stock and/or by transferring amounts from the undivided profits account to surplus. However, the average loan demand seems to increase much faster than the loan limit; therefore banks are sharing or participating in loans to an increasing extent. When a loan is shared by two or more banks, it is necessary for the lenders to share their experiences concerning the borrower.

In selecting a bank, a business firm may consider its needs for services associated with deposits first and those associated with loans second. Since the 1930's, the financial officers of large corporations have become increasingly aware of the importance of dealing with sound banks; and, when the treasurer of such a corporation asks a banker for financial information concerning his bank in addition to that contained in its published financial statement, the request is no longer regarded as presumptuous or unnecessary.[2]

Deposits in banks participating in the Federal Deposit Insurance Corporation are insured up to $10,000; but, many corporations maintain deposit accounts far in excess of $10,000. Therefore the financial officer of the corporation ought to analyze the assets and earnings of a bank prior to depositing his company's funds therein.

[2] J. W. St. Clair, "Rating Ratio for Evaluating Bank Condition Statements," *Present Day Banking, 1953* (New York: American Bankers Association, 1953), pp. 387–403.

While banks are usually thought of as lenders, they are simultaneously debtors of depositors. In rating banks, corporations may check the different ratios of their banks against those found in the annual reports of Federal Deposit Insurance Corporation. Ratios, which are to be used as "norms," may be selected from those appearing for all insured banks, all insured commercial banks, national banks, state member banks, nonmember state banks, and banks grouped according to amounts of deposits ($500,000 or less, $500,000 to $1,000,000, and so on), insured commercial banks as reported by states, or two or more of the above. Other "norms" may be established from reports of the Federal Reserve System for central reserve city banks, reserve city banks, and country banks. The Comptroller of the Currency also publishes statistics of national banks which may be used in computing ratios for national banks.

The three most common ratios used to check banks' financial positions are (1) the "quick assets" ratio (cash and short-term government securities as a percentage of deposits or assets),[3] (2) the earnings ratio which may be expressed as a percentage of total capital accounts with a breakdown to show earnings per $100 of loans, securities, service charges, and so on; and (3) the ratio of net worth to total deposits or to total "risk" assets (all assets minus cash and short-term government securities).

Banks whose ratio ratings are higher than the average for banks in the same class may be selected more safely as depositories by a corporation. Usually, if a bank's assets are predominantly quick assets, it is a better credit risk than one wherein risk assets predominate. However, a bank may hold quick assets because of the presence of volatile deposits (bankers' balances, government deposits, and other large deposits subject to immediate withdrawal); thus the corporation's treasurer must know something about the bank's liabilities as well as its assets. When quick assets predominate, it may be that the bank management is ultraconservative or merely too inefficient to find a more profitable earning outlet for funds. Under such management the bank may lose earnings and become an unsafe depository; therefore the treasurer of the business concern may want to see the bank's profit and loss statement. Customarily, banks do not publish operating or profit and loss statements, but prospective de-

[3] Government bonds are included among the risk assets of banks because of the money market risk. Since the price of government bonds outstanding may decline sharply when interest rates increase, as during 1953 and part of 1954, they are excluded in computing a bank's quick asset ratio.

positors (if their accounts are important enough) may obtain such information directly from banks.[4]

In selecting depositories for their funds, large corporations must emphasize safety more than small firms because the $10,000 insurance coverage is usually sufficient to cover the accounts of small firms. In addition, small companies are more dependent on banks for loans than are large firms; therefore a small company may use the right of "offset" and apply its deposit to its bank loan (debts are used to offset debts). Other things being the same, if the net worth of a bank is smaller relative to its deposits or risk assets than that of the average bank in its class, it may be "trading on equity" to an excessive degree. Such a bank could improve its credit rating by selling more stock or by retaining more earnings. On the other hand, a bank with a favorable net worth–deposit ratio or net worth–risk assets ratio may be following policies which are so conservative as to repel business customers.

While many businessmen have no choice in selecting their banks because three fourths of all towns and cities in the United States are dependent upon the services furnished by one bank, they are in a position to influence the policies of their banks.[5] Usually, the owners of small business firms have little to gain by shopping around in other communities for bank connections; also, the disadvantages of banking outside one's community are so numerous and serious as to offset any possible advantage accruing from superior services offered by an out-of-town bank.

LINES OF CREDIT

Business firms, whose seasonal operations follow a fairly definite pattern, customarily arrange for lines of credit with their banks wherein the banks fix definite maximum limits up to which the firms may borrow. The line of credit may be for the fiscal year, six months, or to cover some given period of production. An application for a line of credit is not an application for a loan but simply an arrangement whereby the bank agrees to make such loans if and when funds are needed. Before passing upon the request for a line of credit, the banker will examine the balance sheet and operating statement of the applicant and may request additional informa-

---

4 For a form designed for this purpose, see J. W. St. Clair, *op. cit.*, pp. 395–97.

5 See Joint Committee on Economic Report, *Monetary Policy and the Management of the Public Debt*, Part 1 (Washington, D.C.: U.S. Government Printing Office, 1952), p. 571.

tion such as the budget of the firm for the coming year. In addition to analyzing this information, the bank will check with others doing business with the applicant (including suppliers and other banks).

If the applicant for a line of credit is an old customer of the bank, a check will be made of the firm's record, such as borrowing and repayment record, deposit balances maintained, record of returned checks and overdrafts, analysis of the checking account, and use of services of the bank not related to deposits and loans. The credit file will yield information obtained from personal inspections of the firm by a representative of the bank; from other banks; from trade and mercantile agency reports; and from information found in official records, newspapers, trade bulletins, and other miscellaneous sources. If the bank grants the line of credit, the borrower will sign promissory notes as funds are needed. The bank may recheck the credit position of the applicant when funds are requested; but, if the applicant's position has not deteriorated, the loan will be made as a matter of course. When a line of credit is granted, the bank is under obligation to meet its commitments.

A business which has a line of credit with its bank may be required to maintain a deposit balance which bears a specified relation to the amount of the line of credit. This so-called compensatory balance may vary from 10 to 20 per cent of the line of credit (or a similar percentage may be required when other types of loans are granted). The percentage required may vary with the money situation—a higher percentage may be required when money is "tight" than when it is "easy." Because a business firm may keep deposits in several banks, one effect of the compensatory balance rule may be that the bank which opens the line of credit expects to be favored over other banks as the firm's depository.

When the needs for funds of a business firm are irregular, the line-of-credit arrangement may be dispensed with; instead, the firm may make formal application for loans when funds are needed. Usually, such an application will be approved when the business firm is an old customer whose financial affairs are satisfactory, as shown by financial statements, or if acceptable security can be pledged. In negotiating the amount of a loan, the interest rate, maturity, presence or lack of security, and other terms, bankers are influenced by the average deposit balance which the business firm has maintained with the bank.

Even when not required to do so, business firms tend to maintain adequate deposit balances with banks. In determining the appropriate size of these balances, one "rule of thumb" is that one tenth of a business firm's current assets should be in the form of "cash on hand or in banks." If the line of credit is five times this balance, it would be about the same as total current liabilities of the business firm. For example, if total current assets equal $200,000, current liabilities $100,000, the line of credit $100,000, and the compensatory balance $20,000, the business firm would have a current asset ratio of 200 per cent, a cash to current assets ratio of 10 per cent, and would be keeping a 20 per cent compensatory balance against the line of credit. While this illustration may oversimplify the situation, it illustrates the fact that when granting a line of credit, a bank may require borrowers to do things that it would be advantageous for them to do even if no compensatory balance were involved.

The "application for loan" form usually filled out by applicants for loans contains spaces for the name of the borrower, date, business activity, bank balance, amount of loan, collateral or endorsers offered, amount already owed the bank, details as to the purpose of the loan, terms (demand, 60 days, etc.), renewal provisions if any, borrower's source and amount of income, and how the borrower expects to repay the loan. If the business firm is incorporated, the names of the officers must be given; if the firm is a partnership, the names of the partners and information as to how ownership is divided must be supplied. Loan applicants will be expected to file copies of recent financial statements and sometimes operating statements are requested. When financial statements are prepared by professional public accountants, their value is enhanced; and, to an increasing extent, such statements are expected of loan applicants.

Banks screen loan applications both formally and informally and the reason for rejecting them throws considerable light on what is expected of loan customers. In interviews conducted by the Federal Reserve System on small business financing, bankers' reasons for rejections included those involving the credit worthiness of applicants, banks' over-all loan policies, and federal and state banking rules and regulations. The lack of credit worthiness was by far the most frequent reason given for rejection of loan applications.[6]

When loan applications were rejected on the basis of lack of credit worthiness, the specific reasons included insufficient owner equity in the business, poor earning record, questionable managerial ability, inadequate or inferior collateral, record of slow and past

[6] Federal Reserve System, "Survey of Credit and Capital Sources," *Financing Small Business*, Vol. I, Part II, Survey III (1958), pp. 37–48.

due trade or loan payments, inadequate accounting system, lack of established earning record, and poor moral risk. It is logical to assume that in individual cases, two or more of these factors led to rejection of loan applications; for illustration, a specific firm may have insufficient equity capital, little or no collateral of satisfactory quality, an inadequate accounting system, and no earning record. Because banks must avoid becoming permanent investors in business firms, the lack of adequate equity capital would be a major reason for rejecting a loan applicant. While banks are interested in lending, their survival necessitates loans being repaid; therefore, a poor earning record, questionable management, insufficient collateral, a slow payment record, and other unfavorable conditions which have a bearing on the safety of a loan would be sufficient reason for rejection.

When applications for loans by small business firms were rejected because granting them would have been in conflict with bank policy, the specific reasons for rejection included these: requested maturities were too long, applicants had no established deposit relationships with the bank, the type of loan sought was not handled by the bank, and the bank's loan portfolio for the requested type of loan was already filled.

While banks still prefer to make short-term loans, they are less reluctant to make long-term loans than was true in the past. Because banks depend on deposits for the assets needed in their operations, they prefer to make loans to their own deposit customers, and when loanable funds are scarce, they will reject loan applications of outsiders rather than curtail those of their own depositors. Thus, small local business firms tend to be favored by their local banks during periods of credit restraint. Their loans are usually in the $1,000 to $5,000 bracket, but they may be larger or smaller. When banks find it necessary to ration loanable funds, small loans may slip through; as a result, the burden of loan rationing tends to fall on large borrowers.

Although a business firm may obtain a bank loan to avert technical insolvency, more often the purpose of borrowing is to enhance profits. The proceeds of a bank loan may be used to build up accounts receivable, to underwrite advertising and sales promotion programs, to expand production by making repairs and modernizing facilities, to finance other projects, to effect operating economies, and to increase volume of sales. While most of the funds borrowed are used to finance short-term and intermediate needs, sometimes such funds are used to finance new buildings, to buy out partners, and to finance other so-called long-term outlays.

SHORT-TERM BANK LOANS

A short-term bank loan is one which calls for repayment of the principal in less than one year. The obligations of the borrower and the rights of the lender are covered in a promissory note. The interest may be taken at maturity or the note may be discounted—interest taken in advance with only the principal amount payable at maturity. When a loan is made to finance seasonal needs, the note is usually single-name paper based on the financial statements of the borrower. The borrower is expected to retire the note when due and a short-term borrower is usually out of debt to his bank for the greater part of the year.

In addition to short-term loans to finance seasonal needs, business firms also obtain warehouse receipt loans, accounts receivable loans, equipment loans, collateral loans, installment loans, and term loans from their banks. The names of the first four of these indicate the nature of the assets pledged as security. Term loans have a maturity of more than one year; installment loans are repaid in equal amounts over a period of time. At one particular time, a business firm may have a term loan, an installment loan, a warehouse receipt loan, or one of many other types of loans.

Percentage-wise, most short-term bank loans are secured; but, when dollar amounts are considered, unsecured loans represent a greater volume of funds. A maxim of bank lending is that "all loans for more than $500 must be made against collateral or against financial statements," and large firms with good accounting systems are able to provide their banks with complete financial statements while small firms are more likely to depend on security.

By definition, endorsed and co-maker loans are not classified as secured loans; nevertheless, endorsement of a second party may facilitate borrowing. At one time, businessmen exchanged endorsements as an accommodation (accommodation loans) with the result that when the credit position of one firm deteriorated, that of others was impaired. While this practice of exchanging endorsements has declined, officers and directors may personally endorse the obligations of their corporations, and the promises to pay of unincorporated business firms may be guaranteed by a third party. In order to carry out a government project, a governmental agency may guarantee loans made by banks to business firms; but, while guaranteed business loans have been important during wars and other national emergencies, they are of minor importance during normal times.

Commercial banks also make specialized business loans, reflecting the particular merchandising and production processes being financed. For illustration, in financing specific items of equipment commercial banks sometimes require that such equipment be pledged as security. Banks have lent against warehouse receipts for decades, but a newer development is the practice of lending against field warehouse receipts (that is, goods warehoused on the premises of the borrower). Banks also purchase accounts receivable (with or without recourse) and make loans to business firms with accounts receivable assigned under a formal arrangement as security for loans.

Short-term business loans may be either time or demand loans. The usual maturity of time loans is 60 days (it has been suggested that one of the reasons for the popularity of the 6 per cent–60-day loan is the ease of computing interest. The interest charge is found by moving the decimal point two places to the right. Interest at 6 per cent for one sixth of a year is 1 per cent); however, renewals are common. Thus the time for which promissory notes are drawn may have little significance. Usually, banks permit prepayment of loans without penalty and allow rebates if the loans have been discounted (interest taken in advance).

Although bank loans may be renewed freely when they mature, a more modern practice is for both borrowers and lenders to be more realistic as to the true nature of underlying business transactions and to negotiate term loans when circumstances warrant loans for more than one year. Term loans are usually made for general financing purposes such as strengthening permanent working capital positions and purchases of equipment, machinery, or facilities. Usually, term loans are retired with funds obtained through the operation of the business—for example, depreciation allowances and earnings retained in the business.

A demand or call loan made to a business firm is one that may be called by the bank or repaid by the borrower at any time. Such loans are common when manufacturers or wholesalers pledge warehoused goods as security for loans. Often borrowers cannot ascertain the time that will be needed to manufacture, process, package, and sell the goods. Nevertheless, they desire to time repayment of funds so as to coincide with proceeds from sales of goods. On the other hand, the bank may want cash or continued protection for the loan prior to removal of the pledged goods from the warehouse; this can be arranged by substituting documents (bill of lading or trust receipts) for the warehouse receipt.[7] Demand loans may be repaid piecemeal as warehoused goods are withdrawn for manufacturing or processing in the normal course of business.

FINANCING WITH A PLEDGE OF INVENTORIES

The Federal Reserve System, in commenting on bank-loan policy, noted that "because of their size and the environments in which they operate, most commercial banks are strongly oriented toward small business."[8] This is not surprising in view of the fact that 80 per cent of all commercial banks have deposits of less than $10,000,000 each. Most bankers want to make loans to small business borrowers who can meet their credit requirements, but small firms often have greater difficulty meeting these standards than do large firms. The same forms and tests of credit worthiness are used for both large and small firms; usually, the main difference in terms is that small loans carry a higher interest rate than large loans.

Loans made to carry inventories are often secured by the goods being financed. For goods which are easily identifiable, it is a common practice to use trust receipts, chattel mortgages, and conditional sales contracts as discussed in other chapters. Another arrangement is to finance inventories through warehousing arrangements and the assignment of title to the lender. A warehouse receipt acknowledges storage of the goods and indicates the terms and conditions on which they will be delivered. When the receipt is nonnegotiable, goods will be delivered only to the person specified in the receipt; when negotiable, delivery may be made to the bearer or a person designated by the holder of the receipt. The warehouse receipt customarily states the quantity and the quality of goods stored (neither is absolutely necessary but the best warehousing practice is to state both). When the banker grants the loan, he must be sure that the warehouse receipt is valid, so that in the event of bankruptcy, his bank will have a legal claim to the goods pledged. The Uniform Warehouse Receipt Act and the United States Warehouse Act provide certain standards that must be met by a bona fide warehouseman who is defined as "a person lawfully engaged in the business of

---

[7] A trust receipt is a contract which "recites" (states) that one, the trustee, receives and holds title to certain goods in trust for another, the entruster. The bank permits the debtor to take possession and title to goods in trust for the bank for the purpose of resale. Upon resale, he must account to the bank for the amount of the debt.

[8] Federal Reserve System, *op. cit.*, p. 83.

storing goods for profits." Use of a warehouse receipt permits the lender to have title to goods stored while the warehouseman or warehouse company has possession of the goods. When the goods are not fungible (a term applied to certain grades of wheat or similar goods, a unit of which is interchangeable with another), the goods warehoused must be so controlled and segregated that they may be identified by a specific warehouse receipt. Release of the goods in whole or in part will be authorized by the lender on payment of the loan in whole or in part. The cost of warehousing is borne by the business enterprise.

In order to reduce the cost of storage and the inconvenience of not having goods on the business premises, so-called "field warehousing" has been developed. Therein goods are stored on the premises of the business firm under conditions that permit them to be segregated, controlled, and supervised by the lender. When pledged as security, title is transferred to the bank. Upon payment of the loan in whole or in part, goods will be released with a designated bank official supervising the physical release. When surrounded by proper physical safeguards and adequate insurance, field warehousing may provide adequate safeguards to the lender and may result in lower costs and greater convenience to the borrower.

Field warehouses are established almost exclusively for credit purposes, while "general storage" and "cold storage" warehouses are used to hold goods awaiting marketing and distribution. Over the last ten years, field warehousing has been a factor in the rapid growth of inventory debts which rank first among secured loans of manufacturing, mining, and wholesale merchandising enterprises. Among the goods that are field warehoused, bulk commodities predominate. Usually goods are held for but a short period of time, pending resale or use in manufacturing.

Among the risks associated with lending on goods stored in warehouses and evidenced by warehouse receipts are those associated with safeguarding the goods (collateral risks) which include protection against spontaneous combustion and germination for grains, suitable refrigeration for perishable goods, protection against moisture for most goods, and fire protection for all goods. Since warehouses do not always carry complete insurance coverage, complete coverage must be maintained by the borrower.

The warehouseman should be honest and qualified to handle the simple but necessary accounting associated with storage and release of goods, and the lender should occasionally make spot checks for quality and condition of goods. Greatest protection is provided when the warehouse is being operated under state and federal laws. Bonds are deposited by warehouse companies to protect owners against theft of goods, and unless stored as fungible, the identical goods must be held and returned.

In addition to collateral and bailment risks, there are other risks which are associated with fluctuations in the value and the nature of the goods stored. Adequate protection is assured when the loan is for only a percentage of the current or anticipated future value of the goods—varying from 50 to 80 per cent. If a hedging contract could be arranged, it would be possible to lend without the danger associated with a decline in market value of the goods. Particular attention is given to the market for the goods pledged and consideration is given to such factors as whether or not the goods are traded on an organized exchange, government price supports, current and anticipated supply and demand, price trends, presence or lack of substitutes, processing costs, and value at forced sales. Advances tend to be highest for staples that are traded on national commodity exchanges and lowest for manufactured goods.

Since all seasonal loans are dependent primarily on the ability of the borrower to repay them out of the normal receipts of business, the credit risk is present when warehouse receipt loans are made as it is in all other credit transactions. If a moral risk is present or if there is serious doubt as to the proposed loan being repaid in the usual course of business, the loan should not be made. While banks may make spot checks on warehoused goods, it is impractical for the bank to inspect every item of goods pledged; thus considerable reliance must be placed on the borrower's description of the goods and their value. The credit analysis work is similar to that entailed in making unsecured loans. If the current ratio of a business firm is low, the loan value of the goods may be reduced to give a higher margin of protection to the loan. In addition to interest, the cost of borrowing includes the expenses associated with handling the warehousing of the goods.

BORROWING ON ACCOUNTS RECEIVABLE

Among the current assets of a business firm, accounts receivable rank next to inventories in being used as security for bank loans. Although regarded as an inconvenient type of security, assigning accounts receivable may be less expensive and more convenient to the business firm than pledging goods if public warehousing is required.

Other things being equal, the nearer the asset is to cash in the flow of funds through the stages of production, the better it is as security for a loan, and receivables are but the collection or payment stage away from cash.

When a business firm obtains a loan against assigned accounts, it may be upon a notification or a nonnotification basis; that is, those whose accounts are assigned may or may not be notified of the assignment. The terms under which loans are obtained are covered in a written form that may include the following: (1) a promissory note or the regular collateral note form on which the words "assigned accounts" are written in the space provided for the description of the property pledged; (2) when the borrower is a corporation, a copy of the resolution authorizing certain officers to obtain the loan and to pledge the accounts receivable as security for the loan; (3) a document known as the assignment of accounts receivable which covers details for administrating and collecting the receivables and for depositing cash receipts in the bank; (4) a list of the accounts pledged; and (5) a remittance sheet which lists the names or numbers of the accounts on which payments are received each day. If a loan is made upon a notification basis, the invoice sent to the trade buyer by the seller may be stamped: "For value received this account is transferred to [name of lender]. Please make remittance direct to them when due."

Although the courts are generally hostile to secret liens, loans may be made on a nonnotification basis because some trade customers may resent having their accounts assigned to a second party. The assignor will continue to receive remittances from trade customers, as for any nonassigned account; but, by agreement between the lender and borrower, some individual employed by the borrower will act as special agent of the lender to keep the records and to handle payments on the assigned accounts. When payments are made by trade customers on assigned accounts, they will be applied to the loan or deposited in a special account created for this purpose. Detailed records of payments are kept on a remittance sheet; and provisions are made for handling returned merchandise so that the interests of the lender will be protected. Provisions may be made for substitution of new accounts receivable for those previously assigned.

Most accounts-receivable loans are made on a nonnotification basis. The assignment is stamped on the original and two copies of the invoices which are pledged (not on the copy that goes to the buyer). If items on the borrower's ledger sheet have been assigned, the word *pledged* is stamped at the top of the sheet and the name of the lender is stamped beside the individual items. Selection of invoices or ledger balances to be pledged is made by a representative of the lender and agreed to by the borrower. In addition to interest, the costs of borrowing include the expenses incurred in administering the collection of accounts receivable plus those for bookkeeping services. The loans obtained by business firms on assignment of accounts receivable may be for as much as 80 per cent of the dollar value of the accounts assigned.

When business firms assign accounts receivable, they are faced with several practical problems which arise from the fact that accounts receivable are but entries on the books of suppliers of goods and services. In other words, there is no written evidence of the obligation of the debtor which may be delivered to the lender (as in the case of promissory notes or bills of exchange). Neither is there any title to goods or a quantity of goods that may be delivered to lenders. Borrowers are required to sign lengthy assignment-of-accounts-receivable agreements. These agreements, drawn up in great detail so as to protect creditors, state the rights and privileges of the lender and the duties and responsibilities of the debtor.

When Congress passed the Assignment of Claims Act of 1940 (U.S. Code Title 31, Sec. 203), it stimulated accounts-receivable financing by permitting business firms to assign claims due or to become due from the United States or from any agency or department thereof under a contract providing for payments aggregating $1,000 or more to a bank, trust company, or other financial institution (unless the claims arise under a contract which forbids such assignment). If an assignment is made, the assignee (lender) must notify (1) the general accounting office, (2) the contracting officer or head of his department or agency, (3) the surety or sureties upon the bond or bonds, if any, in connection with the contract, and (4) the disbursing officer, if one is designated in such a contract. This act, which for the first time permitted assignment of government obligations to financial institutions, was designed to help small subcontractors in obtaining working capital so that they could participate in the defense effort.

In addition to this federal statute, states have passed laws that have strengthened the prior claims of creditors to assigned assets. In New York (and twelve other states) the rule is that the first assignee of an account receivable is entitled to collect the proceeds thereof if the assignment is made in writing for a valuable consideration. Other states recognize the prior claims of assignees provided the lender files a record of the assignment with the Secretary of State or the appropriate recording office of the county in which the assignor's principal place of business is located. Georgia and Pennsylvania provide that the assignee's (lender's) title is perfected when the assignor makes a notification of the assignment on his books. In another group of states, the assignee's title is perfected only upon notification of the debtors owing the accounts receivable. If the courts do not recognize the priority of the claims of secured lenders to borrowers' accounts receivable, the position of the lender is the same as that of other unsecured creditors with reference to accounts receivable.

In some cases, lenders purchase accounts instead of making loans on assignments of accounts receivable. In such cases, promissory notes are not used, but the remainder of the procedure is similar to that followed when loans are made on assigned accounts. Accounts receivable may be purchased "with recourse" or "without recourse." If the paper is purchased with recourse, in case the debtor (customer) does not pay, the lender may collect the unpaid obligation from the seller of the paper. If the paper is purchased without recourse, the seller is relieved of all credit risks (being responsible only if misrepresentation or fraud is present). Such outright purchasing is called "factoring" (see also next chapter).

At one time it was assumed that only financially weak companies assigned or sold accounts receivable, but this is no longer true. Banks have entered the business of lending on accounts receivable in competition with the specialists in order to reduce the risks encountered while meeting the credit needs of small and medium-sized business firms. The three major disadvantages of this type of lending are (1) the amount of attention that must be given by the lender to such loan transactions; (2) the question of validity of claims if and when the nonnotification plan is used; and (3) from the borrower's point of view, even when nonnotification is involved, in some states, customers may become aware that accounts receivable are being used as collateral through the recording of this information. Usually, bank loans of this type are either demand loans or loans which mature within 90 days. Longer maturities are sometimes used with loans on a revolving credit basis. (Revolving credit means that while the original loan is being repaid, new funds may be obtained from the bank under conditions and in such amounts as provided for in the loan agreement.) Because of the risk of fraud, banks frequently audit the accounts of those customers who assign or sell their accounts receivable. This factor, plus the risk item, helps to explain why bank loans based on assignments of accounts receivable bear the highest interest rate among their secured short-term loans to business concerns.

SUMMARY

Most business firms are dependent in part on commercial banks for borrowed funds. With the exception of the periods during World War I, the early 1930's, and World War II, the principal credit extension activities of commercial banks have involved making loans to individuals, partnerships, and corporations on either a secured or unsecured basis.

In recent years, bankers have increased their emphasis on a satisfactory compensatory deposit balance as a requisite for borrowing. Analysis of underlying credit factors has become more thorough and closer adherence to repayment schedules is being required. Generally, bankers are trying to upgrade the quality of their loan portfolios by requiring more collateral and by withdrawing credit from a firm that is not building up its equity and making some progress in its financial affairs. Usually, established customers receive preference over those coming to a bank for the first time.

In selecting a bank, a business firm considers such factors as the size of the bank, the services available, location, and other facilities and conveniences. Other factors include loan policies, loan limits, the size and nature of the bank's assets and liabilities, and various credit ratios.

When the seasonal operations of a business firm follow a fairly definite pattern, the firm may arrange for a line of credit with its bank wherein the bank sets a maximum limit up to which the firm may borrow during a specified time period. Before granting a line of credit, the bank makes a careful study of the record of the business firm; usually, after the line is granted, a compensatory deposit balance of from 10 to 20 per cent of the line is required to be maintained by the borrower. Other business loans are made without the use of lines of credit.

The typical business loan made by a commercial bank is short term, with repayment due in less than one year and with the obligation of the borrower and the rights of the lender covered in a promissory note. Percentagewise, most short-term bank loans are secured, but unsecured loans represent a greater volume of funds. Among the things most commonly pledged or assigned are inventories; stocks, bonds, and other securities; equipment; accounts receivable and assignment of claims; and plants and other real estate.

QUESTIONS AND PROBLEMS

1. Comment on the following: "A good banking connection is necessary for any modern business firm."
2. (*a*) What factors should a business firm consider in selecting a bank? (*b*) Why do some business firms find it necessary or expedient to use two or more banks?
3. "An important factor is that although business loans are down only mildly, total loans are off substantially . . . To a substantial extent, these loan repayments have been financed by the sale of securities to the investing public, so that they do not represent that much change in total demand for credit. . . ." ("Appraisal of Current Trends in Business and Finance," *Wall Street Journal* [New York: February 15, 1960], p. 1.) Discuss the managerial policy suggested by this quotation.
4. "First National . . . invites big corporate and personal accounts." (*New York Times,* March 2, 1955, p. 1.) What is the significance of this quotation for a small business firm in its selection of a bank?
5. Explain the maxim of bank lending that "all loans for more than $500 must be made against collateral or against financial statements."
6. What things are most commonly pledged by business firms for bank loans?
7. Distinguish among time, demand, and term loans and indicate the purposes for which each is most commonly made.
8. "Over the last ten years, field warehousing has been a factor in the rapid growth of inventory debts. . . ." What advantage to the borrower does field warehousing have over general storage warehousing?
9. Identify the documents commonly used in financing with a pledge of inventories.
10. Identify the following risks: (*a*) collateral, (*b*) bailment, (*c*) commodity, and (*d*) credit.
11. Discuss the legal aspects of assignment of accounts receivable for bank loans.
12. Distinguish between (*a*) loans on accounts receivable made on a notification and on a nonnotification basis, and (*b*) purchase of accounts receivable "with recourse" and "without recourse."
13. "National City [bank] raised its lending ability last year through an increase in capital. The merger would help to provide National City with more big borrowers." ("National City Bank Plans to Buy the First Na-

tional," *New York Times*, March 2, 1955, p. 1.) Explain how this would attract big borrowers.

14. Identify the financial policy suggested by the following: "After reaching a mid-year peak of $69 billion, as corporations borrowed to meet June 15 tax payments, total loans dropped gradually until the latter part of August." (The First National Bank of Chicago, *Business and Economic Review*, October, 1960, pp. 2–3."

CHAPTER 13

Financing through Factors and Specialized Finance Companies

Because of the importance of receivables among the assets of business firms, as indicated in the preceding two chapters, it is not surprising that specialized financial institutions have been developed to assist business firms in financing these assets. Among the more important intermediaries in this field are old-line factoring companies, commercial finance companies, and sales finance companies. This chapter deals with the practices and procedures used by these companies in extending credit to business firms.

FACTORING ACCOUNTS RECEIVABLE

In some foreign countries, the word *factor* still retains its earlier meaning, as one who acts or transacts business for another; but, in the United States, it refers more specifically to one who purchases accounts receivable from business firms and assumes all the risks of collection except those due to fraud and misrepresentation. A factor assumes many of the functions associated with sales of goods on credit—including, in whole or part, the selection of clients, credit terms, collection, maintenance of the accounts receivable ledger, and other bookkeeping duties. Factors also assist business firms by making market surveys, determining sources of new business, giving advice as to production, displays, and in other areas of operations.

While old-line factoring is still most deeply embedded in the textile industry, the increase in installment selling and the growth in the volume of charge accounts have led to a broadening of receivables financing to include financing retail accounts receivable as well as mercantile accounts receivable. Many of the old-line factors have discontinued or curtailed their sales activities (acting as selling agents for their clients) and are concentrating on their financing services.[1] Annually, these financial factors provide about $5 billion in financial assistance to business firms. At the present time, the typical factoring agreement is a continuing one whereby the factor purchases the factored company's receivables without recourse as they arise. In effect, the factored company operates on a cash basis and the factor assumes the credit, collection, and bookkeeping work associated with receivables.

Financial Services. At one time, except in the textile industry, it was considered a sign of financial weakness for a business firm to sell or assign its accounts receivable, and a firm that resorted to this practice suffered impairment of its credit standing. This attitude was doubtless created because many firms did not resort to factoring until they were faced with immediate financial collapse. Today, the typical factored company is a fast-growing concern with a large portion of its working capital tied up in accounts receivable. Although accounts receivable are being paid, they are being replaced with new accounts; as a result, the firm is continuously short of cash. Such a firm may need additional equity capital which might be obtained by selling stock if incorporated or by inviting others to participate as partners if unincorporated. However, many proprietors are reluctant—and understandably so—to share ownership with outsiders for fear of losing control or diluting their interests in the firm.

Most small corporations are unable to utilize the securities market in financing because investors are unwilling to buy stock in little-known and untried business concerns. In most cases, small corporations find the expenses entailed in preparing and marketing securities to be prohibitive. When firms are unincorporated, equity investment may require partnership status; this creates risks and responsibilities that many individuals are unwilling to assume. Consequently, a business firm may sell its accounts receivable to avoid having to curtail operations.

These are the chief characteristics of factoring: The client sells

---

1 Among the better-known factoring companies are James Talcott, Inc., New York; Walter E. Heller and Co., Chicago; Mill Factors Corporation, New York; Shapiro Bros., Factors Corporation, New York; and Factors Corporation of America, Philadelphia.

his accounts receivable to the factor without recourse, which means that the factor assumes all credit risks. The factor assumes responsibility for the credit and collection work of the factored client, makes credit investigations, helps to select customers, fixes sales terms, keeps records, and assumes losses if accounts are uncollectible. The factor notifies the clients' customers that they are to make payments directly to the factor and new invoices with shipping receipts are sent through the factor to the buyers of the factored firm's goods. The factor pays the factored company the full value of the factored accounts receivable minus a "reserve"—usually 20 per cent—which is used to absorb collection losses and expenses (the unused portion of this is refunded when the accounts are collected).

To a business firm, factoring means that its accounts receivable are converted into cash, but the transaction differs from that of obtaining a loan by pledging accounts receivable as security. A firm may improve its working capital position through factoring to a greater degree than through a loan because when accounts receivable are factored no matching current liability is created. When a business firm finances through a factoring company, it is subject to the same type of analysis that it would receive if application were made to a commercial bank (character of management, ability to earn profits, nature of the product, reputation in the trade, bank relations, and progress relative to other firms in the industry). If the factor is to buy existing accounts receivable, the accounts are thoroughly examined to determine their collectibility. Not only must the genuineness of the accounts be assured, but the factored company's financing practices must also be checked to make sure there are no other claims against the debtor that might weaken the claims of the factor. Successful financing depends on collecting funds when due and following up on past due accounts to see that they are either paid or written off if uncollectible. As a result of careful checking of accounts and effective collection practices, credit losses of factoring companies are usually very low—a fraction of 1 per cent of the total accounts factored or financed.

The cost of factoring varies with the risk assumed and the amount of work done by the factor. Charges are in terms of interest on the funds lent plus a factoring commission or service fee. Traditionally, the interest rate on funds which the factor invests in receivables has been 6 per cent per annum, but the amount of the commission or service charge depends on the quality of the client's accounts, the terms of sale, volume of receivables, and the number of invoices.

The quality of a client's accounts, and therefore the credit risk, will depend in part on the product (staples, seasonal items, novelties, etc.), the types of business firms to whom goods are sold (wholesalers, distributors, sales agents, department stores, other retailers, manufacturers, etc.), the credit standing of the client's customers, and the credit terms offered by the client (the longer the terms, the greater the risk). The amount of administrative work required will depend in part on the client's annual sales volume (percentagewise it costs less to finance a large volume than a small volume of sales), the average size of the client's invoices (1,000 invoices averaging $1,000 will require less detailed work than 10,000 averaging $100), and extra services demanded by the client (such as handling all billing and bookkeeping operations). The commission may range from less than 1 per cent to 2 per cent or more, and the exact rate is determined by negotiation between the factor and the client.

When large sales predominate, as in manufacturing and wholesale merchandising, rates of 1½ per cent are considered fairly high; factoring rates of 1 per cent are not unusual when the average account is large, the risks are small, and the amount of bookkeeping and collection work is not excessive. The total cost of factoring is sometimes given as a percentage of total credit sales, but it is difficult to compare this cost to that of borrowing because of other services that accompany factoring. However, interest charges are usually computed monthly on daily debit balances averaged over the preceding month, and commissions are figured as a percentage of the face value of all receivables or the total amount of accounts receivable minus discount credit for merchandise returned and allowances granted by the firm to its customers. The commission is primarily a reward for assuming the credit risk plus compensation for the factor's credit, collection, and bookkeeping work.

Usually, the factored company's chief cost of financing is the commission charged. For illustration, if a factor charges 6 per cent per annum on funds advanced before the due date of receivables and a service charge of ¾ of 1 per cent on the gross volume of receivables factored, the total factoring cost, when the annual volume of receivables is $200,000 and the average amount advanced is $25,000, will be $3,000 or 12 per cent of the average amount advanced. If the service charge were increased to 1¾ per cent, the total cost would be $5,000 or 20 per cent of the average amount advanced; if the service charge were increased to 3 per cent, the total cost would be increased to $7,500 or 30 per cent of the average amount advanced.

	¾ Per Cent	*1¾ Per Cent*	*3 Per Cent*
Interest	$1,500	$1,500	$1,500
Service charge	1,500	3,500	6,000
Total	$3,000	$5,000	$7,500

Dividing these total costs of factoring by $25,000 will give rates of 12, 20, and 30 per cent, respectively. However, the savings in bad-debt losses, credit and collection work, and bookkeeping expenses may be considerably more than the added costs of factoring; but service charges should be weighed against savings.

When considered from the viewpoint of a business firm, the advantages of factoring depend upon the position of the firm in question. At the time of the initial contract, the firm will receive a cash advance which is usually equal to 80 per cent of the factored accounts (the 20 per cent of receivables being the reserve for expenses, returned goods, disputes, offsets, and uncollectibles). As new shipments are made, the factored firm receives 80 per cent of each invoice. As a result, most of the firm's receivables are turned into cash immediately. When factoring is arranged on a continuing basis, the factored firm is assured of cash following sales. This cash may be used to care for its accounts payable, to take advantage of cash discounts, and to finance other needs. Thereby, the costs of factoring may be offset in whole or part by cash discounts (which is the same argument used to justify mercantile borrowing from commercial banks).

A business firm, whether it is financing its accounts receivable through factoring or by other means, may increase its working capital available for other purposes by decreasing the amount of funds invested in accounts receivable. On the other hand, a business firm may be able to increase its volume of sales by offering longer credit terms; by factoring its accounts receivable, it may be able to operate on a near cash basis, and obtain loans at more favorable interest rates because a smaller debt and better balance sheet will tend to strengthen its borrowing position. If a factored business firm has unencumbered inventories, plant, equipment, and other property, these assets may be pledged to obtain a loan from a bank, a factor, or a finance company.

Credit Services. The amount of credit which any business firm may extend is limited, and it must bear some relationship to the amount of its capital. In view of the size of its operations, a factor may spread the risk of loss over a broader base and approve the extension of credit to customers whom the factored company may regard as not being good credit risks. There are many specialists on the staff of a factoring company, and their files are used not only as a source of potential customers for their business-firm clients but also as an index of those with whom it would be undesirable to do business.

The credit services that business firms obtain from factors include assuming credit risks on factored accounts receivables and making credit decisions which are often more liberal than a factored client could afford if he were assuming the risk. In addition, the transfer of the business firm's credit functions to the factor may bring about an improvement in the relationship between the business firm and its customers.

Collection and Bookkeeping Services. A factor assumes much of the clerical and collection expenses associated with the use of open-book accounts by the factored business firm. This arrangement permits the business firm to economize on its staff—a type of expense that has become more burdensome because of higher salaries, more expensive equipment, and higher rents. Although these costs are shifted to the factored company by way of the factoring charge, the per unit cost is usually less because the factor's volume of accounts justifies the use of labor-saving devices such as bookkeeping machines designed for this purpose, employment of skilled operators, and development of efficient collection techniques. Thus, the factor is in a position to handle the collection of accounts receivable more efficiently than the factored company.

By using the collection services of a factor a business firm may avoid the conflicts as to policy which often arise between sales and collection departments, may use its personnel to obtain the optimum volume of sales, and may be assured of payment for goods sold. A business firm may antagonize customers by its collection efforts and thus destroy goodwill; therefore, it may be expedient to arrange for a factoring company to assume the collection problem. Since the factor may have several clients in the same industry, the delinquent debtor will be in danger of losing his sources of supply of goods. However, a factoring company is in a position to work with delinquent debtors; if customers have valid reasons for their inability to meet obligations, factoring companies will usually grant extensions.

Advances by Factors. Since factors adjust their terms to meet the needs of their clients, they not only factor receivables (purchase them outright) but also purchase accounts receivable with recourse, discount installment notes, make loans on assigned accounts and other forms of property, and make unsecured loans. When funds are made available, it may be in the form of temporary or seasonal over-advances or in the form of term loans to be repaid over a period of years in fixed installments.

Over-advances, which are made more frequently than term loans, are related to anticipated accounts receivable out of which they are repaid. They are obtained most commonly by business firms whose products are seasonal in nature (such as seasonal apparel, woolen blankets, and so on) and those whose shipping season is limited to one period during the year. The funds obtained are used to purchase raw materials, to defray labor and manufacturing costs, and to carry the finished products until the time for shipment arrives. If security is required for over-advances, inventory is most commonly pledged. In planning for financing, the cash flow or cash budget is developed jointly by the business firm and the factor. Business firms sometimes arrange for term loans from factoring companies to purchase equipment, enlarge facilities, refinance long-term debts, and acquire other assets. (These loans are considered in detail in a later chapter.)

Factoring Agreements. Factoring agreements are based on written contracts between business firms and factors. These contracts usually contain a clause permitting either party to terminate the arrangement at any time subject to 60 days prior notice. After factoring arrangements have been established they may continue for years if the factored firm remains satisfied with the services obtained and the factor retains confidence in the firm. Under factoring arrangements, the factor agrees to render monthly accounting to the client for the sales assigned to it each month and to credit the client with the net amount of all receivables assigned to it. Except for a reserve to care for possible returns, claims, or defenses by customers, the credit may be withdrawn by the client at any time. The net amount of receivables is the face amount of the invoices less the factor's commission and discounts and credits granted by the business firm to its customers. Either the factored firm may arrange for the factor to deposit the proceeds from accounts daily or weekly with the firm's bank, or it may draw upon these balances while they are held by the factor as funds are needed. After offsetting interest and other charges due the factor, such balances may draw interest.

Clients of Factoring Firms. Factoring has little appeal for those business firms whose credit is based on letters of credit or other secured documents, those whose output is taken by a few customers of unquestioned credit responsibility or by other firms where no unusual credit risk is present, and those who have adequate lines of credit with banks. On the other hand, there are many business firms that are not desirable clients for factoring companies because modern factoring is not a distress type of operation.

Factors are not interested in business firms whose management is basically unsound; concerns with extremely limited working capital, net worth, or sales volume; firms whose products are of such poor quality as to lead to excessive complaints and returns; and firms whose operations are static or declining in importance. Among the companies using the services of factors are rapidly growing manufacturing concerns, which tend to be short of cash because their working capital is tied up in accounts receivable and inventories, and small and medium-sized firms that need permanent working capital but are reluctant to raise it by issues of stocks and long-term obligations. Factoring services are not available to business firms that sell to the ultimate consumer.

Objections to Factoring. In conclusion, factoring is more than a method of financing because factors perform basic services which are not obtainable elsewhere. It is the collection services offered by factors that lead some business firms to reject selling accounts receivable and to finance instead with loans. In some lines, the main argument against factoring is the resulting loss of personal contact with customers. Also, many factored companies retain their own collection and bookkeeping work because they believe that the periodic statements sent to customers are more than "billing arrangements" in that advertising matter and personal-note communications may be inserted along with the statement (such as, "our records show that you have not used your account . . ." or "thank you for your past patronage. . ."). For the same reasons that some firms have discontinued factoring their accounts, other firms refuse to factor theirs.

Factoring is opposed by some businessmen who want to sell even if making sales entails taking risks which factors would not allow. Conflicts over selling policies have led to compromises between factors and factored companies: one such compromise may be an arrangement whereby the factor purchases all sales credit up to a certain amount for a stated period of time and if more than that amount is sold on credit, the seller assumes all the credit risk for the excess.

FINANCING THROUGH COMMERCIAL FINANCE COMPANIES

Business firms may obtain loans secured by working capital assets, particularly accounts receivable, from commercial finance companies which seldom assume all the credit risks.[2] Currently, business firms in the United States may use the services of several thousand commercial finance companies, many of which have extended their activities beyond the commercial credit field to include the financing of goods sold by retailers.

Small and medium-sized business firms are the chief users of the financial services of commercial finance companies. Usually, these services consist of purchasing accounts receivable with recourse or making loans secured by accounts receivable, and less frequently making loans on inventories and other assets. These companies have developed special procedures, many of which have been adopted by commercial banks in their financing of business firms. Customarily, credit is granted only after careful review of the finances and operations of the borrowers. Emphasis is not only on the estimated value of the collateral but also on anticipated cash flow within a reasonable period of time. Loans are followed closely, collateral is checked regularly, and collections are made promptly.

Business firms may make revolving credit arrangements with commercial finance companies, in which case the accounts-receivable contracts are drawn so as to provide the lender with security while protecting the operations of the business firm from interference. As in all types of lending, the success of the operation depends primarily on the ability of the debtor to meet his obligations during the normal course of business operations.

The basic agreement between the business firm being financed and the commercial finance company sets forth the rights and liabilities of both together with the over-all conditions under which each account receivable is pledged. Assignments are made when the business firm needs funds. The borrower prepares the schedule of accounts to be assigned and executes a demand note, and the lender

---

[2] Contracts may be made whereby the commercial finance company will buy a group of accounts receivable on a "reserve" basis. The percentage paid for the accounts receivable purchased and the percentage of the purchase price making up the reserve will vary; but if losses exceed the reserve, the burden falls on the commercial finance company.

stamps the assigned accounts in the borrower's ledger (required in most states to validate the assignment). Assignments of accounts may be made on a notification basis, but they are made most commonly on a nonnotification basis.

When accounts-receivable financing is on a notification basis, the original invoices or bills are sent to the customers of the business firm after being stamped showing that the accounts have been assigned and that they are to be paid directly to the finance company. When assignments are made on a nonnotification basis, the customers of the business firm being financed are not informed of the assignment, and their relationships with the business firm will not be affected because the business firm will continue to collect payments of assigned accounts and will remit the proceeds to commercial finance companies in their original form.[3] Usually the nonnotification method is preferred by both the business firm and the customers of the firm. Many of the customers would object to paying their accounts to commercial finance companies, and many business firms prefer to maintain a close relationship with their customers through their own bookkeeping and collection operations.

The written agreement between the business firm being financed and the commercial finance company contains the interest to be paid and other charges, and these may vary both as to percentage and the method used in calculating and collecting interest and service charges. The loan may be discounted, or interest charges may be computed, on the average daily balance over a specific period of time, such as a month. The service charge may be based on the face amount of the receivables handled, the total number of accounts, or a combination of the two. The interest rate charged is commonly 1/30 of 1 per cent per day (12 per cent per annum) on the outstanding loan balance, but it may be more or less, varying with the risk assumed and the cost to the lender.

Commercial finance companies, since they are specialists in accounts-receivable financing, contend that they can perform these functions more economically than commercial banks. They assert that they can be more liberal in lending than commercial banks because they are staffed to appraise the collateral more accurately (which necessitates periodic examination of the books of their customers). In addition, banks usually operate locally while many

[3] For legal as well as financial reasons, commercial finance companies require their clients to remit the actual checks received by them in payment of accounts receivable (proceeds in kind) that have been assigned.

finance companies and factors are regional and three finance companies are national in their scope of operations. As a result of their size and mode of operations, finance companies may be able to make larger loans and to provide services over a geographical area as broad as the market covered by their clients. Factors and finance companies have a more diversified clientele than do commercial banks and they may offer financial, advisory, and other services not offered by local banks.

In financing business firms, commercial finance companies stress accounts-receivable financing, but they also make loans secured by merchandise and—to an increasing extent—income-producing equipment, plants, and fixtures. A business firm whose activities are highly seasonal or irregular may obtain loans secured by inventories evidenced by warehouse receipts, factors' liens, or bills of lading. Even when purchases are not seasonal, a business firm may arrange for advances on a continuing basis. In the automobile industry, dealers may obtain loans from commercial finance companies by having cars warehoused or placed on the floor and title to them transferred to the finance company by a trust receipt (floor planning).

Most of the institutional distinction between accounts-receivable financing companies and factoring companies has disappeared. Most of the old-line factors have accounts-receivable departments, and many of the commercial finance companies are doing some factoring. In addition, many commercial banks make loans on accounts receivable and they sometimes participate with finance companies in financing business firms. In the latter case, the business firm being financed may receive equal amounts from the commercial bank and the finance company; however, the loan will be serviced by the finance company.

Manufacturing companies and wholesalers are the preferred clients of accounts-receivable financing companies because their open accounts are against products that can be readily identified, their customers are business firms, their average invoices are large, and their sales and profits can be expanded as the result of improvement in cash flow. When retail firms finance through commercial finance companies, their interest rates are higher and the terms are more stringent than those paid by firms in the fields of manufacturing and wholesale trade.

Presumably, factors and commercial finance companies compete with commercial banks; but, in practice, they tend to complement rather than to compete with commercial banks in financing. Factors and commercial finance companies obtain a large percentage of their loanable funds from commercial banks and use them to finance business firms whose credit positions are too weak to finance directly through banks or whose credit needs are of a fixed capital type which commercial banks would be reluctant to provide. Although a business firm financing through a factor or commercial finance company pays a higher rate of interest for funds obtained than the rates charged by commercial banks, the difference in financing costs may be partly offset by savings in other areas of operations.

FINANCING RETAILERS

Many retailers use commercial finance companies to finance their sales to consumers, which means that these companies are invading the field dominated by sales finance companies, the specialists in financing such sales. Sales finance companies have grown in response to the needs of business firms in financing sales of durable consumer goods having a relatively high value—including automobiles, radios, television sets, sewing machines, and motor boats. A large percentage of these and other durable goods items are sold on the installment plan wherein obligations are evidenced by installment notes; the retailers' problem is primarily that of financing notes receivable. However, time sales to consumers that are not evidenced by installment notes are growing in volume; hence, business firms in these fields are turning to sales finance companies, commercial banks, and other financial intermediaries for assistance in financing consumer credit in forms other than installment notes. Approximately one third of retail sales are made on credit, and about 35 per cent of these credit sales are handled on an installment basis.

Charge Accounts. In recognition of the promotional effects of selling on credit, many retail stores open credit accounts for prospective customers (most of whom were previously unknown to management). Some credit managers feel that customers resent retail firms "probing into their personal affairs" and ask their customers only for enough information to permit identification. In such instances, decisions as to credit worthiness will be based on information obtained from local retail credit bureaus or other sources. The most important factors in determining credit worthiness of individuals are stability of income, tenure of employment, years of residence in one place, and ownership of life insurance, savings accounts, bonds, and other assets. These factors indicate the stability of the applicant's character and habit, which are the best tests of credit worthiness of an applicant for a charge account or other forms of consumer credit. Other supporting factors are income from wages and other sources, personal wealth, and absence of fraudulent dealings and criminal record.

For charge-account financing, the plan which is growing in use today is the one which permits stores to borrow with receivables pledged or assigned as security. Larger stores with gross annual sales of over $5 million often use the financial assistance of banks, while smaller stores more commonly use the services of finance companies. When consideration is given to interest rates and service charges, borrowing may be the most economical method of obtaining credit. Factoring entails taking over the entire credit checking function of the factored store and putting in the factoring company's own personnel. If sales-conscious store management objects to the credit restraint imposed by the factor, conflicts as to sales policies result. Some firms use a modified plan in which the factor assumes responsibility for selection of credit risks only after sales credit has passed a certain figure. Because store management generally regards factoring as too expensive (and too restraining if sales are expanding rapidly), the preferred method of obtaining credit is borrowing with receivables pledged or assigned as collateral.

Merchants are justified in financing their own receivables with net worth or borrowed capital when net profits are greater than the cost of financing. If profits are not adequate to finance outstanding debts, the financial position of the firm will be weakened. Even if profits are adequate, the cash position of the firm may be unsatisfactory because cash receipts must be used to replace inventories and to meet accounts payable, payrolls, taxes, and other current obligations. As a firm's sales and net profits increase, its cash demands increase; therefore the firm may be continuously short of cash. This means that the retailer may have the same need for financial help from sales finance companies or other financial institutions as recognized earlier in the case of financing mercantile firms.

The average size of accounts receivable and other receivables arising from retail credit is smaller than those from mercantile credit, which increases the task of checking collateral. Customarily, the loan value of retail receivables is less than that of mercantile receivables. Thus a store specializing in consumer goods may not be able to borrow more than 60 to 75 per cent of its accounts receivable while one which assigns mercantile accounts may borrow 80 per cent or more of them. After a careful credit analysis of a store's management, the nature of its business, its location, and its financial statements, the lender may fix a loan limit for the store, which may be twice the net worth of the firm.

While old-line factoring companies do not finance consumer credit, one of the newer developments in this field is the factoring of retail accounts receivable by commercial banks. In co-operation with participating stores and service firms, the factoring bank accepts applications from customers for credit cards; then, when these applications are approved by the bank, the credit cards are honored by merchants and others participating in the charge-account plan. When a charge-account sale is made, the buyer signs a sales slip which is in an assignable form. The sales slip is sent to the bank where it is discounted—usually at the rate of 5 per cent—thereby giving the merchant immediate credit. Some business firms obtain credit at a lower discount rate, but they pay a service charge for bookkeeping and collection which is deducted when sales slips are deposited. All original sales slips of participating firms are included in the monthly statements rendered by banks to their charge-account customers. When customers settle their monthly accounts with their banks within 10 days of billing, no additional charges are made. Cycle billings may be used, and customers are permitted to use a budget plan of payment provided monthly payments exceed a specified minimum. When consumers elect to extend payments over a period of time, usually for a maximum of five or six months, they are charged so much per month (usually 1 per cent) on the unpaid balance.

In the bank-factored charge-account plan, a consumer has the advantage of buying on credit and the convenience of paying for all purchases with one check. A merchant, who has been selling on a cash basis, may participate in a bank-factoring plan to increase his volume of sales; but a merchant selling on a credit basis may have additional justification for factoring charge accounts because it would reduce bookkeeping and collection expenses. The services offered by bank plans for factoring retail accounts may be most valuable to small businessmen such as the skilled mechanic who operates his own service shop but who has no experience in granting credit or bookkeeping and collection work and who cannot afford to employ others.

In many lines of trade, stores are using a modification of the monthly payment plan to allow two or more months for payment. In the budget-payment plan, the minimum payment is specified (for illustration, $10 per month) and the number of payments is limited (for illustration, nine months). Such installment-payment terms were originated by appliance dealers and furniture stores. At the present time, such terms are being offered by many clothing and department stores and other stores selling "soft" (nondurable) goods. In making such sales, stores are using coupon books, letters of credit, and other techniques (lay-away plans and so on).

Installment Sales Financing. By nature, selling on the installment plan necessitates financing at both the wholesale and retail level. When dealers purchase durable consumer goods such as automobiles, they are required to pay cash to the manufacturers, and most dealers are unable to care for the large cash need with their own capital resources. When the floor-planning type of financing is used in automobile financing, the risk is not large, assuming that the dealer is honest and does not overestimate his volume of business. The amount of credit extended usually ranges from 65 to 80 per cent of the invoice price of the cars plus freight, taxes, and extra charges. The dealer's obligation is evidenced by a note that runs for the term of the loan, usually at an interest rate of 1 per cent per month. When cars are sold prior to the maturity of the note, the dealer receives a rebate; but nonpayment at maturity of the note may result in the finance company repossessing some of the new cars. In addition, there are factory arrangements such as repurchase guarantees that will protect the finance company when necessary.

A consumer may either pay cash for an item of durable goods—such as an automobile—with funds accumulated for the purpose or obtained from a cash-lending agency, or he may sign an installment purchase contract at the dealer's place of business. Although some dealers finance their own paper, most of them depend on sales finance companies and commercial banks. Sales finance companies accept installment sales contracts either with recourse or without recourse. When the recourse plan is used, the dealer guarantees the transaction and agrees to assume any loss; when the no-recourse plan is used, the finance company assumes the collection risk. The cost of a car bought on the installment plan is known as the *time price*, and it includes the retail price plus interest, insurance, and other charges.

When sales are made on the installment plan, the buyer may be asked to sign a conditional sales contract whereby the title to the goods purchased is not vested in the buyer until he makes the final installment. This arrangement gives the seller protection; namely, the ability to repossess the goods in the event of default. Many billions of dollars worth of cars, refrigerators, air-conditioning equipment, radios, television sets, and other durable consumer goods are sold annually by means of conditional sales.

The installment note signed by the buyer states that the principal and interest are payable in specified installments on certain dates until the amount is paid in full. Usually, an installment note contains a provision which permits the holder of the note to consider the unpaid principal and accrued interest payable immediately if the maker defaults on any installment of either interest or principal (called the "acceleration" clause). Usually, the conditional sales contract and promissory note appear as part of the customer's application form.

Sales finance companies assume much of the burden of credit investigation as a service to their customers, and their decisions as to credit worthiness are based on the same principles as those applicable to charge-account customers. However, the amounts are usually larger, and the time period is usually longer than for charge-account sales. This means that there are greater risks associated with such sales and that the collection procedure must be more vigorous on installment-note sales than on charge-account sales.

While installment-sales terms lack uniformity, merchants desire substantial down payments and periodic payments sufficiently large so that the secondhand value of the repossessed goods will, at all times, be at least sufficient to cover the remaining claims of the seller. But some things have little secondhand value and the presence of the repossession option is used more as a disciplinary measure to collect payment than for any other reason. As in the case of other forms of credit, modern emphasis is on the ability and willingness of the obligor to meet his debt contracts rather than on the value of the thing pledged as security. Therefore, the modern practice is to base sales terms primarily on credit worthiness of the buyer rather than primarily on the protection offered by the repossession option. Sometimes, legal documents in forms other than the conditional sales contract are used to protect the interest of the seller. For illustration, a chattel mortgage may be used and it may be drawn to cover other goods owned by the buyer in addition to the goods purchased on the installment plan.

Personal property may be delivered to a second party under a contract of bailment in which the bailee receives personal property that must be returned to the bailor or disposed of according to the bailor's directions. In selling, possession of goods may be transferred without transfer of title; such arrangements often appear when goods are leased or rented with an option to buy, when goods are delivered by a business firm to a commission merchant or agent to be sold, and when goods are sold on approval or trial. In the service industries, bailment customarily necessitates the return of personal property; the more common of such cases include warehousing of goods; bailment for repairs, alterations, or changes in form (watches, automobiles, clothing, and so on); delivery of goods to a public or private carrier for shipment; and many other transactions taken for granted in every-day life such as checking a hat in a restaurant or hotel and leaving a car in a public garage.

Trust receipts are also used as a security device, but this arrangement differs from bailment in that the trustee not only takes possession of the property left in trust but also acquires legal title thereto. Unlike bailment, both real and personal property may be transferred in trust.

FINANCING WITH LOAN CREDIT

Personal loan credit refers to advances of cash to individuals primarily for the purpose of buying consumer goods and services as distinguished from sales credit which results from buying goods on time. The ability of stores to sell for cash depends in part on the amount of loan credit that consumers may obtain from banks, credit unions, small-loan or personal finance companies, and other lenders in the personal loan field. Many of these lenders also purchase installment notes from automobile dealers and others who sell on the installment plan. Sometimes proprietors of small business firms use the specialists in the personal loan field as a source of funds. This suggests the existence of the same type of overlapping of financial functions in this field as that found in the case of commercial banks, factors, retail finance companies, and so on. Credit analysis and sources of credit information for personal loan credit are similar to the procedures used for charge accounts and installment credit.

Borrowers obtain personal loans, other than for business purposes, in order to obtain funds for cash purchases of consumer goods as an alternative to installment-plan purchases, consolidate or refinance existing obligations, and meet tax bills, medical expenses, and other emergency needs. Usually, personal loans are repaid on the installment plan, but many involve single payments. Interest rates and other charges vary considerably, depending on the type of lender (whether a regulated or nonregulated financial institution) and many other factors.

Personal loan agencies include commercial banks, many of which operate personal loan departments; credit unions; licensed small-loan or personal finance companies; industrial or "Morris Plan" banks; industrial loan companies; pawnbrokers; and nonregulated lenders. In terms of dollar amounts, commercial banks are the leaders in the personal loan field.

The credit instruments used by different agencies include the simple promissory note, installment note, collateral form note (which combines the promise to pay and a "pledge"),[4] and chattel mortgage note (a promise to pay secured by a chattel mortgage executed by the maker on specific personal property, such as an automobile). Some lenders have devised other forms that may be used in making secured or unsecured loans. Provisions may be made on the face of the note for the signature and address of comakers as well as the maker. The chattel mortgage may be a separate document or a part of the installment note form. If a loan is secured, the thing pledged may be an automobile, bonds or stocks, cash surrender value of a life insurance policy, savings-deposit pass book, household furniture, or any form of personal property.

Loan-Check Accounts. Many commercial banks have installed a type of overdraft credit plan for their noncommercial customers. The various "ready-credit" or "loan-check" plans differ as to details, but the illustration which follows is typical of how these plans operate. When a loan check account is granted, the credit is figured as 12 times the amount to be repaid each month (if $50 is to be repaid each month, the credit is $600). After approval of the application, the bank customer may use his credit by writing checks which will be honored by the bank as long as the maximum credit is not exceeded. Each month that a repayment is made, the amount repaid will be added to the credit remaining in the account; thus, the loan-check credit agreement is a revolving or continuous one until it is cancelled by either the customer or the bank. The customer pays interest on the average outstanding balance of his loan (assume a rate of 5/6 of 1 per cent per month), a service charge on each check written (assume 25 cents), and usually a fee for insurance carried to repay the bank in case of the customer's death. Monthly statements

---

[4] A *pledge* is a bailment of personal property as security for a debt.

sent to the customer show the checks drawn, payments made on the loan, unpaid balance outstanding, and charges for interest, service, and insurance. Since the loan-check plan tends to increase merchants' cash sales, their needs for working capital to finance accounts receivable should tend to decline. This is also the case with credit obtained by consumers from other personal loan agencies which enable retailers to increase cash sales relative to credit sales.

SUMMARY

There are specialized financial institutions in addition to commercial banks which are of interest to business firms as sources of working capital; they include factors, finance companies, and other specialists who purchase, discount and/or make loans against accounts receivable.

Factoring consists of outright purchase of accounts receivable; thus the factor usually assumes other activities for his clients. These activities include analyzing credit and market conditions, keeping records, and offering advice as to production plans and sales policies. A factor subjects his clients to the same sort of credit analysis as does a commercial bank when making a loan. Factoring of the revolving credit type may be advantageous in that it allows the firm to operate on the equivalent of a cash basis, but it also entails close supervision by the factor. Now, most factoring companies are functioning more like general finance companies than like old-line factors.

As an alternative to factoring, many business firms are selling their accounts receivable "with recourse" or assigning them as security for loans made by finance companies or banks. When financing in this way, the business firm borrows against receivables and retains the credit risk as well as the collection function.

Many retail sales are made by using charge accounts, budget accounts, installment notes, and other devices of "buying on time." While some retail stores have sufficient working capital to carry their charge-account and installment-account customers, some stores find it necessary or expedient to borrow from commercial banks or retail sales finance companies. Others discount or assign accounts receivable to banks, finance companies, or other financial institutions.

The ability of retail stores to sell for cash depends not only on the income and savings of their customers but also on the amount that their customers may borrow from banks, credit unions, small-loan or personal finance companies, and other lenders in the consumer credit field. Many lenders in the personal loan field also purchase installment notes from automobile dealers and others, and many proprietors of small business firms use lenders in the personal loan field as a source of funds. Credit analyses and the sources of credit information for personal loan credit are similar to those utilized for charge-account and installment credit.

QUESTIONS AND PROBLEMS

1. (*a*) Identify: (1) factor, and (2) factoring in the United States. (*b*) What are the chief characteristics of factoring?
2. Describe the credit analysis work done by a factor.
3. Discuss: "At one time, except in the textile industry, it was considered to be a sign of financial weakness for a business firm to sell or assign its accounts receivable."
4. What are the advantages and disadvantages of factoring?
5. How does discounting accounts receivable differ from factoring them? Are the risks the same as when loans are made with receivables pledged as security? Why?
6. (*a*) What are the most important factors used in determining the credit worthiness of individuals? (*b*) What plans of selling on credit are used by retail merchants in your locality?
7. (*a*) Compare the risks present in charge-account sales to those present in sales of durable consumer goods by use of installment notes. (*b*) What devices are used to protect creditors?
8. (*a*) Explain bank factoring of retail accounts. (*b*) To what extent is it being used in your locality?
9. (*a*) For what purposes do businessmen obtain personal loans? (*b*) What are the agencies in this field? (*c*) What credit instruments are used?
10. "When hundreds of separate credit and collection departments are eliminated by firms transferring the job to . . . a factoring company, there may be a gain to society. . . . But what does factoring do for the business firm using it?" (Clyde Willion Phelps, *The Role of Factoring in Modern Business Finance* [Educational Division, Commercial Credit Company, Baltimore, 1956], p. 17.) What would be your answer to this question?
11. How would an increase in the use of loan-check plans tend to affect the working capital needs of retailers?
12. "Firms which sell their receivables without recourse to factors enjoy certain advantages over those not utilizing this service." (Ernest W. Walker, "Factoring: Its Function and Technique," *Texas Business Review* [January, 1960], p. 9.) What are these advantages? Are there disadvantages? Explain.

13. "About half the resources of commercial finance companies and factors come from short-term bank loans." ("12-Billion Business Done in Financing," *New York Times* [January 11, 1960], p. 61.) Does this mean that commercial finance companies and factors are middlemen in supplying business firms with bank credit? Explain.

CHAPTER 14

Short-Term Open-Market Financing

A MONEY market is the place where the supply of and demand for short-term funds meet; and, although there are a great many money markets, the one of major interest to large business firms is located in New York City. The money market is used by business firms to acquire not only short-term United States government securities and other near-cash assets but also working capital funds. There are several divisions of the money market, but the two of interest to business firms in search of working capital funds are the commercial paper market and the commercial bill market. These markets wherein promissory notes and commercial bills may be purchased are open to any investor or qualified borrower, which explains the term *open market.*

COMMERCIAL PAPER MARKET

Open-market commercial paper refers to single-name, unsecured notes of business firms and finance companies which are sold on a discount basis to investors. The notes appear in different denominations, usually starting at $5,000; and, although their maturities vary from one to ten months, those with maturities of four, five, and six months are most common. Business firms may use the commercial paper market as a substitute for short-term bank loans or to supplement them, and their decisions in this respect are influenced by the relationship between the prime rate on customer loans of banks and rates in the open market.

In the business loan market, the prime rate is the key to which other interest rates are related, including the rate on promissory notes bought and sold in the commercial paper market. The prime rate is the interest rate on short-term loans of business firms that borrow in large amounts without security. Primarily, they are the rates charged the largest business borrowers whose credit standings are such as to permit them to shift their financing between the customer loan market and the commercial paper market.[1] The open market for commercial paper is dominated on the demand side by firms having national credit ratings, and they include the financial intermediaries considered in the preceding chapter, the most important of which are the sales finance companies.

Business firms that borrow in the commercial paper market usually use the services of commercial paper dealers or commercial paper houses, but some of the large sales finance companies have created their own sales organizations which handle the sale of their companies' open-market promissory notes. When a business firm deals through a commercial paper house, the latter takes an issue of promissory notes on a commission basis or buys the issue outright. The notes, being drawn payable to bearer, are sold without the endorsement of the commercial paper house or other holders. If a second name appears on the notes, it is usually the endorsement of an officer or someone closely associated with the borrower. Most notes are unsecured, but in a few cases where they are secured, the collateral is held by a trust company or trust department of a bank.[2] The commercial paper house guarantees the genuineness of all notes that it sells, but it does not assume the credit risk.

A business firm's success in open-market financing depends upon the willingness of investors to buy and hold its notes. The market is an impersonal one, which means that no favors as to renewal are asked or expected upon maturity of the issue. Although the open market and the customer loan market are sometimes regarded as

---

[1] The prime rate is fixed by the large New York banks, and at the present time it is 4½ per cent. When one of these banks announces a change in its prime rate, the others will announce similar changes within a day or two. The effects are not limited to New York banks because in a matter of days, banks in Chicago and other large cities will change their prime rates.

[2] Of the total number of borrowers—398—in 1951, 97 per cent used one-name unsecured promissory notes. Endorsed or guaranteed notes were given by nine borrowers, and in three cases, the notes were secured by collateral. See C. H. Kreps, Jr., "The Commercial Paper Market," *Money Market Essays* (Federal Reserve Bank of New York, 1952), p. 17.

being a common credit pool, this is not the case because the open market taps sources of credit other than those provided by commercial banks.

From time to time there is considerable variation in the relative importance of classes of investors in open-market commercial paper; in recent years, the more important ones have been commercial banks outside of New York and other metropolitan areas, business firms, and other financial institutions including trust and endowment funds. Business firms have found purchasing commercial paper to be a profitable substitute for investing in United States Treasury bills and tax-anticipation certificates because the yield has been higher. This means that business firms are lending funds to other business firms in competition with commercial banks; however, in terms of volume the customer loan market is far more significant than the open market.

Business firms find it advantageous to borrow in the open market for a number of reasons, one of which is economy. Generally, the interest rate (technically, the discount rate, because notes are sold on a discount basis) is about ½ of 1 per cent below the prime rate—the lowest rate charged large business firms by metropolitan banks. Now, commercial paper houses customarily acquire issues of notes on a dealer basis; therefore, the spread between the purchase price and the sale price represents the direct cost of financing. This cost may be no more than ⅛ or ¼ of 1 per cent computed on an annual basis. When commercial paper houses handle paper on a commission basis, they charge a flat commission which is a small fraction of 1 per cent. Sales finance companies often handle their own paper and tailor it to meet the needs of business firms and others seeking short-term investments.

Although the credit standing of borrowers in the open market is not seriously questioned, commercial paper houses sell promissory notes with the understanding that they may be returned within a week or ten days after the original distribution. However, the notes are not to be returned except for credit reasons. Commercial paper houses thoroughly investigate the credit positions of the business firms whose paper they handle; also, during the option period, additional checking may be done by commercial banks and other investors. Such investigations may be a burden to the business firm financing in the open market, but it has the advantage of advertising the firm's credit standing, which facilitates future borrowing. In addition, general interest may be stimulated in the company and its products, which would benefit the company in other ways.

During a credit investigation, if anything is amiss with the borrower's credit position, it is almost certain to be uncovered and advertised widely in financial circles (a calculated risk that open-market borrowers must take). Since less than 5 per cent of notes are returned to commercial paper houses—presumably for credit reasons only—the high quality of open-market borrowers' credit positions is beyond dispute. But more important, buyers of commercial paper have suffered no loss thereon since 1936 (the loss in 1936 was 0.0078 per cent of the total paper outstanding as of June of that year).

A business firm may find it advantageous to borrow in the open market, thereby eliminating the necessity for keeping a compensatory balance with its bank as required when obtaining customer loans. While a business firm which borrows in the open market may be able to reduce the volume of bank deposits, good banking relations must be maintained. There is always a possibility that a business firm will be short of cash when its open-market commercial paper notes mature; thus it is desirable for a firm to have a line of credit under which it may borrow if and when necessary. Usually, a line of credit is a requisite for open-market borrowing, and a commercial paper house will check this before contracting to buy or act as distributing agent of a business firm's paper. In fact, it would be virtually impossible to sell commercial paper if the borrower could not give proof that bank loans were available.

One of the chief advantages of borrowing in the open market is the ability to obtain larger loans than could be obtained by borrowing directly from banks. Because of the 10-per-cent rule, even the largest banks may be unable to care for the needs of some open-market borrowers. On December 31, 1959, the statutory loan limit for the First National City Bank of New York (the second largest among American banks) was $62,000,000, which would be adequate for most open-market borrowers provided the bank would want to place this amount of funds with one business firm.

Although many banks are increasing their individual loan limits by building up surplus out of retained earnings, building up capital by the sale of stock, and combining with other banks, the credit needs of many individual borrowers are increasing more rapidly. However, commercial banks are participating with other banks to an increasing extent in short-term lending to business firms, and when one bank is unable to handle all of a customer's loan needs, it may arrange with other banks to provide part of the funds.[3] As a group, commercial banks are growing less rapidly than other financial institutions, and it seems apparent that in the future, business firms will turn more frequently to the open market for funds in order to tap the resources of non-bank investors.

Business firms that now borrow in the open market are the "cream of the crop" among short-term borrowers. Although there are only a few hundred firms that borrow in the open market, there are undoubtedly thousands of others that could meet the credit standards required. The business firms that borrow in the open market include manufacturers (particularly textiles, foods and related products, metal products, leather goods, lumber, wood, paper, chemicals, drugs, and paints); wholesalers (particularly groceries and food products, hardware and paints, and textiles and leather products); and retailers (particularly department and chain stores). In addition, this market includes sales finance companies, small loan companies, and other finance companies whose volume of borrowing exceeds that of all business firms.

The typical business firm that sells commercial paper in the open market has an estimated net worth of between one and five million dollars. However, some of them have a net worth of as little as $250,000, while in others it exceeds $25 million.[4] The "bill-board," as designated by commercial paper houses, includes Brown Shoe Company, Bulova Watch Company, Burroughs Corporation, General Mills, Gimbel Brothers, H. J. Heinz Company, Manhattan Shirt Company, Sylvania Electric Products, Wesson Oil Company, and others. There are many lesser-known but equally fine companies that borrow in the open market. It is considered an accomplishment to qualify for open-market borrowing, and valuable business and financial contacts are derived from selling open-market paper. The dealer's commission on notes at a rate of 1/4 of 1 per cent per annum on $1 million maturing in six months is only $1,250; because of

[3] For illustration, in October, 1959, the Consolidated Edison Company of New York announced that it had arranged a $100 million line of credit to run from October 6, 1959, to October 5, 1960, with thirteen banks. Borrowings were to be at the prime rate upon notes up to ninety-days maturity. The borrowing was planned in anticipation of permanent long-term financing. The First National City Bank of New York acted as the clearing agent for the banks.

[4] C. H. Kreps, Jr., *op. cit.*, p. 18.

this low rate, if the dealer is to make a profit, the name on the note must largely sell it.[5]

Although the standards are high, there are a large number of business firms that could finance in the open market if they so desired. Many refrain from doing so for fear of impairing their established relationships with commercial banks. Also, the terms of financing in the open market are less flexible than the terms obtainable when borrowing from commercial banks. Ordinarily, open-market promissory notes cannot be prepaid, extended, or renegotiated like bank loans.

While business firms often use open-market financing as an alternative to bank borrowing, during some seasons of the year these firms may borrow from commercial banks to pay off open-market obligations as they mature. Although business firms derive benefit from the advice of commercial paper brokers and their contacts in the open market, when the "chips are down" there is no substitute for banking contacts. Some commercial banks buy open-market commercial paper; but, in an emergency, they will withhold funds from this market and take care of their own customers' credit needs. This is true because an open market is a place for lending surplus funds, and the commercial paper market is best regarded as a supplement to the customer loan market rather than as its substitute. Since 1930, when the number of borrowers in the open market exceeded 3,000, the number has declined but the dollar amount of loans has increased.

COMMERCIAL BILL MARKET

A commercial bill is a bill of exchange most commonly used in payment for shipments of goods. At one time, this method of financing was expected to replace the open-account cash discount system. After World War I, the American Acceptance Council was organized by American businessmen to promote this method of extending trade credit. Despite the merits of the case and the efforts of the council, little progress was made in changing business credit habits. In the future, however, business firms may find it desirable to use commercial bills more freely in meeting their working capital problems.

In 1912, the National Monetary Commission in its report to Con-

---

[5] The commercial paper houses which have been active in recent years include Goldman, Sachs & Company (the largest in the field) and Lahey, Fargo & Company, both of New York; Weil Pearson & Co., Boston; Ashwell & Co. and A. G. Becker & Co., Inc., Chicago; McLuney & Co., St. Louis; and Piper, Jaffray & Hopwood, Minneapolis.

gress included among its criticisms of the American Banking System: "The lack of commercial paper of an established standard, issued for agricultural, industrial, and commercial purposes, . . . hinders the development of the productive forces of the country."[6] Since then, national banks have been given the right to accept bills of exchange drawn on them under certain conditions, and the Federal Reserve Banks have been authorized to discount eligible bills. Although the use of trade bills in domestic trade has been disappointingly small and the American Acceptance Council was liquidated in 1937, acceptance credit is widely used in financing foreign trade of the United States. In financing the working capital needs of business firms, the two types of bills used are the trade bill of exchange or trade acceptance and the banker's bill or bankers' acceptance.

Trade Bills. A trade bill of exchange is one drawn by the seller of goods on the buyer to cover payment. It is an order to pay as distinguished from a promise to pay (promissory note, bond, certificate of deposit, and so on). A trade bill may be either a demand or time bill. If it is a time bill, it is usually accepted by the purchaser (which makes it a trade acceptance), and the buyer of the goods becomes primarily responsible for the trade acceptance as would be the case if he had signed a promissory note for the goods purchased.

Before the Civil War, most merchandise sold on credit terms was financed with promissory notes and trade acceptances running for six to nine months. During and following the war, suppliers reduced the credit period and began to offer generous discounts for cash payments. This step was taken by suppliers in order to protect themselves from losses caused by the fluctuating value of the "greenback," and one of the aftermaths was to establish the open-book account method of selling. Because of the lack of trade paper, commercial banks made unsecured loans to buyers to enable them to pay cash and to take the generous discounts when purchasing goods. While the trade bill has not disappeared, the volume of such paper outstanding at one time is small compared to the volume of accounts payable.

The use of a commercial or sight draft may be illustrated by the experience of a business firm in Texas which ships cotton to a firm in Massachusetts. On delivery of the cotton to the railroad, the seller receives an order bill of lading as a receipt. The seller draws a sight

---

[6] National Monetary Commission, *Letter from Secretary of the National Monetary Commission Transmitting, Pursuant to Law, the Report of the Commission, 62nd Congress,* Senate Document No. 245, Vol. XXIV (Washington, D.C.: U.S. Government Printing Office, 1912), p. 8.

draft on the buyer for the purchase price of the cotton (plus freight, insurance, and other costs if they are to be assumed by the seller), makes out the commercial invoice, and endorses the bill of lading. All of the documents are mailed to a bank in Massachusetts, as previously requested by the buyer. When the documents arrive, the buyer is notified by the bank so that he may complete arrangements for payment and get the bill of lading in order to obtain the goods from the railroad. The bank will obtain the money from the buyer and will remit it to the seller. The bank acts merely as a collecting agent and charges a small fee for its services. Although this is virtually a cash transaction, the seller has the advantage of retaining title to the goods until payment is made and the buyer has the advantage of not being required to remit until the goods have been shipped.

A buyer who cannot pay for goods immediately upon receiving them may arrange for use of a trade bill with a specified maturity; that is, the bill will run for a stated period of time after presentment of the bill of exchange for acceptance. In this case, the buying and selling arrangement may be similar to that noted above with the exception of the time interval between the receipt of the bill of lading and payment. Before the agent of the seller releases the bill of lading to the buyer, he asks for and receives the buyer's signature on the face of the draft. The buyer (drawee) writes the word *accepted* across the face of the bill, followed by the date of acceptance and then his signature. The trade acceptance will come due at the end of a period of time which varies—it may be thirty days from the date of acceptance. In some instances, the trade terms may specify that the draft will run from the date it is drawn rather than from the date of acceptance.

The facilities of commercial banks are commonly used for presentment, with the buyer being notified of the arrival of the documents by telephone or otherwise. A local bank receiving the bill of exchange either asks the buyer to call for it at the bank or presents it to him at his place of business. The commercial invoice, bill of lading, and other documents accompanying the bill of exchange are checked by the buyer to see that the sales terms are met. If something is wrong, the drawee may either accept the bill of exchange with qualifications or refuse to accept it. If, after signing the draft, he finds that the papers misrepresent the goods or merchandise (papers will come by mail, goods more slowly by freight), he is liable for the draft which he has accepted but may sue the seller for violation of his contract and/or misrepresentation or fraud.

If the trade acceptance is returned to the seller, the latter may discount it for cash, hold it until maturity in thirty days, or use it as security for a loan. A trade acceptance remains a secondary liability of the drawer, and the signature of the acceptor usually adds to its credit standing. If held until maturity, it is superior to an account receivable as evidence of a sale, and it is more acceptable than an account receivable as security for a bank loan.

Unfortunately, instead of the trade bill developing as a preferred credit instrument in domestic trade, it has become associated in its use with firms that have weak financial positions. The trade acceptance has been used as a device to strengthen doubtful accounts and to speed up the turnover of receivables. When a buyer wants extra time beyond that normally given by the seller, the latter may grant the request provided the buyer acknowledges his debt immediately by signing a trade acceptance. In other cases, when a book account is past due, the seller may grant an extension provided the debtor signs a trade acceptance. While this use of the trade acceptance to close out past due accounts is in violation of the theory that the trade bill be accepted at the time of the sale, it is not unusual for trade acceptances to be used in this way.

Bankers' Acceptances. In general, bankers' acceptances originate in the same way as trade bills do, with drafts or bills of exchange drawn by sellers on buyers or their banks. In fact, a trade acceptance may become a bankers' acceptance if a bank endorses the bill and thereby guarantees its payment at maturity. The advantages of having a bank name on a bill of exchange is that it becomes, in effect, a post-dated check that can be sold by the payee before the maturity date. When the buyer's credit position is uncertain as in foreign trade, the seller may request that the bill of exchange be accepted by a bank more as a measure of security than as a method of increasing the paper's liquidity. If the buyer honors the request to provide bank acceptance credit, he contacts his bank and arranges for the acceptance terms. This necessitates signing an acceptance agreement contract, whereby the buyer assumes responsibility for the credit risk and agrees to have funds in his bank to meet the accepted draft when due. The bank may ask for collateral as security for the line of acceptance credit, but usually this is not necessary because the goods being financed provide security for the basic transaction. The accepting bank charges a commission of about $1/8$ of 1 per cent per month for lending the bank's credit standing to the bill of exchange.

After arrangements for acceptance credit have been made, the bank either (1) sends a wire or cable to its correspondent bank nearest the seller requesting the bank to notify the seller of the terms, or (2) sends a letter (called a commercial letter of credit) directly to the seller stating the terms of the acceptance agreement. The terms may be revocable or irrevocable and confirmed or not confirmed by a second bank (usually one near the supplier). The wire, cable, or commercial letter of credit authorizes the drawing of the draft which originates with the seller; it stipulates that the draft will be accepted and paid at maturity if it is drawn according to the stated terms and accompanied by the required documents, such as the bill of lading, commercial invoice, insurance policy or certificate, consular invoice (when movement is across international borders), certificate of origin, weight note, inspection certificate, and/or quality certificate.

The seller will follow the terms of sale, arrange for shipment, deliver the goods to the carrier, obtain and endorse an order bill of lading from the steamship company or other carrier, obtain a consular invoice from the consul in his community, make out the commercial invoice, buy the insurance, and arrange for any other necessary documents. If he wants cash, he may take all the documents to his bank, endorse the bill of lading, draw the bill of exchange as authorized in the letter of credit, and leave the bill of exchange with his bank for collection. Then the bill of exchange with the documents attached will be sent for acceptance by air or regular mail to the bank that granted the acceptance credit. Often, the bank will advance the seller the amount due on the transaction (the face amount minus a discount), place its name on the bill as the drawer, and forward it through banking channels for acceptance. When the buyer's bank receives the bill of exchange with the papers attached, it will check and compare the papers with those on file at the bank (particularly, the copy of the letter of credit sent to the seller); then, if all is in order, the bank will accept the bill of exchange.

Following acceptance of the bill of exchange, the documents are usually retained by the acceptor, who gives them to the buyer of the goods in exchange for a trust receipt. The key document is the bill of lading, without which the buyer cannot get the goods when they arrive.[7] The accepted draft, which still has a stated number of days to

[7] A bill of lading is a receipt for goods or some other form of personal property and evidences the holder's title to property when it is in the possession of a carrier (railroad, steamship company, airline, and so on). There are "straight" and "order" bills of lading. A straight bill of lading is usually made out to the buyer of the goods, who is the one to whom the goods are to be delivered. It is not an acceptable form in financial circles because the buyer can claim the goods irrespective of whether or not he accepts

run prior to maturity, may be sold immediately for cash in the acceptance or bill market or to the accepting bank, which may discount its own acceptance. The one who presents the draft for acceptance (called the presentor) will act on instructions from the owner, who may be the supplier, the supplier's bank, or someone else who has acquired the draft.

Bankers' acceptances are popular with foreign investors who are familiar with this instrument since it is more widely used in Western Europe than in the United States. The holder of the bill is the one who provides the credit used in the transaction, and quite often this is a foreign bank or individual. Accepting banks often buy their own bills to hold in their files, trade for bills of other banks, sell to correspondent banks, or sell in the commercial bill market. The technical reasons for exchanging bills with other banks is that a bank's "own bills" must be reported as bank loans. When banks sell their bills to dealers, the spread between the bid and ask price of 1/8 of 1 per cent is the dealer's profit.

At the end of World War II, over 80 per cent of the dollar amount of bankers' acceptances originated from financing imports and exports; but now, because of the increased use of bankers' acceptances for other purposes, financing exports and imports represents approximately 60 per cent of the total. However, the volume of export acceptance credit outstanding has increased threefold during the last five years, reflecting both the growth in merchandise exports and the increase in the use of private credit (rather than government credit) in this area. Since American imports have not been subsidized by government credit, the increase in the volume of acceptance credit for imports has been more modest—about 40 per cent over the same period.

Since buyers usually take the initiative in arranging for acceptance credit, the growth in the amount of export acceptance credit means that foreign business firms have been taking the initiative in obtaining acceptance credit from American banks to finance their imports from the United States, with the sellers (American business firms)

---

or pays a time draft drawn on him (an exception being when the bill of lading is made out in favor of a correspondent bank or agent who withholds possession of the title to the goods until acceptance or payment of the bill of exchange). An order bill of lading is one that permits delivery of the goods to the holder of the order bill of lading. An agent of the seller, such as a shipping company or a bank, may withhold possession of the goods by merely retaining possession of the bill of lading. When acceptance or payment terms have been met, the bill of lading is released to the buyer of the goods or to his bank.

being the chief beneficiaries. Sometimes American exporters draw trade drafts on foreign buyers as authorized in sales contracts; then the American business firms pledge these drafts at their banks as security for the issuance of time drafts which will be sold for cash in the acceptance market. Acceptances resulting from the financing of the foreign and domestic storage of goods (such as cotton, sugar and other agricultural products) prior to shipment, represent about one third of the total dollar acceptances.

Many American banks in small communities do not grant acceptance credit but depend on their correspondent banks for assistance in financing the foreign purchases of their customers. Metropolitan banks customarily finance the foreign trade needs of both their own customers and the customers of their correspondent banks. In addition, some American banks issue letters of credit for customers of their foreign branches and correspondent banks who wish to buy in the United States or in other foreign countries.

Business firms may arrange with their banks for the honoring of drafts for payment of goods being imported under a revolving acceptance agreement. The bank pays the drafts and notifies the firm of the arrival of the documents, and the firm will either make cash payment for the credit advance and receive the bill of lading in return, or more commonly, it will sign a trust receipt. The trust receipt permits the business firm to take possession of the bill of lading—and therefore the goods—but not the title to the goods until advances made by the bank have been repaid. The firm is usually limited in using the goods and the proceeds from the sale (such as being required to sell them and to pay off the advances with the proceeds). The goods imported may need processing (tanning in the case of hides, or roasting in the case of green coffee) which will be covered in the trust agreement. A more expensive procedure would be for the bank to insist on placing the goods in a public warehouse from whence it would be withdrawn as needed in exchange for a trust receipt or repayment of the bank's advances.

American business firms may use acceptance credit to finance the storage of commodities at home and abroad. If a firm needs temporary working capital, readily marketable staples may be stored in a warehouse and pledged as security for a grant of acceptance credit. This credit arrangement permits the firm to draw time drafts which will be accepted by the bank provided the drafts are secured at the time of acceptance by a warehouse receipt or some other document conveying title to the bank.[8] Then the accepted drafts or bills will be sold in the market at a discount from face value, giving the business firm cash with which to operate. While outstanding, bankers' acceptances of this type must be secured by a warehouse receipt or similar document. The goods may be withdrawn from storage prior to maturity of the bills provided acceptable security, such as an order bill of lading, is substituted. The total cost of borrowing will include warehouse expenses, the commission charged by the accepting bank, and the discount on the acceptance when sold in the bill market. According to the federal law, the term *readily marketable staple* includes articles of commerce bought and sold in a market in which a price may be determined and sales may be made at any time the market is open.

Assuming that a business firm has been financed by its bank up to the full amount permitted the bank under the law for direct loans, arrangements may be made for acceptance credit in an amount in excess of 10 per cent of the bank's paid-in and unimpaired capital and surplus if the transaction being financed permits a grant of acceptance credit. However, the 10 per cent rule would apply if the bank were to discount its own acceptance because such a transaction is treated as a loan and not as a grant of acceptance credit. Banks may accept in excess of 10 per cent for one name provided the amount in excess of 10 per cent is secured by attached documents or other legal instruments arising out of the same transaction as the acceptance. However, a trust receipt that permits the customer to retain control over or to have access to the goods is not considered "actual" security. Although the 10 per cent rule may not be a factor, a business firm applying for additional credit may be referred by the loan department of its bank to the foreign department, which handles both foreign and domestic acceptance credit transactions.

Generally, business firms seek new sources of cheap credit and banks seek new sources of income; hence, an expansion in the volume of commercial bills may be expected in the future. The total cost of

[8] When goods are placed in a warehouse, the warehouseman gives the holder of the goods a warehouse receipt which is evidence of title to the property in the possession of the warehouseman. A warehouse receipt is similar to a bill of lading in that it is either an order or a straight warehouse receipt. An "order" warehouse receipt permits the goods to be delivered to the bearer or to the order of any person named in the receipt; a straight warehouse receipt permits delivery of the goods only to a specified person named in the receipt. In financial circles, there is a preference for the order warehouse receipt for the same reason that the order bill of lading is preferred over the straight bill of lading.

financing with acceptances includes commissions and fees paid to banks for accepting and handling the documents and the interest on the borrowed funds, the rate thereon being determined by money market conditions. To some extent, the amount of open-market financing is influenced by governmental regulation, but the current provisions are sufficiently liberal to permit expansion in the volume of acceptance credit without any change in the law. A business firm may obtain acceptance credit to finance the import and export of goods, shipment of goods within the United States and between foreign countries, and storage of readily marketable staple commodities either in the United States or in foreign countries; but, to be eligible for acceptance, the bills of exchange may not have a maturity in excess of six months.

Because of regulations pertaining to security and purposes, bankers' acceptances are usually related to specific transactions at the time of acceptance. (The major exception to this is grants of acceptance credit to a foreign bank in order to permit it to create dollar exchange.)[9] A member bank, which accepts any commercial draft growing out of the import or export of goods to or from the United States or between foreign countries, is expected before acceptance to obtain and retain in its files satisfactory evidence as to the nature of the transaction underlying the credit extended. In domestic shipment or storage of goods and for storage abroad, a business firm must provide the accepting bank with title-conveying documents—a bill of lading, warehouse receipt, or some similar instrument—or physical possession of goods underlying the credit transaction.

Rates in the Money Market. Whether it is cheaper to finance in the money market or by direct loans depends on the rate at which bills may be discounted plus other costs as compared to the interest

---

[9] Acceptance credit granted by a member bank to a second bank so that it may furnish its customers with dollar exchange is subject to special regulation by the Board of Governors of the Federal Reserve System. Unlike other grants of acceptance credit, there is no direct link between the goods being financed and the acceptance credit. The borrowing bank in the foreign country builds up its deposit balance in New York or elsewhere in the United States by drawing a time draft on its accepting bank, presents the draft for acceptance, and then sells the acceptance draft for cash which it deposits with its bank. Then, the bank is able to sell dollar drafts to its customers who will mail them to their suppliers in the United States for goods purchased. American banks must obtain special permission from the Board of Governors of the Federal Reserve System to grant this blanket type of acceptance credit; banks that may be serviced in this way are located in selected political subdivisions where foreign exchange markets are not well developed and where dollar exchange may be needed (Haiti and Dutch West Indies, Australia, New Zealand, and Indonesia).

charges on direct bank loans plus other costs. Like all open-market rates, those on bankers' acceptances fluctuate, but the fluctuations are less than those on most forms of open-market credit instruments. Although the averages may be misleading, they are suggestive of the relationship that exists between the money rates for different types of paper. For this reason Table 19 is inserted.

TABLE 19

ANNUAL AVERAGE OF MONEY RATES
Per Cent per Annum

Types of Paper	*1958*	*1959*	*1960*
Prime bankers' acceptances, 90 days	2.04	3.49	3.51
Prime commercial paper, 4–6 months	2.46	3.97	3.85
U.S. Treasury bills, 3 months (market)	1.78	3.37	2.87
Short-term loans to business (19 cities)	4.30	5.00	5.20
Corporate bonds, 30 issues Aaa ratings	4.16	4.65	n.a.

Source: *Federal Reserve Bulletin* (January, 1961), pp. 59–60.

If and when a bankers' acceptance is sold in the market, the credit of the accepting bank is the determining factor in the market ratings of the time draft. As a result, bankers' acceptances are bought and sold at the lowest discount rate of any type of business paper in use and second only to short-term Treasury bills of the United States government. If a business firm can sell against bank acceptance credit, it is using the nearest thing possible to selling for cash because a time draft, after acceptance, can be sold for cash in the money market at just below par value.

SUMMARY

In financing their working capital needs, business firms are making considerable use of the services offered by factors, commercial finance companies, sales finance companies, and commercial banks; however, at the present time, they are making little use of the commercial paper market and the commercial bill market. Generally, these open markets offer funds at lower rates than can be obtained from banks or other specialized financial institutions. The cost of borrowing includes commissions and fees, and the terms of borrowing are less flexible than those available when financing through banks.

Companies with excellent credit standings find that issues of unsecured short-term negotiable notes sold through the open market are the cheapest way to meet seasonal or temporary needs for cash without exploiting or disturbing their normal lines of credit at banks. Borrowing by issuance of commercial paper has been used by business firms not only as a means of raising cash but also as a device for establishing their credit standing on Wall Street with an expectation of future intermediate or long-term security issues. The high credit standard prevailing in this market is shown by the fact that there has been no default on commercial paper since 1936. Issues vary in size from a minimum of about $200,000, but there is no maximum set. Most of the commercial paper is handled by a few large dealers, but there are smaller firms which handle paper for smaller business concerns. The larger dealers' profit is usually the spread between buying and selling prices (1/8 or 1/4 of 1 per cent), but smaller issues are usually handled on a commission basis (1/4 of 1 per cent is the usual commission). The large sales finance companies handle the sale of their own open-market commercial paper.

The commercial bill market includes both the trade and bankers' acceptance market, but it is dominated by the latter. The development of the trade acceptance in the United States has been disappointing, primarily because buyers prefer the open-book cash discount system and suppliers in most industries and lines of trade respect their wishes. However, the demand bill is being used by manufacturers in the automobile industry to collect from dealers for new cars and parts on delivery; it is also being used to finance shipments of American goods to foreign countries. The trade acceptance is sometimes used as a device to collect past-due accounts, but this use is in violation of the principle that acceptance should be at the time of delivery of goods.

Generally, bankers' acceptances are related to financing specific shipments of goods between countries, domestic shipment of goods, and storage of readily marketable staples at home or abroad. Financing with open-market paper permits business firms to tap sources of funds other than bank credit at low interest rates; in recent years, corporations have been lenders as well as borrowers in this market.

QUESTIONS AND PROBLEMS

1. Identify: (*a*) open-market commercial paper, (*b*) open-market borrowers, (*c*) commercial paper houses, and (*d*) buyers of commercial paper.
2. (*a*) What are the advantages of financing in the open market with commercial paper? (*b*) What is the significance of the fact that buyers of commercial paper have sustained no losses thereon since 1936?
3. Analyze: "The trade acceptance technique differs from nonnotification

accounts receivable financing chiefly in that a negotiable instrument evidences the debt, and in the fact that the purchaser of the goods recognizes that his debt is likely to be assigned to a third party." (Federal Reserve Bank of Chicago, *Business Conditions* [March, 1958], p. 8.)

4. "Funds obtained from the commercial paper market are best regarded as a supplement to bank loans and not as a substitute for them." Explain.
5. "Commercial paper dealers buy and sell these notes (commercial paper) in the open market. Big finance companies, however, sell their paper directly to investors." (*New York Times,* January 18, 1955, p. 39.) Comment.
6. Identify: (*a*) bills of exchange, (*b*) bills of lading, and (*c*) warehouse receipts.
7. How may a seller in your community use sight drafts when purchasing goods from a manufacturer in another part of the country? Compare with the use of trade acceptances.
8. How does financing with bankers' acceptances differ from financing with trade acceptances?
9. For what purposes may member banks accept drafts or bills of exchange drawn on them?
10. "You can protect your credit in overseas transactions by requiring the overseas buyer to obtain a First National City Bank Export Letter of Credit." (The First National City Bank of New York, *How Our Overseas Division Can Help You Do Business Abroad.* n.d. n.p.) How? Explain how a business firm may establish its credit with foreign buyers with the help of the bank.
11. "If a business firm can sell against bank acceptance credit, it is using the nearest thing possible to selling for cash." Explain.
12. In 1960, the annual average rate on prime bankers' acceptances was lower than on commercial paper. Why? (See Table 19.)

CHAPTER 15

Financing Intermediate Credit Needs of Business Firms

BUSINESS firms finance their needs for intermediate-term (one to five years) credit by negotiating direct loans from commercial banks, insurance companies, factors, commercial finance companies, governmental agencies, and other lenders; by borrowing in the open market wherein the intermediaries between the business firms and their creditors are investment bankers and dealers; and by lease arrangement. This chapter deals with term loans of business firms, characteristics of term loans, intermediate notes of corporations, financing purchase and lease of equipment, and governmental sources of business funds.

TERM LOANS OF BUSINESS FIRMS

During the last twenty-five years, one of the most important developments in the field of finance has been the increase in the use of term loans. A term loan is defined as one made to a business firm for a term in excess of one year. The fact that they are made to business firms distinguishes them from other loans maturing in more than one year (such as credit extended to financial institutions, consumers, and farmers). In some cases, term loans are made to replace short-term loans which had been renewed periodically; hence, the statistics of term lending now as compared with the past may be misleading. Experiences of businessmen during the depression of the 1930's caused them to be wary of the uncertainties of renewals of bank loans, and experiences of bankers caused them to welcome term loan contracts having provisions for installment repayment of principal—a common feature of term loan contracts. However, even without the impetus given by the depression, the development and growth of term lending would have taken place.

Term loans have come into prominence for a number of reasons, the most important of which is the need for credit to finance durable producers' goods. That this need has increased can be seen by comparing the amount of capital needed to equip a store, shop, factory, or any other business unit today to the amount needed to equip such a unit two generations ago. Larger business firms are usually able to satisfy their needs for intermediate funds by sales of notes in the investment market; therefore, they may choose between negotiating term loans with banks and other lenders and borrowing in the open market. Middle-size and small business firms not having access to the open market are usually limited to commercial banks, commercial finance companies, and other lenders as sources of intermediate funds.

When business firms arrange for term loans with their banks, it is usually done to replace or to supplement working capital. Manufacturing companies whose production cycles run for months (such as those in the fields of equipment and heavy machinery) are unable to liquidate their products seasonally; even though a firm in this field may receive some advance payments to meet payrolls and other short-term expenses, it will not be able to pay off its creditors until delivery of its products. Usually, these intermediate term needs for funds do not justify permanent financing with stocks or bonds; therefore, an increasing number of such firms are arranging for term loans with their commercial banks or insurance companies.

Business firms also arrange for term loans to finance expansion—development of new products; purchase of new or enlarged facilities, machinery, or equipment; and/or acquisition of a second business firm. The chief reason that middle-sized and small business firms arrange for term loans is to purchase equipment or other fixed assets. Sometimes large business firms, finding the market unfavorable at the moment, arrange for term loans pending permanent financing through a public offering of securities or the placement of a long-term mortgage. Many large companies, however, have a policy of using both sources of funds—arranging for term loans with banks and/or insurance companies and offering security issues with the assistance of investment bankers.

The purposes for which business firms obtain term loans may be unproductive in nature in that they may not add to gross income or the cash flow. These include term loans made to refund outstanding debt or preferred and common stock. The motive in such refinancing may be to reduce interest costs, to simplify the corporation's capital structure, or to eliminate a bond issue or a loan because of the restrictive provisions embodied in the bond indenture or loan contract. The purpose of management in retiring preferred stock may be to save on income taxes because interest paid on a loan is deductive as an expense for tax purposes while dividends on stock are not deductible. Also, any reduction in the shares of common stock outstanding would increase the "leverage" on the remaining shares.

War and defense spending has stimulated term lending. The credit needs of defense contractors are temporary, and loans obtained by them have the same characteristics as other loans with maturities of more than one year which are made for productive purposes. The new element in such loans is that the credit is guaranteed by the federal procurement agency which contracts for the goods being produced. The Federal Reserve System administers the guarantee feature for the federal government; and *Regulation V*, issued by the System, enumerates the credit insurance policies and procedures (hence the name "V-loans"). The fee paid by the insured lender increases with the percentage of the loans that is guaranteed. Different loan values are given to receivables, finished inventories, and goods in process.

When term loans are made to finance working capital assets and business expansion, management will appraise the financial situation in terms of anticipated "cash flow." A cash budget showing anticipated cash receipts and disbursements in detail over the life of the loan is generally required by the lender, and it is also desirable when considered from the viewpoint of management. Project budgets, *pro forma* balance sheets, and income statements are more helpful in planning term borrowing than they are in short-term borrowing.[1] Earning power and depreciation allowances are emphasized in term loans, while working capital strength is stressed in short-term loans.

The increase in term loans, which reflects the demand for longer term loans by business firms, has been accompanied by a change in the attitude of commercial bankers toward the uses of bank assets. At

---

[1] A project budget is separate from the general budget of a business firm, and it contains estimates for a contemplated activity such as a new product. A *pro forma* ("for the sake of form") statement is used to describe financial and other statements or conclusions based upon assumed or anticipated facts.

one time bankers stressed the commercial loan theory—making short-term self-liquidating business loans. Later, commercial bankers emphasized the shiftability theory—selling marketable securities to others to obtain cash in case of need. (Amendments to the Federal Reserve Act liberalized the conditions under which member banks can borrow at Federal Reserve banks.[2] The increase in the national debt has made it easier for banks to acquire assets that can be turned into cash without loss or delay.)

Now, bankers realize that they can meet their depositors' demands for money by selling assets to or borrowing from their Federal Reserve banks. In lending bank funds under term loan agreements, they are accepting the anticipated income theory—that loans will be liquidated out of future earnings of the business enterprise. Banks are willing to lend to business firms for longer periods, and from the point of view of the banks, such loans are highly desirable provided borrowers' earnings are adequate to meet interest charges and installment principal payments as they become due. (After 1938, bank examiners shifted emphasis away from "marketability" to "normal value" as the test of the quality of bank assets; this made it possible for bankers to make longer term loans without being criticized by examiners.)

The growth in term lending by commercial banks has caused some concern among central bankers. Alfred Hayes, president of the Federal Reserve Bank of New York, has warned banks against becoming "so heavily committed in the form of longer-term advances that they cannot adequately meet the legitimate short-term needs for which commercial banking provides rather unique facilities."[3] The fear is that American banks will be borrowing short (deposit liabilities) and lending long, which will reduce their liquidity and make them unduly dependent on the Federal Reserve System.[4] Another danger is

[2] The Banking Act of 1935 permits member banks to obtain advances from the Federal Reserve banks when secured to the satisfaction of the Federal Reserve banks. Lending is subject to regulations of the Board of Governors of the Federal Reserve System, at a penalty rate of not less than ½ of 1 per cent per annum above the discount rate in effect on the date of the advance or loan. This means that, in addition to the use of federal government securities and short-term eligible paper, other assets may be pledged as security for a loan obtained from a Federal Reserve bank. Most of the advantages associated with this permissive provision have been psychological because Federal Reserve policy has emphasized open-market operations, and most member banks have had government securities to pledge when borrowing at Federal Reserve banks.

[3] "Lending Problems: Banks Don't Want to Make Term Loans," *Business Week* (July 30, 1960), pp. 114 and 117.

[4] See also, A. L. Mills, Jr., "Longer Term Loan Implications for Banking," *Commercial and Financial Chronicle* (November 12, 1959), pp. 3 and 32.

that banks' term lending will bring inflationary pressures on the economy by financing an excessive capital goods expansion.

The attitute of central bankers toward term lending by commercial banks may have considerable effect on the way business firms may finance their intermediate term needs in the future. In term lending, it should be noted that commercial banks are competing with the capital market and shifting away from their traditional function of supplying short-term credit needs of business firms. This shift is also indicated by the growth in consumer and homeowner loans among commercial banks' assets. Hence, it may be expected that in the future business firms will become more dependent on insurance companies, pension funds, and other noncommercial bank lenders for their intermediate-term loans and on open-market financing for intermediate and long-term funds.

CHARACTERISTICS OF TERM LOANS

Maturities of term loans to business firms vary, but there is a tendency for maturities to be longer when interest rates are low and loanable funds are abundant and to be shorter when interest rates are high and loanable funds are scarce. In the 1930's, when term loans to business first became common, initial maturities were usually for three, four, or five years; but, by 1940, about one half of the volume of term loans had maturities exceeding five years. A survey conducted by the Federal Reserve System indicated that 47.5 per cent of term loans made by member banks had maturities of from five to ten years and 6.8 per cent in excess of ten years.[5] Today, term loans make up over 50 per cent of the business loans of New York City banks and only a slightly lower percentage of those of other large city banks.

Although there are many exceptions, the provision for amortization of term loans is common. One of the characteristics of term lending is the flexibility of repayment terms. The terms may be regular, calling for annual, semiannual, quarterly, or monthly installment payments; or they may be irregular, depending on the nature of the business, the regularity of income, and maturity dates of other obligations such as corporate income taxes and debt obligations. A business enterprise may arrange for retirement of only a part of the loan during its life, with the bulk of the obligation to be refinanced

[5] "Term Lending to Business by Commercial Banks in 1946," *Federal Reserve Bulletin* (May, 1947), p. 499; and "Member Bank Term Lending to Business, 1955–57," *Federal Reserve Bulletin* (April, 1959), pp. 353–68.

at the end of the loan period. Since some term loans are made in anticipation of a more permanent form of financing at a later date, a business firm may borrow for a given number of years with no provisions for repayment of the loan on the installment plan.

In term lending, banks usually permit prepayment without penalty, but insurance companies usually attach a penalty to prepayment which is similar to that used when preferred stocks or bonds are called before maturity. In case of prepayment of part of a loan, the proceeds are usually applied to the installment notes having the longest maturities. The term loan agreement may require the borrower to repay all or part of the loan if fixed assets are sold. If and when earnings justify doing so, borrowers may welcome the privilege of prepaying loans, but lenders do not relish reinvesting at lower interest rates. For companies whose earnings are better than anticipated, profitable refinancing may be possible; however, if earnings are less than anticipated, then lenders may be left "holding the bag." Usually, term loan agreements contain detailed provisions for installment payments, prepayment, and the allocation of funds.

To care for intermediate credit needs, arrangements for term loans are frequently made by large business firms as an alternative to financing in the capital market, as well as by small and middle-sized business firms that find it too expensive or impossible to finance in the capital market. The competition among banks and/or insurance companies makes it possible for even small business enterprises to arrange for term loans under favorable conditions. Nevertheless, analysis of interest rates indicates that bankers normally charge lower rates on large loans than on small ones because in term lending as in other forms of lending, the risks and the costs of administration are proportionately less on large loans. Interest rates on term loans vary from less than 5 per cent to as high as 10 per cent per annum in individual cases where risks are large.

Usually, interest rates on term loans are higher than on short-term loans, but the margin of difference is surprisingly small (from ¼ to ½ of 1 per cent per annum). Some term loan agreements contain an "escalator" clause which provides for higher interest rates under certain conditions. Since term loans require more supervision than short-term loans, from the viewpoint of the lender, the higher interest rate may be offset by the higher cost of administration.

Business firms may facilitate borrowing by pledging assets such as land and buildings, machinery, equipment, stocks and bonds, and working capital assets. In term lending, the most important factor in determining the safety of loans is anticipated earnings. In analyzing the credit position of a borrower, emphasis is on the market for the firm's product; the competitive position of the firm; the firm's inventory position; the influence of cyclical, seasonal, and other price changes on the net profits of the company; depreciation, depletion and obsolescence charges; and the financial position of the officers and chief stockholders. The longer-term loans require application of security analysis techniques with emphasis on future earnings as well as credit techniques with emphasis on cash or "liquidity." The capital nature of such loans is illustrated by types of business firms that account for a high percentage of funds borrowed —metal and metal products firms; petroleum, coal, chemical, and rubber companies; and transportation and public utility corporations—all of which have heavy fixed capital requirements.

In term loan contracts, two documents are important—the promise to pay and the term loan agreement. The term loan agreement covers the manner in which the borrower is to conduct his financial affairs until the loan is repaid. The agreement is signed at the time the loan is negotiated and is one of the conditions under which the loan is made. The details of the agreement are drawn so as to fit the needs of the particular business firm, but the objective is always to keep the anticipated earnings of the borrower unimpaired so that he will be able to meet the interest and installment payments on his term loan. To have these details in writing and agreed to before a loan is made reduces the possibility of misunderstandings and protects not only the lender but also the borrower (changes in the lender's loan policies could be embarrassing to the debtor).

The provisions most frequently found in term loan agreements include prohibitions against (1) paying excessive dividends, (2) borrowing from other sources, (3) guaranteeing or assuming obligations of other companies, (4) selling business assets or specific assets such as accounts receivable (if selling fixed assets is permitted, the proceeds must be applied to the term loan in reverse order of repayment), (5) investing liquid assets and repurchasing the firm's own shares, and (6) merging or consolidating with other firms. Usually, the borrower is required to (1) maintain a certain current ratio, (2) keep property in good condition, (3) use the proceeds of the loan as prescribed, (4) carry adequate insurance, (5) keep adequate accounting records and make them available for audit and verification, and (6) furnish regular financial statements to lenders. Additional clauses commonly found in term loan agreements are to the effect that (1) property hereinafter acquired is included in the agreement (after-acquired property clause), (2) the entire obligation becomes due and payable upon failure of the firm to comply with any provisions or standards set forth in the agreement (acceleration clause), and (3) the interest rate will increase or decrease under certain circumstances, such as the increase or decrease in the prime rate of a particular city bank or rediscount rate of the district Federal Reserve bank (the "escalator" clause).

Since most banks are prohibited from lending more than 10 per cent of their capital and surplus to one business firm, large term loans made by banks in small communities must be syndicated, and this may also be necessary for extraordinarily large loans made by city banks.

When a term loan is syndicated, it is divided among several banks and/or insurance companies. One lender serves as leader for the group and the amounts lent, the repayments, and the losses if any, are prorated among the members. The borrower deals with the syndicate leader, who is compensated for his work by being paid a service fee. Serial notes may be issued or the entire loan may be represented by one promissory note with each member receiving a participation certificate. If serial notes are used, those of shorter maturity customarily bear a lower interest rate than those having longer maturities. If both banks and insurance companies participate, the latter usually select the longer-term notes. When multiple lending is used, notes are retained by members rather than sold to the public as would be the case in open-market financing through investment bankers.

Flexibility is one of the most interesting aspects of financing with term loans: maturities, installment payments, etc., may be tailored to meet the needs of individual borrowers. Usually, the term loan is for five years and seldom for more than ten years, but Chrysler Corporation has borrowed for 100 years.[6] Terms may be arranged so that the proceeds of the loan may be taken in installments

[6] On March 1, 1954, the Chrysler Corporation announced that it had arranged with the Prudential Insurance Company for a $250,000,000 loan due July 1, 2054. The interest rate was 3¼ per cent and the proceeds were to be taken in installments over a three-year period starting July 1, 1954. At any time after July 1, 1962, the one hundred-year note could be converted by either party into twenty-year notes with equal sinking-fund payments and with a reduced interest rate. The corporation also has the privilege of repaying out of its own funds up to one fifth of the total borrowed in any one year. The proceeds are to be used for expansion purposes. (In 1953 and 1954, Chrysler Corporation purchased most of the assets of Briggs Manufacturing Company.) When net receipts are considered, the terms are a little more favorable to the corporation than those obtained by General Motors Corporation on the sale of debentures in January, 1954. While this could be used as an argument in favor of private placement, the difference may have been due to the slight decrease in interest rates between January, 1954, and March, 1954.

as funds are needed by the borrower. Sometimes, the term loan agreement amounts to a kind of standby credit arrangement as during World War II, when business expansion depended on obtaining war contracts. When credit is made available on a call basis, a standby fee (usually $\frac{1}{4}$ of 1 per cent per annum) is charged on the average amount of the unused credit commitment.

A term loan offers many advantages to a business firm which requires loan funds that need not be liquidated in a year or less in the normal course of business. If the need for funds is permanent, the business firm should plan to finance with equity capital as soon as conditions make such financing feasible; otherwise, repayment of loans should be in installments.

The development of term loans has made it possible for bankers to meet the political pressure from various government officials who claimed that bankers were not co-operating in solving the financial problems of small business firms. Term lending has benefited business firms—small firms have access to more bank funds than formerly, but they still have intermediate term financing problems which will be considered in greater detail in a later chapter.

INTERMEDIATE-TERM NOTES OF CORPORATIONS

Intermediate-term notes and other credit instruments may be sold directly or indirectly by business firms in the capital market with the assistance of investment bankers. For large corporations seeking credit, this method of financing is an alternative (and sometimes a supplement) to arranging for a term loan with one or more lenders. (Central bankers would favor greater use of this market by qualified business firms.) Large firms may shift from term borrowing to open-market financing and vice versa for intermediate credit in the same way that they may shift from direct borrowing from banks for short-term loans to open-market financing with issues of commercial paper and vice versa. This choice of the source of funds permits large corporations to shift from one market to the other for interest and other reasons. Commercial banks could make the open market more attractive to business firms by increasing their interest rates on term loans, which are at the present time just a fraction of 1 per cent above the prime rate for qualified large borrowers.

Open-market financing with intermediate-term notes usually makes use of promissory notes that are identified by numbers and with dates arranged so that a certain number mature annually in approximately equal installments. Corporate notes may be secured or unsecured and they may be offered publicly or sold by private placement. If corporate notes are offered publicly, they are usually issued under a trust indenture which contains most of the clauses found in term loan agreements. The trust indenture is held by a trust company which acts for both the debtor corporation and investors. Some of these notes will be purchased by insurance companies, pension funds, and other lenders without there being a public distribution.

Corporations may arrange for private placement of notes with one or more insurance companies and/or banks; but, when sold by private placement, these notes may not be offered for resale to general investors. In private placement, terms are arrived at by direct negotiation between the corporation and the prospective lenders. This tends to speed up the transaction because it avoids registration of the issue with the Securities and Exchange Commission. (After registration, there is a twenty-day waiting or "cooling" period, subject to shortening under some circumstances, before the securities may be sold publicly.)

By private placement, the corporation also avoids payment of a registration fee, a federal issuance tax of 11 cents per $100, a trustee's fee for holding the trust indenture, and an investment banker's commission (for all or part of the gross spread between the price paid by investors and the amount received by the corporation). These advantages of private placement may be offset in whole or part if the interest rate is higher than it would have been if the notes had been sold publicly. Generally, private sales of notes are more common than of bonds because note issues are smaller and the maturities shorter than for bonds. The techniques in financing with bonds are similar to those in financing with notes, and they will be considered in later chapters.

The reasons for issuing corporate notes are similar to the reasons for financing with term loans—namely, to refund preferred stocks, bonds, and other obligations; to increase working capital; to finance plant and equipment costs, and so on. The use of corporate notes to increase working capital is illustrated by the borrowing experiences of the United States Steel Corporation during the summer of 1954. By the end of 1953, the working capital of the United States Steel Corporation was down to $346 million, and the corporation was faced with federal corporate income and other tax payments of over $400 million which had to be met in full by June 15, 1954. While the corporation had been financing its post-World War II working capital needs with retained earnings and depreciation allowances, plant replacements and corporate income taxes as well as outlays for wages and other needs resulted in a shortage of working capital.

The United States Steel Corporation's issue of corporate notes or debentures consisted of ten distinct series totaling $300 million of which $75 million was sold privately to the United States Steel and Carnegie Pension Fund. A banking syndicate headed by Morgan, Stanley & Company offered the remaining $225 million to the public. The chief purchasers were commercial banks which sought the notes for their own accounts and in behalf of pension and trust funds under their management. (Interest on the serial notes varied from 1.30 per cent to 2.65 per cent but averaged about 2 per cent—$6 million for the first year.) This was the first public issue made by the United States Steel Corporation since 1940, and it illustrated that even the strongest corporations may need to borrow to improve their working capital positions.

FINANCING PURCHASE AND LEASE OF EQUIPMENT

As previously noted, modern equipment and machinery used by business firms are often purchased with funds borrowed under term loan arrangements. Property of this type also lends itself to installment sales financing. The terms of sale vary widely, depending on the kind of equipment being financed, custom, and other factors. Maturities of equipment loans tend to fall into the intermediate credit class, usually being five years or less but also for as long as ten years. In the case of rolling stock of railroads, the time period is from ten to fifteen years.

Bankers and other lenders prefer to lend on equipment that is not too specialized, does not depreciate rapidly, and has a secondhand market. The size of the loan which a business firm may obtain relative to the cost of the equipment varies from two thirds to three fourths of the cost of new equipment and from one half to two thirds of the appraised value of used equipment. For a small business firm, the cost of borrowing may be high and loans are usually repaid on the installment plan. Customarily there are other charges that the borrower must bear; and, in terms of simple interest, the rates may vary from 10 to 24 per cent or more.

The "Philadelphia" plan of financing is a special arrangement for protecting lenders (similar to the equipment trust certificate used in financing railroad rolling stock). Under this plan, the buyer of equipment makes a down payment and agrees to make periodic payments sufficiently large to meet interest and other charges and to retire the principal over the life of the loan. The lender is given title to the property until the loan is retired. In other cases, the buyer of the equipment signs a lease–purchase contract which requires him to pay taxes on the property, to keep it in good physical repair, and to carry adequate insurance against fire, theft, public liability, and other hazards. This type of term loan is used widely in airline financing.

OBTAINING EQUIPMENT THROUGH LEASE ARRANGEMENTS

Any business firm, regardless of size, which has a shortage of cash may find it advantageous to lease rather than to buy equipment. Leasing shifts the burden of financing the equipment to the supplier whose superior financial resources and credit position make such financing feasible.[7] In addition, lease arrangements may offer the business firm a short-term advantage in that lease–rental fees are deductible for tax purposes. However, there may be no long-run advantage for the lessee because the cost of such equipment may be recovered over its useful life in the form of depreciation allowances. For business firms that are able to obtain capital funds at low interest rates, leasing equipment may be unprofitable when the total cost of leasing is considered (rental fees, installation, maintenance, service, and insurance charges).

Through lease arrangements, business firms may obtain the use of needed plants, stores, fixtures, and equipment such as typewriters, adding machines, computers, bookkeeping machines, furniture, and laboratory, office, and factory equipment. Thereby they may avoid tying up capital funds which may be used more profitably to finance growth and expansion. Although this method of obtaining fixed assets has been used for many years to obtain specialized types of equipment, in recent years there has been an expansion in the items which may be leased to include all forms of capital equipment having depreciable lives.

The two most commonly used leasing plans are the straight lease and the equity lease plans. Under the first, the lessee acquires no proprietory interest in the assets leased; under the second, the lessee

---

[7] One area of the leasing business entails leasing goods at the consumer level. In the car rental field, the user of a rented car saves the expenses of maintaining, financing, washing, painting, garaging and other items. For former car owners in metropolitan areas, the savings on insurance, garaging, licensing, depreciation, and property taxes are considerable. In some areas, a rent-a-plane plan is being tried. Many university students are familiar with rental arrangements for typewriters and other items of school equipment.

acquires an interest in the assets leased and is given an option to buy the assets at the end of the lease period. When a lease arrangement contains an option to buy the equipment at the end of the lease period, the lessee is usually permitted to deduct lease payments as operating costs. In effect, this is similar to the provision permitting rapid depreciation of fixed assets. However, unless care is taken, such an arrangement may be considered a conditional sale wherein there would be some question as to the deductibility of payments for tax purposes.

A business firm may increase its liquidity by leasing equipment rather than buying it, using the difference in cash outlays to generate more income by increasing inventories and receivables. Although a firm's balance sheet would show lease arrangements in footnotes, the volume of its current assets relative to fixed assets would give a picture of greater liquidity. A final advantage claimed for leasing is that the lessee thereby obtains the use of up-to-date equipment and avoids the risk of expensive replacement of equipment due to obsolescence.[8]

In 1959, the American Machine & Foundry Company announced that it had signed a record number of leases for automatic pinspotters (automatic pinboys for bowling alleys); General Electric Company was leasing television studio equipment on a five-year rental basis; and currently there are an estimated 1,000 companies in the business of leasing fleets of trucks and automobiles to business firms. Among the items of equipment available today on a lease basis, in addition to those already mentioned, are earth-moving and road-building machinery used by construction companies; all kinds of tools and equipment used in various industries (drilling, cutting, and grinding tools; milling, baking, laundry, restaurant, mining, sewing, and candy-making equipment); and air-conditioning, sprinklers, electronic equipment, transportation, and many other miscellaneous types of equipment.

A survey conducted in 1960 by *Mill & Factory* indicates that corporations lease equipment for the following reasons: to avoid large initial outlays of capital (40 per cent), to deduct payments for tax

---

[8] The tax income approach used by firms in the business of leasing equipment may be illustrated by the following: When a business firm in the 52 per cent bracket is shown a comparison of the lease method and the purchase method of acquiring the use of a $1,000 piece of machinery, the following statistical analysis may be used. The total cost of the machine under lease arrangement would be $1,260, total cash price $1,000. In a 52 per cent bracket, the firm must earn $2,080 in order to buy the machine. What the firm must earn to pay for the machine ($2,080) less the firm's cost if it leases it ($1,260) means a saving of $820.

purposes (21 per cent), to stay modern (18 per cent), to simplify maintenance procedure (13 per cent), to obtain equipment available only on a lease basis (6 per cent), and to obtain the use of equipment which will be needed for only a short time (2 per cent).[9] In this survey the types of assets being leased by the business firms included in the report were office machines (31 per cent), transportation equipment (23 per cent), material-handling equipment (18 per cent), machine tools (17 per cent), special machinery equipment (9 per cent), and lighting and maintenance equipment (2 per cent).

Of the business firms covered in this survey, 69 per cent reported that they had obtained equipment on a rental basis, 7 per cent stated that their lease payments were being applied toward the purchase price of the equipment, and of the remainder, some were using a combined rental–purchase plan, others were renting with an option to buy, and a few were leasing equipment from the government. According to the statements of these firms, 56 per cent of them planned to continue leasing at the present rate, 30 per cent expected to expand lease arrangements, and 14 per cent planned to curtail lease arrangements.

The increase in the cost of equipment, the quest of business firms for liquidity, and the high tax rates on corporate income have all been factors in the expansion in the leasing of equipment by business firms. The practice of leasing equipment has a history of almost one hundred years; and the pioneers in this field include the Bell Telephone Company, which began to lease its equipment to customers during the 1870's. Other corporations which pioneered in leasing their products are the United Shoe Machinery, International Business Machines, Remington Rand (now Sperry Rand Corporation), and the Pullman Corporation.

Since World War II, the growth in technology which has resulted in the production of many new and expensive machines and other equipment has been a major factor in the increase in lease arrangements by industrial and other business firms. For illustration, it has been estimated that 90 per cent of all electric computers are being leased as compared with only 3 per cent of typewriters. When business firms lease such equipment, they not only avoid capital outlays of sizable proportions but also obtain expert servicing of equipment leased; at the same time, they protect themselves from the risk

---

[9] "Does Industry Lease Capital Equipment?" *Mill & Factory*, Vol. LXVII, No. 1 (July, 1960), pp. 73–75.

of obsolescence which ownership entails. An example of the relative costs is presented in the following illustration of rental and selling prices of electric data-processing equipment marketed by the Univac Division of Sperry Rand Corporation.[10]

Model	*Monthly Rental Range*	*Selling Price Range*
Univac Solid State 80, 90, and STEP (Simple Transition to Electronic Procession)	$3,500 to $12,600	$175,000 to $678,850
Univac III	$14,400 to $35,000	$695,000 to $1,609,000
Univac 490 Real Time System	$20,000 to $40,000	$1,000,000 to $2,000,000
Univac 1107	$40,000 to $60,000	$1,800,000 to $2,700,000

Business firms in some fields have a choice of leasing equipment either from the manufacturer or an independent lessor. Some manufacturing companies organize subsidiary corporations which operate as captive finance companies to lease equipment to users. On the other hand, since most manufacturing companies are interested primarily in profits from manufacturing rather than from leasing equipment, their subsidiaries may offer more favorable terms than independent lessors.

The manufacturer, interested in broadening the market for his product, may include selling items related to the equipment leased. Since rental fees will replace installment payments, the effect may be to give the lessor more stable income over the life of the equipment. Part of the return from leasing will be accounted for as depreciation allowances which will write off the cost of the equipment during its useful life.

The lessor also contracts to service equipment leased (maintenance and repair), and the fact that the equipment is kept in good repair should lengthen its life and also, should promote better customer relations. However, these advantages to the lessor may be offset by the cost of financing, a decline in the rate of capital turnover, and possibly excessive servicing expenses. Usually lessees are less careful in the use of leased property than in the use of property which they own, but the lessor may lessen this risk by clauses in lease contracts requiring that certain standards be met in the use of property and imposing penalties for violations of lease agreements.[11]

---

[10] Sperry Rand Corporation, *Report to Stockholders, Nine Months Ended December 31, 1960* (New York, 1961) p. 3.

[11] Lease contracts of International Business Machines specify that only authorized personnel may service their machines and that their use is limited to eight hours per day. If used for sixteen hours per day, the rental fee is increased by 50 per cent.

An independent lessor purchases the equipment or machinery that he leases to users directly from the manufacturer, often having it delivered directly to the lessee. An independent lessor's profits are derived from brokerage fees, agency or dealer discounts, and mark-ups on the list price of the equipment. Much of his profit results from selling the equipment to the user at the end of the lease period or selling it in the open market for used equipment. Many of the independent leasing companies are national in their scope of operations with branch offices throughout the United States.[12]

A business firm may reduce its obligations to the lessor by agreeing to finance insurance costs, taxes, and maintenance charges, but whether or not this would result in any net saving would depend on many factors. Common lease periods for machinery and equipment vary from three to five years. Under a three-year lease contract, payments may be 50 per cent the first year, 30 per cent the second year, and 20 per cent the third year; under a five-year contract, they may be 33 per cent the first year, 27 per cent the second, 20 per cent the third, 13 per cent the fourth, and 7 per cent the fifth year. Customarily, payments are in monthly installments. In some cases, credit up to 75 per cent of lease payments is allowed on the purchase price. However, terms are flexible enough so that a business firm may obtain a contract tailor-made for its requirements. Often leasing companies have franchise distributors who may add a leasing commission of 5 per cent to the unit cost plus attachments and freight charges.

In considering a lease proposal, a business firm should examine all costs including rental fees, service and maintenance charges, installment payments, and insurance fees, and compare them to the cost of owning the assets—cost of capital, tax savings available, annual depreciation, and real loss in value as the equipment becomes obsolescent. Even if a close examination of relative costs is made, different firms may not reach the same conclusion. For illustration, the variance in costs of borrowing funds may result in one firm deciding to lease and another deciding to buy.

A high-profit company may prefer to lease rather than to buy because of its high earning rate on operations, while a low-profit company may prefer to buy rather than to lease because its earning rate is below the rate paid on leasing equipment. During the early years of a lease contract, tax savings may be high because the rental cost is

---

[12] Among the leasing companies are the Rento Company of Philadelphia, the United States Corporation, Booth Leasing Company, and Nationwide Leasing Company.

deductible as an expense, while on equipment purchased deductions are limited to depreciation allowances. Although there is usually a short-term tax savings when equipment is leased, there may be a long-run tax advantage in buying equipment. In addition, when such purchases are made with borrowed funds, the interest paid thereon is deductible as an expense. In either case, the value of tax savings will vary with the income tax rate to which the firm is subjected.

When business firms make use of the 1954 provisions for rapid depreciation, which permit rapid recovery of the purchase price tax free, it is generally to their advantage to purchase rather than to lease equipment. However, management should weight the advantages of buying against the immediate effect of doing so on their company's cash position, uncertainties of the future, and the possibility of premature obsolescence of equipment. (Usually the lessor can better afford the risk of premature obsolescence than the user because he may be able to transfer the equipment to other users more readily and to recover a greater salvage value by finding a market for parts of the equipment.)

Business firms, in addition to leasing machinery and equipment, are also leasing plants and buildings. The sell–lease technique is used extensively in the retail field wherein some chain stores follow the practice of selling their buildings to insurance companies under lease-back arrangements. At the present time, companies in practically every industry are using this lease arrangement. In financing the leasing of land and buildings, most of the capital funds are provided by life insurance companies, but some may be provided by local investors.

SUMMARY

Intermediate debts of business firms, those running from one to five years (and sometimes up to ten years), may be in the form of term loans; installment paper arising from installment-plan purchases of equipment, machinery, and other forms of business property; and notes and other forms of credit instruments having maturities of from one to five years. Customarily, term loans are repayable on the installment plan, and they are made chiefly by commercial banks and insurance companies. Term lending is accompanied by a term loan agreement which specifies the conditions under which the business firm is to operate. A term loan that is too large for any one bank in a community to make may be participated in by other banks and/or insurance companies.

Some business corporations are able to finance in the open market with intermediate-term notes. These corporate notes may be secured or unsecured; they usually appear in serial form with denominations designed to enhance their marketability; customarily, they represent debts that are repayable on the installment plan. The financing of purchase and lease of equipment and machinery often involves intermediate credit arrangements. Usually maturities of loans are five years or less; but, as in the case of rolling stock of railroads, they may be from ten to fifteen years.

Lease arrangements for machinery and equipment have increased in importance during recent years. Under such arrangements, manufacturers may lease equipment or machinery to users and assume responsibility for financing. This procedure is used by manufacturers of shoe making and repair equipment and manufacturers of accounting and statistical machines and other specialized equipment (as illustrated by the United Shoe Machinery and International Business Machine Corporation). In some cases, manufacturers sell their equipment to independent leasing companies who lease it to users; and, in other cases, they sell to subsidiaries (captive finance companies) who sell or lease it to users.

When manufacturers sell equipment or machinery on the installment plan, they may either hold the installment notes or sell them to banks or finance companies. The equipment or machines serve as security for the debt; where state laws permit, a conditional sales contract is commonly used. In other cases, a chattel mortgage or a lease–purchase contract—with the title held in trust by a trust company—may be used. The last arrangement is used most widely in financing the rolling stock of railroads which is considered in a later chapter. When a business firm has the option of leasing or purchasing equipment, the decision is usually a difficult one because there are advantages and disadvantages inherent in each. However, the fact that the volume of leasing is increasing more rapidly than the amount of investment in plants and equipment suggests that at the present time the advantages of leasing seem to outweigh those of purchasing for many business firms.

QUESTIONS AND PROBLEMS

1. Identify intermediate debts of business firms. Compare them to short-term and long-term debts of business firms.
2. When may it be advantageous for a business firm to replace a short-term loan contract with a term loan contract?

3. What factors explain the increase in term lending by banks to business firms?
4. In term lending, an important factor in analyzing the safety of a proposed loan is appraising anticipated earnings of the borrower. Why?
5. What restrictive clauses are usually found in term loan agreements? What requirements, in addition to those included in ordinary promises to pay, are usually found in term loan contracts?
6. Identify: (*a*) "after-acquired property" clause, (*b*) "acceleration" clause, and (*c*) "escalator" clause.
7. Why are term loans sometimes syndicated?
8. Analyze: "The main reason for the volume rise [in equipment leasing] is that working capital remains tight for most businesses. Even though the credit situation eased slightly in 1960, corporate liquidity declined by 13 per cent." ("Equipment Leasing Up," *New York Times*, January 9, 1961, p. 61.)
9. Distinguish between financing purchase of and lease of equipment.
10. "One thing is clear about the computer systems industry in 1961. Only large, well-financed manufacturers will continue in the production of complete systems. Development and tooling costs are staggering. Moreover, profits come primarily from rentals rather than sales and producers must wait to recoup huge investments." ("Computers Join the Billionaires," *New York Times*, January 9, 1961, p. 62.) Assume that sales were made on the installment plan; would the financing problems differ materially from those present when computers are leased? Explain.
11. A study made by Libby, McNeill & Libby showed that in their expansion plans, immediate long-term financing was not required when funds available from depreciation allowances and retained earnings were taken into account, but that because of the "tightening of the money market and as insurance against unexpected developments" the company "took advantage of a favorable opportunity . . . to negotiate a $10,000,000 loan agreement with five Chicago banks." Under terms of this agreement, the company may borrow any portion of the amount before December 1, 1961, and "on that date the amount borrowed may be converted to a term loan repayable over the following five years in equal annual installments." (Libby, McNeill & Libby, *Annual Report for the Year Ended June 27, 1959* [Chicago, 1959], p. 5.) What management policy is suggested by the foregoing? Discuss.
12. Analyze: "Borrowings from the Bank by apparel producers and retail establishments were among lines showing an increase. Moreover, the aggregate of installment credit outstanding rose . . . smaller business concerns employed this means to finance purchases of needed equipment on an increasing scale." The Chase Manhattan Bank, *Annual Report 1960* (New York, 1961), p. 14.

PART V

Owners' Equity

In considering the financing of business firms, it is difficult to treat one aspect of the problem without taking others into account. For illustration, a discussion of how and why business firms finance with funds from operations and ignoring the effects of using funds from external sources would tend to lead to incorrect conclusions. Also, the relationship between financing short-term, intermediate, or long-term needs with equity capital and long-term obligations cannot be ignored. In other words, all aspects of financing business firms are interrelated.

In business finance, the term *capitalization* is used to include the total dollar value of bonds and par value of stock outstanding; but, in some case, it would be more accurate to include also term loans, debentures, and notes because these credit instruments are being used to an increasing extent in financing business corporations.

This section, financing with owners' equity, emphasizes the services of investment bankers in the sale of equities, financing with common stock, the sale of stock through preemptive rights and privileged subscription, and financing with preferred stock.

CHAPTER 16

Corporate Financing through Investment Bankers

WHILE SMALL business concerns must usually depend upon their commercial bankers for financial advice and services, large corporations have, in addition, the assistance of investment banking firms. A corporation which has not previously financed in the capital market may approach (or be approached by) a representative of an investment banking house with a proposal to underwrite a new security issue. Among the proposals commonly presented are those for funding the floating debt,[1] refunding outstanding issues of long-term bonds with other issues, raising new capital with stock or bond issues, and financing combinations or mergers of two or more corporations. Large investment houses are able to assist corporations in working out these and other plans for raising new funds and revising their financial structures.

A business firm may negotiate with an insurance company or other financial institution for a long-term loan or for the private placement of a bond issue. When two or more lenders participate in a capital loan or in buying a bond issue, the promissory notes or bonds seldom reappear in the capital market; however, when stocks or bonds are sold through investment bankers in the capital market they may change ownership many times before their retirement. This chapter deals with the role of investment bankers and others who aid business firms in placing long-term obligations and equities, and with

[1] Floating debt is any debt not yet funded; that is, not formally evidenced by a bond issue.

dealers and brokers who make a secondary market for the securities issued by business corporations.

DISTINCTIVE FEATURES OF INVESTMENT BANKING

Raising Fixed Capital. The primary economic function of investment bankers is providing long-term capital funds for business enterprises and governments. They do this by purchasing issues of securities from business corporations and governments and selling the securities to institutional and individual investors. In effect, investment bankers are middlemen between sellers and buyers of securities; but, because of the nature of the merchandise handled, investment bankers are expected to act as financial advisors not only to the business firms whose securities they originate and distribute but also to the investors to whom they sell the securities (which raises the question of whether both can be served impartially at the same time).

When investment bankers assist in raising new capital for a business corporation, they advise the corporation as to the type and form of securities that should be offered: if a stock offering is to be made, whether preferred or common stock should be issued; and if bonds are to be issued, whether they should be convertible or nonconvertible. Because the methods used to raise capital funds may be varied and because market conditions are subject to change, the advice of investment bankers will depend not only on the requirements of the corporation and its capital structure but also on the prevailing conditions in the capital market. In some cases, a public offering may be preferred over private placement; in others, private placement with a small number of institutional investors may be advisable. Under other circumstances, an offering may be made to old stockholders or an entire issue may be sold to the highest bidder.

While investment bankers are primarily interested in purchasing and selling entire issues of new securities, they also contract with corporations to assist in selling new issues of stock or convertible bonds which are offered first to old stockholders through subscription rights. Under a contract, called a stand-by agreement, investment bankers help corporations by buying the portion of the issue for which old shareholders have not subscribed.

Investment bankers may contract with corporations to sell new issues on a "best effort" basis. Under this arrangement, an investment banker acts as an agent and his compensation is in the form of commissions (just as brokers are compensated when they buy and sell securities for others). As agents, investment bankers do not take title to the securities which they sell, thus avoiding the risks associated with outright purchase. An investment banker, because of his established clientele, can usually distribute securities more effectively than the issuing corporation could.

Sometimes a family or a few owners of a business corporation will seek the assistance of investment bankers to market their stock. (For illustration, in 1956 over 10 million shares of Ford Motor Company stock held by the Ford Foundation were sold to the general public through investment bankers). Usually, these so-called "secondary distributions" or "registered secondary offerings" of stock are primarily for the benefit of stockholders. However, for a growing business corporation public ownership is valuable because it tends to facilitate raising new capital, stimulate investors' interest in the product of the corporation, and attract the attention of potential investors in future issues of the company's stocks or bonds.

Investment banking houses, because of their broad experience, and close contacts with many different business firms, are in a position to facilitate the acquisitions, mergers, and combinations of business corporations. The major investment houses keep one list of corporations which wish to diversify their products by purchasing other business firms or by merging with them and another list of firms which meet the specifications of the first group. This knowledge, together with their facilities, makes it possible for the investment houses to assist in bringing about these combinations and to handle the financial details resulting from such mergers and acquisitions. In other cases, an investment banker may search out business firms and promote a merger by bringing the parties together, helping with the negotiations, giving advice as to the details of financing, and handling the sale of the securities to the public.

Investment bankers must consider the interests of both buyers (investors) and issuers (corporations) of securities. Apparently the interests of issuers have been represented more adequately than those of the thousands of widely scattered investors because the federal and state governments have found it necessary to make provisions for regulation of new security issues in order to protect investors. The better investment banking houses, realizing that their futures as "merchants of securities" depend upon having satisfied investors as clients, negotiate with corporations for provisions in bond issues as to interest rates, sinking funds, redemption and call prices, maturities, and other features that would have investor appeal. When a preferred stock issue is to be offered, the negotations pertain to the dividend rate, redemption or call price, conversion feature, and possibly sinking-fund provisions.[2]

Investment bankers are sometimes classified according to the nature of their merchandising business as wholesalers and retailers. While no investment house necessarily limits itself to a wholesale business, there are a few investment houses that originate and participate in underwriting new securities but do practically no retail selling. Such investment houses act as managers of underwriting syndicates and also as dealers in placing large blocks of securities with other dealers, retailers, and large institutional investors. A few such wholesalers have sales representatives who sell some securities at retail.

A larger number of investment houses in the wholesaler-retailer group are primarily interested in selling securities, but they also participate in underwriting activities and sometimes act as originators of new security issues. On occasion they may head purchasing syndicates that acquire issues; but, for the most part, they obtain the merchandise which they sell by participating in purchasing and/or selling syndicates originated and managed by larger houses.

The largest group of investment bankers are primarily retailers of securities. Because their financial resources are usually limited and their staffs small, they are unable to assume the risks of originating or participating in underwriting new issues and acquire most of their merchandise (at a discount from the offering price) from other houses who are members of purchasing syndicates or selling groups.

Most managers of business corporations which finance with security issues have established contacts with originating houses; therefore, a proposal for a new issue may come from either the investment house or the corporation. Investment houses keep close watch on the capital needs of their customer corporations and may anticipate their requirements and help to crystallize corporate management's plans for issuing securities.

There is a tendency for investment banking firms to become specialists in originating issues in certain fields such as transportation,

---

[2] The services that investment bankers offer investors must meet high professional standards because so many of the investors are insurance companies, pension funds, banks, educational foundations, religious and charitable associations, and other institutional investors as well as individuals. The major investment houses offer investment advisory and portfolio management services including continuous review of investments, conferences with portfolio managers, collection of dividends and interest, and safekeeping services. The staff of a large investment firm will include lawyers, accountants, economists, and research specialists.

public utilities, petroleum, aviation, rubber, and so on. This development is based in part on the fact that once a house has successfully underwritten an issue of a corporation, it often becomes its permanent investment banker. After having acquired the techniques and skills essential for handling an issue in a certain industry, the banker's services may be sought by or offered to others in the same industry. Other investment houses may solicit the services of such an investment banker to originate an issue, to manage the underwriting syndicate either alone or with a second house, or to be a member of the underwriting and/or selling syndicate. Once a banking house has established a reputation in a certain field, it may have established a clientele not only among business corporations in this field but also among investors interested in that class of securities (which would facilitate retail sales of new securities).

Negotiated Issues. The oldest and most common method whereby investment bankers obtain new issues is by direct negotiation with financial managers of corporations. Usually an established corporation has had past experience in selling security issues with the help of investment bankers; and, if the relationship has been mutually advantageous, a partner or officer of the investment banking firm may have been elected as a director of the business corporation. (Although less common, the opposite may be true: an officer of the corporation may be invited to be a director or officer of the investment banking house.)

If a business firm has contacted or been contacted by an investment house relative to its first public issue of securities, the investment house will make a survey of the available financial information pertaining to the firm. If the proposed financing seems worthwhile, a contract will be drawn up giving the investment house an option on the new issue for a specified period of time. During this option period, a more comprehensive analysis will be made of the corporation's affairs. Following this analysis, the investment banker and the corporation will work out the details covering the financial transactions. At this stage most of the work of the investment banker is advisory.

If an agreement can be reached as to terms of sale, a detailed formal purchase contract will be signed. The engraving of securities will be arranged for by the investment banker. The corporation is responsible for contracting for the services of a trustee, but the trustee is usually selected at the suggestion of the investment banker. The purchase agreement sets forth the plan, time, and method of payment for the securities along with provisions for delivery of the securities (either temporary or permanent bonds or stock certificates).

Often several plans for financing are considered and conditions in the capital market will affect both the details of the plan selected and the actual timing of the issue. While market conditions may be unsatisfactory for a short-term issue, they may be favorable for a long-term issue. At any particular time, there is a best plan for financing a specific company's capital needs; however, there is no specific plan that is best for financing any company's need at all times.

Since the passage of the Securities Act of 1933, most purchase agreements have contained a "market-out" clause which allows the purchase agreement to be terminated by the underwriter or purchasing syndicate prior to the offering of securities if certain unfavorable conditions develop. These conditions may be due to a change either in the company's affairs, such as legal proceedings against the company by stockholders, or in general market conditions, such as outbreak of war or a national bank moratorium. Fortunately the market-out clause is seldom used, but it usually appears in purchase agreements when securities are registered with the Securities and Exchange Commission because much can happen during the required twenty-day waiting period.

In the last stage of negotiation, the corporation and the investment banker will agree upon the offering price (the price at which the securities are to be offered to the general public) and the price paid to the corporation by investment bankers. The difference between the two prices is the "gross spread." The offering price must be selected to meet anticipated market conditions, and it will be influenced by market prices of the corporation's outstanding securities and of similar securities of other corporations in the same industry as well as by general market conditions. The gross spread is the underwriter's compensation, but the underwriter may also receive cash and/or securities as compensation for expenses incurred. When the issuer is a new corporation, an allotment of common stock is often made to the underwriter.

A best-effort commitment is a contract between the corporation and investment bankers in which the latter agree to use their best efforts to sell securities. The investment bankers assume no liability for the unsold portion of the issue and they do not take title to the securities as is done in a purchase agreement. Thus, the investment banker acts merely as an agent and the corporation carries the risk that the securities may not be sold. Although he assumes no risks in a best-effort commitment, the investment banker acts in an advisory capacity and assists in working out the details of placing the securities on the market. The investment banker is compensated for advisory assistance and he receives a commission on the securities which he sells. Other things being the same, the commission paid in a best-effort commitment is less than the gross spread plus fees in a purchase contract or stand-by underwriting contract.

Non-Negotiated Issues. The high quality of some securities justifies their sale to the highest bidder. This method has been used for many years in selling state and municipal issues, railroad equipment obligations, and—in some states—certain securities of gas and electric companies. In 1941, the Securities and Exchange Commission adopted Rule U–50. This rule, with certain minor exceptions, requires the securities of corporations subject to the Public Utility Holding Company Act of 1935 to be sold by competitive bidding.[3] In 1944, the Interstate Commerce Commission took a somewhat similar position in regard to the sale of railroad debt issues.[4]

Competitive bidding has been used by other companies even though there were no legal or regulatory requirements. For illustration, on August 18, 1954, the American Telephone and Telegraph Company announced that it would sell $250 million of new bonds at competitive bidding on September 21, 1954. The registration statement covering the issue was filed with the Securities and Exchange Commission on September 1. Thus, the sales date conformed to the effective date of the registration statement; that is, at the expiration of the twenty-day waiting period.

When corporations sell securities by competitive bidding there is always the possibility that there will be no bids or that the bids will be so low as to make the costs of financing prohibitive. However, to date, experiences with competitive bidding have been satisfactory, and those corporations that have been able to dispose of securities in this way have attracted bids which have reduced their costs of financ-

[3] Competitive bidding in accordance with the provisions of Rule U–50 became effective on May 7, 1941. The Commission retained the right to grant exemptions by order where it appears that competitive bidding is not necessary or appropriate to carry out the provisions of the Public Utility Holding Company Act. For a summary statement of financing pursuant to Rule U–50, see *Nineteenth Annual Report of the Securities and Exchange Commission, Fiscal Year Ended June 30, 1953* (Washington, D.C.: U.S. Government Printing Office, 1954), pp. 79–80.

[4] The Interstate Commerce Commission has regulatory authority over the issuance of securities by the railroads and can withhold approval if its policies are not followed. See Interstate Commerce Commission, *Ex Parte 158.* In the Matter of Competitive Bidding in the Sale of Securities Issued Under Section 20a of the Interstate Commerce Act, 257 I. C. C. 129.

ing. In the published invitation for bids, the time, place, and other conditions are indicated. Usually, investment bankers withhold bids until the deadline in order to set their bid prices in accordance with the latest prevailing market prices. At closing time, investment bankers exchange information about their bid prices and those in Wall Street may know who the successful bidder is even before the vendor can open the bids, determine the highest bidder, and make the announcement. The successful bidder may even sell the issue at retail on an "if-and-when-acquired basis" before his purchase has been confirmed.

From the viewpoint of investment bankers, the development of competitive bidding has tended to weaken the relationships between investment houses and corporations that had been built up over years of direct negotiation for security issues. On the other hand, competitive bidding has permitted other investment houses to participate in the underwriting of the securities of companies which formerly dealt exclusively with particular investment banking firms. However, even when an issue is to be sold through competitive bidding, the issuer customarily uses the advisory services of an investment banking firm during the preoffering stage, and often this investment house is the successful bidder for the issue.

By private placement of a security issue is meant the purchase and retention of the securities by one, two, or a small group of investors. One of the purposes of private placement is to eliminate the expenses of the middleman—the investment banker. Nevertheless, an investment banker usually assists a corporation in working out details of the security issue and in approaching prospective buyers such as insurance companies, private pension funds, and other large investors. Generally a bond issue is more suitable for private placement than a stock issue.

Private placement permits the sale of issues of securities without registration of the issue with the Securities and Exchange Commission as required by the Securities Act of 1933. However the main factor causing the increase in the volume of direct placement since 1933 has been the ability of one or a few insurance companies and other institutional investors to absorb entire issues. The competition for securities has led many institutions to negotiate directly with issuers or to submit bids when bonds are sold to the highest bidder. In negotiating directly with corporations, institutional investors have many advantages over investment bankers. In their negotiations, institutional investors may emphasize the facts that in private placement, the corporation saves the expense and effort incidental to registering the issue with the Securities and Exchange Commission; principal officers and directors of the issuing corporation avoid the personal liability for incomplete, misleading, or untrue statements assumed in filing registration statements with the Securities and Exchange Commission; the corporation avoids the twenty-day waiting period normally required before the registration statement becomes effective; management avoids an underwriting agreement and the market-out clause therein; and the corporation avoids the underwriting fees and other expenses associated with financing through investment bankers. Thus the chief advantages of this method of financing are the speed with which transactions may be completed, the savings in costs compared with public offerings, and the avoidance of disclosure concerning financial affairs required when other methods are used.

Investment bankers are able to assist business firms in obtaining capital funds under favorable terms through private placement because they are aware of the types of securities in which institutional investors are interested. To issuers, the chief disadvantage of private placement is that the securities so placed lose some of the marketability associated with public sales and this may be a handicap when they attempt to refinance through public offerings. In addition, public issues commonly sell at higher prices than those privately placed; therefore issuers must weigh the savings in financing through private placement against the higher interest rates paid on bonds placed privately.

Regardless of the method used to raise capital funds, business corporations may have the assistance of investment bankers in preparing bond indentures, selecting corporate trustees, making charter amendments in the case of stock issues, obtaining approval of the appropriate state regulatory agencies when needed, preparing applications for listing securities on exchanges, and preparing registration statements and other documents required by the Securities and Exchange Commission and/or state agencies.

INTERRELATIONSHIPS AMONG INVESTMENT HOUSES

In the preceding section, emphasis was on the relationships between issuers and investment banking firms; in this section, emphasis is on the relationship among investment houses in processing an issue.[5] This interrelationship necessitates agreements between the issuer of the securities and the members of the underwriting or purchasing group, among underwriters or purchasers, and between members of the purchasing or underwriting syndicate and other investment houses participating in the selling group.

In investment banking, underwriting refers to the guarantee by investment bankers to a business firm of a definite sum of money on a specified date in return for issues of bonds or stock. Because such issues are usually for large amounts, two or more investment banking houses form underwriting syndicates to handle most bond or stock issues. The number of participants in such a syndicate varies with the size of the issue, the resources of the investment houses, the degree of risk of the issue, and the condition of the market wherein the securities are to be sold at retail. Because many issues have to be carried several days before distribution is complete, it is important for investment houses to be able to obtain short-term loans from commercial banks.

Let us assume that the negotiation between the corporation and an investment banker (called the originating house) has reached the stage where the corporation is ready to sign the mutually agreed upon purchase agreement. Now the investment houses that have been invited to join in the financing will be asked to participate by signing the purchase agreement. This agreement is usually drawn so that each member of the syndicate participates separately in the purchase of the issue. If an investment house agrees to take $1 million of bonds in an issue of $10 million, his liability to the issuer is limited to that figure. In other words, he may not be held by the issuer for the purchase of the remaining $9 million of bonds. (However, for some securities, the contract may be drawn so that each investment house shall be jointly and severally liable.)

When investment bankers contract among themselves for handling an issue, their liability may be limited or unlimited. If the limited form of contract is used, an investment house meets its obligation when it sells its portion of the issue; but, if the unlimited form of contract is used, each house is expected to assume its prorata responsibility for the unsold balance at the end of the syndicate period.

---

[5] In October 1953 Harold R. Medina, United States Circuit Judge for the Southern District of New York, dismissed civil charges brought by the government against seventeen investment banking houses. It had been charged that "defendants entered into a combination, conspiracy and agreement to restrain and monopolize the securities business of the United States and that such business was thereby unreasonably restrained and in part monopolized." *United States* v. *Morgan*, 118 F. Supp. 621 (S.D.N.Y. 1953).

The limited or divided account is most popular among investment houses that have a strong sales organization; but, if there is an excellent market for the securities, it is a matter of indifference whether the divided or undivided account form of contract is used. When serial bonds are issued, there may be a strong demand for maturities at both ends of the issue with little demand for the middle maturities. Thus a participant could discharge his obligation to the syndicate by selling the popular securities. This difficulty may be overcome either by using the undivided account system or prorating the bonds of each maturity among the investment houses.

The purchasing syndicate may offer other investment houses an opportunity to participate in selling the issue. In this way, the syndicate manager, as agent for the purchasing syndicate, may mitigate the disappointment of other houses who were unsuccessful in obtaining membership in the underwriting syndicate (at competitive bidding or otherwise). Among the "outsiders" there may be houses with good distributing facilities and with customers interested in the issue.

The syndicate manager may offer selected dealers a specified amount of securities, subject to acceptance within a specified time, or he may offer them the privilege of subscribing for a part of the issue. If a dealer accepts a specific allotment, he makes a definite commitment; but, if he merely subscribes for a part of the issue, the transaction is subject to rejection or confirmation, in whole or part, at the discretion of the manager of the underwriting syndicate or his representative.

The members of the underwriting syndicate can usually sell small corporate issues without help from other dealers; but, selling groups are usually organized for large corporate issues. The selling-group agreement covers the terms of public offering, the dealers' commission (a portion of the gross spread between the price to the issuer and the offering price), and the provisions for terminating the selling group. Corporate management is vitally interested in the proper functioning of the investment house. If an investment house is successful in distributing a corporation's securities among many investors, it will facilitate public financing in the future.

ROLE OF THE SYNDICATE MANAGER

Much of the success of a security issue depends upon the syndicate manager and how well he performs his functions. When there is direct negotiation for a corporate issue, the originating house customarily acts as syndicate manager, but the manager may be a larger investment house that has had more experience in obtaining participation of other houses. After the purchasing contract has been signed, the underwriters assume all of the risks arising from inability to resell the securities to investors and possible losses arising from a decline in the securities market during the underwriting period; hence there is a need for organizing a group of outstanding firms to assure rapid distribution.

After the organization of the purchasing or underwriting syndicate, the duties of the syndicate manager depend upon the nature of the issue; they are fairly simple when he is handling corporate issues that are to be sold by competitive bidding and they are more difficult when he is managing negotiated issues. If the issue is to be sold by competitive bidding, the participating houses will designate one of their number as syndicate manager to work out the price to be offered. Usually the investment house so designated is one whose previous experience justifies its selection. Many such groups may be formed for competitive bidding, and unless the successful bidder has appraised the market accurately, severe losses may be incurred. Because investment houses want to be associated with the successful group, they are inclined to follow the leadership of those with whom they have had successful experiences in the past. A new underwriting group is formed for each security issue; therefore an individual house may be associated with different investment houses for each new issue. Investment bankers who are specialists in handling issues in certain fields tend to have an advantage over others in bidding on issues in their respective fields.

The members of the purchasing syndicate expect the syndicate manager to provide them with papers and documents pertaining to the issue; see that the issue is properly qualified under the laws of different states, registered with the Securities and Exchange Commission if necessary and/or approved by the Interstate Commerce Commission if required; prepare and supply sales material that will be helpful in selling the securities, give opinions as to the eligibility of the issue as legal investments for life insurance companies, pension funds, trust funds, and savings banks, and provide statistical comparisons to other securities in the market; attend meetings and assume leadership in fixing the bid price paid the issuer and the offering price to the general public; arrange settlement with the issuer, accept delivery of securities, and arrange for their distribution among underwriters and others; handle repurchase of securities that reappear on the market during the distribution period; and make a final accounting to members and initiate plans for the sale of securities still on hand. Customarily, the manager is reimbursed for expenses out of the syndicate earnings; in addition, he may receive a management fee.

When securities must be registered with the Securities and Exchange Commission, the underwriters must depend on the business corporation to see that certain provisions of the law and regulations of the Commission are met. Therefore, the syndicate manager requires the corporation in the covenants to do certain things such as prepare and file a registration statement and prospectus that meets the requirements of the law and the regulations of the Commission; provide properly certified copies of the corporation's most recent financial statements; assert that there has been no adverse change in the corporation's affairs since the date of the last balance sheet; use the net proceeds of the issue for the purpose stated in the registration statement; and attest that there are no pending lawsuits against the corporation except as specifically stated. The corporation also agrees to indemnify the underwriters against any liabilities (under provision of the Securities Act of 1933) because of any untrue, misleading, or incomplete statements in registration statements or in the prospectus.

Actually, the essential documents used in financing are drawn up prior to signing the underwriting contract, and the corporation will have worked closely with the syndicate manager or originating house in their preparation. In addition, the investment bankers will have been advised as to the contents of the bond indenture, the selection of a corporate trustee, the charter amendments in case of a stock issue, the listing application in case of registration on a securities exchange, and other matters.

At any particular time, a typical originating investment banking firm will have several issues in different stages of processing, and the ideal situation is one wherein a steady stream of issues is going through investment banking channels into the hands of investors.

REGULATION OF SECURITY ISSUES

Although many assume that regulation of security issues originated with the Securities Act of 1933, states had anticipated most of the provisions found in this federal law. In 1911, Kansas passed the first "blue-sky" law; today, every state except Nevada has some type of regulatory statute covering the sale of securities. Some state statutes require licensing of brokers and dealers, other require registration of securities to be sold in the state, and still others are of the antifraud type which provide penalties for and prosecution of fraudulent acts.

Although the state laws were beneficial, they could not stop the flow of securities from one state to another because states have no jurisdiction over interstate commerce (which has its counterpart today in the flow of worthless securities across international boundaries—from Canada into the United States).

The Securities Act of 1933, as amended, is based upon the premise that full, fair, and accurate disclosure of the character of securities offered publicly for sale in interstate commerce or through the mail will prevent fraud in the sale of securities. The procedures required by the act include filing a registration statement with the Securities and Exchange Commission and securing its approval of the prospectus which is to be made available to the public. The Security and Exchange Commission permits or refuses to permit the registration statement to become effective; however, it does not pass on the quality of the securities and any representation to the contrary is a criminal offense (which is something for sellers of registered securities to remember).

The registrant (corporation) pays the Securities and Exchange Commission a fee of 1/100 of 1 per cent of the aggregate price of the proposed issue, but in no case less than $25.00. The effective date is twenty days after the filing date unless shortened by the Securities and Exchange Commission (as the Commission was authorized to do in 1940). If the statement must be amended, the waiting period starts from the date of filing the amendment. Amendments may be required to meet objections raised by the Securities and Exchange Commission in a "letter of comment." If the registration is already in effect, the Commission may issue a stop order suspending the effectiveness of the registration statement. In this case the issue must be withdrawn or withheld until the registration statement and prospectus meet the standards set by the Securities and Exchange Commission.

During the twenty-day waiting period, the investment bankers may place a so-called "red herring" prospectus in the hands of prospective investors. This preliminary prospectus contains most of the information that will be in the final prospectus except the offering price. It gets its name from a statement that it is not an offer to sell or solicit a purchase stamped thereon in red ink. This prospectus is used to place information in the hands of investors before the actual offering date.

The Securities Act of 1933 makes the sponsors of registered securities accountable for misrepresentations, omissions, and untrue statements of material facts. Persons who may be held accountable include directors, officers, and partners of the issuer; underwriters; accountants, engineers, appraisers, and other professional persons who have been named in preparation or certification of any part of the registration statement (how much professional fees have increased as a result of this contingent liability is not known); and all others who sign the registration statement. Civil and/or criminal liabilities may also arise because of illegal acts such as selling a security before the registration becomes effective, engaging in any fraudulent scheme, and using the mails to defraud (a provision of the federal law before the passage of the Securities Act of 1933).[6]

The Securities Act of 1933 provides for the exemption from registration of certain types of issues. From the viewpoint of business finance, the most important of these issues are those which are privately offered and railroad securities, which like all securities issued by common carriers are subject to regulation by the Interstate Commerce Commission. Among other issues exempt from registration are (1) direct and guaranteed obligations of the United States Government, any state or territory thereof, and political subdivisions of states and territories, (2) national and state chartered banks, (3) nonprofit organizations, (4) short-term commercial paper, (5) insurance policies and contracts, and (6) receivers' and trustees' certificates.

SECONDARY MARKETS FOR SECURITIES

After their primary distribution, bonds and stocks may be traded in one or both of the secondary markets for securities—over-the-counter market and securities exchanges. The Securities Exchange Act of 1934 defined the over-the-counter market so as to include all transactions in securities which take place otherwise than upon national securities exchanges.

A securities exchange is an unincorporated association or incorporated company wherein brokers and dealers trade in securities for others and themselves. Since 1934, securities exchanges whose business is predominantly interstate, called *national securities exchanges,* have been under the general supervision of the Securities and Exchange Commission. At the present time, sixteen exchanges

[6] See the latest annual report of the Securities and Exchange Commission for litigations under the Securities Act of 1933 and the Securities Exchange Act of 1934.

are registered with the Securities and Exchange Commission and four others are exempt from registration. The largest and most important national securities exchange is the New York Stock Exchange, where stocks and bonds of national and international importance are bought and sold. The ability of business corporations to raise capital funds through the sale of bonds or stock is enhanced if the owners can resell them to others. While not equally important to all investors, the quality of marketability adds to the investment status of securities. For this reason, large investment banking firms maintain trading departments and memberships on the leading securities exchanges.

Acting as principal rather than agent, an investment banking firm makes a market not only for the securities in which it has acted as underwriter but also for others in which its clients are interested.[7] As a distributor of securities, an investment banking firm also handles sales of large blocks of securities that cannot be sold on securities exchanges in the regular way. Such shares are usually sold after the close of trading on an exchange or a nonauction basis at a price that is fixed at or near the prevailing one when the exchange closed for the day. Under the terms of the Securities Act, a "secondary offering" must be registered with the Securities and Exchange Commission if the seller has a controlling interest in the business firm. An investment banking firm's trading department also facilitates the purchase and sale of stocks and bonds not listed on securities exchanges.

The securities of most of the business corporations in the United States are bought and sold in the over-the-counter market, but those of major business corporations are listed on national securities exchanges. A corporation may register a security on a national exchange by filing an application for registration with the exchange and giving a copy of the application to the Securities and Exchange Commission. This application contains comprehensive information about the issuer, and if the corporation's application for listing is approved, the corporation is required to keep this information up to date by filing periodic reports. The information required for listing

---

[7] Some investment houses are active in the primary and secondary markets for government securities—the obligations of the federal government and its agencies and those of states and their political subdivisions (municipals). While the United States Treasury offers its securities through the Federal Reserve banks, most of the large investment houses participate in the secondary market for these securities. Some firms also act as underwriters of issues of foreign governments, central banks, development companies, and other foreign corporations.

is the same as that required for registration of a new security issue; therefore investors in stocks and bonds who limit their purchases to those listed on a national exchange have access to more complete information than may be true for other investors.

The purpose of the Securities Exchange Act of 1934 is to insure fairness and honesty in securities transactions on the organized exchanges and in the over-the-counter markets. The Act forbids trading in a security on a national exchange unless it is registered (exclusive of federal government and other exempt securities that include corporate issues which were previously admitted to unlisted trading privileges because of a request made by a member of an exchange and not by the corporation). In 1910, the New York Stock Exchange adopted a rule that abolished unlisted trading. The Securities Act of 1934 provides for continuance of unlisted trading privileges for those issues admitted prior to March 1, 1934; an amendment of the law in May, 1936, provided for unlisted trading privileges for securities already listed on other national exchanges and further extension of unlisted trading privileges to unlisted securities (provided information substantially equivalent to that required for listing on a national exchange is available).

An application for listing is usually refused if the anticipated trading in the issue is small. To be accepted for listing on the New York Stock Exchange, annual earnings of a company are expected to be at least $1 million after all charges and taxes; net tangible assets applicable to common stock should have a minimum aggregate market value of $8 million; the number of common stockholders should be at least 1,500 after substantially discounting odd lots (less than 100 shares) and they should hold 400,000 shares exclusive of centralized or family holdings; there should be a broad national interest in the security so that an adequate auction market in the security can be expected. Standards for listing on other exchanges are less stringent; in many cases, these exchanges are used as seasoning markets prior to listing on the New York Stock Exchange.

The advantages of listing a company's securities on a national exchange include advertising value because the corporation's name appears on ticker tapes, in newspapers, and on the boards in brokers' offices. Listed securities are more attractive to many investors; hence listing usually results in wider distribution of securities and this tends to stimulate nation-wide sales of the firm's products. Another argument in favor of listing is that it creates public goodwill and adds prestige because it indicates that the corporation wishes to co-operate with the Securities and Exchange Commission and securities exchanges by providing the public with information about its affairs and desires to be associated with outstanding corporations whose securities are already listed.

The "blue-sky" laws of most states waive their state registration requirement for securities listed on a national exchange, and for some corporate managers this is an important reason for listing securities.

Securities may be withdrawn from listing on applications originated either by the securities exchange or the issuer. The chief reason for withdrawing or delisting a security is a decline in trading activity owing to a decrease in the volume of securities outstanding because of retirement or redemption of bonds and preferred stock and concentration of ownership of the securities in the hands of a few. Most commonly, bonds that are being retired either by redemption or by conversion into other securities are removed from listing simply by certifying their delisting with the Securities and Exchange Commission.

Although listing securities on a national exchange has advantages, management may not apply for listing because of failure to meet some of the tests noted above, objections to providing the information required, the existence of current satisfactory trading on an unlisted basis or in the over-the-counter market, and the expenses associated with listing.

The costs incurred in listing securities on a national exchange include a registration fee, expenses of preparing forms that must be submitted to the securities exchange and the Securities and Exchange Commission, and payment of an annual fee if the issue is stock. If the issue is listed on the New York Stock Exchange, the corporation must also bear the expense of having a transfer agent and registrar in the Borough of Manhattan. Once a stock is listed, delisting requires a favorable vote of two thirds of the shareholders and even then this approval may be vetoed if 10 per cent or more of the shareholders object.

SUMMARY

Investment bankers are middlemen between issuers and investors; in this capacity, they are advisors of both issuers and investors. While some investment houses are primarily underwriters, others primarily retailers, and others participants in originating, purchasing and selling syndicates, there is a considerable overlapping in their functions. Investment bankers customarily assist in financing business firms by advising the corporation on its financing problems and assisting it in solving them. The investment banker may purchase an issue from the corporation through negotiation or competitive bidding, make a stand-by commitment which involves purchasing any part of an issue not sold by the issuer, or agree to use their best efforts to sell a new issue of securities. Competitive bidding is required for certain classes of securities and may be used in other cases when the quality of securities is high enough to warrant this method of selling.

In some cases, entire issues may be placed privately, thereby bypassing the investment banker and avoiding the expense and delay incurred in registering the issue with the Securities and Exchange Commission.

Underwriting and distributing corporate securities calls for cooperation among many investment houses and usually entails three distinct agreements: one between the issuer and members of the underwriting or purchase group, a second among the members of the underwriting syndicate, and a third between the purchasing or underwriting syndicate and the selling group.

Most new corporate issues are subject to registration by state or federal agencies. The Securities and Exchange Act of 1933, as amended, requires full, fair, and accurate disclosure of the character of securities offered publicly for sale in interstate commerce or through the mail. The Securities Act of 1933 is implemented with the requirement that a registration statement and a prospectus be filed with the Securities and Exchange Commission. The Commission either permits or refuses to permit the registration to become effective but does not pass on the quality of securities. The Securities Act of 1933 provides for exemption of certain transactions including those privately placed and certain issues including those of railroads and domestic governments.

After the primary distribution of a security issue, the securities may be traded on one of the secondary markets—securities exchanges or over-the-counter markets. Of the national securities exchanges, the New York Stock Exchange is the most important. Listing in securities of a corporation on a stock exchange necessitates registering the issue, meeting the standards set by the exchange, and fulfilling the requirements of the Securities and Exchange Commission. These standards have to do with the size of the issue, the annual earnings and assets of the corporation, the number of stockholders, and the amount of trading interest in the security.

QUESTIONS AND PROBLEMS

1. "The machinery for distribution of new securities is complex, but it is fundamentally only merchandising on a broad scale." Explain.
2. How may investment houses be classified? Explain.
3. (*a*) How do investment bankers serve issuing corporations in an advisory capacity? (*b*) Why must the investment banker consider the wishes of investors?
4. Identify: (*a*) security issue, (*b*) investment house, (*c*) underwriting, (*d*) stand-by underwriting, and (*e*) best-effort commitment.
5. (*a*) How does a corporation tend to benefit from the sale of its securities by competitive bidding? (*b*) Does the sale of securities by competitive bidding deprive the issuing corporation of the advice of investment bankers? Explain.
6. Account for the increase in private placement.
7. In handling a large corporate issue of bonds, what three types of contracts or agreements are involved? Why?
8. How has public financing been affected by regulations of the Securities and Exchange Commission?
9. Distinguish between primary and secondary markets for securities.
10. What are corporate management's reasons for (*a*) listing securities, (*b*) delisting securities, and (*c*) not listing securities?
11. Explain: "Major investment firms perform many financial services for corporations on the same confidential, professional basis as legal or accounting firms. The two best known of these functions are raising long term capital and establishing markets for stocks of closely held companies." (Glore, Forgen & Co., *What an Investment Banker Can Do For You* [Chicago, 1960], p. 7.)
12. Analyze: Most "of these 'new money' common stock offerings are small ones for lesser known companies in the so called 'growth' industries, rather than big issues for the nation's industrial giants." (*Wall Street Journal* [New York], November 28, 1960, p. 9.)
13. In the United States, about one adult in eight owns stock. About 52.5 per cent of the stockholders are women and 47.5 per cent are men. Among all shareholders more than two thirds hold stocks listed on the New York Stock Exchange. Account for the popularity of stocks listed on the New York Stock Exchange.

CHAPTER 17

Financing with Common Stock

OWNERS' EQUITY or proprietory capital consists of capital contributed by shareholders and earnings retained by a business. The distinction between the two is not always clear on a corporation's balance sheet because of stock dividends that have been paid, recapitalization, reorganization, and mergers. The word "stock" which appears frequently in business finance has two connotations: to a corporation, it refers to capital acquired through the sale of shares to investors; to an investor, it refers to the actual certificates of ownership interest in a corporation. Different classes of both common and preferred stock as well as various types of debt obligations may be used because of their effects on control, risk, and income. This chapter treats various aspects of equity capital and the problems associated with common stock.

NATURE OF EQUITY CAPITAL

The term "capitalization of a firm" refers not only to capital contributed by stockholders but also to long-term debt. The capitalization of most companies is dominated by common stock, but that of companies with stable earnings such as public utilities will often have a higher proportion of preferred stock and debt. Some corporations adopt a policy of maintaining a predetermined relationship between debts and equities in their capital structures, some shifting among the several sources of funds is likely to occur (see Chart 6). For illustration, the American Telephone and Telegraph Company has adopted a policy of keeping "the proportion of debt to total capital, whenever possible, somewhere between 30 and 40 per cent."[1]

The first characteristic of equity capital is that a business concern is not legally bound to pay any return to those who provide it. For business firms in formative stages as well as for those in operation, this relief from any contractual obligation to pay out funds to

CHART 6

EQUITY CAPITAL AND LONG-TERM DEBT AS PERCENTAGES OF TOTAL CAPITALIZATION

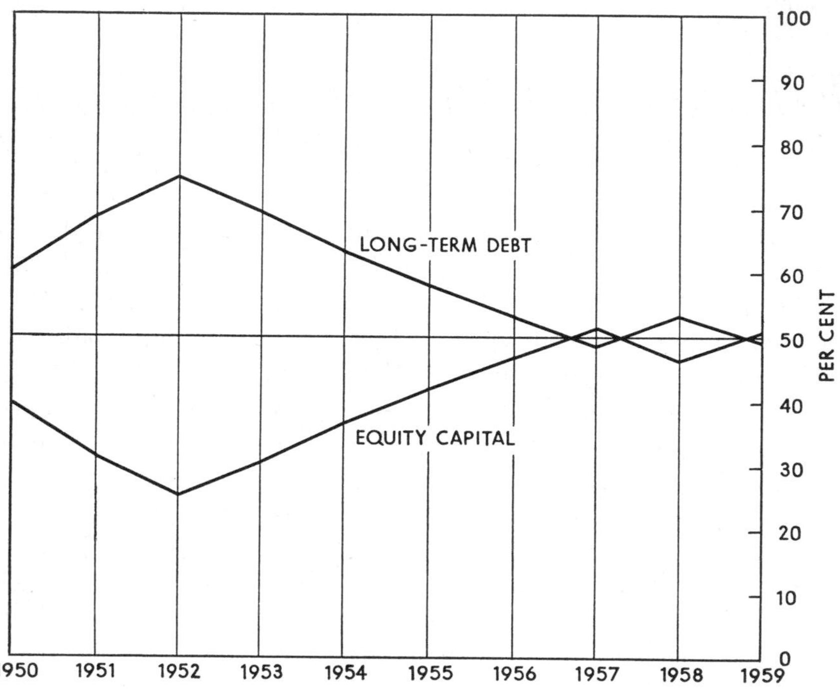

Source: Reynolds Metals Company, *32nd Annual Report* (Richmond, Va.: 1959), p. 7.

owners is advantageous. If a business firm could be operated exclusively with funds supplied by owners and derived from operations, management would have no interest payment problem to consider.

The second characteristic of equity capital is that usually there is no stated time when the funds supplied by owners must be returned. If a business firm is financing with borrowed capital, it may be adversely affected when funds must be withdrawn to repay loans at maturity; but, if a business firm is financing exclusively with

[1] American Telephone and Telegraph Company, *75th Annual Meeting of Share Owners* (New York: April 20, 1960), p. 8.

equity capital, the risk of being weakened by the withdrawal of funds on a prearranged date is absent.

The third characteristic of equity capital is that those who provide it are responsible, at least in theory, for the control and management of the business enterprise. Some equity capital may be supplied under contracts that limit the control rights of those who supply it, such as limited partners in partnerships, preferred stockholders of corporations, and beneficiaries of trusts. Stockholders of corporations usually permit their elected representatives, the members of the board of directors, to select the officers and other agents to manage the affairs of their corporations. This does not invalidate the owner-control aspect of equity capital, but owners of equity capital may surrender their rights to exercise control by failure to use voting rights or by waiving them by contract.

In view of the advantages to be gained by a business enterprise from financing exclusively with equity capital, what justification is there for calling equity capital *risk capital?* From the viewpoint of the business enterprise there is no risk, unless one assumes that it becomes a risk of transfer of ownership to others—which is a risk associated with control but not a business risk. When the term *risk capital* is used to mean equity capital, it refers to the risk assumed by those who supply the capital—not by the business firm.

The owners of equity capital are entitled to net earnings after taxes, interest, and all other obligations of a business are met. They are the residual claimants to the income of a business enterprise, which may be much, little, or nothing. In practice, net earnings may be retained in the business rather than being paid to owners; therefore, despite large net earnings, owners assume the risk of receiving no return on their equity capital.

Presumably, proprietors make permanent investments in their business concerns. True, owners may sell their ownership interests to others, the business firm may be liquidated and the proceeds divided among owners, the business may be recapitalized and the amount of equity reduced, and so on; but none of these possibilities is prearranged except in cases where special contracts are in force (such as prearranged retirement plans for preferred stock, twenty-year trusts, etc.). When a business venture is liquidated, equity owners have residual claims to what is left. In all arrangements between business enterprises and suppliers of capital funds, those who provide the proprietary or equity capital assume the greatest risks.

In analyzing the position of stockholders a distinction should be made between holders of common stock and holders of preferred stock. Although a corporation is under no legal obligation to pay a return to either class of shareholders, if earnings are available holders of preferred stock have a preference over holders of common stock up to a stated amount or percentage per share ($5 or 5 per cent preferred stock). Like common stock, preferred stock usually has no maturity date; but common stock may be issued with or without par value, while preferred stock is usually issued with par value. In exchange for their preferential position over common stockholders in case of liquidation of a corporation, preferred stockholders usually surrender their rights to vote for directors. With these exceptions—prior rights over common stockholders in the case of earnings and to assets in case of liquidation—preferred stockholders' claims, like those of common stockholders, are subordinated to those of creditors of a corporation.

EVIDENCE OF OWNERSHIP

The proprietory rights of owners are usually evidenced by written documents which tend to become longer and more complicated as the number of owners increases. Because of the nature of proprietorships and partnerships, the instruments indicating the rights of proprietors and partners are less formal than those of stockholders of corporations. These instruments may include documents indicating title to real and personal property; and, in case of a partnership, there is usually a written agreement covering each partner's rights, obligations, and privileges. Ownership in business trusts, joint stock companies, or corporations is usually evidenced by transferable certificates, and the units into which proprietary interests are divided are called *shares*. Thus, a stock certificate is written or printed evidence of ownership indicating that the holder whose name appears on the face is the lawful owner of a designated number of shares of capital stock. But the issuance of a stock certificate is not necessary to make one a stockholder of a corporation. Legally, one becomes a stockholder as soon as one's subscription has been accepted and the consideration has been paid (usually in cash but sometimes in exchange for other assets). A person who buys stock in the open market is entitled to vote or receive dividends thereon only after the shares have been transferred to his name on the books of the corporation.

Stock Certificates. Customarily, a stock certificate contains the following: the name of the issuing company and the state wherein it is incorporated; the amount of "par value" if par value stock, or a statement that it is "no par value" stock; a statement that the stock is "fully paid and nonassessable"; the name of the owner; and the name of the officers and others authorized to sign for the company (such as president, treasurer or secretary, transfer agent, and registrar). The back of the certificate will contain provisions for transfer of title with spaces for dates, name of transferee, and signature of the owner. If the company has several classes of stock, the certificates of each class may summarize the rights and privileges pertaining to it, but these provisions are usually found in the articles of incorporation or bylaws of the corporation. Each share of stock within a class carries the same rights and privileges. Among those who have claims to the assets and earnings of a corporation, common stockholders are last in point of priority. Common stock represents the final equity in a corporation; that is, common stockholders have claims to whatever capital or income remains after all prior claims are satisfied.

Since certificates may be issued for any number of shares, an owner may have his total ownership in a corporation represented by a single certificate; but, if he acquired interest in the company at different times by additional purchases or by stock dividends, he may have several stock certificates.

Ownership of Record. The shares of stock of major companies are bought and sold on organized stock exhanges and in the over-the-counter market. The resulting turnover in ownership creates a continuing problem—namely, that of determining owners who are entitled to receive dividends (when declared by the board of directors) and to vote at annual and other meetings of stockholders. The details for handling this problem are usually covered in the bylaws of the corporation rather than left to the discretion of management.

When dividends are declared by the board of directors, they are payable on dates specified in the bylaws to those whose names appear on the books as owners on predetermined dates (usually a specified number of days prior to the dividend dates). This is the explanation for items such as the following on financial pages of newspapers: "Dividends Announced" and in columnar arrangement below, "Company" as General Motors; "period" as quarterly; "amount" as 50 cents; "payable date" as 12–10–'60; and "record date" as 11–17–'60. This means that the board of directors of General Motors Corporation has declared a quarterly dividend on its common stock which is payable on December 10, 1960 to those

ILLUSTRATION 5

EXAMPLE OF COMMON STOCK

(Less than 100 Shares)

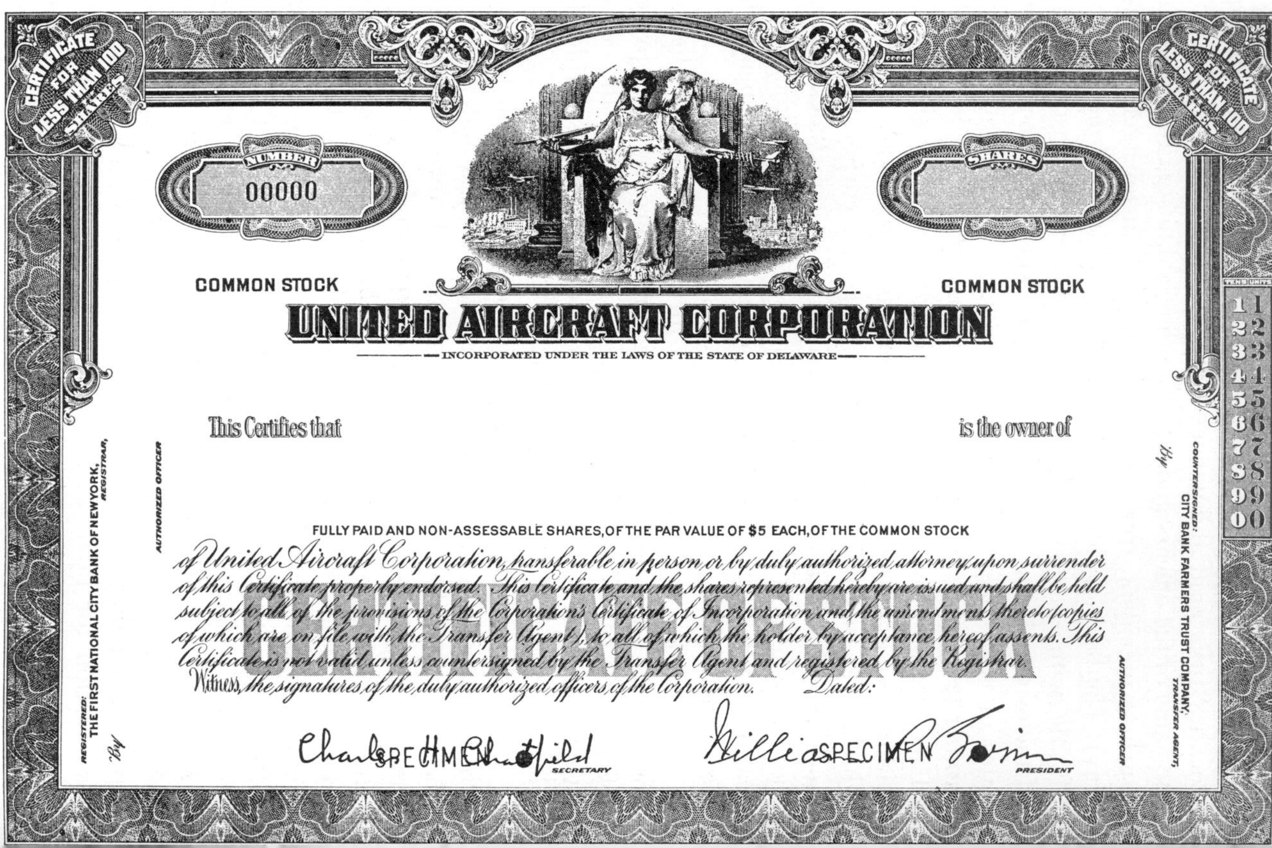

CERTIFICATE FOR LESS THAN 100 SHARES

NUMBER

00000

SHARES

COMMON STOCK

COMMON STOCK

UNITED AIRCRAFT CORPORATION

INCORPORATED UNDER THE LAWS OF THE STATE OF DELAWARE

This Certifies that

is the owner of

FULLY PAID AND NON-ASSESSABLE SHARES, OF THE PAR VALUE OF $5 EACH, OF THE COMMON STOCK

of United Aircraft Corporation, transferable in person or by duly authorized attorney upon surrender of this Certificate properly endorsed. This Certificate and the shares represented hereby are issued and shall be held subject to all of the provisions of the Corporation's Certificate of Incorporation and the amendments thereto (copies of which are on file with the Transfer Agent), to all of which the holder by acceptance hereof assents. This Certificate is not valid unless countersigned by the Transfer Agent and registered by the Registrar.

Witness, the signatures of the duly authorized officers of the Corporation. Dated:

CERTIFICATE OF STOCK

SPECIMEN — SECRETARY

SPECIMEN — PRESIDENT

REGISTERED: THE FIRST NATIONAL CITY BANK OF NEW YORK, REGISTRAR, By AUTHORIZED OFFICER

COUNTERSIGNED: CITY BANK FARMERS TRUST COMPANY, TRANSFER AGENT, By AUTHORIZED OFFICER

TENS UNITS 1 1 2 2 3 3 4 4 5 5 6 6 7 7 8 8 9 9 0 0

ILLUSTRATION 6

EXAMPLE OF BACK OF COMMON STOCK SHARE

UNITED AIRCRAFT CORPORATION

The designations, preferences and relative, participating, optional or other special rights, and the qualifications, limitations and restrictions thereof, of the several classes of stock of the Corporation are set forth in the Certificate of Incorporation and the amendments thereto of the Corporation.

The Corporation will furnish without charge to each stockholder who so requests the designations, preferences and relative, participating, optional or other special rights of each class of stock or series thereof of the Corporation and the qualifications, limitations, or restrictions of such preferences and/or rights. Such request may be made to the Corporation or the Transfer Agent.

For Value received, ___ hereby sell, assign and transfer unto

____

PLEASE PRINT OR TYPEWRITE NAME AND ADDRESS OF ASSIGNEE

____

____

__________________________ *Shares of the capital stock represented by the within Certificate, and do hereby irrevocably constitute and appoint* ________________

__________________________ *Attorney to transfer the said stock on the books of the within-named Corporation with full power of substitution in the premises.*

Dated, ______________

____

NOTICE: THE SIGNATURE TO THIS ASSIGNMENT MUST CORRESPOND WITH THE NAME AS WRITTEN UPON THE FACE OF THE CERTIFICATE, IN EVERY PARTICULAR, WITHOUT ALTERATION OR ENLARGEMENT, OR ANY CHANGE WHATEVER.

THIS SPACE MUST NOT BE COVERED IN ANY WAY

ILLUSTRATION 7

Example of Common Stock

(100 Shares)

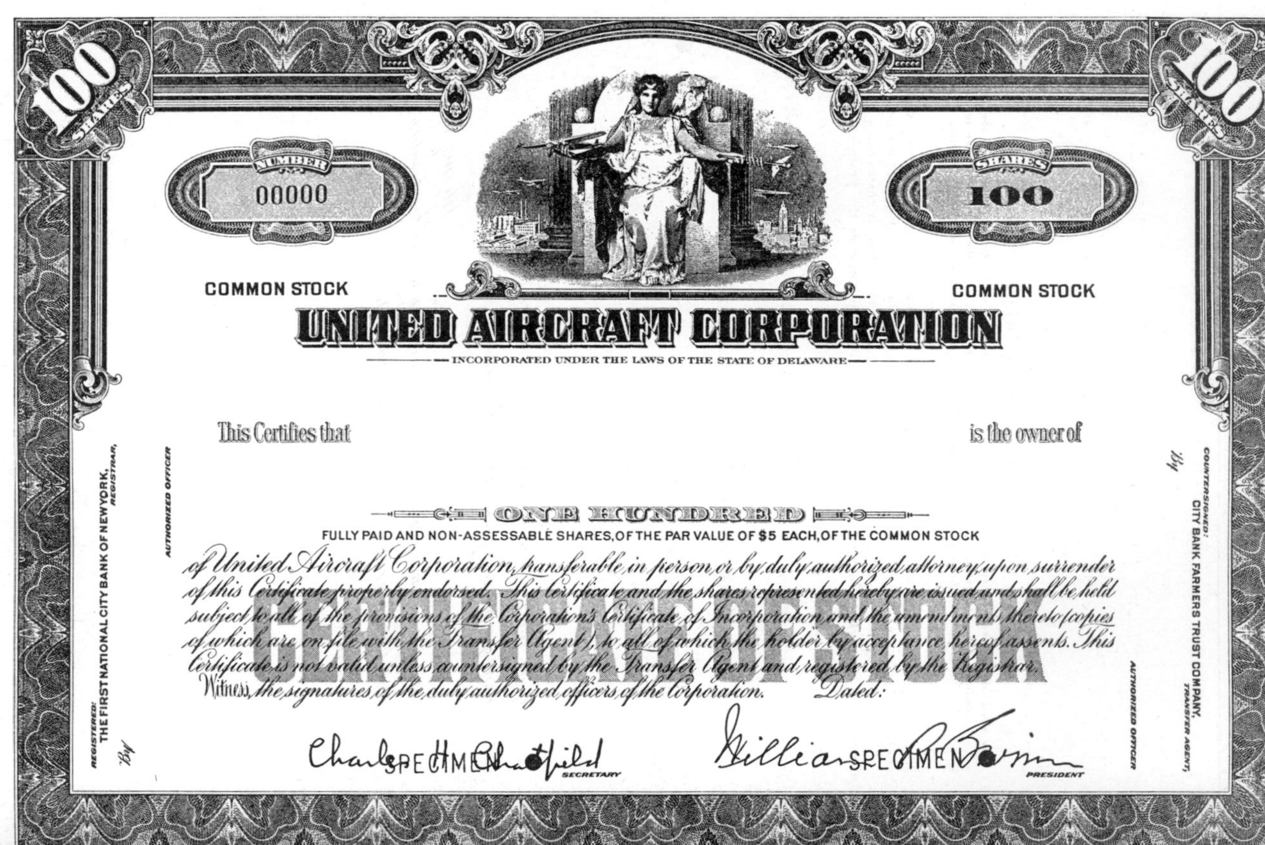

100 SHARES

NUMBER 00000

SHARES 100

COMMON STOCK

COMMON STOCK

UNITED AIRCRAFT CORPORATION

INCORPORATED UNDER THE LAWS OF THE STATE OF DELAWARE

This Certifies that is the owner of

ONE HUNDRED

FULLY PAID AND NON-ASSESSABLE SHARES, OF THE PAR VALUE OF $5 EACH, OF THE COMMON STOCK

of United Aircraft Corporation, transferable in person or by duly authorized attorney upon surrender of this Certificate properly endorsed. This certificate and the shares represented hereby are issued and shall be held subject to all of the provisions of the Corporation's Certificate of Incorporation and the amendments thereto (copies of which are on file with the Transfer Agent), to all of which the holder by acceptance hereof assents. This Certificate is not valid unless countersigned by the Transfer Agent and registered by the Registrar.

Witness, the signatures of the duly authorized officers of the Corporation. Dated:

CERTIFICATE OF STOCK

SPECIMEN — SECRETARY

SPECIMEN — PRESIDENT

COUNTERSIGNED: CITY BANK FARMERS TRUST COMPANY, TRANSFER AGENT, By AUTHORIZED OFFICER

REGISTERED: THE FIRST NATIONAL CITY BANK OF NEW YORK, REGISTRAR, By AUTHORIZED OFFICER whose names appear on its stock book as owners on November 17, 1960. However, those who plan to buy or sell shares must remember that a stock listed on the New York Stock Exchange on which a dividend has been declared will be purchased or sold "ex dividend" (literally, without dividend) three full business days before the date of record of ownership. This rule is applied because of the time required to deliver the stock and to record it in the name of the new owner in the stock ledger. This means that during a period beginning three days before the record date and extending to the payment date, a buyer acquires the stock without the dividend that has been declared and the seller receives the dividend after it has been sold.

Stock Transfer Procedure. Since stock certificates are not credit instruments, they are not negotiated under the provisions of the Uniform Negotiable Instruments Act; but all states have adopted the Uniform Stock Transfer Act which gives stock certificates some of the characteristics of negotiable instruments. Title may be transferred by delivery of the certificate endorsed by the owner (either in blank or to a specified person) or by delivery of the certificate and a separate written assignment drawn either in blank or to a specified person and signed by the owner. When stock certificates are sold through brokers, they are usually endorsed in blank. But the transfer of title to a stock certificate does not mean that title to the stock represented by the certificate is transferred. To complete the transaction, the books of the corporation must be changed to show the transfer of title to the stock, the old certificate must be cancelled, and a new one issued in its place.

A large corporation may have its own stock transfer department or office or it may employ a trust company to supervise transfers of its corporate stock and other securities. The transfer agent or office keeps the stock certificate book, cancels surrendered certificates and attaches them to their proper stubs in the stock book, and issues new stock certificates to the transferees. These new certificates must be signed by the designated officials and, if required, imprinted with the corporate seal. The bank or trust company, employed as registrar, supervises the work of cancellation and issuance of stock certificates and countersigns them. The transfer agent of the corporation will deliver the new certificate to the transferee. Corporations whose shares are listed on the New York Stock Exchange must have both a registrar and either a transfer office or transfer agent in the Borough of Manhattan. The duties of the transfer agent—or the transfer office operated by the company—and those of the registrar are distinct and must be performed by different companies.

TERMS INDICATING EQUITY OF BUSINESS FIRMS

In the shareholders' equity section of a corporation's balance sheet, the first item is usually a statement of preferred stock with par value, including the amount authorized and outstanding and the dividend rate. The second item is a statement of common stock with par value (or without par value) and the amount authorized and outstanding—including or excluding treasury stock, depending on company policy. This is followed by one statement showing capital surplus and another one indicating earnings employed in the business (see Table 20).

TABLE 20

"X" COMPANY AND SUBSIDIARIES
LIABILITIES AND SHAREHOLDERS' EQUITY

	Dec. 31, 1960	*June 30, 1960*
Current Liabilities:		
Accounts payable and accrued expense	$ 43,709,088	$ 49,026,986
Provision for federal income taxes	48,962,669	49,999,001
Total Current Liabilities	$ 92,671,757	$ 99,025,987
Funded Debt:		
3% Purchase money obligations, due 1960 to 1970	$ 1,054,000	$ 1,267,000
2¾% Sinking fund debentures, due 1965	16,250,000	16,750,000
3¾% Promissory notes, due 1977 to 1987	75,000,000	75,000,000
Total Funded Debt	$ 92,304,000	$ 93,017,000
Incentive compensation contingently payable—net	$ 2,836,194	$ 2,206,869
Minority Shareholders' Equity in Foreign subsidiaries	$ 782,359	$ 707,103
Common and cumulative preferred stocks issuable to employees under purchase contracts	$ 12,552,210	$ 14,370,792
Shareholders' Equity:		
Cumulative preferred stock—par value $100:		
Authorized—650,000 shares		
Outstanding—Series D. 3½%—1,585 shares	$ 158,500	$ 105,500
Common stock—par value $10:		
Authorized—30,000,000 shares		
Outstanding—21,388,991 shares including 131,196 treasury shares	213,889,907	213,525,557
Capital surplus	7,392,379	5,995,398
Earnings employed in the business	212,566,498	201,128,138
Total Shareholders' Equity	$434,007,284	$420,754,593
	$635,153,804	$630,082,344

The term *authorized shares* means the total number of shares of all classes which a corporation is authorized to issue. Corporations usually begin operations with but one class of common stock, and the amount authorized is usually greater than the amount issued.

Later, the authorized but unissued shares may be distributed; but, unless the charter is amended, no more shares may be legally issued. In drawing up the articles of incorporation, if the founders of a corporation provide for a large number and varied types of shares, management will have greater latitude in fashioning classes and types of securities with which to finance in the future without the necessity for asking shareholders to approve amendments to the articles of incorporation. Shares authorized may consist of one or more classes; each class of shares may be issued in a series; shares may be issued with or without par value; and shares may be issued with such limitations, preferences, and relative rights as are stated in the articles of incorporation (subject to the provision that a class of nonvoting stock may have the right to vote on any proposal which would change its rights or status).

Issued stock, as the name implies, is the amount of authorized stock actually issued. The difference between the amount of issued stock and authorized stock is called "unissued" stock or "authorized but unissued" stock. Issued stock which has been reacquired by the corporation is called "treasury" stock. The difference between the amount of issued stock and treasury stock, called "outstanding" stock or "stock outstanding," is the amount of stock in the hands of owners other than the corporation.

At the time of organizing a corporation, stock may be given to incorporators in exchange for real property, personal property, patents, and/or services; the laws pertaining thereto usually state that the "consideration" may not be less than the par or stated value of the stock. If assets are given to a corporation without the issuance of stock, the credit should be recorded as donated capital and should appear as part of stockholders' equity. Shares given incorporators in exchange for property are sometimes returned to the corporation either as a gift or at a nominal price so that they may be sold at a price acceptable to management.

A corporation may reacquire its own stock after it has been issued. The resulting treasury stock is then treated as a deduction from the total stock account unless the shares were acquired for a specific purpose, such as to meet sales of stock to officers under an incentive plan (in which case the stock would be treated as an asset). During the 1930's, when prices of both common and preferred stocks were low, many corporations reacquired outstanding shares and justified the action on the basis of need for reducing dividend requirements, lowering the amount of capital to conform to business requirements, finding a profitable outlet for funds on hand, supporting the market for stock in order to protect stockholders' interests, and acquiring stock for future corporate needs at bargain prices. It may be argued that corporations were, in effect, speculating in their own stock, which could result in subsequent losses to the company. In addition, management was criticized for repurchasing issued stock because using corporate assets in this way might weaken protection of creditors (bond indentures usually prohibit the use of corporate assets to reacquire stock except under special conditions that give adequate protection to creditors); dissipate cash and delay payment of dividends; provide a means for showing favoritism in subsequent treasury-stock distributions; and permit insiders to perpetuate their control to the disadvantage of minority interests.

To meet the criticisms noted above, modern business corporation acts limit the right of a corporation to purchase its own stock except out of earned surplus or out of capital surplus contingent upon the affirmative vote of holders of at least two thirds of the shares entitled to be voted thereon. Common exceptions to these limitations include acquisitions of stock to eliminate fractional shares, to pay dissenting shareholders entitled to payment for shares, to affect the retirement of redeemable shares, and to collect or compromise debts owed the corporation. Treasury stock is not permitted to be voted and it may not be counted to obtain the necessary number of shares required by many provisions of business corporation acts such as a quorum of shares for legal meetings of stockholders.

When a corporation issues stock that has par value, the "stated capital" of the corporation is the aggregate of the par value of shares issued. The term is used to remove the ambiguity which has frequently resulted from the use of the terms *capital* and *capital stock*. For illustration, if Corporation A has issued 1,000,000 shares, with each share having a par value of $10.00, the stated capital of the corporation is $10,000,000. If the stock was originally sold for more than $10.00 per share, assume $12.00, there would be $2,000,000 which would be accounted for as "capital surplus" in the balance sheet.

When a corporation issues stock without par value, the corporation's stated "capital" is the aggregate of the "stated value" of the shares issued. In case of no-par stock, the stated value of a share is the dollar amount per share as stated by a resolution of the board of directors or by the charter of the corporation. At the time of issuance, if the price paid (the consideration) is in excess of the stated value, the excess is carried to capital surplus. For illustration, if a corporation which issued 1,000,000 shares of no-par stock sells such stock at $50 per share and specifies that the stated value is $40 per share, it will have a stated capital of $40,000,000 and a capital surplus of $10,000,000.[2]

The common practice of exchanging stock for services or property at the time of organizing a corporation may result in the corporation's stated capital having little meaning even though the law may specify that shares are to be issued for a consideration (expressed in terms of money) of not less than par value or stated value. In the absence of fraud, the judgment of the board of directors as to the value of lawyers' and promoters' services and property received for shares is conclusive (the "good faith" test for valuation by the board of directors).

Because "stated capital" is the par or stated value per share times the number of shares outstanding, any change that would increase the total would increase the amount of stated capital. This may result from the distribution of a stock dividend, sale of new stock, an increase in par or stated value of each share, or some combination of the above. Conversely, any change that would reduce the number of shares outstanding and/or the par or stated value would reduce the stated capital. Stated capital is not available for dividends until the stated value is reduced.

The balance sheet item *surplus* is defined as the excess of a corporation's assets over the sum of its liabilities and capital stock. If creditors contribute the amount represented by liabilities and owners contribute the amount represented by capital stock, who contributes the remaining assets? Before this question is answered, there is a second one—who owns the assets represented by surplus? Stockholders have residual claims to all business assets; therefore, the answer is that stockholders own the assets represented by surplus. This explains why surplus is considered in this chapter on equity or proprietary capital, which is defined as that contributed or owned by proprietors or owners.

Surplus is most commonly divided into two classes: "capital surplus" and "earned surplus." Capital surplus (all surplus except earned surplus) may result from the premium paid by stockholders

---

[2] While modern business corporation acts give corporate management wide latitude in fashioning classes and types of stock, they also contain provisions that prevent old stockholders' interests from being "watered" without their prior approval (usually an affirmative vote of two thirds or more of the shares).

when they paid more than par value or stated value for stock (as discussed above), gifts or donations of stock or assets to the corporation, profits from repurchasing shares or reduction in par or stated value of stock, writing up the value of assets, and so on.

Earned surplus or accumulated earnings is defined as the retained profits resulting from the ordinary operations of the business plus gains of a more extraordinary nature from other sources. At any one time the earned surplus is equal to the corporation's net profits, income, realized gains or losses from the date of incorporation (or the last date from which there has been a readjustment of the capital surplus or capital account whereby a deficit was eliminated or for other reasons), minus transfers to "stated capital" and "capital surplus," and disbursements to stockholders.[3]

Any change in the amount of authorized stock or in its par value requires an amendment to the articles of incorporation or charter of a corporation by a vote of the stockholders of the class of stock affected. Such action is customarily taken after the passage of a resolution by the board of directors recommending the change and the procedure that is to be followed in exchanging the old stock for new. Usually, an affirmative vote by at least two thirds of the class of stock affected is necessary to amend the articles of incorporation and before the recapitalization plan may be put into effect.

If the par value of stock is reduced, as was done by General Motors in 1950 and 1955 and by American Telephone and Telegraph Company in 1959, the change is referred to as a stock split. No consideration is involved. Such a change will increase the number of shares outstanding, reduce the book value and tend to reduce the market value of each share, and may lead to a more favorable market for the shares because the lower price may attract more buyers. If the par value remains the same and new shares are issued, consideration is

---

[3] Corporations may show an earned surplus deficit as illustrated by Atlanta Laundries, Inc. and wholly owned subsidiaries statement:

Capital:	*January 2, 1960*	*December 27, 1958*
Common Stock—		
Authorized issue 30,000 shares of no par value outstanding—28,617.4 shares at $5.00 per share stated value**	$143,087.00	$143,087.00
Capital surplus	718,103.12	718,103.12
Earned surplus (deficit)	(64,886.45)	(88,372.95)
Net Capital	$796,303.67	$772,817.17

** "The number and stated value of outstanding shares of common stock reflect an issued 1,030 and 180/200ths shares actually not issued but reserved for shareholders entitled thereto, upon demand, under terms of the company's recapitalization as of January 1, 1937." Atlanta Laundries, Inc., *Annual Report Year Ending January 2, 1960* (Atlanta, 1960), n.p.

involved (services, cash, or other property). The consideration is an amount equal to the sum of the par value or stated value of the shares transferred from surplus to stated capital. If a corporation has issued 1,000,000 shares having a par value of $10.00 per share, the stated capital of the corporation is $10,000,000. If the surplus is $10,000,000 and 1,000,000 shares are issued as a stock dividend, the surplus is reduced to zero and the stated capital is increased to $20,000,000. Such shares would be fully paid and nonassessable. In 1953, General Electric changed its common stock without par value into common stock having a par value of $5 per share on a three-for-one basis. The common stock had a stated value of $6.25 per share (market value about $102 per share when the conversion was announced). This action required the capitalization of $252,000,000 of earned surplus ($8.75 per old share).

The policy of management in reducing the par or stated value of stock is usually motivated by the desire to make the stock more attractive to investors and to widen the market for it. As stated by the president of the American Telephone and Telegraph Company in regard to the proposed split of three for one (effective April 24, 1959), this "will strengthen our position in competing for the large amounts of capital needed in the future to meet the nation's requirements for telephone service in our expanding economy."[4] The number of shareholders at the time of the proposed stock split was 1,629,000, of which 96 per cent were individuals and the average holdings of all shareholders was 43 shares. Prior to the offering of additional shares to stockholders of record on February 23, 1961, the number of shareholders was 1,900,000.

STOCK VALUES

Par Value Stock. The par value of stock is the value as stated on the stock certificate in terms of money (for illustration, $33⅓ for American Telephone and Telegraph Company, $1.66⅔ for General Motors common stock, $1 for North American Aviation Inc., and 10 cents for United Piece Dye Works). The legal significance of par value is that it purports to represent the minimum original investment in cash, property, or services behind each share. This amount, often called legal or dedicated capital, is regarded as having been paid in for protection of creditors; therefore it is not available for dividends to stockholders.

[4] American Telephone and Telegraph Company, *Share Owners' Quarterly* (Winter, 1959), n.p.

The par value of each share is determined at the time of incorporation; but this, like other provisions in a business corporation's charter, may be changed by following the proper legal procedure (usually by a vote of stockholders holding two thirds of the shares). At one time, the par value was customarily $100.00, but the current practice is to select a low par value. The use of stocks with low par value makes it possible for management to attract a wider market for the shares, and sometimes to sell them at a premium and thereby to accumulate a capital surplus. Some state business corporation laws require that par value stock be issued for no less than par value; but, if par value stock is sold for less than par value, the future owners assume a contingent liability for the difference—the amount that the original owners did not pay. Par value stocks sold or issued for no less than par customarily have on the face of the certificate "full paid and nonassessable shares."

Stock Without Par Value. The issuance of stock without par value —or no-par stock—by business corporations was first authorized by New York in 1912, and similar enabling acts have been passed by all other states. The use of stock without par value has several advantages for management. At the time of incorporation, the board of directors indicates the consideration (price) for which shares of no-par stock will be issued. Later, part of the authorized but unissued shares may be sold at a price above or below the original consideration as determined by the board of directors. If the old stockholders are given the right to buy such shares, they will be in a position to protect their investments against dilution; but, if the board of directors is not bound by the pre-emptive right rule, the shares may be sold under terms that are disadvantageous to the old stockholders. The same is true for stocks with par value, except that such shares may not be sold for less than par value.

The use of stock without par value gives management greater freedom in accounting for "capital." The amount of flexibility depends upon the rules which govern the consideration for which the stock is issued. If the price of the stock is prescribed in the articles of incorporation, the situation may be similar to that existing when par value stock is issued. If emphasis is on fair market value, the judgment of the board of directors is conclusive (assuming absence of fraud). If the consideration is subject to approval by stockholders, the use of stock without par value may differ but little from the use of stock with par value which may be changed by a vote of the stockholders. But if the articles of incorporation authorize the board of directors to fix the consideration from time to time, management has greater freedom in determining the stated capital of the corporation than it would if par value stock were used. Nevertheless, courts of equity will protect stockholders against dilution of their equity by preventing sales of new shares to others below the prevailing market value.

The reasons for the authorization of stock without par value are to remove the restriction upon the selling price of newly issued shares at less than par, to permit the sale of fully paid and nonassessable stock at prevailing market prices, to emphasize that there may be no relationship between par value and true value of stock, and to permit an issue of more shares by simply lowering the "stated" value. The use of stock without par value is a well-established practice in American business finance. However, incorporation and state franchise taxes may be higher when no-par stock is used than they would be if low par value stock were used. Furthermore, owners may be subject to a higher stock transfer tax on no-par stock.

The insistence of the courts that the capital of a corporation must be kept intact raises many important accounting problems that must be solved by management if no-par stock is used. Finally, such stock may be less attractive to potential shareholders who may fear that their equity would be diluted if the stated value of the stock were reduced and new shares were sold to others. Today, the advantages associated with financing with no-par stock may be secured by issuing stock with par values of $5.00 to $10.00 or even 5 or 10 cents. From an accounting and legal point of view, the use of par value stock entails fewer problems than the use of no-par stock and the modern tendency is to substitute low par value stock for no-par stock.

The use of par value stock, as compared to no-par stock, is important to those who may wish to sell such shares because substantial savings in federal transfer taxes are possible. No-par stock is treated as if it had a par value of $100; therefore the federal transfer tax would be twenty times as much for no-par stock as for $5.00 par value stock (a tax base of $10,000 instead of $500 for 100 shares).

Book Value. The book value of a business firm is its net worth, the difference between its assets and liabilities, as shown by the accounting records. If this amount measures the proprietary interests of the owners, the book value of one share of stock is this figure divided by the number of shares outstanding. The book value of a share of stock may be above or below its par or stated value. If a corporation has issued preferred stock, the aggregate of the par or stated value of such stock outstanding must be subtracted from net worth before computing the book value of a share of common stock.[5]

Book value does not necessarily indicate market value because a corporation may have assets that are worth substantially more or less than their book value. While no criticism is meant of accounting practices, there is considerable variation among accounting methods employed by different business concerns which may result in either an overstatement or understatement of their assets. Another factor is that much of the proprietary value of a firm's stock will be determined by the net income of a corporation which may not be reflected in the book value of the stock.

Capitalization of Earnings. A widely used method for determining the value of stock is one in which the earnings of the company are capitalized. This necessitates the selection of a rate at which to capitalize as well as the determination of the earnings per share. If the earnings per share of common stock amount to $10.00, a capitalization rate of 15 per cent would mean that the value of each share of stock is $66.67 ($10.00 ÷ .15 = $66.67); but if the capitalization rate were 10 per cent, the capitalized value would be $100.00. In choosing the capitalization rate, the best procedure would be to use the rate which best reflects the market price for similar stocks in the market.

Market Price. Market prices usually reflect future expectations, both current and expected earnings and current and expected dividends, general prospects of the industry, and the company's position within the industry. When there is a broad market for the stock, its market price is usually the best index of its value. At a particular time, however, there may be temporary factors at work which may mean that current prices would not be representative of the true value of the stock of the company. Adjustments may be made for such situations by averaging quotations of the stock over a period of time. The market price of the stock of a corporation will be influenced by the amount of earnings assignable to the stock; this will depend in part on the capital structure of the corporation.

TYPES OF COMMON STOCK

Common stock is the general stock of a corporation sold, at least in part, by those responsible for the incorporation of the business enter-

---

[5] In arriving at book value for each share other adjustments may be made, including those for preferred stock which has a nominal book value per share but has a high callable price and is selling in the market at a premium. Aggregate values used may be for only tangible assets as shown by the company's books.

prise. Generally common stock has no fixed rate of dividends and owners are the last to share in the property when a corporation is dissolved. After a corporation is established, management may sell additional shares of common stock if provided for in the original charter or in the bylaws or by subsequent amendments to the charter. The terms and conditions under which common stock is sold are looked upon as an indication of good faith of those responsible for the financial policies of a corporation and also as an index of the soundness of the business venture. Stock offerings by corporations having meager or nonexistent assets have declined because of federal and state regulations.

Classified Common Stock. During the 1920's many corporations provided for more than one class of common stock. The two most common terms used to designate classes of common stock are Class A and Class B. Although both classes share equally in earnings and —upon liquidation—in assets of a corporation, usually one class, such as Class B, has voting preference or sole voting rights. The amount of voting stock is usually small compared with the amount of nonvoting stock; as a result control is vested in a few. Voting stock may be issued to management, former creditors if the corporation has undergone a financial crisis, and bankers who have purchased bonds or other securities of the corporation. In practice, voting common stock may be used as a substitute for a voting trust.

The issuance of nonvoting common stock, to be sold to the general public in order to acquire assets has been criticized as being out of step with public policy.[6] Nevertheless, business corporation acts customarily give corporate management wide latitude in classes of stocks and types of securities that may be offered. Even though the voting rights of a class of stock may be limited or denied, the owners of this stock cannot be deprived of the privilege of voting on issues that affect their interests (such as the right to vote on consolidations and mergers, on sale or mortgage of assets not in the regular course of business, and on voluntary dissolution).[7]

---

[6] The New York Stock Exchange, Securities and Exchange Commission, and Bankruptcy Courts not only frown upon but also take measures to prevent issuance of nonvoting stock when such action falls within their provinces.

[7] The common stock of the Philadelphia Electric Company includes a small amount of $1 dividend preference common stock which has preference over common stock in payment of dividends. The company's charter requires that the common stock equity represented by the $1 dividend preference common stock and surplus must be greater than the involuntary liquidating value of the preferred stock of the company in order to avoid restrictions on the payment of dividends on the common stock. Since the liquidating value is more than three times that of preferred stock of the company, the provision is meaningless but it does illustrate the type of restriction current in preferred stock agreements. In

Disadvantage of Common Stock Ownership. Investors who own common stock or other types of proprietory interests assume certain risks. A corporation's board of directors is under no legal obligation to pay dividends but the members of the board are agents of the stockholders who own the corporation. Stockholders are not helpless—they may change the membership of the board of directors. Furthermore, a stockholder may sell his shares; when enough stockholders do so, the value of the stock will be depressed and this reflects unfavorably on the corporation's management.

Legally dividends may be paid only from current or retained earnings except in cases wherein a corporation is in process of being liquidated (for illustration, a consuming-assets corporation exploiting a natural resource which is subject to depletion.) In contrast, before anything is available for dividend payments, all prior claims, including interest, installment payments on debts, and sinking funds as provided for in debt agreements, must be met out of earnings. In case of failure, common stockholders take what is left after all other claims are met. In reorganization procedures, stockholders may lose all of their equity or may be permitted to retain an interest in the reorganized company or to purchase new stock in proportion to their current holdings (which, in effect, may be a voluntary assessment on their stock).

Advantage of Common Stock Ownership. The prospect of large returns on an investment in the common stock of a corporation may far outweigh the disadvantages of stock ownership. In any business venture, the creditor and preferred stockholder, in effect, "pay" for their more secure positions by accepting a limited return on their investments and surrendering control over corporate assets. In buying credit instruments, individuals must compete with institutional investors (commercial banks, savings institutions, insurance companies, trusts, and others), and the demands of these investors for credit instruments is a factor in their low yields. Owing to changes in some state laws, institutional investors are competing more actively with individuals for preferred and common stock; but not to the extent that is true for bonds and other credit instruments.

While a business corporation's board of directors is under no contractual obligation to pay dividends on common stock, a board may

---

case of liquidation, the $1 dividend preference common stock would share in remaining assets after payment of claims of creditors and preferred stockholders on the same basis as common stockholders. The holders of the $1 dividend preference common stock have no pre-emptive rights but are entitled to one vote for each share held.

feel morally (and sometimes legally) obligated to do so and the dividends actually voted and paid may exceed the yield on other forms of a corporation's securities. When earnings are retained temporarily rather than paid out as dividends, an increase in earnings tends to follow; as a result, more earnings may be available for dividend payments at a later date. If retained earnings are capitalized by a stock dividend, the common stockholders' investments in terms of the number of shares will be increased. Pre-emptive rights to subscribe to new securities may be given to old stockholders under conditions which are valuable (see Chapter 18).

Inflation tends to reallocate the value of assets of corporations among their security holders by reducing the real value of fixed-income securities and increasing the real value of variable-income securities. If a corporation with assets of $1,000,000 has creditors' claims against it for $500,000, its stockholders' share in assets is $500,000. Assuming inflation of 100 per cent, the corporation's assets will have a value of $2,000,000, creditors' claims will be $500,000, and the stockholders' share in assets will be $1,500,000. If one assumes a similar division of income before inflation, the ratio of creditors' interest payments to stockholders' dividends would change, from one-to-one, to one-to-three after inflation.

In addition to enjoying the prospects for larger returns, common stockholders customarily have the right to elect the members of the board of directors and to vote on other matters presented at annual and special meetings of stockholders. If a corporation finances with a single type of security, it is almost always common stock. Common stock is the type of security most widely used by American business corporations. But, lest we forget, holders of common stock have residual claims to both assets and earnings and they are the chief risk-bearers of modern industry. The fact that their risks are real is reflected in the wide fluctuations in prices of common stocks.

PROPRIETARY CAPITAL AS A BASE FOR FINANCING

Proprietary or equity capital is sometimes identified as a business firm's net worth, but net worth may include some temporary funds retained in the business pending distribution to owners. Proprietary capital is considered to be the more permanent form of capital which includes stated capital or capital stock, capital surplus, and earned surplus, or simply capital stock and surplus. A business firm may use debts as well as proprietary capital in meeting its long-term capital needs. Debt financing may be used for a number of reasons which will be discussed in later chapters, but the aspect of debt as linked to proprietary or equity capital, called "trading on equity," is discussed here.

Trading on Equity. If a business firm borrows large amounts, it can expand its trading or business operations without increasing its equity. That is to say, it is, in effect, doing a great deal of trading on relatively little equity—hence the term or expression, *trading on equity*. Trading on equity may also be described as follows: When a business firm is financing exclusively with proprietary capital, its owners have sole claims to the earnings and assets of the firm; but when a business firm borrows, it is "trading away" to creditors the prior rights of owners to its assets and earnings. Other things remaining the same, the legal position of owners (their prior rights to assets) of equity capital of a business concern will progressively become less favorable as the concern goes further into debt. Trading assumes that something is given as well as received; when funds are borrowed by a business concern, creditors supply capital and equity owners receive the use thereof under conditions that should be mutually advantageous.

Owners of a new business concern may not be able to supply all the funds needed from their accumulated savings and going concerns in need of funds may be unwilling to share control or future profits with new partners or new stockholders. On the other hand, some individuals with funds at their disposal are unwilling to assume the risks of ownership and may prefer to have a prior claim to earnings and assets even though it may entail foregoing larger returns in the future. Therefore to secure needed funds, owners and proprietors of business enterprises customarily "trade" part of their prior claims to earnings for the use of funds of those who prefer to be creditors rather than assume the hazards of ownership. Because creditors want to be fully protected from the hazards that proprietors should assume, there are limits to the degree of trading on equity that a business firm may do. Unless proprietors and owners invest substantially in their business enterprises, creditors may be unwilling to lend to them on any terms.

A significant aspect of "trading on equity" is the leverage factor —that is, the greater-than-proportionate change in return to common stock when there is a change in operating income. Assume that two companies have been earning 4 per cent (or $100,000) on their annual sales of $2,500,000 and that "X" Company is financing with debt which bears a 5 per cent interest rate. The earnings assignable to common stock before income taxes would be as follows:

	X Company	Y Company
Total debt (interest 5%)	$ 500,000	
Capital and retained earnings	500,000	$1,000,000
Total Liabilities and Capital	$1,000,000	$1,000,000
Earnings	$ 100,000	$ 100,000
Less interest	25,000	
Total Earnings	$ 75,000	$ 100,000
Per cent earned on total capital	15	10

If earnings increase to 5 per cent ($125,000) on annual sales the following year, without any change in volume, earnings will have been increased by 25 per cent ($25,000); but the amount assignable to total capital would be as follows:

	X Company	Y Company
Earnings	$125,000	$125,000
Less interest	25,000	
Total	$100,000	$125,000
Per cent earned on total capital	20	12.5

While the increase in earnings has been 25 per cent, the per cent earned on total capital by X Company has increased from 15 to 20 per cent—that is, one third; earnings on total capital of Y Company have increased from 10 to 12.5 per cent, or one fourth, which is in proportion to the increase in total earnings. A second aspect of financing with debt rather than with owners' equity is the tax advantage—which is not considered here because the emphasis is on leverage.

The leverage factor is a double edged sword, resulting in a greater proportionate decrease (or increase) in return to common stock than the decrease (or increase) in operating income. For illustration, a decline in operating earnings noted above to $25,000 the third year would mean that X Company would have no earnings on total capital and Y Company would earn 2.5 per cent on total capital.

There is no rule as to the correct proportion between debt and equity in the financial structure of business firms. However, when a corporation's financial structure becomes top-heavy with short- and long-term debts, it may find itself forced to liquidate current assets under unfavorable conditions to meet its debt obligations. If this situation becomes widespread among business firms, it may lead to a large amount of forced selling which, in turn, could set off a chain reaction leading to a business recession.

It is practical for "public" corporations to raise funds by selling securities to old stockholders, but this may not be possible for a small business firm with a small number of owners. In rare cases, a partnership or small corporation may be able to obtain new capital from a financial "angel"; but in general, small business firms are dependent on retained earnings as a source of new equity capital. As noted previously, the trend among most business firms, including large corporations that are able to finance publicly, has been to finance to a considerable extent with retained earnings. During periods when business is most profitable, the ability to finance with retained earnings is greatest. Therefore, during good times, most firms increase their net worth by retaining earnings; but, because it is easy to borrow during such times, many firms increase their debts out of proportion to the increase in net worth and fail to improve their equity positions.

A business firm may become insolvent as the result of a sharp decline in earnings which is not offset by a decline in fixed charges (interest payments and commitments to repay principal or to earmark earnings for this purpose as in sinking-fund agreements). Usually, financial difficulties are reflected first in a company's working capital which may reveal a shrinkage in the value of inventories owing to a decline in prices, a decline in the value of receivables as more become uncollectible, and/or a decline in operating income due to a decrease in sales. Under such circumstances, the pressure for repayment of outstanding loans together with the inability to arrange for new ones may force management to liquidate assets under unfavorable conditions.

One of the first rules for management to follow is to conform to practices which will maintain a balanced relationship between debts and net worth. Usually this means testing the financial position of a business concern by constructing ratios (such as current liabilities to tangible net worth, total liabilities to tangible net worth, and net worth to total assets) and comparing them to those considered standard for the type of business and to those of other firms in the same field.

SUMMARY

There are two main sources of capital funds: owners and lenders. Equity or proprietary capital refers to that provided by owners and has the following distinguishing characteristics: the firm is under no contractual obligation to pay a return thereon, there is no stated date on which the funds must be returned to the investor, and those who provide funds are responsible for the management and control of the firm. Sometimes the term *risk capital* is used; this emphasizes the fact that owners of equities assume risks to a greater degree than do lenders. Even though owners must assume risks inherent in stock ownership, this may be more than offset by prospects for high returns.

Evidence of ownership in a business will vary according to the form of organization. If the business is incorporated, ownership is evidenced by stock certificates. In most instances, stock can be sold at will by the owner; even though a stock certificate is not a credit instrument, the Uniform Stock Transfer Act has given stock certificates some of the characteristics of negotiable instruments.

The charter or bylaws will usually specify the amounts and types of stock which may be issued. The total amount which a firm may issue is called "authorized stock." The amount that is actually issued is referred to as "issued stock." If a company repurchases or otherwise acquires some of its own stock, it is called "treasury stock." The stock issued and not reacquired by a corporation is the "outstanding stock."

Shares of stock may or may not have a par value. No-par stock may give greater freedom to the management of a concern than does par value stock, but there may be higher franchise and stock transfer taxes. At the present time, the trend seems to be toward using par value stock, but selecting a low figure for that value.

There may be more than one class of common stock. A fairly common practice during the 1920's was to divide common stock into classes A and B and to vest sole voting rights in the Class B stock. This may facilitate control by a small group.

Trading on equity occurs when a company finances with senior securities: bonds and other credit instruments. This may have the effect of increasing earnings on the equity capital; but, at the same time, it increases the fixed commitments which the firm must make and hence may jeopardize its financial position.

QUESTIONS AND PROBLEMS

1. Capitalization or the financial structure of a business enterprise is sometimes thought of as the long-term debt and capital stock of a business firm. How does this concept of capital compare to others previously considered?
2. What are the most important characteristics of equity capital?
3. From the viewpoint of a business firm, what justification is there for calling equity capital "risk capital?" From the viewpoint of those who supply it?
4. What is a stock certificate? Is it negotiable? Transferable? Explain.

5. (*a*) When is a stock "ex dividend?" (*b*) What is meant by "holder of record?"
6. Identify the following types of stock: (*a*) authorized, (*b*) issued, (*c*) unissued, (*d*) treasury, and (*e*) outstanding.
7. Was management justified in reacquiring shares by open-market purchases during the early 1930's? Explain your answer.
8. (*a*) Distinguish between surplus and capital surplus. (*b*) How may a corporation increase stated capital and decrease capital surplus?
9. (*a*) Distinguish between stock splits and stock dividends. (*b*) May the earned surplus be affected by each? Explain.
10. (*a*) What is the legal significance of par value? (*b*) What are the advantages and disadvantages in the use of no-par stock? (*c*) Under current federal transfer taxes, what is the advantage of par value stock over no-par stock?
11. (*a*) Identify book value. (*b*) How may the earnings of a corporation be capitalized to determine the value of stock?
12. Distinguish between Class A and Class B common stock.
13. Smaller firms trade on equity more than do large firms. Is this from choice or necessity? Explain.
14. "The Texas Utilities Company declared yesterday a dividend of 53 cents a share, payable on April 3 to holders of record of March 1. (*New York Times*, February 18, 1961, p. 23.) How early must the stock be purchased in order to receive the next dividend? Explain.
15. Analyze: "The point that we bankers should make in our dealings with small business firms is that if a company wants to grow, sooner or later some type of equity or long-term debt financing becomes inevitable." (J. W. Remington, "Small Business is Banking's Business," *Banking, Journal of the American Bankers Association* (August, 1960), p. 161.

CHAPTER 18

Financing through Pre-emptive Rights and Privileged Subscription

A HOLDER of common stock has a common-law right to subscribe for new issues of common stock and other securities that are convertible into common stock of his corporation. The financial significance of this *pre-emptive right* is that, after the original issue of common stock, a corporation must first permit the old stockholders to purchase new issues before offering them to others. However, the prior rights of common stockholders may be waived either by statutory law or by a vote of common stockholders. When waived, management has more discretion in planning new common stock offerings.

This chapter deals with the problems associated with common stock offerings under pre-emptive rights and other privileged subscription offerings to employees, officers, and others.

THE PRE-EMPTIVE RIGHT

Justification for the Pre-emptive Rights Rule. The pre-emptive right of a common stockholder permits him to participate proportionately in any increase in the capital stock of his company. Hence, he is given the opportunity to maintain his percentage interest in his company and if he uses his privilege to buy new stock when offered, he protects his interest in the company from being diluted. The financial abuses current during the post–Civil War era included the issuance of new shares to insiders in order to perpetuate their control to the disadvantage of existing shareholders.

The first argument in support of the common-law pre-emptive right principle is that it permits old common stockholders to protect their voting positions. Assume that an individual owns 10 per cent of the 20,000 shares of voting stock of a corporation through ownership of 2,000 shares. If a new issue of stock were sold to outsiders in an amount equal to the shares outstanding, the voting rights of the original stockholder would be reduced from 10 per cent to 5 per cent. The only way in which the original stockholder could restore his relative voting position would be to acquire 2,000 additional shares, which he may or may not be able to do. But, if he had been given the right to subscribe to an additional 2,000 shares before they were offered to others, he would have had the first opportunity to do so.

A second argument in support of the pre-emptive right principle is that the shareholders must be permitted to retain their proportionate share in the surplus or net worth of their corporation. Over a period of years, a corporation may have retained earnings so as to have a surplus equal to the par value or stated value of the stock outstanding. If we assume that this value is $100, each share of common stock outstanding has a book value of $200 (capital stock, $2,000,000 + surplus, $2,000,000 ÷ shares outstanding, 20,000 = $200 book value per share). If we assume that 20,000 shares of a new issue are sold for the old par or stated value of $100, it would mean that the book value of each share of common stock outstanding would be reduced from $200 to $150 (capital stock, $4,000,000 + surplus, $2,000,000 ÷ shares outstanding, 40,000 = $150).

In effect, selling new shares at par value transferred $50 "on the books" from old stockholders to new stockholders. The only way that the original stockholder could protect himself against such a "paper" loss would be to buy shares in amounts equal to his original holdings. If he had been given the right to acquire new shares in an amount proportionate to his holdings before the stock was offered to others, he would have had the opportunity to protect himself against the dilution of his interest. If the rights were actually worth $50 per share and if the stockholder had chosen not to acquire more shares, he could have sold his rights and thus recaptured his capital loss but he would not retain his proportionate voting power.

The third argument in support of the common-law pre-emptive right principle is that the old stockholders must be permitted to retain their proportionate interest in the earnings of their corporation. If the corporation is earning $160,000 or 4 per cent on the net worth of $4,000,000 ($160,000 ÷ $4,000,000 = .04), it would amount to $8 per share ($160,000 ÷ 20,000 = $8). If 20,000 new shares are sold for $100 per share, the assets of the corporation would be increased by $2,000,000 which would earn $80,000 at the rate of 4 per cent and would thereby increase total earnings to $240,000. When these earnings are divided by the number of shares outstanding, the earning rate per share would be $6 ($240,000 ÷ 40,000 = $6). In effect, the old stockholders' interest in earnings would have been reduced from $8 to $6 per share and the interest in earnings of the new stockholders would have been increased from $4 to $6 per share. In this case, as in the foregoing, the use of the common-law principle of pre-emptive right would permit the old stockholder to protect his position with reference to earnings by subscribing to the new shares in proportion to his existing holdings of stock.

Applicability of the Pre-emptive Rights Principle. If the common-law principle pertaining to the pre-emptive right of old stockholders to buy new common stock is justified, the pre-emptive right principle is equally applicable to issues of preferred stock, bonds, and other securities which are convertible into common stock. If the right to exchange preferred stock, bonds, or other securities for common stock at the option of the owner has any value, the rights of old common stockholders as to voting, equity, and earnings of the corporation will be diluted at the time of conversion in the same way as noted above in the case of sales of new common stock to new stockholders.

At the time of organizing a corporation, there are no equity, net worth, or similar rights to protect. Therefore, common stock may be sold to anyone. But, when a corporation begins operations after selling only a part of the shares that it has the right to issue, the problem becomes more complicated. If the company begins operating after selling 100,000 shares of the 200,000 authorized, it will have 100,000 "authorized but unissued" shares. After operating a few years, the board of directors may vote to sell the remaining shares as a second installment of the original issue. Under the pre-emptive right rule, must these shares be offered first to the old stockholders? If the time between the two installments is long enough for the old common stockholders to have acquired additional equity or net worth, the answer is apparently "Yes"; otherwise, "No."

Modern business corporation acts provide that the pre-emptive right is applicable to reissued treasury stock of a corporation unless limited or denied in the articles of incorporation. With a two-thirds or more affirmative vote of the shares entitled to vote thereon, treasury as well as other stock may be offered to officers and employees without first being offered to shareholders.[1] As long as such stock is held by the corporation, it can neither participate in dividends nor vote.

The pre-emptive right rule does not apply when new stock is issued in exchange for property. A corporation may wish to obtain control of a second company by exchanging authorized but unissued shares for the stock of the second company, or a corporation may acquire the property of a second company by giving such stock rather than by paying cash. While the law recognizes the right of corporate management to exchange stock for property, management may find it expedient to protect itself by asking for prior approval of stockholders if the amount of property is large. By doing so management recognizes the right of creditors and/or stockholders to sue the board of directors, jointly or individually, if their rights and privileges are impaired or violated (a contingency which they may anticipate by obtaining prior approval of shareholders).

In order for management to sell new stock not previously authorized by the corporation's charter, approval of stockholders entitled to vote thereon must be obtained. Actually, this amounts to approval of an amendment to the articles of incorporation and the same general procedure (filing with the Secretary of State, etc.) used in obtaining the original certificate of incorporation must be followed. While the charter may require that shares be offered to old stockholders, a waiver of pre-emptive rights may be obtained from old stockholders (usually by at least a two-thirds affirmative vote of those entitled to vote on the question). Most commonly, stockholders are asked to waive their pre-emptive right to permit purchases of stock by officers and employees.

Pre-emptive rights are based on common law but they may be withdrawn by statutory law. To an increasing extent, business corporation acts make provisions for the waiver of pre-emptive rights in the articles of incorporation of corporations. The Indiana, Delaware, and California codes go even further and provide that no pre-emptive rights exist unless they are specifically included in a corporation's charter. More commonly, the statutes require incorporators to specify in the articles of incorporation "any provision limiting or denying the shareholders the pre-emptive right to acquire additional or treas-

[1] See Sections 24 of both the Model Business Corporation Act and the Illinois Business Corporation Act.

ury shares of the corporation." On the other hand, business corporation acts also permit the articles of incorporation to be amended so as to "grant to shareholders of any class the pre-emptive right to acquire additional or treasury shares of the corporation whether then or thereafter authorized." Old stockholders are protected, irrespective of their previous voting status, by being permitted to vote on any amendments which affect their existing pre-emptive or other rights.

PRIVILEGED SUBSCRIPTIONS

Privileged subscriptions exist when old stockholders, employees, officers, and/or others are given the first right to buy new securities of their corporations. Usually, the term "privileged subscription" suggests that only certain ones may subscribe for the securities and that special advantages are associated with offering terms which make the privilege valuable. The term is usually used when new securities are being issued, but it could be applied to sales of treasury stock. When considered as a financing device, privileged subscription is most important when new securities are offered to old stockholders. Such offerings under pre-emptive rights may be voluntary or they may be mandatory as when required by common law, statutes, or charters of issuing corporations.[2]

Problem of Pricing in "Public" and Privileged Subscription Offerings. When a corporation plans to make a public offering of new stock, the market price of the outstanding stock should be expected to decline as soon as, or even before, the board of directors announces the subscription price and other terms. This decline will tend to be in proportion to the size of the issue or, in other words, the amount that the claims to earnings represented by each old share are expected to be decreased by the new issue. This market reaction should be anticipated in setting the offering price of the issue; the closer the price is to the market on the offering date, the smaller will be the decline in the market price. The penalty for overpricing the stock is failure of the issue; the penalty for underpricing (below market price) is loss in net proceeds per share of stock sold.

Market for Pre-Emptive Rights Offerings. The market for securities sold under pre-emptive rights is assumed to be limited to old stockholders; but purchase warrants or rights are transferable,

---

[2] Regardless of the provisions of states' business corporation acts pertaining to pre-emptive rights, stockholders have the right to sue members of the board of directors of their corporation if their interests are being affected adversely by a public sale of securities. The strength of their case will depend on the amount of dilution of their claims to earnings and net worth and the reduction in their proportionate voting power.

and they are often sold. If most of an issue were acquired by new investors instead of old stockholders, one may assume that a direct sale to the public through investment bankers would have been preferable, as the corporation would have obtained a higher price as well as an increase in the number of stockholders. By having more stockholders to whom to sell future offerings of stock and other securities, the corporation's financial position would be strengthened.

In financing with subscription rights, management assumes that most of the old stockholders will use their rights to increase their investments in their company (an assumption that is not always justified). The size of a new issue is an important factor in the success of a rights offering in that old stockholders are in a better position to absorb all of the shares offered when the ratio of new to old securities is small—assume one to twenty as compared to one to one. In the first case, the stockholders would be asked to increase their investments by about 5 per cent; in the second case, they would be asked to double their investments. A careful analysis by management of the distribution of existing shares would throw light on the question of the size of the issue that could be absorbed by existing stockholders. In planning a corporation's expansion program, arrangements may be made for financing over a period of years with the relative size of successive issues small enough to permit existing stockholders to acquire their proportional share of new stock. A policy of permitting stockholders to buy their shares on the installment plan is sometimes used to make issues sold under pre-emptive rights more attractive.

Before offering new issues to old common stockholders, management customarily analyzes this market to determine whether or not it is composed of investors able to absorb the issue. The stock may be owned by a few large stockholders who are unable to purchase more shares or are unwilling to do so because they want to diversify their investments. On the other hand, there may be a small number of institutional investors including investment companies that are both able and willing to acquire new shares at "bargain prices." Generally speaking, the best market for privileged subscription sales of new securities exists when there are a large number of satisfied shareholders.[3] Previous sales of new securities by privileged subscrip-

[3] American Telephone and Telegraph Company's latest offering of common stock was for more than $961 million to more than 1,900,000 shareholders. Each shareholder was permitted to buy one new share of stock at $86 for every 20 shares held on February 23, 1961; thus the holders of 223.5 million shares were permitted to subscribe for more than 11,175,000 new shares. The last previous offering by A. T. & T. was in 1956 on a one-to-ten basis.

tion may have demonstrated to stockholders that the degree of dilution of each share was negligible and that the depressing effect on the market price of the stock was temporary. Pre-emptive offering tends to make stockholders feel that management is genuinely interested in them and wants them to have all the advantages associated with being shareholders. The reaction of existing stockholders will be most satisfactory if the old dividend rate is to be continued because, as investors, they are primarily interested in income from their investments.

On the assumption that everyone is interested in purchasing at "bargain prices," the key to successful financing is the spread between subscription and market prices. In other words, a new issue is certain to be a success if the subscription price is sufficiently below the market price. If we assume a market price of $150 and a subscription price of $125, one could expect an offering of new stock to old stockholders to be successful. Of course, the lower the subscription price the smaller will be the return to the company for each new share sold, and a greater number of new shares will have to be sold to raise a given amount of funds. The greater the number of new shares sold, the greater will be the dilution of value of each old share and the more depressing will be the effect on the market price of each share. This will be reflected in the market price of the subscription rights or warrants considered in the next section.

Management may set an unusually low subscription price in order to adjust the market price of the stock downward; if so, management may be guided in part by the same motives which lead a corporation to declare a stock dividend or stock split. In fact, if there is no objection to reduction in market price of the stock and no pressure on management to maintain the old dividend rate, there is no reason why the subscription price for a new issue may not be at a substantial discount. For illustration, a stock selling for $100 may have its market price adjusted downward to a more popular level by offering old stockholders new shares at a subscription price of $10 (an unrealistic approach).

Legal and Routine Procedures. After financing plans are drawn for a new stock issue, they must be approved by the corporation's board of directors. This approval takes the form of a resolution stating the amount of stock to be sold and the purpose of the issue. When authorized but unissued stock is available, the financing plan may be put into operation directly; otherwise, the board of directors will instruct the officers to submit a charter amendment to increase the authorized capital to shareholders for their approval (at a regular or special meeting). Following approval of the charter amendment, the resolution customarily states that new shares will be offered to stockholders and that transferable subscription warrants evidencing their rights to subscribe for new shares will be distributed.[4]

After the charter amendment has been filed as required by law and a registration statement has been filed with the Securities and Exchange Commission, an officer of the corporation will notify the shareholders of the action taken and the details of subscription rights offered to stockholders, including the record date for determining who will receive subscription warrants, the offering period (when the offering will open and when it will end), the date warrants will be mailed, and how rights for less than enough to acquire one share will be handled. This letter is issued for information purposes only and is in no way a formal offering or commitment on the part of the corporation to sell securities.

As soon as practical after the record date, the corporation will transmit to stockholders of record the subscription warrants together with a letter of transmittal containing instructions as to the use of the warrants and a copy of the prospectus which contains the basic facts about the company and the issue. Since the warrants are transferable, they customarily state the terms of the issue, the number of shares for which the stockholder is entitled to subscribe, the subscription price, the office which will receive payment for the stock, the final date for using the rights, and the date of issue of the new stock. On the back of the warrant there is a form for the assignment of the warrant (in case the shareholder wishes to transfer it to others) and also a subscription agreement to be signed by the one exercising the subscription right.

Usually two or more rights are needed to purchase one new share; therefore most stockholders will have more or less rights than the number needed to purchase one or more shares. For illustration, if seven rights are needed to purchase one share, the owner of 25 shares will have four extra rights in addition to those needed to subscribe for three shares. To prevent the stockholder from losing his extra rights, management may arrange for a trust company or bank

---

[4] The preliminary notice of financing is made available through the press and/or the current publications of the corporation. For illustration: "The Company is planning to offer additional shares of stock to the share owners. Under these plans, share owners would be entitled to buy one new share for each 20 shares held on February 23, 1961, and "rights" to purchase the additional shares would be mailed early in March. The purchase price for the shares would be fixed by the Board of Directors shortly before the offering and would be somewhat below the market price at that time." American Telephone and Telegraph Company, *Share Owners Quarterly* (Winter, 1961), n.p.

to act as agent to sell the four rights or to buy three additional rights at the market price according to the request of the owner when he exercises his subscription rights. Also management may arrange to have subscription warrants listed on a stock exchange, where they would be traded until the end of the offering period. Thus those wishing to buy or sell additional warrants (seven or more in our assumption) would have to make such purchases or sales in the open market through regular brokerage channels.

Customarily, the formal offering documents will contain a copy of the prospectus together with a description of the securities offered and the rights and warrants and their uses. Also provided will be information pertaining to the company's planned use of the funds, its financial statements, the nature of the business, litigations involving the company, and any special information (for example, regarding license or other contracts) that may affect the company. As a matter of policy, management usually states what the anticipated dividend rate will be. Here is the statement made by the American Telephone and Telegraph Company in connection with its 1961 stock offering: "It is also anticipated that the quarterly dividend to be paid in July 1961 (on all shares including the ones sold under the offering) would be at the rate of 90 cents per share."[5] Since the quarterly dividend prior to the announcement had been at a rate of 82½ cents per share, the timing of the announced increase had the effect of enhancing the market price of the stock prior to the new financing.

VALUE OF SUBSCRIPTION RIGHTS

The announcement of a corporation's financing plans will be followed by setting the offering date of the new stock and the date of record. (For example, the American Telephone and Telegraph Company announced that the offering period would start "about March 10," and end April 14, 1961, and that the warrants would be sent to holders of record on February 23.) Prior to the record date, subject to the qualification below, the stock will be selling with "rights on"; that is, the buyer of the stock will also purchase the rights. When management does not announce the subscription price until the beginning of the offering period, buying and selling the stock and/or "rights" is on a "when issued" basis. (American Telephone and Telegraph Company announced the subscription price of its common stock at $86 on February 16, 1961 and trading in the rights started

[5] *Ibid.* n.p.

at around \$1.28 per share based on the preceding closing price of the stock at \$112.875.)

Stockholders are mailed their transferable subscription warrants at the closing of the transfer books (similar to the closing of the book prior to dividend payments) for as many rights as they have shares of stock. The shares of old stock listed on the New York Stock Exchange will be selling ex-rights (three full business days prior to the date of record), and the market price will have declined by the value of the rights. The loss in market price of the stock will be offset by the value of the subscription warrants which the stockholder may sell or use to purchase stock at the subscription price. The value of the "rights" is at parity when it is a matter of indifference whether one buys the stock at the market price or buys warrants so as to buy stock at its subscription price. If the market price of the stock falls below its subscription price, the "rights" will have no value. The market price of rights will fluctuate with the market price of the stock only as long as the market price is above the subscription price.

The value of subscription warrants during the "rights on" period may be determined by the following formula:

$$R = \frac{M - S}{N + 1}.$$

Using the figure \$112.875 for market value (M), \$86 for subscription price (S), and 20 for the number of rights needed to buy one share (N), makes the value of each subscription warrant (R) = \$1.28

$$\left(R = \frac{\$112.875 - \$86}{20 + 1}\right).$$

Since subscription warrants may be bought and sold on a "when issued" basis, investors may participate in the new financing either by buying the stock until the record date (as modified by the New York Stock Exchange rule) or the stock purchase warrants.

On the date fixed by management, those entitled to receive subscription warrants will receive them with full instructions as to their use or disposal. Other things being equal, the price of the stock should be the same as during the "rights on" period minus the value of the subscription right. Under the circumstances assumed above, the market price will tend to fall to \$111.60 because one could buy 20 rights for $25.60 and subscribe for one share at the subscription price of $86 (total cost $111.60). During the period when the new stock is being sold, the market value of the subscription warrants will be determined by this formula:

$$R = \frac{M - S}{N}\left(\frac{\$111.60 - \$86}{20} = \$1.28\right).$$

Normally, the offering period (during which rights have value) is limited to two or three weeks; thereafter, all stock-purchase warrants lose their value. Rights not used by old stockholders may be sold to others before the expiration date. If the company's stock is listed on a stock exchange, the stock rights are usually listed for trading.

The illustrations used above assume a rigidity of prices for stock before and after "ex-rights" that does not exist in practice because there are many factors that influence stock market prices in general and the market price of any one stock in particular. Because there are arbitragers in the securities market who buy subscription warrants and sell stock when the market price of the stock is above the price of the rights plus the subscription price, the price of the rights will tend to move up and down with the market price of the stock. Assuming that the stock is selling for $112 per share and the rights are selling for $1.25, the arbitrager might sell 1,000 shares short for $112,000 and buy 20,000 warrants for $25,000 and subscribe for 1,000 shares at $86,000, for a total of $111,000. He would use the shares to cover his short position and would make a gross profit (less commissions and taxes) of $1,000 on the transaction. From the viewpoint of the securities market, the sale of 1,000 shares would tend to lower the market price of the stock and the purchase of 20,000 warrants would tend to raise the market price of the warrants and to bring the two in line.[6]

Although the value of the stock right is merely a compensation given to shareholders for the loss in market value of their shares,

[6] However it is fairly common for stock rights to be priced above their actual value based on the current market price of the shares to which the rights to purchase apply. This may be caused by one or a combination of the two following reasons: (1) traders may establish a short-term speculative position in the issue by buying the stock rights and (2) a special provision of the Board of Governors of the Federal Reserve System allows a generous loan value of any new shares subscribed for through the exercise of stock rights (75 per cent as compared to 30 per cent on ordinary margin transactions at the present time).

some stockholders tend to regard their subscription warrants as something like a bonus that may be turned into cash. In effect, the subscription warrant is similar to a stock dividend. However, if the old dividend rate is maintained, the stock will tend to return to its old market price. So, under certain circumstances, investors may be correct in considering stock rights as a kind of bonus. Since management of a corporation is usually inclined to set the subscription price of a new issue low enough to insure its sale, the company's shareholders will usually find it advantageous to use their subscription rights or warrants. Under ideal conditions, the value of rights will be exactly equal to the loss in market value of the stock; but there are always some uninformed stockholders who neither use nor sell their subscription rights with the result that an advantage will tend to accrue to those who do use their rights.

When a corporation plans to sell stock by privileged subscription, the success of the financing may be enhanced by permitting stockholders to oversubscribe for new shares. Thus if a common stockholder has rights for ten shares, he may subscribe for ten shares and request an additional ten shares if and when available. All such requests will be added and the shares not subscribed for by those holding rights will be prorated among those requesting additional shares. It does not follow that the subscriber will receive all of the additional shares requested, but he may get part of them because no matter how attractive the subscription privilege may be, there will be some who will not use their rights.

Corporate management may arrange for "standby" or "price" underwriting; that is, it may negotiate a contract with an investment banking syndicate to purchase the unsold portion of an issue to be offered to its stockholders. Under such an arrangement, the corporation may pay either a flat commission on the entire issue or a smaller commission on the issue plus a higher one on each bond or share not subscribed for by stockholders. When planning to offer an issue under subscription rights, the corporation may use the services of its investment banker in preparing forms, pricing the stock, registering the issue with the Securities and Exchange Commission, preparing the prospectus, and handling other details associated with distribution of the securities. In case of refinancing, the corporation may contract with an investment banking syndicate to guarantee the sale or exchange of an entire issue; and, if the old security holders request cash in place of new securities, the underwriters will purchase the portion not sold to former security holders.

SPECIAL SOURCES OF EQUITY CAPITAL

Customers and Suppliers. The customers of some corporations are among the special groups to whom stock may be offered. In some lines of business, such as public utility companies, approaching customers with stock offers is not difficult. Some public utility companies, such as those providing gas, electricity, water, communications, and transportation services, originate as community projects with much of the venture capital provided by potential users of the services. In other cases, the companies are organized as mutual companies with all the stock owned by customers. So, a tradition of stock ownership in local utility companies was strong in the 1920's when public utility companies were being consolidated into larger units. In some cases, control of operating companies was obtained by exchanging stock of holding companies for the stock of operating companies. In addition, new capital was obtained for expansion by selling new securities to existing customer-stockholders and others.

The primary reasons for selling stock to customers of public utility companies during the 1920's were financial; but, in some cases, "goodwill" was considered to be of equal or greater importance. It was assumed that a customer who was a stockholder would be less critical of rates or rate increases than a nonstockholder, and that the customer-stockholder would be on the side of the company if and when unfavorable legislation was being considered by Congress or the state legislature. Most of the shares sold to customers were preferred stock on which heavy losses were incurred during the depression beginning in 1929. As a result, the expected "goodwill" became "ill will" which was a factor in the passage of the Public Utility Act of 1935 (Title I is called the "Public Utility Holding Company Act of 1935").

Manufacturing companies have sought to expand the sales of their products by selling stock to retail and wholesale distributors so as to give them a direct interest in the company. The same sort of customer relationship may result when the customer takes the initiative in providing new capital to the manufacturer in order to be assured a source of supply. Today, some large corporations assist small business firms in order to be assured of an outlet for their products or a source of supply. However, when such relationships are developed, it usually means a loss of part of its independence for the smaller company, which may ultimately become a subsidiary of the investing company.

Employees. The United States Steel Corporation, E. I. duPont de Nemours & Company, Proctor and Gamble Company, Commonwealth Edison Company, and the Illinois Central Railroad Company were among the first companies to attempt to break down the barrier between employers and employees by encouraging the latter to become co-owners. Now almost one half of the companies whose stocks are listed on the New York Stock Exchange have adopted stock-buying plans for their employees.

It is not surprising that employee-ownership plans enjoy great popularity during stock market booms when stock ownership seems to be a short cut to riches. Nor is it surprising that only one in five of the major employee stock-ownership plans initiated during the 1920's survived the stock market collapse of 1929–30. The revival in popularity of such plans since World War II has been caused by several factors. Many employee-investors recognize that common stock can be a hedge against inflation and sponsors of employee-ownership plans realize that wage earners may be an important source of investment funds as was demonstrated by their purchases of Series E bonds under payroll deduction plans during World War II.

The present-day employee stock-purchase plans are of two basic types: one operates under privileged subscription plans wherein stock is sold to employees below market prices; the other operates under arrangements whereby stock is purchased in the open market and sold to employees at market prices. The sponsors of both types of plans seem to assume that the company's stock has investment merits because employee stock-purchase plans are presented as savings plans.

Stability and height of dividends are the first tests of the suitability of corporate stock for employee investment; and, if the earnings of a corporation are stable and large enough to permit regular payment of dividends, one requisite for a successful employee stock-purchase plan is present. The dividend rate should be high enough to make investment in the stock attractive as compared to other investments (Series E bonds, deposits in the United States Postal Savings System, savings deposits, and savings and loan association accounts), or the securities should be issued by companies having excellent growth records and policies of declaring stock dividends or stock splits. In some cases, employees may purchase special issues of securities having an assured dividend rate, but usually ordinary common stock of the company is sold.

A second test of the investment quality of a security suitable for purchase under an employee stock-purchase plan is marketability—the ability to sell with little or no capital loss and with little or no delay. Because the price of common stock is subject to considerable fluctuation, some companies make loans to employees with their stock pledged as security which may eliminate the necessity to sell stock at a possible loss when funds are needed by the employee.

The third and most important test of investment quality is safety. As noted above, most of the employee-ownership plans initiated during the 1920's were discontinued as a result of the stock market collapse beginning in the fall of 1929. Employees, like other investors, lost heavily when the market prices of their companies' shares declined. When this loss was accompanied by unemployment, employees lost not only their chief source of income (jobs) but also most of the value of their savings when they were forced to sell their securities. This danger of double loss (income and savings) is inherent in any employee stock-purchase plan of any corporation.

If the market price of a company's stock is subject to wide fluctuations, it may be wise for management to refrain from inaugurating any company-sponsored employee stock-purchase plan unless the corporation is willing to risk serious losses by agreeing to repurchase all stock sold to employees. Even when a company's stock has all the qualities which make it a safe investment, management should at least provide for repurchase of stock sold to participants in the company-sponsored plan during the first year after its sale.

Although a company's stock may meet all the tests of a good investment, the average employee does not purchase stock through regular brokerage channels either because he lacks knowledge of investments and investing machinery or because he is unable to buy more than one or a few shares at a time and considers the minimum brokerage fee (usually $6) to be excessive. Although one of the obstacles to purchasing securities through regular channels was removed in 1954 by the Monthly Investment Plan of the New York Stock Exchange which all members are required to make available, the payroll-deduction device with which employees are familiar has been incorporated in many of the employee stock-purchase plans; consequently, the average employee may be less hesitant to participate in a company-sponsored stock-purchase plan than to purchase stock through a broker. After an employee signs the original stock-purchase or savings contract under a payroll-deduction plan, the company or its agent or trustee buys the stock and makes delivery as soon as the contract terms have been met.

When stock is sold to employees under privileged subscription plans, the stock may be treasury stock or a new issue specifically authorized by the stockholders who, in their approval of the proposed plan, have waived their pre-emptive rights to the stock issue. In some cases, part of an issue sold under pre-emptive rights to stockholders may be earmarked for sale to employees. The major value to employees of privileged subscription offerings may be the difference between the subscription price and the market price.

As in the case of any privileged subscription plan, if the subscription rights given to employees are valuable, the plan will sell itself. However, the problems associated with administering an employee stock-purchase plan are more complicated than those associated with privileged subscription sales to old stockholders because of the longer period of time over which employees may subscribe to stock and the absence of negotiable warrants. One of the major problems confronting management in selling securities to employees is that of preventing employees from abusing their privileges—buying securities at bargain prices today and selling them at a premium tomorrow.

Customarily only those employees who have been with a company for a year or more are eligible to participate in an employee stock-purchase plan. Usually, employees are permitted to buy stock on a weekly or monthly investment plan; but, in order to avoid some of the speculative aspects that might follow, there is usually a provision that payments must be completed within a definite period in order to prevent "overtrading." Management may also limit the amount of the subscription to a specific number of shares and may also refuse prepayment for shares purchased. Dividends on shares in process of being acquired are usually credited to the account of the buyer, but interest may be paid on the cash balances being accumulated for stock purchases in order to discourage borrowing at a lower rate and using the proceeds to acquire stock that pays a higher rate. (If a plan functions properly, it will encourage saving rather than speculating.) If an employee desires to withdraw from the plan, he may request either shares of stock equivalent to the amount paid in, plus any remaining cash balance, or a return of the cash paid in plus the interest accrued thereon.

When stock is sold to employees at less than market price, restrictions are usually placed on its resale. One restriction may be a requirement that the stock must either be held for a specified number of years or be sold back to the company. Restrictions are usually stamped across the face of the stock certificate; therefore, a purchaser of such shares cannot disclaim knowledge of the restrictions and cannot use the claim of being an "innocent" holder as a legal defense.

The current trend is for corporations to arrange for purchase of securities through payroll-deduction plans at market prices rather than through fixed-price contracts which are a feature of privileged subscriptions. When a buy-at-the-market plan is administered by a "disinterested" trustee, the sponsoring company avoids the charge of paternalism directed by labor unions at employee stock-purchase plans. The stock purchased may be delivered to the employee as soon as practicable after the end of the calendar year or it may be held by the trustee in a trust fund until the employee terminates his service with the company. For illustration, 98 per cent of the eligible employees are participating in the trust of the Sears, Roebuck & Company which now holds over one fourth of all the shares of the company's outstanding stock. Of the 15,000,000 individuals who now own stock, one in every five got into the market through company stock-purchase plans. Experiences with payroll-deduction plans during and since World War II suggest that it would be possible for employees to acquire ownership of many large American corporations in a relatively short time if all employees' savings were used for this purpose.

In buy-at-the-market plans the stress is on dollar buying or weekly commitments to buy rather than on the number of shares purchased. If the price of the stock declines, more shares may be purchased with the same number of dollars; if the price rises, fewer shares may be purchased. However, the average cost per share purchased will be lower than the average market price at which the shares were bought (note last two columns in Table 21). What is true during falling prices in regard to "average market prices" being higher than the "average cost per share purchased" is also true during rising prices.

TABLE 21

"DOLLAR AVERAGING"

Dollars Invested per Month	*Market Price*	*Shares Purchased Each Month*	*Total Shares Purchased*	*Average Market Price*	*Average Cost per Share Purchased*
$50	$50	1	1	$50	$50
50	25	2	3	37½	33⅓
50	10	5	8	28⅓	18¾
50	25	2	10	27½	20

The dollar averaging formula is among the simplest plans for investing and it gives surprising results over a period of time if the same dollar amounts are invested regularly. However, it is assumed that the securities being purchased have investment qualities as noted in another section of this chapter.

When considered from the viewpoint of management, the primary purposes of employee stock-purchase plans are to improve labor-employer relationships, to reduce labor turnover, to increase the efficiency and responsibility of labor, and to obtain new funds.[7] The chief risk assumed by management is that any decline in the prosperity of the corporation may cause employees to lose on their investments for which management may have to assume moral and perhaps financial responsibility.

While employee reaction to stock ownership varies with individuals, participants in periodic savings plans are usually persons who are the most dependable and ambitious among the labor force. While the conflict between management and labor over the distribution of earnings—as salaries to wage earners and dividends to stockholders—may be reduced by employee-ownership, it is doubtful if this conflict could ever be eliminated short of 100 per cent employee-ownership of a company's stock—and then only for very small companies. Unquestionably, ownership of their company's stock stimulates the interest of employees in their company. An employee need not be a student of business finance to appreciate the quarterly, annual, and other reports of the company to its shareholders—and particularly his quarterly dividend check.

While a stock-purchase plan may be arranged so that a participant loses something if he leaves the company for another job (or gains something if he stays), it does not follow that being a stockholder makes him a more subservient employee. The mere fact that he is a stockholder may make him more independent in his views because he is not solely dependent on his pay check as a source of income. In addition, he is usually better informed about the financial affairs of his company and this permits him to speak with more au-

---

[7] The preamble of the employee stock-purchase plan of the United Gas Corporation and participating subsidiary companies summarizes its purposes as follows: "(1) to assist employees to acquire a proprietary interest in the United Gas System through stock ownership; (2) to encourage and assist employees to adopt a regular savings program; (3) to promote greater productivity and job stability; and (4) to promote the best interests of the stockholders of the companies through retention of the service of employees."

thority than his nonstockholder co-workers. As long as earnings are good and dividends are being paid, the corporation tends to receive favorable publicity from its stockholding employees who, like other shareholders, are inclined to talk about their financial affairs.

As part owners of their corporation, it is assumed that employees will have a feeling of responsibility for the property and problems of their corporation. Certainly any practice that leads to greater responsibility for tools, machinery, and other forms of property and to an improvement in the quality of services rendered is beneficial; but modern "incentive" plans, rewards for profitable suggestions, wage increases, promotions, and other practices that reward individual employees seem to have greater merit.

While the financial advantage to a corporation of selling stock to employees is usually placed last among the advantages of stock-ownership plans, it may be among the first for small companies. That the ability to obtain funds from employees is always a valuable asset to any company is illustrated by the purchase of stock of the Endicott Johnson Corporation in January, 1961, which was an important factor in keeping the company under the control of existing management.

Loyal stockholders are an asset for any company regardless of size because satisfied stockholders are ready investors in new issues. Unless sales of new stock are justifiable on financial grounds alone (a need for equity capital), employee stock-purchase plans should limit the purchases of securities of the employer-corporation to outstanding stock. Stock ownership by wage earners is not a novelty and some employees buy stock in their companies independent of employee stock-purchase plans. In general, diversification of investments is desirable in any investment program; therefore the investments of wage earners should include securities other than those of the employee's company. This need for diversification is recognized in some of the corporation-sponsored open-market or "dollar averaging" plans.

Through stock-purchase plans, corporations permit their employees to share in the prosperity of their companies and the nation and to acquire assets which provide them with a hedge against inflation. The safeguards against stock losses and the contributions to stock-purchase plans provided by sponsoring corporations not only protect and enrich employees but also improve morale, foster loyalty, educate workers as to the virtues of capitalism, encourage thrift, and provide a means whereby workers may diversify their assets to include common stocks as well as savings accounts and United States savings bonds.

Privileged Subscription for Officers. The various plans under which officers acquire stock usually include the right or privilege to purchase a given number of shares of the company's stock at a certain price within a certain time. This option varies from the ordinary type of "call" contract bought and sold in the securities market in being for a number of years rather than for thirty, sixty, or ninety days—the typical call option contract. Options may be granted for shares that are authorized but unissued, held as treasury stock, or reacquired at the market price on the date the option is granted.

The primary purpose of stock-option plans is to promote the interests of the company by encouraging key personnel to remain with the company and to provide them additional "incentive for unusual industry, efficiency, and loyalty by enabling them to acquire a proprietary interest in the company." Since key officers often acquire shares through regular brokerage channels, the value of a stock-purchase option depends on the difference between the option price and the market price of the stock when the option is used. If the option period is ten years, the value of the option increases (or decreases) as the market price increases (or decreases). In order to retain the stock purchased under officer stock-purchase plans, the participants are under contract not to leave the company except under certain specified conditions (such as ill health and reaching retirement age).

Usually, the salaries of key personnel increase as corporations grow in size; but, because of high personal income taxes, "take home pay" increases only moderately.[8] To accumulate an estate, of-

[8] Typical of the statement of remuneration of directors and officers appearing in proxy statements are the following (with names deleted):

Position	*Aggregate Remuneration*	*Federal Tax on Remuneration*	*Net Amount after Tax*
Chairman of the Board	$130,000	$80,272	$49,728
President and Director	94,900	53,107	41,793
Vice President and Director	71,500	36,316	35,184
Comptroller, Treasurer and Director	51,480	22,857	28,623
Vice President and Secretary	40,300	15,701	24,599

ficers must depend on capital appreciation. This has been a factor in the decision of many former executives to start their own businesses, usually in the same field as that in which they obtain their practical experience. This was doubly disadvantageous to the former employer —the services of a key official were lost and a new competitor was created. The stock-option-purchase plan seems to be the most practical solution to this problem. By linking the financial interest of key personnel to the future growth of the company, management anticipates that both the company and the officers will benefit. Today approximately 60 per cent of the corporations whose shares are listed on the New York Stock Exchange offer executive stock-option plans. The price and other conditions under which stock may be purchased are usually arranged so as to make acquisition of stock most advantageous in terms of the federal income tax law in effect when the option is obtained. Usually, the option period varies from two to ten years and the option price is not less than 95 per cent of the market price of the stock at the time the option is given, so that any profit resulting from the use of the option will be taxable only at the 25 per cent rate for capital gains provided the stock is held for six months.[9]

Because executives sometimes lack the funds necessary to exercise their options, some corporations (General Motors, for illustration) give cash and stock bonuses in addition to the options. Stock-option plans are usually effective in holding key men, and those given by small companies are often more valuable than those given by large corporations because the market price of the stock of a successful expanding small company tends to rise more rapidly than that of a large older corporation. This has been the case with some electronic companies which have used options to lure outstanding scientists away from large companies.

Often, a side effect of officer stock-option plans is to make the optionee interested in reducing costs (particularly true in the case of scientists, many of whom have never before been interested in expenses). However, if stock options are used too freely they lose their incentive effect—being taken for granted as are other "fringe bene-

---

[9] The Commissioner of Internal Revenue customarily rules on stock-option plans before they are put into effect. Management usually arranges the options to qualify as "restricted stock options" as defined in Section 130A (d) (1) of the Internal Revenue Code. Section 130A provides for special tax treatment, with the issue being whether profits resulting from the use of options are to be taxed as "capital gains" or as income at the rates prevailing in the higher income brackets as compared to the relatively low rates for capital gains.

fits"—hence the policy of management should be to restrict their application to top executives who have a direct effect on the corporation's earnings.

Each option granted specifies the option price and the period during which it may be exercised (most commonly ten years, but it may be shorter to prevent its running beyond the retirement age of the holder), and the longer this period, the more favorable it is to the option holder. The "Stock Option Incentive Plan" of the United States Steel Corporation does not permit the use of an option during the first year it is granted except on the death or retirement of the optionee; but, with this exception, an option may be exercised in whole or part at any time or over a period of time during ten years from the date the option is issued. While options are not negotiable, some arrangement may be made whereby all or part of those not exercised may be transferred to the optionee's estate in case of death. There have been cases wherein stock option committees have cancelled outstanding options or replaced them at a lower price when the company's stock dropped in price, but this is unusual and not recommended for obvious reasons.

In case of stock splits, stock dividends, and/or other changes in a corporation's capital structure, the board of directors may make appropriate adjustments in the number of shares and the price per share for outstanding options. At one extreme, continued ownership of stock acquired through options may be contingent upon the officer's continuing in the service of the company until he reaches the compulsory retirement age and thereafter if he refrains from engaging in competition with the company. At the other extreme, the beneficiary of an option plan may be free to dispose of his stock at any time (but in order for capital gains to be considered long-term and taxable at the 25 per cent rate, shares must be retained for a minimum of six months).

Plans of companies which have been in operation long enough to eliminate defects usually place restrictions on the options that may be granted during a fiscal year. The number of rights granted may not exceed a specific number of shares, or the value of shares optioned may not exceed a specific percentage of net earnings above the rate of earning on the capital investments of the company. For illustration, a company may earn a specified rate of 5 per cent plus an additional $10,000,000. Then the company may issue options that will permit key executives to buy $1,000,000 worth of stock (that is, 10 per cent of the earnings above the specified rate on total capital).

This type of restriction stresses the importance of having satisfactory earnings before granting options and also lessens the danger of diluting earnings per share if stock options are exercised. More often, stockholders are asked to approve future sales of stock to key officials without restrictions except as to the total number of shares to be issued.

From a social point of view, options that permit officers to acquire stock may be the answer to the criticism that modern corporations lack the desirable initiative present when management and ownership are closely linked. Most progressive corporations in the United States are using some type of executive-incentive plan. At one time, the offering of stock purchase warrants was used most frequently by "sick" corporations as an inducement to acquire the services of capable officials of other corporations. Because of accumulated retirement benefits and for other reasons, a salary differential was often insufficient inducement to an official currently employed by another company; but, when the right to acquire stock under an option was added, the inducement to change positions was often sufficient.

One of the advantages that has been claimed for the use of options is that "it costs the company little or nothing"—in fact, it brings cash into the company when the option is used. However, when a corporation purchases stock in the open market at the time of issuing an option, it is deprived of the use of assets during the option period while the stock is being held as treasury stock; and the situation is but little different when authorized but unissued stock is held during an option period because the corporation is foregoing the use of assets which it might have had if the stock had been sold when authorized. So directly or indirectly, the stock option "costs the company something" even though it brings in cash when the optioned stock is sold. Another fallacy in the assertion that stock options cost nothing is that it ignores the effect of stock purchased under options on old stockholders' rights to earnings. As the number of shares distributed under stock option plans increases, the proportionate interest of stockholders decreases; in addition, the market price of the stock tends to decline.

When stock options are exercised, stockholders' rights to earnings and assets and voting privileges are diluted. Therefore it is important to balance the cost of stock options to the corporation and the dilution of old stockholders' interests against the extent to which the benefits bestowed on optionees are reflected in higher net profits. Presumably, boards of directors regard the potential dilution of stockholders' earnings and other rights to be more than offset by past, current, and anticipated contributions of optionees. Because "inside" directors dominate the boards of directors of many corporations, they may be able to obtain favorable stock-purchase options for themselves. Some have attempted to justify stock-option plans on the basis of increased net profits which accrue as a result of the activities of the optionees; while this may be true to some extent, it must be pointed out that many times external factors are more important in explaining the prosperity of a company than are the internal factors for which management is responsible.

Perhaps the most conclusive evidence of the merit of stock-option plans is the fact that many corporations whose boards of directors are dominated by "outside" directors are using them. The authority to issue new shares and/or to distribute shares under conditions proposed in executive stock-option plans must be obtained from stockholders; when stockholders have been asked to vote thereon, they have customarily approved by considerably more than the required number of affirmative votes. When such plans have been brought before the federal and state courts, they have been upheld.

SUMMARY

The justification for the common-law pre-emptive right principle is that old common stockholders should be given the right to protect their proportionate voting power and commensurable share in the net worth and earnings of their company. The term privileged subscription implies that the offering is limited to certain individuals and that it is valuable. As a financing device, such an offering is most important to old stockholders when the value of subscription warrants is substantial. For "rights" to have value, the market price of the stock must be above the subscription price. While one of the arguments in favor of offerings by privileged subscription is avoidance of underwriting fees, management may arrange for standby underwriting by investment bankers or for their services as agents to assure the sale of shares not subscribed for during the offering period.

Many corporations provide for sales of their stock to employees and officers under special stock-purchase plans and a relatively few companies offer stock to their customers. While all such plans have the effect of raising funds, they are usually employed in an effort to build better relations. To make an ideal security for an employee stock-purchase plan, a stock should be marketable, safe, and have a stable dividend rate. Many corporations have stock-option plans for officers which are used as an inducement to obtain and keep key personnel. When such plans result in increased efficiency and better management, they are justified. However, in both employee stock-purchase plans and officer stock-option plans care must be exercised to prevent abuse of the plans.

QUESTIONS AND PROBLEMS

1. Identify: (*a*) pre-emptive right, and (*b*) privileged subscription.
2. (*a*) Give the arguments in support of the common-law pre-emptive right principle as applied to offerings of new common stock. (*b*) When is this principle applicable to other securities?
3. From the viewpoint of management, may the presence of pre-emptive rights be a hindrance to financing? Explain.
4. Compare the problem of pricing in public offering with that in privileged subscription.
5. (*a*) How may the value of subscription rights be computed during the "rights on" period and during the "ex-rights" period? (*b*) In what way is a subscription warrant similar to a stock dividend?
6. Why do corporations usually arrange for stand-by underwriting contracts when offering securities by privileged subscription? Are such contracts expensive? Explain.
7. In employee-ownership plans, emphasis is usually on the savings aspects of such plans. Are common stocks a satisfactory form in which to invest savings of members of the working class? Explain your answer.
8. Summarize the problems faced by management when a stock offering is made to employees under a privileged subscription plan.
9. Identify the "buy-at-the-market" plans offered by some corporations to employees. How are they administered? Compared to privileged subscription plans, do they seem to offer more advantages to a corporation? To employees?
10. How does management justify the use of stock-option plans for officers? Are they expensive? Explain.
11. Explain: "Lone Star Gas Company is offering its common stockholders rights to subscribe for 655,733 common shares at $40 a share on the basis of one new share for each ten held on Jan. 5." (*New York Times*, January 9, 1961, p. 65.)
12. Discuss the management policies suggested by the following: "Polaroid Corp.—Carlton P. Fuller, vice president and treasurer, on Dec. 15 exercised a stock option to purchase 6,080 shares. He now holds 31,180." . . ."Twin Coach Co.—William H. Coleman, president, acquired 13,400 shares through a stock option increasing his interest to 14,450 shares." ("Insiders' Stockholdings," *New York Times*, January 12, 1961, p. 47.)

13. The president of General Electric Company justified the company's stock option plan as "meeting competition with other companies" for executive talent, as giving key employees "incentive of proprietorship," and as resulting in "benefits to all shareowners." (General Electric Company, *General Electric, 1960 Annual Meeting, A Report to General Electric Share Owners*, p. 9.) Do you agree? Why?
14. Analyze: "In some respects, the stock option problem is primarily a tax problem. However, it also becomes a problem of corporate management —and to a very considerable extent, or so it seems to me, one of corporate morality." (E. N. Griswold, "Are Stock Options Getting Out of Hand?" *Harvard Business Review*, November–December, 1960, p. 49.)

CHAPTER 19

Financing with Preferred Stock Issues

WHEN THE objective of the organizers of a corporation is to give management considerable latitude in capitalizing the corporation, the articles of incorporation may contain provisions authorizing the issuance of one or more classes of preferred stock in addition to common stock. Preferred stock represents ownership and is placed with common stock in the owners' equity section of the balance sheet. This chapter deals with the nature and use of preferred stock and the many variable features that may be present in preferred stock issues.

CHARACTERISTICS OF PREFERRED STOCK

Preferred stock is stock which the charter of a corporation has given preference over common stock in claims to dividends and usually to assets in case of liquidation of the corporation. Although preferred stockholders have no contractual rights to dividends, they come first if and when dividends are declared. Until their claims are settled, common stockholders may not receive dividends. Of course, the creditors have prior claims over both common and preferred stockholders to income and assets; hence, those who want the maximum protection in their investments will purchase bonds rather than preferred or common stock.

The typical preferred stock is a hybrid type of security; it is neither common stock nor bond, but it possesses certain characteristics of both. As a stock, it represents equity capital, and as such it entails no interest obligations or maturity contract. Just as it has a legal obligation to pay interest on bonds at a specified rate, the corporation has a moral obligation to pay dividends on preferred stock at the rate specified in the articles of incorporation.

Position of Preferred Stockholders. The preferred stockholders of a corporation which is prosperous and well managed receive income just as regularly as they would if they had legal claims to income. In fact, preferred stockholders themselves are often confused as to the nature of their investments—calling the income thereon "interest" rather than "dividends." However the risks assumed by a preferred stockholder are greater than those assumed by a bondholder (assuming other things are equal) because there is a difference between a "moral" and a "legal" obligation. Therefore a corporation's dividend rate on preferred stock is usually higher than its interest rate on bonds.

The market for preferred stock includes the more conservative investor who wants a greater return than offered by bonds and a more stable return than offered by common stock. When the laws of the state of incorporation permit such investments, this market includes insurance companies, savings institutions, and other institutional investors (that are usually given greater freedom in investing in preferred stock than in common stock). This situation permits the corporate issuer to "tap" a wider market than could be reached by an issue of common stock.

Preferred Stock As A Financing Device. Preferred stock is the least important of the three major classes of corporate securities issued each year (see Table 22). Preferred stock is issued most often by corporations whose earnings are stable, as illustrated by public

TABLE 22

NEW CORPORATE SECURITY ISSUES, 1952–1959*
(In Millions of Dollars)

Year	*Bonds*	*Preferred Stock*	*Common Stock*	*Total*
1952	7,601	564	1,369	9,534
1953	7,083	489	1,326	8,898
1954	7,488	816	1,213	9,516
1955	7,420	635	2,185	10,240
1956	8,002	636	2,301	10,939
1957	9,957	411	2,516	12,884
1958	9,653	571	1,334	11,558
1959	7,190	531	2,027	9,748

* Figures are Securities and Exchange Commission estimates of new issues maturing in more than one year and sold for cash in the United States.

Source: *Federal Reserve Bulletin*, October, 1960, p. 1154.

utility companies. Although preferred stock is seldom used by manufacturing companies as a financing device, some major industrial companies have preferred stock issues outstanding as illustrated by General Motors Corporation and the United States Steel Corporation. The latter corporation reported the value of its three major instruments of long-term finance as follows: common stock—$2,823,446,282, preferred stock—$360,281,000, and long-term debt—$454,447,447, which means that preferred stock represents about 10 per cent of the corporation's capital structure.[1]

Since those with the largest financial stake in a corporation—the officers and members of the board of directors—are usually large common stockholders, why do they favor the issuance of preferred stock which forces their claims to earnings farther down the ladder? Obviously, it would be illogical for them to give something of value without receiving something in return, and usually preferred stock is subject to limitations as well as preferences. The justification for issuing preferred stock is primarily financial, being a means whereby a corporation may acquire assets more economically than by use of common stock and with greater safety than by borrowing.[2] The use of a type of stock that does not have the right to vote may be one of management's reasons for issuing preferred stock, but this is usually a secondary one. Preferred stockholders usually retain certain permanent voting rights and they are often able to obtain temporary ones because of statutory requirements or investment bankers' insistence when underwriting issues of preferred stock. In fact the demands of underwriters of a preferred stock issue for representation on the board of directors may be such as to endanger the position of existing management more than would the sale of a new common stock issue to old stockholders.

Dividends. Customarily the dividend rate on preferred stock is provided for in the corporate charter, being fixed by management at a rate that will assure the sale of the stock at the time of issuance. Although a so-called "regular" dividend may be paid on common stock—such as the $3.60 per share per annum dividend on the common stock of the American Telephone and Telegraph Company—the dividend to be paid is set by the board of directors at its dividend

---

[1] United States Steel Corporation, *Annual Report 1959* (New York, 1959), p. 32. Income reinvested in the business was $1,924,096,165.

[2] Preferred stock is used by corporations for purposes other than raising funds with which to operate. For illustration, American Cyanamid Company issued 765 shares Series A preferred stock under stock purchase contracts with employees. American Cyanamid Company, *Forty-Second Annual Report, 1953*, p. 9.

meeting and it does not have the legal status possessed by a preferred stock dividend rate. When preferred stock has par value, the dividend rate is expressed as a percentage; when it is no-par stock, the rate is expressed as a specific amount per share. The name of a preferred stock includes the dividend rate: for illustration, American Tobacco Company, 6 per cent cumulative preferred stock with $100 par value; United States Steel Corporation, 7 per cent cumulative preferred stock with a par value of $100; and General Motors Corporation $5 cumulative preferred stock with no par value and $3.75 cumulative preferred stock with no par value.

On the typical preferred stock, the dividend rate is limited to the specified rate, but on common stock there is no limit on the amount of dividends that may be declared if earned. For illustration, if a corporation has net profits after interest and taxes of $200,000 and has outstanding 10,000 shares of 5 per cent preferred stock and 10,000 shares of common stock, the preferred stock has prior claims to $50,000 of net profits and the remaining $150,000 will be available for dividends on the common stock.

The often-stated advantage to the issuer of financing with preferred stock—that dividends may be passed and cash retained—is a technical rather than a practical advantage. Management usually finds it equally necessary to meet dividend payments on preferred stock and to meet periodic interest payments on bonds so as to prevent the corporation's credit standing from being adversely affected. When preferred stock is cumulative—a common feature—the pressure to pay dividends thereon is magnified because unpaid dividends accumulate as claims against future earnings of the corporation which must be met before dividends can be paid on common stock. (When dividends have not been paid on cumulative preferred stock, dividends are referred to as being in arrears.) Corporations try to avoid dividend arrearages on preferred stock issues because they have a depressing effect on the corporation's credit and on the market price of its common stock as well as on its preferred stock. The amount of preferred stock outstanding is usually small as compared with the amount of common stock; hence it is more important to maintain the market value of the common stock than to pass dividends on preferred stock so as to prevent the cash drain entailed. Although corporations have a legal option to pass dividends on preferred stock, such action is rarely taken except in cases of unusual financial difficulty (as happened many times during the 1930's).

If preferred stock dividends are postponed for any length of time, the amount in arrears may be so great as to make it almost impossible for earnings to catch up.[3] In this case the board of directors may propose a settlement such as giving some cash and preferred stock for the dividends in arrears. However, unless expected earnings are sufficient to meet the dividends on the new as well as the old preferred stock, such financing would be meaningless. Another means of solving the dilemma would be to capitalize dividends in arrears and to exchange the preferred stock plus the accumulated dividends for noncumulative preferred stock or for common stock. Then dividends could be passed without accumulating and the position of the corporation would be strengthened. Such changes would need the approval of at least the required percentage of the shares affected to be binding on the stockholders.

The articles of incorporation may permit the avoidance of the risk of preferred stock dividend arrearages by specifying that dividends on a preferred stock issue are noncumulative. During periods of low earnings, dividends on noncumulative preferred stock may be passed as freely as on common stock without creating future claims to dividends that are prior to claims to dividends on common stock. Although noncumulative preferred stock is commonly issued by railroad companies, other companies sometimes issue it as illustrated by the American Locker Company, United States Tobacco Company and Curtiss–Wright Corporation. Many of the preferred stock issues outstanding, having the noncumulative feature, have resulted from involuntary reorganization of corporations in which bondholders had

---

[3] The New York Stock Exchange listed eleven preferred stock issues with dividend arrearages totaling $27,671,112 (down from $158,858,804 a year earlier). On November 21, 1960, the Exchange listed ten preferred issues with dividend arrearages of which five were obligations of railroad companies. They were as follows: Amalgamated Leather Co., 6 per cent cumulative convertible (accumulated arrearages $12.00 per share on October 1, 1960); Chicago & North Western Railway, 5 per cent Series A convertible (latest payment $3.30 on March 5, 1954); Erie-Lackawanna Railroad, 5 per cent cumulative Series A (arrearages $5.00 on September 1, 1960); International Railways of Central America, 5 per cent cumulative participating (latest payment $1.25 on November 15, 1957 with arrearages of $60.00 on October 5, 1960); New York, New Haven & Hartford Railroad, 5 per cent convertible Series A (latest payment $1.25 on May 8, 1955); Reading Company, 4 per cent noncumulative 2nd preferred (latest payment 0.50 January 14, 1960); Reis & Co., $1.25 cumulative convertible (arrears $14.06 on October 1, 1960); Studebaker–Packard Corporation, $5 cumulative convertible (convertible into 33⅓ common shares from January 1, 1961); Van Norman Industries, $2.28 cumulative convertible (cumulative to extent earned, each share convertible into two common—dividend arrears $2.85 on September 30, 1960); and Virginia Carolina Chemical, 6 per cent cumulative participating (paid $1.50 on arrearages on October 1, 1958—with dividend arrears of $85.50 on October 1, 1960).

been required to exchange bonds for preferred stock of this class. When noncumulative preferred stock is sold, it customarily has a higher dividend rate than would otherwise be necessary.

Since the proprietary interest of those in managerial positions is usually represented by common stock and since the noncumulative feature works to the advantage of common stockholders, directors may be tempted to pass dividends on preferred stock even though the earnings of the company justify their payment. In general, directors have not done so except in rehabilitation cases wherein the temporary retention of large earnings is justified. In the classic case on this subject, the court ruled in part: "When the net profits of a corporation out of which a dividend might have been declared for the preferred stock, are justifiably applied by the directors to capital improvements, the claim of the stock for that year is gone, if by the terms of the articles of incorporation and the certificates, the preferential dividends are not to be cumulative."[4]

As noted earlier, the typical preferred stock does not participate in dividends beyond the rate specified on the stock certificate. Since there is some doubt as to rights of preferred stockholders to participate in dividends beyond the stated rate, the board of directors may remove any uncertainty by inserting a provision in the stock certificate such as "preferred as to dividends at the rate of 5 per cent annually (or $5 per share) and no more." On the other hand, in order to make a preferred stock more attractive to investors, the corporation may make specific provisions for participation in dividends beyond the rate stated in the preferred stock certificate (illustrated by American Locker Co., $0.30 noncumulative participating Class A preferred stock).

In the absence of specific provisions for participation, there is doubt as to the right of preferred stock to participate in dividends beyond the rate stated for preferred stock. However, the assumption is that the stated preferential rate is at the same time a "statement of limitation." When a participation clause exists in preferred-stock contracts, the most common form is one that permits it to share equally with common stock if and when a dividend in excess of the rate provided for preferred stock is declared on common stock. If the dividend rate on preferred stock is 5 per cent and a 7 per cent dividend is declared on common stock, the preferred stockholders would

---

[4] *Wabash Ry. Co. v. Barclay*, 250 U.S. 197.

receive 7 per cent rather than 5 per cent. The rule for participation is subject to various adjustments, such as a provision that each increase in dividends on common stock beyond 3—or some other—per cent is to be matched by a similar increase in the rate on the preferred stock, or that the preferred stock may receive no more than 8—or some other—per cent irrespective of the rate paid on common stock.

Generally, preferred stockholders have no prior or pre-emptive rights to subscribe for new shares of convertible preferred or common stock. In other words, they are usually treated as "outsiders" when the corporation issues new securities convertible into common stock. Customarily, preferred stockholders must approve proposed stock splits—when old preferred stock is to be retired and a larger number of new shares are to be issued in its place. For illustration, on May 1, 1952, American Can Company 7 per cent cumulative noncallable preferred stock was split four for one and the par value was reduced from $100 to $25. Preferred stock may be par or no-par stock, and among current issues stock with low par value (less than $100) seems to be preferred. Among other rights of old preferred stockholders, the most important may be the right to determine the conditions under which new preferred and other senior securities may be issued.

Preferred stock of a corporation may consist of different issues; for illustration, the Philadelphia Electric Company has provided for different issues of $100 par value cumulative preferred stock as follows:[5]

	Number of Shares		
	Authorized	*Outstanding*	*Amount*
4.68% Series	150,000	150,000	$15,000,000
4.4% Series	500,000	274,720	27,472,000
4.3% Series	150,000	150,000	15,000,000
3.8% Series	300,000	300,000	30,000,000
Unclassified	400,000	......	....
Premium on preferred stock	......	......	1,213,910
Total Preferred Stock	1,500,000	874,720	$88,685,910

The preferred stock is redeemable at the option of the company at the following prices per share plus accrued dividends: 4.68 per cent Series—$105 to December 31, 1962, and $104 thereafter; 4.4 per

[5] Philadelphia Electric Company, *Annual Report for the Year 1959* (Philadelphia, 1960), p. 29.

cent Series—$112.50; 4.3 per cent Series—$102; and 3.8 per cent Series—$106.

Liquidation and Dissolution Status. In case of liquidation or dissolution of a corporation, corporate charters usually give preferred stockholders priority over common stockholders as to assets as well as dividends. But if the articles of incorporation give them preference as to dividends only (being silent in regard to priority as to assets), preferred stockholders share pro rata with common stockholders in case of liquidation or dissolution. The purpose of giving preferred stock priority as to assets is to facilitate financing by making the stock more salable, in the same way that pledges of property make bonds more salable.

The preferred stockholders' preference to assets, like the preference to dividends, is subject to limitations. Usually, in the case of involuntary liquidation or dissolution, priority to assets of preferred stock is limited to the par value, stated value, or call price of the stock. If the corporation is reorganized, the preferred stockholders may be permitted to exchange old preferred shares for new preferred and/or common stock in the new corporation while the old common stockholders' claims may have no value. If the corporation is liquidated, preferred stockholders have the first claim to any cash remaining after debts are paid. In case of liquidation, if one assumes that after paying debts the amount of equity per share of stock—both common and preferred—is $25 and that there is an equal number of shares of each kind of stock, the owners of preferred $100 par value shares will receive $50 a share and the common stockholders would receive nothing.

Sometimes the corporate charter will make a distinction between the right to assets of preferred stock in voluntary and in involuntary dissolution. If so, preferred stock's right to participate in assets is usually higher when the dissolution is voluntary. The general rule seems to be that if there is any uncertainty, preferred stock is entitled to a "fair investment" value which may be more than par or stated value. But, if there is a statement to the effect that preferred stock has a preference as to assets in an amount equal to par value or in some other specified amount, a contract exists that limits the claims of preferred stockholders to that amount. The current and future value of preferred stock will depend primarily on the earning record of the corporation, because investors are interested secondarily, if at all, in what preference they have to assets in case of liquidation or dissolution.

VOTING RIGHTS OF PREFERRED STOCKHOLDERS

Voting rights refer to the privilege of voting for directors and on policies and other matters brought before annual and special meetings of stockholders. Unless specifically stated to the contrary in the articles of incorporation, preferred stockholders have the same voting rights as common stockholders. Since the right to vote is a fundamental one, any limitations placed upon preferred stockholders regarding this right must be permitted by the state business corporation act as well as included in the articles of incorporation and printed on the preferred stock certificate. Usually, this disfranchisement is modified by law and/or by agreements covering temporary circumstances. In other words, complete disfranchisement is unusual.

Consent Voting Rights. Among the more common circumstances whereby preferred stock is permitted to vote is one in which the assets of the corporation or the rights and privileges of the preferred stock are involved. This means that consent of the preferred stockholders must be obtained before any such proposed action is taken. In limiting or denying any class of stock the right to vote, most state business corporation acts prohibit corporate charters from denying the right to vote on sales or mortgages of assets not in the regular course of business, voluntary dissolution, a change in the corporation's name, mergers and consolidations, and amendments to the charter that would affect the contract of any class of shares (par value, aggregate number of authorized shares, pre-emptive rights, cancellation of accrued dividends, preferences, limitations, etc.).

Since preferred stockholders vote as a class on proposals affecting their rights and privileges, it means that a proposal is defeated unless favored by the required percentage of the stock affected (usually two thirds) even though a much larger number of common stockholders favor it. If management is insistent on the proposal in spite of its rejection, it may be necessary for the parties representing management to acquire the preferred shares, to obtain a court ruling to permit the corporation to proceed with its plans, or to amend the proposal to make it acceptable to preferred stockholders. The existence of preferred stock may be a serious obstacle to management in new financing if the proposed new shares have rights and preferences superior or equal to those of old preferred shareholders.

Variation in Voting Strength of Preferred Stockholders. If and when preferred stock is given temporary or permanent voting rights as to the election of directors and on other matters, the effect of these rights is determined by the relative voting strength of preferred stockholders. The number of shares of preferred stock relative to common stock may be such that the preferred stockholders are able to select all or none of the directors. If cumulative voting for directors is permitted, the minority group may obtain representation. In all cases, shareholders must vote in person or by proxy. If the voting arrangement is "one share, one vote," preferred stock is usually outnumbered and so special charter provisions may be made to give preferred stock representation on the board of directors. Preferred stockholders may be given two or three votes per share; but, most commonly, the principle of class voting is applied to selection of directors, with preferred stockholders being permitted to select a given number or a given percentage of directors.

As provided for in the articles of incorporation, preferred stockholders' rights to vote may be temporary or permanent. Management may take the position that common stockholders are the risk takers and, as such, should have the entire responsibility for management. To the extent that preferred stock dividends are being paid regularly, as provided for in the corporate charter, the status of preferred stockholders is different from that of common stockholders. But, if preferred stock dividends are passed, preferred stockholders are in the same relative position as common stockholders and should have a share in management. Customarily, preferred stockholders are entitled to vote if dividends on preferred stock are passed a specified number of times (usually four consecutive quarters). In some cases, when dividends on preferred stock are in default in an amount equivalent to four full quarterly dividend payments, the preferred stockholders may be authorized to elect a majority of the board of directors until all the arrearages have been paid.

Providing for preferred stockholders' representation on a board of directors or the right to vote may not follow any definite pattern or principle. The deciding factor may be the position of the board of directors, whether strong or weak, when arrangements are made with investment bankers for underwriting a specific issue of preferred stock. Since shareholders rarely vote except by proxy, the discussion of voting rights may appear to be academic; but this has not been the attitude of regulatory agencies.

The Securities and Exchange Commission has been instrumental in securing protective charter provisions for preferred stockholders. In the past, the abuses associated with the issuance of preferred stock by operating and holding public utility companies resulted in heavy losses to investors in these securities. Now, the issuance of preferred stock by such companies is prohibited except under limited circumstances subject to approval by the Commission.[6] The New York Stock Exchange has been instrumental in increasing the practice of giving temporary voting rights to preferred stockholders when dividends are in default by refusing to list preferred stock that, as a class, does not have the right to elect at least two directors when the dividends have been in arrears or default for six quarters.

In considering the voting rights of stockholders, it was noted that their consent is necessary before a corporation may authorize a new stock issue. Since financing with shares not previously authorized requires a charter amendment, the question submitted to shareholders is one of approving or disapproving a change in the corporate charter. A list of the proposals which must be submitted to preferred stockholders suggests the extent to which legislators are trying to protect old preferred shareholders. This protection is greater when "class voting" is required.

Proposals Requiring Class Voting. Class voting is required on proposals to increase or decrease the authorized number of such shares, to permit an exchange or create a right of exchange whereby another class of stock may be converted into this preferred class, to create a new class of shares having rights or preferences prior to those of existing preferred shares, to increase the rights and preferences of any class that has inferior rights so that they become equal to or prior to those of the preferred shares, to limit or deny any existing pre-emptive rights, and to cancel or otherwise affect dividends on shares which have accrued but have not been declared. While this list is not complete, it suggests the difficulties that a cor-

---

[6] The Securities and Exchange Commission has insisted that the articles of incorporation of companies in the public utility field must contain various features to protect the rights of preferred stockholders.

"These usually consist of the right to elect a majority of the board of directors in the event of default in the payment of four quarterly preferred stock dividends, and certain voting rights in connection with the following matters: the issuance of short-term debt in excess of prescribed amounts, mergers and consolidations, the authorization of any class of stock ranking prior to or on a parity with the outstanding preferred stock, the amendment of the charter to change the express terms of the preferred stock in any substantially prejudicial manner, the issuance of authorized but unissued preferred stock and increasing the amount of authorized but unissued preferred stock. In addition, the Commission has required that the charter limit the amount of initially authorized but unissued preferred stock and contain certain provisions with respect to the payment of common stock dividends which will reasonably safeguard the interests of the preferred stockholders."

Tenth Annual Report of the Securities and Exchange Commission Fiscal Year Ended June 30, 1944, A Ten Year Survey 1934–1944 (Washington, D.C.: U.S. Government Printing Office, 1945), p. 103.

poration may encounter in financing with a second issue of preferred stock (assuming that preferred stockholders would be reluctant to approve any change which would affect their interests adversely).

SPECIAL TYPES OF PREFERRED STOCK

Convertible Preferred Stock. In addition to the features of preferred stock already discussed, management may add a number of "fringe" provisions which are included at the time of issuance in order to enhance the attractiveness of the stock. The title of preferred stock may indicate that it is convertible into common stock at the option of the holder (for example, Air Reduction Company, 4.5 per cent cumulative convertible preferred stock, par value $100, may be exchanged for 3¾ shares of common stock until December 1, 1961). Management expects to make preferred stock more salable by giving the conversion privilege to enable holders to share in the future growth of the company. In effect, holders are given an option to acquire common stock at a fixed price in exchange for preferred stock. At the time of issuance of convertible preferred stock, shares of authorized common stock are reserved to be issued upon conversion of preferred stock.

The conversion option may be expressed as a price—for illustration, two shares of common stock may be acquired for $50 in exchange for one share of preferred stock; or it may be expressed as a ratio—for illustration, one share of preferred may be exchanged for two shares of common stock. The conversion price or ratio may be variable, with the value of the conversion privilege being lowered progressively over a period of years. Usually a date is fixed beyond which the preferred stock is no longer convertible into common stock (as above on December 1, 1961). The ratio of conversion may be fixed so as to make immediate conversion profitable, but this is not the usual practice. So the conversion feature usually adds only a speculative value to the preferred stock.[7] The fact that there are many convertible preferred stocks outstanding suggests that in many cases owners have not found conversion sufficiently attractive. Nevertheless it may be valuable (see below).

When one share of $20 par value preferred stock may be ex-

[7] Illustrations of conversion ratios are Abbott Laboratories, 4 per cent cumulative convertible, $100 par value, preferred stock into 1.7 shares of common until January 1, 1962; Allegheny Corporation, 6 per cent cumulative convertible, each share convertible into 4.7 shares of common on payment of $3.75 a common share; and Allis-Chalmers Manufacturing Co., 4.08 per cent cumulative convertible, par value $100, each share convertible into 3½ shares of common.

changed for two shares of common stock with a market value of $10 or more, conversion may take place. Investors in common stock may purchase common stock directly or may purchase convertible preferred stock to exchange it for common stock. The cheaper method of obtaining common stock will be used; therefore the market value of the preferred stock will tend to be at the same ratio to common stock as the conversion ratio when the market price is above the conversion price. If one assumes that one share of preferred stock is convertible into two shares of common stock, the preferred position of the preferred stock may cause it to sell for $20 while common stock may be selling for $8 or $9 per share; but if the common stock is selling for $11, one would expect the preferred stock to be selling for about $22.

If and when conversion is profitable, shifts of buying and selling orders between common and preferred stock will tend to eliminate any differential with the result that the price of the preferred will reflect the price of the common stock. In practice, arbitragers in securities will sell the common stock "short" and make delivery by buying the preferred and converting it into common (depressing the price of the common and increasing the price of the preferred stock, thereby eliminating the price differential).

The conditions under which an owner of convertible preferred stock may convert it into common stock are determined primarily by the market prices of the two issues and how long this situation is expected to continue. Owners may decide to use the conversion privilege when dividends on common stock are so much larger than on preferred stock as to offset the added risk, when the conversion privilege is about to expire and the value of the preferred stock without the conversion right will be less than the value of the common stock into which it is convertible, when the convertible preferred stock is to be redeemed and the value of common stock is greater than the redemption price of the preferred stock, and when other advantages possessed by common stock justify conversion (voting rights, privileged subscriptions, etc.).

One factor in the reluctance of the preferred stockholder to convert is the fact that he may receive a fractional share for part of his preferred shares. This situation arises when one share is exchangeable at a ratio other than 1 to 1. Usually fractional shares have neither voting rights nor rights to dividends and expire at the end of a specified time. The board of directors may be authorized by the corporation's charter to sell all of the common stock represented by certificates for fractional shares and to distribute proceeds thereof to the holders of the "scrip" certificates.

As noted above, the conversion privilege is inserted into charter provisions for preferred stock to make it more salable; but what is to be the long-run effect on the corporation's capital structure and the rights and privileges of old common stockholders? While issuance of convertible preferred stock may permit the corporation to finance more cheaply with temporarily beneficial effects on common stockholders, subsequent conversion may have a depressing effect on the price of common stock because of the increase in the number of shares and resulting dilution of earnings and assets represented by each share. However, a reduction in the amount of senior stock outstanding will strengthen the claim to earnings of common stockholders when the corporation's earnings decline. Furthermore, the elimination of preferred stock will simplify the corporate financial structure, will broaden the market for common stock, and finally, will clear the way for future issues of preferred stock under market conditions which may be more favorable to the corporation.

Preferred Stock with Warrants. Sometimes preferred stock is issued with warrants attached that permit the stockholder to purchase common stock at a price, or prices, stated in the contract. At the time of issuance, this price is usually above the market price, but this may cease to be the case at some future time. The stock purchase warrant is an option similar to that of the conversion privilege, but it has an additional advantage to the corporation in that it brings in additional cash when it is exercised. The warrant usually elapses at the end of a stated time, but during the interim the option price of common stock as stated in the warrant may have been increased progressively ($20 until a certain date, then $22 until a second date, etc.). Warrants may be detachable or nondetachable. If detachable, the warrant may be separated from the stock certificate and sold at any time; if nondetachable, it may be separated when presented to the corporation together with cash for common stock. Corporations issue preferred stock with warrants attached for the same reason that they issue convertible preferred stock—to enhance their attractiveness to investors.

Preferred Stock of Different Series. If the articles of incorporation so provide or such powers are specifically vested in the board of directors, a corporation may issue special classes of different series of any preferred stock. Shares of the same class are identical, but there may be variations between different series as to the rate of dividends, the price and terms under which shares may be redeemed, the amount payable upon shares in the event of voluntary or involuntary liquidation, sinking-fund conditions, and the terms and conditions under which the shares may be converted.[8] This permissive feature facilitates raising capital from time to time under varying market conditions. However, if these provisions are used, it may be necessary to file a statement of the terms and conditions, together with a copy of the resolution of the board of directors, with the Secretary of State for review to see that the provisions of the statutes are met. On approval, the resolution establishing the series and designating the terms becomes part of the articles of incorporation.

Special Protective Features. It is not unusual for management to issue preferred stock that has special features that provide additional protection for investors. For example, the terms under which preferred stock is issued may make it obligatory for a corporation to limit long-term borrowing, forego expenditures which would reduce working capital, and refrain from additional issues of preferred stock. However, if such provisions are needed it would be well for investors to avoid the issue; if they are not needed, their inclusion is meaningless "window dressing." Nevertheless, there are cases wherein such restrictions are important to investors. For illustration, when a large issue of preferred stock is offered in order to increase the equity base for future debt financing, investors may be interested in features that limit the debts of the corporation.

When attempting to finance with additional issues of preferred stock, corporate management may be faced with restrictions in addition to those already discussed which come under the heading of "preferences and limitations" protected by law. These restrictions may cover paying dividends on common stock; purchasing or redeeming junior securities; and selling, leasing, or transferring assets. The terms under which senior preferred stocks and bonds are issued may prohibit the issuance of new securities until earnings and other standards have been met; when such standards have been set, even long-term indebtedness may be allowed. In the case of rapidly

[8] For illustration, Union Electric Company has outstanding preferred stock which is cumulative and without par value, with stated value per share as follows: $4.50 series, 213,595 shares; $4.00 series, 150,000 shares; $3.70 series, 40,000 shares; and $3.50 series, 130,000 shares. A subsidiary, Missouri Power & Light Company has two similar preferred stock issues outstanding: 4.30 per cent series, 20,000 shares, and 3.90 per cent series, 40,000 shares. The total capital stock and long-term debt as reported for the company and its subsidiaries was as follows: preferred stock, $59,359,500; common stock, $114,026,220; and long-term debt, $276,035,000. (Union Electric Company, *Annual Report for the Year Ended December 31, 1959* [St. Louis, February, 1960], p. 25.)

expanding companies, the limitations embodied in outstanding preferred stock issues may necessitate retiring the issues; management usually makes preparations for such retirement at the time of the original offering.

REDEMPTION OR RETIREMENT OF PREFERRED STOCK

Management may provide for the retirement of preferred stock at the time of issuance by inserting the call feature and/or making provisions for sinking funds. The investment bankers who underwrite an issue of preferred stock may insist on the sinking-fund provision in order to assure improvement in the quality of the securities over the years. They may also insist on a provision to retire a specified percentage of the shares over a series of years. The preferred stock certificate, the contract between the corporation and the shareholder, may contain a clause permitting the corporation to repurchase the stock at a specified price at the option of the corporation or according to some prearranged plan. The purpose of including such an option is to permit the corporation to retire these securities if management finds it desirable to do so. In other cases, preferred stock is noncallable.[9]

The legal procedure for redemption of preferred stock usually requires that the owners receive thirty days (or some other specified number of days) prior notice that the preferred stock is being called on a certain date for redemption, the place where stockholders are to receive payment upon surrender of their stock certificates, and the call or redemption price. Arrangements may be made with a bank or trust company in the United States to make payment with funds deposited by the corporation for this purpose.

The call price is of interest to preferred stockholders because the call option would tend to be used when it is to the advantage of the corporation to do so. In order to finance economically, management must keep this call price as low as possible without seriously reducing the salability of the preferred stock. The call price is above the par or stated value of the stock; the amount above par or stated value, called the call premium, will be largest when financing in the capital market is most difficult and lowest when least difficult.

[9] Illustrations of noncallable preferred stock are American Can Company, 7 per cent cumulative preferred, par value $25; American Snuff Company, 6 per cent noncumulative preferred, par value $100; Cluett, Peabody & Co., Inc., 7 per cent cumulative sinking-fund noncallable (sinking fund 125) par value $100; and Great Western Sugar Company, 7 per cent cumulative preferred, par value $100. See footnote 10 for illustrations of callable preferred stock.

Therefore, the same factors that necessitate a high dividend rate also necessitate a high call premium.[10]

The most important advantage to corporations in issuing callable preferred stock is the ability to replace an issue carrying a high dividend rate with one carrying a lower dividend rate. However, refinancing may be expensive and even unprofitable. At the time of refinancing, the corporation must issue enough new preferred stock not only to finance repurchase of the old shares but also to pay for the premium thereon plus underwriting and legal fees and other costs of refinancing. Since many of the preferred stocks issued during the 1920's had a call price of $120, the amount of new shares issued would have to exceed the old by at least 20 per cent. But if the dividend rate on the new shares is reduced enough, eventually the refinancing will be worth while in spite of the fact that dividends must be paid on more shares.

At the time of issuance of preferred stock, a corporation may make provisions for its retirement. Instead of planning to refinance the preferred stock issue if and when market conditions are favorable, the terms under which the stock is issued may require the corporation to redeem a specified amount of the stock each year and/or to set aside a definite sum for this purpose. The pool of assets earmarked to retire preferred stock is called a sinking fund. Usually, funds required for redemption purposes must be set aside before dividends are paid on common stock. The use of sinking funds to retire preferred stock provides for orderly liquidation when the capital needs represented by such securities are but temporary. Provisions for sinking funds appear most commonly for preferred stock issues of industrial companies.

The provision for a retirement or sinking fund places corporate management under obligation to retire the preferred stock for which the fund was created. The provisions of the sinking fund may link the amount to be retired each year to net earnings by specifying that a minimum percentage of net profits after taxes is to be used for this purpose, specify that a certain percentage of the original issue is to be retired each year, provide for periodic contributions to a fund to be used to retire preferred stock when most advantageous to the corporation, or provide for a combination of the above. In most cases,

---

[10] Illustrations of call prices for preferred stock are Christiana Securities Co. 7 per cent cumulative preferred, callable 120; General Mills, Inc., 5 per cent cumulative preferred, callable $114, and West Penn Power Company, 4½ per cent cumulative preferred, callable $110.

there is a provision that the reacquired preferred stock is to be retired or cancelled on or before a specified date.

In using the assets set aside to retire preferred stock, the corporation may purchase the stock directly from stockholders or in the open market at or below the redemption price; purchase those preferred shares as determined by lot (placing serial numbers in a container and retiring the numbers drawn); or retire stock on a pro rata basis, each shareholder being required to surrender stock equal to a certain percentage of his holding. At the time of issuance, these terms are agreed to by those purchasing the stock; therefore, stockholders would have no choice but to surrender their shares in return for the redemption payment when offered under the conditions cited above. Retiring preferred stock by lot is more commonly used than the pro rata method.

As in the case of callable preferred stock, the sinking-fund redemption price is customarily above the par or stated value of the shares. This price may be adjusted downward with the passage of time because the preferred stockholder's cost of investing will gradually have been "amortized" out of dividends on the preferred stock. The justification for the downward adjustment in the redemption price is that the higher premium during the early life of the stock is a compensation to the investor for reinvesting; the investors who hold preferred stock for twenty years have less claim to compensation than those who hold it for but one year. Sometimes sinking-fund retirement provisions are arranged so that assets will not be used until the passage of a specified number of years (deferred sinking-fund plan). The provisions may also prevent corporate earnings from being used for the purpose of retiring preferred stock as long as any dividends on preferred stock are in arrears. Otherwise management may withhold dividends to depress the market price of the stock so as to reacquire it at "bargain" prices to the disadvantage of shareholders.

The primary purpose of management in providing for sinking funds when issuing preferred stock is to obtain capital under more favorable terms (higher price for the stock or a lower dividend rate). Many insurance companies whose market for preferred stock is thin expect the purchases of the preferred stock by the managers of the sinking fund to keep up the market price (or at least to maintain an orderly market for it). However, sinking-fund provisions at the time of issuance of preferred stock may not have the expected beneficial effect on the market for the stock in future years unless total authorization is limited. Many corporations issue preferred stocks in series; while old stock is being retired, larger amounts of new stock may be issued to the detriment of the market price for all of the company's preferred stock issues.

Provisions for compulsory sinking-fund contributions may be disadvantageous to a corporation at a time when it would be more profitable to retain earnings or when cash is needed for other purposes. At the time when a corporation's earnings are largest, it may lose the use of cash; at the time when its earnings are smallest, it may have to choose between withdrawing cash or defaulting on its sinking-fund contributions. If the latter is chosen, the corporation is usually subject to certain restrictions on its activities such as borrowing, paying dividends on common stock, and reacquiring stock already issued.

In some cases, a corporation merely establishes the right to redeem or call stock without making any specific provisions as to sinking funds or other details except a call price. There may be a provision that the corporation may not pay more than par or stated value plus the accrued unpaid dividends for the preferred stock. The conditions under which a corporation may provide for the retirement of its preferred stock may be similar to those used in the case of sinking funds except that retirement would be on a voluntary basis, with the corporation purchasing the securities in the open market or directly from stockholders. The corporation may announce to preferred stockholders that it will repurchase some of the preferred shares at a stated price or merely that it will buy a certain number of shares, requesting that preferred stockholders notify the company as to the price at which they will sell their shares. The last method permits the corporation to buy shares of preferred stock from those who "tender" their stocks at the lowest price.

After a corporation has reacquired redeemable shares, the shares are cancelled (which should not be confused with the cancelling of old stock certificates and issuing new ones when ownership of stock is transferred "on the books"). Later, such shares may be restored to the status of treasury stock or "authorized but unissued shares"; sometimes, however, the provisions under which the shares are issued call for their permanent retirement. In either case, when shares are cancelled, the corporation is required to file a statement of the cancellation with the Secretary of State. Since permanent retirement necessitates a change in the amount of authorized capital, the filing of the statement of cancellation amounts to an amendment to the articles of incorporation.

SUMMARY

In return for giving preferred stock priority over common stock as to dividends and usually as to assets in case of liquidation, corporate management usually places limitations on the dividend rate and on the right to vote for directors. Corporations issue preferred stock when it is more advantageous than issuing bonds or additional shares of common stock. Preferred stock may be cumulative or noncumulative; that is, when dividends are passed, they may or may not accumulate as claims to future earnings which will have to be paid before dividends may be paid on common stock. Preferred stock may or may not participate in dividends beyond the rate specified on the stock certificate.

Although preferred stock usually has limitations placed on voting rights, complete disfranchisement is rare. Preferred stockholders have the right to vote on any proposals which affect their rights and privileges, and it is not uncommon for them to have a temporary or permanent right to vote for representation on the board of directors.

Corporate management may issue convertible or nonconvertible preferred stock if provided for in the charter. The objective of management in issuing convertible preferred stock is to make the stock more salable by giving holders an opportunity to benefit from future growth of the company by use of the conversion privilege; however, the long-run effects on the corporation's capital structure are uncertain. While mass conversion of preferred stock may affect the status of common stock adversely, the corporate financial structure will thereby be simplified, the market for common stock broadened, and the way cleared for future issues of preferred stock under market conditions which may be more favorable. Corporations sometimes issue preferred stock with warrants attached which permit the holders to purchase common stock at a price stated in the contract.

Redemption or retirement of preferred stock issues may become desirable at some future time and corporate management may anticipate this situation by making preferred stock callable. The most important advantage to corporations in issuing callable preferred stock is the ability to replace an issue carrying a high dividend rate with one carrying a lower rate. The corporate charter may also provide for issuance of various series of preferred stocks differing as to the rate of dividends, price and terms under which shares may be redeemed, amount payable upon shares in case of voluntary or involuntary liquidation, sinking-fund provisions, and terms and conditions under which shares may be converted.

The conditions under which preferred stock is issued may later place restrictions on management's attempt to finance with additional issues. Instead of planning to refinance preferred stock issues if and when market conditions are favorable, corporate management may issue stock under terms requiring redemption of a specific amount each year and/or may set aside assets to retire the stock. The provision for a retirement or sinking fund places management under obligation to set aside net earnings even though such earnings might be used profitably by the corporation. In some cases, a corporation merely establishes the right to redeem or call stock without making any specific provisions as to sinking funds or other details except call price.

In practice, the use of preferred stock in financing the needs of business corporations has few of the advantages associated with the nominal legal characteristics of such issues. In addition preferred stock lacks the flexibility in regard to dividend payments offered by common stock issues. Corporate management would be wise to treat dividends on preferred stock as a fixed charge. This suggests that it may be preferable to issue bonds rather than preferred stock for two reasons. First, interest rates on bonds are usually lower than dividend rates on preferred stock (the total cost may be about the same if sinking-fund provisions are made for the first and not for the second). Second, interest payments on bonds represent a cost of business and are deductible for tax purposes, while dividend payments on preferred stock represent a distribution of net profits to owners and therefore are not deductible. Both the flexibility associated with dividend payments on common stock and the tax advantage associated with bond financing could be obtained by the use of income bonds.

QUESTIONS AND PROBLEMS

1. Is one justified in calling the typical preferred stock a "hybrid type of security" that possesses certain characteristics of common stock and certain characteristics of a long-term bond? Explain.
2. Why does management use preferred stock in financing?
3. May the covenants for a preferred stock issue be drawn so that the securities will have more of the characteristics of a bond than of common stock? Explain. May the opposite be true? Explain.

4. What justification would there be for assuming that many of the high-grade, high-dividend, noncallable preferred stocks now outstanding represent a financial mistake by the issuing corporations? Explain.
5. Identify the following features of preferred stock: (*a*) cumulative, (*b*) participating, and (*c*) callable.
6. Explain the status of preferred stock when a corporation is liquidated and dissolved.
7. (*a*) Under what conditions do business corporation acts or corporations' charters prohibit limiting or denying any class of stockholders the right to vote? (*b*) Under what special conditions may preferred stockholders have the right to vote? (*c*) Considered from a legal point of view, is it easier to borrow or to issue preferred stock? Why?
8. What preferences and limitations are suggested by the following titles: (*a*) "American Machine & Foundry, 3.90 per cent cumulative preferred" stock, and (*b*) "Western Maryland Railroad, 4 per cent noncumulative convertible second preferred" stock?
9. What is meant by the statement that the conversion option may be expressed as a ratio or as a price? If the option is used, how would the position of old common stockholders be affected? Would the capital structure of the corporation be strengthened? Explain your answers. Is there justification for concluding that conversion is frequently offered by management to divert attention of investors from some corporate weakness?
10. Assume that financing is difficult and that it is necessary to offer attractive terms to investors. What features would you include in order to make preferred stock offered attractive and still keep the dividend rate in line with outstanding preferred stock issues? Explain. Assume that financing is easy and that it is possible to negotiate favorable terms; would your answer differ?
11. What is meant by the statement that a stock purchase warrant is an option similar to a conversion privilege? How may a corporation gain more from the former than the latter?
12. If management regards preferred stock as a temporary part of the corporation's financial structure, what features would you expect to find in the charter provisions for preferred stock?
13. Analyze: "Flintkote Co. said it would borrow about $30 million this year, . . . Holders of the 4½ convertible second preferred, the $4.50 series A convertible second preferred, and the $2.25 series B convertible second preferred stocks will vote on the proposals [to increase the company's authorized funded debt]." (*Wall Street Journal* [New York], February 6, 1961, p. 13.)
14. Most of the new preferred stock issues, forty of the fifty-eight sold in 1959, were offered by public utility companies. Why is this type of security of greater popularity with public utility companies than with industrial companies?

PART VI

Long-Term Debts of Business Corporations

THE LONG-TERM debts of business corporations include bonds, debentures, and long-term notes. The relative importance of bond financing as a means of corporate borrowing has declined in the last thirty years. The emergence of large financial institutions not only has made the reliance on long-term notes possible but also has permitted increased use of private placement of bond issues. One of the common uses of long-term notes is in connection with real estate mortgage financing, an important source of funds for many business firms.

The use of the term *bond* implies a mortgage bond; however other special types of bonds are used. Such bonds include those secured by equipment (equipment trust bonds); those secured by the general credit of the issuer with no specific assets pledged (debenture bonds); those secured by stocks and bonds owned by the issuer (collateral trust bonds); those based on the credit of one or more corporations (guaranteed, assumed, and joint bonds); and those on which there is no requirement to pay interest unless earned (income or adjustment bonds). When compared to other credit instruments, bonds show the greatest variations as to maturity, security, interest payments, negotiability, repayment provisions, and special features including call options and convertibility privileges.

Being credit instruments, bonds have maturity dates and plans must be made for their extinction. The methods of extinction are redemption or retirement, refunding, and conversion. The selection of the method will be determined by many factors including capital structure of the firm, condition of the capital market, and other variables.

This section deals with the general nature of corporate bonds, mortgage debts, special types of corporate bonds, and extinction of long-term debts.

CHAPTER 20

General Nature of Corporate Bonds

AMONG THE instruments of long-term finance, bonds are used commonly by corporations in open-market financing.[1] A corporate bond issue is usually distributed to investors or lenders through the facilities of middlemen—bond houses or investment banks. This chapter deals with the nature and characteristics of bonds, the functions of the corporate trustee, and the various classes of bonds.

NATURE OF A BOND

A Promise to Pay Money. A bond is a written promise to pay the holder a specific sum of money after a term of one year or more after issuance. A bond has been called a "glorified" long-term promissory note. It may be issued by an individual, partnership, or public or private corporation. Customarily, a bond is one of a series of similar credit instruments, all of which may or may not be of like denominations and/or maturities. If a corporation borrows $10,000,000 for 25 years, the resulting debt may be represented by 10,000 bonds of the standard $1,000 denomination. The aggregate is called a bond issue, and it is supported by the general credit of the obligor (debtor) and any security that may be specifically pledged. The

[1] For illustration, Swift and Company considered raising additional funds in 1961 by using debentures, convertible debentures, and sale of common stock—or a combination of securities. In its proxy statement, the company asked shareholders to authorize an increase in common stock and to waive pre-emptive rights to a convertible issue (because so many stockholders owned but a few shares and to pro rate the offering would be too expensive). See also *New York Times*, December 29, 1960, p. 33.

great bulk of corporate bonds are in $1,000 denominations or multiples thereof; but $500 and $100 bonds, commonly called *baby* bonds, are also issued. While baby bonds may appeal to small investors, they are not favored by corporations because of the costs of engraving certificates and the handling fees charged by trustees (which may be a set amount for each bond certificate transferred or registered regardless of denomination). Now the demand side of the corporate bond market is dominated by institutional investors who usually prefer large denomination bonds. In fact, under the rules of some securities exchanges, a bond having a denomination under $500 may be refused by the purchaser.

Bonds are usually thought of as long-term credit instruments with maturities of ten years or more; however, to some extent there is a connection between maturity patterns and the industry of the issuer, with railroad and public utility companies' bonds having the longest maturities and "industrial" bonds having the shortest. In a serial bond issue, some of the bonds may come due in one year, some in two years, and so on, with the result that maturities from one to fifteen years may be included in a fifteen-year serial bond issue. Although seldom if ever issued in the United States, bonds may be issued with no maturity dates (called perpetual or annuity bonds on which interest is paid in perpetuity). However, bonds with maturities of more than ninety-nine years at the time of issue have been distributed (most commonly in connection with the financial reorganization of railroad companies).

Provisions for Interest Payment. Usually, a bond contains a promise to pay interest on stated dates: quarterly, semiannually, or annually. The discount type of bond (such as the Series E savings bond) is seldom issued by American corporations. Some business corporations, as a result of financial reorganizations, issue a type of bond that requires the obligor to pay interest only when it is earned during any one interest period after other expenses have been met. The misleading term *income bond* is usually applied to such bonds, but the term *income adjustment bond* would be more suitable. For other so-called income bonds, the term *preference* bond would be more appropriate because of their resemblance to preferred stock. Income bonds of either type may be cumulative or noncumulative as to interest payments.

A business corporation may make its periodic interest payments by checks which are mailed to registered holders (those in whose names bonds are registered on the corporation's books as of a certain predetermined date—for illustration, the last business day in June and December). A second method is to meet interest obligations by keeping deposits in certain conveniently located banks to be used to pay interest coupons as they are presented (customarily by other banks acting as collection agents for the holders of the bonds to which the coupons were previously attached).

Since bond coupons are only about twice the size of an airmail stamp, banks use especially prepared "window" envelopes in which they are enclosed for collection. Only matured coupons of the same issue are to be enclosed in each envelope. The envelope also contains spaces to be filled in by the depositor, including the name of the issuer, place of payment, due date, name of depositor, and the dollar value of coupon or coupons enclosed. The envelope also carries the name and address of the bank and a request "If not paid when due, please return in this envelope" or a similar statement. The interest rate, expressed as a percentage of the face or a par amount of the bond, is usually included in the title of the bond along with the name of the debtor corporation and the maturity date of the bond; for example, Dow Chemical Company 3s 82 (that is 3 per cent bonds, due in 1982).

INDENTURE PROVISIONS

Rights in Mortgage Deed and/or Trust Indenture. In addition to being a promise to pay, a bond is also an instrument representing the rights of the owner to participate in the mortgage deed and/or trust indenture. Bonds may be unsecured promises to pay or they may be secured by a mortgage on real property, a pledge of tangible personal property, or a pledge of intangible personal property.

When a mortgage bond is issued, a mortgage deed or trust deed will be drawn up and deposited with a trustee. When tangible personal property is pledged, a mortgage or some other legal instrument (such as a conditional sales contract or trust receipt) will be used to enable the trustee to protect the interests of bondholders. If intangible personal property (such as stock and bonds) is pledged, the trustee may take physical possession of the collateral used as security. For unsecured bonds, called debenture bonds, the bondholders are dependent on the promise to pay of the obligor plus certain things which are enumerated in the indenture (meaning contract) that is signed by the debtor and held by the trustee. In the more complicated forms of financing, a trust indenture will be used along with the mortgage deed or other documents.

A bond usually makes reference to the mortgage deed or trust indenture and may embody some of its terms; but, if the language used in the reference is not correct, it may destroy the negotiability of the bond. Therefore a business firm normally follows legal advice in preparing a bond issue so that its salability will not be impaired.

Trust or Bond Indenture. A bond indenture customarily contains a preamble giving the purpose of the indenture, the proceedings taken by the corporation to make the issue legal (such as a resolution by the board of directors), and something about the nature of the bonds, bond coupons (if any), and other details. The indenture names the two parties of the contract—the debtor corporation (issuer) and the trustee—and also indicates the fees, commissions, and other payments to be received by the latter. The bond indenture states the conditions covering the issuance of the bonds (amount, form, certification, delivery, registration, and so on), callable features, right to convert into common stock, and other features which are discussed in the next chapter.

Many of the restrictive provisions found in bond indentures are applicable to pledged property. The trust indenture contains a complete description of the pledged property and a statement as to whether or not property acquired in the future is to be included in the mortgage. The debtor customarily agrees to keep mortgaged property in good repair, to insure it against loss from fire and other risks, to pay all assessments and taxes levied upon it, to defend the title and to see that the mortgage is properly recorded, to maintain a replacement fund for protection of the property, and to make provisions for a sinking fund.

The covenant entered into by the corporation usually prevents it from creating any debt having priority over the claims of creditors covered in the indenture, paying dividends until earnings exceed interest and sinking-fund requirements by a specified amount or percentage, permitting net working capital to fall below a certain figure, and selling fixed assets unless the proceeds are applied to retiring the debt. Other restrictions cover the lease of property, consolidations, and mergers.

The bond or trust indenture also specifies the actions that may be taken by trustees and bondholders in the event of default on any of the conditions laid down. These conditions are far more inclusive than paying interest when due and meeting principal obligations when they mature. In case of default, the bond or trust indenture may permit the trustee to take possession of the mortgaged property and operate it for the benefit of the creditors, to sell the property to the highest bidder without suit, to foreclose the mortgage and dispose of the property under judicial sale, to bring suit for specific performance of any agreement, and to declare the principal due (the acceleration clause) and take action to recover the unpaid portion of the debt. The trustee may be given discretion in applying any of these remedies or he may be forced to take action by a written request of 10 per cent or more of the creditors.[2] As may be surmised from this brief summary, a bond or trust indenture may be a long document; the length of the average trust indenture is slightly over one hundred pages.

CORPORATE TRUSTEE

When a business concern borrows directly from a bank or other lender, the lender holds the promise to pay and other documents, and it is his responsibility to see that the debtor meets the terms of his contract. In contrast, when a bond issue is sold, hundreds of investors may participate in lending; hence provisions are made for their protection during the life of the bond. Business corporations employ trust companies or banks to act as agents for them and also as trustees for bondholders.[3] Because the trust company or bank is compensated for its services by the debtor corporation, one might assume that the corporation would be favored in case of conflict between the interests of the corporation and the bondholders. However, there are certain basic principles that a qualified and disinterested trustee will not violate. Because of its length, the trust indenture is generally not printed and distributed to bondholders, but its chief provisions are usually summarized in the prospectus—the document given to those interested in buying the bonds. Most bondholders are dependent upon trustees to care for their interests; consequently Congress has set standards that trust companies and banks must meet before they can serve as trustees of bond issues in which a wide public interest is expected.

[2] Sometimes a trust indenture will contain a clause which permits the company and the trustee to modify the terms of the trust agreement within limits. If this power is used, it appears as a supplement to the original trust agreement. Often, modifications of indenture provisions necessitate approval of holders of two thirds (or some other percentage) of the bonds or debentures.

[3] For illustration, the trustees for the long-term debts of the Union Electric Company are the St. Louis Union Trust Company of St. Louis for the company's mortgage and deed of trust obligations, and the Mercantile Trust Company of St. Louis for the company's debenture obligations.

Trust Indenture Act of 1939. The Trust Indenture Act of 1939 requires business corporations to select trustees that are disinterested and competent. (In practice, the trustee selected by the corporation is the one recommended by the investment banker.) To be "disinterested" a trustee must have no financial or other interest in the issuer that would be in conflict with the interests of investors. A copy of the indenture is filed with the Securities and Exchange Commission when the nature of the security issue or the method of financing brings it under the Commission's supervision. Before a trust company or bank selected to hold the bond indenture is permitted to act as trustee, approval of the Securities and Exchange Commission must be obtained. Like other provisions for registration, there are exceptions to the registration requirement. These exceptions include domestic government securities and corporate securities when the principal amount of the issue is less than $1,000,000.

According to the Trust Indenture Act of 1939 (with minor exceptions), if there are one or more trustees, one of the trustees must be a corporation with capital and surplus of not less than $150,000 and all conflicting interests must be eliminated (such as when a trustee is acting under another indenture for the same debtor, is affiliated with the issuer, or is the owner of securities previously issued by the issuer). In performing their functions, trustees must provide bondholders with periodic and special reports on the status of the trust, conditions of property held in trust, and other matters, and must notify bondholders of any default within ninety days. After default, the trustee must exercise his powers with the same degree of care and skill as a prudent man would conduct his affairs under similar circumstances (the "prudent man" theory).

CLASSIFICATION OF BONDS OF BUSINESS CORPORATIONS

A bond may be classified in many ways depending upon the type of issuer, purpose of borrowing, presence or absence of pledged security, provisions for payment of interest and repayment of principal, and other terms in the trust indenture.

Type of Borrower. One of the most common methods of classifying bonds issued by business enterprises is according to type of borrower (hence railroad bonds, public utility bonds, and industrial bonds). Within each major category there are two or more possible subdivisions; for example, in the public utility industry the subdivisions are gas, power and light, communications, and water. Although our interest is primarily in the bonds issued by business corporations, the greatest volume of bonds being bought and sold in the capital markets are those issued by governments—federal, "municipal" (state, city, county, school district, and other political subdivisions of the state), and foreign. Government-owned corporations, federal agencies, certain mortgage banks, and some nonprofit organizations also raise capital by selling bonds. Many business corporations are engaged in several lines; when this is true, they are customarily listed according to the type of business from which they obtain the largest proportion of their earnings.

Purpose of Borrowing. In issuing bonds, the primary purpose of the borrowing corporation is to raise money. However, it does not follow that all bond issues give the corporation additional funds with which to operate, because the funds so raised may be used to repay short-term or floating debts, refund other long-term debts, or retire preferred stock. Some public utility and railroad companies regard their long-term debts as a permanent part of their capital structures; at least part of the funds they raise from the sale of bonds is used to pay other bonds when due or when called (a refunding bond issue). When a short-term debt is retired with funds from the sale of bonds, the so-called "floating debt" has been "funded"; that is, converted into a more or less permanent interest-bearing debt.

During periods in which the national economy is expanding, the amount of borrowing by business concerns to obtain new capital will exceed the amount of borrowing to retire other securities (including short-term loans, term loans, notes, bonds, and preferred stock); but during periods when business is depressed and interest rates are low, refunding issues may be larger than those for "new money." New capital may be used to build or purchase plants and other forms of real property, to purchase machinery and/or equipment, and to increase working capital assets. Sometimes the title of a bond will indicate the purpose for which it was issued. For illustration, a consolidation and refunding bond is one that is issued by a corporation formed by consolidating two or more corporations to replace bonds previously outstanding; railway equipment obligations are those issued to finance the purchases of equipment by railroads.

Presence or Absence of Security. Corporate bonds are classified according to the presence or absence of something specifically pledged as security. Unsecured corporate bonds, called debenture bonds, are based on the general credit of the borrower. Secured bonds are classified according to the type of property pledged or assigned—such as those based on real property (mortgage bonds), tangible personal property (as railroad equipment bonds), and intangible personal property (as collateral trust bonds based on stocks and bonds). Debenture bonds and each of the three major classes of secured bonds are treated in the chapters which follow.

Bearer and Registered Bonds. A corporation may issue either bearer bonds which are payable to the bearer and negotiable or registered bonds which are promises to pay money to those whose names are registered in the books of the corporation. Like a stock certificate, a registered bond has the name of the owner on its face. Ownership may be transferred by written assignment by the registered owner only when presented at the office of the corporation or the designated transfer agent. In order to complete the transfer of ownership, the corporation's bond register must be changed to indicate the change in ownership. A corporation's bonds may be "fully registered"; that is, registered both as to principal and interest. Then, interest is paid by check to the owner of record upon a predetermined date (as in the case of preferred stock dividends except that bond interest dates are fixed in the trust indenture rather than in the corporation's bylaws), and the nuisance of handling and accounting for bond coupons is avoided. A bond certificate has a place for entering the date of registration, the name of the registered owner, and the signature of the transfer agent. When bonds are transferred, the entries are recorded on the bond certificate and the records of the company or its transfer agent.

Some bonds are registered as to principal only and not as to interest. In this case, provisions for interest payment take the form of dated coupons which are attached to the bonds and payable to the bearer. They are the corporation's promises to pay as of certain dates. As each interest payment date arrives, the bondholder customarily clips the proper coupon and sends it to his bank to be collected by the bank from the obligor. The name and location of the paying agent appears on each coupon, but a change in the location of the paying office during the life of the bond does not invalidate the coupon or principal obligation. Coupons are payable to order or bearer, and this is true after the bond has been paid unless the coupons refer to the bond for their terms and conditions. This relationship is pertinent in cases wherein bonds have been called and a number of "ragged" bonds appear (bonds from which coupons not yet due have been detached).

Unlike registered bonds which are payable only to the registered holder, bearer bonds are payable to any person having possession of them. The fact that ownership passes by mere delivery—no endorsement is needed—facilitates purchase and sale of such bonds but adds to the hazards of ownership. If nonregistered bonds are lost or stolen and subsequently sold, the new owner may have a valid claim to them (as would be true for similar "bearer" negotiable credit instruments); unless previously notified, a debtor corporation which has paid interest or principal to holders other than true owners is not liable for the loss. Provisions for replacement of bonds which have been lost or stolen are included in the trust indenture. Usually a corporation will replace lost or stolen bonds with duplicate bonds, and the trustee will authenticate them if the bondholder gives satisfactory evidence of their loss or destruction and furnishes a bond of indemnity for the amount required by the company and trustee.

In deciding whether to issue fully registered bonds, bonds registered as to principal only, or bearer bonds, corporations are guided by preferences of investors as indicated by investment bankers. Obviously, fully registered bonds necessitate more work in keeping records of changes in ownership than do straight coupon bonds. Because corporations try to please creditors, they customarily make provisions for changing the status of their bonds if desired by owners. Thus a bearer bond may be changed to a registered bond, and a registered bond of the coupon type may be converted into an unregistered bond by simply making the bond payable to "bearer" and so recording it in the bond register. A fully registered bond can be converted by either attaching coupons to the old bond certificate or replacing it with a new bond certificate with coupons attached.

A provision for interchangeability of bonds (registered bonds exchanged for "bearer" and vice versa, large denominations for small ones, etc.) may or may not be included in the trust indenture; but a better market for the bonds may be expected by the corporation if such privileges are offered. Fully registered bonds appeal to institutional investors, endowment funds, and others who expect to hold them for a long period of time but the negotiable type appeals to those who trade in bonds.[4] In order to reduce the amount of paper to be handled, bonds may be issued or reissued in multiples of the standard $1,000 denomination ($5,000, $10,000, etc., but denominations of $1,000,000 are more common for federal government bonds than corporate bonds). The cost of issuing a new bond certificate is about $2.

[4] A registered bond is a promise to pay money to the one whose name is registered on the books of the corporation. It may be transferred only when presented to the corporation with a written assignment executed by the registered owner. It is neither payable to the bearer nor to the order of the registered owner and so it is not a negotiable instrument; however, registered bonds can be transferred as easily as common stocks.

Provisions for Extinction. Bonds are classified according to provisions for their extinction as sinking-fund bonds and serial bonds. A sinking fund for retirement of bonds is created by appropriations of cash earmarked for reacquiring the bonds of the issue on or before maturity. Usually the trust company that administers the trust indenture also serves as the sinking-fund trustee. Serial bond issues consist of a number of bonds issued at the same time with individual bonds having different maturity dates (serially due). Thus the maturities of the bonds are arranged so as to necessitate retirement of the bond issue on the installment plan.

When no special provisions are made by a corporation for the extinction of a bond issue, the corporation may plan to refinance it on or before maturity with funds obtained from a sale of new securities, a term loan, a sale of property, or with cash obtained in some other way. In some cases, new securities may be offered in direct exchange for the old securities. Usually bonds are issued with a provision that they may be called or redeemed at the option of the corporation (callable bonds), but there are other issues of bonds (noncallable bonds) which do not give management this option.

Option Provisions. The marketability of most bonds depends on their status as credit instruments; however, some bonds are issued with warrants and others are issued with the provision that they may be converted into other securities, usually common stock, at the option of the bondholders. When bonds are issued with warrants, the owner acquires a promise to pay and an option to buy some other security of the corporation (usually common stock). The warrant permits the holder to buy the security at a fixed price within a specified period of time. Warrants may be detachable or nondetachable. Detachable warrants may be bought and sold as separate instruments; but nondetachable warrants must be sold along with the bond until the option is used.

Corporations may issue bonds having the conversion privilege; that is, the bonds may be exchanged for some other security (usually common stock) of the issuing corporation at a fixed price within a specified period of time.[5] When warrants are used, the corporation

[5] The 5 per cent convertible sinking-fund debentures of Libby, McNeill & Libby are convertible into common stock of the Company at $14.80 per share to December 15, 1966, $16.70 per share thereafter to December 15, 1971 and $18.75 per share thereafter to December 31, 1976. On June 27, 1959, 707,257 shares of the Company's common stock were reserved for conversion of the debentures. (Libby, McNeill & Libby, *Annual Report for the Year Ended June 27, 1959*, p. 12.)

receives cash in payment for the new securities. When bonds are converted, there is a direct exchange of the new security for the one being extinguished. In some cases, conversion may require some cash in addition to the surrender of the old bond. For illustration, the American Telephone and Telegraph Company's 12-year, 3¾ convertible debentures, dated December 10, 1953, were issued under provisions which permitted their conversion into stock on or after February 9, 1954, at the conversion price of $136 per share, "payable by surrender of $100 principal amount of debentures and payment of $36 in cash."

Provisions for Trading. Corporations may arrange to have their bonds listed on securities exchanges. At present, the New York Stock Exchange lists some 1,500 bond issues, and the American Stock Exchange (formerly New York Curb Exchange), the Midwest Stock Exchange, and other exchanges list a smaller number of issues.[6] Over the last twenty-five years, the aggregate value of listed bonds has increased, largely due to the increase in United States government securities; but the volume of trading on organized exchanges has declined. The issues of railroad companies are the most important group of corporate issues listed on the New York Stock Exchange. To increase bond trading on the floor of the New York Stock Exchange, the Exchange adopted the "fourteen bond rule." This rule requires members to buy and sell listed bonds on the exchange, unless a better price can be obtained for the customer in the over-the-counter market, when the orders are for less than $15,000 par value. Trading is on an auction basis with the unit being one bond with a par value of $1,000; however, smaller denomination bonds may be traded if buyers can be found.

Corporations may avoid the expense of listing their bonds because most of the trading in corporate and other bonds, whether listed or not, is in the over-the-counter markets (a term covering trading outside organized national securities exchanges). Usually, purchases and sales of bonds are negotiated over the telephone through dealers who quote "bid" and "asked" prices; that is, they buy at the bid price and sell at the asked price. The spread between the bid and asked price is the dealer's gross margin of profit; the more actively a bond is traded the smaller is the spread. Quotations on bonds are in terms of percentages of face value; for illustration, when a $1,000

[6] For illustration, all Philadelphia Electric Company securities are listed on the Philadelphia–Baltimore Stock Exchange and the New York Stock Exchange. Philadelphia Electric Power Company bonds are listed on the Philadelphia–Baltimore Stock Exchange.

bond is quoted at 94.5, the price is $945.[7] Accrued interest is added to the purchase price computed from the last coupon or interest payment date to the date of the purchase. Bonds on which interest is in default and income and adjustment bonds are quoted "flat"; that is, without the payment of accrued interest by the purchaser.

BONDS BASED ON THE CREDIT OF TWO OR MORE CORPORATIONS

Businessmen sometimes guarantee or endorse the promissory notes of their corporations so as to obtain credit on more favorable terms from their banks. This practice of making two or more parties responsible for debts has been extended to include bonds which may be guaranteed by a second party, assumed by a second corporation, or issued jointly by two or more corporations.[8]

Guaranteed Bonds. A guaranteed bond is one guaranteed by an individual, a government, or a corporation other than the issuing corporation. The relationship between the guarantor and the corporation whose obligations are guaranteed is usually close, such as a parent company and a subsidiary company. Customarily, the guarantor assumes full responsibility for fulfillment of the debt contact, and in case of default by the party whose obligations are guaranteed, the guarantor is responsible. Sometimes an individual who has an important financial interest in a corporation guarantees the bonds; certain issues of semipublic corporations have been guaranteed by the federal government.

The value of a guaranty depends on the financial standing of the guarantor and the terms of the guarantee; the credit standing of a bond is enhanced when the credit of the guarantor is better than that of the issuer. A guaranty may apply to either interest or principal or both, and it may be secured by a deposit of collateral which would give the bond some of the characteristics of a collateral trust bond. A guaranty may be covered by a lease agreement, by a special contract with the debtor corporation, or by endorsement of the bonds

---

[7] Customarily, United States government bonds are sold in terms of dollars and fractions (32nds) rather than dollars and cents. Therefore, bid and asked prices of 98.18 and 98.20 mean $\$98\frac{18}{32}$ and $\$98\frac{20}{32}$.

[8] For illustration, the Chesapeake and Ohio Railway Company, *1959 Annual Report*, page 36, under "Notes to Financial Statements," it is noted that "The Company has guaranteed $16.0 million of loans payable by certain of its wholly-owned subsidiaries. In addition, the company is contingently liable as guarantor of certain obligations of other companies. These relate to normal operating arrangements and are not material in relation to the Company's financial position."

by the guarantor.[9] In the last case, the guarantee is direct; in the other two cases it is indirect. Most commonly guaranteed bonds result when one corporation leases property of a second corporation and guarantees the interest and principal payments on its long-term debt.

Assumed Bonds. An assumed bond is one which has been issued by one corporation and made the liability of a second corporation or individual who has voluntarily assumed responsibility for it. The party assuming the obligation customarily makes no changes in the indenture as signed by the original issuer; but, when any changes are made, they must have the approval of the bondholders or trustee. In addition, such a contingency must have been provided for in the bond indenture (covering mergers, consolidations, and sales of assets, as by a subsidiary corporation to a parent corporation).

Assumed bonds are common in American business finance where business combinations are prevalent. They are of the same dual nature as guaranteed bonds, usually being secured obligations of the original issuer but involving only the general credit of the second corporation. If the bonds have a better investment status following assumption by a second corporation, it is because of the greater earning power of the corporation which has taken over responsibility for the bond indebtedness.

Joint Bonds. Bonds which are the joint obligation of two or more corporations at the time of original issue are known as joint bonds. Sometimes the term "joint and several" is used, and this means that the signers are bound jointly as well as individually for the full amount of the debt. Joint bonds may be secured or unsecured. When several railroad companies in large cities use the same terminal facilities, a subsidiary corporation may be organized to own and manage these facilities. When bonds secured by a mortgage on this property are issued by the subsidiary, the parent corporations severally and jointly may guarantee the bonds either on the face or in an operating or lease agreement. In some cases, where the terminal property is owned by one operating company, the other roads using

---

[9] Over the signatures of the proper officers and seal of the grantor, this guarantee may read as follows: "For value received, the *X* corporation hereby guarantees the punctual payment of the principal and interest of the within bond, at the time and in the manner therein specified, and covenants, in default of payment of any part thereof by the obligator to pay the said principal and interest of the within bond, as the same shall become due, upon the demand of the holder thereof."

the facilities may guarantee the bonds secured by a mortgage on the terminal facilities.

MISCELLANEOUS TYPES OF BONDS

Participating Bonds. On rare occasions, bondholders are permitted to share in the earnings of a corporation in an amount in excess of the fixed rate of interest, thereby receiving—in excess of a minimum stated amount—additional sums depending on the earnings of the issuer. Such bonds are called participating bonds. Participation may be cumulative or noncumulative; it may be limited to a maximum rate; or the provision in the trust indenture may be so stated as to give bondholders a stated proportion of the earnings of the corporation before federal income taxes. Participation gives to bonds a speculative feature which some investors find attractive.

Stamped Bonds. Stamped bonds, an uncommon type, are those which have been modified in some way after having been issued. These bonds are stamped on the face with the legend, "Subject to the provisions set forth on the back hereof." The back of the bond will be stamped with the changes which have been made with the consent of the bondholders (such as changes in the sinking fund, interest rate, maturity, and/or provision for security).

Treasury Bonds. Treasury bonds are those which have been reacquired by the issuing corporation to be disposed of as the corporation desires. Treasury bonds exclude those in sinking funds which have been acquired by the sinking fund trustee and are no longer under the control of the corporation. If the purpose of the corporation is to resell them, treasury bonds may be shown on the balance sheet as an asset; otherwise they may be deducted from the total amount of bonds outstanding.

Voting Bonds. Ordinarily, bondholders have no voice in the management of the corporation; but, under certain circumstances, bondholders may be permitted to select a given number of directors. Provisions for voting may result from concessions made to investment bankers at the time a bond issue is negotiated; but, more often, this provision results from reorganization of the corporation and the replacement of other debts with income or adjustment bonds. The indenture under which the income bonds are issued may provide for bondholders' representation on the board of directors if interest is passed for a specified number of successive interest payment dates.

Income Bonds. Income bonds may be unsecured or secured by a pledge of property; they may be cumulative or noncumulative as to interest payments; they may be registered or coupon bonds. The bond indenture customarily provides that interest must be declared by the board of directors when earned after certain specific deductions, but the decision as to whether or not interest is paid if not earned is left to the discretion of the board of directors. While income bonds bear a stated interest rate, the board of directors may vote to pay whatever funds are available even though it may be only a fraction of the amount due bondholders. If income bonds are cumulative, interest that has been passed becomes part of the amount that must be paid when the principal comes due. Holders of noncumulative bonds lose all claims to interest not paid unless there is a provision that they have claims to whatever interest has been earned. Then that part of their claims to earned interest will accumulate as in the case of cumulative preferred stock.[10]

While most of the income bonds now outstanding are of the income adjustment type, the preference type of income bonds may be used to advantage by new or established companies having uncertain or widely fluctuating incomes. Established companies that have fairly steady income may find institutional investors willing to buy the preference type of income bonds when they are not permitted to buy preferred stock. The main advantage to the issuing corporation in the use of preference bonds in place of preferred stock is the tax saving; interest paid on such bonds is deductible as an expense in computing the base for federal income tax payments, while dividends paid on preferred stock are not.

The legal problem is to see that the conditions under which income bonds are issued are such that the courts will treat them as debts rather than as preferred stock. If an income bond is legal, there is no reason why corporations should not replace preferred stock with income bonds in financing, particularly when preferred stock is to be redeemed. This would be advantageous even if the interest rate on income bonds were no less than the dividend rate on the preferred stock. In presenting the case for income bonds, note the amount of income available to common stockholders in Case 1 as compared with

---

[10] For illustration, the provisions for interest payments on the income bonds of the Beacon Hotel Corporation of New York under the amendatory indenture now in effect are cumulative if earned up to 3 per cent per year from 1959–1964 and fixed interest thereafter until June 30, 1969 (when the bonds mature). (Beacon Hotel Corporation, *Twenty-Second Annual Report for the Year Ended June 30, 1960* [New York, 1960], p. 2.)

Case 2. Some companies have replaced preferred stock with income bonds, and others have considered doing so.[11]

Case 1		
Assumed level of earnings	$2,000,000	
Federal corporate income tax (52%)*	1,040,000	
Net after federal income taxes	$ 960,000	
Less dividends on preferred stock (100,000 shares at $5)	500,000	
Available to common stock (100,000 shares)	$ 460,000	
Earnings per share of common stock		$4.60
Case 2		
Assumed level of earnings	$2,000,000	
Interest ($10,000,000 bonds at 5%)	500,000	
Earnings less interest	$1,500,000	
Federal corporate income taxes (52%)*	780,000	
Net after federal taxes	$ 720,000	
Available to common stock (100,000 shares)	720,000	
Earnings per share of common stock		$7.20

* To simplify the illustration, the lower rate applicable to the first $25,000 of earnings has been ignored.

Receivers' or Trustees' Certificates. If new cash is needed for working capital purposes when a business enterprise is under the supervision of the court, the court may authorize the receiver or trustee of the bankrupt corporation to issue new certificates which are obligations of the corporation. Usually the holders of these debt instruments, called receivers' or trustees' certificates, are given priority over other creditors of the corporation.

Stabilized Bonds. Stabilized bonds are those whose principal and interest are adjusted to changes in the price level as measured by an index number (such as the index number of wholesale commodity prices prepared by the Bureau of Labor Statistics) to allow for changes in the purchasing power of the dollar. Proposals for this type of bond are given attention during periods of inflation, but little use has been made of such bonds in financing American business firms.

Considered from the viewpoint of investors whose incomes have been affected most adversely by inflation, a stabilized bond would offer compensation for the decrease in value of their investments; however, considered from the viewpoint of the economy as a whole, there is danger of accelerating the inflationary spiral by the expan-

[11] In 1956, the board of directors of the Chicago Great Western Railroad wrote to the company's preferred stockholders to say that the board was considering the advisability of offering a new issue of 5 per cent unsecured 100-year subordinated income debentures in exchange for the outstanding 5 per cent preferred stock and "wondered" if the stockholders were interested (enclosing a post card on which to reply).

sion of interest and principal payments. The only solution to the problem seems to be to return to sound monetary and fiscal government policies and a stable dollar. In the past, American corporations have sometimes issued stabilized bonds; a recent illustration of such bonds is those issued by the Christiansen Corporation, producers of aluminum and magnesium alloy ingots.

SUMMARY

A bond is usually one of a series of similar credit instruments which make up a bond issue. The individual bonds are not necessarily of like denomination or maturity. For illustration, in a serial bond issue, some bonds come due in successive years. The most common corporate bonds are those in $1,000 denominations or multiples thereof.

A bond usually contains a promise to pay interest on stated dates. The exception among bonds issued by business firms is the income bond, on which interest is paid only when earned. Bonds may be registered as to principal and interest, as to principal only, or unregistered. When bonds are fully registered, interest payments are made through the office of the corporation or through a paying agent. Nonregistered bonds are coupon bonds with the interest date printed on each coupon. The coupons may be mailed to designated payees when the interest date arrives or they may be deposited in the holder's bank to be collected for him.

A mortgage bond is one secured by a mortgage on real property. When the security for a bond issue is stocks and bonds, the bonds are known as collateral trust bonds. Unsecured bonds are called debenture bonds or debentures. The bond indenture or contract signed by the debtor and held by the trustee states the conditions covering the issuance of the bonds, the restrictions on management, and the remedies of trustees and bondholders in the event of default on any of the conditions laid down. The trustee, who must be qualified and disinterested, holds the indenture and administers the terms of the bond covenant.

Bonds of business enterprises may be classified according to the type of borrower (whether a railroad, public utility, or industry); the purposes of borrowing (whether to repay short-term or floating debts, to refund or consolidate debts, or to obtain new capital); the presence or lack of security (whether unsecured bonds, known as debentures or debenture bonds, or secured bonds, which include mortgage bonds, equipment bonds, and collateral trust bonds, depending on the type of security); the registration provision (whether fully registered, registered as to principal only, or bearer or coupon bonds); the provision for retirement (whether sinking-fund or serial bonds); and the provision for redemption (whether callable or noncallable).

Bonds based on the credit of one or more corporations include guaranteed bonds, assumed bonds, and joint bonds. Income bonds, on which there is no requirement to pay interest unless earned, are more accurately called *adjustment bonds* when issued as the result of corporate reorganizations. Income bonds may be secured or unsecured, cumulative or noncumulative, and registered or coupon bonds. From the viewpoint of the corporation, the issuance of preference type income bonds may have advantages over the issuance of preferred stock because some institutional investors may be willing to buy income bonds whereas they would be prohibited from buying preferred stock; interest payments on income bonds are deductible as an expense when computing federal income taxes while dividend payments on preferred stock are not; and the interest rate on income bonds is usually lower than that on preferred stock.

QUESTIONS AND PROBLEMS

1. Identify: (*a*) bond, (*b*) bond issue, (*c*) perpetual bond, (*d*) discount type bond, and (*e*) issuer.
2. What provisions are usually found in a bond or trust indenture? Compare to those found in a term loan agreement. Which document is usually the most restrictive to the corporation? Why?
3. What are the functions of a trustee under provisions of a bond indenture? How did the Trust Indenture Act of 1939 affect the work of trustees under bond indentures?
4. How may bonds be classified on the basis of provisions for interest payments? Distinguish between bearer and registered bonds. Give the advantages and disadvantages of each type to the issuer.
5. Give examples of bonds classified according to (*a*) type of security, (*b*) purposes of borrowing, and (*c*) type of borrower.
6. Distinguish between serial and sinking-fund bonds.
7. What are the advantages to the issuer of (*a*) call feature, (*b*) conversion privilege, and (*c*) warrants? What type of company most frequently uses them?
8. Identify: (*a*) guaranteed bonds, (*b*) assumed bonds, and (*c*) joint bonds. What do they have in common? When and why are they used?
9. Identify: (*a*) participating bonds, (*b*) stamped bonds, (*c*) treasury bonds, (*d*) voting bonds, and (*e*) trustees' and receivers' certificates.

10. (*a*) Distinguish between cumulative and noncumulative income bonds. (*b*) What would be the main advantage to a corporation in replacing preferred stock with preference type income bonds? Why?
11. Large business firms that raise funds by public financing usually depend more on bond issues than on sales of common or preferred stock. Why?
12. Keeping in mind that 1959 was a "boom" year, explain the following: "Bond financing by corporations in the first eight months of this year (1960), at $5,156,516,000, easily exceeded the $4,552,504,000 total for the like period of 1959, . . ." (*Wall Street Journal* [New York], November 28, 1960, p. 4.)
13. Analyze: The American Telephone and Telegraph Company borrowed in the capital market yesterday "at an interest cost of 4.686 per cent . . . through a competitive sale of $250,000,000 of thirty-two–year debentures carrying a five-year protection against a lower-cost financing. An investment group led by Morgan Stanley & Co. won the issue on a bid of 101.0599 for obligations bearing 4¾ per cent interest coupon." (*New York Times*, October 26, 1960, p. 53.)
14. "Corporate stock is serviced out of profits and, because they are a 'residual' share of income, they fluctuate widely with general business conditions." (Federal Reserve Bank of Minneapolis, *Monthly Review*, February 29, 1960, p. 16.) Analyze.

CHAPTER 21

Mortgage Debts of Business Firms

DIRECT negotiation between business firms and banks for long-term loans is as old as commercial banking; now, as in the past, real property is the most common form of fixed assets pledged as security for such loans. The promise to pay may be either a mortgage note or a mortgage bond; and, for a particular mortgage loan transaction, there will be one or more notes which will be held by one or more investors. In the case of a mortgage bond issue, there may be hundreds of bonds held by numerous investors.

During the last thirty years, there has been a tendency for large business firms to finance more with promissory notes and less with bonds. Now, large institutional investors have such an abundance of funds available that they negotiate directly with borrowers for loans that in the past would have necessitated open-market financing with bond issues. The ability of institutional investors to lend such amounts reflects the preference of savers for live insurance, deposits in savings institutions, and other forms of indirect investments (savings which go through institutions into the capital market rather than being invested directly).

The mortgage device is used when real property is pledged as security for loans; it is sometimes used when equipment and other forms of tangible property are pledged as security, giving rise to chattel mortgages. In this chapter, emphasis is on business firms' use of real property as security for loans, evidenced by real estate mortgage notes and mortgage bonds.

REAL ESTATE MORTGAGE NOTES AND BONDS

A real estate mortgage note is one secured by a mortgage on specific real property. In some states as well as in financial circles generally, a mortgage deed given to secure a note is considered to be a lien on the pledged property rather than an actual conveyance of title. Mortgage bonds are similar to real estate mortgage notes; however, the conditions under which mortgage bonds are issued are similar to those under which other bonds are issued, and the mortgage deed is included among the provisions of the trust or bond indenture.

A Real Estate Mortgage Defined. In some states, a real estate mortgage is still considered to be a conditional conveyance or transfer of title to real property by the mortgagor (borrower) to the mortgagee (lender) as security for payment of a debt. The conditional aspect of the transfer is removed if the debt is not paid as promised in the note. On the other hand, when the note is paid, the title to the mortgaged property goes back to the borrower. In effect, the borrower who signs the mortgage remains in possession of the mortgaged property as long as he makes the required interest and principal payments on the loan. At one time, if all mortgage payments except the last had been made, title would have been vested unconditionally in the mortgagee if the last payment were delayed. Gradually, the lender's automatic right to a "clear title" to mortgaged property in case of default was changed. First, the courts gave mortgagors relief by permitting delayed payments; now, in many states, the law has developed to a point where the mortgagee has only the right to file a suit to foreclose the property under terms of the mortgage. In other words, the mortgage merely gives the mortgagee a lien upon the mortgaged property.

Foreclosure Sale. Following judicial proceeding to foreclose, the court renders a judgment for the debt and directs the sale of the property at public auction. Usually, the lender attends the auction to protect his interest in the property (bidding up to the amount of his claim). If the property is sold for less than the debt, the deficiency is charged against the debtor; but, if the property is sold for more than the mortgage debt, the amount in excess of the debt is refunded to the debtor (minus foreclosure costs). If there is a deficiency so that the creditor (mortgagee) is not paid in full, he may obtain "execution" of a "deficiency judgment" that permits seizure of the nonexempt property of the debtor to satisfy the unpaid balance.

Mortgage Obligations in Reorganizations. In many instances, business firms which are unable to meet their obligations on mortgage bonds are not liquidated. Upon the request of either the debtor or the creditors, the federal courts may appoint a receiver to operate the business pending financial reorganization. When a reorganization plan is completed and accepted by the required number of security holders involved, the plan is put into effect by the court without a foreclosure sale. Reorganization plans must protect the contractual rights of security holders; this means that the first mortgage holders must be given preferential treatment and that other secured creditors will be given consideration according to the priority of their claims. In other words, the courts are accepting the "absolute priority doctrine" in business reorganizations. However, first mortgage liens do not have preference over the actual and necessary cost of preserving and administering the property in receivership. Claims having priority over first mortgage liens include receivers' certificates (if any), unpaid wages earned within three months prior to filing the petition of bankruptcy not exceeding $600 per person, and taxes due the United States government and state governments or political subdivisions thereof.

Multiple Mortgage Structures. If acceptable to lenders, a business concern may give as many first mortgages as it has separate pieces of property. At one time, railroads issued separate first mortgages on different terminal buildings and divisions of the railroad; but, to some extent, these smaller issues have been refunded and replaced by fewer but larger issues covering more real property.

If acceptable to lenders, a debtor may mortgage some pieces of property and not mortgage others; but, more often, lenders insist that the first mortgage deed be drawn to cover not only all existing property of the debtor but also all property subsequently acquired by him (the "after-acquired property" clause). A first mortgage may be an open-end or closed-end mortgage; that is, it may permit or may prohibit new financing with bonds of equal rank under the mortgage. The use of open-end mortgages tends to simplify the debt structure of the business firm (see below).

If acceptable to new lenders, the debtor may give a second, third, and subsequent mortgages on the same property. Second mortgage holders have claims to interest and principal payments after the first mortgage creditors have been paid; third mortgage holders have claims after first and second mortgage creditors have been satisfied; and so on for subsequent creditors. Sometimes the situation is so complicated that a holder of a mortgage bond may have a first mortgage claim to a particular piece of property, a second mortgage claim to a second piece, a third mortgage claim on another piece, and so on.

Recording of Mortgages. Ordinarily mortgages are recorded in the office of the county clerk or recorder; but the procedures for recording corporate mortgages, which are used as the basis of bond issues, vary among the different states. In some states, such mortgages may be filed in the county where the principal business office of the corporation is located or with the Secretary of State. The purpose of recording a mortgage is not only to give notice to other investors of the existence of the mortgage but also to protect the prior claim of the mortgagee. If there is an unrecorded mortgage outstanding when a second mortgage is created and recorded, the unrecorded first mortgage becomes junior to the second mortgage. The only defense that the holder of the unrecorded mortgage has is to prove that the holder of the recorded mortgage knew of the existence of the unrecorded first mortgage (which may not be possible to prove).

When a business concern buys property, it may take title "subject" to the existing claims against the property, including any mortgages, unpaid taxes, and other public and private encumbrances. As an alternative, a business concern may "assume" a mortgage on the property purchased. In either case, the purchaser pays the interest on the mortgage and the principal when the mortgage matures. However, there is a distinction between acquiring property subject to a mortgage and assuming a mortgage, and this distinction becomes important in case of a foreclosure sale. If the property is sold for less than the debt, the mortgage holder can hold the purchaser liable for the deficiency if he assumed the mortgage; but, if the property was purchased subject to a mortgage, the mortgage holder may sue the person who originally borrowed the money but may not sue the one who purchased the property subject to the mortgage. If property is acquired as the result of the foreclosure of a first mortgage, the buyer gets the property clear of all encumbrances except taxes, foreclosure expenses, and generally, special assessments; but, if property is acquired as the result of the foreclosure of a junior mortgage, the senior mortgage is unaffected.

Mortgage Covenants. The mortgage document contains the names of the lender and the borrower, a legal description of the property, and the amount, interest rate, maturity date, and terms of repayment of the debt; in addition, it contains a statement of the things that the borrower contracts to do—to pay taxes, special assessments, and other public charges against the property; to keep the property in good repair; to keep the property fully insured against fire, tornado, and other hazards; and to make no substantial changes in the property without the prior consent of the lender. Other clauses may be inserted to cover special circumstances (such as the release of mortgaged property prior to payment of the debt, substitution of property for the released property, application of cash to the debt in case of sale of the released property, and so on).

Value of Mortgage Liens. A business firm may give a mortgage lien on real property in order to obtain funds at lower cost; however, if the earnings of the debtor are inadequate to meet interest and principal payments on the debt, the value of the assets pledged as security will probably be inadequate to meet the same obligations in case of a foreclosure or liquidation sale. Nevertheless, the creditors have prospects of collecting something of value from the sale of the mortgaged assets; in addition, they also participate on the same basis as the unsecured creditors in the distribution of the remaining assets of the corporation.

Originally, mortgages were associated with financing purchases of farms, homes, and other small properties that had relatively stable market value. If the mortgage loan amounted to 50 or 60 per cent of the appraised value of the property, it was assumed that creditors would be fully protected even if some shrinkage in value took place at a foreclosure sale. This same assumption cannot be made in regard to the foreclosure value of mortgaged property of modern business enterprises which may have little value except when being used by a "going concern."

The chief value of a first mortgage lien to creditors is that it gives them a prior claim to the earnings of the debtor corporation. Earnings must be available for the accumulation of funds to retire debts and to meet interest obligations. A prior lien is important because it indicates the relative treatment in reorganization or liquidation, but earning power is essential to the preservation of values. When a company, such as a railroad, is being operated under supervision of the court, the receiver may continue to meet interest payments on senior obligations while junior obligations are in default.

The holders of first mortgage notes or bonds have the same type of prior claim to earnings as creditors have over stockholders, or preferred stockholders have over common stockholders. It is true that a corporation may pass a preferred or common stock dividend without exposing itself to legal proceedings as would be the case if it failed to pay interest on a junior debt, but the essential difference among the securities of a company is in the priority of claims to earnings and assets. As in the case of all types of long-term lending, lenders are customarily repaid with funds from operations accounted for as depreciation allowances and profits resulting from the use of fixed assets. Without earning power, the assets of a corporation have little value other than for scrap. Another aspect of a mortgage lien on business property is that it gives the lender a device to restrict or discipline the borrower.

Title of Mortgages or Mortgage Bonds. The title of a mortgage or a mortgage bond ought to give information about the terms of the mortgage or mortgage bond issue; for illustration, a first, second, or third mortgage or mortgage bond issue should indicate the priority of claims of the holders to earnings and assets of the borrower. However, in order to enhance their investment appeal, issuers may give misleading titles to mortgages or mortgage bonds. There is investment appeal to the words *first* and *general;* hence, issuers may use titles such as first refunding, first consolidated, first general, and first and refunding, when any one of these mortgages may represent junior liens. Any mortgage that has a secondary claim to property is a junior mortgage and the term "junior" is usually applied to all except first mortgages. When the term "underlying" is used to designate senior mortgages and the term "overlying" is used to designate junior mortgages, the emphasis is on the proximity of the lien to the property pledged.

As the title suggests, a consolidated mortgage or unified mortgage is one created to replace or unify two or more mortgages already in existence. The new mortgage may result from the unification of the mortgages of several creditors or the unification of several mortgages of the same creditor. The consolidated mortgage is often associated with a merger or consolidation of two or more companies. A general or blanket mortgage is one that covers several pieces of real property. A specific mortgage is one on a particular property. A participating mortgage is one in which two or more lenders share.

Mortgages are also classified according to the type of property pledged as security—equipment, bridges, leaseholds, and plant and office buildings; how the funds are to be used—construction, improvement, and refunding; and business of the borrower—commercial, industrial, public utility, railroad, and real estate company.

SPECIAL TYPES OF MORTGAGE PROVISIONS

Closed Mortgages. A mortgage may limit the amount of notes or bonds of equal rank that may be issued under its provisions. Once this amount of debt has been created, the mortgage is said to be closed. The typical terms in closed mortgage covenants cover cases where the entire amount of the authorized debt is to be created at once. In some cases, the terms permit creation of debts at different times until the entire amount authorized has been created. Sometimes, the debtor may take action through creation of a supplementary indenture to close the mortgage before the entire amount authorized has been exhausted.

When a closed mortgage is used, the prior claims to assets of the first mortgage creditors must be recognized in supplementary financing. There may be additional borrowing on an unsecured basis, with junior mortgages, or on pledges of any property not covered in the first mortgage covenant. With the exception of small companies, financing with closed-end mortgages has been replaced by the use of open-end or limited open-end mortgages.

Open-End Mortgages. A mortgage which is not limited to a specified amount of debt is called an open-end or indeterminate mortgage. The new bonds or notes issued under an open-end mortgage have the same priority as to assets as those previously issued under its provisions. First mortgage bonds of the same rank may be issued provided certain prescribed conditions are met. The original issue of first mortgage bonds may be for $65 million, which may be followed by later issues of similar bonds, thus increasing the total amount of first mortgage bonds outstanding (see Table 23).

TABLE 23

SCHEDULE OF LONG-TERM DEBT—DECEMBER 31, 1959

PHILADELPHIA ELECTRIC COMPANY	
First and Refunding Mortgage Bonds	
2¾% Series due 1967	$ 65,000,000
2¾% Series due 1971	20,000,000
2¾% Series due 1974	65,000,000
2⅞% Series due 1978	25,000,000
2¾% Series due 1981	35,000,000
3⅛% Series due 1983	20,000,000
3⅛% Series due 1985	50,000,000
4⅜% Series due 1986	50,000,000
4⅝% Series due 1987	40,000,000
3⅜% Series due 1988	40,000,000
5% Series due 1989	50,000,000
Total Philadelphia Electric Company	$460,000,000
PHILADELPHIA ELECTRIC POWER COMPANY—A SUBSIDIARY	
First Mortgage Bonds	
2⅝% Series due 1975 (excludes amount due within one year)	$ 30,613,000
Total Long-Term Debt	$490,613,000

Source: Philadelphia Electric Company, *Annual Report for the Year 1959* (Philadelphia, 1960), p. 29

Usually the mortgage indenture covers in detail the conditions under which a debtor corporation may finance under an open-end mortgage. Among the more common provisions are those which limit additional financing on the basis of the relationship between interest charges and earnings, new debt and property acquired, mortgage debt and net current assets, and mortgage debt and net worth.

A typical indenture provision is one which requires earnings available for interest payments to be at least twice the interest charges upon the existing funded debt plus the debt to be created. Usually earnings for a stated period are considered because the stability of earnings is equally as important as the amount as of a certain date. The trust indenture may specify that the corporation must have earned each month for the preceding twenty-four months an amount equal to at least twice the computed interest charges.

The trust indenture may specify that the property acquired must have more value than the new debt which is created (for example, the new debt may be only 50, 60, or 70 per cent of the fair value or actual cost of the new property). The position of old creditors will not be weakened by the issuance of new bonds if assets are being acquired more rapidly than debt (assuming that the same margin of protection is being maintained).

Debts may be related to net current assets of a business concern; as the latter increase, the amount of new bonds may increase. The indenture provision may specify that funded debt must not exceed net current assets or some percentage thereof. This restriction stresses the liquidity of a business firm's assets as related to its long-term debts.

A corporation may not be permitted to borrow with additional mortgage notes or bonds if the mortgage debt in existence and to be created exceeds the capital stock and surplus or net worth of the business firm. Also included may be restrictions as to the amount of new mortgage debt that may be created in any one year and specifications as to the standards that must be maintained before dividends can be paid.[1]

---

[1] For illustration, the mortgage indenture of the Philadelphia Electric Company "requires that the Company's maintenance expenditures plus provisions for depreciation and amortization plus earned surplus remaining after deducting dividends, all on a cumulative basis from December 31, 1940 to the end of each calendar year, shall be not less than 16% of the Company's Base Operating Revenues for each such period." Since these items have always exceeded the 16% specified, it has not interfered with the payment of dividends on the common stock. (Philadelphia Electric Company, *Prospectus* [pertaining to issue of 640,306 shares of common stock], June 2, 1959, p. 11.)

Usually, one or more of the above restrictions are found in the mortgage deed or trust indenture of any company borrowing under provisions of either an open-end or limited open-end mortgage. Under such a mortgage, a corporation may issue bonds at different times under the same indenture (the interest rates and maturities of different series may vary). This is illustrated by the first mortgage bonds of the Union Electric Company which are as follows:[2]

First mortgage bonds—	
4⅜% Series due 1988	$ 35,000,000
3¾% Series due 1986	40,000,000
3⅜% Series due 1971	90,000,000
3¼% Series due 1982	30,000,000
2⅞% Series due 1980	25,000,000
2¾% Series due 1975	13,000,000
3% Debentures due 1968	20,000,000
Total Union Electric Company	$253,000,000

Limited Open-End Mortgages. Limited open-end mortgages permit new issues of notes or bonds of the same rank up to a stated amount; when that amount is issued, the mortgage is closed. Limited open-end mortgages have two characteristics that are similar to open-end mortgages; both permit a larger authorization of bonds than the amount outstanding and the issuance of additional bonds of equal rank if prescribed conditions are met. Limited open-end mortgages have one characteristic that is similar to a closed-end mortgage—once the total amount of bonds authorized has been issued, no more bonds of equal rank may be issued. If the limit set is far in excess of the present and anticipated future needs of the borrower, the mortgage may be no more restrictive than an open-end mortgage. From the viewpoint of the business firm, the chief advantage of an open-end mortgage is that additional borrowing is permitted without the use of junior mortgages which normally carry a higher interest rate. While it may be assumed that a debtor would not borrow unless he could meet his obligations, management may be too optimistic about the future of the business venture and may borrow excessively. In mortgage covenants and trust indentures, business concerns are required to follow sound financial procedures which should be followed irrespective of specific requirements.

MORTGAGES ON AFTER-ACQUIRED PROPERTY

After-Acquired Property Clause. Sometimes the after-acquired property clause is inserted in the mortgage agreement. This clause

[2] Union Electric Company, *Annual Report for the Year Ended December 31, 1959* (St. Louis, 1960), p. 26.

means that the creditors are given the protection provided by not only existing property but also property subsequently acquired by the debtor. Most commonly, this clause has been interpreted by the courts to include all real property and, in some cases, all personal property affixed to the mortgaged property. To avoid confusion, the terms of the mortgage should indicate clearly that personal property subsequently acquired does not constitute a part of the building or plant and that it is to be excluded from the mortgage. The mortgage deed or trust indenture may be even more explicit by stating that only property which is acquired with the proceeds of the present or future sale of first mortgage notes or bonds is to come under the lien of the mortgage.

When the after-acquired clause is inserted in a closed-end mortgage, it tends to raise the standard of security by bringing more and more property behind the same amount of mortgage notes or bonds; when used with open-end mortgages, it tends to maintain the existing standard of security by requiring new property purchased to come under the mortgage to secure the additional notes or bonds. If a company is expanding, a closed-end mortgage with an after-acquired clause tends to be a handicap when arranging for a new loan; however, the after-acquired clause is less restrictive when used with open-end mortgages.

The history of financing in the railroad and public utility fields indicates that emphasis has shifted from closed-end to open-end or limited open-end mortgages. Now, closed-end mortgages are most common among small companies. Customarily smaller companies, whose mortgages outstanding are of the closed-end type, finance with retained earnings and equity capital; but, when these mortgages are for fifteen years or less, a second mortgage loan or bond issue may be negotiated.

Methods of Circumventing After-Acquired Clause Restrictions. There are ways whereby the after-acquired clause or the restrictions resulting therefrom may be circumvented. These include—in addition to calling or refunding bonds—giving the vendor of property acquired a purchase-money mortgage, acquiring the use of additional property by a lease, organizing a subsidiary corporation to hold title to newly acquired property, and merging or consolidating the debtor corporation with another company or other companies.

A purchase-money mortgage, which may be used to circumvent the after-acquired property clause, gives the seller a prior lien on the property for the amount represented by the mortgage. For illustration, if a down payment of 50 per cent is made for property valued at $2,000,000 and a purchase-money mortgage (so called because it is used in lieu of part of the purchase price) is given for the remainder, the mortgage would be for $1,000,000. The purchase-money mortgage is treated as if it were attached to the property at the time of transfer. Thus, the property would be acquired with a first mortgage already on it. Only the equity that the corporation has invested in the property would be affected by the after-acquired property clause.

A lease arrangement may be made as a substitute for a purchase of new property when such property would come under an existing mortgage because of the after-acquired property clause. A lease arrangement requires the use of a contract which gives the lessee the right of possession and use of the property for a specified period of time. A survey made by the Department of Commerce indicates that more than one half of the retailers and wholesale distributors rent their business premises, and over one half of the retailers and two thirds of the wholesalers have leases. Manufacturers and other industrial companies, as well as railroads and public utility companies, use leases of different types.

In order to prevent new property from coming under an existing mortgage, a corporation may organize a subsidiary corporation to take title to such property. Then, the subsidiary may arrange for a mortgage loan or an issue of mortgage bonds with the property pledged as security. The use of this legal subterfuge to avoid the after-acquired property clause is but one minor reason for the creation of subsidiaries.

Merger or consolidation, "legal suicide," may be used by a corporation as a device to overcome the restrictive effects of the after-acquired property clause in an outstanding mortgage indenture. By consolidation or merger, the debtor corporation loses its identity, and its obligations become the obligations of the successor corporation. Modern corporation laws specifically state that "neither the rights of creditors nor any liens upon the property of any such corporation shall be impaired by such merger or consolidation."

Thus liens on property taken over by consolidated corporations have priority over liens subsequently executed. Nevertheless, the covenant in the mortgage deed to place "all its property owned or hereafter acquired" in the mortgage lien is not interpreted as being an obligation of the successor corporation. Thus the mortgage lien of a selling company, containing the after-acquired clause in the mortgage indenture under which assumed bonds were issued, does not apply to property acquired after the acquisition of assets of the selling company by the buying company.

On the other hand, most mortgage indentures have provisions that limit the merger or consolidation of the debtor corporation as long as the mortgage lien is in effect (which illustrates how creditors tend to plug up loopholes in the law that work to their disadvantage).

BUSINESS USES OF REAL ESTATE LOANS

Use by Small Firms. Probably at least 60 per cent of all direct business loans outstanding are secured; and, according to available statistics on secured business loans, approximately 25 per cent of the number and 20 per cent of the dollar value of these loans are secured by real property. Real estate loans are more common among small business firms than large ones.[3] A small firm may have inexperienced management, no previous borrowing record, and no adequate financial statements or records. These factors may cause a bank to demand security, and the only acceptable security which many small business firms have to offer is real estate.

Cost of Borrowing. Interest rates on real estate loans to business firms are usually higher than the rates on other types of business loans. In addition, there are other costs of borrowing such as title search, appraisal of property, recording of the mortgage, insurance, and other fees. The lender expects the borrower to provide either an abstract of title (a history of the title to the property) and an attorney's opinion based on the abstract of title or a mortgagee's title insurance policy; evidence of payment of all taxes other than those for the current year; fire, tornado, and other types of property insurance policies; and a written appraisal showing the dimensions, exact location, and other details of the property signed by a qualified appraiser. Because these added costs are large, real estate loans are rarely made for short terms such as six months. (It would be more appropriate to borrow on an unsecured basis or to pledge working capital assets for short-term funds.)

Use in Financing Commercial Property. Among the business enterprises using real property as security for long-term debts are real estate and other companies which build and/or own office buildings, large apartment buildings, hotels, store buildings, and

---

[3] Small business enterprises are defined as those with total assets of less than $750,000 for firms in the manufacturing field, $250,000 in the wholesale trade field, and $50,000 in the retail, service, construction, and other fields of industry.

other commercial properties as investments (not occupancy). When a retail store (or other business firm) buys its own building, the purchase is financed in part with a mortgage loan made by a commercial bank, mutual savings bank, savings and loan association, or life insurance company. In some cases, two or more lenders may participate in a single real estate mortgage loan. Loan values usually vary from 50 to 60 per cent of the appraised value of the property. Thus, substantial equity is required of real estate companies who own property as investments; and if the company is incorporated, these funds may be obtained by the sale of stock.

Practically all real estate loans on commercial property are amortized with the first installments being larger than those for later years. The loans may run from five to thirty years, depending on the location, nature and use of the property, the credit of the borrower, and the lender. The amortization schedule for shorter-term loans may not provide for complete repayment of the loan; and, as a result, the unpaid balance may be refinanced with a new mortgage loan at maturity. Prepayment of the principal may be permitted under certain circumstances as stated in the mortgage covenant. Under certain conditions, a company (particularly a real estate company) may not be allowed to pay dividends on its common stock during the period of amortization of the loan; in other cases, the amount of dividends may be limited.[4]

Use in Financing Industrial Property. To an increasing extent, both large and small manufacturing and other industrial companies are financing the purchase and/or construction of office, warehouse, and factory buildings with ordinary real estate loans. Industrial buildings usually have specialized use and therefore are poorer security than structures having less limited use. As a result, compared to commercial property, industrial property usually has less loan value, loan maturities are shorter (often ten years or less), and amortization schedules are more rigorous. The amortization schedule may call for repayment of one half of the loan during the first five years in monthly or quarterly installments. The mortgage covenant may contain those clauses which are common for real estate mortgages plus many of those found in term loan agreements (maintenance of working capital, restrictions on payment of dividends, etc.).

---

[4] In the 1920's, large office buildings, hotels, and other commercial buildings were financed with issues of real estate bonds similar to those issued by railroads and public utility companies; but, because of the poor record of such bonds during the 1930's, real estate bonds of this type are now rarely issued.

BUSINESS USES OF REAL ESTATE MORTGAGE BONDS

Financing with real estate bonds necessitates open-market financing, while the use of real estate loans permits direct negotiation between borrowers and lenders. Thus, a small business firm is faced with the same difficulties when attempting to finance with a real estate bond issue as noted previously for other types of open-market financing by small unknown firms. Therefore, most of the long-term credit needs of small business firms are met by real estate mortgage credit provided by insurance companies and savings institutions.

Large nationally known corporations with relatively large fixed assets, as compared to working capital assets, are the chief users of mortgage bonds in raising capital in the open market. When classified according to major groups, public utility companies are the most important users of mortgage bonds, ranking ahead of manufacturing companies which make more use of debenture bonds and stock. Among the other major groups financing with mortgage bonds are communication and transportation companies.

Customarily, corporations issue secured bonds rather than unsecured bonds in order to reduce the cost of financing, to satisfy investment bankers' demands for security when negotiating for the purchase of bond issues, and/or to follow established custom. The ability to obtain a higher price for a secured bond issue (or to borrow at a lower interest rate) is due to the fact that investors are willing to pay for their preferential position over unsecured creditors to earnings and—in case of reorganization or liquidation—to assets of the debtor.

While investment bankers have an important role in determining the terms that appear in bond issues, neither the investment banker nor the issuer dares to ignore the wishes of investors who determine the success or failure of an issue. Most investors in corporate bonds are conservative; and, if they have been accustomed to buying secured obligations, the issuer and investment banker will offer such securities when it is the normal practice. Now, bond offerings must meet the professional standards set by institutional investors—insurance companies, trust and pension funds, mutual savings banks, and others. Although individual investors are important buyers of goverment obligations (such as savings bonds) and common stock, they have practically disappeared from the corporate bond market.

In appraising the investment merit of corporate bond issues, individual and institutional investors now have access to more information upon which to base their decisions. The Securities Act of 1933 requires corporations financing under its provisions to file certain information with the Securities and Exchange Commission. This information about the issuer and the securities being offered is available to the general public. Since the 1920's, there have been improvements in financial accounting and reporting. The three primary financial statements (income, balance sheet, and earned surplus) have been refined and modified to fulfill their functions more effectively. In keeping with the stress on income rather than on assets as being the best determinant of investment value, there has been greater emphasis on the use of income statements in investment analysis.

The position of some bondholders has also been strengthened by their corporations' financing more with equities and less with debts. The fact that certain corporations in the railroad and public utility fields must obtain approval of governmental agencies before selling new issues of bonds has contributed to this development. For illustration, statistics provided by the Securities and Exchange Commission show that regulated holding companies and their subsidiaries have a higher proportion of new common stock issues than unregulated public utility companies.[5] Any change in the capital structure of a corporation that indicates that trading on equity has declined means that the security of bondholders has improved. Nevertheless, for the last decade, borrowing with bond issues has been the largest on record. This has been true in spite of the fact that there has been an increase in the use of term loans and in financing with retained earnings in addition to some financing with common and preferred stock. Lower interest rates and the corporate income tax advantage have been factors in the preference for debt financing over equity financing; but the chief reason for the expansion in bond financing has been the increase in business, as measured by the gross national product.

Sources of Mortgage Funds. Sources of mortgage funds include commercial banks, insurance companies, personal trusts, savings institutions, private pension funds, and other financial institutions. One principle of commercial bank lending is that a commercial bank's demand deposits should not be tied up in the capital structure of the business firms of its customers. However, most commercial banks accept time deposits as well as demand deposits, and the funds received

[5] *Seventeenth Annual Report of the Securities and Exchange Commission Fiscal Year Ended June 30, 1951* (Washington, D.C.: U.S. Government Printing Office, 1952), pp. 107–8.

from savings depositors may be lent or invested in longer term obligations than those received from demand depositors. Hence, many small business firms find their local banks to be an important source of mortgage credit. In some states, where statutes provide for "business homesteads," this type of lending is handicapped because such statutes restrict creditors from resorting to forced sales in order to satisfy their claims. As a result, business firms may have to limit their mortgage loans for the purpose of purchasing business property or financing improvements thereon.

Relative to the maturities of mortgage loans made by lenders other than commercial banks, mortgage loans made by commercial banks are short term. Although loans for as long as ten years are not unusual, studies of commercial banks' loans indicate that typical maturities are from three to five years. However, such loans are frequently renewed in whole or part; therefore, the stated maturities of banks' mortgage loans may be misleading. Continuous bank loan renewals are most frequent for borrowers in the transportation, communication, and public utility industries, wherein the long-term capital needs are larger than in industries such as commodity dealers and finance companies.

Lenders other than commercial banks are subject to fewer legal and operating restrictions; therefore insurance companies, personal trusts, savings banks, private pension funds, and other financial institutions are more important sources of long-term mortgage funds for business firms than are commercial banks. The most important external or outside source of long-term business funds is insurance companies, whose investment of all types in business firms amount to about $50 billion. About one half of these investments are in the form of corporate bonds, notes, and debentures of industrial and other companies exclusive of public utility and railroad companies. Life insurance companies hold approximately one third (over $16 billion) of the debts of electric light, gas, and communication companies of the United States and about $3.8 billion of the railroad bonds outstanding. To an increasing extent, life insurance companies are acquiring corporate bonds and notes through direct negotiations with business firms. Statistics are not broken down to show the percentage of bonds and notes secured by real property, but the volume of such credit instruments held by life insurance companies is large. (In addition, life insurance companies have investments of over $4 billion in preferred and common stock of utility, industrial, and railroad companies.)[6] Some individual companies now obtain most of their loan capital from insurance companies. For illustration, all of the long-term debt obligations of the Anaconda Company (excluding obligations of subsidiaries) are held by insurance companies.[7]

About three fourths of life insurance companies' business loans outstanding are in amounts of less than $250,000. Those in amounts of $10 million and over are participated in with other life insurance companies or banks; the average participation is about $2.5 million for each participant. The interest rate is usually higher on small loans because the administation costs are higher and the credit risk is greater than on large loans.

Most life insurance company loans to small businesses are based on real estate mortgages. Although almost any type of business building may be pledged, the most common types pledged are retail stores, general office buildings, and manufacturing plants. The average loan on office buildings is the largest—over $500,000—and those on hotels, theaters, and garages are second in average amount —about $350,000. Some insurance company business loans are made to finance purchase and installation of heavy machinery and equipment which is usually pledged as security.

By making policy loans, life insurance companies provide funds that may be used for working capital needs and for other purposes. On such loans, the companies are under contractual obligation to lend upon the security of the cash surrender value of a life insurance policy, but relatively few loans of this type are made (less than 4 per cent of the assets of life insurance companies are in policy loans). Since the interest rate on these loans is fixed by contract, one might expect businessmen to make greater use of them as a source of funds when money markets are tight and when it is difficult to borrow at low interest rates.

In evaluating the importance of insurance companies as a source of business funds, the statistics should include investments in commercial and industrial rental properties which are held under leaseback arrangements with business firms (such as those of office buildings, shopping centers, industrial parks, and research centers). Finally, an unknown quantity of capital used for business purposes

[6] See also, Institute of Life Insurance, *Life Insurance Fact Book, 1959* (New York, 1959), pp. 71–80.

[7] The $65,000,000 insurance loans of the Anaconda Company are being repaid in equal installments of $4,600,000 on September 1st of each year from 1965 to 1977 and the balance on September 1, 1978 (with certain options available that permit prepayment). The Anaconda Company, *Annual Report 1959* (Butte, Montana, 1960), p. 22.

is obtained through loans on life insurance policies and loans secured by homes and other nonfarm properties.

Personal trusts that are managed by trust companies and commercial banks provide a surprisingly large volume of business funds (over $50 billion), but most of these funds (over two thirds) are invested in corporate stock and only a small amount in corporate bonds and mortgages. Personal trusts are far more important in the ownership of corporate stock than investment companies, the specialists in the field. However, private pension funds are second only to insurance companies in the ownership of corporate bonds, and they are almost as important as investment companies in the ownership of common stock. The latter's investments are chiefly in common stock, but they hold some corporate bonds. Although mutual savings banks and savings and loan associations specialize in home mortgage financing, they make some mortgage loans to business firms. Most of the resources of sales finance companies, personal finance companies, and credit unions are used to finance the personal needs of consumers rather than the capital needs of business firms.

SUMMARY

The decline in public relative to private offerings of bonds has been due to two major developments: (1) the abundance of funds available to large institutional investors and (2) the regulation of open-market financing. The real estate mortgage loan is the most common form of long-term loan, and the principles involved therein are adapted for use in financing with real estate mortgage bonds.

The two basic documents in a simple real estate mortgage loan are the note and the mortgage; in a mortgage bond issue, the documents include a mortgage, a bond indenture, and a bond. A real estate mortgage is more generally regarded as a lien on the mortgaged property than as a conditional conveyance or transfer of title to real property given by the borrower to the lender as security for payment of a debt. In many cases, failure to meet mortgage debt obligations does not result in liquidation of the business firm but rather in its financial reorganization. The reorganization plans are customarily made to protect the contractual rights of security holders, which means the first mortgage holders are given preferential treatment.

When a mortgage bond indenture limits the amount of notes or bonds of equal rank that may be issued under its provisions, the mortgage is said to be closed when this amount of debt has been created. A mortgage that permits more borrowing under the mortgage is called an open-end mortgage; when a limit is fixed for new issues of notes or bonds, it is known as a limited open-end mortgage. The mortgage indenture covers the conditions under which the debtor may finance under an open-end or limited open-end mortgage. These restrictions may be related to earnings of the corporation, value of the new property, net current assets, or net worth of the firm.

The after-acquired property clause may appear in mortgage agreements. There are several ways whereby this clause may be circumvented, such as giving the vendor of the property acquired a purchase-money mortgage, acquiring the use of property by a lease, organizing a subsidiary corporation to hold title to the newly acquired property, or merging or consolidating a debtor corporation with another company.

Real estate loans made by commercial banks, insurance companies, and other lenders are most common among small business firms. Interest rates on real estate loans to business firms are usually a little higher than those on other types of business loans, but the cost of borrowing includes other expenses in addition to interest charges. Unless guaranteed or insured, mortgages vary from 50 to 60 per cent of the appraised value of the property covered; practically all real estate loans on commercial property are made on an amortization basis. The loan value for industrial property is usually less than for commercial property, the maturity of the loans is usually shorter, and the amortization schedule is usually more rigorous. Mortgage bonds issued by a corporation are secured by a mortgage conveying or assigning all or a specific part of the corporation's assets to a designated trustee as security for the payment of the bonds. The mortgage bond indenture includes the mortgage and the trust indenture containing the covenants and provisions found in a typical contract of this type. This indenture also covers the procedures to be followed in case of consolidation, merger, and sale of assets; it usually contains provisions or clauses drawn so as to protect the rights of creditors.

QUESTIONS AND PROBLEMS

1. Identify: (*a*) real estate mortgage; (*b*) open-end, limited open-end, and closed mortgages; (*c*) terms found in a mortgage document; and (*d*) legal aspects as to transfer of title.
2. Explain the chief value of a first mortgage lien to bondholders in terms of income and property rights.
3. Identify: (*a*) consolidated mortgage, (*b*) blanket mortgage, (*c*) specific mortgage, (*d*) participating mortgage, and (*e*) multiple mortgage structure.

4. What are the advantages to a corporation of using open-end or limited open-end mortgages? Are there clauses in trust indentures to protect bondholders? Illustrate.
5. (*a*) Identify the "after-acquired property" clause. (*b*) What is the purpose of using it and how does it tend to affect the borrower? (*c*) Give four methods whereby a corporation may circumvent the restrictions resulting from the after-acquired property clause in an outstanding mortgage.
6. (*a*) What classes of business firms are the chief users of real estate mortgage notes and bonds? (*b*) Why do corporations issue secured rather than unsecured bonds?
7. Note and explain the role of life insurance companies in financing business firms.
8. Justify the policy of management in offering two security issues at the same time as indicated by the following: "Southwestern Public Service Co. registered $15 million of 30-year first mortgage bonds and 120,000 shares of $25 par cumulative preferred stock with the Securities and Exchange Commission." (*Wall Street Journal* [New York], February 13, 1961, p. 9.) What are the characteristics of each of these security issues?
9. Analyze: "Atlantic City Electric Co. registered $10 million of 30-year first mortgage bonds for public sale at competitive bidding." (*Wall Street Journal* [New York], February 13, 1961, p. 9.)
10. Explain: "Lake Superior District Power Co. awarded its $3 million of single-A rated first mortgage bonds to Saloman Bros. & Hutzler and Baxter & Co." (*Wall Street Journal* [New York], February 8, 1961, p. 11.)
11. Explain why the dollar amount of securities in the form of debts is generally larger per issue than the amount in the form of preferred or common stock, as shown in problem 8 above.
12. "Georgia Power plans $29.5 million of new financing this year, including $15.5 million of first mortgage bonds, $8 million of preferred stock and $6 million of common stock. . . . the balance of the 1961 construction budget will be met from depreciation reserves, deferred income taxes and cash on hand." (*Wall Street Journal* [New York], January 27, 1961, p. 5.) Explain.

CHAPTER 22

Special Types of Corporate Obligations

MANY CORPORATIONS issue unsecured long-term obligations called debentures or debenture bonds. Although such bonds are supported only by the general credit of the issuing corporation, if they are the only outstanding obligations of the issuer, their owners have first claim to earnings and assets of the corporation. Because of the ready marketability of rolling stock of railroads and of stocks and bonds owned by corporations, corporations may issue special obligations using these assets as security. Often the probability of recovery by creditors is greater in the case of default on railroad equipment (secured by rolling stock) and on collateral trust bonds (secured by stocks and bonds) than on mortgage bonds. This chapter deals with three special types of obligations: equipment obligations, collateral trust bonds, and debentures.

EQUIPMENT OBLIGATIONS

Business concerns often pledge tangible personal property as security for debts in order to obtain funds at a lower interest rate, in larger amounts, or for longer periods of time. The pledged property should be easy to identify; consequently, such items of equipment as automobiles, tractors, and locomotives having serial numbers—and other types of property to which labels may be attached—are often used. In many cases, the sum required in one purchase transaction is sufficiently large to justify open-market financing with bonds, notes, or trust certificates. Although techniques differ, many of the principles used in mercantile and installment sales are applicable to railroad equipment financing.

Terms of Sale of Equipment. Like individuals purchasing durable consumers' goods on the installment plan, buyers of railroad equipment are expected to make down payments of from 10 to 25 per cent and to pay the balance plus interest and other financing charges on the installment plan. In addition, buyers contract to keep the property in good physical condition; to carry adequate fire, public liability, and other insurance; to pay all taxes; to attach a metal plate on each piece of equipment showing that the trustee is the owner or holds title; periodically, to provide statements showing the location and condition of the property; and to indemnify the trustee for claims arising out of use of any of the property.

In arranging for amortization of the principal, the payment period is shorter than the expected life of the equipment so that there will always be some value behind any part of the debt still outstanding. The payment period for rolling stock of railroads may be from ten to twenty years, but is usually about fifteen years.

Methods of Financing Unpaid Installments. The manufacturer or vendor may carry the financing burden if his funds are adequate or he may sell his unpaid balances to a large bank or insurance company, as in receivables financing. In other cases, the purchaser may raise funds by open-market financing. When the amount needed is large, open-market financing may be more feasible and more economical than other methods. Although there are extra financing charges associated with open-market financing (for example, trustees' fees, investment bankers' fees, and other fees and charges), the interest rate is usually lower.

In order to appeal to a large number of investors, notes, bonds, or trust certificates are issued in convenient denominations, such as $1,000 or multiples thereof, when open-market financing is used. Usually, maturities are arranged so that a given number mature the first year, the same number the second year, and so on throughout the life of the issue. For illustration, if an issue consists of 1,500 bonds, notes, or trust certificates, 100 units may mature each year over a 15-year period. During the interim, the railroad, like a consumer buying a car on the installment plan, will have possession and use of the rolling stock but may not have a clear title to it. Equipment notes, bonds, or trust certificates are issued under one of three plans: the equipment mortgage plan, the conditional sales plan, or the trust lease plan.

Equipment Mortgage Plan. The equipment mortgage plan uses an ordinary note or bond secured by a chattel mortgage on specified tangible personal property. A chattel mortgage note or bond is one executed by the maker (borrower) on specific personal property owned by him. This means that the issuer of the equipment notes or bonds must have title to the property before he can use it in financing as security for a loan irrespective of the form of the borrowing (direct or open-market). If the railroad takes title to property, it may mean that the property will come under any "after-acquired property clause" in an outstanding bond contract. Therefore, the railroad company may want to arrange for obtaining possession of the equipment without acquiring title (see below). However, some railroads may be in a position to take title without the property being subject to a prior lien, and this is the assumption in the following case. The railroad company makes a down payment on the equipment and takes title and possession of the equipment from the manufacturer. Then the railroad company executes a trust indenture agreement with a trust company or bank conveying title to the railroad equipment to the trustee (in trust for creditors) in the same manner as under ordinary mortgage financing as previously explained. There will be special covenants in the mortgage pertaining to payment of the debts, taxes, and insurance, as well as maintenance of property, action to be taken in case of default on the debt, etc.

In order to raise cash to pay the amount owed, the railroad company issues notes or bonds which are sold under competitive bidding to investment bankers, insurance companies, or other investors. If an underwriting syndicate is the successful bidder, the securities are usually resold to other investors; but, if institutional investors acquire the issue, the securities are usually held by them as investments. Competitive bidding is the standard procedure for selling issues of railroad equipment obligations, including trust certificates as well as bonds and notes. Because of the use of serial notes or bonds, the total debt will decline progressively as the issue approaches maturity.

The trust company holding the trust indenture handles the routine details of collecting installment payments from the railroad, paying interest and principal when due, and—in case of default—taking possession of the equipment. In addition, the trust company must see that recording fees and taxes are paid, that the railroad equipment covered by the issue is properly marked with a metal plate for identification purposes, and that the railroad files periodic reports as to location and condition of the equipment.

Conditional Sales Plan or New York Plan. In the preceding section, it was noted that railroad companies may want to avoid taking title to equipment which they wish to pledge as security for a bond or note issue; one legal device used in this case is the conditional sales or purchase contract. A conditional sale is one wherein title to goods or equipment is not vested in the buyer until fulfillment of some specific condition, which is usually payment of the final installment of the buyer's contract. There is no outright sale; the user has a conditional rather than a clear title. Although the goods are in the buyer's possession, he is not the owner until he has fulfilled the required conditions.

Under a conditional sales arrangement, after the railroad places the order with the manufacturer and makes the down payment (earnest money), the trustee takes title to the equipment, sells the equipment obligations, completes the payment to the manufacturer, and makes a conditional sale of the equipment to the railroad company. The conditional sales contract will require the railroad company to make a given number of deferred payments, with title to the equipment remaining with the trustee until all payments have been made. Thus, a conditional sales plan of financing railroad equipment is arranged so that the trustee is the one who buys the equipment from the manufacturer and then makes a prearranged conditional sale to the railroad company.[1]

Cash to pay the manufacturer is obtained by an issue of serial notes or bonds which is sold to the highest bidder. The trustee assumes responsibility for the serial notes, and collects money from the railroad company in regular installments and uses it to meet interest charges and principal payments on the serial notes or bonds. When the last payment has been made, the railroad company takes title to the equipment.

The responsibilities of the trustee are the same under a conditional sales contract as under a chattel mortgage arrangement. Since the basic procedures for raising funds and administering the debt are the same, one may question why the conditional sales plan is used in preference to the chattel mortgage plan. The advantage claimed for the

---

[1] Sales may be arranged so that the railroad buys the property directly from the manufacturer, who then transfers the property to the trustee, which executes an agreement to sell it to the railroad for an initial cash payment and a number of deferred payments. The deferred payments are represented by bonds or notes. It is stipulated that title to the equipment rests with the trustee until all payments have been made when title passes to the railroad. If this method is used, it necessitates assuming the same legal hazard as noted when a railroad takes title when financing with a chattel mortgage.

conditional sales plan is that the railroad company does not acquire title to the equipment; thereby it avoids the possibility that the courts may rule that the equipment comes under the after-acquired property clause. Such a ruling would result in investors in the serial notes or bonds having but a secondary lien on the property.

Unfortunately, railroads may be faced with a similar problem of ownership when using conditional sales contracts; in certain states, the reservation of title in the seller (the bank or trust company) as provided in conditional sales contracts as described here may not be recognized. These state courts may rule that title is vested unconditionally in the railroad. The fact that rolling stock of a railroad company may pass through many states and does not "stay put" helps to explain the development of the lease purchase plan, or Philadelphia Plan, as a substitute for both the chattel mortgage and conditional sales plans.

Lease Purchase or Philadelphia Plan. The lease purchase or Philadelphia Plan was developed in order to evade the after-acquired property clause in railroad mortgages by making equipment obligations an indirect obligation of railroads and to meet the objection that conditional sales contracts are not legal in some states. The lease purchase plan consists of two parts: a trust agreement and a lease purchase agreement. This plan is usually referred to as the *lease plan* but the term *lease purchase* is used to distinguish it from the straight lease arrangement discussed below.

In the lease purchase arrangement, the railroad leases the property but the terms of the lease permit the railroad to take title to the property when principal payments and other obligations have been met. The trust company sells trust certificates in an amount sufficient to cover the cost of the equipment purchased. Rental payment (technically called dividend payment) schedules are arranged to meet the interest on the trust certificates and part of the principal. The railroad usually makes an "advance rental" payment equal to 20 per cent of the cost of the equipment which is, in effect, a down payment.

In the trust agreement, there are three parties: a trust company, which takes title to the equipment as trustee and becomes the issuer of equipment trust certificates; the manufacturer or seller, who receives a down payment in cash and the balance in cash from the sale of share certificates or equipment trust certificates for the remainder of the purchase price of the equipment; and the railroad company, which leases the equipment and provides the trust company with enough cash as advance rental to make the down payment to the manufacturer. Technically, the trust company and not the railroad sells the trust certificates to the highest bidder (competitive sales are required for equipment trust certificates as well as for railroad equipment notes and bonds), but customarily, the railroad is reported as the seller.[2]

The trust certificates are obligations of the trustee, but the railroad company may guarantee their payment by endorsement or otherwise. The advance rental reduces the amount of public financing and gives the margin of protection commonly required in installment financing. The terms of the lease require the railroad to pay taxes on the leased property, to keep it in good physical condition, to carry adequate insurance, to indemnify the trustee from all claims arising out of use or ownership of the property, to attach metal plates to the property to show that the trustee is the owner, and to make periodic reports on the location and condition of the property.

At one time, the lease purchase plan was by far the most important of the plans for financing rolling stock of railroads; but, in recent years, the conditional sales plan has gained in importance—air lines as well as truck lines use this plan relatively more than they use the other plans.[3] When railroad companies are faced with modernization expenditures of billions of dollars, the more liberal terms permitted by the conditional sales plan may account for the increase in its popularity. The bid and ask yield rates on equipment trust obligations indicate their strong investment position (see Table 24). The chief explanation for the difference in prices for different issues is the maturity—those with shorter terms being quoted at lower yield rates. Although some railroads are in receivership and are being reorganized, this situation is not reflected in the prices of their equipment bonds.

Equitable Life Lease Plan. An economical way whereby railroads may obtain the use of equipment is to lease it without any obligation to purchase the equipment. Although the laws of many states prohibit or limit insurance companies' investments in common stock, they permit the purchase of credit instruments and property. In 1949, the

[2] For illustration, on February 3, 1954, "the Pennsylvania Railroad" sold $5,265,000 serial trust certificates maturing over a 15-year period at public sealed bidding to a banking syndicate headed by Halsey, Stuart & Co., Inc. The borrowing cost was about 2.8 per cent (the bid having been 99.5626 for certificates bearing an interest rate of 2¾ per cent).

[3] According to the *New York Times* (January 4, 1954, p. 83), in 1953 about one half of the new railroad equipment purchased by railroad companies was financed under the conditional sales (New York) plan with practically no down payment.

Equitable Life Assurance Society of the United States announced a plan to purchase equipment outright and then lease it to railroads. This plan, which permitted a lease arrangement without a down payment and periodic interest and capital payments required under the Philadelphia Plan, was attractive to railroad companies and was accepted immediately.[4]

TABLE 24

RAILROAD EQUIPMENT BONDS

Name	*Maturities*	*Rates*	*Bid*	*Asked*
Atlantic Coast Line	1961–72	2½–4¼	4.65	4.35
Baltimore & Ohio	1961–73	1½–4¼	4.65	4.35
Chesapeake & Ohio	1961–74	1⅛–4⅝	4.40	4.20
Erie Railroad	1961–72	1⅝–4¾	5.50	5.00
Missouri Pacific	1961–73	2⅜–4¾	4.65	4.35
Texas & Pacific	1961–69	1¾–3⅞	4.60	4.30
Wabash Railroad	1961–72	1⅞–4½	4.60	4.30

Source: *New York Times*, January 26, 1961, p. 47.

In the Equitable Life lease plan there are two contracts: (1) the purchase sale contract between the insurance company and the manufacturer of equipment and (2) the equipment lease contract between the insurance company and the railroad. The insurance company buys the equipment directly from the manufacturer, paying 80 per cent cash and the remainder in installments maturing over a five-year period. Although the purchase terms are less favorable to the manufacturer than those under the older plans, the assurance of an increase in sales volume caused many manufacturers to accept it.

The lease signed by the railroad runs for fifteen years, with the per day rental for the equipment being largest during the first years and lowest during the last year. For illustration, the rental may be $1.55 per day for a $5,280 freight box car for the first three years, 50 cents per day for the last three years of the lease, and 20 cents per day thereafter if the lease is renewed. Rentals paid by the railroad are deducted as operating expenses in computing tax returns, and this item is large compared to the small depreciation allowance usually permitted on equipment purchased. However, railroads may acquire equipment under "certificates of necessity" which permit amortization of the investment for emergency facilities out of earnings over a

[4] See *Sixty-Fourth Annual Report of the Interstate Commerce Commission* (Washington, D.C.: U.S. Government Printing Office, 1951), pp. 38–41; and *Sixty-Fifth Annual Report of the Interstate Commerce Commission*, pp. 35–38.

five-year period. This arrangement may make outright ownership more attractive than the rental system.

Use of Equipment Obligations in Other Fields. The successful experiences of the railroad industry in financing with equipment obligations has led other industries to experiment with this method of financing. Air transport companies are financing, to some extent, with equipment trust certificates, bonds, and notes. Oil companies, chemical companies, and other industrial firms have used equipment obligations in financing special types of equipment (oil and chemical cars, fleets of cars and trucks of construction companies). But most of the equipment of these companies is being financed by finance companies, insurance companies, banks, and other lenders by direct installment loans.

COLLATERAL TRUST OBLIGATIONS

Collateral Notes. A popular form of direct borrowing from banks is by means of collateral notes secured by stocks and bonds. Usually such loans are for only a part of the value of the securities pledged (the amount depends on the securities pledged, the purpose of the loan, and the credit standing of the borrower). A collateral note contains a pledge of securities in addition to a promise to pay. One requirement in connection with a pledge is delivery of the pledged property to the pledgee (lender). In case of default, the lender is authorized to sell the pledged securities and to apply the proceeds to the loan. The borrower is entitled to any part of the net proceeds in excess of the obligation and is responsible for any deficiency. Unless there are specific provisions to the contrary, interest and/or dividends on the securities pledged are paid to the owner in the same manner as they would be if the securities were in his possession. Practically the same procedures are used in open-market financing with collateral trust bonds.

Collateral Trust Bonds. Collateral trust bonds are secured by pledges of stocks and/or bonds. As in other bond issues, a trust indenture held by a trustee includes the standard provisions of the bond indenture. Therefore, emphasis in this discussion is on the collateral aspects of this type of financing.

As provided for in a collateral trust indenture, the pledged property will be delivered by the corporation to a trustee to be held for the protection of bondholders. Customarily, the trustee will not authenticate (give authority, as by legal proof) the collateral trust bonds until the pledged securities are deposited with him. Stocks and registered bonds may remain in the name of the debtor or they may be transferred to the name of a nominee, such as an employee in the trustee's office. (The purpose in using a nominee is to facilitate the transfer of securities, which is easier when the securities are registered in the name of a person rather than a trust company or corporation.) In the case of a default on interest or principal payments on the collateral trust bonds, pledged securities remaining in the name of the debtor corporation are transferred to the name of a nominee or the trustee.

As long as interest and principal payments on collateral trust bonds are being met, the income from the pledged securities will be turned over to the pledgor (debtor); but, in case of default, all interest and dividend payments on securities held as collateral will be retained by the trustee. Usually all forms of capital distribution such as stock dividends, cash received as principal payments, and liquidating dividends on any securities held as collateral will be retained by the trustee as security for the collateral trust bonds.

Release of Securities. The collateral trust indenture may authorize the trustee to release pledged securities to the debtor corporation or to individuals who must own shares to qualify as directors, provided the securities are replaced in each case with others of equivalent or higher value. From a practical point of view, it is difficult to make this substitution provision foolproof. Sometimes, the indenture will specify the procedure to be used in determining if the securities offered as substitutes have equivalent or higher value; in other cases, the indenture may specify that only certain securities may be substituted (for illustration, United States government bonds).

Other Indenture Provisions. The collateral trust indenture usually permits the pledgor to vote pledged stock on all routine matters and the proxies are turned over to the debtor corporation as a matter of course, but the pledgor's right to vote is usually restricted if there is to be a vote on a fundamental change in the corporate structure (such as those pertaining to new financing, reorganizations, mergers, and consolidations). In case of default on interest or principal payments on the collateral trust bonds, the power to vote pledged stock reverts to the trustee.

Securities Pledged for Collateral Trust Bonds. Although a business corporation with large investments in stocks and bonds could avoid borrowing by selling these securities, there are many reasons why this is not done. The corporation may own stock in other corporations for control purposes, as best illustrated by a pure holding company. If such a corporation is to borrow in order to buy more stock, it may pledge the shares it holds as security for an issue of collateral trust bonds.

Many holding companies assume responsibility for financing their subsidiaries by buying their issues of bonds and then pledging these bonds as security for an issue of collateral trust bonds which bear a lower interest rate than those of the subsidiary. By using a mortgage loan, the subsidiary could avoid the expense of originating a bond issue and the holding company could pledge the mortgage loan to raise funds in the open market.

A corporation may even use its own bonds as security for an issue of collateral trust bonds (seemingly one of the many absurdities of corporation finance wherein a corporation uses its debt instruments as security for other debts). Long-term mortgage bonds may be pledged as collateral to secure an issue of short-term bonds. This use of liabilities (bonds) to secure other liabilities is a device to neutralize the restrictions on maturity and interest rates found in open-end mortgage bond provisions.

A corporation may be permitted to issue new first mortgage bonds of the class outstanding which may be twenty-year bonds. The bond indenture may permit such bonds to be sold if and when the yield thereon is 4 per cent or less. Let us assume that the capital market will not purchase at par or more a twenty-year, 4 per cent mortgage bond; then the bonds may be issued and deposited (not sold) with a trust company as security for a ten-year issue of collateral trust bonds which are sold to investors. The ten-year collateral trust bonds will probably sell at a better price than the twenty-year, 4 per cent mortgage bonds for two reasons: (1) for approximately twenty-five years the interest rates on shorter maturities have been lower than on longer maturities, and (2) the collateral trust bonds are better secured than the mortgage bonds. If the bonds pledged exceed those sold by 50 per cent, the basic security behind the collateral trust bonds has been increased by 100 per cent. When collateral trust bonds are redeemed, the pledged mortgage bonds would be returned to the pledgor and retired.

Because it is a common practice for one corporation to invest in the securities of other corporations, collateral trust bonds may be secured by bonds and stocks of corporations which are entirely independent of the pledgor.

Reasons for Use of Collateral Trust Bonds. If and when a corporation pledges stocks and/or bonds as security for a bond issue, the basic reason is to obtain a more favorable interest rate than could be obtained on an unsecured loan or debenture bond issue. While the credit rating of collateral trust bonds depends primarily on the credit standing of the borrower, a pledge of securities will improve the credit rating if the pledged collateral has sufficient value. Thus, in addition to the credit standing of the borrower, the factors determining the credit rating of collateral trust bonds include: the earning power behind the pledged securities, the marketability of the collateral during adverse conditions, and the protection provided by the terms of the trust indenture. In bond financing there seems to be a preference for real property as security; but, in an emergency, real property may lack the marketability possessed by stocks and bonds. In recapturing investments, marketability may be the most important quality possessed by pledged property. Because of court decisions in bankruptcy reorganizations, creditors may be entitled to damages resulting from the postponement of the sale of pledged collateral. Therefore, holders of collateral trust bonds may be in a stronger financial position when a corporation is being reorganized in bankruptcy than are mortgage bondholders.

DEBENTURE BONDS

A debenture or debenture bond is a certificate issued as evidence of a debt. In its broadest meaning, the term includes all bonds issued by corporations; in fact, the terms *debenture* and *bond* are sometimes used interchangeably, as both are promises of corporations to pay debts. In its more restricted meaning, a debenture is a direct obligation of the issuing corporation based solely on the general credit of the issuer without the assignment, mortgage, or pledge of property. But debenture bonds are more than mere promises to pay because they are issued under bond indentures containing provisions which restrict the issuer for the protection of creditors. The bond or trust indenture is held by a responsible and disinterested trustee who supervises the execution of the provisions found in the trust indenture.

Adequate earnings plus a willingness of the debtor to pay are by far the most important protection that any creditor could have; but other things being equal, debtors are able to borrow more economically if they provide security. However, there is a limit below which interest rates may not be reduced, and there are extra administrative costs when property is assigned or pledged which are not present when loans are unsecured. In practice, unsecured debt instruments bear a lower interest rate than secured obligations—but not because they are unsecured. This seeming paradox is explained when cognizance is taken of the fact that borrowing without security requires a higher credit rating than borrowing with security; it is this higher credit standing that accounts for the fact that interest charges are lower.

The fact that debenture bonds are unsecured by any specific lien on property is less important than their status with reference to other securities issued by the corporation. If the issuer (debtor) has no senior obligations outstanding and no sizeable amount of short-term debt, the status of its debenture bonds is about the same as that of a first mortgage bond. Involuntary liquidation or reorganization usually results from failure of the business concern to meet interest and principal obligations. Under these conditions, unsecured creditors may sue, obtain judgment, and attach specific property to satisfy their claims; and, in practice, this amounts to the same thing as when property is assigned or pledged under a mortgage or other lien. Debenture bondholders, as creditors, have a claim to earnings and assets which is senior to that of preferred and common stockholders.

Protective Features in Debenture Bond Indentures. The status of debenture bonds is usually protected by provisions in the bond indenture which forbid or restrict the issuance of any debt having a prior lien. The issuance of mortgage bonds may be permitted if the outstanding debenture bonds are given prior or equal coverage. If the corporation subsequently issues mortgage bonds, the debenture bondholders in effect become first mortgage bondholders even though their bonds are still called debenture bonds.

The bond indenture may permit a corporation to pledge or assign assets to secure current loans of less than one-year duration to finance normal business operations. Although there is a possibility that a corporation may need to pledge all its assets to obtain working capital, this exception may be unimportant if the bond indenture also requires the debtor corporation to maintain a current ratio of 2 to 1, to keep total debt below net worth, to refrain from paying dividends if earnings are less than twice interest charges, and so on for other standard provisions found in term loan agreements and bond indentures. A debenture bond indenture may contain provisions for a sinking fund, call option, conversion privilege, and other features found in mortgage bond indentures.

The use of special features in issuing debentures may be illustrated by the Brunswick Corporation's 20-year, 4½ convertible subordinated debentures which were offered publicly in January, 1961. As the word *convertible* in the title suggests, they are convertible into common stock (at $51 per share), and they may be exchanged for common stock at any time within fifteen days prior to the redemption date for debentures that have been called for redemption. The use made of this privilege will depend on the market price of the common stock.

While some corporations may depend exclusively on the conversion feature as a selling device for debentures, the management of the Brunswick Corporation also made provisions for "compulsory" and "voluntary" contributions of cash to a sinking fund. The trust indenture requires the company to contribute cash in an amount equal to $1.5 million on January 1 each year, starting in 1971, for ten years. The company has the option of providing cash for retirement of the debentures up to $1.5 million on January 1 each year from 1966 to 1980 inclusive. In the provision for the mandatory part of the sinking fund, management is permitted to make adjustments in cash contributions for debentures that have been converted into common stock, reclaimed, or otherwise cancelled. When a provision is made for use of sinking funds in debt retirement, it is usually accompanied by giving the company the right to call the debt in whole or part at prices stated in the indenture and on the bonds or debentures. Management of the Brunswick Corporation made the debentures subject to call and set the redemption price at 104½ per cent for the first year (1961) and at declining prices thereafter until 1979, at which time the price will be 100 per cent and will remain thus until maturity of the debentures. The call premium makes debentures and/or bonds more attractive to investors because it reduces the likelihood of their being called at an early date; if they are called, the premium is a compensation for having to reinvest the funds. However, if interest rates fall far enough to make refinancing by corporations profitable despite paying the premium on outstanding obligations, investors will be at a disadvantage despite the premium because the return on new investments will probably be lower than on those redeemed.

Customarily, corporations provide for the payment of interest and principal on their obligations at metropolitan banks as well as at their own offices. The Brunswick Corporation made provisions for the payment of interest and principal at the American National Bank and Trust Company of Chicago (this bank is also the trustee) and the Irving Trust Company in New York as well as at its Chicago and New York offices. The corporation's debentures were to be made available in denominations of $100, $1,000, and in multiples of

$1,000 when approved by the corporation. The debentures have coupons attached but are registered as to principal.

The word "subordinated" in the title of the Brunswick Corporation's debentures suggests another quality common to corporate debentures. Not only are debentures unsecured obligations but they are also subordinated in claims to interest and principal payments to "senior indebtedness" of the issuer as defined in the indenture. In the case of the Brunswick Corporation, "senior indebtedness" was defined as "indebtedness of the Company now outstanding or hereafter incurred for money borrowed by the Company or guaranteed to others or for money borrowed by others for which the Company is responsible, and . . . renewals, extensions and refundings of any such indebtedness provided that such indebtedness is not superior in right of payment to the Debentures."[5] Thus, the corporation did not impair its credit position with C.I.T. Corporation (a finance company), banks, and long-term creditors by the issue of the subordinated debentures.

The Brunswick debentures contain restrictions on the payment of *cash* dividends on common stock and on the repurchase of common stock outstanding (prohibited if the effect is to reduce the consolidated net worth below $23,500,000 and limited in the aggregate amount under other circumstances). However, these restrictions neither limit payments of cash dividends on preferred stock outstanding nor prohibit purchase of preferred stock for retirement under terms of a sinking fund previously set up for this purpose.

Debentures are more common among issues of industrial companies than railroad and public utility companies because industrial companies usually have fewer fixed assets to pledge as security. In addition, because of its specialized nature, industrial property is not considered high-grade security for mortgage bonds (this has not prevented insurance companies from making loans on industrial property). When industrial corporations having high credit standings finance with bond issues, they usually issue debentures or unsecured bonds. Now, companies financing with debentures represent practically every industry.

However, the more formal type of debenture is being replaced to some extent by ordinary promissory notes held by banks, insurance

---

[5] Brunswick Corporation, *Prospectus, Brunswick Corporation, $25,634,400 4½% Convertible Subordinated Debentures, Due January 1, 1981* (January 11, 1961), p. 15.

companies, and other lenders, with the term-loan agreement taking the place of the trust indenture. This situation may be illustrated by the statement of the *financial structure* of the Dow Chemical Company (see Table 25). Dow's promissory notes are held by insurance companies with repayments due annually; 3% debentures are convert-

TABLE 25

FINANCIAL STRUCTURE—DOW CHEMICAL COMPANY AND SUBSIDIARIES

	May 31 1960	1959
Current Liabilities:		
Notes payable	$ 3,905,385	55,532,713
Long-term debt due within one year	22,500,000	2,500,000
Accounts payable	43,150,125	33,599,147
United States and foreign taxes on income	41,866,637	37,996,563
Accrued and other current liabilities	48,428,664	38,934,818
	$159,850,811	$168,563,241
Long-Term Debt:		
Promissory notes, 2.7% (due Jan. 1, 1972)	$ 11,000,000	$12,000,000
Promissory notes, 3.25% (due July 1, 1977)	40,500,000	42,000,000
Debentures, 2.35% (due Nov. 1, 1961)	14,557,000	14,892,000
Debentures, subordinate 3% convertible (due July 1, 1982)	29,033,000	43,428,000
Bonds, 4¼% (Swiss subsidiary)(due Nov. 30, 1971)	13,921,114	
Notes payable—banks	45,000,000	60,000,000
	$154,011,114	$172,320,000
Minority interests in subsidiary companies	$ 1,676,168	$ 1,391,499
Stockholders' Interest:		
Common capital stock (1960—outstanding 27,362,631 shares)	$136,813,158	$131,785,452
Capital surplus	359,540,307	295,789,345
Earned surplus	89,352,635	89,231,804
	$585,706,100	$516,806,601
Total	$901,244,193	$859,081,341

Source: The Dow Chemical Company, *Annual Report for the Year Ended May 31, 1960* (Midland, Michigan, 1960), p. 21 and 24.

ible into common stock and 4¼% bonds are obligations of Dow Chemie A.G., a Swiss subsidiary (the principal and interest guaranteed by the Dow Chemical Company). The company's loans from banks are included under both long-term debt and current liabilities. In addition to borrowing under a loan agreement at 4½ per cent interest, repayable in four equal semi-annual installments, the company has a credit agreement that provides for maximum credit of $100,000,000 with interest determined by the prime rate for 90-day maturities.

SUMMARY

Business firms, particularly those in the railroad industry, often finance the purchase of equipment by pledging it as security. The strong credit position of these equipment obligations is explained by the fact that, even when railroads are in bankruptcy or in process of reorganization, trustees continue to meet the payments on equipment obligations so that the railroads may continue to function.

In states that regard a chattel mortgage as giving the mortgagee merely a lien upon the pledged property (not as transferring title to the mortgagee), equipment being financed may be subject to the after-acquired property clause in outstanding mortgages. Therefore the chattel mortgage plan is often rejected in favor of the conditional sales plan wherein title to the equipment remains with the trustee until all payments have been made. Under this plan, the railroad company makes a down payment and signs a contract to make deferred payments; and, in order to pay off the vendor of the equipment, serial bonds or notes are issued and sold to the highest bidder. The so-called Philadelphia Plan is a trust lease arrangement using a trust agreement and a lease purchase agreement. In 1949, the Equitable Life Assurance Society of the United States originated a plan whereby equipment is purchased by the insurance company and leased to the railroads on a per day rental basis.

Collateral trust obligations are secured by pledges of intangible personal property—stocks and/or bonds. The collateral trust indenture customarily contains provisions relative to substitution of securities, voting of pledged shares, and others designed to protect bondholders. To finance a subsidiary company, a parent corporation may issue collateral trust bonds secured by securities of its subsidiary because a bond issue of the parent corporation will command a larger market and a lower interest rate than would a bond issue originated by the subsidiary. Factors in the credit rating of collateral trust bonds include: the earning power of the issuer, the credit ratings of the issuers of the pledged securities, the marketability of the securities pledged during adverse economic conditions, and the protection provided by the terms of the trust indenture.

Debenture bonds are protected by the earning power of the debtor corporation without being secured by any lien on specific property. The indentures under which debenture bonds are issued contain provisions designed to protect bondholders including restrictions on the issuance of any debt having a prior lien unless the debentures are given the same secured position. While debtors pledge property to reduce the cost of borrowing, unsecured debt tends to bear a lower interest rate because a higher credit rating is required when borrowing without security and the administrative costs of servicing unsecured debts are lower than when collateral or other property is pledged.

QUESTIONS AND PROBLEMS

1. Identify: (*a*) equipment bonds, (*b*) equipment notes, and (*c*) equipment trust certificates.
2. What are the advantages claimed for the conditional sales (New York) plan of financing railroad equipment?
3. (*a*) Account for the development of the lease purchase (Philadelphia) plan of financing railroad equipment. (*b*) How does a lease purchase arrangement differ from a straight lease plan?
4. What factors determine the credit rating of collateral trust obligations?
5. What provisions may be made for release or substitution of securities held by the trustee?
6. Explain how a parent holding company may use collateral trust obligations to finance a subsidiary.
7. (*a*) "Debenture bonds are more than mere promises to pay." Explain. (*b*) What protective features are usually found in debenture bond indentures? (*c*) Under what circumstances may debenture bondholders be or become, in effect, first mortgage bondholders?
8. It has been stated that corporations offer security when borrowing in order to obtain lower interest rates. It has also been stated that unsecured debt instruments bear a lower interest rate than secured instruments. Reconcile these two seemingly contradictory statements.
9. What types of corporations most commonly issue debenture bonds? Why?
10. Explain: "Illinois Central Railroad Co. awarded $4,500,000 equipment trust certificates to Halsey, Stuart & Co. and associates on a bid of 98.8066 for a 4% coupon." (*Wall Street Journal* [New York], February 8, 1961, p. 11.)
11. Explain: "The Missouri-Kansas-Texas Railroad asked the Interstate Commerce Commission to guarantee a $16 million loan . . . from a group of banks, insurance companies and retirement funds at 5% for 15 years." (*Wall Street Journal* [New York], February 3, 1961, p. 11.)
12. Analyze: "Consolidated Natural Gas Co. obtained a 4.38% annual net interest cost in selling its $45 million triple-A rated 4⅜% debentures, due February 1, 1986." (*Wall Street Journal* [New York], February 8, 1961, p. 11.)

13. Identify the types of long-term debts listed below:

2⅞% Sinking fund debentures, due 1967	$ 8,500,000
3% Promissory notes, due serially to 1969	5,400,000
3½% Sinking fund debentures, due 1979	12,300,000
5% Convertible sinking fund debentures, due 1976	10,467,400
	$36,667,400

Source: Libby McNeill & Libby, *Annual Report for the Year Ended June 27, 1959* (Chicago, 1959), p. 11.

CHAPTER 23

Extinction of Long-Term Debts

AT THE SAME time that borrowers make provisions for the issuance of bonds and other forms of long-term debts, they customarily make provisions for their extinction. By extinction of bonds and long-term notes is meant the elimination of particular obligations but not necessarily the elimination or reduction of the total debt of the issuer. Among the methods employed in debt extinction are redemption, refunding, and conversion. Redemption of bonds and long-term notes is the payment of cash to the holders of the credit instruments; refunding is the issuance of new bonds or other securities to replace those outstanding; and conversion is the exchange of outstanding long-term debts for some other security. In some cases, an issue of bonds or long-term notes may be retired by using a combination of the three methods of extinction.

DEVICES FACILITATING DEBT EXTINCTION

Significance of Maturity Date. Among the various reasons given by business management for making provisions for the extinction of bonds are the following: to meet the demands of investment bankers, to strengthen the financial position of the corporation, to offset the decline in property values due to depreciation, and to comply with the American tradition which demands that debts be paid. Without question there is a bias against perpetual bonds—issues that never come due. Therefore, practically all bonds issued by American corporations have a due date or maturity date. The significance of using a maturity date is that management must face the problem of bringing about extinction of bonds on or before maturity. In the case of bonds convertible into common or preferred stock, if bondholders use the conversion privilege, no repayment is necessary; however, management has no assurance that bondholders will use the conversion privilege.

Retirement of a bond issue may take place at maturity when all the bonds come due, on a call date as set by management, periodically as provided for in serial bond issues, piecemeal by open-market purchases or direct negotiation with individual bondholders, or through the use of two or more of these methods. When cash is exchanged for bonds at maturity, the debtor meets his contractual obligation to repay the principal. For the convenience of bondholders, bonds are usually redeemed at designated banks in financial centers as well as at the principal office of the debtor.

"Call Date" Method of Retirement. Today, practically all issues of bonds of corporations are covered by trust indentures containing a section that permits the bond issue to be called and redeemed in whole or part at the option of the issuing corporation. The call privilege is inserted at the request of the corporation so as to permit adjustments in the capital structure. Corporations may also use the call privilege to take advantage of a decline in interest rates, to eliminate bond issues with unfavorable indenture clauses, to reduce debt, and to replace long-term bonds with term loans or short-term obligations (and vice versa). Because interest rates fluctuate with the business cycle, the call option has been exercised most often during recessions to replace bonds bearing high interest rates with bonds bearing lower interest rates. Over a period of years a corporation may refinance its bond indebtedness several times in order to reduce interest charges.[1]

When corporations finance with callable bonds, management must anticipate a less favorable reaction from investors than when financing with noncallable bond issues. Obviously, if a corporation gains from refunding at lower interest rates, investors lose. Buyers of callable bonds anticipate having their bonds redeemed at a time when it is more difficult to obtain the same rate of return on new investments.

Bond indentures require that trustees or issuing corporations notify bondholders when bonds are to be called, and unless bonds are surrendered promptly, bondholders incur a loss of interest. When

---

[1] In March, 1954, the Detroit Edison Company sold $40,000,000 of general and refunding mortgage, 2⅞ per cent bonds due in 1984 to a banking syndicate headed by the First Boston Corporation at a price of 98.6499 (per cent of par) which were offered to the public at 99.25 to yield investors 2.91 per cent. The bonds were issued to replace higher cost obligations issued in 1953.

thousands of bonds are outstanding, it is inevitable that some will not be presented on the redemption date after which all interest ceases. Holders of registered bonds will be notified by letter, but holders of nonregistered bonds must depend on notices in newspapers and financial publications. Usually prior notice of from thirty to sixty days is given along with announcement of the details included in the redemption plan. Bond indentures usually provide that bondholders will receive a premium (more than par value) if and when bonds are called before maturity.

The call or redemption price is negotiated when bonds are issued, and it will vary according to capital market conditions and the credit position and bargaining power of the issuing corporation. A well-known corporation having a high credit rating may offer a low call premium such as 2 per cent, but a less well-known corporation may have to offer a higher one, such as 5 or 6 per cent. Sometimes the call privilege is restricted so that bonds may not be called until the lapse of a specified number of years, but more commonly a declining schedule of call prices is provided (for example, 105 during the first 3 years, 104 during the next 3 years, etc.) in order to increase compensation to investors if bonds are called during the early part of the debt period.

The influence of the call price on the market price of bonds reflects the interest rates prevailing in the market. When the market rate is below the coupon rate, corporate management will consider the advantage of refunding at a lower interest rate; but if the market rate is above the coupon rate, no savings in interest would result from refunding. In the latter case, if refunding is planned it would be for reasons other than savings on interest charges.

If callable bonds are issued when interest rates are extremely low, there is less likelihood that bonds will be called. (If and when the interest rate changes, it should be upward.) Hence, a low call premium can be used because it will have little effect on the offering price of bonds. If interest rates are high and are expected to decline, the call feature will tend to depress the market price of bonds for the obvious reason that investors would expect the debtor corporation to refinance when interest rates decline. In this case, the call premium will have to be substantial (which in later years may be a serious deterrent to refinancing).

Before deciding to call bonds, the issuing corporation will compare the savings on interest over the remaining life of the bonds with the costs of refinancing including call premium, underwriting fees, legal expenses, cost of engraving new bonds, routine expenses of retiring old bonds and issuing new ones, cost of preparation of the registration statement, and extra interest payments. (Refunding necessitates extra interest payments because a corporation will not call an old issue until the new issue has been sold and because old bondholders must be given thirty or sixty days' notice prior to the redemption date which means that interest will be paid on both issues for the thirty- or sixty-day period.) Unless the extra cost items are taken into account, any computation of savings based on the difference in interest rates will be inaccurate.

For corporations desiring to amortize their debts out of funds from operations instead of refunding them at lower interest rates, the call feature permits the use of funds—when advantageous to the debtor corporation—that otherwise might be tied up in sinking-fund investments. The call feature may also be used to implement other methods of debt retirement; for illustration, when a corporation notifies bondholders that their convertible bonds are being called on a certain date, the holders have the option of using their conversion privilege immediately or selling their bonds to someone who will convert them. If the conversion privilege is valuable, the bonds may be sold at a premium. Finally, the call feature may be used to facilitate redemption of bonds for which sinking funds have been created.

Today, business corporations are financing their long-term capital needs to an increasing extent by long-term loans from banks, insurance companies, and other institutional investors. The loan agreement may permit prepayment of the loans, in whole or part, at the convenience of the debtor. Usually commercial banks permit prepayment without penalty, but insurance companies and others are inclined to attach a premium to prepayment which is similar to the excess of a bond call price over par. Most lenders will permit prepayment of debts without penalty out of earnings, but they will assess a penalty if prepayment is accompanied by refunding at a lower rate of interest. During the years when there is the greatest uncertainty as to the future of the borrower's business success, the lender is assuming the greatest risk. If the borrower's credit position improves sufficiently to enable borrowing at a lower interest rate, the lender who assumed the risk originally may feel that if the loan is repaid it means the loss of the loan when it is most attractive. (Conversely, if the borrower's credit position does not improve as anticipated, the loan may not be repaid and the lender's risk will increase.) This situation explains the existence of the practice of attaching penalties for prepayment.

SINKING FUND AND SERIAL DEBTS

Sinking Funds for Debt Retirement. A sinking fund for debt retirement requires periodic appropriations of cash by the debtor to redeem the bonds or long-term notes before or at maturity.[2] Customarily, sinking funds are provided for in the trust indenture or loan agreement, but the board of directors of a corporation may establish sinking funds by resolution at any time. Usually a sinking fund for a bond issue is administered by the trustee who holds the bond indenture, but it may be administered by a second trust company or some other agency. Sometimes in lieu of cash, a debtor corporation is permitted to deposit reacquired bonds of the issue being redeemed to fulfill sinking-fund requirements. This provision is advantageous if and when bonds can be acquired at less than par or less than their call price. The trustee administers bond redemption according to the provisions set forth in the trust indenture or other contract. When they are on a contractual basis, contributions of a corporation to the sinking fund are usually compulsory. Therefore, a corporation is technically insolvent when it fails to meet its sinking-fund obligations as well as when it fails to meet interest and principal payments when due.

Types of Sinking Funds. Sinking funds are sometimes classified according to the method used in determining the annual appropriation. According to this classification, they are the fixed annual amount, variable annual amount, percentage of earnings, and per unit of output sinking funds.

When a corporation's contribution to the sinking fund is in fixed annual amounts, the amount may be fixed in terms of either dollars or amount of bonds; for illustration, $100,000 in cash or 100 bonds having a par value of $1,000. This method of retiring bonds means that the debt burden will be largest the first year and will decline pro-

[2] For illustration, among the long-term debts, less current maturities of the Hooker Chemical Corporation and subsidiaries on November 30, 1960 were: $24,444,800 of 5 per cent convertible subordinated debentures due September 15, 1984 with annual sinking-fund payments of $1,000,000 commencing in 1960 and $1,500,000 commencing in 1979; $3,480,000, 3½ per cent sinking-fund debentures, due January 1, 1974 with annual installments of $260,000; and $1,360,000, 3 per cent sinking-fund debentures, due February 1, 1967 with annual installments of $200,000. Hooker Chemical Corporation and Subsidiaries, *Annual Report for the Year Ended November 30, 1960* (New York, 1961), p. 10.

gressively in successive years because interest payments are on all the bonds the first year and decrease as bonds are retired.

A corporation's sinking-fund payments may be in variable annual amounts to fit into other financial plans of the corporation. For illustration, if the proceeds of a bond issue are spent for construction of a plant, the effects of the improvement of the company's income would tend to be gradual; and, for several years, the increase in income may be insufficient to cover average annual sinking-fund requirements. Therefore, management may arrange to postpone sinking-fund contributions for a number of years, keep constant the total of sinking-fund contributions and interest payments throughout the life of the bond issue (annuity method), or fit the "carrying charges" of the new debt into those already in existence so as to smooth out the total debt burden of the corporation (all sinking funds and interest charges).

The annuity method necessitates determining first the sum to be set aside periodically to provide the required amount at maturity, and then the life span of the bond issue. However, a corporation could decide on the life span of the bond issue first and then compute the amount of the sinking-fund contribution. In either case, the assumption is that no part of the debt is to be eliminated until maturity. The first year the corporation pays the interest on its bonds and the amount contracted for to the sinking-fund trustee, who promptly invests it in the bonds. The second year the corporation makes the same interest and sinking-fund payments, but now the trustee is able to invest in a larger amount of bonds because it has both the sinking-fund contribution and the interest on bonds that were reacquired the first year. At maturity, the trustee will have accumulated the amount needed to retire the debt. In practice, the bonds may be retired as they are reacquired; but the annuity principle may be maintained if the corporation increases its sinking-fund contribution each year by the amount that its interest charges are reduced (thereby keeping the annual combined installment constant).

Payment of interest is a fixed charge and a business firm may arrange for contributions to the sinking fund so that they will not interfere with this obligation. After provisions have been made for taxes, interest, and other charges, a corporation may provide that all net profits up to a designated amount will be paid to a sinking-fund trustee. Funds above this amount would be available for dividends, debt retirement, and retention in the business. Even when the sinking-fund contribution is a percentage of earnings, there may still be a specified minimum amount that must be contributed regardless of earnings.

In the case of wasting-assets corporations (for example, mining and petroleum companies), provisions for sinking-fund contributions may be in terms of output: the greater the rate of depletion, the greater the amount paid into the sinking fund. For illustration, the contribution would increase in direct proportion to output—a specified number of dollars for each ton of coal or copper, each barrel of oil, or each 1,000 feet of lumber. However, such a plan may call for a minimum annual contribution plus a variable one based on output.

Uses of Sinking Funds. Sinking-fund contributions are usually invested in the bonds of the issue for which the sinking fund was created, but they may be invested in other securities or assets of the issuing corporation or in securities of other corporations. If invested in the bonds for which the sinking fund was created, the method whereby the sinking-fund trustee may reacquire the bonds must be determined. Because open-market purchases of bonds would be expensive when bonds are selling above par, provisions may be made at the time of issuing the bonds for calling the bonds by lot or calling a certain percentage of those held by each bondholder at specified intervals. (The latter method may be impractical because it could entail fractional parts of bonds.)

When bonds are selling at a discount, it would be profitable to reacquire them through open-market purchases. If bonds are non-callable and the market for them is inactive, the trustee or issuing corporation may request bondholders to offer (tender) their bonds for redemption. In this case, bondholders who are willing to sell make sealed offers and the trustee accepts those having the lowest offering prices up to an amount sufficient to exhaust the cash available for this purpose.

The ultimate purpose in creating a sinking fund is to protect the credit of the issuing corporation; to this end, the sinking-fund trustee may invest in any obligation of the debtor corporation. In some cases, the trust indenture may permit or require the annual contributions to the sinking fund to be invested in additions, improvements, or acquisitions of property of the debtor corporation. These sinking-fund investments tend to improve the corporation's debt-paying ability and to strengthen the position of its outstanding bonds.

A trust indenture may specify that sinking-fund contributions are to be invested in specific securities such as obligations of the federal, state, and local governments, or it may permit investments in securities of other corporations. If investments are limited to low-yielding securities, the corporation may lose the difference between the rate paid on bonds outstanding and the rate earned on its investments; but, if investments are in municipal securities on which interest is tax free, these savings on income tax payments may be enough to offset the interest differential. When the decision as to investing sinking-fund contributions is left to the discretion of the trustee, he may follow a policy of trying to make a profit from investments.

A provision in the bond indenture permitting the corporation to deliver bonds rather than cash to the trustee to fulfill sinking-fund requirements may expedite bond redemption. (The trustee may be required to accept such bonds at par or at the call price, irrespective of the price paid to reacquire them.) Although sinking funds provide for an orderly reduction of the debt of the issuing corporation, equally orderly procedures for retirement of corporate bonds may be achieved by issuing serial bonds. Sinking funds may be used in providing for retirement of long-term notes, but usually debts of this type, when held by one or a few lenders, are retired on the installment plan.

Serial Bonds. A serial bond or note issue is one made up of a series of bonds with maturities arranged so that a specified number of bonds come due each year throughout the debt period. Management may sell the bonds of a serial bond issue with a different coupon rate for each maturity or with the same coupon rate for all maturities. If bonds are sold so that the coupon rates reflect the yield curve in the market, all the bonds sell at par. If the bonds have the same coupon rate, the market price of each maturity will reflect the yield curve in the market (see Table 26).

Since the use of bond tables permits ready estimates of bond prices under varying yield curves, it is a matter of indifference whether varying or fixed coupon rates are used.[3] If a corporation wants a definite number of dollars, interest rates are negotiated at the time the bonds are issued; but, if the corporation sets the interest rate in ad-

[3] If the yield curve appearing in the second column of Table 26 were charted, it would be an upsweeping yield curve. It would show, as of one date, that the interest rate on each maturity of the same class of credit instrument increases with its maturity, with the lowest rate on one-year obligations and the highest on twelve-year obligations. A downsweeping curve is just the opposite, with the highest rate being for the shortest maturity and the lowest rate being for the longest maturity. Yield curves or "patterns of interest rates" are as of one time, and are not a time series.

TABLE 26

YIELD CURVE, COUPON RATES, AND PRICES OF SERIAL BONDS

Maturity Year	Price Constant—Varying Coupon Rates			Coupon Rate Constant—Varying Prices		
	Yield Curve in Market (Per Cent)	Coupon Rate (Per Cent)	Price	Coupon Rate	Price	Yield Curve (Per Cent)
1.	1.00	1.00	100	3%	101.99	1.00
2.	1.50	1.50	100	3	102.94	1.50
3.	2.00	2.00	100	3	102.90	2.00
4.	2.25	2.25	100	3	102.85	2.25
5.	2.50	2.50	100	3	102.34	2.50
6.	2.75	2.75	100	3	101.37	2.75
7.	3.00	3.00	100	3	100.00	3.00
8.	3.10	3.10	100	3	99.30	3.10
9.	3.20	3.20	100	3	98.45	3.20
10.	3.30	3.30	100	3	97.46	3.30
11.	3.40	3.40	100	3	96.35	3.40
12.	3.50	3.50	100	3	95.13	3.50

vance, dollar receipts from the sale of the issue will be unknown until the actual sale of the bonds.

In determining the number of serial bonds that will mature each year, corporations are faced with the same problems as in determining the annual appropriation to a sinking fund. Maturities may be arranged to come due in equal amounts each year or they may be arranged so that the total amount needed for interest and principal payments will be the same each year. Usually, the serial bonds having more distant maturities are callable; this gives flexibility to the redemption plan. When longer-term bonds are callable, more rapid retirement than originally anticipated may be effected if conditions are favorable. The bond indenture may require the creation of a sinking fund for the bonds having the longest maturity; it also may require that the bonds be called in reverse order when calls are made (that is, the first call will be for bonds having the longest maturities).

Market conditions, as reflected in yield curves, may be a factor in the decision whether to issue serial bonds or sinking-fund bonds. When short-term interest rates are relatively low (an upsweeping curve), there is a preference among investors for short-term obligations. This would indicate a good market for a serial bond issue because it includes short-term and intermediate bonds as well as long-term bonds; therefore the total interest charges would be less than on an equivalent issue of long-term bonds. It is sometimes said that if long-term sinking-fund bonds are issued, the higher interest paid may be offset by savings when the bonds are reacquired; for this to be true, however, the sinking-fund trustee of the corporation would have to reacquire the bonds at a discount. When the yield curve is upsweeping—as it has been for many years—and the credit position of the issuing corporation is sound, the market price of long-term bonds is usually high until they mature.[4]

While sinking-fund contributions may be more flexible than serial bond maturities, the maturities of serial bonds may be arranged so that none mature in the years that other obligations become due. The number of bonds in each series may vary, the maturities of the earlier years may be omitted, and other arrangements may be made so that bond maturities may be fitted into the over-all debt-retirement plan of the corporation. Serial bonds are issued by corporations in all major industries. They are used in financing railroad equipment obligations and real estate when there is a fairly steady rate of depreciation of the property pledged and fairly steady income.

Although long-term loans are usually repaid in equal annual or semiannual installments, there are many variations in such arrangements, as when plans call for refinancing loans at maturity either by negotiating for new loans or by issuing new stock, bonds or other debt obligations to be sold in the capital market.[5] In other cases, business corporations may contract to repay part of the principal periodically and to leave a part of the loan unpaid at the end of the loan period to be refinanced at that time. A business firm may make such an arrangement when the useful life of the asset being financed substantially exceeds the loan period. For illustration, a corporation may arrange for a loan of $20,000,000, with a maturity of ten years, and with principal repayment of $1,000,000 (plus interest) annually. In this case, a debt of $10,000,000 would remain at the maturity of the loan; although the corporation would be faced with a financing problem, the amount to be financed would be only half of what it would have been if no provisions had been made for repay-

[4] If the upsweeping curve prevails and there is no change in the level or shape of the curve, the market yield on an outstanding security goes down with the passage of time. So, a fifteen-year bond which had a 3 per cent yield at the time of issuance will sell at a higher price, or lower yield, after five years of its term have elapsed.

[5] Approximately one half of the long-term debt, minus current maturities, of $59,684,-800 of the Hooker Chemical Corporation and Subsidiaries are in the form of unsecured notes repayable on the installment plan. As of November 30, 1960, they included $16,-000,000, 3¼ per cent notes due May 1, 1977 with annual installments of $800,000; and $9,200,000, 3⅝ per cent notes due January 1, 1966 with semiannual installments of $400,-000 to January 1, 1962 and $600,000 thereafter. (Hooker Chemical Corporation and Subsidiaries, *Annual Report for the Year Ended November 30, 1960*, p. 10.)

ment. Debt retirement policies are linked to depreciation policies, and funds from operations accounted for as depreciation allowances as well as retained earnings after taxes are used to meet interest and principal payments.

REFUNDING BOND ISSUES

When bonds are refunded at or before maturity, either new securities are issued to obtain cash with which to repay those outstanding or new securities are offered directly to bondholders in exchange for those they hold. In the latter case, bondholders who are unwilling to exchange their bonds are paid off in cash. Because refunding is debt replacement rather than debt liquidation, the procedures in refunding operations differ from those used in sinking-fund and serial bond repayment plans.

As noted previously, certain corporations (particularly those in the railroad and public utility fields) regard their long-term debts as a permanent part of their capital structures; therefore, refunding is usually for purposes other than the reduction of corporate debt. Depression experiences have caused students to question the assumption that the public demand for services of railroad and public utility corporations will always be sufficient to provide an amount of earnings which will be adequate to meet their debt obligations. Nevertheless, railroads and public utility companies commonly refund their bonds on or before the maturity date, although some debt reduction may take place in some cases.

Refunding at Maturity. To meet maturing bond obligations, a corporation may issue new bonds, preferred or common stock, or it may negotiate for a direct loan from insurance companies and/or banks. Old bondholders may accept new bonds in exchange for old ones if offered one or more special inducements such as a cash bonus, better security, a sinking-fund provision, conversion privilege, or the right to elect one or more directors. Since most corporate bonds are held by institutional investors, the chief bondholders may negotiate with the debtor corporation for a direct exchange of old bonds for new, and doubtless this practice would be more common were it not for the regulation requiring that new bond issues of certain companies be sold to the highest bidder.

When a large bond issue matures, the credit position of the issuer and the conditions in the capital market will influence the method of refunding. It would be fortuitous if both the credit position of the corporation and the situation in the capital market happened to be favorable on the maturity date of the old debt. In the face of an unsettled capital market, a corporation would normally reappraise and postpone new financing plans; but this option of postponement is not present when obligations mature. If the capital market is unfavorable (as during much of the period from 1958–59 and particularly in 1959, when interest rates were the highest since World War II), stopgap financing may be favored. This may take the form of issuing short-term notes in the capital market or obtaining loans from commercial banks or insurance companies.

Refunding before Maturity. Although a corporation may plan to keep bond indebtedness as part of its capital structure, it customarily inserts the call option in the bond indenture in order to be free to refund such bonds when market conditions are favorable. This privilege is usually acquired at a price—a higher interest rate or lower price for callable bonds. Management seemingly considers the price reasonable because most modern corporate bonds are callable.

In picking the time to call bonds, management is influenced not only by current interest rates but also by expected interest rates. Although current capital market conditions might justify immediate refunding, it may be postponed if more favorable conditions are expected in the near future. Because call prices usually decline progressively as bonds approach maturity, the call date may be postponed in order to refund at a lower call price. It may even be desirable to postpone refunding until maturity.

Refunding permits arranging for a more remote maturity date and "freezing" the interest rate at a new level for additional years. However, these advantages must be weighed against the possibility of covering the same time period with the existing bond issue plus notes of shorter maturity, which usually bear a lower interest rate than do long-term bonds.

Although elimination of restrictive clauses in trust indentures may be one of the reasons for retiring old bond issues, management must face the possibility that the same or equally restrictive clauses may be inserted in the trust indenture of a new issue. In addition, as compensation for a lower interest rate on the new issue, investment bankers may demand a sinking-fund provision, the conversion privilege, a better pledge of security, a higher call premium, a more liberal margin of current assets over liabilities, and/or restrictions on payment of dividends on common stock.

Extensions. In the event that a corporation cannot meet its maturing bond obligations, management may ask bondholders to extend the maturity of an issue. If there are but a few bondholders, some plan of extension may be agreed upon; however, if there are many bondholders, arranging for an extension becomes difficult. If an extension is arranged, the debtor corporation is usually required to make substantial concessions to bondholders. In effect, a creditors' committee may replace the board of directors when an extension is arranged. Creditors may prefer to agree to an extension in the hope of averting principal losses that would tend to result if the corporation were forced into bankruptcy. However, during the 1930's, there were changes in the bankruptcy laws and provisions were made for reorganizing business firms under supervision of the federal courts.

CONVERSION OF BONDS

In addition to redemption and refunding, a third method whereby corporate debts may be eliminated is by conversion into stock. The conversion privilege gives a bondholder the right to convert his bonds into another security of the issuing corporation, usually common stock, within a given period of time and at a specified rate of exchange. However, the option lies with the bondholder rather than with management, and whether or not bondholders use the conversion privilege depends largely on the terms of conversion and the market price of the stock.

Conversion Rate or Price. The conversion clause in the trust indenture may be expressed as a ratio or as a price; for illustration, it may permit either the exchange of a $1,000 bond for 20 shares of stock or the use of the bond to buy shares of stock at $50 per share irrespective of the market price. In the latter case, a $1,000 bond could be exchanged for 20 shares of stock. The conversion ratio or price may vary from year to year; if so, it is usually most favorable to bondholders during the first years of the bond, becoming progressively less favorable with the approach of the maturity date.

The conversion ratio or price may be fixed so that conversion will be profitable when the bonds are issued or when the conversion period goes into effect;[6] but usually, the conversion price is fixed above

---

[6] From the beginning of the conversion period (February 9, 1954), the right to exchange American Telephone and Telegraph Company 12-year, $100 3¾ per cent convertible debentures (due December 10, 1965) was valuable. These debentures, which were callable, were exchanged at the ratio of one debenture plus $36 in cash for one share of common stock. For as long as the common stock is selling for more than $136 per share, the value of the conversion privilege will be reflected in the market price of the debentures. Within six months from the beginning of the conversion period, most of the debentures had been converted. Later, the remainder were called.

the market price of the stock into which bonds may be converted. So, bondholders usually wait until the market price of the common stock makes conversion profitable—the market price of the stock at least equals the conversion price. However, some bondholders may use their conversion privilege when the market price is slightly less than the conversion price because it is less expensive to convert a bond than to buy stock through regular brokerage channels.

If the market price of a corporation's common stock rises above the conversion price of its convertible bonds, this increase will be reflected in the market price of the bonds. For illustration, if a $1,000 bond may be exchanged for 20 shares of stock or has a conversion price of $50 per share, when the market price of the stock is $60 per share the market price of the convertible bond will be about $1,200. When common stock is selling below the conversion price, the market price of the bonds depends primarily on their investment value as credit instruments.

The conversion price may be set so that it is least favorable to bondholders when business is good, common stock prices are rising, the conversion privilege is popular, and investors are optimistic about the future and less conservative about their investments. In this case, the motives of management may be to discourage dilution of the old common stockholders' interests and to maintain the leverage factor. Conversely, the conversion price may be set so that it is most favorable to bondholders when the company's earnings are poor, the price of its stock is low, the earning prospects are unfavorable, and investors are less optimistic about the future and more conservative about their investments. In this case, the purpose of management is to encourage conversion in order to reduce the corporation's debts and to increase its equity capital.

Conversion Period. The conversion period may, and usually does, run throughout the life of the bond. However, in some cases it may not become effective until several years have elapsed, while in other cases it may expire at the end of a stated number of years before the bond matures. Making such bonds callable adds an element of uncertainty to the value of the conversion privilege. The conversion clause has been compared to subscription "rights," with the former running for years while the latter is in effect only during the "offering period." However, the use of "rights" brings cash to the corporation while the use of the conversion privilege usually only changes the form of the capital structure—decreasing debts and increasing equity capital. More appropriately, subscription rights should be compared to stock purchase warrants which are sometimes attached to bonds. However, both stock warrants and the conversion privilege tend to add a speculative element to bonds.

Protective Clauses. Since the conversion feature would lose part of its value if the issuing corporation's board of directors were to declare a stock split or stock dividend, the bond indenture may include an antidilution clause to protect bondholders. For illustration, assume that the bond indenture contains an antidilution clause and that the conversion ratio is a $1,000 bond for 20 shares of common stock; if the stock is split 3 for 1, the bond may be exchanged for 60 shares of common stock. Assuming the presence of the antidilution clause, if the corporation capitalizes surplus and gives each old stockholder one share of new stock for each share held, the bond becomes exchangeable for twice the number of shares originally provided for in the trust indenture. In addition to covering stock splits and stock dividends, the trust indenture may also cover subscription rights, sales of additional stock, sales of other securities having conversion rights, and priority in the case of redemption, mergers, dissolution, and consolidations.

When convertible bonds are callable, the corporation customarily gives bondholders call notice of thirty or more days prior to the redemption date. Because the conversion privilege expires with the redemption of the bonds, it must be used before the redemption date. A corporation may encourage conversion by declaring an extra dividend on common stock and then notifying holders of convertible bonds so that they may participate in the extra dividend by converting their bonds into stock before a specified date. Management may also provide for a new issue of stock and may offer holders of convertible bonds subscription rights if they exchange their bonds for stock within a stated period. Although holders of convertible bonds are not obligated to convert them, they usually do so if the inducements offered are sufficiently attractive.

Arguments For and Against Convertible Bonds. The arguments in favor of the use of convertible bonds by corporations include the following: (1) The cost of borrowing is lower, the assumption being that investors will pay more for a bond, or accept a lower interest rate, if they have the option of converting it into common stock in the future. If stock prices are high and there is an active market for such convertible securities, convertible bonds may have a special appeal to the more speculative-minded bond buyer. (2) If and when bonds are converted into common stock, the capital structure of the corporation will be simplified, fixed interest charges will be reduced, and the way will be cleared for additional bond financing. (3) Conversion will tend to increase the number of common stockholders and thus broaden the market for future financing. (4) The terms under which the bonds are sold (pre-emptive rights) give management an opportunity to develop the "goodwill" of old common stockholders. (5) Although timing of debt retirement is controlled by creditors and it may or may not coincide with the financial plans of management, conversion usually takes place when debt reduction is desirable. Since the price of common stock is highest during the peak of the business cycle, there will be a tendency to use the conversion privilege at this time, when debt reduction is desirable.

The chief argument against conversion privileges in bond issues is that they tend to narrow rather than broaden the market for the issuer's securities, because old common stockholders have a pre-emptive right to buy bonds convertible into common stock (unless pre-emptive rights are waived by charter provisions, a vote of shareholders, or the statutes under which the corporation is chartered). "Rights" may be purchased by others including some institutional buyers; but, to the latter, the conversion privilege is of secondary importance as compared to the investment status of bonds.

Buying bonds with a speculative feature may be discouraged by regulatory agencies. For illustration, the Comptroller of the Currency specifically forbids national banks to purchase "securities convertible into stock at the option of the holder or with stock warrants attached . . . if the price paid for such security is in excess of the investment value of the security itself, considered independently of the stock purchase warrants or conversion feature."

Conversion tends to dilute the voting rights, equity, and earnings per share of stock to the disadvantage of old shareholders. Dilution of voting power may result in voting control passing from old to new shareholders. Unless the tendency to dilute equity and earnings per share is offset by an increase in earnings and the maintenance of the same dividend rate, the market price per share of stock will tend to decline. Reduction in the amount of debt would tend to decrease the tax advantage associated with the right to deduct the interest paid from earnings before computing the federal income tax, and corporations would lose the advantage associated with "trading on equity" if and when bonds were converted into common stock.

SUMMARY

The issuance of bonds with maturity dates necessitates making plans for their extinction. Such plans may provide for redemption, refunding, or conversion. Redemption or retirement of a bond issue may take place when all bonds come due, on a call date as provided in the bond indenture, periodically over the life of the issue when serial bonds are issued, or piecemeal by repurchase of bonds in the open market or by negotiation with individual bondholders. Sinking funds may be set up to redeem bonds, other debt obligations may be created to obtain funds with which to redeem the original issue, or extinction may be brought about by exchanging the bonds for other securities (conversion).

The call feature in bonds permits corporations (1) to reduce interest charges by replacing high interest-bearing bonds with obligations carrying a lower interest rate, (2) to eliminate bond issues having unfavorable indenture clauses, and (3) to expedite conversion when bonds have the conversion feature. A sinking fund for debt retirement provides for periodic appropriations of cash for redeeming bonds on or before maturity. During the interim, sinking-fund contributions are invested by the trustee in accordance with provisions in the trust indenture or sinking-fund contract. Both sinking-fund and serial bond issues provide for an orderly reduction in debts, and market conditions or yield curves may determine which type will be issued. When bonds are refunded at or before maturity, the corporation will issue new securities which may be sold to obtain cash to redeem those outstanding or may be offered directly to bondholders in exchange for those they hold. The conversion privilege gives bondholders the right to convert their bonds into another security, usually common stock, of the issuing corporation; but whether or not bondholders use this privilege depends largely on the terms of conversion and the market price of the stock. The conversion rate or price as well as the conversion period are set forth in the trust indenture.

QUESTIONS AND PROBLEMS

1. (*a*) What are the reasons given by management for making provisions for the extinction of bonds? (*b*) What devices may be employed to facilitate bond extinction?
2. (*a*) Why is the call feature of bonds valuable to the issuing corporation? (*b*) What factors determine the call or redemption price?
3. How is the call feature of value to a corporation interested in amortizing debts out of earnings rather than in refunding them?

4. (*a*) Identify the four main types of sinking funds classified according to the method used to determine the annual contribution. (*b*) Why is the annuity method most commonly used?
5. (*a*) What are the duties of a sinking-fund trustee? (*b*) When is the provision that reacquired bonds may be deposited in lieu of cash to fulfill sinking-fund requirements most advantageous?
6. How may sinking-fund contributions be used? How may they be used so as to improve the corporation's debt-paying ability and to strengthen the position of its outstanding bonds?
7. Explain: "Under the provisions of the trust indenture for the 3¼% Debentures due 1979, the [General Motors] Corporation is required in each year beginning with 1958 to make annual cash payments to the sinking fund agent of $10,000,000 for the redemption of outstanding debentures on the next succeeding January 1; or in lieu of all or any part of such cash payments, the Corporation may deliver to the sinking fund agent reacquired debentures at the cost of such debentures to the Corporation or at the applicable sinking fund redemption price, whichever is lower." (General Motors Corporation, *Annual Report 1959*, pp. 36–37.)
8. "If serial bonds are sold so that the coupon rates are the same for all maturities, bond prices will reflect the yield curve in the market." Explain.
9. When financing with serial bonds, how may flexibility be provided in the redemption plan?
10. Is the type of long-term financing indicated by the following unusual? "Certain insurance companies have loaned $65,000,000 to The Anaconda Company. Interest is at the rate of 4% per annum. The principal amount is to be paid in equal annual installments of $4,600,000 on September 1st of each year from 1965 to 1977 and the balance on September 1, 1978. Certain options for prepayment are available to the Company." (The Anaconda Company, *Annual Report for the Year Ended December 31, 1958* [New York, 1959], p. 28.) Explain.
11. (*a*) "Refunding is debt replacement rather than debt liquidation." Explain. (*b*) How do the procedures in refunding operations differ from those used in sinking-fund and serial bond repayment plans?
12. "Debts may be eliminated by conversion into stock" but the option lies with the bondholders. Does the time when bondholders tend to use the conversion privilege coincide with the time when doing so would be most beneficial to the corporation? Explain.

PART VII

Business Promotion and Expansion

THE EASE of entering business in the United States is evidenced by the fact that 1,300 new firms are launched each business day; however, the risk of failure is high as evidenced by the fact that approximately 40 per cent of new businesses fail during the first few years of operation. The process of organizing a new business unit is referred to as promotion and includes the steps required to assemble the funds, facilities, and materials needed in preparation of business operations.

One of the paramount problems faced by operators of small firms is that of financing, because ordinarily, they are unable to tap the sources available to large firms. Once a business is organized, it is logical to expect it to grow, and growth itself brings with it additional financing problems. The economies resulting from size often create additional incentive for growth and expansion. In the past, the general public has been prone to identify expansion in size with monopoly, and this attitude is reflected in the enactment of antitrust laws and provisions for regulation.

The right of one business firm to own stock in others is well established, whether the ownership be for purposes of investment or control. When the purpose is that of control, a holding company may be created. However, because of public interest in the activities of large business units, holding companies, especially those in the public utility field, are subject to regulation.

This section covers organizing and financing a new business firm, financing small business firms, growth of business enterprises, and control of corporations by other corporations.

CHAPTER 24

Organizing and Financing a New Business Firm

EACH BUSINESS day, 1,300 new firms are launched in the United States, wherein the free enterprise economy permits virtually everyone to engage in business. Along with the privilege of starting a new business goes the risk of failure. One indication of the magnitude of this risk is the failure of 40 per cent of all new firms within the first few years of operation, and many among the organizers of the 60 per cent that do not fail could probably earn more with less effort as employees. However, many business firms which have been highly profitable were founded by men who ignored the odds against them.

A new business which prospers is usually one started by an individual who has confidence in his own ability, has had years of experience as an employee of a firm in the same industry, has appraised the situation realistically, is convinced that he has something better to offer the public, and is willing to work harder and longer than would be expected of him as an employee.

When any new firm is launched, the process is referred to as promotion; this term may be used to describe the formation of a new company in an established field, the creation of a company to manufacture or market a new product, the consolidation of several existing corporations, and the process whereby an existing privately owned business (or closely held corporation) is converted into one in which the stock is to be publicly owned. Promotional projects of the third and fourth types receive the attention of professional promoters, and they are closely related to problems of business growth, transfers, consolidations, mergers, and holding companies which are considered in later chapters. This chapter deals primarily with the problems associated with launching new business firms in either established or new fields. Although the typical new business is small, the large number of such firms makes the aggregate economic consequences of their organization more significant than those of the industrial giants which receive the attention of professional promoters.

ENTRY INTO BUSINESS

Operating one's own business has appeal for many reasons. Those most frequently expressed are independence—the opportunity to utilize one's capacities and give expression to one's ideas; profits—the belief that profits received will exceed income derived from working for others; and prestige—a businessman enjoys a position of respect in an economy such as ours. These are among the motives that have brought the 4.5 million business firms in the United States into existence.

There are, however, serious deterents to entering business; the emotional and psychological characteristics of some individuals make them unqualified to assume the accompanying responsibilities, and the risks associated with entering business deter others. Many have a sense of security in working for others (their skills, aptitudes, or previous experience may enable them to earn an income by performing a job) and this security may be jeopardized by going into business. In addition to risking security of occupation, entry into business usually requires an investment of savings and the assumption of debt by the would-be businessman.

Since many individuals are not mentally, emotionally, or financially equipped to assume the role of a businessman, one might ask "what are the characteristics required of a founder of a business firm?" Unfortunately, there is no exact answer to this question because the qualities required for business success are not easily identifiable. There are, however, traits which may be indicative of the chance of success or failure. Most successful businessmen have the ability to see opportunities for profit, and they have enough initiative to take advantage of them. In addition to having imagination, they have analytical minds and faculties for critical thinking which prevent them from substituting blind optimism for a sound appraisal of business facts. Few individuals are equally enthusiastic about all fields of endeavor; consequently, a successful businessman is usually working in an area in which he is genuinely interested. Although aptitude tests have been used in an effort to determine the area in which an individual would be most likely to succeed, the results have not been conclusive.

Probably the best preparation for a person interested in entering business for himself is experience with an existing firm in the same line of business. This is evidenced by the stock-option, pension, and profit-sharing plans of large corporations which are designed not only to keep key men from moving to competitors but also to deter them from organizing their own businesses. Business is called an art because skill or proficiency is acquired by experience as well as by study and observation. Business firms must be managed with discretion, but no set of rules or scientific procedures for doing the whole job have been devised. Anyone who has taken an elementary course in chemistry knows that everyone in the class will achieve the same results if instructions are followed precisely during an experiment; however, in the operation of a business, application of equal factors of production by different firms will not assure like results.

The rate of new business firm formations was exceptionally high during the early post-war years, but since 1948, the rate of increase (ratio of the number of new businesses established during a year to the number in operation at the beginning of the year) has been fairly stable. However, statistics which indicate only the increase in the number of firms in the United States hide the fact that many are started, many are discountinued, and many change ownership during the year. For illustration, over the 10-year period ending in mid-1957, 3.9 million new firms were organized, 3.2 million were discontinued, and 4.2 million changed ownership. The conclusion is obvious—although starting a new business entails risks, the lure of success is strong enough to cause thousands to be formed each year.

One indicator of the "health" of business firms is the number of business failures per 10,000 firms in operation. In Chart 7, the two lowest points in the failure rate of firms occurred during wars when fewer new firms were organized and inflation magnified dollar profits. The high points in the number of failures, as shown in Chart 7, occurred during periods of recession or depression. However, over the span of years since 1900, there has been an improvement in the general health of business firms as measured by the rate of failure. During the first three decades of this century, the failure rate exceeded that which has prevailed since then. Business failures can be lessened by careful planning; to paraphrase the marketing state-

CHART 7

Rate of Business Failures (Failures Per 10,000 Business Firms)

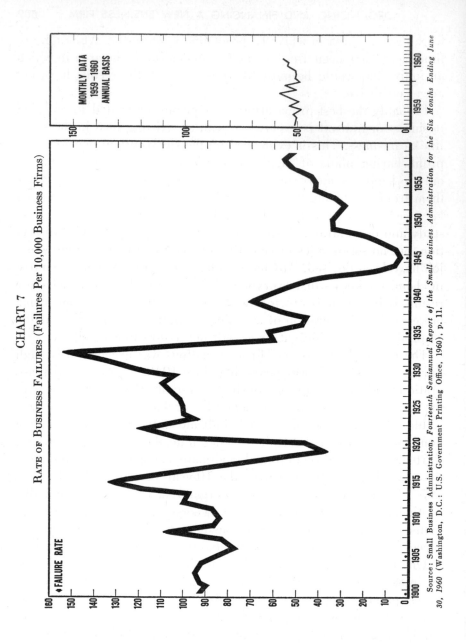

Source: Small Business Administration, *Fourteenth Semiannual Report of the Small Business Administration for the Six Months Ending June 30, 1960* (Washington, D.C.: U.S. Government Printing Office, 1960), p. 11.

ment, "a product well bought is half sold," one may say that a business firm that is well planned has moved half way toward success—certainly the chances of its failure are reduced.

STAGES IN LAUNCHING A BUSINESS FIRM

Promotion is defined as the initial step in launching a new business; the promoter is the one who assembles the men, money, and materials and carries the firm through the initial stages before turning it over to the managers. However, a promoter may continue as manager of the firm he organizes. The promoters of most new firms are individuals who have been employed in the same industry prior to going into business for themselves. The objective of most of them is the management of the firms which they promote, finance, and establish.

The four stages of promotion are birth of the idea, investigation to determine its practicality, assembly of facilities, and financial organization preceding operations. When control is released to those who are to operate the business, the promoter's work ceases and management takes over. The promoters may become the proprietors and managers because many new business enterprises are promoted by those who intend to operate them. The same person does not necessarily execute all four steps of promotion; one may have the idea but may need the assistance of others in order to form a business to use this idea.

Birth of the Idea. The first stage in promotion of a business firm is an idea of a business undertaking that seems to offer possibilities for profits. The idea may be a simple one such as a service business to repair radios, television sets, and household appliances, or it may be a complex plan for consolidating a number of railroad systems under a single management.

In order for the idea to materialize, it ought to be one in which others can believe. It may be one of manufacturing candle burners, using a new chemical process developed in a private laboratory, building a new natural gas pipeline, manufacturing television receivers, or operating a "tot" shop, a day nursery, a "do-it-yourself" shop, or some other manufacturing, merchandising, or service company.[1] Most new business firms as well as old ones conduct a

---

[1] The United States Department of Commerce publishes a number of pamphlets to aid veterans and others in starting new businesses. Among the titles which may be ordered from the Superintendent of Documents, Washington 25, D.C., are some of general interest such as *Your Own Business, The Small Businessman and His Bank, The Small*

merchandising or service business, but the percentage increase in the number of new companies since World War II has been greatest in the construction industry and wholesale trades. The great increase in the number of construction firms can be explained by the increase in demand for new homes, roads, sewer lines, schools, hospitals, plants, and other forms of construction, and the relatively small capital needed to set oneself up in business.

Some postwar ideas for business undertakings have been more spectacular than the average or typical one. For example, Mr. Claude A. Williams conceived the idea of a new natural gas line from the Rio Grande Valley to the Hudson River, and out of this idea was born the $240,000,000 Transcontinental Gas Pipe Line with a main line 1,840 miles long. The postwar housing shortage led to the creation of almost two hundred companies to construct prefabricated homes (most of these companies have disappeared). The electronics industry, an infant ten years ago, is now in fifth place among the nation's manufacturing industries (outranked only by automobiles, steel, aircraft, and chemicals). The products of electronic firms now enter most phases of American life (defense with use of missiles and space satellites; production with automation of factory and office operations; and the home with use of television and newly developed sound reproduction techniques based upon electronics).

In modern industry, many new products are the result of findings of research laboratories of large business corporations—sometimes as by-products of other lines of research. As a result, there is a tendency for independent inventors to be replaced by well-organized research laboratories. In the past, corporations have been charged with stifling progress by buying up and not using inventions in order to prevent their fixed assets from becoming obsolete. This may still happen; but today, the most profitable and progressive companies are those fostering research. The success and even survival of many firms depends on the efficiency of their research and development programs.

During recent wars, shortages of raw materials led to dismal forecasts of the economy's productive abilities; but industry produced more than had been anticipated. This can be explained, in part at

---

Businessman and Sources of Loans, and *The Small Businessman and His Financial Statements.* Other pamphlets deal with such subjects as licenses, retail policies, trade-marks, and government regulations. In addition, others discuss problems of special lines of business such as book stores, dry cleaning businesses, grocery stores, laundries, shoe repair shops, and so on for a total of about forty different lines.

least, by the ability of research departments to find substitutes for scarce products. One ought not underestimate the number of ideas worthy of exploitation conceived in research laboratories of industrial concerns; at the same time, one must not assume that going concerns are responsible for all new products and hence there is no room for newcomers. The first ingredient for promotion is creative imagination—something which may be developed.[2]

Investigation as to Practicality. The second phase in promotion is to try to determine if earnings would be adequate to justify investment of the estimated capital necessary to establish the new venture as a going concern. (The same type of analysis is involved when a new idea arises within a company—the question being, "Will anticipated earnings justify the increased expenditures required to develop it?") Temporarily, the answer may be "no" but may change to "yes" following refinements in process or changes in the general economic situation. Over a period of time, the number of new firms formed tends to increase as business activity increases.

The steps taken to arrive at an estimate of the profit potentiality of a proposed business enterprise depend somewhat on the type of business. However, an appraisal should be made of the demand for the service or product; nature of the competition which would have to be met; amount of income and expenses based on anticipated demands (at different sales volumes); investments required in fixed and working capital assets; availability of buildings, equipment, labor, and other assets needed in the venture; character and ability of potential officers; and interest of investors if public financing is planned. For each specific venture there may be special problems such as checking on the validity of a patent or determining the ability to obtain a license.

The prospects for a business concern may be clearer if they are in written form (the promotion report). The most common errors made in estimating prospects are failures to allow for adverse changes in general business, changes in consumer preferences, delays in starting the venture, and appearance of new competitors. Since every promoter is enthusiastic about his venture (or should be), the best safeguard against errors is to have the promotion report checked by a competent outsider. Still, the "experts" can be wrong. Nevertheless, there is need for careful screening of proposed companies. Impartial

---

[2] Alex F. Osborn, *Applied Imagination* (rev. ed.; New York: Charles Scribner's Sons, 1957).

advice may be provided by professional firms organized for such purposes.[3] Also, the Small Business Administration, state and local development companies, investment banking houses, commercial bankers, and lawyers may be consulted.

Often, instead of starting an entirely new firm, an individual who wants to enter business will buy a going concern (the number of annual transfers usually exceeds the number of new firms organized). In the event that a business is purchased, a local banker may be able to furnish information to the purchaser, and assistance from the local Chamber of Commerce, trade associations, and businessmen may prove helpful.

Assembly of Facilities. If the promotion report is favorable, the next step is to decide on the form of legal organization and to assemble the facilities. Option contracts may be arranged to buy or lease required properties and tentative arrangements may be made for skilled services. The promoter may arrange for trade credit and even tentative sales contracts may be made if the product is of a specialized type. The simpler the product, the easier it is for the promoter to assemble the necessary facilities and to get it into successful operation. Where there are many individual patents on parts of a complicated product, such as an automobile, the ability of a newcomer to compete successfully with established companies is almost impossible. The Tucker Corporation tried unsuccessfully to enter the automobile manufacturing field during the period following World War II when automobiles were scarce. Another illustration is the original Kaiser-Fraser Motor Company which was unable to operate at a profit while the other Kaiser companies, producing aluminum, steel, and ships have been able to do so. But the nature of the goods or services being produced is only one factor in the success or failure of a new business firm.

Sometimes the problem of assembly consists of taking over existing facilities and converting them to a different use. For illustration, the Texas Eastern Transmission Corporation of Shreveport, Louisiana was organized to transmit natural gas over pipelines constructed during World War II to transmit oil and refined products from the South and West to the harbors of New York and Philadelphia. On January 30, 1947, the government sold the pipelines (called the

---

[3] *The Directory of Consultant Members* may be obtained from the American Management Association, 1515 Broadway, New York 36, New York (price $2.00); a list of member firms of the Association of Consulting Management may be obtained from Consulting Management Engineers, 347 Madison Avenue, New York 17, New York.

"Big Inch" and the "Little Inch") as surplus property to the highest bidder—the Texas Eastern group—for over $143,000,000. (The original cost was $146,000,000.)

Patents pertain primarily to inventions and processes used in production. Patents granted by the federal government to encourage inventions give the owner a monopoly right for a period of seventeen years from the date the patent is granted, and it may be renewed by a special act of Congress. The owner of a patent may sell or lease it to others. The buyer may be a corporation which may acquire it from the original owner for cash or stock. Those who have business ability as well as inventive talent may provide for the production of their patented product by having it manufactured on a contract basis.

The description of a patent should be broad enough to prevent the production of a substitute product and still specific enough to prevent difficulty in getting approval of the application for the patent. Usually both legal and engineering skills are needed. There are thousands of patented products that never get into production because of high production costs, the absence of a current or a continuing or repeat market for the product, and the high costs of advertising and selling. Promoters may expect vigorous competition from established firms who are most seriously affected by the new product or process.

A copyright is granted by the federal government to protect authors, publishers, and creators of artistic works. Copyrights are for a period of twenty-eight years and may be renewed for a like period of time. Trade-marks, trade names and names of corporations may be registered.[4]

Before launching a business enterprise, promoters need also to check on licensing and other legal requirements. Practically every form of lawful business necessitates a license of some type from the federal, state, or local government.[5] The title given to the license may be a certificate to do business, a registration, a license, an occupational tax, or a permit, for which a fee is usually required. When the purpose of licensing is to enforce certain standards as to equipment and qualifications of employees (education, moral, training, experience, and/or competence), examinations may be required. A

---

[4] See United States Department of Commerce, Office of Small Business, *Small Business and Trade-Marks* (Washington, D.C.: U.S. Government Printing Office, 1949).

[5] See United States Department of Commerce, Office of Small Business, *Small Business and Government Licenses* (Washington, D.C.: U.S. Government Printing Office, 1950).

license is customarily issued for a period of one year and is usually renewed if the standards required for the business are maintained.

License fees or occupational taxes may be required for manufacturers and dealers in certain products such as oleomargarine, butter or cheese, ammunitions and firearms, narcotics, and alcoholic beverages. Promoters must also meet the registration and other requirements when operating bowling alleys, pool rooms, and gaming devices, dealing in tobacco and petroleum products, operating public carriers, customs warehouses, radio and television stations, etc.

Some licenses, like patents and copyrights, have monopolistic aspects. A government franchise or privilege to operate an electric light and power company, a telephone system, a railroad or bus line would be in this category. Automobile manufacturers, brewers, and others may give a sales agency a contract for a certain area which may have the same type of franchise value as one issued by a government. A concession, the right to use public or private property for a certain purpose, may be needed by a promoter (for examples, to sell food or souvenirs in a national park or in a privately owned ball park or to search for and exploit mineral resources).

At the present time, "franchising" appears in practically every industry and is particularly important in the service industries which are characterized by small business units.[6] A franchise is, in simple terms, a contract permitting the holder to sell and distribute goods or services in a specified area. A franchise holder pays the parent company a franchise fee or commission for the privilege of using its trade name, selling its products, or serving as its agent in leasing its equipment. A small firm, by obtaining a franchise, benefits from national advertising, use of trade secrets, established products, production procedures, cost control, and other services offered by the parent company.

In effect, many parent companies are promoters in that they find potential franchise holders and assist them in selecting business sites, planning layouts, training employees, and financing. Early in 1961, the third annual "Start Your Own Business Exposition" was held in New York City and was participated in by over one hundred exhibitors who had representatives on hand to explain their franchise opportunities and arrangements. Before granting a franchise, a re-

[6] Franchise holders include those operating automatic coin-operated laundries; dry cleaning establishments; car wash firms; income-tax record service companies; drive-in restaurants and stores; mobile units for distribution of ice cream, coffee, and other foods; automobile accessories; and personal improvement services including health equipment and products, dance studios, and reducing salons.

sponsible parent company checks an applicant's personality, education, and business experience as they relate to the type of business operation under consideration, and the amount of capital available to the applicant that may be used to purchase the franchise, to set up the business, and to keep it functioning.

Financial Organization Preceding Operations. After the blueprints of the business firm are drawn, options are arranged, legal form of business organization decided upon, and the charter or license arranged for or obtained, the enterprise is ready for the financing phase. For new business ventures, most of the capital will or should be provided by owners. In case of partnerships and single proprietorships, equity capital is provided by the partners and the single proprietor; in case of corporations, by the stockholders.

The financing of the Texas Eastern Transmission Corporation of Shreveport, Louisiana (see above) has become a classic in the field. The promotional group bought the initial issue of 150,000 shares of common stock (later split 7 to 1 into 1,050,000 shares), which provided the venture capital needed by the group. After the corporation's bid for the pipelines had been accepted by the government, $120,000,000 in bonds were sold to institutional investors and 3,550,000 additional shares of common stock were sold to the public at $9.50 per share. The fact that such a large amount of the original purchase price of the property was obtained from bonds sold to institutional investors is indicative of the investment aspect of the venture. At the other extreme are the current issues of common stock of companies that are taking advantage of the public interest in uranium and more recently in electronics.

There are many established mining and other companies that have acquired interests in mines and mineral lands in Utah, Arizona, Colorado, and other areas. In addition, there are many new companies that have been formed to develop property; some companies being formed have merely acquired leases; and others are being formed to look for uranium. New stock may be issued by such new companies for a penny, a nickel, a dime, and so on per share, with the result that single issues have been for 30 million shares. Most reputable bankers and brokers advise against the purchase of such shares.

For the ordinary small business unit, about the only capital that proprietors can be sure of is the amount that they, themselves, are able and willing to contribute. Sometimes an organizer of a small business firm by-passes conventional financing and raises the necessary funds from members of his family and from business associates. When the business operation is one which uses a franchise, the parent company may provide a plan which will reduce the original cash investment required (a major automobile manufacturing company owns a subsidiary corporation which helps dealers set up operations, and many distributors use the leasing services of the parent company).

If prospective proprietors have savings and securities, their capital contributions may be substantial; but if their assets are in nonliquid form (or of such a nature that they do not want to sell them), their ability to contribute to the venture will depend on what they can borrow by pledging their assets or arranging for an unsecured loan. Home mortgages are sometimes refinanced in order to obtain additional funds for business purposes. Veterans have used their borrowing privileges in negotiating loans with banks and other lenders (guaranteed in part by the Veterans Administration). Promoters may also use the Small Business Administration, small business investment companies, and other lenders as sources of funds (see Chapter 25). However, prior arrangements may have been made for trade credit, sales contracts may have been made with buyers to become effective when the firm is established, and lease arrangements for buildings and equipment may have been arranged for in advance so as to reduce the amount of fixed capital needed for operations. Usually, a promotional period is considered over when a business commences operations.

PROMOTION

Types of promoters include, in addition to those interested in starting their own businesses, professionals who make careers of starting business firms, and institutions—chiefly investment houses. Most promoters are in the first category and they usually limit their promotional efforts to one successful venture, but if that fails, they may attempt a second. In some cases, a businessman who has been successful in promoting a business firm will sell it and use his talents and profits to start another. If this type of operation becomes a common and frequent practice, the promoter might well be classified as a professional who is more interested in promoting new companies than in operating them.

Many new companies are created as a result of transfers of titles that occur when existing companies are combined or merged. Behind such transfers there may be an independent professional promoter, but more often such combinations are promoted by investment houses. Although promotion is rarely the primary activity of an investment banking firm, such a firm is equipped to perform such functions more efficiently than could an independent professional promoter or any other financial institution.

In some cases, manufacturing and distributing companies help to organize and finance smaller firms in order to promote their products, but they have little or no interest in deriving a profit from promotion of the smaller firms because their profits are derived from the sale, distribution, or franchising of their products. On the other hand, professional promoters are primarily interested in securing profits from the promotion of business firms; it is the activities of such promoters that are dealt with in the remainder of this chapter.

ACTIVITIES OF THE PROFESSIONAL PROMOTER

A professional promoter is usually a good salesman and organizer who has acquired the reputation of being able to launch new companies. He often has some funds available for investment in opportunities that he considers worth developing and promoting. If the opportunity is in the form of an instrument which has been patented and for which there is a potential demand, he may enter into a contract with the owner to produce it on a royalty basis if the reports of his patent lawyer, engineers, and other specialists are favorable.

The contract with the owner (or inventor) for manufacturing the instrument will be followed by an investigation of the patent to see that it is drawn correctly and does not infringe on other United States patents. A contract will be made with a manufacturer to produce a sample or working model and the instrument's performance will be tested by an independent laboratory. With the assistance of specialists in the field, the promoter will make a survey of the market in which it is to be sold. If the market is a highly specialized one, displays or demonstrations before interested parties may be arranged. An investigation may then be made of the possibility of selling the instrument through national, regional, or local distributors on a commission or some other basis.

The cost of manufacturing the instrument will be considered in establishing a retail price. The extent to which it will be competitive at that price must also be determined. Even if the price is lower than that of competitive instruments, the promoter's company formed to sell the instrument will be faced with problems that are common to all new firms. One of the most important tasks of the promoter is that of arranging for the financing of his company, usually through the sale of common stock to the public. If the stock is to be distributed only within one state, the standards set for security offerings by the state regulatory agency must be met; if the stock is to be sold in two or more states, the standards set by the Securities and Exchange Commission must be met.

The prospectus announcing the offering of new stock contains a description of the offering, the plan for using the proceeds, a description of the business, anticipated earnings and dividends, capitalization of the company, description of the capital stock, options held by the promoter and others to purchase stock, legal proceedings that involve the company, options held by lawyers and other experts, and a report of an independent public accountant. Before the offering, the details contained in the prospectus and supporting documents must be amended to meet the standards set by the supervisory agency.

The problems faced by promotors are often complex and the different stages in promotion are usually participated in by several men or groups. For illustration, Mr. E. Holley Poe is given credit for conceiving the idea of using the government-built pipeline to transmit natural gas to the northeastern market (Texas Eastern Transmission Corporation of Shreveport, Louisiana). Mr. R. H. Hargrove, a veteran of the natural gas industry, was consulted on the feasibility of the idea. Legal guidance was provided by Attorney Charles I. Francis, a former counsel for the Petroleum Administration. Technical advice was provided by a well-known geologist, E. L. De Golyer. Engineering and financial backing came from George R. and Herman Brown (Brown & Root, Engineers and Contractors). Later this group was joined by George T. Naff, lawyer and engineer with experience in the gas industry.

Risks in Promotion. The risks assumed by promoters are many because many ideas for a new business never reach the launching stage. First of all, the time of the promoter is used in trying to develop a proposed company. Also, his cash outlays for options to buy or lease buildings and other things may be substantial and there may be no hope for recovery if the project fails to materialize. Cash payments for professional advice—legal, accounting, engineering and others—are often paid by the promoter. An individual or group of individuals may work for years developing an invention or process on which it is difficult to place a valuation in terms of hours or dollars spent; but, nevertheless, the costs are real.

Usually, a promotional venture may be terminated at any time by mutual agreement. In case of termination, there may be obligations which would have to be settled by the participants according to previous agreements. In addition, there may be valuable assets to dispose of, the proceeds of which would have to be applied to meeting current obligations. It is generally held that the promoter who executes a contract is personally liable if the corporation is not thereafter created. Long before the venture is ready for public financing, the funds of the promoter and other participants may be exhausted. At this stage, the promoter and those who have their funds invested in the project may lose control unless they are able to obtain financial aid from others by selling stock on a "when, as, and if issued basis," or by obtaining funds in the form of a loan from others who agree to join the promotional group.

Not only do a number of firms fail to survive the first few years of operations but many that do survive operate at a loss for many months or years. If the business venture is organized as a sole proprietorship or partnership, the promotional expenses are the responsibility of the individual proprietor or partners; but, when a firm is incorporated, a number of legal questions arise as to the rights of promoters.

After a corporation has been created, directors and officers are agents; but how can a promoter be an agent for a corporation which is not in existence? Sometimes directors are thought of as controlling the property of the corporation as trustees; but how can a promoter be considered a trustee when he holds no property in the ordinary sense of the word? Nevertheless, many of the principles involved in a trust relationship are applied in determining the rights and the compensation of promoters of new corporations. The new corporation customarily assumes all costs of promotion; but the costs may seem excessive to some of its stockholders. In some cases, management may disallow the promoter's claims; but when management of the new corporation and its promoter or promotional group are the same, arm's length bargaining is lacking. Out of this situation and judicial decisions thereto, certain rules applicable to promoters have been developed.

Among the rules that have been developed to cover the legal status of the promoter are the following: A promoter may not make a secret profit at the expense of the corporation. There is no objection to the promoter's making a profit provided there is full disclosure of the material facts to a board of directors which is independent or not subservient to the promoter. Later, if secret profits are disclosed, the corporation may sue the promoter to recover them. The action taken may be to rescind a contract or to recover cash and/or stock given in payment. The suit may be for damages without changes in existing contracts. In the past, these common-law procedures for recovering unreasonable amounts paid to promoters proved inadequate. Now, all states except Nevada have so-called "blue-sky" laws or antifraud laws to protect buyers of securities.

In some stock offerings, state agencies have forced changes such as reductions in the offering price and in the allotment of stock and stock purchase options to the organizers for services. Occasionally, the securities commission or regulatory agency places the shares of the promoter and others closely linked to the promoter in escrow until the company has earned a specified amount per share of stock. These stockholders may also be required to subordinate their claims to those of other shareholders in the event of liquidation during the term of the escrow.

The Securities Act of 1933 calls for full disclosure of all pertinent information on a proposed issue, requires registration of the security issue with the Securities and Exchange Commission (with many exceptions), and provides for civil and criminal action against violators for omissions of pertinent information. When there are material omissions or misstatements, the Commission may prevent or delay the distribution of securities by refusing to permit the registration to become effective. Although the Commission does not pass on the investment value of securities, it is required by law to see that the information provided prospective investors is accurate, complete, and not misleading. State and federal regulatory agencies also insist that prospective investors are informed as to the compensation of the promoters, the organizers, investment bankers, and others closely associated with the promotion.

Compensation of Promoters. Usually, a promoter will receive an allotment of common stock in the new project as compensation, but sometimes his compensation will consist of option-warrants that give him the right to buy a specified number of shares of common stock at a stated price for a specific period of time. The promoter may also receive cash, a salary contract for a number of years as president or manager, a contract for professional services, or some combination of awards and privileges.

Promotional expenses may be as much as 10 or 15 per cent of the capital of the business firm in addition to costs of financing, and these costs as well as those for assets purchased by the promoter are absorbed by the new company. For illustration, Glenn McCarthy, Inc., a Delaware corporation, acquired from the promoter, Mr. Glenn McCarthy, "the right to direct and control operations for the exploration and discovery of oil and gas on approximately 970,000 acres covered by a lease granted Mr. McCarthy by the Republic of Bolivia . . ."[6] Payments of $47,500 were made to Mr. McCarthy for the Bolivian lease plus $62,500 to Mr. B. V. Christie, "who was instrumental in Mr. McCarthy securing the Bolivian lease, as a finder's fee." The company also assumed the expenses associated with incorporation, the maintenance of an office and a staff during the promotion period, and an advance by the promoters to acquire a drilling rig and other equipment for use by the company in its proposed Bolivian operation.

The public financing consisted of an offering of 10,000,000 shares of common stock with a par value of 25 cents at a price of $2 per share. The underwriter or investment banker was B. V. Christie & Co. of Houston, Texas. The underwriter (under the assumption that all of the shares of common stock "offered hereby are sold") agreed to purchase 1,000,000 shares and to use his best effort to distribute the remaining 9,000,000 shares to the general public at $2 a share. The underwriting discount or commission to be collected by the investment banker was 30 cents per share, which would mean that the proceeds to the company were $1.70 per share or $17,000,000 (assuming that all shares were sold and before deducting the estimated expenses of the company in connection with the offering in the amount of $125,000 plus certain underwriting expenses not to exceed $15,000).

The amount of shares authorized was 25,000,000 of which 1,251,000 were outstanding before the public offering. Ownership of these shares was divided as follows: Glenn H. McCarthy, president and director, 1,000,000; B. V. Christie, director, 250,000; and Ralph E. Fair, vice-president and director, 1,000. The shares acquired by Mr. McCarthy and Mr. Christie illustrate how promoters are often rewarded for their efforts through stock ownership.

Both Mr. McCarthy and Mr. Christie had acquired their shares at 25 cents per share. At the time that Mr. McCarthy signed his rights over to the company, he had an agreement that would reimburse him for his expenditures; and, upon the signing of the agreement, he re-

---

[6] This quotation and other statements of facts are taken from *Prospectus Glenn McCarthy, Inc. 10,000,000 Shares Common Stock Par Value $.25 Per Share* (dated October 16, 1953).

ceived $250,000 and Mr. Christie received $62,500. Although Mr. McCarthy's $250,000 was not called a "promoters fee," it might have been. These sums just equalled the costs of Mr. McCarthy's and Mr. Christie's stock. To quote from the propectus, "as a result of the transaction above described, Messrs. McCarthy and Christie will receive an aggregate of 1,250,000 shares of Common Stock of the Company at no cost to them."

In addition to being given stock in a new venture, sometimes promoters are permitted to share in the prospects of their company in other ways. For illustration, Mr. McCarthy was given a ten-year employment contract by the company under which he is to receive a salary not in excess of $60,000 per annum plus an amount equal to 10 per cent of the corporation's net profits after the payment of federal income taxes and excess profits taxes, if any. Shares of a new company, such as Glenn McCarthy, Inc., are speculative in nature, and they are so labeled in the prospectus. Since Mr. McCarthy has had wide experience in the petroleum industry, the issue had a wide appeal to speculators.

SUMMARY

Promotion of a business enterprise includes all the steps from the conception of the idea to the birth of the firm. The idea must be practical whether it is for a ten-cent gadget or a billion-dollar atomic blast furnace. Its production must give promise of being profitable to those risking their capital resources to put it into operation. Some of the factors analyzed in estimating profit potentiality include anticipated production costs, public demand for the product or service, and competition in the field.

The next stage in promotion is that of assembling the facilities (arrangements for acquiring fixed assets and services, licenses or permits, etc.) and may even include arrangements for trade credit and sales contracts. The final stage before the business firm begins operations is that of financing with consideration given to the pros and cons of using equity and/or loan capital and the amounts and types of each. Unless the new enterprise, especially if a new invention is being utilized, gives promise of large profits, it is difficult and expensive to raise needed capital from the general public.

The professional promoter's interest in a new firm often ends when the project is launched. Then he may sell his proprietory interest to obtain funds with which to promote another enterprise. While the services of a professional promoter are expensive, the risk he assumes are substantial. Many ideas considered and worked on by a promoter never reach the launching stage. His expenses may include cash outlays for options and for other things; if the project fails, he has little hope for reimbursement. Because the legal status of the promoter may be in question when the business venture is a publicly financed corporation, certain rules have been developed. "Blue-sky" laws in states' statutes, antifraud laws, and the Securities Act of 1933 have as one of their objectives "to prevent misrepresentation, deceit or other fraudulent practices in the sale of securities."

QUESTIONS AND PROBLEMS

1. Distinguish among the different types of promotion.
2. Identify the four steps in promotion of a new business firm.
3. What should be covered in a promotional report?
4. (*a*) What are the advantages of financing a new firm with equity capital? (*b*) If equity capital is inadequate, may loan capital be used? (*c*) Is trade credit usually available to new firms?
5. What traits or characteristics should the organizer of a new firm have if the venture is to succeed? In your opinion what factors account for the vulnerability of new business firms?
6. (*a*) What risks are assumed by a professional promoter? (*b*) In addition to cash, how may a promoter be compensated for the risks assumed and the expenses incurred in promoting a new business firm?
7. Identify "blue-sky" laws. What are the different types?
8. "What are the odds against survival for a newly born business? A great deal greater than the average person might think—in fact, about 5 to 1 against a life span of ten years." (*New York Times*, January 10, 1956, p. 39.) Identify the factors which account for these odds.
9. What is the significance of the following statement? "There were 774 registration statements filed with the Securities and Exchange Commission in the . . . year ended June 30, 1960, by companies that had never before sold stock publicly. This compares with 297 such registrations for fiscal 1959." (*Wall Street Journal* [New York], February 17, 1961, p. 1.)
10. Analyze: "The conventional wisdom says that uncontrolled enterprise is the economic key to the general welfare; but enterprise is most free in the medium-sized companies and on the peripheries of industry, in the small, local, and retail businesses. As the number of stockholders grows, the old ideas of private property alter and become dim." (W. H. Ferry, *The Corporation and the Economy* [Santa Barbara, California: Funds for the Republic, Inc., 1959], pp. 8–9.)

CHAPTER 25

Financing Small Business Firms

ALTHOUGH the same principles of business finance are applicable to all business firms irrespective of size, the application of those principles may not be the same for small firms as for large business units. Consequently, the problems associated with the financing of small business firms demand separate treatment (although they are often neglected). To an increasing extent, public corporations are under the control of professional managers; in many cases the gap between management and proprietorship is a wide one. The failure of a large corporation may mean little more than the loss of a job to a professional manager, but the failure of a small business firm usually means both the loss of a job and of personal assets to the owner-manager of a small firm.

The relationship of small business firms to the capital and money markets, the customer-loan market, and the market for equity capital is not the same as that of large corporations. The differences in the availability of capital between large and small firms have been recognized not only by students and writers concerned with this subject but also by Congress, which has made provisions for the Small Business Administration and small loan investment companies.

Small business firms handle about one third of the total business done in the United States, and most of these firms operate in fields which come closest to the ultimate consumer—the fields of retailing and service. This chapter deals with the characteristics of small businesses, sources of financing help from large business firms, the Small

Business Administration, small business investment companies, and development companies.

CHARACTERISTICS OF SMALL BUSINESSES

Management. One of the outstanding characteristics of small business enterprises is the fact that ownership and management are combined in the same individual or group of individuals. Owner-operators or their families usually provide the capital used in the venture in contrast to large corporations wherein ownership is widely dispersed and managers own but a small percentage of the capital. The owner of a small business is usually a resident of the community in which the firm operates and is usually active in the affairs of the community, while the principal stockholders of a large corporation may live anywhere in the world.

Customarily the operations of a small firm are local in nature, while those of a large corporation may be national or international, with plants and/or outlets scattered throughout the country or the world. The working relationship between an owner-manager and his employees is usually a close one, and the employees usually know considerably more about the business than do the majority of the employees of large corporations. Strikes, which occur because of breakdowns in labor-management relations of large corporations, are seldom among the problems which confront the owner-manager of a small business firm.

Incompetent management is the basic cause of business failure. An incompetent manager may have failed to anticipate the scope of the enterprise, the character of the market, the amount of competition, and/or the amount of equipment and other assets that would be required. Often, a business failure is explained on the basis of inadequacy of financial resources; usually, a more accurate appraisal of the cause of failure would be an excess of capital—more credit than the talents of the manager enable him to use profitably. In most cases it is the man who fails, not the business.

Control. Regardless of whether a small firm is organized as an individual proprietorship, a partnership, or a corporation, it will be under the control of the owner or owners. While there are many advantages associated with a small business, there are some disadvantages for which there may be no solution. Its staff is usually small and often consists of a single individual—the owner. When the owner-manager's abilities are spread too thin, improper business decisions tend to occur. Often, it is impossible for such an individual to keep fully informed about general economic, technical, and market conditions. Undermanagement is a characteristic of many small businesses, and among the managerial functions which are most often neglected, accounting and finance are foremost.

Often the owner of a small business devotes his life to building it up; therefore, he is reluctant to share ownership with others by the use of equity capital. Consequently, he resorts to debt financing even though sound business financing principles call for additional equity financing. If such an individual succeeds in obtaining more loan capital than he is capable of using efficiently, the net return from business operations may decline rather than increase and failure rather than expansion may be the result. When the debt to equity ratios of small and large companies in the same industry are compared, such as firms in the field of manufacturing, the debt-equity ratio is larger for small firms than for large ones.

Financing Problems. Most of the original equity capital of a small business is provided by the owner, members of his family, and friends; however, these sources cannot be depended upon for additional funds because most investors diversify their holdings so as to lessen their risks. Thus a small firm may reach a stage in its development at which it will have to depend to an increasing extent on retained earnings if it is to grow. Perhaps the most serious financial problem confronting owners of small businesses is lack of sufficient equity capital; in many cases this is caused in part by an owner's refusal to sell additional equity to those who would be willing to purchase it. Also, small firms have more difficulty in raising equity capital than loan capital.

A survey made by the Board of Governors of the Federal Reserve System of the financing experiences of small corporations in the manufacturing field indicated that many small companies do not need external financing. During the year covered by the survey, more than 40 per cent of the companies reported no need for short-term credit other than trade credit and about 65 per cent reported no need for long-term credit or for additional equity capital. On the other hand, a minority of approximately 38 per cent reported a need for additional short-term credit, 17 per cent reported a need for long-term credit, and 14 per cent for additional equity capital.[1]

Of the small manufacturing firms that reported a need for short-term credit, 75 per cent stated that they were able to obtain external

[1] "Small Business Financing: Corporate Manufacturers," *Federal Reserve Bulletin*, January, 1961, p. 8.

funds on a satisfactory basis; but of those which needed long-term funds, only 38 per cent were able to satisfy their needs on a satisfactory basis. Only 14 per cent of those in need of equity capital were able to obtain it on satisfactory terms. Usually, the firms that had trouble in raising capital in one area also had trouble raising it in other areas; some that needed long-term funds had made no specific effort to obtain them.[2] The experiences of various small manufacturing corporations grouped according to size are summarized in Table 27.

TABLE 27

SIZE OF COMPANY AND TYPE OF FINANCING RELATED TO FINANCING EXPERIENCE
(Percentages of All Manufacturing Corporations in Each Size Group)

FINANCING EXPERIENCE	*Small*	*Medium*	*Large*
	Short-Term Credit		
Total in scope	100.0	100.0	100.0
Total response	81.8	83.9	94.5
No need for funds	44.5	38.7	45.3
Needed funds	37.3	45.2	49.8
Needs met satisfactorily	26.3	39.9	48.3
Experience not satisfactory	11.0	5.2	1.5
No financing efforts made	4.3	1.2	0.5
	Long-Term Credit		
Total in scope	100.0	100.0	100.0
Total response	81.7	84.0	94.5
No need for funds	64.1	66.0	70.1
Needed funds	17.6	18.0	24.4
Needs met satisfactorily	5.9	11.7	20.9
Experience not satisfactory	11.7	6.4	3.5
No financing efforts made	8.4	3.6	2.0
	Equity Capital		
Total in scope	100.0	100.0	100.0
Total response	81.8	83.9	94.5
No need for funds	68.2	69.9	52.7
Needed funds	13.5	14.1	42.3
Needs met satisfactorily	1.4	6.2	36.3
Experience not satisfactory	12.2	7.9	6.0
No financing efforts made	10.7	6.7	3.0

Note: Details may not add to totals because of rounding.
Source: *Federal Reserve Bulletin*, January, 1961, p. 12.

Profitability. Among the small companies those least likely to need external financing are the more profitable companies. Irrespective of the measure of profitability—profits to sales or profits to net worth ratio—the Board of Governors' survey supports the conclusion that the least profitable small business firms are most likely to report a need for external funds. Credit is a paradox in that small firms

[2] *Ibid.*, p. 10–11.

most in need of credit have the most difficulty in obtaining it. Nevertheless about one half of those with below average profitability, participating in the survey, were able to meet all their financing needs satisfactorily.[3]

Balance Sheet Structure. Presumably small business firms may obtain additional funds without difficulty if they have a strong balance sheet structure. The strength of a balance sheet structure may be tested by (1) the quick asset ratio or liquid assets to current liabilities, (2) current ratio or total current assets to total current liabilities, (3) current liabilities to total assets, and (4) net worth to total debts. As might be expected, small manufacturing corporations that reported higher-than-average liquidity or higher ratio of equity to debt needed external financing least, while those needing external funds had the most difficulty in obtaining them. However the balance sheet analysis was not conclusive in proving that it was equally important among all size small firms because the middle-size and larger firms were more successful in financing their needs than many of the above-average small companies.[4]

Credit Ratings. The ability of small business firms to obtain credit is influenced by the credit ratings given them by Dun and Bradstreet and other rating services. Although mercantile rating services are chiefly for trade suppliers, credit rating services are also used by banks and other lenders. Success in obtaining funds from external sources by those small manufacturing companies participating in the Board of Governors' survey was related to their credit ratings. Nonrated companies had the greatest difficulty in obtaining funds while the highest rated companies had the least. But here again there is the credit paradox: those who needed external financing the most had the lowest credit ratings.

SOURCES OF FINANCING

If a business firm is to operate successfully, it should be able to supplement its financial resources from outside sources. The adage "Neither a borrower or a lender be" has no place in present-day business practice; most business firms are borrowers or lenders and sometimes they are both at the same time. There are many external sources of business funds, but generally small businessmen are more dependent on their banks for both short-term and long-term credit

---

[3] *Ibid.*, p. 16.

[4] *Ibid.*, p. 17.

than upon other sources of loan credit. Small business firms' other sources of short-term funds include trade suppliers, finance companies, factors, shareholders, officers of their own companies, and sometimes investors in the commercial paper market.

However, as small companies increase in size they usually become less dependent upon banks for their long-term loans and finance more with nonbank financial institutions and in the securities markets. Small corporations that seek equity financing may rely almost entirely on sales to existing shareholders and funds raised through employee stock-purchase plans or benefit plans.

Most nonmanufacturing companies are smaller than manufacturing companies, and the average small firm will depend primarily on commercial banks for both short-term and long-term credit. The typical small businessman has had borrowing experiences at his bank. These may include obtaining a mortgage loan on his home, a chattel mortgage on his car, or an unsecured personal loan; hence he is familiar with the principles and procedures that banks follow in making business loans. However, it may surprise him to find that the loan officer considers the risks of a business loan to be greater than the home mortgage, car, or personal loan he made previously at the bank. Furthermore, he may find that his business loan will carry a higher interest rate and a shorter maturity and that it may be subject to restrictions that are not present in his mortgage loan.

While the typical homeowner's loan is repaid in monthly installments that include interest and principal payments, insurance, and taxes, a business loan will usually be discounted and have a maturity of sixty or ninety days with or without the right of renewal. Although term loans may be obtained, these are of secondary importance among the loans to small business firms. A small businessman who obtains a business loan from his bank will be expected to keep a deposit account with the bank during the loan period and to use other services of the bank, while the recipient of a homeowner's loan will be under no pressure to use the services of the financial institution which holds the mortgage on his home.

A small business loan is usually secured by a pledge of assets. While some banks will accept almost any type of property as security, others, particularly small banks, are not equipped to handle pledges in the form of accounts receivable or warehouse receipts; consequently, real estate owned by a businessman may be the only acceptable asset that may be pledged for a bank loan. When a bank loan is made for thirty to ninety days without the right of renewal, the businessman is expected to repay the funds in whole or part from funds from operations; hence, the businessman must be prepared to show that such funds will be available at the specified time. A fairly common shortcoming among small business firms is the lack of adequate records upon which a sound credit decision could be based. It is often maintained, and with some justification, that large businesses can obtain funds more easily than can small firms; it must be remembered, however, that part of this apparent ease of obtaining credit can be explained by the presence of more complete financial records and statements. In fact, it might be stated that if large business firms went to their banks and other lenders with no more adequate financial records than those provided by the typical small business firm, they would fare no better. One of the most important financial tools used by the operator of a small business firm is a cash budget.

One of the most generally used methods of computing a cash budget is the cash receipt and cash disbursement method. Its construction may be for any period of time, but a cash budget is usually made on a weekly or monthly basis. A cash budget permits a comparison of actual cash receipts and expenditures with the budget estimates.

Sometimes cash disbursements can be timed to coincide with cash receipts, reducing the need for borrowing and permitting cash balances to be kept at a desirable level. Many owner-operators of small firms lack the accounting help needed for cash budgeting. Hence, the burden of creating a small businessman's first cash budget may fall upon his banker. Any budget is a projection of past accounting records indicating estimated cash receipts (gross income), which usually come from sales; required outlays for the expected level of sales; and adjustments for these and other factors, including plans for capital outlays that affect the cash flow.

Budgetary techniques are discussed in greater detail in books on budgetary accounting, but a form that can be used by small business firms appears in Table 28 (note: a space is provided not only for budget estimates but also for the actual receipts and disbursements that may be added when available.) Thus the sum of cash on hand at the beginning of the month and cash receipts during the month, less cash disbursements during the month, equals cash on hand at the end of the month. When this information is available, arrangements for borrowing and plans for repaying loans may be made.

TABLE 28

ESTIMATED CASH RECEIPTS AND CASH DISBURSEMENTS
April to June

	APRIL		MAY		JUNE	
	Budget	Actual	Budget	Actual	Budget	Actual
Estimated Receipts:						
Cash sales..........						
Accounts receivable.						
Other income.......						
Total Receipts....						
Estimated Disbursements:						
Accounts payable...						
Payroll............						
Expenses...........						
Advertising........						
Interest expense....						
Plant and equipment						
Repayment of bank loan.............						
Total Disbursements.........						
Estimated excess of cash receipts over cash disbursements..						
Estimated balance at beginning of month.						
Estimated bank borrowing during month						
Estimated loan repayments during month.						
Estimated balance at end of month.......						

HELP FROM LARGE BUSINESS FIRMS

The burden of financing small business firms is assumed in part by large companies in the form of trade credit or cash advances made by suppliers, by lease of equipment and real property, and by franchise arrangements. Trade credit, which is more important to small business firms than to large ones, was discussed in an earlier chapter (see Chapter 11).

Most large industrial corporations, such as General Motors for illustration, take paternal pride in the small companies that act as their suppliers. In a study made of 27,500 United States firms that provide General Motors Corporation with goods and services used in the production of automobiles and other products, the interdependence of large and small business firms was emphasized. In 1959 almost $5.5 billion or 48.5 cents out of each dollar received by General Motors was paid to suppliers, 70 per cent of whom employed fewer than 100 persons and 45 per cent of whom had fewer than 25 employees. Among these small suppliers were 6,500 business firms that had sold goods or services to General Motors for over 10 years and another 600 for over 30 years.[5]

Large corporations make a point of refuting the statement that small business firms are disappearing, and they support their contention with statistics from an impartial source, the United States government. Not only do large corporations buy from and sell to small companies but they also sponsor merchandising procedures which tend to increase the number of locally owned small companies. For illustration, many large corporations have shifted their emphasis from direct selling by mail and through their own salesmen to having small independent companies handle their products on a commission basis. In the case of machinery or equipment, the manufacturer makes the local business firm responsible for selling and/or leasing it. In other cases, the economic position of the small business firm is strengthened by franchise arrangements with a larger corporation for the sale and distribution of its goods and services.

Among manufacturers of durable consumer goods (automobiles, household appliances, radios, etc.), machinery, and equipment, franchises between parent companies and small local firms have been used for many years; but, as noted in an earlier chapter, franchising has been extended to include practically all phases of merchandising in recent years.

There is considerable variation in the relationship between parent companies and the smaller firms which handle their products. However, the various services extended by parent companies include supervision of personnel training, centralized buying, and assistance in problems of financing, accounting, and advertising. For its

---

[5] General Motors Corporation, *Shareholders' Quarterly* (First Quarter, 1960), p. 10.

success, the parent company is largely dependent upon the smaller firms through which its products are distributed; hence, the parent company's interest in operations of these firms will continue as long as franchises are in effect.[6]

When a small company needs specific equipment, the parent company may provide it on a lease basis; if financing is required, the parent company will provide assistance either directly or through a subsidiary company created for this purpose. Some parent companies that franchise their products provide the buildings, stores, drive-ins, display rooms and other facilities for merchandising their products; others build stores or other facilities, sell them to local investors or life insurance companies, and rent them back on a lease-purchase basis. Under other conditions, property may be leased by the local operator with the lease guaranteed by the parent company. However, all units that operate under the same name are not necessarily owned by local businessmen (for illustration, only 60 per cent of the more than 550 Howard Johnson Restaurants are owned and/or operated by individuals under a franchise agreement with the Howard Johnson organization).

SMALL BUSINESS ADMINISTRATION

At the present time the Small Business Administration is the only federal government agency created and designed to render aid exclusively to small business firms.[7] Size is commonly measured by the number of employees, the volume of sales, or total assets, but the dividing line between large and small businesses differs for different industries. Thus the dividing line will be higher for manufacturers than for distributors, higher for wholesalers than for retailers, and higher for some retailers than for dealers in personal services.

The Small Business Administration classifies manufacturing com-

[6] L. T. White, in "How Big Companies Help Small Marketers," *Small Marketers Aids*, No. 31 (Small Business Administration, March, 1958), p. 3., gives the following list of financial services provided by large business firms to small companies: "Extend credit, help install time-payment plans, consign merchandise, endorse notes, lend money, teach management of money, assist dealer financing—floor plans, finance dealer receivables, suggest accounts receivable financing and investments, advise on credit and collection, provide credit and collection service, advise on insurance and taxes, analyze financial statements, find investors, buy stock giving owner option to re-purchase it later, provide consumer financing through dealer, organize dealer councils, help in financing new establishments."

[7] At various times, small business firms could obtain assistance from the Reconstruction Finance Corporation, Smaller War Plants Corporation, Small Defense Plants Administration, Federal Reserve banks (Section 13 b loans), Veterans' Administration, Export-Import Bank of Washington, and V-loan program.

panies that employ fewer than 250 persons as small businesses, while firms that employ more than 1,000 persons would be considered large. In between are many firms that would fall in one or the other category depending on circumstances. The Small Business Administration would consider a wholesale firm small if its annual dollar volume of sales is $5,000,000 or less, and a retail or service trade concern small if annual sales or receipts are $1,000,000 or less. However, some retailers may fall into the small-business category if their annual sales are $2,000,000 or less (such as department stores or other general merchandisers, automobile dealers, and grocery stores which handle fresh meat).[8]

In order to be classified as a small business, a firm must not be dominant in its particular field of operations (the government must not encourage monopolies) and it must be independently owned (if it is a subsidiary of a large corporation, it should expect to get its financial aid from the parent company). While other divisions of the federal government use different measures to classify businesses as large or small, there is general agreement in the conclusion that 99 per cent of all business firms are small. Only 150,000 firms would be classified as large and over 4,500,000 would be classified as small businesses.

Most of the financial assistance of the Small Business Administration has been in participation with commercial banks and other private lenders. Participation is of two types: (1) deferred, in which the Small Business Administration agrees to purchase up to 90 per cent of the unpaid balance of a loan on request of the lender; and (2) immediate, in which the Small Business Administration agrees to share in up to 90 per cent of the loan from the beginning. In deferred participation, a bank or a private lender agrees to pay the Administration a fee varying from ½ of 1 per cent to 1 per cent per annum depending upon the portion of the loan which has been underwritten by the Administration.

The Small Business Administration may also make direct loans to small businesses without participation by private lenders. Because the intent of Congress was not to create a government agency that would be a competitor of private lenders, the Small Business Administration is prohibited from making direct loans if arrangements can be made for participation by a private lender. Further-

---

[8] U.S. Cong. House, Select Committee on Small Business, *Definition of "Small Business" Within Meaning of Small Business Act of 1953, as Amended,* H. Res. 56, 85th Cong., 2d sess., 1959, p. 13.

more, the agency is not permitted to make an *immediate* participation loan when a *deferred* participation loan can be arranged.

When an application is made for a direct loan, the agency must try to arrange for a participation loan with others or preferably a loan that will be made by a private lender and underwritten by the Small Business Administration. In many instances, small businesses find that they can finance their needs elsewhere and withdraw their requests for financial help from the Administration.

Since 1953—when SBA was organized—and through June 30, 1960, the agency approved 20,362 business loans for $995,191,000 of which the agency's share was $808,803,000 or 85 per cent of the total. The maximum loan that the Small Business Administration may make to one name is $350,000; and, during the first seven years of operations, the average size loan was $47,000. Private lending institutions have participated in 13,031 of the total number of business loans approved by the agency and the percentage of bank participation has increased slightly since 1960. Although the total amounts involved in the loans of SBA are small compared with the volume of credit extended by private lenders, the agency has responsibilities to small businesses in addition to that of lending. These include giving financial counseling, certifying small firms for government orders, advising small firms on managerial procedures, providing firms with technical assistance, and providing assistance in production.

A small company that obtains a participation loan has the advantage of dealing with his banker. A loan of this type is serviced locally by the loan officer of the bank; and, after the loan has been seasoned, the bank may be willing to assume full responsibility for it. In some cases, loans that have been made by the Small Business Administration have been cancelled before becoming effective and taken over by banks or private lenders.

Business firms that borrow under the Small Business Administration program customarily do so in order to augment their working capital; acquire equipment; consolidate their obligations; or construct, remodel, purchase, or convert a plant or other facility. Manufacturing companies have been the chief users of the financial services of the Small Business Administration, but in the last few years an increasing number of companies in the retail and service fields have used its services.[9]

[9] See also *Semiannual Reports of Small Business for the Six Months Ending June 30, 1960* (Washington, D.C.: U.S. Government Printing Office, 1960), pp. 35–39.

The Small Business Administration is responsible for the federal government's disaster loan program and "post loans" to corporations which have been formed by small business concerns for research and development. The agency also aids other governmental agencies in financing urban renewal and rural development and private or public groups in the construction of hospitals, convalescent and nursing homes, and hangars for airplanes.

SMALL BUSINESS INVESTMENT COMPANIES

In 1958 Congress passed the Small Business Investment Company Act in order to provide for institutions to supply long-term loan capital and equity capital for small businesses.[10] The Act which is administered by the Small Business Administration permits private groups to be licensed by the Administration and incorporated under state law. If a state charter cannot be obtained, the small business investment company may be granted a federal charter. When an investment company is licensed by the Small Business Administration, it may obtain one half of its minimum capital requirement of $300,000 by the sale of subordinated debentures to the Small Business Administration. These debentures bear interest at 5 per cent per annum, mature in 20 years, and must be retired systematically over the last half of the period of indebtedness. The companies operate under the provisions of the federal law and regulations of the Small Business Administration.

At the present time, small business investment companies are permitted to make loans with maturities of from five to twenty years to small businesses or to acquire convertible debentures with similar maturities, invest in equity securities of small business firms including stock of any class (subject to rights and limitations negotiated between the company and small business firms), and purchase debt instruments which give an option to convert any portion of the outstanding debt into stock of the small business firm or has attached thereto a nondetachable or detachable stock purchase warrant.

On June 30, 1960, there were 107 small investment companies which had a combined capital of $70 million. Of this total, the Small Business Administration had committed some 16 per cent and

[10] The purpose of the Small Business Investment Company Act is "to improve and stimulate the national economy . . . and the small business segment thereof . . . by establishing a program to stimulate and supplement the flow of private equity capital and long-term loan funds which small business concerns need for the sound financing of their business operations and for their growth, expansion, and motivation." It was also stated that "this policy should be carried out in such manner as to insure the maximum participation of private financing sources." P.L. 699, 85th Cong., 2d sess., August 20, 1958.

the remainder had come from private sources.[11] Commercial banks are authorized to invest in the stock of small business investment companies but an individual bank's investment is limited to 1 per cent of its capital and surplus. As a result of this provision, many of the companies now in existence have been sponsored by commercial banks. In addition to giving banks a new investment outlet for a small percentage of their resources, the law provides them with a means to assist their loan customers in obtaining equity or long-term loan capital. If thousands of new small investment companies are created, as visualized by the sponsors of the Act, it will probably come about through the co-operation of commercial banks acting individually and in groups with the Small Business Administration. At the present time, the companies that have been organized are too few in number and too recently organized to have had much effect on the financing of business firms; but, in individual cases, the results have been significant although local in nature.[12]

In order to finance through or with the assistance of a small business investment company, a business firm must be qualified for financial assistance by the Small Business Administration. It must be independently owned and operated, not dominant in its field of operation, have assets not in excess of $5,000,000, have net worth not in excess of $2,500,000, and its average net income after federal income taxes for the preceding two years may not exceed $250,000 (average net income to be computed without benefit of any carry-over loss).[13]

DEVELOPMENT COMPANIES

Development companies are institutions that have been set up for the specific purpose of diagnosing the needs of a state or community and of obtaining or supplying financial aid for prospective, new, or expanding local businesses. Emphasis may be both on preserving old companies and on bringing in new ones. There are over 1,500 development companies in the United States which have an estimated capital of about $5 million.[14] Now practically every state has a de-

---

[11] The Electronic Capital Corporation which was organized with an original capital of $305,110 by the Bank of America National Trust and Savings Bank in May, 1959, subsequently sold $18,000,000 of common stock to the general public.

[12] Donald E. Vaughn, "Development of the Small Business Investment Company" (Unpublished Doctor's dissertation, University of Texas, 1961).

[13] *25 Federal Register 10087* (October 22, 1960), Section 121.3–11.

[14] See *Hearings on Small Business Financial Problems* (Report of the Subcommittee of the Committee on Banking and Currency, U.S. Senate, 85th Cong. 2d sess.) (Washington, D.C.: U.S. Government Printing Office, 1958), p. 408.

velopment organization of some type, a few of which are regional in scope of operations but the majority of which are local in nature.

Some of the development companies are organized as corporations which may or may not sell stock and may or may not acquire property. Congress recognized their existence in the Small Business Investment Company Act of 1958 which authorized them to convert into small business investment companies. The Small Business Administration is permitted to lend to a state development company an amount equal to the amount of borrowings by the development company from other sources (little use has been made of this provision to date).

The creation of development companies has been a by-product of the "battle for business firms" among the states which has characterized the period since the end of World War II. The promotional role in the movement to attract new plants of new or old companies may be exercised by the governor of the state, mayor of a city, other state or city official, the Chamber of Commerce, bankers' association, or some other group. Usually behind the activities of such promoters or promotional groups is a development company that does the research work and offers financial and other assistance. Local development companies may be financed in several different ways: some raise funds by soliciting gifts from local businessmen and others, some by selling stocks or bonds on which interest is paid, and some use other devices to raise funds, such as borrowing from banks, holding $100-a-plate dinners, and so on.

Occasionally, local groups oppose businesses owned by outside interests or foreign groups; but usually local communities, states, and regions are interested in attracting business and will offer financial and other inducements to them.[15] The financial assistance given to existing or new firms varies, but in many communities, plants are acquired and rented to the firm (in some cases the city government issues bonds and builds the plants) on a long-term low-rent basis. The local government may also exempt the industrial firm from property taxes or give it preferential rates for a specified number of years.

There are several aspects of this "scramble" for business firms and industrial plants that should be noted, such as the danger of enrich-

---

[15] The southern states have attracted numerous new plants as well as old companies from northern states. In 1954, northern Congressmen, under the leadership of John F. Kennedy, stated that "the Federal Government should classify some of the lures the South holds out as 'unfair competition.' " *New York Times*, July 26, 1954, pp. 1 and 12.

ing one community, state, or region at the expense of another without improving the economy as a whole. Any subsidy provided by a local group may be wasted if it results in financing a business firm that would be unable to operate without the help of the community. Even greater harm would be done if financing and maintaining an inefficient firm in a community results in repelling efficient firms or in retarding the growth of firms already established in the area.

Relocation of plants and business firms and establishment of new firms normally takes place as the result of normal economic forces; to the extent that development companies expedite these changes, the economy as a whole benefits. Capital is more mobile than labor; therefore, in depressed areas wherein there is technological unemployment, the solution may be the establishment of new companies or industries to replace those closed because of technological progress.

SUMMARY

In general, small business firms can obtain adequate supplies of short-term credit but have difficulty obtaining intermediate and long-term credit. Although principles of business finance apply to small as well as large businesses, their applications may vary with the size of business units. Small firms rarely have access to the capital markets in financial centers, but they are able to obtain intermediate and long-term credit from numerous sources—such as banks, insurance companies, factors, commercial finance companies, and other firms which supply the credit needs of business.

While it is commonly stated that inadequate financing is one of the leading causes of small business failures, the opposite may be true. Many instances can be found in which a small business actually had access to greater financial resources (often in the form of credit) than it was capable of managing. In other words, the difficulty arose not because of undercapitalization, but in undermanagement. Between 1946 and 1956 small businesses raised approximately $50 billion in loans and equity capital while large corporations raised about $70 billion; because the former do about one third of the business of the United States, they are relatively better supplied with capital than are large corporations.

Small businesses are usually more dependent upon commercial banks for credit than are large ones; for this reason cash flow statements, budgets, and other statements should be prepared with care. Unfortunately, many small firms do not maintain the accounting and other records necessary for a sound credit decision on the part of a loan officer of a commercial bank. Although banks and other lenders are an important source of credit to small business firms, such firms are also assisted by larger corporations who provide trade credit, financial services and advances to their suppliers, customers, and representatives.

The Small Business Administration, a government agency, was created to aid small businesses in their financing and other problems. The federal government also made provisions for small business investment companies whose primary function is to provide long-term loans and equity capital to small business concerns. In addition, privately owned state and local development companies as well as local development authorities have been established to assist in financing and obtaining new business firms and industrial plants for their communities.

QUESTIONS AND PROBLEMS

1. Is there justification for separate treatment of financial problems of small business firms apart from large firms? Why?
2. Explain how a small firm's ability to obtain external financing is affected by (*a*) its relative size, (*b*) profitability, (*c*) balance sheet structure, and (*d*) credit rating.
3. Analyze: "Last year Western Electric, our manufacturing and supply unit, paid more than a billion dollars to other firms for manufactured goods, raw materials and for services. These 35,000 firms are located in more than 3,000 towns and cities across the Nation." (American Telephone and Telegraph Company, Share Owners' Quarterly [New York, Spring 1960], n.p.)
4. What managerial policy is suggested by the following? "In building up its dealers, one of the major automotive producers found no lack of men able to sell and service. But such men seldom had money, and they rarely knew where and how to acquire growth capital. Company studies resulted in a new type of financing plan. It meets all of the needs stated above and others. When success is assured, the supplier of venture capital is willing to sell back his stock and step out. The dealer then owns it all." (L. T. White, "How Big Companies Help Small Companies" *Small Marketers Aid,* No. 31. [Small Business Administration, March, 1958], p. 3.)
5. What is the Small Business Administration? How does it help in financing small business firms?
6. Analyze: ". . . small and growing business firms have adequate access to short-term [credit]. . . . If a gap in the credit structure exists as regards small business, . . . it concerns lack of equity capital." (Fed-

eral Reserve Bank of Chicago, "Small Business Investment Companies," *Business Conditions* [October, 1958], p. 13.

7. What financial needs of small business concerns may be met in part by small investment companies? How are they organized and financed?
8. Explain: "One bank-owned [small business] investment company . . . plans that its customers shall repurchase the portion of ownership held temporarily by the investment company when financial support is no longer needed. The company's funds thus become a pool of revolving credit for small growing firms." (Federal Reserve Bank of Atlanta, "Small Investment Companies," *Monthly Review* [February, 1960], p. 13.)
9. Explain: "State development credit corporations should not be confused with state development credit authorities, local development corporations, or small business investment companies established under provisions or the Small Business Investment Act of 1958." Federal Reserve Bank of Richmond, "A New Look in Business Finance," *Monthly Review* [March, 1959], p. 2.)
10. "That small business is plagued by a dearth of equity capital is usually taken for granted. A shortage of equity funds for small firms does not mean, however, that none are available." (David Allen Snell, "Financial Problems and the Availability and Adequacy of External Financial Resources for Small Firms" [Unpublished Doctor's dissertation, University of Texas, 1960], p. 73.) Do you agree?

CHAPTER 26

Growth of Business Enterprises

GROWTH IS a normal expectation of a typical business enterprise—the logical and hoped-for result of sound management. The benefits accruing to an economy from prosperous and well-managed business firms are apparent. Over its economic life, a business firm may expand internally, externally, or in both directions. Internal expansion may be financed exclusively with funds from operations or with funds from external sources—or with a combination of both. Often, the same firm will shift from one source to another in response to changes in circumstances. External expansion is accomplished by a combination of two or more companies. This chapter considers growth factors, the forms and types of business expansion, valuation problems arising from business combinations, public policies relative to business acquisitions, legal problems associated with mergers and consolidations, stockholders' acceptance of combination plans, and the flexibility of combination plans.

GROWTH FACTORS

In an expanding economy, growth of business concerns is to be expected; but, after a firm has reached its optimum size, there may be economic justification for creating new firms to care for the expanding needs of the economy rather than increasing the size of existing firms. Although some may argue that existing firms ought to assume the burden of providing more goods and services, management should realize that lower profits result from pushing output and sales beyond the optimum point. The danger of overexpansion in a dynamic economy is less than in a static or declining one, but the danger is there nevertheless.

Social Factors. The optimum size of a business firm is the size that enables it to produce most efficiently at the lowest possible per unit cost, thus permitting its product to be sold at a lower price than those of its competitors. In a competitive society, business firms which cannot meet this competition will tend to be forced out of business. If the output of the lowest-cost firm is sufficient to meet the entire demand of the economy, it could obtain a monopoly. This point looms large whenever the proper size of business firms is debated on social, political, and economic grounds. One of the arguments is that elimination of small business firms entails a loss in social values for which the greater efficiency of large business units does not compensate. Another argument is the possibility that monopolists will exploit the general public by overcharging consumers for their products.

The popular attitude toward large business firms is reflected in public policy which has been directed toward preserving small and medium-size business units in fields wherein they can succeed if properly managed. The approach has been both positive and negative—protection and aid to small business units on one hand and control and regulation of large units on the other. The activities of the Small Business Administration and the United States Treasury's preferential tax treatment of small business units exemplify the positive approach. The negative approach is illustrated by provisions for control and regulation of combinations under the Sherman Antitrust Act of 1890 and the Clayton Act of 1914 as amended.

Unfortunately, the concept of monopoly is usually associated with size and there is often little relationship between the two; for illustration, a small business concern such as a store in an isolated community may hold a much more monopolistic position than a large one in a city where there are many competitors. Perhaps the greater accessibility to different markets, made possible by automobiles and good roads, has done more to break up monopolies than all the national and state antimonopoly laws that have been enacted. At the same time, consumers have profited from the greater efficiency of modern merchandising which has accompanied an increase in the size of stores and other business units.

In some industries, such as public utilities and transportation, service is provided more economically on a noncompetitive basis. Obviously, the cost of telephone service would be higher if ten companies operated in a single city than if a single company provided this service. State and local governments have given monopoly status not only to electric, gas, telephone, water, and public warehouse companies but also to railroads and other transportation companies. The rates and practices of these companies have long been subjected to regulation by federal, state, and local public service commissions. The geographical areas served by such companies is limited by their franchises, and their growth depends in part on finding new customers for their services. Hence, these companies are the chief sponsors of new industries in many areas (see Chapter 25). Usually, regulated companies are not considered growth companies in the sense that their prospects for future expansion are at a rate above the average of other companies.

Since 1917, a change has taken place in the public attitude toward large business units, and this is reflected in some of the laws passed by Congress which have encouraged, rather than discouraged, combinations and expansion of business firms. These acts include the Webb-Pomerene Act of 1918, which permited American firms to form combinations for export purposes, and the Transportation Act of 1920, which directed the Interstate Commerce Commission to draw up plans (which were never carried out) for consolidation of the railroads. In fact, some Acts of Congress even seemed to challenge the effectiveness of competition; this is illustrated by the National Recovery Act of 1933, which encouraged formulation of codes of fair competition (declared unconstitutional by the Supreme Court in 1935). At the same time that growing tolerance and acceptance of large corporations developed, provisions for the regulation of these corporations were strengthened to prevent abuses that could accompany expansion and combinations in business units; for example, the Interstate Commerce Commission, Federal Trade Commission, and Securities and Exchange Commission were created.

The use of cut-throat competition to eliminate other companies in the same field is practically a thing of the past, but the Department of Justice has followed a policy of maintaining competition by enforcement of antitrust laws (including recent legal action against the electrical equipment manufacturing companies). The average size of business firms in the United States, as would be expected in a rapidly growing economy, has increased during the present century; but the tenacity of small locally owned and operated business units is well documented.

Research and Development. The importance of research and development as a factor in the growth of individual business firms has been recognized in earlier chapters. If companies are to remain competitive, new products and new techniques are essential; and financial resources are needed not only to support research but also to care for the extraordinary costs of introducing new products. For example, E. I. duPont de Nemours & Company reported that it had approximately 2,200 scientists working at more than 30 laboratory locations and incurred annual expenditures of $80 million, exclusive of laboratory construction and technical assistance for sales and manufacture.[1] The president of General Electric stated: "As we head into the Sixties General Electric has in place probably the largest staff of technically trained, professional manpower of any Company in the World. Twenty-three thousand hold degrees in the physical sciences. . . . Today, almost 34,000 General Electric employees are college graduates. And 30,000 of our employees—80% of them without college education—are going to school in Company-sponsored courses. . . ."[2]

The Small Business Administration has issued a directory containing the names of 3,000 small business concerns that are interested in performing research and development; therefore, many companies that have no research departments (and others which do) may employ the services of these specialists to assist them in solving their manufacturing, distributing, and other problems. The Small Business Administration also sponsors the formation of companies for the specific purpose of carrying on research and development, production, and the search for raw materials and equipment.[3]

Government sources of information may be used by small as well as large business firms, but the latter have the advantage in that they may supplement the information on research and development from outside sources with their own specialists. It seems unlikely that co-operative research and development, joint leasing, use of expensive equipment, co-operative buying of raw materials, and pooling of productive resources by groups of small companies will do little more than permit them to maintain their current position in manufacturing, a field wherein large firms dominate.

Value of Final Product. In a free enterprise system, a particular firm's optimum size is determined largely by technological, managerial, marketing, and financial factors. Other things being equal,

---

1 E. I. duPont de Nemours & Company, *Annual Report for the Year 1957* (Wilmington, 1958), pp. 9–10.

2 General Electric Company, *1960 Annual Meeting* (New York, 1960), p. 6.

3 These pool companies include the Allied Specialties Company, Philadelphia, Pennsylvania, in which there are fifteen companies, and Production Research Engineering Pool Corporation, North Hollywood, California, in which there are seventeen companies. See also *Fourteenth Semi-Annual Report of the Small Business Administration for the Six Months Ending June 30, 1960* (Washington, D.C.: 1960), p. 89.

the optimum-size business unit tends to vary directly with the value of the final product—large if the value of the final product is large, as in the shipbuilding, aircraft, and automotive industries, and small if the value of the final product is small, as in the service industries such as barber shops, beauty parlors, and shoe repair shops. This does not mean that there will be no large business units in the service industry because there are giant public utility and transportation companies. Nor does it mean that the value of the final product of large companies is always large because just the opposite is often the case. So, the value of the final product is only one of many factors that influence the optimum size of a business firm.

Technological Factors. Labor-saving machines and division of labor which may be employed for economic advantage tend to increase the size of business firms. The minimum-size business unit will be relatively large if its operations entail production that (1) requires large outlays for machinery, (2) may be subdivided, and (3) is suitable for "occupational specialization" (for illustration, production of automobiles, locomotives, and other durable producers' and consumers' goods).

The trend is toward designing and building more and better machines; but their purchase by a business firm must be justified on the basis of their income productivity. For example, an individual press used in the automobile industry costs as much as $250,000 and the interest, depreciation, and other fixed charges thereon may be $250 per day. If the daily capacity of the press is 1,000 parts, fixed charges are 25 cents per part; but, if only 100 parts can be used per day, fixed charges are $2.50 per part. If other operations can be stepped up to use 1,000 parts daily, it may be profitable to acquire the press. Therefore, such a business firm is under pressure to increase production to the point where expensive machines can be utilized to capacity. Thus, a firm should be large enough to utilize machinery profitably; or conversely, a firm should limit acquisition of fixed assets to those which it can utilize profitably (which may result in its being at a competitive disadvantage compared to a larger firm).

In practice, the problem is more complex than the foregoing illustration suggests because there are many kinds of expensive machines used in production and this necessitates balancing output of each kind against all others. In order to operate one major machine fully, it may be necessary to operate fifty machines of another type, thirty of still another type, and so on. Therefore, the amount of capital necessary to equip the optimum-size plant in some fields may run into millions of dollars.

The pressure on business firms to expand will increase in the future because of the development of commercial-type data-processing equipment. The Univac Division of Sperry Rand Corporation has developed data-processing equipment whose selling price range is from a low of $175,000 to $678,850 for smaller models and from $1,800,000 to $2,700,000 for the largest model—Univac 1107.

The optimum size of a single business unit, considered from a technological point of view, does not prevent the formation of business concerns that operate several plants, stores, and other outlets under one management. Technological factors tend to determine the minimum rather than the maximum size of individual units as illustrated by chain stores in grocery, drug, and general merchandise lines and multiple plants and outlets operated by manufacturing firms such as General Electric Company and General Motors Corporation.

Influence of Marketing Factors. The cost of marketing a product rather than its value is sometimes the only justification for business expansion. Among the most expensive activities of some business firms is sales promotion, and this entails marketing research, study, advertising, and planning. Brand-name goods, regardless of the price of individual items, are sold in a national or international market; the marketing process requires large outlays for advertising, selling, and marketing organizations throughout the trade area. Some products, such as cigarettes, could be produced economically by small firms; however the marketing costs may be so great as to necessitate their allocation over a large volume of sales, best achieved by a large business firm. Sometimes a business concern can increase and/or stabilize its sales volume by adding other products that appeal to the same market and that can be distributed through existing facilities.

Influence of By-Products. In order for a business firm to maintain its competitive position, management may be forced to increase the size of the business unit so as to utilize the by-products of production profitably; but these by-products must be available in quantities sufficient to justify expenditures for facilities to process them. This tends to put additional pressure on management to expand operations not only to utilize by-products but also to increase the output of the primary product to be assured a sufficient amount of by-product to make its utilization profitable.

Influence of Managerial Skill. In achieving the optimum-size business firm as distinguished from the optimum size of individual plants or units, management may capitalize on the economies which result from the use of specialized skills in production, distribution, research, and financing that may be denied small firms. By using specialized skills, a business firm may find it advantageous to operate multiple plants, chains of stores, hotels, or service stations under one management. However, if top management is too far removed from the operations of individual units, this type of combination may be unprofitable. In other words, the cost of co-ordinating and formulating general policies must be weighed against the advantages of unified management and services of specialists.

Industrial companies manufacturing tens of thousands of individual products for consumers, producers, and the government have been able to meet the challenge of size through decentralization of management. Under decentralized management arrangements, individuals have been made responsible for organizing and managing divisions or units of large business firms on a semi-independent basis. Along with such responsibility goes the authority to plan and budget, formulate production schedules, establish inventory levels, estimate the cash flow and cash needs, and so on. On the other hand, decentralized management must conform to policies established by corporate management that are binding on all employees, and those responsible for management in the decentralized plan are provided with instruction manuals as to the company's policies and matters of over-all interest to the company. Company policies pertain to items such as appropriations for major improvements, compliance with antitrust laws, maintenance of the company's salary structure, and use of the company's name and symbols. The divisions or units operate under the principle of reserve authority which permits the corporation's officers at the top level to change policies when appropriate.

Influence of Financing Costs. The cost of financing is a problem common to all business firms. However, large well-known firms have the advantage of being able to borrow in the capital market (where interest rates tend to be lower than those charged by banks and other lenders) and to increase equity capital through the public sale of stock. Although interest charges are usually a small item in the cost of operating a business firm, the ability to obtain funds is of prime importance. As noted in preceding chapters, the larger firms have decided advantages over small firms not only in costs of borrowing but also in availability of funds. Growth is seldom determined wholly by the ease and cheapness of external financing because a successful business firm will have profits in a comparatively short time and will be able to use these funds from operations to finance expansion.

The decision of management as to the appropriate size of any individual business enterprise may differ from the optimum as determined by technological, managerial, marketing, financial, and other factors. However, at any one time, management will be making adjustments because of the influence of one or more of these factors. As already noted, if there is a conflict between the ideal technological unit and the ability of centralized management, the solution may be to appoint divisional managers for plants, stores, or other units and to give them the power to operate these units, in large part, as separate business entities. However, failure to find or conform to the various optima may result in failure of a business firm or at least in its functioning at an uneconomical level. The problem is a challenging and continuing one because of fluctuations in the economy caused by changes in general prices or individual and group prices within the general price structure, in technology, in the tax structure, and in the demands of the general public. In some cases, expansion is not based on socially beneficial factors but on the desire of management to eliminate competition and/or to control prices through control of supplies, marketing facilities, or patents. The attitude of key executives of a business firm may be the most important factor in explaining expansion and the direction it takes.

FORMS AND TYPES OF EXPANSION

Direction of Expansion. Expansion of business firms customarily takes one of the following directions: horizontal, vertical, circular, and conglomerate or heterogeneous. Horizontal expansion is exemplified by the combination of similar stores, plants, or other business units under one management. Vertical expansion consists of bringing together two or more successive stages in production under one management—in the steel industry this would include iron mining, transporting and refining the ore, converting ore into steel, and distributing steel and steel products. Circular expansion entails bringing together different products that can be distributed through the same channels under one management. Conglomerate or heterogeneous expansion consists of bringing under one management products or activities that have no apparent similarity either in the nature of the products or their marketing requirements.

Plans for Expansion. Most well-managed business enterprises have plans for expansion and these will vary with the size of the business firm, the field in which it operates, and its position within the field. A common objective of expansion is to develop, improve, and increase the use of potential or existing products. In order to achieve the goal of increased sales, management may improve and expand marketing facilities and services offered to customers. The expansion policy may be influenced by research directed toward lowering the costs of production and/or distribution so that the profit margin may be maintained or increased. Plans for business expansion may have as their objective improvement of the market position of the firm through advertising campaigns, acquisition of patents, and/or elimination of competitors.

Internal and External Growth. Expansion of business firms may result from internal or external growth or from a combination of both. Internal growth may result from the application of retained earnings and/or funds raised from outside sources.[4] In other words, internal growth, as defined here, includes all growth except that resulting from complete or partial absorption of other business units. External growth may result from acquisition of assets by merger, by consolidation or fusion, by lease, by the holding company device, or by some modification of one or more of these methods.

In a merger, the absorbing firm retains its identity and the firm absorbed loses its identity; in a consolidation, all participants lose their identities and a new firm emerges; in a lease or holding company arrangement, all participants retain their identities but control passes, to a great extent, from the lessor or subsidiary companies to the lessee or holding company. Although there are technical differences among the devices used to achieve external growth, the terms "merger," "consolidation," "fusion," "amalgamation," and "combination" are often used without distinction; perhaps the word "combination" could be used with some degree of accuracy to cover all forms of expansion resulting from transfers of ownership or control of other business units.

Sometimes the advantages accruing from external growth may be obtained in whole or part by the establishment of a "community of interest" through interlocking directorates and/or ownership of common stock in several corporations by one or more persons; voluntary chains of retail units linked by contract to a central organization in

[4] Over a period of years, the growth traced to combination may affect the competitive position of a business firm which, in turn, will be reflected in its earnings and therefore the amount of expansion financed with retained earnings. For illustration, when "organized fifty years ago, American Can acquired virtually a monopoly of can-making by merging more than 100 can-making firms. Its size gave it unique bargaining power and for many years it obtained secret rebates in buying tin plate from the U.S. Steel Corporation." (George W. Stockings, "Book Reviews," *Journal of Finance*, Vol. IX, No. 4 [December, 1954], pp. 942–43.) As recognized previously, the point is that it is impossible to distinguish between the effects of combination and internal expansion in explaining the size of modern business units.

order to obtain the benefits of unified management; trade associations wherein business firms join in research projects, studies, and publications on matters of mutual interest; cartels wherein members contract among themselves to divide the market and to otherwise reduce competition; and/or pools wherein participants, without written agreement, limit competition by controlling traffic, by sharing patent rights, and so on.

Internal versus External Expansion. Internal expansion has advantages over external expansion in that it avoids valuation problems and alteration costs incurred in remodeling facilities acquired; permits locating new facilities to take advantage of low taxes, abundant labor supply, cheap power, low-cost raw materials, and convenient transportation facilities; and avoids the necessity for obtaining stockholders' consent to combination and dealing with dissenting minority stockholders and creditors of the firm or firms to be transferred. On the other hand, time and money are required to build, equip, and staff new plants; if new products are included in the expansion, time and money will be required to advertise and to develop a market for them. Finally, additional funds may be needed to finance working capital assets such as inventories and receivables.

External expansion has advantages over internal expansion in that little or no time is lost in putting plants and facilities into operation because a going concern usually includes an experienced staff, outlets for products, goodwill, and a ready market. Usually, combinations do not increase an industry's total productive capacity, and so external expansion may lessen the danger of cut-throat competition.

Timing of Expansion. Since external expansion represents changes in ownership and internal expansion represents capital formation, there may not be any relationship between the timing of the two. Internal expansion tends to coincide with movements of the business cycle but this is not necessarily true of combinations. If, as one group contends, the chief motive behind combination is the achievement of economies of operation, the combination movement should be greatest during periods of business depression. If, as a second group contends, combinations are due to the activities of promoters, the combination movement would be greatest during stock market booms when common stock is easier to sell. If, as a third group contends, combinations follow or coincide with movements in the commodity market, the peak in combinations would coincide with the peak in wholesale commodity prices. No one of these factors explains the various combination movements, but one or more have been important to some degree in the three major merger movements in the United States (along with political atmosphere, stage in economic development of the United States, tax factors, and other reasons noted below).

Three Major Combination Movements. An analysis of the three major merger or combination movements in the United States (1898–1903; 1917–29; and 1940 to date) shows that distinct sets of forces explain each of these movements.[5] The important factors in the first combination movement include relaxation of business corporation laws to permit corporations to hold stock in other corporations; achievement of combination without violation of the Sherman Act, which prohibited collusive activities but permitted combinations if the issue of monopoly was not raised; development of transportation facilities and national markets, which permitted economical operations of large-scale multi-unit business concerns; improvements in managerial techniques; and development of financial markets.

The first wave of business combination was one wherein many business firms in the same line of activity were brought under one management. Destructive competition was greatly reduced and the stage was set for cost reductions, price increases, and profit expansion. Some combinations were of the vertical type but most of them were horizontal in nature (such as tinplate and shoe manufacturers and sugar refining companies). Promoters made use of the holding company device as well as the old charter (merger) and new charter (consolidation) methods in bringing together different business units under one management. Very little thought was given to diversification and the apparent aim of management was to reduce costs and obtain better control over markets. The merger movement of this period proved to be beneficial to the promoters, investment bankers, founders of absorbed or consolidated companies that received stock in the absorbing or new company, the general public that invested in the new companies, and consumers who obtained better products (although there were exceptions).

The predominant factor in the merger movement of the 1920's was the stock market boom that facilitated the sale of securities issued by new combinations. The fact that many of the combinations were vertical and circular types of expansion seems to suggest that the motives for expansion were to assure the growing firm an adequate supply of raw materials and to make advertising, selling, and distributing or-

[5] J. Fred Weston, *The Role of Mergers in the Growth of Large Firms* (Berkeley and Los Angeles: The University of California Press, 1953), pp. 81–84.

ganizations more effective. In the second merger movement, economies in business operations were basic—economies in buying and selling, in the use of personnel, etc.—but promotional opportunities and underwriters profits were also important factors.

The background for this merger movement is found in developments that occurred during World War I, when pressure was brought to bear on firms to combine in order to increase production by increasing efficiency in the use of labor, capital, and other resources (even the federal government found it expedient to take over and operate the railroads under a unified system and under centralized control). The War Industries Board insisted on standardization of products and elimination of competition among agencies purchasing war supplies—and even resorted to price fixing. These wartime controls demonstrated the advantages of centralized management; the combination movement of the 1920's, which reached its peak during 1927–29, was but an extension of this movement under private control. Among those affected were public utilities, mining and oil industries, manufacturers, hotels, motion pictures, retail chain stores, and other divisions of the service industry. One of the most significant aspects of expansion during this period was the growth in holding companies in the public utility field (see Chapter 27). At the beginning of 1930, the 200 largest nonfinancial corporations controlled about 50 per cent of nonbanking corporate wealth.

In the merger movement beginning in the 1940's, the motivating factors included tax advantage, relatively low prices of common stock, and postwar shortages and a seller's market, which made it expedient to form combinations rather than to await plant construction. The desire to secure market control seems to have been relatively unimportant during this merger period. Perhaps the decrease in monopoly-type mergers can be explained by a realization that many of the economies of size had already been achieved—limitations on management, technological changes, etc.; more vigorous enforcement of antitrust laws; and a decline in the influence of investment bankers who had, in the past, not only instigated plans for combinations but also helped finance them.

The third wave of mergers, consolidations, and acquisitions is still in progress, and scarcely a day passes without press notices of one or more proposed or pending combinations of two or more business firms. The principle that seems to be motivating most of these combinations is the need for diversification so as to stabilize income over the business cycle. The result is a conglomerate type of combination which has brought under the control of one management producers of such unrelated items as cigarette lighters and aircraft parts; anthracite coal and men's and boys' underwear; road building equipment, fishing rods, steel, and glass; woolen and worsted fabrics and precision sheet metal goods; etc.[6]

In the current combination movement, which is expected to extend well into the Sixties, vertical combinations seem to be designed to economize on marketing and management resources and expenditures (note the variety of products that are advertised by one company during a TV program). The railroad industry is expected to spawn combinations that will reduce the number of companies and place the remaining firms on a sound financial basis. Some industrial companies are still looking for ailing concerns to absorb so as to obtain the advantage of carrying forward a tax loss that can be applied against future earnings. Thus, many business firms are either trying to improve their positions in their own industries or taking on the output of entirely new products in a line not related to their original business activities. However, the Justice Department has been successful in preventing certain rumored or proposed mergers as exemplified by those of Bethlehem Steel and Youngstown Steel and Tube Company, and Texaco, Inc., and Superior Oil Company of California—"when the effects may be substantially to lessen competition or to tend to create a monopoly."

VALUATION PROBLEMS IN BUSINESS TRANSFERS

The problem of evaluating business property is present in all transfers of business concerns. Valuation may stress book value, as found from the balance sheet; experts' appraisals, based on the concept of replacement cost new, minus depreciation; substitution value; liquidation value; capitalization of anticipated income or going concern value; market value of securities; or a combination of two or more of the above.

Book Value. Since accounting practices vary widely, book value may have little significance in determining the value at which a business firm is to be transferred. Book value is most meaningful when applied to current assets; that is, cash and near cash items, and least significant when applied to intangible assets which may have little or no value after being transferred to a second company.

Book value is usually the basis on which sales, mergers, or consoli-

[6] Under consideration at this time are plans to merge the National Distillers and Chemical Corporation and the Bridgeport Brass Company.

dations of banks are arranged; and, in combinations of nonfinancial business units, book value has a place if for no more than psychological or subjective reasons (owners tend to be reluctant to accept a price that is less than book value). The greatest weakness of the book-value method is that it tends to show historical costs which may have little relation to current values.

Appraisal Value. Generally, those interested in acquiring, merging, or consolidating companies have an appraisal made of the value of the properties under consideration. Often equally "expert" appraisers representing the various companies or interested groups arrive at such different valuations as to lead unbiased observers to question all of their findings. The principle of replacement cost new, minus depreciation, is most commonly used in appraising plants and equipment; but other methods must be used in the appraisal of land and intangibles. The market value of adjacent similar properties may be used in evaluating land; the valuation of intangibles (goodwill, franchise, etc.) will be influenced by their nature and status.

Substitution Costs. When a business firm's motive in acquiring business property is expansion of plant or other facilities, the firm may evaluate the property by estimating the cost of a new plant and facilities which may be substituted for the existing one. The comparison is between old and new properties; thus an allowance must be made for depreciation and obsolescence of the old property and the cost of putting it into shape for production. As a basis for negotiation, cost of new assets could be used in arriving at an offering price. However, the offering price would be less than the cost price of a new plant or other assets, unless the need to meet production schedules that cannot be handled by sub-contracting or lease arrangements makes immediate acquisition imperative.

Liquidation Value. The seller as well as the buyer may balance the business transfer against alternatives. From the seller's viewpoint, the alternative to selling may to be liquidate the business through piecemeal sale of assets. Ordinarily, valuation of a business firm is based on the "going concern" concept; that is, the assumption is that the business will be operated over a reasonable period of time. If a firm is operating under conditions which seem to justify discontinuance, the alternative to a transfer may be voluntary or forced liquidation. The liquidation valuation arrived at by the seller is usually the minimum offer that he will accept in a transfer.

Capitalized Earning Value. Among the most frequently used methods of evaluating property in business combinations is that of capitalizing the estimated earnings of the company or companies.[7] This requires the answers to the questions: How much will the property earn? And at what rate shall these earnings be capitalized? In estimating earnings, the usual procedure is to consider the company's record over the last three to five years (which is no different from the method used in estimating the performance of a baseball player, race horse, etc.). If the firm's average yearly income is estimated to be $100,000 and the selected rate of capitalization is 12 per cent, the company will be valued at $833,333 ($100,000 divided by 12 per cent).

The rate at which estimated earnings are capitalized should reflect what similar companies' stocks are selling for in the market in terms of net earnings after federal income taxes. If such earnings are $10 per share and the stock is selling around $80 per share, the rate of capitalization of net earnings after taxes is 12.5 per cent ($10.00 ÷ $80 = .125 or 12.5 per cent). There will be variations in the rates at which the market capitalizes the stock of individual companies, reflecting the difference in stability of earnings, dividend policies, and other factors; but, if the emphasis is on similar companies, an acceptable rate may be found. Usually, it will be best for the buyer to be guided by the rate of earnings of his company; and if this is 15 per cent, it would be logical to use the 15 per cent rate in evaluating property to be acquired. In this case, the estimated earnings of $100,000 would be capitalized at 15 per cent and the capitalized value would be $666,667 ($100,000 divided by 15 per cent). After arriving at this figure, the market value of redundant assets may be added to obtain the maximum offering price (see below).

Market Value of Stock. In valuation procedures, the objective is to arrive at a price which will be acceptable to both the buyer and seller. Sometimes this figure may be arrived at by using the market price of the corporation's securities. If equity is represented by 10,000 shares of common stock selling at about $75 per share, the net

---

[7] In commenting upon its wide experiences with the fairness and feasibility of reorganization plans under Chapter X of the National Bankruptcy Act, the Securities and Exchange Commission wrote as follows: "the Commission has consistently stated that the proper method of valuation for reorganization purposes is primarily an appropriate capitalization of reasonable prospective earnings." The Commission commented further "In recent years the Commission has encountered difficulties because the parties are disposed to base values and capital structures upon inflated war earnings, either because they overlook the extent to which earnings are inflated or hope such earnings will continue long enough to permit debt to be scaled down to manageable proportions." *Tenth Annual Report of the Securities and Exchange Commission for the Fiscal Year Ended June 30, 1944* (Washington, D.C.: U.S. Government Printing Office, 1945), pp. 150 ff., *passim.*

value of the property would tend to be about $750,000. If the corporation has preferred stock outstanding, the total market value of both the common and preferred stock might be considered as the value of the property. However, the market price of securities may reflect some temporary factor which might justify the use of the average market price for weeks or months preceding combination negotiations. Often, the rumor of a combination causes the market price to increase. In arriving at a fair price, it may be necessary to base it on the market price prevailing before the negotiation period.

Negotiated Exchange. In evaluating assets of a firm involved in an anticipated combination, both buyer and seller will use one or more of the methods discussed above and each will use the method or methods most advantageous to him. The original figures may be far apart, and in the negotiations that follow, the skill and bargaining positions of the negotiators will determine the terms under which the combination is arranged. When fixed assets are predominant, historical costs, substitution costs, or replacement costs may be most helpful; however, when intangible assets are predominant, capitalized earnings or market value of securities may be most helpful in determining valuation. The last two methods recognize the importance of the "going concern" concept, the rate of growth of earnings, ability of management, and strategic position of the firm because of patents, location, new processes, banking connections, and so on.

Capitalization of earnings should contribute to answering the buyer's questions as to how much the assets are worth to him, but it may not provide the complete answer. Some of the assets included in the prospective transfer may be unnecessary to the combination. These redundant assets may be in a highly liquid form such as cash, investments, and/or cash surrender value of life insurance policies; or they may be less marketable in nature. The funds obtained from the sale of redundant assets could be applied to the purchase price; thus the total valuation may include the capitalized value of estimated earnings plus the market price of redundant assets.

A public notice of a combination usually reveals the price in case of an acquisition or the exchange ratio of shares in case of a merger or a consolidation, but very little of what goes on behind the scenes prior to a combination is revealed. Management is generally more informative in placing merger plans before the stockholders for approval, but usually management emphasizes expected advantages to the company and details as to changes in the charter and bylaws that accompany the proposed merger.

PUBLIC POLICY AND BUSINESS ACQUISITIONS

In selecting the form that a business acquisition is to take (merger, consolidation, etc.), management is influenced by public policy which has the preservation of competition among industrial companies as one of its aims. By their nature, public utility and railroad companies are so-called "natural monopolies of organization"; therefore, public policy has stressed regulation rather than preservation of competition in these fields. In addition to being uneconomical and unprofitable, it would not serve public policy for two or more telephone, light and gas, and water companies to operate within a city. Therefore, no effort has been made to maintain competition in such instances; however some effort has been made to maintain competition among railroads serving customers between distant points such as New York and Chicago, St. Louis and San Francisco, etc.

In general, the antimonopoly movement has been directed toward preserving competition in industrial fields; but, as evidenced by legislative action, there has been a lack of consistency in public policy. In fact, the federal government has passed laws that have decreased competition in certain fields as illustrated by statutes providing for price support of agricultural products, bituminous coal, oil, fluid milk, and labor.[8] The National Recovery Act of 1933 was declared unconstitutional by the Supreme Court in 1935, but it was the most sweeping of the acts passed by Congress to stabilize prices. During the first month after passage of this act, 400 "codes of fair practice" were approved in spite of the fact that many of them included provisions of a monopolistic nature. An industry which is subject to a high degree of cyclical instability or is undergoing a secular decline apparently can obtain congressional permission to use monopolistic devices such as restricting output and fixing minimum prices.

Prior to 1890, cases involving the issue of "restraint of trade" came before state courts which sometimes ruled that contracts having control of prices as their purpose were unenforceable and that there was criminal conspiracy against public interest. To avoid the legal

---

[8] Among other acts permitting monopolistic practices are the Bituminous Coal Conservation Act of 1935, declared unconstitutional and replaced by a second Act in 1937 which has withstood the test of constitutionality; the Connally Hot Oil Act of 1935, forbidding interstate commerce in excess of state petroleum quotas; the Railway Labor Act of 1926; the Norris-La Guardia Act of 1932; the National Labor Relations Act of 1935; and the Taft-Hartley Act of 1947. Fair-trade laws of states, having as their purpose elimination of price cutting on brand-name goods, have been supported by Congressional legislation in the Robinson-Patman Act (1936) and the Miller-Tydings Enabling Act (1937). Other acts of Congress have placed parity price floors under agricultural prices.

hazard of being a party to unenforceable agreements and/or being charged with criminal conspiracy, business combinations were formed by organizing voting trusts—issuing trust certificates by a common-law trust in exchange for the stock of competing companies. The trustees became the legal owners of the corporations; as such, they had the right to make all decisions concerning them. If the rights of trustees were challenged in one state, they could reorganize in a second state and continue operations.

The Sherman Antitrust Act of 1890 was directed at monopoly and restraint of trade in interstate commerce, and, the Antitrust Division of the Department of Justice is responsible for the enforcement of federal antitrust laws.[9] With the realization that mere size is not necessarily an indication of unreasonable restraint of trade or unfair trade practices, there has been a change in the attitude of Congress, the courts, and the general public toward combinations. In their effects on competition, some mergers are bad, some good, and some neutral. If all mergers or combinations were bad, making them illegal would be a simple way to handle this problem.

While public policy may be served by increasing or preserving competition through prevention of combinations, a monopolistic situation may result from internal growth. This may be accomplished by building additional capacity for supplying an expanding market in new as well as old areas, developing new products for diversification or replacement of old ones, and obtaining customers of other companies and employing their key personnel. Although combinations account for the origin of some large firms, their current positions within their industries may have been due as much to internal as to external growth. A second aspect of the combination movement is that some of the ends sought may be attained by means short of formal combination. Price stabilization and limitations on competition may be achieved in industries wherein there is considerable concentration through trade associations; pools or sharing-the-market arrangements; informal contacts through publications, letters, and dinner meetings; interlocking directorates and interlocking officers; and price leadership, governmental regulation, or other miscellaneous means.

---

[9] The Assistant Attorney General for the Antitrust Division of the Department of Justice is charged with the enforcement of the antitrust and thirty kindred acts. The Division receives complaints and conducts investigations (in co-operation with the Federal Bureau of Investigation) which may lead to criminal prosecutions or suits in equity to break monopolies or restraints of interstate or foreign trade.

Federal Trade Commission. The Federal Trade Commission was created in 1914, and its powers have been enlarged by subsequent acts of Congress. At present the functions of the Federal Trade Commission include promoting "free and fair" competition in interstate trade by preventing price fixing agreements, boycotts, combinations in restraint of trade, and unfair or deceptive acts including false advertising, price discrimination, and so on; safeguarding the life and health of the public by preventing the dissemination of false advertisements of drugs, cosmetics, and food; and making available factual data concerning economic and business conditions as a basis for legislation and for the protection and guidance of the public. The Clayton Act (1914) was passed "to supplement existing laws against unlawful restraints and monopolies." As amended, the Clayton Act makes illegal any practices that may decrease competition, including acquisition of stock and interlocking directorates. The Federal Trade Commission issues complaints, holds hearings, and enters "cease-and-desist" orders in case of proved violations. A business firm may appeal such an order to the Circuit Court of Appeals, which may affirm, modify, or set aside orders of the Commission.

Interstate Commerce Commission. The Interstate Commerce Act of 1887 provided for regulation of transportation companies but gave more or less tacit admission that certain monopolistic aspects are present in this type of business. Subsequent legislation by Congress broadened the scope and strengthened the authority of the Interstate Commerce Commission; at present, it has jurisdiction over common carriers (railroads, water, motor), express companies, sleeping car companies, pipelines, and freight forwarders engaged in interstate commerce and foreign commerce to the extent that it takes place in the United States. At the same time that the Commission protects the public interest by preventing overcharging for services and so on, it must assist in developing, co-ordinating, and preserving a national transportation system.

The Interstate Commerce Commission has the following powers in dealing with companies coming under its jurisdiction: it may permit pooling or division of traffic, service, or earnings; it supervises the use of rolling stock and special equipment by various companies (exchange, interchange, and return); it passes upon proposed consolidations, mergers, and acquisitions of control; and it requires annual reports and prescribes the forms of the accounts, records, and memorandums to be kept.

Federal Power Commission. The Federal Power Commission was created in 1920, but its present form of organization dates primarily from June, 1930. The Commission is responsible for licensing hydroelectric projects on government lands (excluding power projects in national parks or national monuments) and on navigable waters of the United States. The Commission has jurisdiction over the transmission and sale at wholesale of electric energy in interstate commerce and public utilities engaged therein (Title II of the Public Utility Act of August 26, 1935) and the transportation and sale of natural gas in interstate commerce for resale and natural gas companies engaged therein (Natural Gas Act of June 21, 1938 as subsequently amended).[10]

The Federal Power Commission prescribes and enforces a system of accounts to be maintained by companies under its jurisdiction and passes upon the issuance of their securities and the transfer of their assets. In arriving at rates or charges for electric energy or power sold at wholesale in interstate commerce and for natural gas sold by companies under its jurisdiction, the Commission co-operates closely with state regulatory agencies.

Federal Communications Commission. The Federal Communications Commission was provided for by the Communications Act of 1934 and the Commission now administers that Act as amended. Its jurisdiction pertains to wire, radio, and television companies that operate in interstate and foreign communication. Charges and practices are subject to review by the Commission, which is authorized to issue licenses, classify radio and television stations, prescribe the nature of their services, assign frequencies, and make regulations to carry out the purposes of the Act. The Federal Communications Commission may issue and revoke or modify licenses, the assignment or transfer of control of which is prohibited except upon the written consent of the Commission.

STATUTORY MERGERS AND CONSOLIDATIONS

The business corporation law of the state of incorporation is one of the most important factors considered by a corporation in decid-

---

[10] The Commission's powers have been enlarged by the Flood Control Acts of 1938 and subsequent years, River and Harbor Acts of 1945 and subsequent years, and other acts including the Tennessee Valley Authority Act, Bonneville Project Act, and Fort Peck Project Act. See also the latest edition of the *United States Government Organization Manual* (Washington, D.C.: U.S. Government Printing Office).

ing on the form to be used in acquiring another business firm. State business corporation acts customarily cover lease or transfer of corporate property, mergers, and consolidations. In general, these laws require approval of plans for business transfers by not only the board of directors but also shareholders holding two thirds of the shares.

The sale or lease of all or most of a corporation's assets differs from a merger or consolidation in that the corporation retains its legal existence. In some cases, such a corporation may change the nature of its business and continue its existence; in other cases, the corporation's board of directors and stockholders may follow the legal provisions for voluntary dissolution to end the life of the corporation.

After approval by the boards of directors of all corporations concerned, a plan for merger or consolidation must be presented at annual or special meetings of shareholders for their approval or disapproval.[11] The plan must contain names of the corporations in the proposed merger or consolidation; name of the surviving or new corporation; terms and conditions of the proposed merger or consolidation; appropriate changes in the articles of incorporation of the surviving corporation or complete charter provisions for a new corporation; method and basis for converting the shares of each corporation into shares, other securities, or obligations of the surviving or new corporation; and any other provisions with respect to the proposed merger or consolidation which are deemed desirable or necessary.

Before a merger or consolidation becomes effective, the proper papers must be filed with the Secretary of State, who issues the certificate of merger or consolidation and thus brings to an end the corporate existence of all participants other than the surviving or new corporation. If one of the participants is a foreign corporation, it must follow the appropriate provisions prescribed in the laws of its state of incorporation and must file a certified copy of the documents with the Secretary of State of the state that issues the certificate of merger or consolidation showing that these requirements have been met. When the certificate of merger or consolidation is issued, the surviving or new corporation takes title to the property of the absorbed companies and assumes responsibility for their debts and other obligations.

---

[11] Mergers of corporations customarily involve parent operating and subsidiary corporations. Some of the major ones make the headlines on financial pages (for illustration, General Dynamics Corporation absorbed Consolidated Vultee Aircraft Corporation in 1954 after acquiring 17 per cent of its stock in 1953).

COMPLETION OF COMBINATION PLAN

One of the greatest difficulties encountered in a merger or consolidation is that of securing an acceptable arrangement for converting the shares of each corporation into shares of the surviving or new corporation. This requires a relative or proportionate evaluation of each class of shares to insure equitable treatment of all shareholders. In some cases, negotiations for mergers or consolidations have lasted for years; in other cases, proposed transfers have never been completed either because the valuation problem could not be solved to the satisfaction of a sufficient number of stockholders or because of dissension among the chief executives of participating companies (they could not all hold equivalent positions in the new company as there would be only one presidency and one chairmanship of the board of directors to be filled).

The complexity of the problem of relative valuation increases in geometric progression as the number of corporations combined increases. The assets and earning power of a corporation will be the same irrespective of the number of shares distributed, so each shareholder is interested in getting his proportionate share. In order to obtain the necessary affirmative votes, the promoter must convince the required number of shareholders in each group that they are receiving their proportionate shares and that all participants will benefit from the anticipated higher earnings which will follow as a result of the merger or consolidation.

The exchange of shares may be on the basis of assets contributed, respective earnings, one of the other valuation methods previously noted, or a combination of any of the methods used to measure the contribution of each corporation. In arriving at the respective value of each corporation, the valuation methods used may be book value of assets; appraisals by engineers, accountants, and others; capitalization of net income; capitalization of the market value of securities; and a combination of two or more of these methods (see above).

If Corporation *A* is allotted 40 per cent of the value of the new corporation, Corporation *B* 30 per cent, Corporation *C* 20 per cent, and Corporation *D* 10 per cent, then the shareholders of each company will receive the same proportionate number of shares in the new corporation. Assuming that the plan necessitates the distribution of 100,000 shares, if Corporation *A* has but 4 stockholders each holding 25 per cent of the stock, 10,000 shares would be distributed to each stockholder; if Corporation *B* has 10,000 stockholders, they would receive an average of 3 shares; if Corporation *C* has 2,000 shareholders, they would receive an average of 10 shares each; and if Corporation *D* has 10 shareholders, they would receive an average of 1,000 shares. If the promotional group decides to issue more or fewer shares, the same allocation of interest would be followed with the same proportionate interest being given to each group and then the shares would be reallocated according to each shareholder's interest.

When a plan for a merger or consolidation is acceptable to all stockholders, the amount of funds needed to bring the combination into existence will be limited to "behind the scenes" promotion expenses and legal costs. However, if some shareholders dissent from the merger, as they have a right to do, cash may be needed to meet their claims.[12] If a settlement is not reached out of court, either the dissenting stockholders or the corporation may file a petition in the appropriate court asking for a finding and determination of the fair value of such shares by an appraiser appointed by the court. After appraisal and notification, dissenting shareholders are bound by the final judgment of the court. During the interim, dissenting shareholders customarily retain the rights and privileges represented by their shares.

When a merger is effected through an exchange of stock, the capital gains tax is avoided and for tax purposes the absorbing company reports acquired assets at the seller's book value—although the purchase price is usually higher than the book value. (Often equipment that has been written off the owners' books has remaining value and the use of historical costs usually understates the book value of plants and equipment.)

When stock of a company to be merged is acquired in the capital market, rumors of the pending merger tend to inflate the market price and to make acquisition of the company unduly expensive.[13] The anticipated effect of a merger is improvement in operating effi-

[12] The procedure here stated reflects the holding of most state business corporation statutes that have been revised since about 1932. In most other states, dissenting shareholders are bound by the decision of the majority or the affirmative vote of the required percentage which may be two thirds or three fourths of the shares.

[13] The process of acquiring shares of other companies, which seems to be going on at all times, cuts across national boundaries as illustrated by the acquisition of its British subsidiary, the Ford Motor Company, Ltd., by the Ford Motor Company of the United States late in 1960, when $354 million was paid for publicly held shares. The acquisition price of $20.67 per share was much higher than the price for which the shares had been selling prior to the offer to buy by the American company.

ciency through property consolidation, combined staff, and other savings that will permit larger and more stable income, higher profits, more cash dividends, and higher market price for the stock.

ALTERNATIVES TO MERGERS AND CONSOLIDATIONS

A group promoting a merger or consolidation may expedite acceptance of their plan by purchasing or acquiring voting shares of the corporations which they wish to acquire. If these promoters secure representation on the boards of directors of the respective corporations, they may create an atmosphere friendly to the merger or consolidation and may assist in drawing up the plan. Sometimes, after obtaining control of other corporations, a group may find it expedient to operate the corporations as separate entities rather than to effect a formal merger or consolidation. The 1950 amendment of the Clayton Act prohibits acquisition by a corporation of stock or assets of another corporation if "the effect of such acquisition may be substantially to lessen competition or tend to create a monopoly," but the presumption is that such acquisitions will not be disapproved unless economic evidence can be shown that competition would thereby be "substantially" reduced or that monopolistic elements are present.

The lease method is perhaps the easiest way to acquire assets of other corporations, and a large number of railroad systems have been created by this means. In the industrial field, the lease arrangement is limited largely to rental contracts covering real property. However, a few companies rent or lease machines of different types. Lease agreements are not considered business transfers because they do not represent a change in ownership of business assets.

The degree of ease in acquiring assets is often the predominant factor in determining the procedure that will be followed in effecting combinations; however, other factors such as the permanency of the combination are considered. If the problem faced by management is a temporary one, such as catching up with current and/or anticipated demand, it may be better to subcontract for parts or other units needed rather than to resort to external expansion. Because the economies resulting from operating multiplant firms are limited and the threat of antitrust legal action may be present, the permanent policy of management may be to contract with independent firms for many of the things needed in operations. The ability to make such contractual arrangements has been a factor in the decline of vertical expansion. However, if the motive of management is to stabilize output, avoid duplication of marketing facilities, prorate advertising or sales costs over a larger sales volume, or obtain the benefits of centralized research, a more permanent type of combination may be sought. Thus a circular or horizontal combination may be arranged in order to use a single sales force or to achieve heterogeneous or conglomerate combinations. Combinations of firms that are dissimilar in production or sales activities may be justified on financial or other grounds.

Business arrangements whereby control rather than absorption of business units is acquired have greater flexibility than permanent combinations. In a merger or consolidation, uneconomic plants or other units may be sold; but a corporation that controls an uneconomic plant or other unit may dispose of it by selling the stock of such a unit. Although lease arrangements offer certain advantages, such contracts are usually long term and rental charges may become burdensome during business depressions. Burdensome fixed charges may be avoided when control is secured through stock ownership. Control through acquisition of voting shares is the most flexible method of acquiring other business firms because the resulting combination can be dissolved by a parent corporation simply by selling the shares of the subsidiary.

The holding company, a corporation which holds shares of other companies in order to vote the stock and thereby achieve a common group policy, is the best illustration of the flexibility of the corporate form of business enterprise. The holding-company device is used to keep control of existing companies, to promote a new venture through creation of a new corporation, or to set the stage for a merger or consolidation at a future time. As compared to the total risks assumed in permanent combinations, a holding company's risks are limited to its investments in its subsidiary companies. The right of business corporations to acquire stock of other corporations is usually conferred by statute; it is at variance with the common-law principle that stock ownership by one corporation of a second corporation is not in keeping with the purposes for which the corporation was created. A pure holding company is a corporation organized for control purposes; it is not, at the same time, an operating company. A pure holding company may assume managerial, research, financial, and other activities which would make it similar to the head office of an industrial or merchandising enterprise having multiple plants, stores, or other outlets.

SUMMARY

A business firm's optimum size is influenced by social, technological, managerial, distributional, and financial factors as well as the profitableness of using machines and processing by-products. To ignore these factors may result in failure of the business concern. Because these factors—as well as those of public demand and general prices—are subject to change, the problem is a continuing one. To achieve or maintain its optimum size, a business firm may find it necessary to expand either through external or internal growth.

External growth results from acquisitions of assets by means of merger, consolidation, or combination with other business units by use of the lease, holding company, or some other device. Internal growth results from the application of retained earnings and/or of funds raised from outside sources. The expansion of a business firm may take any one of the following directions: horizontal, vertical, circular, or conglomerate—or it may entail a combination of these.

In all business transfers, the problem of valuation is present. The basis for evaluating business assets may be book value, replacement cost, substitution cost, liquidation value, capitalization of earnings, or the market value of stock; the transfer may be effected by negotiating an exchange of securities, purchase of assets, or purchase of stock.

The forms of business transfers and the methods used to effect them have been influenced by public policy as reflected in statutes such as the Interstate Commerce Act of 1887, the Sherman Antitrust Act of 1890, and the Clayton Act of 1914. In the industrial field, public policy has stressed the preservation of competition; but, as evidenced by legislative action, there has been a lack of consistency in public policy with the result that, in some instances, competition has decreased as the result of legislative action. Public policy as to the public utility and railroad fields has been directed toward providing regulation rather than preserving competition, and the Federal Trade Commission and Interstate Commerce Commission were created to protect the public by preventing abuses which could stem from the monopolistic aspects of the "public necessity" companies under their jurisdictions.

QUESTIONS AND PROBLEMS

1. "Historically, Americans have been antagonistic toward 'big business' and this attitude is reflected in our statutes." Explain.

2. Identify: (*a*) optimum-size business firm, (*b*) factors influencing optimum size, (*c*) direction of expansion, (*d*) internal growth, and (*c*) external growth.
3. What were the important factors in the combination movement of (*a*) 1898–1903, (*b*) 1926–29, and (*c*) 1940 to date?
4. When the United States Tobacco Company acquired Circus Foods, Inc. (canned nuts) and Tuckershape Pin Company (pens, pencils, and desk sets), what type of combination was formed?
5. In explaining sales of closely held companies, the tax structure has had an influence because of the impact of estate taxes and the lower tax on capital gains. Could the same results be achieved if all or part of the owners' shares were distributed publicly?
6. (*a*) In evaluating business property to be transferred, what valuation methods may be used? (*b*) What is the weakness of "book value" valuation method? (*c*) Account for the fact that "capitalization of anticipated earnings" is the valuation method so frequently used.
7. "The antimonopoly movement has been directed toward preserving competition in industrial fields; but, as evidenced by legislative action, there has been a lack of consistency in public policy." Justify this statement.
8. Distinguish between a "merger" and a "consolidation."
9. "The complexity of the problem of relative valuation increases in geometric progression as the number of corporations combined increases." Explain.
10. "Business arrangements whereby control rather than absorption of business units is acquired have greater flexibility than permanent combinations." Explain.
11. Discuss the type of combination illustrated by the following: "Allied Laboratories, Inc., a manufacturer and distributor of human and veterinary pharmaceutical and biological products, became the newest member of the Dow [Chemical Company] family December 30, 1960." (Dow Chemical Company, *Dow Diamond* [Winter, 1961], p. 6.)
12. Mr. H. M. Shattuck said that "All restaurants attached to motels will have resident operators . . . and the motel franchise in no way replaces the franchise division for restaurant operations." (Shattuck, "Richmond Firm to Build Series of Schrafft's Motels," *Wall Street Journal* [New York], February 23, 1961, p. 10.) Explain the type of growth illustrated by the above quotation.
13. Explain: "Our ability to acquire [plants, machines, mills, furnaces, mines, and other capital facilities necessary for production and sale of finished products] depends upon our success in generating the funds with which to buy them." (Roger M. Blough, *Business Has A Mandate Too* [United States Steel Corporation, 1960], p. 11.)
14. What management policy is indicated by the following? "The McCrory Corporation and H. L. Green Company said yesterday that their directors were discussing merger or another kind of consolidation. McCrory owns more than 47 per cent of H. L. Green stock. Both companies have chains of variety stores." (*New York Times*, January 24, 1961, p. 36.)

CHAPTER 27

Control of Corporations by other Corporations

A CORPORATION may gain control of another corporation by purchasing shares of voting stock and voting such shares through its representatives, as prescribed by the bylaws or the board of directors. The power to acquire and to vote shares in the name of a corporation has permitted control of corporate assets with a relatively small investment. A corporation may acquire the assets of a second company without acquiring the corporate entity, thereby leaving the old company as a going concern. For example, the Graham Paige Corporation has sold its automobile manufacturing assets and now operates as an investment company. Sometimes the assets of a second corporation are acquired under a lease arrangement without destroying the entity of the lessee. This chapter deals with corporate investments in securities of other corporations, holding companies, and regulation of public utility companies.

CORPORATE INVESTMENTS IN SECURITIES

Question of Legality. At one time the legality of corporate ownership of stock of another corporation was questioned on the ground that it was foreign to the purpose for which the corporation was created. If a corporation held stock of a second corporation, it was under implied powers—the means of accomplishing the purpose for which the corporation was formed. For illustration, in order for a corporation to protect its interest, it was considered entirely reasonable and necessary to take title to stock that had been pledged as security for a debt, provided it had no intention of keeping the stock as a permanent investment or controlling the other corporation; under different circumstances, it was considered legal for one corporation to accept stock of another corporation in payment for property.

Today, however, the general powers of business corporations, as provided for in statutes, customarily include the right to acquire and otherwise deal in shares or obligations of other domestic and foreign corporations. (There are many corporations, such as investment companies, which have been formed for no other purpose.) Holding companies are customarily organized to obtain control of other corporations through ownership of their voting stock. The same results may be obtained by use of voting trusts, as demonstrated by their use toward the end of the last century when voting trusts gained control over competing companies in the petroleum, sugar, and other industries.

Prior to 1888, some corporations were given the power to own stock of other corporations by special acts of state legislatures. In 1868, the Pennsylvania legislature chartered a corporation which was organized for the specific purpose of owning shares of other corporations. Twenty years later, the New Jersey legislature enacted a law permitting corporations to own shares in other corporations. This pioneer statute has been amended and broadened; subsequently, its provisions pertaining to stock ownership have been adopted by other states.

The New Jersey statute appeared at the time that "trusts" were under attack in the courts and many of these so-called trusts were reorganized as New Jersey corporations with the new corporations acquiring the stock formerly held by the trustees. In exchange for their trust certificates, the former beneficiaries of the voting trusts received shares in the new corporations organized as holding companies. The shift from the use of a voting trust to a holding-company control device met the legal objection that voting trusts were illegal because they deprived stockholders of their voting rights.[1] However, the combination resulting from a holding company may be challenged if the results are not in the public interest (if it reduces competition, restrains trade, creates a regional or national monopoly, and so on).

---

[1] Today, the voting trust is provided for in some business corporation acts and it is considered legal when not used in restraint of trade. It is most frequently used to retain control of a particular company. For illustration, in 1952 three directors of the Hamilton Watch Company established a voting trust in which about 40 per cent of the voting shares were deposited in order to prevent the Benrus Watch Company from obtaining control. The latter owned about 25 per cent of the voting stock of the Hamilton Watch Company. The voting trust agreement was for ten years.

In 1904, the Supreme Court ordered the dissolution of the Northern Securities Company because it constituted a restraint on interstate commerce as defined in the Sherman Antitrust Act. The subsidiary companies included two competing lines, the Northern Pacific and Great Northern railroads. Lawsuits were brought against holding companies with varying results. The legal shelter sometimes resorted to, when an unfavorable decision was anticipated, was a merger or consolidation into one corporation. Obviously, if there is only one corporation, there cannot be collusion, but the undesirable competitive situation which court action was designed to correct may still be present (see below). The ownership by one corporation of the stock of a second corporation is, in itself, legal; but the situation resulting therefrom may make the ownership illegal.

One of the more important aspects of the "merger" movement of 1918–1929 was the extensive use of the holding company device in the public utility field and to a lesser extent in other industries. By 1930, ten groups of holding companies controlled about three fourths of the nation's electric light and power industry. Promoters were able, with relatively small investments, to control vast networks of companies by owning small amounts of voting stock and by pyramiding holding companies on holding companies (layers of three or more above operating companies were not unusual). During the depression, dividends of operating companies were greatly reduced or eliminated and the funds needed to pay the charges on the various securities of holding companies shrank or disappeared. Even before the federal government made provisions for the reorganization of the electric light and power industry, many of the systems were reorganized and some had disappeared.

Investment Purposes. A corporation's cash in excess of its current needs may be invested to secure income; and, because of their high quality and marketability, short-term government obligations are favored for such investments. However, when investments in these securities are adequate to cover all anticipated needs for near cash, a corporation may choose to invest the remainder in securities of other corporations. Presumably, a corporation making such investments is able to justify the retention of earnings for expansion purposes, otherwise it may be subject to penalties under Sections 531–536 (old Section 102) of the Federal Revenue Act. A second question that may be raised in connection with a corporation's investments in the securities of other corporations pertains to the effect of such stock ownership on the relationship between the two corporations.

In December 1950, Congress amended the Clayton Act so that the Federal Trade Commission could rule against the acquisition by one industrial corporation of the stock of a second corporation if adverse effects on competition are expected; the Interstate Commerce Commission passes upon acquisition of stock by railroad companies; and the Securities and Exchange Commission passes upon acquisition of stock by public utility holding companies.

The extent to which a corporation which has invested in a second corporation may influence the latter's policies is difficult to appraise. If the investing corporation follows the typical small investor's policy of assigning proxies to management, it may avoid any outward evidence of influencing management. On the other hand, this passive approval of existing management may indicate that the investor and management are in agreement and that a satisfactory relationship exists between the two corporations. If the investing corporation holds stock in a corporation which is a competitor, a supplier, or a customer, it may be more difficult to prove that competition will not be adversely affected. In 1954, after having been in the court for about five years, the federal court dismissed the case brought by the Justice Department against E. I. duPont de Nemours & Company, General Motors Corporation, United States Rubber Company, Christiana Securities Company, Delaware Realty & Investment Company, and more than 100 individuals.[2] This decision was appealed by the government to the Supreme Court for reversal of Judge LaBuy's decision, argued before the Supreme Court, and remanded to the Chicago United States District Court with instructions to eliminate "the effects" of the stock ownership.[3] The basic issue in the du Pont case

---

[2] Judge Walter J. LaBuy in the United States District Court in Chicago ruled that the government's complaint in the so-called General Motors suit should be dismissed because, to quote from the "Conclusion" of the opinion:

"It may be that a violation of the Clayton Act can be made out in the absence of an actual restraint of trade where it is established that there is a reasonable probability that a condemned restraint will result from the acquisition of stock. The acquisition challenged by the Government—duPont's investment in General Motors—took place over thirty years ago. In those many intervening years the record discloses that no restraint of trade has resulted. . . . The Government has failed to prove conspiracy, monopolization, a restraint of trade, or any reasonable probability of a restraint, and for these reasons the Amended Complaint should be dismissed." Source: Letter to the Stockholders (E. I. duPont de Nemours & Company, Wilmington, Delaware, December 8, 1954).

[3] Under the Court's ruling, du Pont is permitting its stockholders to vote its holdings of General Motors stock (1.37 shares of General Motors common stock for each share of duPont owned). Disinvestment has not been ordered by the Court because of the anticipated depressing effect on General Motors stock and tax problems. If a property dividend were declared by duPont and distributed in the form of General Motors stock, the personal income tax burden that would fall on du Pont stockholders is regarded as being unfair. A property dividend seems most reasonable and least disturbing to the market,

is whether General Motors stock (63 million shares or about 23 per cent of the total number of shares outstanding) was acquired for investment purposes or to give du Pont a dominant position as supplier of automobile finishes and fabrics to General Motors Corporation. The acquisition raises the question of the applicability of the law to *vertical* stock acquisitions as well as to already accepted *horizontal* acquisitions, and the majority of the Supreme Court ruled in favor of including vertical acquisitions.

The suspicion of collusion between two or more corporations because of stock ownership may be impossible to prevent except by prohibiting corporations from buying stock of other corporations. However, commercial banks and other financial institutions, whose investments in corporate stock are prohibited or greatly limited, influence the policies of corporations because of debtor-creditor relationships. Thus, the same suspicion of collusion could exist because of debtor-creditor relationships between corporations selling goods on credit or making loans to other corporations. The opportunity for antisocial practices is present whenever two or more individuals, business firms, and/or corporations deal with one another; it would be undesirable to forbid all intercorporate financial relations although it may be desirable to subject them to administrative and judicial review.

Under certain circumstances, a combination may increase competition rather than decrease it. For illustration, there may be more competition in the automobile industry as the result of the consolidation of Nash-Kelvinator Corporation and Hudson Motor Car Company to form the American Motors Corporation and the combination of Studebaker Corporation and Packard Motor Car Company to form Studebaker-Packard Corporation. Perhaps these new combinations can compete more effectively with the "big three" than they were able to do when they were operating as four independent companies. The American Motors Corporation has a close working agreement with Willys Motors, Inc., a wholly owned subsidiary of Kaiser Industries Corporation, which may lead to a merger between the two. Sometimes one company invests in the common stock of a second company for defensive reasons—to prevent a competitor from assuming control and taking its business. For example, Union Pacific Railroad was reported as having purchased a sizable block of common stock of

but action may be delayed until Congress makes special tax provisions for cases of this type. Antitrust suits of similar types may be expected if and when this tax situation is worked out so as not to penalize innocent common stockholders.

Denver & Rio Grande Western Railroad to protect itself from loss of freight in case the Atchison, Topeka & Santa Fe Railway should win its battle with the Southern Pacific Company for control of Denver & Rio Grande Western Railroad. Previously, Southern Pacific announced it had purchased 10 per cent of Western Pacific's outstanding stock and intended to seek control of the road.[4] Moves by management of one company to seek control of a second company by investing in its stock is not always approved by its stockholders, and management of the second company may take legal or other action to prevent it.

Community of Ownership. When two or more corporations co-operate to finance a new corporation, co-operative ownership results (a situation that is being encouraged by the Small Business Administration, as was previously noted). A corporation may be created to carry on a research project, to facilitate a buying program, to collect and disseminate information, to develop a new process or invention, or to develop mutually owned or collectively used real estate such as terminal facilities of railroads. In some cases, the mutually owned corporation may be created to comply with some provision in a state law (such as gas collecting and processing corporations formed to use waste products of the petroleum industry where "flaring" in oil fields has been prohibited).

The concept of mutual ownership of one corporation by several corporations exists in reverse when one holding or operating company owns the controlling interest in several other companies. Between these two extremes, there may be an intermingling of ownership wherein operating companies may own and be owned by all the other companies in a group. If the small amount of stock which a director may be required to own to qualify as a director is disregarded, theoretically a perfect corporate community of ownership could be achieved by prorating 10 per cent of the common stock of each of eleven corporations among the other ten corporations in the group. Dividends on stock would be paid only to other corporations and no natural person would receive an investment income from the common stock of any of the eleven corporations. Although such intermingling of corporate stock to exclude natural persons from ownership is possible, usually a "community of interest" is one formed by a small group of persons who, through stock ownership in

[4] See also, *Wall Street Journal* (New York), February 17, 1961, p. 16.

different corporations, elect directors and otherwise influence the policies of the corporations.

HOLDING COMPANIES

A holding company is usually organized as a corporation (but it may be a business trust or joint-stock company) which controls one or more corporations through stock ownership. Sometimes a corporation may control a second corporation by owning but a small percentage of its stock; but control can only be assured by ownership of 50 per cent plus one share of the voting stock. However, as defined in the Public Utility Holding Company Act, "any company which directly or indirectly owns, controls, or holds with power to vote, 10 percentum or more of the outstanding voting securities of a public-utility company" is a holding company. Investment companies customarily limit their investments in any one company to 5 per cent or less of the voting stock in order to prevent their being classified as holding companies and to meet the requirement contained in the Investment Company Act to qualify as a diversified company.

Types of Holding Companies. At one time the classification of holding companies as "holding" and "holding-operating" companies was descriptive, but it is no longer the case. More accurately, holding companies are managerial corporations that perform the same services for their subsidiaries as the head office of a large company performs for its divisions, stores, or other units; and operating-holding companies are operating companies that control one or more subsidiary companies. Most large American industrial corporations may be classified as operating-holding companies rather than as holding-operating companies to give the proper emphasis on operations. Even a small bank may own subsidiary corporations, one of which may own the bank building, a second which may own and operate the safe deposit business, and a third which may operate the bank's trust business.

Superholding Companies. The corporate structure of a combination may consist of several layers with a superholding company controlling holding companies which control holding companies—until eventually we come to the operating companies which produce the income to support the superstructure of corporations, controlling corporations, *ad extremum.* Congress inserted the "grandfather" clause in the Public Utility Holding Company Act of 1935 and thus limited the number of layers of corporate entities to three—a superholding or holding-operating company, one or more subsidiary "holding" or "hold-operating" companies, and operating companies. However, this law is applicable to only those corporations covered by the Public Utility Holding Company Act of 1935, whereas holding companies exist in all fields of business—public utility, railroads, and other industries and their subdivisions.

Financing-Holding Companies. In its simplest form, a holding company has assets that consist of the voting stock of its subsidiaries (in amounts sufficient to assure control), office equipment, cash, and sundry assets. Some holding companies are at the same time financing companies—financing their subsidiaries by purchasing their bonds or stock. In this case, the financing-holding company may pledge the bonds of its subsidiary for a bond issue of its own. For illustration, if the smaller subsidiary agrees to pay 4½ per cent on its bonds, the parent company might pledge them together with those of other subsidiaries for a larger bond issue bearing an interest rate of perhaps 3 or 3½ per cent. If and when a holding company acts as a financing company in this way, the result is an expansion of its assets to include more than the voting stock of its subsidiaries. The greatest change in the assets of a holding company occurs when the assets of subsidiaries are absorbed by merger or consolidation and the company becomes a holding-operating company.

When a wholly owned subsidiary sells stock, it will be to the parent company. For instance, the New York Telephone Company may announce plans for the sale of additional stock, all of which will be purchased by the American Telephone and Telegraph Company. The funds received for the stock will be given back to the American Telephone and Telegraph Company in payment for advances made by the parent company. Last year the Superior Oil Company of California, which owns 51.6 per cent of the stock of the Canadian Superior Oil, Ltd., announced that it would advance $10.8 million to the Canadian Superior Oil, Ltd., interest free in order to enable it to retire its bank indebtedness. The Canadian Superior Oil, Ltd., is to repay the loan from the proceeds of a stock sale subject to the approval of stockholders and the government.

Operating-Holding Companies. In addition to being holding companies, operating-holding companies produce goods and services which are sold to the general public. If Corporation *A* owns all the stock of operating company *B*, it will be simple to obtain approval of Corporation *B* for a merger of *A* and *B*. The accounting procedure would be to delete corporation B stock as an investment of corporation *A* and replace it with "plant, equipment, and other assets" formerly owned by the acquired corporation. Adjustment for the difference between value may be made by crediting or charging the "capital surplus" of corporation *A*. If there are minority stockholders, their shares may be purchased for cash or exchanged for new stock, usually at the option of the minority stockholders. If there are dissenting shareholders, their claims may, if necessary, be settled through court proceedings as previously noted. Subsidiary corporations are being absorbed practically every day by operating-holding companies (with the general public taking little notice of the fact). Many corporations such as General Motors and United States Steel, which were organized as holding companies, have become operating-holding companies with the emphasis properly placed on their operating activities.

Decline in Pure Holding Companies. The factors in the decline of pure holding companies may be summarized as follows: corporate income tax; court decisions, which permitted use of the merger or consolidation device to avoid antitrust action; and improvements in managerial techniques, which permit units or divisions to function as efficiently as separate corporations. If Corporation *A* is buying from Corporation *B*, there may be intercorporate profits which could be avoided if Corporation *B* were absorbed by Corporation *A* (and so on for other intercorporate transactions). In addition, the dividend paid by Corporation *B* to Corporation *A* would be subject to taxation as corporate income (hence "double taxation" as already explained). However, some of the tax disadvantages associated with the operation of subsidiary corporations are avoided if the parent company owns 80 per cent of the voting power of all the classes of stock and at least 80 per cent of the nonvoting stock of the subsidiary and files a consolidated return for federal income tax purposes.

Consolidated Financial Statements. The extent to which parent corporations are treating their subsidiary corporations as units within the company is indicated by the growing practice of consolidating financial statements which show combined income and assets. Customarily, these statements cover all subsidiaries, provided that the business units are not dissimilar in nature, the parent company's investment is 50 per cent or more (if less, the subsidiary is sometimes referred to as an "affiliate"), the intercompany transactions are large; and the fiscal years are similar. Special situations may justify the exclusion of a subsidiary when the situation is the opposite of those cited above, when it is located in a foreign country, or when it is in the process of being liquidated or sold.

Among the best-known operating-holding companies in the United States is the American Telephone and Telegraph Company System, which provides long-distance telephone service for its customers, controls its telephone and other subsidiary companies through stock ownership, and has investments in other companies affiliated with it (see Table 29). The American Telephone and Telegraph System consists of the American Telephone and Telegraph Company, twenty subsidiary telephone companies, certain subsidiaries not consolidated, and an investment interest in other companies. The subsidiaries which are not consolidated include the Bell Telephone Laboratories, Inc., which is the research and development company; the Western Electric Company, Inc., which is the manufacturing company for the American Telephone and Telegraph System; and the 195 Broadway Corporation, the realty company.

Increases in telephone rates have been a minor factor in the increase in earnings of the American Telephone and Telegraph System (the Federal Communications Commission insisted on a reduction in interstate long distance rates in 1959); but new markets and increases in operating efficiency have been important factors. The "Bell System" is one of the leaders in "electronics" and "space research" and is now classified as a "growth company." In addition to the Bell System, there are over 5,000 independent telephone companies in the United States served by the American Telephone and Telegraph long distance communciations system.

As a result of a series of mergers, the United States Steel Corporation is classified as an operating-holding company. Today, many of the properties that were operated by subsidiary corporations are being operated as divisions. The parent corporation still owns about fifty subsidiary corporations, some of which are not active.[5] It also has substantial investments in nine other companies but in no case more than 50 per cent of their voting stock. The United States Steel Corporation is the largest steel producer, a major coal and chemical

---

[5] After the assets of a corporation have been transferred to the parent company, the latter may pay the annual franchise tax in order to keep the corporate name which may have trade value. For illustration, the United States Steel Corporation is keeping as subsidiaries, although they are not active, corporations such as Chapin Mining Company, Carnegie-Illinois Steel Corporation, H. C. Frick Coke Company, and United States Coal & Coke Company.

TABLE 29

BELL SYSTEM COMPANIES

December 31, 1959

COMPANIES INCLUDED IN CONSOLIDATED STATEMENTS

AMERICAN TELEPHONE AND TELEGRAPH COMPANY

	Capital Stocks Owned by A.T.&T. Co.		Advances from
Principal Telephone Subsidiaries	% Owned	Cost (a)	A.T.&T. Co. (a)
New England Tel. & Tel. Co.	69.33	$ 310,641	$ 31,300
New York Tel. Co.	100.00	1,304,280	......
New Jersey Bell Tel. Co.	100.00	513,667	8,200
Bell Tel. Co. of Pennsylvania	100.00	626,316	9,000
Diamond State Tel. Co.	100.00	41,700	1,200
Chesapeake & Potomac Tel. Co.	100.00	101,000	12,800
Chesapeake & Potomac Tel. Co. of Maryland	100.00	226,468	25,750
Chesapeake & Potomac Tel. Co. of Virginia	100.00	220,000	37,100
Chesapeake & Potomac Tel. Co. of West Virginia	100.00	97,000	26,900
Southern Bell Tel. & Tel. Co.	100.00	1,181,817	15,500
Ohio Bell Tel. Co.	100.00	511,042	15,000
Michigan Bell Tel. Co.	99.99	409,399	14,700
Indiana Bell Tel. Co., Inc.	100.00	189,587	4,800
Wisconsin Tel. Co.	100.00	218,224	10,000
Illinois Bell Tel. Co.	99.32	610,882	59,800
Northwestern Bell Tel. Co.	100.00	401,040	15,800
Southwestern Bell Tel. Co.	99.99	1,243,243	25,100
Mountain States Tel. & Tel. Co.	86.75	366,230	67,600
Pacific Tel. & Tel. Co.	89.62	1,273,651	161,000
Bell Tel. Co. of Nevada (b)	.....	......	......
Total		$9,846,187	$541,550
SUBSIDIARIES NOT CONSOLIDATED			
Bell Telephone Laboratories, Inc.	(c)50.00	$ 25,000	$......
Western Electric Co., Inc.	99.82	631,721	......
195 Broadway Corporation	100.00	23,015	3,200
Other (d)	.....	27,980	7,376
Total		$ 707,716	$ 10,576
OTHER COMPANIES			
Southern New England Tel. Co.	19.21	$ 36,990	$ 300
Cincinnati & Suburban Bell Tel. Co.	29.83	21,065	......
Bell Tel. Co. of Canada	3.57	18,855	......
Miscellaneous Investments (d)	.....	18,194	......
Total		$ 95,104	$ 300

(a) Thousands of dollars.
(b) Wholly-owned subsidiary of Pacific Tel. & Tel. Co. Cost of capital stock—$31,500,000.
(c) Remaining shares owned by Western Electric Company.
(d) Includes investments of Principal Telephone Subsidiaries.

Source: American Telephone and Telegraph Company, *The 1959 Annual Report* (New York, 1960), p. 29.

producer, and, through a subsidiary, the largest cement producer in the United States.

ADVANTAGES AND DISADVANTAGES OF HOLDING COMPANIES

Although there has been a tendency for large holding companies to simplify their organizations by eliminating some of their subsidiary corporations by absorption or other means, there has also been a minor development in the opposite direction wherein some operating companies have organized and operate new subsidiary corporations. The holding-company device may also be used to acquire control of an existing company which is an important supplier, customer, competitor, or a firm whose products or services will complement or complete those of the acquiring corporation. The holding-company device also offers a means whereby the promoters may embark on a new venture without assuming any risks other than the amount invested in the venture. At the same time, there may be legal, administrative, tax, and/or other advantages in using the holding-company device to acquire and operate subsidiary or affiliates as compared to other ways of arranging combinations.

Managerial Aspects. Few holding companies limit their activities to the original objective, that of assuming control and managing operating companies through puppet boards of directors and officers. Most parent companies are supplying their subsidiaries with specialized services in different fields such as accounting, advertising, law, engineering, finance, personnel direction, and research. While small subsidiary companies are not able to employ a great number of experts, they may obtain the benefits of their services and advice "at a price" by using the pool of specialists employed by the holding company (see below). The parent company may assume complete responsibility for financing, establishing sales outlets, arranging employee benefit plans, and handling other problems of group interest. Where the individual business units are predominately small with no serious production, marketing, and financial problems, the holding-company device may be justified even though the same services could be obtained through the head office if the individual firms were combined to form a large business concern.

Without question, there is an optimum size for each technical unit; but other factors may be sufficiently important to justify a consolidation or a merger. Some large corporations have achieved the advantages of decentralization without creating subsidiaries. For illustration, General Motors operates divisions such as Buick Motor, A C Spark Plug, Delco Products, Fisher Body, Chevrolet Motors, Frigidaire, and about thirty other divisions, each of which has its own self-contained administrative unit with a general manager responsible for all functional activities.

Expansionary Aspects. When expansion is considered, it is agreed that it is cheaper to acquire control over a second corporation than to effect a merger, consolidation, or outright purchase. All that the holding company needs to do is to acquire, by purchase or exchange, enough of the voting stock of a second corporation to assure control. When the voting stock of an operating company represents only a small part of its capital structure, control can be obtained by a relatively small investment. If management of the holding company can arrange an exchange of its bonds, preferred stock, or nonvoting common stock for the operating company's voting stock, control could be obtained with no cash outlay and no dilution of voting rights of the holding company's stock.

The holding company's management may be able to obtain control of an operating company without being confronted with the problems often encountered in effecting mergers and consolidations, wherein a minority group may block the transfer or demand payment through court proceedings which are time consuming and expensive. Although this argument has merit, stockholders may raise objections in any type of business transfer; lawsuits based on charges of fraud, misrepresentation, and mismanagement may be and have been instituted by stockholders of subsidiary companies against holding companies.

Risk and Legal Aspects. When subsidiary companies are operated as separate legal entities, the holding company may liquidate its investment in an unprofitable subsidiary with a minimum of loss; and if a subsidiary fails, the loss of the parent corporation is usually limited to its investment in the stock of the subsidiary. For illustration, many merchandising and service companies minimized their losses during the 1930's by incorporating their real estate properties separately; but today, as a result of several court decisions, the responsibilities of a parent corporation for the debts of its subsidiaries are better defined. No longer may a parent corporation be sure that it is not responsible for the debts of a bankrupt subsidiary corporation. Sometimes the debts of a subsidiary have been incurred for the benefit of the parent corporation or other subsidiary companies in the system or combination. If it can be shown that the subsidiary was used as the "agent," "adjunct," or instrumentality of the parent corporation, the latter may be held responsible for the debts of the subsidiary (the so-called "instrumentality rule").

When a parent corporation is guilty of unfair treatment or mismanagement of a subsidiary corporation, it cannot avoid responsibility for the debts of the subsidiary. However, as noted by the Securities and Exchange Commission, each case wherein the issue of mismanagement or unfair treatment of a subsidiary arises calls for careful analysis of a complicated set of facts to determine the degree of responsibility of the parent corporation. In order to prevent creditors of a subsidiary from collecting assets from the parent corporation when those of the subsidiary are inadequate to cover claims, the following steps should be taken: (1) the subsidiary should be set up as a separate unit sufficiently strong to bear any financial strain to which it would normally be subjected; (2) managements of the two corporations should function separately and the day-to-day business and financial records should be kept separately; and (3) those with whom the two corporations come in contact should be kept aware of the fact that they are separate entities.

A corporation may organize a subsidiary company to evade some legal provision in a contract with creditors, as illustrated by forming a new subsidiary to hold title to property in order to evade the after-acquired property clause in trust indentures covering mortgage bond issues. In other cases, a corporation may organize separate subsidiaries incorporated in the states or foreign countries wherein they operate in order to offset restrictions placed on business activities of foreign corporations. If one or several different activities carried on by a corporation are subject to special regulation, all of the corporation's affairs might be brought under review and state supervision. In addition, carrying on several different activities may be in violation of the "purpose clause" in the company's charter. In either case, legal difficulties may be avoided by incorporation of separate subsidiaries to carry on the various activities.

Tax Aspects. Sometimes, a parent corporation may avoid paying taxes on earnings outside its state of incorporation by operating through a subsidiary corporation which would limit state taxes paid in that state to those on the earnings from operation within the state. The tax advantages derived from separate incorporation must be weighed against the expenses incurred in creating and maintaining separate corporate organizations, paying state organization and franchise taxes, reporting to state regulatory agencies, and paying higher federal income taxes.

The greatest penalty associated with operating separate corporate units are probably those due to the federal income tax laws. To file a consolidated tax return, a parent company must own 80 per cent of its subsidiary company's voting stock and at least 80 per cent of the nonvoting stock.[6] In a consolidated tax return, the parent corporation is able to adjust its income and expenses by cancelling out intercompany transactions. The savings which would result may make it desirable for the parent corporation to increase its equity holdings in its subsidiaries.

Goodwill Aspects. After being acquired by a holding company, a subsidiary company may continue to operate under its own corporate name to preserve existing goodwill of customers, employees, and others. In some cases, the acquisition of a subsidiary can be arranged by purchasing the stock of a few large stockholders without the general public becoming aware of the transfer of control. In other cases, a parent corporation may avoid the resentment against "outside interests" by incorporating subsidiaries separately; sales organizations, warehouses, factories, and other outlets or units located in other states and foreign countries are often incorporated separately under the laws of the state or country wherein they operate. If some of the stock of such a subsidiary is sold locally, goodwill may be created to the advantage of the parent corporation as well as the subsidiary.

REGULATION OF PUBLIC UTILITY HOLDING COMPANIES

Public utility and railroad companies differ from other corporations in that they render necessary services, are "natural monopolies" insofar as they render their best service when operating under monopolistic conditions, require large capital outlays, have incomes that tend to be fairly steady, and are subject to service and rate regulations. The principle of rate regulation is based on the concept that the general public must be protected from excessive rates which could be charged by a company having a monopoly; at the same time, the companies must be permitted to earn a fair return on capital. Rate regulation necessitates evaluation of assets, as previously discussed, because net income of $1,000,000 may be "fair" on a valuation of $16,000,000 but inadequate on a $22,000,000 valuation.

Customarily, the jurisdiction of state public service commissions is limited to operating companies, and certain information which they need may be in the files of holding companies over which they have no jurisdiction. In the past, financial practices originating with holding companies and their promoters often led to inflated value of assets and expenses of operating companies. Following intensive investigation of public utility holding companies from 1928 to 1935

[6] See *Internal Revenue Code of 1954,* Section 1504 (a).

by the Federal Trade Commission, Congress passed the Public Utility Holding Company Act of 1935. This law pertains only to holding companies and their operating subsidiaries in the electric and gas industries which hold properties in more than one state. The Securities and Exchange Commission was empowered to supervise the financial practices of the public utility holding companies and their operating subsidiaries and to pass upon their proposed security issues.

Congress prohibited organization of holding companies above the second level and required that the corporate structures of the different systems be simplified and regrouped along regional lines. The electric light and power and gas industries are essentially local in nature and the most economical operations thereof are obtained on a local or regional basis.

Electric light and power and gas holding companies are required to register with the Securities and Exchange Commission. The Commission has the power to approve or disapprove the issuance of securities by the holding companies and their subsidiaries (and to place a ban on unsecured bonds, preferred stock, no-par stock, and nonvoting stock without the Commission's specific approval); control intercompany transactions, such as loans, sales of securities, charges for managerial services, and sales and construction contracts; approve or disapprove the acquisition of subsidiaries; and require periodic reports and the use of prescribed accounts, records, and statement forms.

In giving the Securities and Exchange Commission detailed powers over the business activities of public utility holding companies, Congress sought to correct inefficiencies resulting from the growth of uneconomical systems, creation of top-heavy capital structures, and inflation of operating costs and capital values. When a holding company deals with an operating subsidiary company, bargaining at arm's length is absent; in the past, this situation sometimes led to "upstream" loans (from operating companies to the holding company) and to service, interest, and other intercompany charges that were not related to actual costs (with the operating companies' customers and minority stockholders being exploited). The abuses that were prevalent included keeping the books of the holding company out of the jurisdiction of state regulatory bodies, padding and manipulating expenses, creating secret reserves, releasing inaccurate information about financial positions of subsidiary companies, and manipulating market prices of stocks.

One of the most serious problems faced by the Securities and Exchange Commission was that of rehabilitating holding company systems. The excessive prices paid for operating units led to over-capitalization which broke down during the depression of the 1930's and resulted in heavy losses to investors. An extreme case was the "billion dollar" Associated Gas & Electric Company, which issued three classes of common stock, six classes of preferred stock, four classes of preference stock, 24 classes of debentures, seven issues of secured notes, four issues of investment certificates, and various warrants and rights. Being a holding company, the chief assets of the Associated Gas & Electric Company were the securities of subsidiary companies (it controlled about 175 companies directly or indirectly).

The irresponsible financial practices of holding companies were harmful to their operating subsidiary companies, and the latter were left with large fixed charges, dividend arrearages on preferred stock, and excessive issues of preferred and common stock. During the early 1930's, some holding companies depended on their operating companies for loans and dividends; and, in most cases, the loans were made and the dividends were voted even though doing so was not warranted. In other cases, the holding companies used the credit of the operating companies to obtain funds for ventures which were not related to the activities of the operating companies.

Since 1935, considerable progress has been made in "squeezing the water out of inflated valuations," reducing costs of operations, increasing net earnings, and simplifying holding company systems. Both disinvestment in nonintegrated properties and simplification of corporate structure are still taking place—but at a much slower rate because integration of public utility companies is almost complete. When completed, each holding company system will resemble operating-holding companies such as Commonwealth Edison Company, Consolidated Edison Company of New York, and other large companies of this type. Because of better organization and management, the public utility industry has been able to keep pace with the rapid growth in demand for its services. In addition, it has been able to provide services at only slight increases in rates while general commodity prices have increased more than 100 per cent.

SUMMARY

The right of corporations to own stock in other corporations has been established by statutes, and the development of both investment companies and holding companies stems from these enabling acts.

When the purpose of acquiring stock of other corporations is control, a parent-subsidiary relationship results; when the purpose is investment, the investor corporation usually limits its stock ownership in any one corporation to avoid being classified as a holding company.

A pure holding company is a nonoperating company which controls the operations of subsidiaries through voting privileges obtained by stock ownership; an operating-holding company, as the name suggests, is both a holding company and an operating company. Most of the major corporations in the United States are of the latter type. In financial reporting, subsidiaries are sometimes treated as units of a system and sometimes consolidated financial reports are made. The practice followed depends on factors such as the percentage of ownership of the parent in the subsidiary, the volume of intercompany transactions, and the degree of similarity in operations. The relative advantages and disadvantages of large holding companies depend on managerial, expansionary, risk, legal, and tax factors.

The Public Utility Holding Company Act of 1935, which pertains to registered electric and power and gas holding companies and their operating subsidiaries having properties in more than one state, limited the layers of corporate entities to three (the so-called "grandfather" clause) and gave the Securities and Exchange Commission detailed powers over the financial activities of public utility holding companies. The objectives of the Commission have been (1) to correct the inefficiencies and inflation in operating costs and capital values that resulted from the growth of uneconomical holding-company systems with top-heavy capital structures and (2) to supervise intercorporate transactions. Since 1935, a great deal of progress has been made in simplifying capital structures, deflating valuations of corporate assets, reducing operating costs, and increasing net earnings; as a result, the industry has been able to keep pace with the increased demand for service at only a slight increase in rates relative to the increase in general commodity prices.

QUESTIONS AND PROBLEMS

1. Identify: (*a*) holding company, (*b*) subsidiary company, and (*c*) affiliated company.
2. Distinguish among the different kinds of holding companies.
3. Identify: (*a*) community of ownership, (*b*) consolidated financial statements, (*c*) "grandfather" clause, and (*d*) "integrated" public utility system.

4. May it be cheaper to acquire control over a second corporation by stock ownership than to effect a merger, consolidation, or outright purchase? Explain.
5. (*a*) What is the "instrumentality rule"? (*b*) How may a holding company avoid invocation of the instrumentality rule if and when a subsidiary fails?
6. What is the tax advantage of operating a unit as a subsidiary company? The tax disadvantage?
7. Why was the Securities and Exchange Commission given detailed powers over certain business transactions of public utility holding companies?
8. If you were a director would you approve of Montgomery Ward & Company's plan to form a finance company to help carry the company's accounts receivable? Why? See also Glore Forgan & Co., *Montgomery Ward & Co.* (Chicago, 1959).
9. Are there special reasons why the United States Steel Corporation operates some of its properties through subsidiary corporations such as the Quebec Cartier Mining Company, Orinoco Mining Company, United States Steel Export Company, Carnegie Natural Gas Company, and Birmingham Southern Railroad Company?
10. Analyze: "A stockholder filed suit yesterday to block the purchase by the Bates Manufacturing Company, a textile concern, of the stock of Fruit of the Loom, Inc. . . . The action was brought by . . . a shareholder of Windsor Industries, Inc., which is said to own 57 per cent of the voting stock of Bates . . . Bates is sparring with the Philadelphia and Reading subsidiary, Union Underwear Company, which is the largest licensee of Fruit of the Loom." (*New York Times,* February 16, 1961, p. 43.)
11. "The Supreme Court held that du Pont's ownership of the General Motors stock violated Section 7 of the Clayton Act, which prohibits mergers and acquisitions pending 'substantially to lessen competition.' " (*New York Times,* February 22, 1961, p. 42.) In view of the fact that the right of corporations to own stock in other corporations has been established by statutes, on what basis is this action justified?

PART VIII

Recapitalization, Reorganization, and Liquidation of Business Firms

RECAPITALIZATION, reorganization, and liquidation of businesses are aspects of business finance that reflect changes in the life cycles of business concerns. Recapitalizing a business firm refer to remodelling its capital structure, and this is done for various reasons including attainment of more economical financing, avoidance of financial strain, and preparation for listing on a stock exchange. A business firm's capital may be simple, consisting of a single type of common stock, or it may be complicated, including two or three types of common stock, several issues of preferred stock, a large number of bond issues, debentures, and long-term notes.

The reorganization of a business firm may refer to managerial changes but as used here, it means a revision of the firm's capital structure necessitated by default on interest and principal payments or other obligations. Broadly speaking, the principal difference between recapitalization and reorganization is that the first is voluntary while the second is forced on a business firm by creditors.

Liquidation of a business concern ordinarily means that its assets are converted into cash in order to discharge liabilities with any remaining cash to be distributed to owners. If a firm is incorporated, additional legal steps are necessary in order to dissolve the corporation.

This section deals with recapitalization, reorganization, and liquidation of business firms.

CHAPTER 28

Recapitalization

RECAPITALIZATION of a corporation is the readjustment of the amount of its bonds, long-term notes, and stock not for purposes of raising additional capital but to change its capital structure. For example, a company is recapitalized when it replaces mortgage bonds with debentures or long-term notes, and preferred stock with common stock. Recapitalization as used here does not refer to changes in the capital structure because of financial embarrassment such as failure to meet interest or principal obligations. Once a default occurs, the right of management to take corrective action passes to a large extent from the corporation to its creditors; and the changes in the capital structure that follow are called reorganizations (see Chapter 29).

CAPITAL STRUCTURE

The capital structure of a business firm includes its long-term debts and owners' equity; the relationship between the two is suggested by Table 30. The extent to which companies finance with long-term debts tends to be greatest for public utility companies and least for industrial companies. Although the accounting procedures differ for companies in different industries, financing with funds from operations is usually far more important for industrial than for railroad or public utility companies because the latter are subject to rate regulations.

Irrespective of the industry in which it operates, the total amount of capital needed by a firm depends in part on its cash conversion cycle. The process of turning cash into noncash assets and back to

TABLE 30

CAPITAL STUCTURES*
(Amounts In Thousands)

ITEM	INDUSTRIAL		RAILROAD		PUBLIC UTILITY	
	Amount	*Per Cent*	*Amount*	*Per Cent*	*Amount*	*Per Cent*
Noncurrent debts . .	$ 364,129	19.9	$391,248	39.3	$270,670	52.8
Preferred stock . . .	. . . .	. . . .	4,391	0.4	59,360	11.5
Common stock	441,414	24.2	209,257	21.1	103,660	20.2
Surplus (etc.)	1,046,273	55.9	387,114	39.2	79,185	15.5
Total Liabilities and Equity	$1,851,816	100.0	$992,010	100.0	$512,875	100.0

* Statistics from balance sheets of three companies, the names of which are withheld.

cash starts with the investment in plant, facilities, raw materials, and wages; then into finished products or services; and finally into cash when the finished products are sold. The cash conversion process is a continuous one, and the faster it takes place the smaller is the amount of capital needed to operate a business. Management is interested in the cash conversion cycle, but the responsibility for it rests primarily with the finance officers of a business firm.

A loss of cash results when interest and principal payments on debts are met (which tend to come at the wrong times, unless planned for in advance); hence, "excessive indebtedness" usually appears among the stated reasons for business firms' financial difficulties not only because payments thereon reduce a business concern's resources but also because these obligations place the borrower in a position where creditors can demand payment irrespective of the inconvenience caused the borrower.

Customarily, there are provisions in long-term debt contracts that require assets to be set aside periodically for debt retirement: in sinking-fund bond issues, to retire bonds at maturity; in serial bond issues, to retire bonds as they mature each year; and in term loans, to meet installment payments on the principal. In most cases, the debt contract requires the debtor to meet certain financial standards including maintenance of a specified current ratio. Because a financially strained firm normally exhausts its sources of short-term credit first, a decrease in its current ratio below the standard specified may indicate that a default is imminent.

Finally, a bond indenture or a term loan agreement usually contains an acceleration clause which makes outstanding obligations covered by the contract due and payable at the option of creditors if any term of the contract is violated. If creditors use the acceleration clause to call unpaid balances on outstanding debts, business management may be confronted with a cash demand which may necessitate an adjustment of the debt or liquidation of the firm.

When a business firm has incurred heavy losses, it may be able to prevent default on current obligations by using funds from operations accounted for as depreciation and other allowances; but in so doing, the firm is liquidating assets and this could lead to insolvency in the bankruptcy sense. This type of gradual liquidation is most serious to intermediate and long-term creditors who, in case of forced liquidation, look to receipts from the sale of fixed assets to cover their claims. Term loan agreements and bond indentures usually place restrictions on additional borrowing; therefore a business firm bound by such contracts, while being required to use cash to pay interest and to repay principal, may not be able to borrow when the need for additional funds is greatest.

One of the underlying causes of indebtedness becoming excessive and causing financial strain is failure of management to achieve the increase in earnings anticipated at the time debts were contracted. The amount of earnings may be compared to funded debt, which indicates how much is available for interest payments, or it may be compared to total capitalization (tangible net worth plus funded debt) to indicate the profitableness of funds employed in the business. The ratio of net sales to net worth is indicative of the productivity of each proprietary dollar.

If earnings decline sharply, the resulting situation may be described as one wherein fixed assets are excessive, but it would be more accurate to describe it as a situation resulting from unprofitable expansion. Overexpansion may result from enlarging or improving the appearance of retail establishments or manufacturing plants, constructing new buildings, and so on. If improvements financed with borrowed funds are less productive than anticipated, the combination of lower earnings plus the additional debt charges may cause financial strain. Even when fixed capital expansion is not financed with long-term debt, it may still cause a serious shortage of working capital assets and this may necessitate borrowing under unfavorable conditions.

Poor administration of earnings is a second cause of fixed assets becoming top-heavy. If inadequate allowances are made for depreciation, profits will be overstated, and on the basis of high profits, sole proprietors or partners may make heavy withdrawals from their business firms and boards of directors of corporations may declare excessive cash dividends. This loss of cash causes a business firm's working capital position to be weakened and its net worth to be reduced.

For smaller companies, total debt should not, as a general rule, exceed tangible net worth (net worth minus intangible assets); usually total debt should be much less than tangible net worth. Some strong industrial companies have no funded debt and their current debts will be relatively small—varying from season to season. Although long-term debt financing is becoming more popular, it is not a characteristic of manufacturing companies—the most important component of the industrial group (being less than 16 per cent of total invested capital, defined to include long-term debt, capital stock, and capital reserves).

If bonded debt is linked to real property, the maximum loan should be no more than 50 to 60 per cent of the appraised value of the property. If long-term debt is linked to earnings, earnings after income taxes should equal three times the interest charges on the debt (varying a little with stability of earnings—more if earnings are fluctuating, less if stable). Like all rules, those above are subject to exceptions; but, in general, the larger the number of exceptions made, the larger will be the number of business failures.

Once a business firm is faced with insolvency because of inability to meet long-term obligations, it may use the same remedial devices to obtain cash as used by firms having inadequate working capital (see above). In some cases, the problem may be solved temporarily by obtaining an emergency loan; but it may be solved permanently by increasing net worth—if the business is incorporated, by selling stock, and if unincorporated, by taking in partners. The future prospects of the business firm and the ability of management to attract additional investments in the business will determine whether or not either method is practical. If a business firm's working capital is adequate, bondholders and other long-term creditors may consent to an extension of maturities of debts.

The decline in wholesale commodity prices looms large among the reasons given for the concentration of business failures in certain years. If 20 per cent of business enterprises in the United States are marginal firms, as has been estimated, it is not illogical to assume that losses taken on inventories during periods of falling prices are sufficient to eliminate the margin of profit which has kept them in business during good or normal times. Only those firms with adequate working capital which keep liabilities, inventories, receivables, and fixed assets within bounds will be able to take in stride lower profits and/or losses on inventories during depression periods.

The relationship between a decline in wholesale prices and an increase in business failures is present at the industrial as well as the mercantile level. Every business firm has inventories, the composition and proportion of which vary among industries and firms within the same industry—raw materials, semimanufactured products, durable producers' goods, and durable and nondurable consumers' goods.

All the elements of cost enter into sales prices, and these cost elements vary among industries and among firms within industries. Companies in certain fields buy in markets wherein prices fluctuate and sell in markets wherein prices are relatively stable; and conversely, companies in other fields buy in markets wherein prices are relatively stable and sell in markets wherein prices fluctuate. In the first case, a decline in general prices would subject a firm's profits to less strain than in the second case, if other things remain the same.

During a business depression, a decline in sales volume may be more significant than a decline in prices as a factor in business failures. Even though prices may be fairly stable, as in the durable goods producing industries (machines, tools, equipment, automobiles, etc.), the demand may be so depressed as to cause serious financial strain. For illustration, if an annual sales volume of 10,000 units (or some other figure) is needed to cover a firm's fixed charges, any substantial decline in sales below this figure may cause financial strain. On the other hand, if demand is stable (as for necessities among consumers' goods), part of the strain due to lower prices would tend to be neutralized.

In some industries, labor costs are a relatively high proportion of total costs; in others, they are relatively small. Wage rates are hard to adjust downward; therefore, the degree of flexibility in adjusting operating expenses to meet declining prices varies among industries. A business firm in an industry wherein labor costs are proportionately high is subject to a double squeeze on profits—lower sales receipts and relatively high labor costs. Conversely, a company operating in an industry wherein labor costs comprise a small proportion of total costs is subject to less pressure on profits—lower cost prices tend to compensate for lower sales receipts.

Competent management is aware of the business cycle, the characteristics of its industry and other factors pertinent to the business enterprise; it adjusts production, market, and financial policies to these risks. Although price history is an important factor in explaining periodic fluctuations in the number of business failures, weakness in capital structure probably accounts for much of the correlation between declines in wholesale commodity prices and increases in business failures. A business firm in an industry sensitive to cyclical changes will be subjected to extreme fluctuations in financial needs.

RECAPITALIZATION OF COMMON STOCK

The simplest method of changing the capital structure of a business firm is increasing the number of shares outstanding. Stock splits and reverse stock splits change the par or stated value of shares, but stock dividends increase the number of shares without changing the par or stated value. Customarily, such changes are initiated by resolutions of the corporation's board of directors and approved by the shareholders, being in effect amendments of the charter.

Stock Splits. Recapitalization of common stock by a stock split and a reverse stock split changes the number of shares outstanding; unless the capital account is changed correspondingly, the par or stated value of shares must be changed. Financial management may recommend a stock split for several reasons, one being to increase the number of shareholders. The assumption that the more shares outstanding, the more shareholders, is not always valid; however, there is a tendency for the number of shareholders to increase following a lowering of the market price resulting from a stock split. For illustration, the Atchison, Topeka, and Santa Fe Railway split its common shares 5 for 1 when there were 40,000 common stockholders, and by 1960 the number had increased to 100,000. The specific reasons for attempting to increase the number of shareholders include the following: to meet the qualifications for listing the company's shares on a national stock exchange, to obtain a wider market for shares offered under pre-emptive rights, to increase the interest of the public in the company's products, and to disseminate ownership more widely in order to facilitate control of the company by existing management.

A stock split may be favored by the management of some corporations, such as growth companies, in order to avoid the appearance of excessive per-share earnings. Stock splits of this type are usually accompanied by an increase in dividends. For illustration, when H. J. Heinz Company proposed a three-for-one split of common stock in December, 1960, the board of directors voted an increase in cash dividends from 55 cents to 75 cents per quarter on the old shares (25 cents on the new shares when distributed).

A stock split may be recommended by management in order to create a more attractive market price in anticipation of a planned consolidation or new financing. For instance, if the stock is selling for $300 per share the price could be reduced to approximately $30 by a ten-for-one split. Also, a price decline of a low-priced stock is less apparent than that of a higher priced stock—a decline of 10 per cent or $3 per share on a $30 stock tends to be less disturbing to investors than a $30 decline in a $300 stock. This illusion of stability in market price for low-priced shares is also applicable to earnings.

Stock splits are associated with periods of prosperity and growth; hence there have been many during recent years (in 1959, a good business year, there were 320). After the announcement of an impending stock split, the price of the stock usually increases in expectation of higher cash dividends; but if such a dividend increase does not materialize, the price will tend to decline. A stock split increases the number of shares outstanding, decreases the par or stated value of each share, lowers the book value per share, but has no effect on the total amount of net worth or any of the items in the stockholders section of the balance sheet.

Reverse Stock Split. Reverse stock splits are associated with depressions and with financial difficulties of individual companies evidenced by low earnings and extremely low market prices of shares. A corporation may reduce the number of its shares of common stock outstanding in order to bring the market price of the stock into a more popular trading zone. While the investor type of stockholder may show little interest in the stock of a company selling for $2 or $3 per share, he may become interested if there is a reverse stock split of one for ten and the company's shares are traded in the $20 to $30 price range.[1]

Usually, consolidation of shares is made when they are selling at an extremely low price. For example, the stock of the New Haven Clock and Watch Company was selling on the American Stock Exchange for 25 cents per share; but the next day, following recapitalization of the company and a reverse stock split of one for eight

[1] One of the most famous reverse stock splits occurred on April 26, 1938, when Cities Service Company's authorized common stock was changed from 50,000,000 no-par shares to 5,000,000 $10 par shares—for a one-to-ten reverse split and ½ vote per share. At the same time, 348,000,724 treasury shares were cancelled. Subsequently, in 1955, the authorized shares of the company were increased to 20,000,000 with 1 vote per share.

shares, the new shares were selling for more than $2 (closing at 2⅝). Presumably, management hopes to improve the credit rating of the corporation by increasing the market price of stock; usually, however, something more basic than changing the par or stated value of stock is needed. Since a reverse stock split reduces the number of shares outstanding while it increases the par value, there is no change in the amount in the owners' equity section.

Stock Dividends. A distribution of a stock dividend will increase the amount of stock outstanding, have no effect on the par or stated value of the stock, increase the amount of the capital account, reduce the amount of the surplus account, and have no effect on the net worth. As noted in an earlier chapter, periodic stock dividends are often distributed in lieu of cash dividends; however, the emphasis in this section is on large and irregular stock dividends which affect the capital structure materially. Financial management usually recommends stock dividends of this type for the same reasons that stock splits are recommended. The chief problem associated with stock dividends concerns the amount of surplus to be capitalized, and this subject was discussed in Chapter 9.

By declaring a large stock dividend—20 per cent or more—management may bring about an increase in the number of shareholders, avoid the appearance of excessive earnings per share, and lower the market price to a more popular trading range. Since the effects of large irregular stock dividends are the same as those of stock splits, they are ordinarily treated in financial circles as stock splits.

Increase in Capital Surplus. Recapitalization may result in a decrease in the amount of the common stock account and a corresponding increase in the capital surplus account. This change may be brought about by lowering the par or stated value or by reducing the number of shares of common stock outstanding. Because of the ease of changing par or stated value of common stock, it is the method of recapitalization most commonly used when an increase in capital surplus is desired. For illustration, a decrease in the par value of each share from $20 to $10 with 1,000,000 shares outstanding would permit a reduction of the capital account from $20 million to $10 million and a corresponding increase in capital surplus.

The use of capital surplus is subject to legal requirements, as was noted in an earlier chapter; but its existence permits a corporation to eliminate an "earned surplus" deficit, reduce the book value of tangible fixed assets, write-down goodwill and other intangible assets, and create surplus reserve accounts. A reduction in value of assets would make possible a reduction in depreciation charges; the resulting decline in expenses would cause net income reported to increase and thus make dividend payments possible. However, if the reduction in the valuation of assets is excessive, the resulting understatement of depreciation charges and overstatement of earnings may encourage management to recommend the declaration of excessive dividends.

The amount of capital may be decreased and the amount of capital surplus increased by reacquiring stock at less than par or stated value; this may be done by purchasing stock in the open market, from shareholders in proportion to their holdings, or from individual shareholder in response to a request by management for tenders of their shares. The capital account may also be reduced and the capital surplus account increased by a donation of stock to the company. A reduction in the capital account with no corresponding change in the capital surplus account can be accomplished by the distribution of a "liquidating dividend."

A reduction in the capital account may adversely affect the relationship between the company and its creditors, as it would weaken the debt to capital ratio. If a corporation's outstanding liabilities are excessive, the courts may intervene; in some states capital stock may not be reduced if the assets remaining after the stock reduction are less than the company's debts.

PREFERRED STOCK RECAPITALIZATION

The features and restrictions under which preferred stock is issued may be burdensome to management; in an effort to rid a corporation of the limitations imposed thereby, common stock may be exchanged for preferred stock under a recapitalization plan. Other treatments of preferred stock under recapitalization plans include the consolidation of several series into one preferred stock issue or the exchange of a single preferred stock issue for two or more issues of preferred or common stock.

Recapitalization of preferred stock may be motivated by a desire or necessity to simplify the capital structure, reduce voting stock outstanding, create a better capital structure for future financing, and bring the capital structure into line with earnings (see also Chapter 19). Preferred stock is relatively unimportant in the capital structures of most business firms; but for some companies, its presence has created serious problems.

When business corporations finance with preferred stock, the cumulative feature is usually included to make the securities attractive to investors. Then, if dividends are not paid one year, they accumulate as claims against the corporation which must be paid before dividends can be paid on common stock. This situation may exist in partnerships if claims of limited partners are permitted to accumulate. Although preferred stock dividends are contingent rather than fixed charges, allowing them to accumulate tends to affect the position of the business enterprise adversely.

Arrearages of preferred stock dividends and unpaid claims of limited partners may not cause actual insolvency but they may affect a firm's credit position so adversely as to lead indirectly to financial strain or failure. The existence of arrearages may make it difficult to sell stock or to borrow; as a result, the business firm may be thrown upon its own resources which may not be adequate to meet some emergency need for funds. A business corporation is usually given the power to amend its articles of incorporation "to cancel or otherwise affect the right of the holder of shares of any class to receive dividends which have accrued but have not been declared." However, the holders of two thirds or more of the stock affected must approve any change.

Any plan for recapitalization of preferred stock should have sufficient merit to make it possible for management to sell it to stockholders on the basis that the proposed changes will strengthen the corporation and further the interests of all concerned. If prospects point to a continued weakening in the competitive position of the corporation, the alternative to acceptance of some compromise plan might be reorganization or liquidation. One of the objectives of a plan for eliminating dividend arrearages is to avoid or lessen the cash drain incurred in paying accumulated dividends; but some cash payments may be necessary to satisfy dissenting preferred stockholders. Stockholders are usually offered one or more of the following in exchange for their preferred stock and the dividend arrearages: additional preferred stock of the same class; new preferred stock with a lower dividend rate, conversion privilege, participation feature, and/or seniority over outstanding preferred stock; common stock; and some cash and a combination of two or more of the above. On rare occasions, preferred stockholders may be offered bonds or other credit instruments.

After a plan has been effected, unless earnings are sufficient to pay charges on the obligations that have replaced the old preferred stock, new dividend arrearages will accumulate. If bonds or other types of debt instruments are used, a more serious problem than the former one may result because fixed charges (interest) have replaced contingent charges (dividends). If a recapitalization plan is to provide permanent financial relief, the corporation should recapitalize with common stock or preferred stock with a lower dividend rate.

One of the more popular recapitalization plans entails the offering of a small amount of cash, preferred stock, and common stock. The cash is given as a sort of bonus to sweeten the transaction in order to encourage acceptance. The new preferred stock may be given preference over the old, if and when it is not exchanged, and the shareholders may be given the right to convert new preferred stock into common stock. The new dividend rate will be below the old rate and the call feature will usually be added if it was lacking in the old issue. If the old stock had the call feature, the new call price will be more favorable (lower) to the company. Either preferred or common stock may be used to capitalize the dividend arrearages. Because the dividend arrearage is the "consideration," the amount of stock offered will be limited so that the shares are "fully paid and nonassessable." For illustration, if the dividend arrearage on each share is $50 and the par value of the stock is $10, no more than 5 shares would be offered in exchange for the dividend arrearage on each preferred share.

The bargaining position of common stockholders is usually inferior to that of preferred stockholders in recapitalization of preferred stock dividend arrearages because dividends cannot be paid on common stock until dividend arrearages have been eliminated. Nevertheless, common stockholders may be reluctant to accept a settlement plan for dividend arrearages that would give preferred stockholders a share in future earnings above the amount of the old preferred stock dividend rate.

If current earnings are large and the earning trend is expected to continue, common stockholders may take the position that retained and current earnings warrant settling arrearages in cash, thus protecting their interests in future income, surplus, and voting power from the dilution which would occur if old preferred stockholders were given common stock in settlement of their claims. Although common stockholders may object to a proposed plan which calls on them to share their ownership privileges, they realize that elimination of dividend arrearages may permit the corporation to pay cash dividends on common stock at an earlier date.

In voting on a plan to settle their claims to accumulated dividends, preferred stockholders are concerned with their prospects for future dividends on preferred and/or common stock and the proportionate amount of earnings that will be available for this purpose. Their decision to accept or reject a recapitalization plan may rest upon their appraisal of future earnings and how they are to share in them under the proposed recapitalization plan, as compared to their current rights to dividends including arrearages. However, a recapitalization of preferred stock with dividends in arrears is usually followed by an improvement in the market value of the corporation's outstanding common stock, because it places the common stockholders closer to dividend payments.

Corporations rarely settle large dividend arrearages in cash, as provided for in preferred stock contracts; if management fails to work out a recapitalization plan that is acceptable to stockholders, it may use indirect methods to achieve its ends. Management may succeed in gaining shareholders' support for a merger or consolidation in which the dividend arrearages will be absorbed in the exchange of stock. If a majority of stockholders accept such an arrangement, the dissenting minority stockholders can be paid off in cash as is usually done in other mergers or consolidations.

Prior to supervision by the Securities and Exchange Commission of public utility companies, the abuses associated with the use of preferred stock by operating and holding public utility companies were so serious that as a matter of public policy these companies have been prohibited from using preferred stock except under limited circumstances. Although preferred stock issues make up about one tenth of the capital structures of railroad companies, many of these issues are results of financial reorganizations and few of them have the cumulative feature.[2]

RECAPITALIZATION OF DEBTS

Recapitalization of debts in the corporate structure are frequently related to adjustments that are considered under the heading of reorganization (see Chapter 29); in addition, many debt contracts contain provisions permitting prepayment which facilitates voluntary recapitalization of the debt at any time.

The percentage composition of total capitalization—long-term debt, preferred stock, common stock, and surplus—will indicate whether or not a business firm's capital structure is reasonably balanced and how much leverage there is for common stock. The rules

---

[2] In 1952, total railway capital of $18 billion was divided about as follows: common stock, 40 per cent; preferred stock, 11 per cent; and funded debt, 49 per cent (exclusive of long-term debt in default). *Sixty-Seventh Annual Report of the Interstate Commerce Commission* (Washington, D.C.: U.S. Government Printing Office, 1954) p. 168.

pertaining to the use of debts were considered in earlier chapters. Maximum limits may be in terms of the percentage of debts to equity in the capital structure, the proportion of total interest charges to earnings, or other pertinent ratios.

Although capital repayment and sinking-fund contributions are not expenses, they necessitate a cash outlay and must be included in the budget of a corporation. The cash flow—that is, net income after taxes plus depreciation allowances—is related to debts in the sense that both depreciation and obligations are tied to heavy investments in property, plants, equipment, and machines. The steady rise in funds from operations which are accounted for as depreciation allowances permits a more flexible debt retirement program and gives management a stronger bargaining position when renegotiating term-loan agreements and bond indentures that contain prepayment terms or callable features.[3]

Business corporations now depend more on large institutional investors for funds than on small investors; and, when recapitalization of their debts becomes necessary or desirable, institutional investors are easier to deal with than small investors because the latter usually insist upon being repaid according to the provisions in the original debt contract. The practice of using a sinking fund to retire bonds before maturity may be popular with insurance companies and other large investors but not with small investors. Managers of personal trusts (usually small investors) resent the time and expense incurred in returning called bonds and reinvesting the funds. Actually, sinking-fund provisions in a trust indenture may be so exacting as to impair the operations of a company, with the result that the security or earning power behind the issue is weakened; but such provisions may help sell the bonds and maintain the market price.

Bondholders who do not present their bonds when called draw no interest after the redemption date. Bond redemptions are usually advertised in newspapers and financial publications, but small investors often fail to see the notices; even when the bonds to be redeemed are called by lot, small investors may fail to realize that their bonds are in the list.

In addition to bonds which are retired because of sinking-fund provisions, issues may be called in order to refinance at a lower in

[3] ". . . the Company's operations provided all cash requirements. Debt was reduced $31,115,300 during the year. Capital expenditures required $120,804,600, and cash dividends paid to stockholders were $58,406,400, equal to 56% of earnings. Although an increase in capital expenditures is planned for 1960, we anticipate that cash generated internally again will be sufficient to meet our needs." (Phillips Petroleum Company, *Forty-Second Annual Report 1959* [Bartlesville, Oklahoma, 1960], p. 2.)

terest rate or to free the corporation from restrictive provisions. Regardless of the amount of publicity given to the call, many bonds are not presented promptly for payment; this results in loss of interest to the owner and inconvenience to the fiscal agent attempting to "close the books" on the issue. Bonds are usually called at a premium which may be profitable to a large investor but is seldom adequate compensation to a small investor who must find another investment for his funds in a market that may be unfavorable. On the other hand, being close to the market, large investors are prepared for refinancing by corporations and are equipped to meet it at a minimum of cost per bond redeemed.[4] The number of bonds redeemed each year will total approximately $1.5 billion, and a considerable percentage represents sinking-fund activities.

The relaxation of the division between the sources of capital and credit has facilitated the recapitalization of long-term debt and the shift between long-term and short-term obligations. Large corporations also have the option of financing with long-term notes under term loan agreements or in the open market under provisions of bond indentures.[5]

Financing under open-end mortgages permits new financing when conditions are favorable and may contribute to improvement in recapitalization procedures. All of a company's long-term bonds may consist of first mortgage bonds issued under one mortgage indenture and issued in series at different times. For illustration, the Reynolds Metals Company has outstanding $315 million in first mortgage bonds issued in Series A, Series B, and Series C, which are redeemable in whole or part at varying specified premiums and for which different sinking-fund provisions were made.[6]

SUMMARY

Financial difficulties may be caused by inadequacy of working capital as revealed by a deterioration in a business firm's working

[4] As an aid to investors, some newspapers each week (usually on Monday) publish a list of bonds which have been called, the amount, the call price, and the date of redemption. For example, the *New York Times* (February 20, 1961, p. 38) published a list of twenty-four bonds which have been called for redemption (most of these were obligations of states and their political subdivisions).

[5] Note the following: "During the past year, short-term borrowing increased from $51,000,000 at the end of fiscal 1958 to $60,000,000 at March 31, 1959. Arrangements also were made for the refunding of $15,000,000, 3¼ Promissory Notes due December 31, 1959, with five-year, 4½ Notes, payable in installments commencing June 30, 1962." Sperry Rand Corporation, *Report to Stockholders for the Year Ended March 31, 1959* (New York, 1959), p. F 6.

[6] Reynolds Metals Company, *32nd Annual Report 1959* (Richmond, Virginia, 1960), pp. 35–36.

capital position. Such deterioration may be due to an increase in disbursements, a decline in receipts, and/or a decline in the rate of flow of working capital assets. Various ratios may be used to aid in determining the point of financial weakness so that appropriate remedial action may be taken.

Excessive indebtedness, commonly given as a reason for financial difficulties of business firms, is the result of overexpansion or the presence of top-heavy fixed assets. When the acquisition of fixed assets is financed by long-term debt, the fixed charges and obligations imposed by debt contracts often bring on a financial crisis when earnings decline or the assets prove to be less productive than expected. As preventive measures a business firm should adopt conservative policies as to withdrawals or dividend payments and should watch its debt to net worth ratio.

Although business depression has been given as a cause of financial difficulties, competent management is aware of the business cycle and the characteristics of its industry and takes precautionary measures to safeguard its business firm.

Capital structure may be a factor in business failures—inability to meet fixed debt charges and dividend arrearages on preferred stock may be the immediate cause of business difficulties. When management fails to work out a voluntary compromise of dividend arrearages satisfactory to preferred stockholders, an adjustment may be effected through a merger or consolidation. While a merger or consolidation requires approval of stockholders holding two thirds of the stock affected (as it true for any proposed change in the corporate charter), a merger or consolidation may be approved when a plan for adjusting arrearages may fail to be approved. Judicious use of preferred stock calls for following rules similar to those pertaining to the use of bonds.

Adjustments in the capital structure may be made in common stock outstanding as well as in preferred stock issues. The number of shares of common stock outstanding may be increased by a stock split or reduced by a reverse stock split. A business firm may increase its "capital surplus" account by decreasing the par or stated value of stock or by reducing the number of shares outstanding.

QUESTIONS AND PROBLEMS

1. "Normally, the chief financial officer watches the net working capital asset position of his business firm closely." Why?
2. What factors may cause the cash position of a business firm to deteriorate?

3. What ratios may be used to check a business firm's working capital position? Explain.
4. (*a*) What devices may a business firm use to obtain cash when financial strain is due to a slowing down in the circuit flow of working capital assets? (*b*) What is the danger in using these devices?
5. Identify: (*a*) provisions in debt contracts that may bring on financial crises; (*b*) "unprofitable" expansion; (*c*) debt rules that may be followed to prevent indebtedness from becoming excessive; and (*d*) policies that management may adopt in regard to cash withdrawals, dividend payments, depreciation allowances, and retained earnings when fixed assets become top-heavy.
6. (*a*) What preventive measures may be taken to prevent losses in inventories during periods of falling prices from causing financial strain? (*b*) Are some business firms more vulnerable to inventory loses than others? Why?
7. What should be the objective of management in working out an arrangement for eliminating preferred stock dividend arrearages?
8. (*a*) What are the rules suggested for financing with preferred stock? (*b*) Do these rules vary with the type of corporation? Explain. (*c*) What adjustments may be made in common stock to improve capital structure of a business concern? (*d*) What is meant by a reverse stock split? When may it be used by management?
9. ". . . for all practical purposes, a capital structure that is top-heavy with contingent claims of preferred stock may, so long as this condition persists, prove to be just as effective an obstacle to profitable operations as one involving top-heavy debt claims. "(Donald A. Fergusson, "Preferred Stock Valuation in Recapitalizations," *The Journal of Finance* [March, 1958], p. 49.) How may a capital structure such as the one described above be corrected?
10. Analyze: "We anticipate that a large part of the funds for the contemplated capital investment program will become available from earnings produced by these investments, from depreciation provisions, retained earnings, and in part from working capital . . ." (Charles S. Bridges, president of Libby, McNeill & Libby, *Address before the New York Society of Security Analysts* [New York: Libby, McNeill & Libby, 1959], p. 13.)

CHAPTER 29

Reorganization of Business Concerns

FINANCIAL reorganization is the revision of the financial structure of a business firm necessitated by its failure to meet interest, debt repayment, or other obligations. Thus a business enterprise that cannot meet its maturing obligations is insolvent in a "temporary," "technical," or "equity" sense. At the same time, if the business firm has liabilities in excess of its assets, it is insolvent in the "true" or "bankruptcy" sense. A business firm could be insolvent in the equity sense without being insolvent in the bankruptcy sense; conversely, it could be solvent in the equity sense and insolvent in the bankruptcy sense. An insolvent firm may operate indefinitely as long as it meets its obligations as they come due.

When a business concern is in default on its obligations, its creditors may take action either out of court or in court to liquidate the business firm (see Chapter 30) or they may adjust the business debts either out of court or in court so that the business firm can continue to function. The most important of the adjustment procedures that may be followed are considered in this chapter.

FINANCIAL STRUCTURE

The financial plan of a corporation is the projected pattern for issues of stocks and bonds and other debts at the time the corporation is organized or reorganized; but owing to numerous factors, at a later date, the financial structure of a business firm may bear little resemblance to the original plan. A study of the financial position of a firm will include a review not only of its capital structure but also of its short-term obligations. There is no longer a sharp division between the credit and capital needs of businesses; hence the presentation in Table 31 of financial structures of business firms seems more

TABLE 31

FINANCIAL STRUCTURES*

(Amounts In Thousands)

Item	Industrial		Railroad		Public Utility	
	Amount	*Per Cent*	*Amount*	*Per Cent*	*Amount*	*Per Cent*
Current liabilities	$ 739,277	28.9	$ 69,958	6.6	$ 39,361	7.1
Noncurrent debts	364,129	14.2	391,248	36.8	270,670	49.0
Total Liabilities	$1,103,406	43.1	$ 461,206	43.4	$310,031	56.1
Preferred stock	....	....	$ 4,391	0.4	$ 59,360	10.8
Common stock	$ 441,414	17.2	209,257	19.8	103,660	18.8
Surplus (etc.)	1,016,273	39.7	387,114	36.4	79,185	14.3
Total Owners' Equity	$1,457,687	56.9	$ 600,762	56.6	$242,205	43.9
Total Liabilities and Equity	$2,561,093	100.0	$1,061,968	100.0	$552,236	100.0

* Statistics from balance sheets of three companies, the names of which are withheld.

appropriate than a presentation of capital structures would be.

As is to be expected, the short-term indebtedness of industrial companies is proportionately larger than the current liabilities of railroads and public utility companies. Compared with industrial firms and railroads, public utility companies are more prone to go into debt and their financial structures are dominated by long-term debt (see Table 31). While railroads and industrial companies may issue preferred stock, this means of financing is used to a much greater extent by public utility companies.

The amount of financing with common stock may seem relatively small, as illustrated by the three companies whose financial structures are presented in Table 31; it must be remembered, however, that large corporations are able to take advantage of other means of financing and that the relationship between equity and debt financing is obscured by the presence of earned surplus, capital surplus, and reserves. While the accounting procedures are not the same for industrial, railroad, and public utility companies, current emphasis on financing with funds from operations by railroad and industrial companies is suggested by Table 31. Companies subjected to rate regulation have a different problem in financing with retained earnings from that of nonregulated companies. In addition, the corporate income tax structure has an impact on what might be considered a normal relationship between debt and equity financing.

In the history of the United States, the most significant peace-time industry reorganization occurred in the public utility industry following the passage of the Public Utility Holding Company Act of 1935. Congress made mandatory the reorganization of public utility systems and the elimination of unnecessary holding and operating companies—a movement which management had started in 1930.[1] Most operating companies had been kept in good condition throughout the depression; hence most attention was directed toward correcting financial abuses that developed during the rapid expansion of the industry during the 1920's.[2] Most of the unnecessary holding and operating companies have been eliminated; at the present time, the companies in the industry are among the most efficiently organized and operated in the country.

INADEQUACY OF WORKING CAPITAL

The capital structure of a business firm excludes its short-term liabilities, but financial difficulties that lead to involuntary recapitalization often originate among current liabilities. Usually, a weakening of a firm's current financial position is one of the first indications that it is encountering financial difficulties. The cash position is particularly important because the continuing operation of a business depends not only upon paying debts when due but also upon acquiring labor and goods and materials with which to operate.

If a business firm prepares a cash budget, management can compare estimated disbursements with estimated receipts plus bank balances to ascertain whether loans will be required during the budget period. A sharp increase in required disbursements or a sharp decline in receipts will have an adverse effect on the cash position of a business firm. An increase in disbursements may be caused by losses resulting from hurricanes, tornadoes, fires, fraud, and other causes

---

[1] In 1930, the North American Company sold to the Pacific Gas and Electric Company its controlling interest in the San Joaquin Light and Power Corporation, the Great Western Power Company, and the Midland Counties Public Service Corporation—a logical development because these companies were physically interconnected with the properties of the Pacific Gas and Electric Company.

[2] The rapid growth of the public utility industry was financed in part by equipment manufacturing and construction companies and holding companies. The public utility companies were among the first to use open-end mortgages freely.

that may be covered by insurance; but the firm may be faced with a costly interruption in operations as well as a sharp increase in expenditures for replacement of property for which adequate funds may not be available. Although governmental agencies may supplement normal sources of credit in such emergencies, some business failures result from so-called "Acts of God."

Financial difficulties are usually caused by a decrease in receipts rather than by an increase in expenditures; for illustration, sales may decline and outstanding receivables may not be collected promptly. The situation is one wherein working capital assets are frozen or at least congealed. If current obligations are small, the firm may be able to "weather the storm;" if they are large, the hackneyed term "excessive short-term indebtedness" may be used to explain the firm's difficulties. In either event, the firm's difficulties are the result of a decline in sales or collections or both.

The explanations offered by management for a decline in sales include competition; changes in customers' buying habits because of new styles, fads, or other innovations; changes in techniques of production and/or methods of distribution; and introduction of substitute products. The objective observer's reaction to these explanations is likely to be that management must expect to lose sales to competitors who are more competent in meeting price reductions, anticipating changes in customers' demands, producing and/or distributing goods more economically, and offering new products.

A decline in sales is usually followed or accompanied by a situation wherein inventories are excessive. Such a situation may result if the business firm has been guilty of "speculation in inventories"; that is, overbuying in anticipation of higher prices. In addition to having misjudged the market, management may have made poor selections of goods or products to be manufactured and/or sold. If goods are returned because of misrepresentation, it may reflect adversely on buying, production, or sales policies. In other cases, excessive returns may be caused by too liberal a policy as to returning of goods or cancelling orders. When customers want to return goods or cancel orders for no other reason than a downward trend in prices, management may counteract this movement by lowering prices or offering larger cash discounts.

Faulty work of the credit and collection department may be a factor in the frozen conditions of working capital. Unwise selection of credit customers and/or inadequate collection policies may be the reason for inability to collect receivables. While sales are important to a business firm, collections are equally important. A deficiency in either is, in the final analysis, the fault of management. When the so-called reasons for business failures are analyzed, most of them point directly or indirectly to poor management. The validity of this conclusion is substantiated by the fact that usually there are other business concerns in the same field that are operating profitably.

Business management may borrow the techniques of credit men to test the soundness of a business firm's current position; self-analysis is valuable in that it may be used to set the course that the business firm will follow. By using comparative balance sheets and ratio analyses, management may ascertain the adequacy of net worth if and when the firm is faced with work stoppages, recessions, and other economic hazards.

Because inadequacy of working capital is a common weakness among business firms, sound managerial procedure calls for giving this problem primary attention. The ratio of current assets to tangible net worth (net worth minus intangible assets) indicates the percentage of equity represented by current assets; a ratio of current liabilities to tangible net worth would indicate the extent to which owners are providing funds relative to current liabilities. (Perhaps it would be more accurate to say that financial difficulties of business concerns are due to "too little net worth" rather than to "excessive short-term indebtedness.")

A businessman may keep his fingers on the pulse of his firm's affairs by computing its "current," "inventory," and "collection" ratios and comparing them to those of other firms in the same line of trade or industry. Otherwise, management may be satisfied with a business concern's rate of growth without being aware of the fact that the firm's position has deteriorated because current liabilities have increased more than current assets.

In addition to giving attention to a firm's current and other ratios, management should examine the quality of current assets and the nature of current liabilities. A current ratio of 1.5 to 1 may be considered unsatisfactory; but, if current assets are in the form of bank balances, the ratio may be adequate. On the other hand, a ratio of 3 to 1 may seem satisfactory; but, if current assets are predominately in the form of inventories of questionable market value, the ratio may be unsatisfactory. Hence, the quality of current assets is as important a factor in appraising the current position of a business as is the amount of current liabilities. Among the ratios that may be used to test the quality of current assets are current assets less inventories to current assets, cash and short-term investments to current assets, cash to current assets, and inventory to current assets.

Recently, at a small-businessmen's clinic, the participants (all owning or representing small business firms) were polled as to how many of them had made a ratio analysis of their company's affairs; only one of the forty had made such an analysis. Although this situation may not be typical, it suggests how little financial analysis is being done on the initiative of management of small business firms.

The tools of financial analysis may include *pro forma* statements, which necessitate not only the construction of profit and loss and balance sheet statements at the end of an accounting period but also the constructions of other statements that project business firms' operations through the next fiscal year. Business management will assume certain results from operations, including the effects of the use of new funds obtained from bank loans, open-market financing, and other sources. After the anticipated effects of new funds are projected on the balance sheet, a ratio analysis of the hypothetical balance sheet should indicate if borrowed funds and the use thereof will strengthen or weaken the business firm.

When the financial position of a business firm becomes strained because of a slowing down in the circuit flow of its working capital assets, it may be able to obtain cash by selling, assigning, or pledging accounts receivable; selling non-essential fixed and other assets; liquidating inventories by using devices such as "clearance" and "end-of-the-month" sales; and applying pressure to collect past-due accounts. The firm may also conserve its cash or reduce cash drain by using trade credit more fully and refraining from taking cash discounts; reducing salaries (in rare instances, employees have accepted temporary delays in receipt of salaries); and reducing operating expenses for items such as maintenance, advertising, etc. A firm that reduces operating expenses may find the reduction helpful not only in easing its financial strain but also in negotiating with creditors for extensions of maturities of debts and for new loans.

Some of the drastic measures used to improve the cash position of a business concern (as noted in the preceding paragraph) may only advertise its strained position and make it difficult to obtain normal amounts of trade, bank, and other forms of credit. This loss of credit would intensify rather than alleviate the firm's need for cash. Under such circumstances, unless a firm can arrange for a temporary loan or obtain new capital, it may have no choice but to secure some form of debt adjustment—extension of maturities, composition settlement, or involuntary reorganization.

Federal and state governments sometimes come to the aid of business concerns as illustrated by the assistance given to companies in the railroad industry when Congress passed the Transportation Act of 1958, providing for a loan guarantee program to be administered by the Interstate Commerce Commission and to be in force until March 31, 1961.[3] In February, 1961, the New York, New Haven & Hartford Railroad was saved from "the brink of bankruptcy" when the Interstate Commerce Commission guaranteed a loan which had been arranged with a group of banks headed by the Chase Manhattan Bank of New York (6 previous loans totalling $21,659,400 had been guaranteed by the Commission). In February, the New Haven Railroad was urgently in need of funds to meet a $1.5 million payroll and other costs. In addition to the "New Haven," other railroads have participated in the Interstate Commerce Commission loan guarantee program.[4] (In July, New Haven was adjudged a bankrupt.)

OUT-OF-COURT ADJUSTMENTS

Extensions. An extension is an arrangement wherein creditors agree not to press for payment of overdue debts until the lapse of a specified period of time. Usually the obligations in default are short term, but they may be long-term debts or even sinking-fund commitments as required by bond or trust indentures. As noted in a previous chapter, about 90 per cent of wholesalers' and manufacturers' sales are made on credit; thus, it is not surprising that trade suppliers are usually the most numerous among the creditors of a financially embarrassed small business firm. Because trade creditors ordinarily advance credit that is unsecured, they tend to be at a disadvantage in both reorganizations and liquidations of debtor firms. Although more numerous, individual trade suppliers usually have less at stake than do financial institutions and other large creditors. This situation gives these small creditors a "nuisance" advantage in dealing with the debtor firm and the other creditors (see below).

Simple Extensions or "Workouts." Customarily, a simple extension or "workout" is one wherein a single financial institution, such as a bank or finance company, assumes the leading role in the rehabilitation proceedings. The assumption is that the chief creditor

---

[3] State and local governments sometimes provide relief for financially distressed companies. For example, the governors of four states (New York, Massachusetts, Rhode Island, and Connecticut) agreed to submit proposals to their state legislatures to reduce the tax bill for the New York, New Haven & Hartford Railroad by $6.2 million for a four-year period. *Wall Street Journal* (New York), February 23, 1961, p. 7.

[4] See *Wall Street Journal* (New York), February 6, 1961, p. 2.

(usually a bank) has decided to "stay with" the debtor rather than to force liquidation of the business firm. When negotiating the extension of credit, the bank is confronted with the choice of extending the maturity of all or a part of the firm's debt. Sometimes the debtor will be able to pay a part of the bank loan, and often the bank will accept a part payment and extend the maturity of the balance.

When many small creditors (such as trade creditors) are pressing for payment, the bank may agree not only to extend the maturity of its outstanding loan but also to make an additional loan so that these creditors may be paid in full. As a result, the business firm's total debt will not be reduced but will be consolidated and owed to a bank that is willing to work with the debtor.

As a condition for advancing additional funds, the bank usually demands added protection; if the firm is incorporated, the officers, directors, and/or large stockholders may be required to endorse the promissory notes of the corporation. This endorsement means that the personal debt-paying ability of large equity holders and/or those responsible for the operations of the business firm has been added to that of the corporation. If the officers, directors, and others closely linked to the firm have claims against the corporation, they may be required to subordinate their claims to those of the bank.[5]

In administering a "workout," a bank usually insists that the debtor curtail business activities. The workout budget usually specifies that all capital outlays cease, that administrative expenses be sharply reduced, and that purchases be adjusted downward to a basis of much lower production and/or sales expectations. When arranging a workout, the bank is hopeful of keeping alive one of its business customers; the average bank is frequently confronted with this problem of saving financially embarrassed business customers.

When a workout does not result in an improvement in the business firm's position during the initial or supplementary extension period, other plans may be made. Often, a bank will change its position toward the debtor firm because of some act of other creditors, the debtor's failure to follow the workout budget, or the firm's disappointing performance, as checked against expectations.

[5] A bank may have a provision in the subordination agreement permitting it to file upon and receive dividends of the subordinated creditors. If a firm has liabilities of $75,000 and assets of $30,000 upon liquidation and the indebtedness is divided equally among the bank, subordinated creditors, and unsecured creditors, each group's "dividend" would be $10,000. Then, if the bank is assigned the $10,000 received by the subordinated creditors, its loss would be reduced to $5,000 ($25,000—$20,000 rather than $25,000—$10,000).

Creditors' Committee. A bank that is one of a number of large creditors cannot afford to stand aside while other creditors receive the major part of the business assets leaving it little or nothing in case of ultimate liquidation. After working with a business firm, a bank may want extensions of maturities of debts to be broadened to include the claims of all creditors; or, at the beginning of negotiations for an extension, a bank and two or more creditors may participate in the proceedings. Later, a meeting of all creditors may be called.

The one who calls the creditors' meeting may be a representative of a trade, credit, or manufacturers' association, or an adjustment bureau (operated by a local association affiliated with the National Association of Credit Men). Adjustment bureaus (now numbering fifty-five) are doing outstanding work in arranging for extensions as well as serving as participants in all types of adjustment and liquidation proceedings.

Either the debtor firm or its creditors may initiate the negotiations for an extension through an adjustment bureau. At the initial meeting of the principal creditors called by the adjustment bureau, the debtor is asked to attend and to provide any requested records or other information. The bureau may be asked to study the debtor's financial situation and to make a report thereon at a formal meeting of the creditors. At this formal meeting, the firm's financial position is discussed and a creditors' committee is usually elected. This committee works out the extension agreement which becomes a valid contract as soon as all creditors agree in writing; but, if some do not sign, the whole agreement may be called off or some arrangement may be made whereby the minority creditors will be paid off in cash.

While there is no specified form for the extension agreement, it must cover the extension period and provide for control of the business by a creditors' committee for as long as the agreement is in effect. The debtor must sign papers permitting the committee to retain control and to operate the business.[6]

In some cases, there may be several contracts; in others a single

[6] The papers used to give the creditors' committee control will depend on the form of business organization. If it is a corporation, a voting trust may be set up giving the trustees power to elect directors and appoint officers and to liquidate the business if it seems desirable to do so. Another arrangement is to deposit 51 per cent of the voting stock in escrow. A partnership or single proprietorship may file a chattel mortgage on assets with the committee and sign documents authorizing the committee to approve purchases, sales, payments, and salaries and to countersign checks of the firm.

contract may be worked out to provide for the extension of old claims, advances of new funds (which may be given priority in repayment), the transfer of management to the creditors' committee, and the return of management to owners when the debts are paid in full. The same contract provisions may be worked out from year to year, provided the firm's financial position is improving, or they may be terminated at the end of one year.

The size of a creditors' committee depends upon the number of creditors, the variety of interests involved, and the size of the business firm. Although existing personnel of the business firm may be retained, the committee assumes responsibility for making policy decisions. The creditors' committee has a chairman, usually a banker, who is responsible for seeing that decisions are carried out. Sometimes, the committee will appoint a trained executive to act as treasurer or controller of the business concern. In a relatively short time, this official should be in a position to tell the committee whether the business ought to be continued or liquidated.

The function of the new or reorganized management is to correct those conditions which precipitated the business concern's difficulties. The financial difficulties of such firms may be solved by changing credit and collection policies; reducing inventories; introducing new products; liquidating advances to directors, officers, or others; and reducing wages, salaries, and other expenses. If the plans of the creditors' committee are carried out successfully, profits will increase, net working capital will be built up, debts will be liquidated, and the firm will be in a position to obtain new credit when needed. Then, the creditors' committee will be discharged and the control of the business firm will be returned to its owners.

The advantages claimed for the creditors' committee method of reorganizing business enterprises include the following: (1) The expenses and costs are usually less than when other methods are used (for illustration, members of the creditors' committee often serve without compensation and any payment made to them usually follows successful reorganization of the business firm). (2) Usually, reorganization takes place without unfavorable publicity that would handicap the firm's normal business operations. (3) Although some changes in the firm's personnel may be necessary, a creditor's committee reorganization has the advantage of keeping intact most of the staff to resume management as soon as the committee's control is released to the owners. (4) A creditors' committee may act promptly in settling claims of creditors and thus expedite return of the business firm to its owners. (5) Usually, the committee's representative will take prompt action in case the plans do not work out as anticipated; under certain circumstances, he may arrange to provide the firm with additional funds to finance new activities; under other circumstances, he may move in the opposite direction—to turn existing assets of the firm into cash as soon as possible in order to minimize creditors' losses.

Among the reasons for the lack of popularity of the creditors' committee form of business reorganization is the inability of such a committee to stop actions of non-co-operative creditors who are trying to collect their claims. When two or more creditors sign an agreement with the debtor for an extension of their claims, a binding contract is created. But, since no creditor is forced to sign such an agreement, those who do not are free to demand payment when their claims come due. Many small and some large nonsigners take advantage of this situation to demand payment; as a result, participants in the creditors' committee sometimes find it necessary to make advances to the business concern to prevent further deterioration in its affairs. Sometimes, creditors are in no position to make extensions, as happened so often during the early 1930's; under such circumstances, the creditors' committee plan for reorganization may not be feasible.

The creditors' committee also lacks the power, possessed by the courts, to exclude questionable claims and to set aside unprofitable contracts such as leases. The success of a creditors' committee reorganization plan depends largely upon two factors: the ability of the chief creditors to negotiate a binding agreement among creditors for extension of most of the debtor's obligations and the full co-operation of the owners of the firm with the creditors' committee.

While most extension agreements pertain to the debts of small business firms, sometimes holders of long-term obligations of large business units are asked to agree to the extension of the maturities of their bonds and notes. If the outlook for the company seems favorable, an agreement can usually be arranged with the large creditors; but often the small dissenting bond or note holders (hold-outs) must be paid in full.

Voluntary adjustments often result in reductions in the interest rate and the amount of the principal. Also, other changes in the indenture agreement—such as elimination of sinking-fund requirements and subordination of existing claims to a proposed new loan or bond issue—may be made. On the other hand, management may find it necessary to offer special inducements to old creditors who agree to an extension—such as a cash premium, a higher call price, larger maturity values, additional security, restrictions on common stock dividends, a common stock bonus, restrictions on senior issues, or a sinking-fund provision when one did not exist previously.

Composition Settlements. Another type of voluntary adjustment which requires the same type of co-operation among creditors and between them and the financially distressed business firm is the composition settlement. A composition settlement is an arrangement wherein the debtor agrees to pay and the creditors to receive a percentage of the obligations as full payment, thus to liquidate the debts of the business enterprise. If a debtor realizes that his business firm's position is in danger of becoming hopeless, he may negotiate with creditors to pay them a part of their claims (such as 25, 50, or 75 cents on the dollar). In other cases, the initiative may be taken by a banker, a group of creditors, or a representative of an adjustment bureau who is fully aware of the debtor's position. (For illustration, a composition may follow termination of an extension agreement.) Often, a composition settlement is negotiated with the assistance of an adjustment bureau as in the case of the extension discussed above. Usually, provisions are made for the supervision of the business firm by a creditors' committee until the settlement is completed.

While the details of a composition settlement usually provide for a reduction in creditors' claims by a uniform percentage, there may be exceptions in favor of small creditors who often take advantage of their "nuisance value" to gain better treatment. Before resorting to the more expensive bankruptcy proceedings, the larger creditors may agree that small creditors be paid in full if their claims do not exceed a certain amount, such as $100.

In some composition settlements, provisions are made for the payment of adjusted claims on a stated date or dates, with no provision for further extensions, and for dissolution of the creditors' committee when all obligations have been met. In other cases, provisions may be made for settlement of part of the adjusted claims in cash and the remainder in notes payable to the individual creditors and for dissolution of the creditors' committee either upon delivery of the cash and notes or when all obligations have been met. In all cases, when the creditors' committee is dissolved, all control documents are returned to the business firm.

Every creditor, when offered a composition settlement, has a difficult decision to make. He will want assurance that the offer represents the maximum that the debtor can pay, that the debtor has done all he can to meet his obligations, and that an accurate picture of the debtor's financial condition has been presented.

Composition settlements may have an advantage over extensions in that creditors receive some cash at once; but, if the settlements include notes that mature in one, two, or more years, creditors are still faced with collection problems just as they would be in extensions. If the business firm is unable to meet these notes at maturity, it may be involved in new financial difficulties before it has extricated itself from the old one. If liquidation of the debtor firm is to take place, creditors might be wise to refuse composition settlement when the offer is made.

The success of any out-of-court adjustment depends upon the willingness of all large creditors to make concessions and of some of them to serve as members of a supervisory committee (usually, a thankless position). In addition, banks and other financial institutions may be expected to advance additional funds to the firm and the major trade creditors may be expected to continue to sell merchandise at regular terms to the business firm. If major creditors refuse to make commitments in extensions or composition agreements, the debtor's financial position will tend to deteriorate.

The current Trans World Air Lines financing case illustrates the difficulty of bringing interested parties together when the amount of new funds needed is large. Under threat of foreclosure, the chief stockholder (Hughes Tool Company) agreed to place its 78 per cent holding of Trans World Air Line stock in a voting trust consisting of three members, two of whom represented the banks and insurance companies that had agreed to underwrite the $265 million refinancing program (the third represented the Hughes interests).[7]

REORGANIZATIONS UNDER THE FEDERAL BANKRUPTCY LAW

Article I, Section 8, of the United States Constitution states that "Congress shall have power . . . to establish . . . uniform laws on the subject of bankruptcy throughout the United States." This power was used by Congress in 1800, 1841, 1867, and 1898; although frequently amended, the Bankruptcy Act of 1898 is still in force. The "Chandler Act," or "Bankruptcy Act of 1938," was the last important revision.

The federal bankruptcy law contains chapters and sections that cover not only liquidation of insolvent business enterprises but also

---

[7] See also *New York Times*, December 8, 1960, p. 53.

their reorganizations. The first seven chapters of the Bankruptcy Act contain statutory procedures for liquidation of insolvent business concerns; the chapters added during the 1930's provide for reorganizations.

Prior to the passage of the Bankruptcy Act of 1938, there were many instances wherein a public need existed for the continuance of services provided by business firms that were unable to pay their obligations or were insolvent in the bankruptcy sense. Examples of such business firms include companies that provide water, gas, electricity, and transportation services. The procedures followed in such cases, wherein the public interest outweighed those of creditors, were developed into a body of rules supplementary to common and statutory law; but, as Congress added new chapters to the Bankruptcy Act, what was formerly called "equity" law became statutory law.

In equity proceedings, a receiver was appointed by the appropriate court (usually a federal court) to operate the business. The receiver was made responsible for operating the firm efficiently and keeping the property intact (preventing seizure by creditors); however, the receiver was not given the responsibility for working out a plan of reorganization. This was usually done by large investors, officers and directors of the corporation, and investment bankers who had underwritten the issues in default. These interested parties took the leadership in the organization of protective committees, but they had to contend with "outsiders" who appointed themselves as members of self-created "protective committees" for the purpose of claiming expenses and fees which were to be paid out of the proceeds from the corporation's assets.

Under the old equity proceedings, there were usually too many protective committees to work efficiently; and, as a result, a reorganization committee was usually selected from among those who made up the stronger protective committees. After the reorganization plan was completed, the next step was to gain approval of its fairness from the court. The final step was the formality of a foreclosure sale from the old to the new company, with the settlement of the claims being made in new securities and with dissenting interests being paid off in cash.

The weaknesses of equity receivership included excessive costs of reorganization which reduced the share remaining for creditors and other security holders, domination by bankers and "insiders" of the reorganization proceedings which worked to the disadvantage of general creditors, and creation of reorganization plans that failed to meet the test of feasibility.

The provisions made by Congress since 1932 for reorganizations do not cover all the possible situations that could confront business firms (such as who may vote a block of stock formerly held in trust and whether a favorable vote on a proposed merger is legal). However, equity proceedings are now almost a thing of the past in reorganizations of business firms because "arrangements" for less complicated cases are provided for under Chapter XI, for more complicated cases and large corporations other than railroads under Chapter X, and for railroads under Chapter VIII.

Arrangements under Chapter XI. An arrangement is defined in the statute as a "plan of a debtor for the settlement, satisfaction or extension of the time of payment of his unsecured debts." The petition to effect an arrangement must be filed by a debtor, not a creditor. It is usually filed in the district court in which the business is located, but it may be transferred to any district court for the convenience of the creditors. The petition will identify the petitioner (name, address, and occupation or place of business), state that bankruptcy proceedings are not pending under other sections of the law, state that the petitioner is either insolvent because liabilities exceed assets or because he is unable to meet his obligations as they mature, contain the proposed plan or arrangement, include annexed schedules containing a full statement of debts and an inventory of assets, and contain exhibits showing executory contracts and a statement of the full and true nature of the petitioner's affairs.

The arrangement may include provisions for treatment of all secured creditors in the same way or division of debts into classes to be treated differently; rejection of contracts; specific undertakings of the debtor during any period of extension including the payment of accounts receivable; termination of any period of extension provided by the arrangement; continuation of the business with or without supervision or control by a receiver, creditors' committee, or otherwise; payment of debts incurred after filing of the petition; supervision by the court until provisions of the arrangement are performed; and other appropriate measures.

Following the filing of the petition, the court may (on application of creditors) appoint a trustee or receiver for the petitioner's property and one or more appraisers to prepare an inventory of its assets. The debtor may remain in possession of his property, and he may be ordered to file an approved surety bond to indemnify the "estate" against subsequent loss, pending confirmation of an arrangement.

The bankruptcy law requires that an official meeting of the creditors be called; but, before proceedings reach this stage, much work will have been done by creditors and an adjustment bureau which may have entered the case. Informal meetings may have taken place and a creditors' committee may have been selected; in this case, the committee may have met with the debtor to review the plan of arrangement and possibly revise it. The creditors' committee or the adjustment bureau may have arranged with the court for an investigation of the debtor's affairs (books, inventories, and records), keeping the court informed as to creditors' wishes and making reports to the creditors.

The referee or judge presides at the first official meeting, allows or disallows claims filed by creditors, and examines the debtor and other witnesses that may be called or that may appear. The plan proposed by the debtor may be accepted or altered; if altered, the debtor must accept the modifications. Creditors, present or represented at the meeting, have the right to examine the debtor and other witnesses and to suggest changes in the arrangement. The proposed arrangement may not be presented for confirmation until it has been accepted in writing by a majority in number and in amount of proven and allowed claims of each class of creditors. If the plan is not accepted, the first official meeting may be adjourned for a stated period of time. If no agreement is reached at later meetings, the debtor business will be liquidated through bankruptcy proceedings (see Chapter 30).

Assuming that an arrangement is accepted in writing by a majority of each class of creditors, it will go into effect when it is confirmed by the court. Before the court confirms the arrangement, it must apply five tests: Have provisions of Chapter XI of the Bankruptcy Act been observed? Is the arrangement to the best interests of creditors? Is the plan fair, equitable, and feasible? Has the debtor been guilty of any acts or failed to perform any duties which would be a bar to the discharge of a bankrupt? Has the proposal and its acceptance been made in good faith and not made or procured by means, promises, or acts forbidden in the Act?

After an arrangement has been confirmed by the court, it becomes binding not only on those creditors who have approved it but also on all others. The referee or judge determines the time when the debtor is to make his payments and directs the receiver, trustee, or some other person to receive and disburse them. The debtor is discharged by the court as to all debts covered by the arrangement, but the confirmation and discharge may be set aside by the court within six months upon petition of a creditor if fraud was employed in obtaining the arrangement. Such a petition would be followed by new hearings and perhaps a new arrangement or the liquidation of the debtor as a bankrupt.

One advantage of an arrangement is that it compels the minority group of creditors to accept a plan approved by the majority. Since the court must approve claims, an additional advantage of an arrangement is that it offers protection against questionable, fraudulent, and unreasonable claims. The disadvantages of arrangements, as compared to extensions or composite settlements outside the courts, are that costs and expenses are greater and proceedings less flexible, more time consuming, and usually unfavorable in that they may involve adverse widespread publicity. However, when there are a large number of creditors and/or a few non-co-operative large creditors, the best solution to the problem may be to work out a reorganization (arrangement) under supervision of a federal court as provided for in Chapter XI of the Federal Bankruptcy Law.

Reorganization under Chapter X. Chapter X of the Federal Bankruptcy Act provides for the reorganization of corporations, other than railroads, under the supervision of the federal courts. This chapter of the Act is obviously designed to cover the reorganization of large corporations wherein there is public interest because of investments in the securities issued by such corporations. The petition to reorganize under Chapter X may be filed by the debtor corporation, three or more creditors having claims of $5,000 or more, or an indenture trustee. The first is called a voluntary petition and the last two are called involuntary petitions; in practice, the first type is the most common.

A voluntary petition, which is usually filed in the district court where the head office is located, must state that the corporation is insolvent or unable to pay its debts as they mature; present facts showing why relief is sought under Chapter X and give details as to the nature of the business; disclose the corporation's assets, liabilities, capital stock, and financial condition; reveal the nature of all pending legal proceedings, including the status of any plan of reorganization, readjustment, or liquidation in connection with or independent of any judicial proceedings; and give the reasons why the petitioner or petitioners ask that a reorganization plan be effected. If the judge is convinced that the petition of a debtor has been filed in good faith and meets the requirements of Chapter X, he may enter an order approving the petition; otherwise, he is required to dismiss it.

If the petition has been filed by creditors or an indenture trustee (an involuntary petition), the debtor may file an answer within ten days or within a longer period if the court permits. Answers may also be filed by other creditors, an indenture trustee, or any stockholder if the company is solvent in the bankruptcy sense (assets still exceed liabilities). Customarily, the judge will reject the petition if the creditors acquired their claims for the purpose of filing the petition, if adequate relief could be obtained under Chapter XI, if a reasonable plan of reorganization cannot be effected, and/or if interests of creditors and shareholders can be served best by a prior proceeding which is pending in the courts.

If the debtor's liabilities are more than $250,000, the judge must appoint one or more trustees to conduct the business pending reorganization or liquidation. For smaller corporations, the judge may leave the debtor in possession and appoint an examiner to perform the functions of the trustees. Trustees and their attorneys must be "disinterested" (this term is defined in the law so as to bar not only creditors, officers, and stockholders of the debtor but also investment bankers, lawyers, and others who have assisted in the issuance of securities of the debtor corporation). In order to assist in management of the business pending reorganization, the judge may appoint an employee, officer, or director as an additional trustee.

After the decision as to management is made, a date is set for the trustees to present "schedules" of assets and liabilities (including liens, contracts, and similar obligations) and names and addresses of creditors and stockholders of each class. The judge may also direct the trustees to investigate past management of the firm and to report any facts pertaining to fraud, misconduct, mismanagement, and irregularities on the part of directors, officers, and others. Out of this investigation, factual information may be brought forth to form the basis for prosecution of individuals for past acts. A hearing of interested parties must be called within not less than thirty nor more than sixty days after the petition has been signed. At this hearing, objections to continuance of existing management or to the appointment of any trustee may be heard.

Unlike proceedings under Chapter XI and the older equity proceedings, the basic responsibility for presenting a plan of reorganization falls upon the trustee rather than upon management and/or security holders. In rare cases wherein the debtor is left in possession (as may be true if liabilities are less than $250,000), an "examiner" may be given responsibility for filing a plan of reorganization. Nevertheless, creditors and stockholders are permitted to submit proposals for reorganization. Thus, not one plan but several may be presented at a second meeting of interested parties.

The plan for reorganization must conform to certain statutory requirements so as to meet the tests of being "fair, equitable and feasible." The plan must specify what claims, if any, are to be paid in full in cash; provisions altering or modifying rights of creditors and stockholders; provisions for rejecting any executory private contracts; exclusion of creditors or stockholders or any class thereof which are not to be affected by the plan; treatment of all or any part of the property of the debtor; and payment of all costs and administrative expenses and other allowances (such as those of committees of stockholders and creditors), which may be approved by the judge.

The judge is required to hold a hearing on the reorganization plan following the expiration of the time given to the trustee to file his plan. At this hearing, objections to the plan may be submitted, amendments may be proposed, and substitute plans of creditors or stockholders may be considered. The committees representing unsecured creditors (often working with adjustment bureaus, as in other types of adjustments), secured creditors, stockholders, leaseholders, and others may work together and arrive at a plan that will be acceptable to all; but, more often, they will submit several plans. Following this hearing, the judge must submit the plan or plans to the Securities and Exchange Commission if the indebtedness exceeds $3,000,000, but he may do so at his discretion if the sum is less than $3,000,000.[8]

The role of the Securities and Exchange Commission under Chapter X of the Bankruptcy Act is advisory, with the Commission having no power to veto or to require the adoption of a reorganization plan. In effect, the Commission's technical staff is placed at the disposal of the judge who may or may not accept its recommendations. The Commission is well prepared for its advisory role, having regional offices staffed with accountants, analysts, and lawyers who keep in close touch with all the hearings, parties, and issues which are involved in reorganizations. While the reorganization is in process, the Commissioner may be called upon by creditors, stockholders, and others for advice and suggestions as to the proper procedures to be followed.

Since the law states specifically that a trustee must be "disinter-

[8] Experience of the Securities and Exchange Commission as participants in corporate reorganizations under Chapter X are summarized in the annual reports of the Commission. In the appendix of the reports, there is a table which lists by name the reorganization proceedings in which the Commission participated during the fiscal year in question.

ested," the Securities and Exchange Commission may present evidence before the judge that will lead to either the resignation or removal of trustees not qualified under the Act. The Commission may object to the appointment of a second trustee (who may be an officer, director, or employee) on the grounds that the appointment is unnecessary; but if an officer, director, or employee is appointed, the Commission may work to prevent his encroachment upon the function of the disinterested trustee.

The Securities and Exchange Commission also insists that trustees comply with that section of the law which requires trustees to give security holders reports on their investigations of property, liabilities and financial conditions of the debtor, and the operation of the business (often the Commission assists in the preparation of such reports). The Commission may undertake investigations as to possible courses of action to be followed in case of mismanagement, fraud, or other types of misconduct by officers, directors, and other insiders. The Commission is also active in investigations of conditions under which creditors' and other committees are selected and function.

In appraising a proposed reorganization plan, the Securities and Exchange Commission must pass upon its fairness, equitability, and feasibility. In judging the fairness and equitability of a plan, emphasis is on legal and contractual priority provisions for settling claims in cash or securities. Junior claimants may participate only to the extent that debtors' property has value after satisfaction of all prior claims or that they make additional contributions necessary to the reorganization of the debtor firm. In arriving at valuation of the property, the Commission stresses the "appropriate capitalization of reasonable prospective earnings."

In arriving at the value of assets, the greatest amount of disagreement arises in estimating future earnings and in arriving at the interest rate at which these prospective earnings are to be capitalized. If anticipated earnings are high and the rate of their capitalization is low, the total value of the property may justify the inclusion of common stockholders in the plan. On the other hand, if anticipated earnings are low and the rate of their capitalization is high, common stockholders may be either excluded or permitted to reacquire an interest in the company by contributing a specific amount of cash for each share of stock held. The Commission is concerned with the adequacy of working capital, the relationship of capital structure and bonded debt to property values, the effect of new capitalization on the company's prospective credit, the adequacy of prospective earnings relative to interest requirements and dividends on preferred and other stock, and the prevention of the need for future reorganization.

After the advisory report of the Securities and Exchange Commission is made, copies of the report are made available to the parties appearing at the proceedings. This report may or may not be the basis for approval, disapproval, or modification of the reorganization plan. Before the judge approves a plan for reorganization, he must be sure that it complies with provisions of the law covering fairness, equitability, and feasibility; and, after approval, he sets a time limit for its acceptance by the security holders.

Acceptance of a reorganization plan under Chapter X requires approval of two thirds of each class of claims (amount of claims, not number of claimants) of those affected. Not included among those affected are security holders whose claims have not been disturbed, as might be the case with first mortgage bond holders, and others such as common stockholders whose claims have been wiped out entirely. A plan is considered to be accepted by a class of security holders if two thirds of the amount of claims filed and allowed are accepted in writing. Although a class of creditors or stockholders votes to reject a plan which is acceptable to other classes, the plan may be put into effect if provisions are made to protect the interest of dissenters.

Customarily each class of security holders has, more or less, its own self-appointed protective committee; for such a committee to be truly representative, it must have either proxies to act for security holders or physical possession of the securities. The latter may be arranged first by contracting with a bank or trust company to accept the securities in exchange for certificates of deposit, if and when deposited, and then by soliciting the deposits of securities.

After accepting a reorganization plan, the judge calls a final hearing. At this point the plan may still be altered upon the proposal of interested parties if, in the opinion of the judge, the change does not have an adverse effect on the interests of other security holders. The judge will confirm the final plan if he is convinced that it is fair, equitable, and feasible and otherwise meets the requirements of the law.[9]

---

[9] Other requirements of the law are (1) claims of the United States Treasury must be satisfied; (2) the proposal and plan must have been made and procured in good faith and not by means or promises forbidden by the Act; (3) costs and expenses incident to reorganization must have been fully disclosed and must be reasonable, or if they are to be fixed after confirmation, they are to be subject to the approval of the judge; and (4) the interests of directors, officers, and others who are to manage the corporation must be compatible with those of creditors and stockholders and consistent with public policy.

Confirmation means that the reorganization plan is binding on the corporation, its creditors, and its stockholders. As in cases under Chapter XI, confirmation and discharge can be set aside within six months if fraud is involved. The judge may specify that claims which have not been filed or presented within five years will be set aside and any securities or cash remaining with the corporation will become its property or the property of any corporation organized to succeed it.

The judge must pass on the claims of creditors, trustees, attorneys, and others for costs and expenses incurred during the reorganization proceedings. Prior to the 1930 amendment under equity proceedings, insiders or others in no way connected with the corporation prior to reorganization proceedings often purchased securities of the debtor corporation and organized and controlled "protective committees" to further their own interests. The present law provides for regulation of indenture trustees and persons or committees representing stockholders in reorganization proceedings. Under oath, every representative is required to file a statement showing the authority under which he is empowered to act for the creditors or stockholders, giving pertinent facts and circumstances under which this power was granted and indicating circumstances under which securities held by persons represented were acquired. The judge may disregard any proxy, power of attorney, indenture, or depository agreement which he finds to be unfair or not consistent with public policy. The court seeks to protect the "estate" from exorbitant charges and at the same time to provide equitable allowances to creditor committees and others when merited.

The Securities and Exchange Commission has been helpful in reorganizations by presenting facts which have resulted in keeping down the costs of reorganizations. These have included exposure of the lack of qualification of members of committees and unreasonableness of claims for services rendered.

Reorganization under Chapter VIII. The provisions for reorganization of railroads are contained in Chapter VIII of the Bankruptcy Act which was added in 1933 as Section 77. Although the general procedures for reorganization of railroads are the same as for reorganization of public utility and industrial companies under Chapter X, the Interstate Commerce Commission has the key role in railroad reorganizations. In some cases, the federal district court cannot proceed with the reorganization proceedings until the Commission has acted.

Reorganization proceedings may be initiated by filing a petition in the appropriate federal district court by the railroad with the approval of the Interstate Commerce Commission, or by creditors whose claims are equal to 5 per cent or more of the company's total indebtedness, 10 per cent of all creditors, or 25 per cent of any class of creditors. After proper notice and a hearing, the court appoints a trustee who must be approved by the Interstate Commerce Commission. The trustee, whose primary function is to operate the railroad, may be a former employee of the company; but in the case of larger railroads, one or more additional independent trustees must be appointed.

The Interstate Commerce Commission is responsible for holding hearings on plans submitted by the trustee or on behalf of 10 per cent or more of any class of creditors or stockholders, and it must submit a reorganization plan to the court. By rulings of the United States Supreme Court, the Commission's findings as to valuation of assets and other facts are final and are not subject to review by the federal district court. Consequently, the jurisdiction of the court is limited to determining that procedures followed conform to the law. However, the court may object to the Commission's plan and insist that it be reconsidered.

Creditors, stockholders, and other interested parties are permitted to file objections to the Interstate Commerce Commission's plan; arrangements will then be made for a hearing at which opposition to the plan will be heard. When the court approves a plan, it will direct the Commission to conduct the voting. Then a certified copy of the plan, which must be accepted or rejected in writing by the different classes of claimants, will be sent to all interested parties. The results will be reported to the court, which will confirm the plan if approval of the necessary two thirds of each class of affected security holders has been obtained. However, the judge may confirm a plan of reorganization which has not been accepted by two thirds of each class of security holders affected if he finds that it makes adequate provisions for fair and equitable treatment of the claims or interests of those rejecting it, if the rejections are not reasonably justified, or if the plan otherwise conforms to all the requirements of the law.

The Mahaffie Act. In April, 1948, Congress enacted the Mahaffie Act, which provides for a simple procedure for a mild reorganization of railroads. By adding Section 20*b* to the Interstate Commerce Act, Congress allowed a railroad, with the approval of the Interstate

Commerce Commission, to propose a recapitalization or readjustment of the company's funded debt to the creditors. When the proposed modification is approved by holders of 75 per cent of the aggregate principal (more than 75 per cent if the principal amount is held by fewer than 25 holders), the Commission may enter an order approving the change. Minority creditors have the right of judicial review as under any other order issued by the Interstate Commerce Commission.

Before the Interstate Commerce Commission permits the readjustment plan to be submitted to secured creditors, it will have had public hearings on the proposals and will have determined if the proposals are within the scope of the law and in the best interest of the public, the carrier, and the different classes of security holders (those directly as well as indirectly affected). If readjustments can be made under the provisions of the Mahaffie Act, it could result in the avoidance of expensive, long, drawn-out proceedings that characterize the reorganizations under Chapter VIII.

Reorganization Plans. In financial reorganizations of corporations under supervision of the courts, the statutes require that plans be "fair and equitable." The United States Supreme Court has interpreted this to mean that the doctrine of "absolute priority" must be followed in treatment of security holders. Thus, senior security holders' claims must be satisfied in full before junior security holders are permitted to participate. After the valuation of property, common stockholders may have no equity in the corporation; therefore they may not be permitted to participate in the reorganization plan. In this case, they may appeal to the United States Supreme Court for modification of the reorganization plan; if they are successful, a new plan may be formulated. (Other security holders have the same privilege of appeal.)

In order to make a new plan feasible, one class of security holders may have to accept two or more classes of junior securities in exchange for those they hold. For illustration, each holder of a $1,000 first mortgage bond may be requested to accept a $500 first mortgage bond and preferred stock or common stock for the remainder of his principal and accrued interest claims against the corporation; second mortgage bond holders may receive only preferred and common stock; old preferred stockholders may receive only common stock; and old common stockholders may receive only the privilege of buying new common stock or they may hold no rights at all in the reorganized corporation. The objectives of a reorganization plan should be to reduce fixed charges, to eliminate burdensome leases and debt obligations, to assure adequate working capital, to permit the raising of new capital in the future, and to pave the way for a sound financial policy.

SUMMARY

When a business enterprise cannot meet its maturing debt obligations, the situation may be handled by an adjustment outside of the courts or by an arrangement or reorganization under supervision of the courts. A firm may be able to meet its obligations if given time; and, if creditors choose to stay with the firm, a credit extension may be worked out. The chief creditor, usually a commercial bank, will be influenced by the size, number, and nature of the debts and by the action taken by other creditors. When there are a number of large creditors, the extension plan may be formulated and administered by a creditors' committee. Either the debtor or creditors may negotiate an extension through an adjustment bureau. The extension plan worked out by the creditors' committee becomes binding on the debtor and those creditors who sign the contract, but nonsigners are free to demand payment when their claims come due.

In other cases, a composition settlement may be effected wherein creditors agree to accept a percentage of the obligations as full payment. Usually, composition settlements are negotiated and administered in the same way as extensions, with a creditors' committee supervising the business firm until the settlement is completed.

During the 1930's, Congress added several sections to the Federal Bankruptcy Act to provide for reorganization of business concerns. Under the provisions of Chapter XI, an "arrangement," defined as a "plan of a debtor for the settlement, satisfaction, or extension of the time of payment of his unsecured debts," may be effected through a petition filed by the debtor. A petition to reorganize under Chapter X of the Act may be filed by the debtor, by creditors, or by an indenture trustee.

In railroad reorganizations under Chapter VIII of the Federal Bankruptcy Act, plans are filed with the Interstate Commerce Commission. Since the United States Supreme Court has ruled that the Commission's finding as to valuation and other facts are final, they are not subject to review by the courts, although questions of law are. When Congress amended the Interstate Commerce Act in 1948, it provided for ways whereby funded debts could be adjusted outside the bankruptcy courts by order of the Commission; however, like other orders of the Commission, such arrangements are subject to judicial review.

QUESTIONS AND PROBLEMS

1. (*a*) Distinguish between insolvency in the equity sense and in the bankruptcy sense. (*b*) What is meant by the following: "there are a lot of 'bankrupts' still doing business in this town"? (*c*) What is a "bankrupt"?
2. Identify: (*a*) an extension of "workout"; (*b*) creditors' committee; and (*c*) adjustment bureau.
3. Discuss the role of (*a*) the creditors' committee and (*b*) an adjustment bureau in an extension.
4. What are the advantages and disadvantages of creditors' committee reorganizations?
5. Identify: (*a*) composition settlement, (*b*) role of creditors' committee in composition settlements, and (*c*) advantages of composition settlements over extensions.
6. Identify: (*a*) Chapter VIII, (*b*) Chapter X, and (*c*) Chapter XI of the Federal Bankruptcy Act.
7. Define an "arrangement." What are the items usually covered in the reorganization plan?
8. (*a*) What five tests are applied before an arrangement plan is confirmed? (*b*) What are the advantages and disadvantages of an "arrangement" as compared to an "extension" or "composition settlement" outside of court?
9. Distinguish between (*a*) a "voluntary" and "involuntary" petition for reorganization under Chapter X, (*b*) an "interested" and "disinterested" trustee, and (*c*) the role of a creditors' committee in reorganizations under Chapter X and Chapter XI.
10. What information must be contained in a plan for reorganization under Chapter X?
11. What is the function of the Securities and Exchange Commission when a corporation is reorganized under Chapter X of the bankruptcy law?
12. Compare reorganizations under Chapter VIII to those under Chapter X regarding (*a*) the agency having the leading role, (*b*) who may file petitions, (*c*) who is responsible for the reorganization plan, and (*d*) the jurisdiction of the court.
13. What alternative to reorganization under Chapter VIII is offered by the Mahaffie Act, as found in Section 20*b* of the Interstate Commerce Act?
14. What are the objectives of any sound reorganization plan?
15. "A plan of reorganization . . . was submitted . . . [and] has been approved by all interested groups, including the Securities and Exchange Commission." (*Wall Street Journal* [New York], May 18, 1959, p. 11.) What characteristics must a plan have in order to obtain the approval of the Securities and Exchange Commission?

16. "At the end of the year, the [Securities and Exchange] Commission was actively participating in 45 reorganization proceedings involving 67 companies." (*25th Annual Report of the Securities and Exchange Commission Fiscal Year Ended June 30, 1959* [Washington, D.C.: U.S. Government Printing Office, 1959], p. 143.) What does the Commission do in these cases?

CHAPTER 30

Liquidation of Business Firms

IN THE AREA of business finance, attention is customarily directed toward the problems associated with the organization, operation, and expansion of going concerns; however, many firms must be liquidated and the likelihood of financial loss to owners or investors and creditors is highly probable. Essentially, liquidation is the process of converting a firm's assets into cash and distributing it in the order of priority of claims of the various classes of creditors and owners. The liquidation of a business firm may be presided over by management, creditors, or an appropriate judicial officer. If the economy is to be strengthened, the buyers of the assets of a liquidated firm must be able to use them more efficiently than the original owners—an economic aspect of business failure that should not be ignored.

This chapter deals with the liquidation of business concerns under the following subtitles: (1) liquidation of solvent business enterprises, (2) liquidation of insolvent business firms outside federal courts, (3) dissolution of corporations, (4) liquidation under the federal bankruptcy law, and (5) greater protection for creditors (including creditor business firms, as provided by current laws).

LIQUIDATION OF SOLVENT BUSINESS ENTERPRISES

Statistics of the number of business enterprises that have been discontinued for any reason appear periodically in the *Survey of Current Business.* Studies based on the statistics of business discontinuations for certain years have revealed the fact that less than one half are due to failure. Although business transfers are not classified as business discontinuations, the purpose in some of these transfers is to prevent or minimize losses; perhaps one fourth of the transfers of business firms are of this type. Dissolutions of old business firms and the formation of new firms is a normal aspect of American business.

The rate of business discontinuations may be much more rapid than the rate at which new business firms are established, as exemplified during the early years of World War II; but the more normal condition is for the number of terminations to be less than the number of new business organizations. While some business discontinuations are due to failure, many are terminated voluntarily for various reasons. Sometimes a business firm disappears not because of inefficiency but rather because of an unusually high degree of efficiency which leads to the firm's acquisition by a second company in order to obtain its trade-marks, patents, products, personnel, or trade customers. In other instances, owners of profitable businesses sell them because there is no suitable succession to present management or because a buyer's offer is too attractive to refuse.

Some business firms are purchased not because of their profitability but rather because they have been operating at a loss. Such acquisitions enable buyers to reap substantial tax benefits under the provisions of the internal revenue code which allows a loss to be carried forward five years or back three years.[1] Although the Internal Revenue Service has made its regulations concerning the acquisition of companies to obtain tax losses more restrictive, the possible tax write-off is often the most valuable advantage obtained in the acquisition of a money-losing company.

Voluntary liquidations are normal in wasting-assets industries. After a natural resource has been fully exploited or depleted, the company's alternative to liquidation is either to shift to some other industry or to acquire new assets in the same field in another location, which most major companies are able to do. A lumber company which follows a policy of replanting rather than one of depleting the supply of timber may be an exception. As noted in a preceding chapter, wasting-assets companies recover capital invested out of

[1] An illustration of the application of the federal tax write-off provision is this: Assuming that X Company has a loss of $1 million in 1960, it may claim a refund on taxes paid in 1957, 1958, and 1959; but if it had no profits and paid no taxes during those three years, it may obtain a tax advantage by carrying the loss forward within the next five years. In effect, the first $1 million of net profit earned before the expiration of five years will be tax free. A second corporation may offer to buy X Company to acquire not only its assets but also its "no-tax on the next $1,000,000."

earnings which are accounted for as allowances for depletion. The distribution of depletion reserves to owners as dividends amounts to a gradual liquidation of the business concern.

For a small firm, a policy of using depletion reserves to acquire new assets in the same field may not be feasible; and, if management is highly specialized, to enter a new field of production may be unwise. The return of capital in the form of depletion-reserve distribution may not be taxed as ordinary dividend distributions; stockholders are usually informed as to what portion of their dividends is being paid out of current profits (taxable) and what portion is capital distribution.

A business enterprise may, for one of a number of reasons, liquidate its business in part by converting some of its assets into cash and reducing its capitalization by retirement of long-term debt, preferred stock, or part of its outstanding common stock. A decrease in capital structure and a corresponding decrease in operations may permit a business firm to concentrate on that part of its business which is most profitable and avoid financial difficulties that could lead to insolvency. In some cases, a company may have no choice as to the disposal of part of its business owing to unfavorable court or legislative action. This is illustrated by the liquidation of many holding companies as a result of the passage of the Public Utility Holding Company Act of 1935.

Sometimes management, realizing that the prospects of a firm are uncertain, will liquidate immediately in preference to waiting until the company becomes hopelessly insolvent. In other cases, when firms encounter difficulties in raising needed capital and meeting current obligations, they will choose to liquidate. Among the common causes for changes in business prospects are new inventions, changes in processes of operation, shifts in public demands for products, and local changes in streets or highways which can completely disrupt the operations of retailers and service companies. Even though business prospects are excellent, an enterprise may be liquidated because of the death or retirement of a proprietor, a partner, a key official, or some one else on whom the success of the business depends. Other reasons for voluntary liquidations include disagreements among owners as to business policy and decisions of owners to start new business ventures, to accept more profitable employment elsewhere, to convert personal assets into liquid form in anticipation of inheritance taxes, or to diversify holdings. The combinations and variations of reasons why business firms are voluntarily liquidated is almost without limit.

LIQUIDATION OF INSOLVENT BUSINESS FIRMS OUTSIDE FEDERAL COURTS

As in the case of reorganization proceedings, insolvent business enterprises may be liquidated either out of court or under the supervision of state or federal courts. Business firms liquidated because of legal action are usually small ones, whereas large firms are usually permitted to reorganize. When the problems are uncomplicated and mutual trust exists between a debtor and his creditors, arrangements may be made for liquidation under supervision of a creditors' committee. If the problems are complicated, the procedure may entail a common-law or statutory assignment or a state court receivership. Since federal law has precedence over state law in bankruptcy cases, either the debtor or creditors may have a case transferred by petition to a federal court.

Creditors' Committee. The problems associated with organizing a creditors' committee and negotiating a liquidation agreement (among creditors and with the debtors) are, in general, the same as those present in formulating an adjustment agreement, extension, or composition settlement. In fact, an adjustment attempt is sometimes followed by a decision of the creditors and debtor to liquidate the business.

If a firm is incorporated, liquidation of assets is followed by dissolution of the corporation; but proprietors and partners continue to live, and to them, obtaining a discharge or release of all liabilities at the time of liquidation is of utmost importance. On the other hand, creditors prefer that liabilities be kept alive because the debtor may acquire assets in the future which could be seized to settle unpaid claims. Unless a release or discharge from the unpaid balances of the debts can be obtained from all creditors, the debtor may prefer to file a petition in bankruptcy and have the proceedings transferred to a federal court. A threat to do so may result in concessions from creditors who are reluctant to sign a release; in addition, non-co-operative or recalcitrant creditors may be subjected to pressure from other creditors who favor an out-of-court settlement which is generally to the advantage of the creditors. As in the case of composition settlements or extension agreements, non-co-operative small creditors may be paid in full; but, in other cases, the only feasible solution may be to resort to the federal courts.

When there are a small number of creditors and they trust the debtor, they may permit him to liquidate his busines and to prorate the cash among them with or without supervision of a creditors' committee. Sometimes, a representative of the local adjustment bureau of the National Association of Credit Men will work closely with the debtor and creditors in liquidation proceedings. The representative will act not only as an advisor but also as a depository and distribution agent for funds to be given to creditors. If evidence of fraud or unfair treatment appears, all proceedings may be stopped by either the creditors or the debtor and federal bankruptcy proceedings may be initiated.

Common-Law Assignments. A debtor who feels that his business is hopelessly insolvent may make an assignment of all his assets to a trustee (also called an assignee) to be held in trust for the benefit of his creditors. Such assignments may be effected under state statutes or under common law. A common-law assignment is usually conducted under a committee of creditors, and thus the publicity associated with statutory assignment is avoided (the latter being a matter of public record). The common-law assignment or one made under the state law is an act of bankruptcy; as such, it permits the creditors to petition the debtor into bankruptcy within four months. Thus, both common-law and statutory assignments require the consent of creditors.

While the initiative in making an assignment of assets is taken by the debtor, it is usually with the consent of his chief creditors; and while the debtor selects the trustee, this advantage is theoretical because so-called "voluntary" assignments are commonly made under pressure of creditors who are instrumental in the selection of the trustee or assignee. The assignee is the trustee for the creditors; and, as in any trust, the beneficiaries have remedies against the trustee for improper or illegal actions in administering trust affairs.

Sometimes a banker who has been closely connected with the business firm (as one who has been active in a previously attempted workout) is selected as the assignee or trustee; but, in other cases, assignments may be made to friends, lawyers, adjustment bureaus, credit men's associations, or trade associations. Since the plan to liquidate a business firm may follow an unsuccessful attempt to rehabilitate the firm under supervision of a creditors' committee, the best results may be obtained by using the same individuals to work out the liquidation proceedings.

To be effective, all creditors must accept the assignment arrangement; and, once creditors have consented to an assignment, they may not file petitions in bankruptcy. Often a representative of an adjustment bureau is selected to be the original or replacement assignee because he is well qualified to obtain the signatures of all creditors.

Willingness of creditors to accept an assignment agreement depends upon their confidence in the ability of the assignee as well as their satisfaction as to the good faith of the debtor.

The legal procedure for the transfer of assets from the debtor to the trustee varies, but it may be done by executing a chattel mortgage, power of attorney, or deed of trust. The function of the assignee is to preserve, collect, and distribute assets for the benefit of creditors without preference, except as may be prescribed in the instrument of assignment.

Although there are certain advantages in the use of an assignment in liquidating an insolvent business firm, there are some disadvantages. Since the assignee is personally liable to all the creditors for his actions, he may be ultraconservative in carrying out his duties despite the fact that he has a great deal of freedom in selling assets and otherwise administering the affairs of the estate. A second disadvantage is the possibility that an assignment may be upset and the proceedings transferred to a federal or state court, which would mean a delay in settling the affairs of the debtor. However, a federal or state court proceeding is less flexible and less economical than an out-of-court settlement. A third disadvantage is that the assignee lacks power possessed by the court, such as the right to examine the debtor under oath and to recover preferential payments made to certain creditors. Although a creditors' committee may work closely with the assignee, its supervision over him may not be as effective as that of a court over a receiver.

Even though assignments may be administered under supervision of state courts, there are territorial limitations on the powers of the assignees and there is a lack of uniformity in the laws and requirements of various states. Considered from the viewpoint of the debtor, the most serious objection to a common-law or statutory assignment may be his inability to secure a release from creditors, particularly those from outside of the state, from the unpaid portion of his debts. (A debtor may bring about a petition in bankruptcy by making an assignment which would cause creditors to take action to have the proceedings transferred to a federal court, thus avoiding the stigma of voluntary bankruptcy.)

Although states have provisions for receivership and liquidation of insolvent business enterprises, the federal bankruptcy law, with its provisions for reorganizations and for the discharge of debtors, has largely superseded these state statutes. There may be no advantage in proceeding under state courts since dissenting creditors may have almost any settlement reached therein transferred to a federal court. In addition, state courts have limited territorial jurisdiction. However, while creditors have the right to transfer a liquidation proceeding from a state court to a federal bankruptcy court, they may choose not to do so because the costs involved are greater.

Statutory Assignments. Although all states have provisions for statutory assignments, they are used less frequently than common-law assignments (see above). Although there are some differences between the two, in general they are similar. In common-law assignments, preferences may be given to certain classes of creditors which may or may not be permitted under state statutes. After assignments have been initiated, the creditors may request the appropriate state court to replace the original assignee. The instrument used in making an assignment is prescribed by law and it must be filed in the appropriate public office (thereby giving publicity to the proceedings). Final accounting must be made by the assignee to the appropriate state court.

State Court Receivership. State laws also may have provisions for liquidation and rehabilitation of business firms and/or for seizure of specific assets which are involved in litigation. To carry out these objectives, receivers may be appointed by an appropriate state court. The purpose of receivership is to protect the interests of majority parties, which may necessitate operating a business even though it means that the legal or contractual rights of minority parties are temporarily set aside (as in seizure of assets, the loss of which would cripple a business firm). In other cases, the situation may be such that the interest of all except certain minority parties are best served if the assets and the business are liquidated. State receiverships may be available only in specified instances and then only when other remedies are not available. In some states, a state court receiver operates in liquidations like a statutory assignee; but being an officer of the court, the receiver is selected by the court and not by creditors or the debtor.

DISSOLUTION OF CORPORATIONS

Business corporation acts provide for both voluntary and involuntary dissolution of corporations, the former being outside the court and the latter being under court supervision. Sometimes a dissolution proceeding that starts on a voluntary basis is shifted to the courts at the request of either the corporation or the dissenting creditors.

Irrespective of how a corporation is dissolved, creditors of the debtor corporation face different problems than those faced by creditors of unincorporated business firms in process of dissolution.

The fact that a corporation ceases to exist upon dissolution means that its creditors must file and collect claims against the corporation before dissolution. As noted previously, single proprietors and partners live on after the liquidation of their business firms and they may be held responsible for unpaid balances unless a release or discharge is obtained from creditors.

The simplest procedure for dissolution of a corporation is by written consent of all stockholders. Since this method of initiating dissolution procedure requires the signatures of all stockholders, it is used only when there are but a few stockholders. In most cases, the initiative for voluntary dissolution is taken by the corporation, and this involves the adoption of a resolution by the board of directors that the corporation be dissolved and subsequently, the affirmative vote of at least the required percentage of shares outstanding (usually two thirds). Irrespective of the method used, a "statement of intent to dissolve" must be filed with the Secretary of State or the appropriate state official.

Filing the "statement of intent to dissolve" gives creditors of the corporation an opportunity to present their claims against the corporation. In addition, the corporation must give written notice to each known creditor or other claimant and must cease doing business except that which is incidental to the winding up of its affairs. Normally, the corporation continues to exist until a certificate of dissolution is issued by the Secretary of State. Some state laws provide that voluntary dissolution proceedings may be revoked at any time prior to issuance of a certificate of dissolution by the Secretary of State. If voluntary dissolution proceedings have not been revoked and if all provisions of the law have been met, the Secretary of State will issue a certificate of dissolution.

Sometimes a corporation is dissolved but the business is not discontinued; in this case, the corporation's legal existence ceases, but the business may be operated as an unincorporated business firm or the assets may be absorbed by a second corporation or a new corporation, as in a merger or consolidation. Section 11 (b) of the Public Utility Holding Company Act of 1935, which requires the public utility systems to dissolve or reorganize companies which do not fit into "a single integrated public-utility system" or which "unduly or unnecessarily complicate the structure," has probably been responsible for the dissolution of more corporations than any act in modern history.

In addition to voluntary surrender of charters, corporations may be dissolved through state judicial proceedings. The Attorney General may take dissolution action in the appropriate state court for such causes as failure to file an annual report as required by law; failure to pay fees, franchise taxes, or penalties prescribed by law; and failure to maintain a registered agent in the state. In addition, legal action to dissolve a corporation may result if the corporation exceeds or abuses the authority conferred upon it by law or if misrepresentation has been made of any material matters in reports and other documents submitted by such corporation as required by the statutes. However, if a corporation eliminates the cause of action before dissolution, usually legal proceedings to dissolve the corporation cease.

Other reasons for involuntary dissolution of corporations may include (1) the occurrence of some contingency provided for in the charter, such as consolidation or merger; (2) failure to commence business within a certain period of time; (3) expiration of the period for which the corporation was chartered; (4) an act of the state legislature; or (5) failure or losses. However, liquidation and dissolution result most frequently because a corporation is technically insolvent.

A state court may appoint a receiver to liquidate a corporation when other remedies available either at law or equity are deemed inadequate. The receiver has all the duties and powers customarily bestowed on receivers. The court will enter a decree dissolving the corporation after the costs and expenses of such proceedings have been paid, all debts and other liabilities have been discharged, and the remaining property—if any—has been distributed to shareholders. If the assets are insufficient to satisfy all costs, expenses, debts, and other liabilities, the court will enter a decree dissolving the corporation after assets are distributed equitably as far as they will go in payment. For reasons already considered, most corporations that are insolvent are liquidated under supervision of the federal courts (see below).

LIQUIDATION UNDER THE FEDERAL BANKRUPTCY LAW

The current bankruptcy law of the federal government dates from 1898, but it has been amended frequently by Congress and interpreted and supplemented by general orders and rules adopted or prescribed by the Supreme Court of the United States. In order to bring about uniformity in procedures, the Supreme Court has adopted seventy official forms to be employed by officers of the bankruptcy courts, debtors, creditors, and other parties. In addition, other supplementary but unofficial forms are available to cover contingencies in bankruptcy proceedings.

Purpose of Bankruptcy Act. With regard to liquidating insolvent business concerns, the Federal Bankruptcy Act has the following two main purposes: (1) to convert the assets of insolvent debtors into cash so as to pay the claims of secured creditors according to the priority of their claims and to distribute the remainder to other creditors in proportion to their claims as filed and allowed by the Court; and (2) to relieve honest but unfortunate debtors of the obligation for unpaid portions of their debts in order to give them the opportunity to renew their business activities without being subjected to past claims which might make continuance in business impossible. This discharge of the bankrupt is now considered to be but a secondary objective of bankruptcy proceedings because modern emphasis is on the protection of creditors against fraud prior to and/or during liquidation proceedings and the equitable distribution among them of debtors' available assets.[2]

Voluntary and Involuntary Bankruptcy Petitions. Bankruptcy proceedings for liquidation purposes under federal law are initiated by a petition filed either by the debtor or by the creditors on an official form in which the petitioners request that the debtor be adjudged a bankrupt.[3] If the petition is filed by the debtor, voluntary bankruptcy is involved; if filed by creditors, involuntary bankruptcy is in-

---

[2] The American Bar Association has been asked to look into the reasons underlying the increase in the number of *nonbusiness* bankruptcies in recent years. Only 10 per cent of the bankruptcies are currently accounted for by business firms; the largest single group of bankruptcies are those incurred by wage earners. Most of the latter reported that they owned no assets. Because of the large proportion of total bankruptcies that consist of personal bankruptcies, there is little relationship between the number of bankruptcies and business conditions. However, bankruptcies tend to increase during depressions. The more common reasons for the recent increase in personal bankruptcies include careless and irresponsible credit practices (which accounts for part of the increase in consumer credit outstanding), extravagance, unrealistic expenditures for housing and durable consumer goods, unexpected emergencies such as loss of jobs or sickness, and counsel recommending bankruptcy as an easy way out of an unhappy financial situation. See also Helen Arnold, "We Went Bankrupt on the Installment Plan," *Readers Digest* (January, 1961), pp. 30–35.

[3] When there are twelve or more creditors, the petition may be filed by three or more creditors having provable claims of $500 or more in excess of any specific security they may have; but, if the number of creditors is less than twelve, one creditor may file if he has unsecured claims of $500 or more.

volved. Petitions may be filed by or against persons, partnerships, and corporations (except municipal corporations, railroads, insurance companies, incorporated banks, or building and loan associations).[4]

Acts of Bankruptcy. An involuntary petition of bankruptcy must allege that the debtor has committed, within the four months preceding the filing of the petition, one or more of the following six acts of bankruptcy: (1) committing fraud while insolvent, such as transferring, concealing, or removing assets with the intent to hinder, delay, or defraud creditors; (2) giving one or more creditors a preference or an advantage over others while insolvent, such as transferring or permitting legal seizure of assets; (3) permitting any creditor to obtain a lien on property while insolvent (a passive way to give preference); (4) making a general assignment for the benefit of creditors, whether or not the debtor is insolvent at the time; (5) permitting appointment of a receiver or trustee to take charge of the property while insolvent in either the bankruptcy or equity sense; and (6) admitting in writing inability to pay debts and willingness to be adjudged a bankrupt whether solvent or insolvent at the time.

Adjudication. If forms are filled out properly, the judicial decision on a voluntary bankruptcy petition is made immediately; but in involuntary proceedings, the debtor (defendant) is given an opportunity to make and answer charges. He may deny having been insolvent at the time the alleged bankruptcy act was committed, or he may question the court's jurisdiction, and so on. A hearing will be held at which evidence may be submitted by creditors in favor of and opposed to the debtor. Then, the case will either be dismissed for lack of evidence or the debtor will be adjudged a bankrupt. If no answer is filed by the defendant, which is the ordinary procedure, he will be adjudged a bankrupt by default. So "bankrupt" companies are those which have been declared bankrupt by a federal court.

Referee in Bankruptcy. After adjudication, the case is transferred to a "referee in bankruptcy." This judicial officer is appointed for a term of six years; but, because appointments may be renewed, his tenure of office may be prolonged indefinitely. Referees may perform all the duties conferred on the courts by the Federal Bankruptcy Act, subject to review by the judge. Among the more important duties of a

[4] The term "corporation," as used in the Bankruptcy Act, includes partnership associations, joint-stock companies, business trusts, and unincorporated companies. Creditors may not file a petition in bankruptcy against persons owing less than $1,000, against wage earners whose compensation does not exceed $1,500 a year, or against farmers engaged chiefly in tilling the soil.

referee in bankruptcy are (1) to see that the bankrupt files his schedule of assets and list of creditors properly, (2) to notify creditors and other interested parties of meetings and actions in the proceedings, (3) to keep and furnish requested information to the court and interested parties, (4) to declare liquidating dividends to be distributed to creditors and to prepare dividend sheets showing dividends declared and to whom payable, and (5) to keep all records of the case until its conclusion and then to transmit them to the clerk of the court where these records will remain open for inspection. (Since real estate is commonly involved, such records are valuable to abstractors in tracing changes in the title to real property.)

Receiver in Bankruptcy. Before the selection of a trustee to take charge of the bankrupt's estate in liquidation proceedings, a receiver may be appointed by the judge to take possession of all or part of the debtor's property and to prevent further deterioration of the estate. Action is usually taken upon petition by creditors either before or after the hearings on the bankruptcy petition. The tour of duty of an appointed receiver may be a short one, but this is unlikely since bankruptcy proceedings are apt to be drawn out over a long period of time. A receiver's primary function is to preserve, and not to administer, the debtor's estate; but he may sell perishable assets and otherwise perform such duties as are defined in the order of the judge or referee who appointed him. If no receiver is appointed, it is the duty of the "bankrupt" to preserve the value of the property pending appointment of a trustee. The appointment of a receiver in bankruptcy can only be justified when such action is absolutely necessary to preserve the estate. Title to the property remains with a bankrupt until a trustee has been selected.

Action by Creditors. The trustee in liquidation proceedings under the Federal Bankruptcy Act is the officer of the court who takes charge of the administration and settlement of the bankrupt estate. He is selected at the first meeting of the creditors, but his election is subject to the approval of the judge or referee. If creditors cannot elect one or more trustees (there may be three) by a majority vote, the trustee or trustees may be appointed by the court. The referee calls and presides over the meeting of creditors soon after the debtor is adjudged a bankrupt. Usually, the creditors select a committee to represent them in later proceedings (such as consulting with and advising the trustee in performance of his duties). Since bankruptcy proceedings are conducted in the interest of general creditors, secured creditors are not permitted to vote except when their claims exceed the probable value of pledged assets. Creditors may be represented at creditors' meetings by proxy or attorney; no given quorum is required at such meetings.

The creditor must file a "proof of claim," which means that he must present a sworn statement setting forth his claim upon forms and in a manner prescribed by the Supreme Court of the United States. It is a crime punishable by imprisonment for a period not exceeding five years to present a false proof of claim against the bankrupt's estate. After claims are filed (proved) they are either allowed or rejected. Before the election of a trustee, either a creditor or the bankrupt may object to a claim, thereby making it subject to reexamination. Such matters are handled by the trustee after his election and confirmation.

Trustee in Bankruptcy. The trustee acquires all the bankrupt's property as of the date of the filing the bankruptcy petition. He has the power or right to reacquire property transferred in fraud of creditors; property held by an assignee; and property committed to or invested in the bankrupt by inheritance, bequest, or otherwise within six months after his bankruptcy.

After taking title to the bankrupt's property, the trustee's duty is to liquidate it as soon as possible under supervision of the court; therefore businessmen who have selling ability and experience in the same line of business as the bankrupt are often elected as trustees. Receipts are deposited in one of the depositories (banks) designated for the receipt of bankruptcy court funds. Obligations are met in the order of their priority, which is as follows: (1) the actual and necessary expenses of preserving the bankrupt estate; (2) wages due workmen and other employees earned within three months before commencement of bankruptcy proceedings but not to exceed $600; (3) creditors' costs incurred in preventing discharge of the bankrupt under an arrangement or some other proceedings and in convicting any person for an offense under the Act; (4) taxes due the United States, state, and local governments; (5) debts given priority by national or federal law; and (6) general creditors.

Following liquidation and distribution of assets, a final hearing is called at which the trustee gives an accounting to the creditors and the referee. If no objections are raised, the trustee's accounts will be approved by the referee and the court will discharge the bankrupt.

Discharge of Bankrupt. The discharge of the bankrupt is a release granted by the court from all debts that remain unsatisfied except (1) taxes due the federal, state, and local governments; (2) liabilities for obtaining property by false pretenses, malicious injuries, alimony, support of wife and child, and similar personal liabilities; (3) unscheduled claims; (4) claims against the bankrupt arising because of fraud, embezzlement, and so on while acting in a fiduciary capacity; (5) wages earned within three months prior to bankruptcy proceedings; and (6) money deposited by employees as security for faithful performance of duties during term of employment.

A discharge may not be allowed if the bankrupt has (1) committed certain offenses which are punishable by imprisonment under the bankruptcy act, (2) destroyed records, (3) made fraudulent transfers of assets, (4) been granted a discharge in bankruptcy within six previous years, (5) refused to obey orders of the court, or (6) failed to explain satisfactorily deficiencies or losses in assets. The judge of the bankruptcy court may reopen the case before the lapse of a reasonable amount of time on the application of the creditors (the common reason for doing so is thc discovery of new assets). In this case, a new trustee will be elected and the foregoing procedures will be repeated.

GREATER PROTECTION FOR CREDITORS

Since the passage of the Chandler Act of 1938, most of the major abuses which formerly marred bankruptcy procedures have been eliminated. No longer are persons relatively safe from prosecution if they participate in fraudulent bankruptcies (as when "rings" made a "racket" out of operating insolvent business concerns). In the past, bankruptcy assets remaining for creditors were greatly reduced because too often referees, trustees, receivers, and creditors' attorneys combined to "milk" the bankrupt's assets for personal gain. Now the remuneration of officials and other participants in bankruptcy proceedings is controlled by law and regulations, and the qualities of ability and integrity are emphasized in selecting appointees. However, if creditors would participate more actively in bankruptcy proceedings, even better administration and more vigorous criminal prosecution of fraudulent debtors might result.

The Chandler Act provides opportunities for closer and more intelligent control by creditors by requiring (1) the selection of a creditors' committee of three or more at the first creditors' meeting and giving the committee official standing to advise and to consult with the trustee; (2) notice to be given of all applications for compensation (attorneys for the bankrupt, the referee, the receiver, the trustee, the creditors, and any others); (3) information to be provided as to sale of assets, compromises of claims if more than $1,000, and other similar matters; and (4) exclusion of creditors with claims of less than $50 in computing the number eligible to vote at creditors' committee meetings when trustees are selected.

The Chandler Act also makes provisions for (1) mandatory examination of bankrupts (instead of merely permissive examination); (2) criminal action applicable to debtors in reorganization as well as in bankruptcy; (3) classification of sections pertaining to liens, preferences, and fraudulent transfers; and (4) appointment of an equity receiver being construed as an act of bankruptcy. As noted in the preceding chapter, greater protection was given to security holders in Chapter X of the Bankruptcy Act by (1) providing for the appointment of a disinterested trustee by the judge (if indebtedness is over $250,000) who is to assume the leading role in evolving a plan of reorganization; (2) requiring the submission of the plan to the Securities and Exchange Commission (if indebtedness exceeds $3,000,000); and (3) when so directed by the court, requiring the trustee to ascertain whether any basis exists for charges of fraud, misconduct, or mismanagement.

Under the most favorable conditions, bankruptcy proceedings are expensive; therefore, trade associations try to hold down the costs of rehabilitation of financially embarrassed business firms and liquidation of others by out-of-court settlements (and these settlements exceed in number those made under supervision of the courts). When nonbankruptcy proceedings are used for liquidation purposes, adjustment bureaus may perform the functions of creditors' committees or at least co-operate closely with them. Usually, adjustment bureaus have both an intimate knowledge of debtors' affairs and contacts with their chief suppliers who are usually most numerous among unsecured creditors. It is due, in part, to the activities of credit adjustment bureaus that more cases are being adjusted out of court and that costs of court cases have been reduced. On the other hand, sight must not be lost of the fact that to the extent that creditors are not permitted to seize assets at random by court proceedings, a business firm is not faced with a situation wherein the seizure of certain assets would prevent the efficient use of all the company's property.

SUMMARY

A business enterprise may be liquidated by procedures involving common consent of the debtor and creditors, common-law or statutory assignments, corporate dissolution, state court receivership, or federal bankruptcy proceedings. During an average year, probably one half of business discontinuations are voluntary liquidation of solvent business enterprises. Obviously, many are proprietorships and partnerships, wherein death or retirement of owners often leads to dissolution of the business firm. In some cases—such as firms in wasting-assets industries—voluntary liquidations are common; sometimes the threat of insolvency may lead to voluntary liquidation to minimize or prevent losses.

Insolvent business enterprises may be liquidated voluntarily or involuntarily either outside of courts or under the supervision of state or federal courts; when liquidated outside of courts, the procedure may be a common-law assignment under supervision of a creditors' committee. Although similar in most respects to common-law assignment, statutory assignment is a matter of public record since it necessitates filing with the appropriate public official.

When insolvent business concerns are liquidated under the Federal Bankruptcy Law, the bankruptcy proceedings may be initiated by a petition filed by the debtor or creditors. An involuntary petition, one initiated by creditors, must allege that the debtor has committed one or more of the six acts of bankruptcy within four months preceding the filing of the petition. If the debtor is adjudged a bankrupt, a referee in bankruptcy is appointed. Before the appointment of a trustee, a receiver in bankruptcy may be appointed to preserve the debtor's estate.

The trustee, selected by creditors, subject to approval of the judge or referee, is the officer of the court who administers and settles the bankrupt estate. After liquidation and distribution of assets, barring objections, the trustee's accounts are approved by the referee and the court discharges the bankrupt from all debts remaining unsatisfied (with minor exceptions, as provided in the statutes).

The Chandler Act of 1938 provided for greater protection of creditors by introducing safeguards against fraudulent bankruptcies and control over remuneration of officials in bankruptcy proceedings. Now, the discharge of the bankrupt is a secondary objective of bankruptcy proceedings and the primary purposes are to protect creditors against fraud prior to and/or during liquidation proceedings and to assure the equitable distribution of debtors' available assets among the creditors.

QUESTIONS AND PROBLEMS

1. Distinguish between (*a*) business failure and business discontinuation, (*b*) liquidation and dissolution of a business concern, and (*c*) voluntary and involuntary liquidation of a business firm.

2. Why is it important for an owner of an unincorporated business firm to obtain a release or discharge for unpaid balances of debts in liquidation proceedings? How does his position differ from that of stockholders of a corporation?
3. Distinguish between common-law assignments and statutory assignments. What are the advantages and disadvantages of each?
4. What is the procedure for voluntary dissolution of a corporation? Why must written notice be given to each known creditor?
5. (*a*) Under what circumstances may the Attorney General take dissolution action against a corporation? (*b*) Cite other reasons for involuntary dissolution of corporations.
6. Why are large corporations most commonly liquidated under the supervision of the federal courts?
7. Identify: (*a*) the six acts of bankruptcy, (*b*) adjudication, (*c*) referee in bankruptcy, (*d*) receiver in bankruptcy, and (*e*) trustee in bankruptcy.
8. When bankruptcy occurs, what is the order of priority in which obligations are settled?
9. (*a*) What are the exceptions to the release granted by the court from debts remaining unsatisfied when a bankrupt is discharged? (*b*) Under what circumstances may a discharge of a bankrupt not be allowed?
10. At one time, the emphasis in bankruptcy proceedings was on the protection of the bankrupt. Explain.
11. How does the Chandler Act provide greater protection for creditors?
12. How have trade associations and adjustment bureaus reduced costs of reorganization and liquidation proceedings?
13. "In the *Ludman Corporation* case, certain creditors petitioned the court to adjudicate the debtor a bankrupt." (*25th Annual Report of the Securities and Exchange Commission Fiscal Year Ended June 30, 1959* [Washington, D.C.: U.S. Government Printing Office, 1959], p. 146.) In order for the creditors to receive favorable action on their petition, what acts must the debtor have committed? Explain.
14. "One of the primary duties of the trustee is to make a thorough study of the debtor to assure the discovery and collection of all assets of the estate, including claims against directors, officers, or controlling persons who may have mismanaged the company's affairs, diverted its funds to their own use or benefit, or been guilty of other misconduct." (*25th Annual Report of the Securities and Exchange Commission Fiscal Year Ended June 30, 1959* [Washington, D.C.: U.S. Government Printing Office, 1959], p. 147.) Is the trustee vested with the power to correct abuses such as those noted above?
15. Explain: "There have been more liquidations of businesses in 1960 than in the previous year, and many of these came under creditors' agreements in which settlements were made without filing of bankruptcy in the courts." (*New York Times*, January 9, 1961, p. 114.)

16. Explain: "Many collapsing companies wind up short of bankruptcy courts by reaching out-of-court agreements to divide their assets among creditors, a tactic which avoids bankruptcy court costs." (*Wall Street Journal* [New York], January 23, 1961, p. 1.)

Index

Index

D

E

F

S

This book has been set on the Linotype in 12 and 10 point Bodoni Book, leaded 1 point. Part and chapter numbers are in 18 point and part and chapter titles in 24 point Bodoni No. 175 italics. The size of the type page is 27 by 46½ picas.